STATE RANKINGS

1992

A Statistical View of the 50 United States

Kathleen O'Leary Morgan, Scott Morgan and Neal Quitno, Editors

Morgan Quitno Corporation
Copyright 1992, All Rights Reserved

P.O. Box 1656, Lawrence, KS 66044
(913) 841-3534

ISBN: 0-9625531-2-3
ISSN: 1057-3623

State Rankings sells for $39.95 ($3.75 shipping). For those who prefer ranking
information tailored to a particular state, we also offer state-specific reports.
"State Perspectives" are available for each of the 50 United States. These
individual state guides provide information on a state's rank for each of the 459
categories featured in the national State Rankings report. These sell for $16.00
($3.75 shipping) or $8.00 if ordered with State Rankings ($4.25 shipping).

Third Edition
Printed in the United States of America

PREFACE

State Rankings 1992 features extensive state and federal government information in an easy to read, easy to understand format. Information from a multitude of state, federal and private sources is presented in rank order so that instant comparisons of the 50 United States can be made in fifteen subject areas ranging from Crime to Transportation, Social Welfare to Agriculture, and Population to Government Finance.

In most cases, states are ranked on a high–to–low basis. Any ties among states that have the same totals are listed alphabetically for a given ranking. All tables list national totals unless otherwise noted. The columns headed by a percent (%) symbol represent each state's percentage of a particular national total.

The information contained in the 1992 edition was derived from U.S. government agencies and private organizations. Original sources are noted whenever possible. Publications cited as sources sometimes contain additional statistical detail and more comprehensive definitions than can be presented in this volume. More information on the subjects covered may generally be obtained directly from the source. For those readers seeking additional information, we have provided a roster of the addresses and telephone numbers of those government agencies which are the most commonly cited sources.

While State Rankings 1992 features the same easy to read format as previous editions, we have made a number of improvements. Most noteable is its increased size. An additional 112 charts are included, for a total of 459 tables of state and national information. At the suggestion of some of our subscribers, we have also included more per capita information, allowing for more equitable comparisons of states.

State Rankings 1992 is the third edition for Morgan Quitno. The book (formerly known as US Statistical Rankings) was published in one form or another since 1967 by Joe and Joan Williams of Elmwood, Nebraska. The current editors became involved when Joe stopped by one of our offices and made a sales pitch so convincing that we not only bought a copy but eventually made an offer to buy the whole operation. We are making every effort to build on the Williams' sound idea of providing researchers with a reference tool that is not only useful but also easy and enjoyable to use.

Finally, we would like to thank the numerous federal government officials who provided us with information and guidance in developing State Rankings 1992. We also are grateful for the help of the librarians at the State Library of Kansas in Topeka who have provided invaluable information and counseling to us about what a truly useable reference book should contain. It is only through the dedication and expertise of these individuals that State Rankings is possible.

We welcome your suggestions or comments.

STATE FAST FACTS

STATE	NICKNAME	CAPITAL	POPULATION*	AREA**	DATE ADMITTED TO UNION
Alabama	Heart of Dixie	Montgomery	4,089,000	52,423	December 14, 1819
Alaska	The Last Frontier	Juneau	570,000	656,424	January 3, 1959
Arizona	Grand Canyon State	Phoenix	3,750,000	114,006	February 14, 1912
Arkansas	Land of Opportunity	Little Rock	2,372,000	53,182	June 15, 1836
California	Golden State	Sacramento	30,380,000	163,707	September 9, 1850
Colorado	Centennial State	Denver	3,377,000	104,100	August 1, 1876
Connecticut	Constitution State	Hartford	3,291,000	5,544	January 9, 1788
Delaware	First State	Dover	680,000	2,489	December 7, 1787
Florida	Sunshine State	Tallahassee	13,277,000	65,758	March 3, 1845
Georgia	Peach State	Atlanta	6,623,000	59,441	January 2, 1788
Hawaii	Aloha State	Honolulu	1,135,000	10,932	August 21, 1959
Idaho	Gem State	Boise	1,039,000	83,574	July 3, 1890
Illinois	Land of Lincoln	Springfield	11,543,000	57,918	December 3, 1818
Indiana	Hoosier State	Indianapolis	5,610,000	36,420	December 11, 1816
Iowa	Hawkeye State	Des Moines	2,795,000	56,276	December 28, 1846
Kansas	Sunflower State	Topeka	2,495,000	82,282	January 29, 1861
Kentucky	Bluegrass State	Frankfort	3,713,000	40,411	June 1, 1792
Louisiana	Pelican State	Baton Rouge	4,252,000	51,843	April 30, 1812
Maine	Pine Tree State	Augusta	1,235,000	35,387	March 15, 1820
Maryland	Free State	Annapolis	4,860,000	12,407	April 28, 1788
Massachusetts	Bay State	Boston	5,996,000	10,555	February 6, 1788
Michigan	Great Lake State	Lansing	9,368,000	96,810	January 26, 1837
Minnesota	North Star State	St. Paul	4,432,000	86,943	May 11, 1858
Mississippi	Magnolia State	Jackson	2,592,000	48,434	December 10, 1817
Missouri	Show Me State	Jefferson City	5,158,000	69,709	August 10, 1821

*1991 Census resident population estimates.

**Total of land and water area in square miles. Revised from previous years due to improved measuring capabilities.

STATE FAST FACTS

STATE	STATE SONG	STATE FLOWER	STATE TREE	STATE BIRD
Alabama	Alabama	Camellia	Southern Pine	Yellowhammer
Alaska	Alaska's Flag	Forget-Me-Not	Sitka Spruce	Willow Ptarmigan
Arizona	Arizona	Saguaro Cactus Blossom	Paloverde	Cactus Wren
Arkansas	Arkansas	Apple Blossom	Pine	Mockingbird
California	I Love You, California	Golden Poppy	California Redwood	California Valley Quail
Colorado	Where the Columbines Grow	Rocky Mountain Columbine	Colorado Blue Spruce	Lark Bunting
Connecticut	Yankee Doodle Dandy	Mountain Laurel	White Oak	American Robin
Delaware	Our Delaware	Peach Blossom	American Holly	Blue Hen Chicken
Florida	Swanee River	Orange Blossom	Sabal Palmetto Palm	Mockingbird
Georgia	Georgia On My Mind	Cherokee Rose	Live Oak	Brown Thrasher
Hawaii	Hawaii Ponoi	Yellow Hibiscus	Candlenut	Hawaiian Goose
Idaho	Here We Have Idaho	Syringa	White Pine	Mountain Bluebird
Illinois	Illinois	Native Violet	White Oak	Cardinal
Indiana	On the Banks of the Wabash, Far Away	Peony	Tulip Poplar	Cardinal
Iowa	The Song of Iowa	Wild Rose	Oak	Eastern Goldfinch
Kansas	Home on the Range	Sunflower	Cottonwood	Western Meadowlark
Kentucky	My Old Kentucky Home	Goldenrod	Kentucky Coffee Tree	Cardinal
Louisiana	Give Me Louisiana	Magnolia	Cypress	Eastern Brown Pelican
Maine	State of Maine Song	White Pine Cone and Tassel	Eastern White Pine	Chickadee
Maryland	Maryland, My Maryland	Black-eyed Susan	White Oak	Baltimore Oriole
Massachusetts	All Hail to Massachusetts	Mayflower	American Elm	Chickadee
Michigan	Michigan, My Michigan	Apple Blossom	White Pine	Robin
Minnesota	Hail! Minnesota	Pink and White Lady's Slipper	Red Pine	Common Loon
Mississippi	Go, Mississippi!	Magnolia	Magnolia	Mockingbird
Missouri	Missouri Waltz	Hawthorn	Dogwood	Bluebird

STATE FAST FACTS

STATE	NICKNAME	CAPITAL	POPULATION*	AREA**	DATE ADMITTED TO UNION
Montana	Treasure State	Helena	808,000	147,046	November 8, 1889
Nebraska	Cornhusker State	Lincoln	1,593,000	77,358	March 1, 1867
Nevada	Sagebrush State	Carson City	1,284,000	110,567	October 31, 1864
New Hampshire	Granite State	Concord	1,105,000	9,351	June 21, 1788
New Jersey	Garden State	Trenton	7,760,000	8,722	December 18, 1787
New Mexico	Land of Enchantment	Santa Fe	1,548,000	121,598	January 6, 1912
New York	Empire State	Albany	18,058,000	54,475	July 26, 1788
North Carolina	Tar Heel State	Raleigh	6,737,000	53,821	November 21, 1789
North Dakota	Peace Garden State	Bismarck	635,000	70,704	November 2, 1889
Ohio	Buckeye State	Columbus	10,939,000	44,828	March 1, 1803
Oklahoma	Sooner State	Oklahoma City	3,175,000	69,903	November 16, 1907
Oregon	Beaver State	Salem	2,922,000	98,386	February 14, 1859
Pennsylvania	Keystone State	Harrisburg	11,961,000	46,058	December 12, 1787
Rhode Island	Ocean State	Providence	1,004,000	1,545	May 29, 1790
South Carolina	Palmetto State	Columbia	3,560,000	32,007	May 23, 1788
South Dakota	Coyote State	Pierre	703,000	77,121	November 2, 1889
Tennessee	Volunteer State	Nashville	4,953,000	42,146	June 1, 1796
Texas	Lone Star State	Austin	17,349,000	268,601	December 29, 1845
Utah	Beehive State	Salt Lake City	1,770,000	84,904	January 4, 1896
Vermont	Green Mountain State	Montpelier	567,000	9,615	March 4, 1791
Virginia	Old Dominion	Richmond	6,286,000	42,769	June 25, 1788
Washington	Evergreen State	Olympia	5,018,000	71,303	November 11, 1889
West Virginia	Mountain State	Charleston	1,801,000	24,231	June 20, 1863
Wisconsin	Badger State	Madison	4,955,000	65,503	May 29, 1848
Wyoming	Equality State	Cheyenne	460,000	97,818	July 10, 1890

*1991 Census resident population estimates.

**Total of land and water area in square miles. Revised from previous years due to improved measuring capabilities.

STATE FAST FACTS

STATE	STATE SONG	STATE FLOWER	STATE TREE	STATE BIRD
Montana	Montana	Bitterroot	Ponderosa Pine	Western Meadowlark
Nebraska	Beautiful Nebraska	Goldenrod	Cottonwood	Western Meadowlark
Nevada	Home Means Nevada	Sagebrush	Single-Leaf Pinon	Mountain Bluebird
New Hampshire	Old New Hampshire	Purple Lilac	White Birch	Purple Finch
New Jersey	Ode to New Jersey	Purple Violet	Red Oak	Eastern Goldfinch
New Mexico	O Fair New Mexico	Yucca	Pinon	Roadrunner
New York	I Love New York	Rose	Sugar Maple	Bluebird
North Carolina	The Old North State	Dogwood	Pine	Cardinal
North Dakota	North Dakota Hymm	Wild Prairie Rose	American Elm	Western Meadowlark
Ohio	Beautiful Ohio	Scarlet Carnation	Buckeye	Cardinal
Oklahoma	Oklahoma!	Mistletoe	Redbud	Scissortailed Flycatcher
Oregon	Oregon, My Oregon	Oregon Grape	Douglas Fir	Western Meadowlark
Pennsylvania	Hail! Pennsylvania	Mountain Laurel	Hemlock	Ruffed Grouse
Rhode Island	Rhode Island	Violet	Red Maple	Rhode Island Red
South Carolina	Carolina	Yellow Jessamine	Palmetto	Carolina Wren
South Dakota	Hail, South Dakota	Pasque Flower	Black Hills Spruce	Ringnecked Pheasant
Tennessee	The Tennessee Waltz	Iris	Tulip Poplar	Mockingbird
Texas	Texas, Our Texas	Bluebonnet	Pecan	Mockingbird
Utah	Utah, We Love Thee	Sego Lilly	Blue Spruce	Seagull
Vermont	Hail, Vermont	Red Clover	Sugar Maple	Hermit Thrush
Virginia	Carry Me Back to Old Virginia	Dogwood	Dogwood	Cardinal
Washington	Washington, My Home	Western Rhododendron	Western Hemlock	Willow Goldfinch
West Virginia	The West Virginia Hills; This Is My West Virginia; and West Virginia, My Home, Sweet Home	Big Rhododendron	Sugar Maple	Cardinal
Wisconsin	On Wisconsin!	Wood Violet	Sugar Maple	Robin
Wyoming	Wyoming	Indian Paintbrush	Cottonwood	Meadowlark

TABLE OF CHAPTERS

Note: Please consult individual chapter dividers for a complete listing of each chapter's tables.

Date Each State Admitted to Statehood*

RANK	STATE	DATE OF ADMISSION	RANK	STATE	DATE OF ADMISSION
1	Delaware	December 7, 1787	26	Michigan	January 26, 1837
2	Pennsylvania	December 12, 1787	27	Florida	March 3, 1845
3	New Jersey	December 18, 1787	28	Texas	December 29, 1845
4	Georgia	January 2, 1788	29	Iowa	December 28, 1846
5	Connecticut	January 9, 1788	30	Wisconsin	May 29, 1848
6	Massachusetts	February 6, 1788	31	California	September 9, 1850
7	Maryland	April 28, 1788	32	Minnesota	May 11, 1858
8	South Carolina	May 23, 1788	33	Oregon	February 14, 1859
9	New Hampshire	June 21, 1788	34	Kansas	January 29, 1861
10	Virginia	June 26, 1788	35	West Virginia	June 20, 1863
11	New York	July 26, 1788	36	Nevada	October 31, 1864
12	North Carolina	November 21, 1789	37	Nebraska	March 1, 1867
13	Rhode Island	May 29, 1790	38	Colorado	August 1, 1876
14	Vermont	March 4, 1791	39	North Dakota	November 2, 1889
15	Kentucky	June 1, 1792	39	South Dakota	November 2, 1889
16	Tennessee	June 1, 1796	41	Montana	November 8, 1889
17	Ohio	March 1, 1803	42	Washington	November 11, 1889
18	Louisiana	April 30, 1812	43	Idaho	July 3, 1890
19	Indiana	December 11, 1816	44	Wyoming	July 10, 1890
20	Mississippi	December 10, 1817	45	Utah	January 4, 1896
21	Illinois	December 3, 1818	46	Oklahoma	November 16, 1907
22	Alabama	December 14, 1819	47	New Mexico	January 6, 1912
23	Maine	March 15, 1820	48	Arizona	February 14, 1912
24	Missouri	August 10, 1821	49	Alaska	January 3, 1959
25	Arkansas	June 15, 1836	50	Hawaii	August 21, 1959

Source: U.S. Bureau of the Census,

"1980 Census of Population" (vol. 1, part A, PC80-1-A)
*First thirteen states show date of ratification of Constitution.

I. AGRICULTURE

Number of Farms in 1990

National Total = 2,143,150 Farms*

RANK	STATE	FARMS	%	RANK	STATE	FARMS	%
1	Texas	186,000	8.68%	26	Oregon	36,500	1.70%
2	Missouri	108,000	5.04%	27	South Dakota	35,000	1.63%
3	Iowa	104,000	4.85%	28	Louisiana	34,000	1.59%
4	Kentucky	93,000	4.34%	28	North Dakota	34,000	1.59%
5	Minnesota	89,000	4.15%	30	Colorado	26,500	1.24%
5	Tennessee	89,000	4.15%	31	Montana	24,700	1.15%
7	California	85,000	3.97%	32	South Carolina	24,500	1.14%
8	Ohio	84,000	3.92%	33	Idaho	21,800	1.02%
9	Illinois	83,000	3.87%	34	West Virginia	20,500	0.96%
10	Wisconsin	80,000	3.73%	35	Maryland	15,200	0.71%
11	Oklahoma	70,000	3.27%	36	New Mexico	13,500	0.63%
12	Kansas	69,000	3.22%	37	Utah	13,200	0.62%
13	Indiana	68,000	3.17%	38	Wyoming	8,900	0.42%
14	North Carolina	62,000	2.89%	39	New Jersey	8,100	0.38%
15	Nebraska	57,000	2.66%	40	Arizona	7,800	0.36%
16	Michigan	54,000	2.52%	41	Maine	7,300	0.34%
17	Pennsylvania	53,000	2.47%	42	Vermont	7,000	0.33%
18	Georgia	49,000	2.29%	43	Massachusetts	6,900	0.32%
19	Alabama	47,000	2.19%	44	Hawaii	4,600	0.21%
19	Arkansas	47,000	2.19%	45	Connecticut	3,900	0.18%
21	Virginia	46,000	2.15%	46	New Hampshire	3,000	0.14%
22	Florida	41,000	1.91%	47	Delaware	2,900	0.14%
23	Mississippi	40,000	1.87%	48	Nevada	2,500	0.12%
24	New York	38,500	1.80%	49	Rhode Island	770	0.04%
25	Washington	37,000	1.73%	50	Alaska	580	0.03%

Source: U.S. Department of Agriculture, National Agricultural Statistics Service,
 "Agricultural Statistics" (April 1991)

*USDA defines a farm as any establishment that sells or normally would sell at least $1,000 worth of agricultural products in a calendar year.

Land in Farms in 1990

National Total = 987,721,000 Acres*

RANK	STATE	ACRES	%	RANK	STATE	ACRES	%
1	Texas	132,000,000	13.36%	26	Georgia	12,500,000	1.27%
2	Montana	60,500,000	6.13%	27	Tennessee	12,400,000	1.26%
3	Kansas	47,900,000	4.85%	28	Utah	11,300,000	1.14%
4	Nebraska	47,100,000	4.77%	29	Florida	10,900,000	1.10%
5	New Mexico	44,500,000	4.51%	30	Michigan	10,800,000	1.09%
6	South Dakota	44,300,000	4.49%	31	Alabama	10,300,000	1.04%
7	North Dakota	40,500,000	4.10%	32	North Carolina	9,700,000	0.98%
8	Arizona	36,000,000	3.64%	33	Louisiana	9,000,000	0.91%
9	Wyoming	34,800,000	3.52%	34	Nevada	8,900,000	0.90%
10	Iowa	33,500,000	3.39%	34	Virginia	8,900,000	0.90%
11	Colorado	33,100,000	3.35%	36	New York	8,400,000	0.85%
12	Oklahoma	33,000,000	3.34%	37	Pennsylvania	8,100,000	0.82%
13	California	30,800,000	3.12%	38	South Carolina	5,200,000	0.53%
14	Missouri	30,400,000	3.08%	39	West Virginia	3,700,000	0.37%
15	Minnesota	30,000,000	3.04%	40	Maryland	2,250,000	0.23%
16	Illinois	28,500,000	2.89%	41	Hawaii	1,710,000	0.17%
17	Oregon	17,800,000	1.80%	42	Vermont	1,510,000	0.15%
18	Wisconsin	17,600,000	1.78%	43	Maine	1,450,000	0.15%
19	Indiana	16,300,000	1.65%	44	Alaska	1,000,000	0.10%
20	Washington	16,000,000	1.62%	45	New Jersey	870,000	0.09%
21	Ohio	15,700,000	1.59%	46	Massachusetts	680,000	0.07%
22	Arkansas	15,500,000	1.57%	47	Delaware	570,000	0.06%
23	Kentucky	14,100,000	1.43%	48	New Hampshire	490,000	0.05%
24	Idaho	13,700,000	1.39%	49	Connecticut	420,000	0.04%
25	Mississippi	13,000,000	1.32%	50	Rhode Island	71,000	0.01%

Source: U.S. Department of Agriculture, National Agricultural Statistics Service,
   "Agricultural Statistics" (April 1991)

*USDA defines a farm as any establishment that sells or normally would sell at least $1,000 worth of agricultural products in a calendar year.

Average Number of Acres per Farm in 1990

National Average = 461 Acres*

RANK	STATE	ACRES	RANK	STATE	ACRES
1	Arizona	4,615	26	Florida	266
2	Wyoming	3,910	27	Louisiana	265
3	Nevada	3,560	28	Georgia	255
4	New Mexico	3,296	29	Indiana	240
5	Montana	2,449	30	Wisconsin	220
6	Alaska	1,724	31	Alabama	219
7	South Dakota	1,266	32	New York	218
8	Colorado	1,249	33	Vermont	216
9	North Dakota	1,191	34	South Carolina	212
10	Utah	856	35	Michigan	200
11	Nebraska	826	36	Maine	199
12	Texas	710	37	Delaware	197
13	Kansas	694	38	Virginia	193
14	Idaho	628	39	Ohio	187
15	Oregon	488	40	West Virginia	180
16	Oklahoma	471	41	New Hampshire	163
17	Washington	432	42	North Carolina	156
18	Hawaii	372	43	Pennsylvania	153
19	California	362	44	Kentucky	152
20	Illinois	343	45	Maryland	148
21	Minnesota	337	46	Tennessee	139
22	Arkansas	330	47	Connecticut	108
23	Mississippi	325	48	New Jersey	107
24	Iowa	322	49	Massachusetts	99
25	Missouri	281	50	Rhode Island	92

Source: U.S. Department of Agriculture, National Agricultural Statistics Service,
"Agricultural Statistics" (April 1991) Calculated by the editors.
*USDA defines a farm as any establishment that sells or normally would sell at least $1,000 worth of agricultural products in a calendar year.

Value of Farmland and Buildings in 1991 *

National Total = $672,235,000,000

RANK	STATE	VALUE	%	RANK	STATE	VALUE	%
1	Texas	$63,492,000,000	9.44%	26	Virginia	$11,526,000,000	1.71%
2	California	55,040,000,000	8.19%	27	Oregon	10,377,000,000	1.54%
3	Illinois	40,841,000,000	6.08%	28	Arizona	10,260,000,000	1.53%
4	Iowa	38,760,000,000	5.77%	29	New Mexico	10,235,000,000	1.52%
5	Minnesota	26,190,000,000	3.90%	30	Mississippi	9,802,000,000	1.46%
6	Nebraska	26,188,000,000	3.90%	31	Idaho	9,028,000,000	1.34%
7	Florida	23,250,000,000	3.46%	32	New York	8,660,000,000	1.29%
8	Kansas	22,369,000,000	3.33%	33	Alabama	8,147,000,000	1.21%
9	Missouri	20,946,000,000	3.12%	34	Louisiana	8,145,000,000	1.21%
10	Indiana	20,783,000,000	3.09%	35	Wyoming	5,324,000,000	0.79%
11	Ohio	19,107,000,000	2.84%	36	Maryland	4,941,000,000	0.74%
12	Oklahoma	16,038,000,000	2.39%	37	South Carolina	4,930,000,000	0.73%
13	South Dakota	15,561,000,000	2.31%	38	Utah	4,554,000,000	0.68%
14	Wisconsin	15,013,000,000	2.23%	39	New Jersey	4,273,000,000	0.64%
15	North Dakota	14,904,000,000	2.22%	40	Massachusetts	2,456,000,000	0.37%
16	Montana	14,702,000,000	2.19%	41	West Virginia	2,313,000,000	0.34%
17	Pennsylvania	14,232,000,000	2.12%	42	Nevada	1,949,000,000	0.29%
18	Colorado	13,571,000,000	2.02%	43	Connecticut	1,781,000,000	0.26%
19	Kentucky	13,564,000,000	2.02%	44	Vermont	1,724,000,000	0.26%
20	Washington	12,768,000,000	1.90%	45	Maine	1,418,000,000	0.21%
21	Georgia	12,438,000,000	1.85%	46	Delaware	1,281,000,000	0.19%
22	Tennessee	12,251,000,000	1.82%	47	New Hampshire	1,053,000,000	0.16%
23	North Carolina	12,057,000,000	1.79%	48	Rhode Island	343,000,000	0.05%
24	Arkansas	11,935,000,000	1.78%	–	Alaska**	N/A	N/A
25	Michigan	11,718,000,000	1.74%	–	Hawaii**	N/A	N/A

Source: U.S. Department of Agriculture, Economic Research Service,
        "Agricultural Resources: Situation and Outlook Report (AR-22, June 1991)
*As of January 1, 1991
**Not available.

Average per Farm Value of Farmland and Buildings in 1991*

National Average = $314,427 per Farm

RANK	STATE	FARM VALUE	RANK	STATE	FARM VALUE
1	Arizona	$1,315,385	26	Indiana	$305,625
2	Nevada	779,640	27	Minnesota	294,270
3	New Mexico	758,148	28	Oregon	284,312
4	California	647,525	29	Pennsylvania	268,523
5	Wyoming	598,247	30	Arkansas	253,936
6	Montana	595,202	31	Georgia	253,827
7	Florida	567,066	32	Virginia	250,554
8	New Jersey	527,585	33	Vermont	246,346
9	Colorado	512,113	34	Mississippi	245,050
10	Illinois	492,054	35	Louisiana	239,559
11	Nebraska	459,432	36	Oklahoma	229,114
12	Connecticut	456,615	37	Ohio	227,463
13	Rhode Island	445,087	38	New York	224,945
14	South Dakota	444,605	39	Michigan	217,000
15	Delaware	441,848	40	South Carolina	201,208
16	North Dakota	438,353	41	North Carolina	194,469
17	Idaho	414,142	42	Maine	194,260
18	Iowa	372,688	43	Missouri	193,941
19	Massachusetts	355,965	44	Wisconsin	187,660
20	New Hampshire	350,840	45	Alabama	173,347
21	Washington	345,081	46	Kentucky	145,852
22	Utah	344,992	47	Tennessee	137,654
23	Texas	341,355	48	West Virginia	112,805
24	Maryland	325,066	–	Alaska**	N/A
25	Kansas	324,193	–	Hawaii**	N/A

Source: U.S. Department of Agriculture, Economic Research Service,
    "Agricultural Resources: Situation and Outlook Report (AR-22, June 1991)
*As of January 1, 1991.
**Not available.

Average Value of Farmland and Buildings per Acre in 1991 *

National Average = $682 per Acre

RANK	STATE	PER ACRE
1	New Jersey	$4,912
2	Rhode Island	4,827
3	Connecticut	4,240
4	Massachusetts	3,612
5	Delaware	2,248
6	Maryland	2,196
7	New Hampshire	2,148
8	Florida	2,133
9	California	1,787
10	Pennsylvania	1,757
11	Illinois	1,433
12	Virginia	1,295
13	Indiana	1,275
14	North Carolina	1,243
15	Ohio	1,217
16	Iowa	1,157
17	Vermont	1,142
18	Michigan	1,085
19	New York	1,031
20	Georgia	995
21	Tennessee	988
22	Maine	978
23	Kentucky	962
24	South Carolina	948
25	Louisiana	905

RANK	STATE	PER ACRE
26	Minnesota	$873
27	Wisconsin	853
28	Washington	798
29	Alabama	791
30	Arkansas	770
31	Mississippi	754
32	Missouri	689
33	Idaho	659
34	West Virginia	625
35	Oregon	583
36	Nebraska	556
37	Oklahoma	486
38	Texas	481
39	Kansas	467
40	Colorado	410
41	Utah	403
42	North Dakota	368
43	South Dakota	351
44	Arizona	285
45	Montana	243
46	New Mexico	230
47	Nevada	219
48	Wyoming	153
–	Alaska**	N/A
–	Hawaii**	N/A

Source: U.S. Department of Agriculture, Economic Research Service,
    *Agricultural Resources: Situation and Outlook Report (AR-22, June 1991)
*As of January 1, 1991
**Not available.

Percent Change in Average Value per Acre of Farmland and Buildings: 1990 to 1991 *

National Percent Change = 2% Increase

RANK	STATE	PERCENT CHANGE	RANK	STATE	PERCENT CHANGE
1	New Mexico	17%	26	Kansas	1%
2	Colorado	15%	26	Missouri	1%
3	Nevada	13%	26	Nebraska	1%
4	Arizona	8%	26	Ohio	1%
4	Michigan	8%	30	Delaware	0%
4	Minnesota	8%	30	Idaho	0%
4	North Dakota	8%	32	Louisiana	–1%
8	South Dakota	7%	32	Tennessee	–1%
9	New Jersey	6%	34	Georgia	–2%
9	New York	6%	34	Kentucky	–2%
9	Wisconsin	6%	34	North Carolina	–2%
12	California	5%	34	Oklahoma	–2%
12	Iowa	5%	38	Pennsylvania	–3%
14	Mississippi	4%	38	Texas	–3%
14	South Carolina	4%	40	Connecticut	–4%
14	Utah	4%	40	Maine	–4%
17	Arkansas	3%	40	Massachusetts	–4%
17	Illinois	3%	40	New Hampshire	–4%
17	Wyoming	3%	40	Rhode Island	–4%
20	Florida	2%	40	Vermont	–4%
20	Indiana	2%	46	Alabama	–6%
20	Montana	2%	47	Maryland	–9%
20	Oregon	2%	48	Virginia	–15%
20	Washington	2%	–	Alaska**	N/A
20	West Virginia	2%	–	Hawaii**	N/A

Source: U.S. Department of Agriculture, Economic Research Service,
   Agricultural Resources: Situation and Outlook Report (AR-22, June 1991)
*As of January 1, 1991.
**Not available.

Net Farm Income in 1990

National Total = $50,831,600,000*

RANK	STATE	FARM INCOME	%	RANK	STATE	FARM INCOME	%
1	California	$7,030,400,000	13.83%	26	Alabama	$822,600,000	1.62%
2	Texas	3,370,700,000	6.63%	27	North Dakota	802,000,000	1.58%
3	Iowa	2,964,400,000	5.83%	28	Louisiana	631,700,000	1.24%
4	Minnesota	2,503,700,000	4.93%	29	Mississippi	616,000,000	1.21%
5	Florida	2,272,900,000	4.47%	30	Arizona	582,300,000	1.15%
6	Nebraska	2,128,000,000	4.19%	31	Virginia	542,200,000	1.07%
7	North Carolina	1,968,400,000	3.87%	32	Tennessee	460,600,000	0.91%
8	Wisconsin	1,863,300,000	3.67%	33	Maryland	427,000,000	0.84%
9	Illinois	1,704,900,000	3.35%	34	Montana	386,600,000	0.76%
10	Washington	1,401,000,000	2.76%	35	New Mexico	337,200,000	0.66%
11	Kansas	1,378,000,000	2.71%	36	South Carolina	273,700,000	0.54%
12	South Dakota	1,284,500,000	2.53%	37	New Jersey	246,600,000	0.49%
13	Arkansas	1,203,800,000	2.37%	38	Utah	239,700,000	0.47%
14	Ohio	1,172,600,000	2.31%	39	Connecticut	188,000,000	0.37%
15	Pennsylvania	1,138,700,000	2.24%	40	Delaware	170,600,000	0.34%
16	Oklahoma	1,109,800,000	2.18%	41	Maine	150,700,000	0.30%
17	Idaho	1,090,000,000	2.14%	42	Massachusetts	148,900,000	0.29%
18	Georgia	1,076,000,000	2.12%	43	Vermont	126,800,000	0.25%
19	Indiana	1,053,700,000	2.07%	44	Wyoming	120,200,000	0.24%
20	Kentucky	1,038,100,000	2.04%	45	Nevada	87,300,000	0.17%
21	Michigan	940,500,000	1.85%	46	Hawaii	84,300,000	0.17%
22	New York	934,500,000	1.84%	47	West Virginia	76,300,000	0.15%
23	Missouri	873,900,000	1.72%	48	New Hampshire	39,600,000	0.08%
24	Colorado	873,100,000	1.72%	49	Rhode Island	36,500,000	0.07%
25	Oregon	851,800,000	1.68%	50	Alaska	7,500,000	0.01%

Source: U.S. Department of Agriculture, Economic Research Service,
Economic Indicators of the Farm Sector: State Financial Summary, 1990" (ECIFS 10-2, December 1991)
*Net farm income is a measure of the net value of production in a given year.

Farm Income: Cash Receipts from Farm Marketings in 1990

National Total = $169,987,155,000*

RANK	STATE	FARM INCOME	%	RANK	STATE	FARM INCOME	%
1	California	$18,858,873,000	11.09%	26	North Dakota	$2,537,350,000	1.49%
2	Texas	11,980,527,000	7.05%	27	Mississippi	2,432,964,000	1.43%
3	Iowa	10,319,173,000	6.07%	28	Oregon	2,311,783,000	1.36%
4	Nebraska	8,845,164,000	5.20%	29	Virginia	2,119,633,000	1.25%
5	Illinois	7,937,793,000	4.67%	30	Tennessee	2,038,610,000	1.20%
6	Minnesota	7,011,173,000	4.12%	31	Louisiana	1,921,224,000	1.13%
7	Kansas	6,994,864,000	4.11%	32	Arizona	1,865,492,000	1.10%
8	Florida	5,708,300,000	3.36%	33	Montana	1,605,731,000	0.94%
9	Wisconsin	5,706,149,000	3.36%	34	New Mexico	1,528,793,000	0.90%
10	Indiana	4,930,668,000	2.90%	35	Maryland	1,345,165,000	0.79%
11	North Carolina	4,866,512,000	2.86%	36	South Carolina	1,175,560,000	0.69%
12	Arkansas	4,259,205,000	2.51%	37	Wyoming	766,767,000	0.45%
13	Colorado	4,213,419,000	2.48%	38	Utah	754,826,000	0.44%
14	Ohio	4,171,818,000	2.45%	39	New Jersey	647,383,000	0.38%
15	Missouri	3,938,589,000	2.32%	40	Delaware	643,661,000	0.38%
16	Georgia	3,842,186,000	2.26%	41	Hawaii	587,689,000	0.35%
17	Washington	3,815,779,000	2.24%	42	Maine	460,387,000	0.27%
18	Pennsylvania	3,767,174,000	2.22%	43	Vermont	446,722,000	0.26%
19	Oklahoma	3,554,437,000	2.09%	44	Connecticut	445,901,000	0.26%
20	South Dakota	3,348,717,000	1.97%	45	Massachusetts	418,462,000	0.25%
21	Michigan	3,183,356,000	1.87%	46	West Virginia	338,132,000	0.20%
22	Kentucky	3,098,398,000	1.82%	47	Nevada	333,435,000	0.20%
23	New York	3,006,046,000	1.77%	48	New Hampshire	133,892,000	0.08%
24	Idaho	2,934,519,000	1.73%	49	Rhode Island	70,793,000	0.04%
25	Alabama	2,737,422,000	1.61%	50	Alaska	26,539,000	0.02%

Source: U.S. Department of Agriculture, Economic Research Service,
"Economic Indicators of the Farm Sector: State Financial Summary, 1990" (ECIFS 10-2, December 1991)
Farm marketings are crops and livestock.

Farm Income: Government Payments in 1990

National Total = $9,298,030,000

RANK	STATE	FARM INCOME	%	RANK	STATE	FARM INCOME	%
1	Texas	$974,702,000	10.48%	26	Alabama	$82,226,000	0.88%
2	Kansas	834,746,000	8.98%	27	Kentucky	81,610,000	0.88%
3	Iowa	753,733,000	8.11%	28	North Carolina	73,255,000	0.79%
4	Nebraska	624,646,000	6.72%	29	New Mexico	63,840,000	0.69%
5	North Dakota	545,378,000	5.87%	30	South Carolina	62,637,000	0.67%
6	Minnesota	511,759,000	5.50%	31	New York	59,304,000	0.64%
7	Illinois	506,603,000	5.45%	32	Arizona	43,349,000	0.47%
8	South Dakota	332,851,000	3.58%	33	Pennsylvania	41,414,000	0.45%
9	Oklahoma	319,040,000	3.43%	34	Florida	37,155,000	0.40%
10	Arkansas	312,696,000	3.36%	35	Utah	34,897,000	0.38%
11	Montana	299,599,000	3.22%	36	Virginia	32,378,000	0.35%
12	Missouri	299,065,000	3.22%	37	Wyoming	31,283,000	0.34%
13	California	252,333,000	2.71%	38	Maryland	17,386,000	0.19%
14	Indiana	244,170,000	2.63%	39	New Jersey	15,744,000	0.17%
15	Colorado	236,723,000	2.55%	40	Maine	6,982,000	0.08%
16	Washington	205,425,000	2.21%	41	West Virginia	6,049,000	0.07%
17	Ohio	197,006,000	2.12%	42	Vermont	5,793,000	0.06%
18	Mississippi	185,969,000	2.00%	43	Nevada	5,347,000	0.06%
19	Wisconsin	181,243,000	1.95%	44	Delaware	3,213,000	0.03%
20	Michigan	168,831,000	1.82%	45	Massachusetts	3,023,000	0.03%
21	Louisiana	154,631,000	1.66%	46	Connecticut	2,123,000	0.02%
22	Idaho	133,431,000	1.44%	47	New Hampshire	1,856,000	0.02%
23	Georgia	130,593,000	1.40%	48	Alaska	1,117,000	0.01%
24	Tennessee	91,029,000	0.98%	49	Hawaii	519,000	0.01%
25	Oregon	89,137,000	0.96%	50	Rhode Island	191,000	0.00%

Source: U.S. Department of Agriculture, Economic Research Service,
"Economic Indicators of the Farm Sector: State Financial Summary, 1990" (ECIFS 10-2, December 1991)

Farm Income: Crops in 1990

National Total = $80,363,701,000

RANK	STATE	FARM INCOME	%
1	California	$13,343,714,000	16.60%
2	Illinois	5,460,821,000	6.80%
3	Florida	4,448,019,000	5.53%
4	Iowa	4,437,024,000	5.52%
5	Texas	4,268,378,000	5.31%
6	Minnesota	3,253,477,000	4.05%
7	Indiana	2,871,067,000	3.57%
8	Nebraska	2,807,674,000	3.49%
9	Washington	2,420,139,000	3.01%
10	Ohio	2,335,424,000	2.91%
11	North Carolina	2,213,714,000	2.75%
12	Kansas	2,098,649,000	2.61%
13	Michigan	1,785,034,000	2.22%
14	Idaho	1,780,841,000	2.22%
15	North Dakota	1,723,899,000	2.15%
16	Missouri	1,667,974,000	2.08%
17	Georgia	1,574,081,000	1.96%
18	Oregon	1,557,088,000	1.94%
19	Arkansas	1,552,776,000	1.93%
20	Kentucky	1,400,075,000	1.74%
21	Louisiana	1,284,157,000	1.60%
22	Oklahoma	1,191,312,000	1.48%
23	Colorado	1,184,074,000	1.47%
24	Wisconsin	1,124,923,000	1.40%
25	Mississippi	1,111,288,000	1.38%

RANK	STATE	FARM INCOME	%
26	Pennsylvania	$1,053,407,000	1.31%
27	Arizona	1,046,246,000	1.30%
28	South Dakota	1,036,068,000	1.29%
29	New York	1,022,887,000	1.27%
30	Tennessee	928,009,000	1.15%
31	Montana	742,052,000	0.92%
32	Virginia	740,881,000	0.92%
33	Alabama	654,909,000	0.81%
34	South Carolina	599,038,000	0.75%
35	Maryland	516,701,000	0.64%
36	Hawaii	499,245,000	0.62%
37	New Mexico	482,814,000	0.60%
38	New Jersey	451,510,000	0.56%
39	Massachusetts	302,525,000	0.38%
40	Connecticut	250,068,000	0.31%
41	Maine	240,492,000	0.30%
42	Delaware	183,829,000	0.23%
43	Utah	178,686,000	0.22%
44	Wyoming	157,193,000	0.20%
45	Nevada	115,085,000	0.14%
46	New Hampshire	70,720,000	0.09%
47	West Virginia	69,517,000	0.09%
48	Rhode Island	58,269,000	0.07%
49	Vermont	48,951,000	0.06%
50	Alaska	18,977,000	0.02%

Source: U.S. Department of Agriculture, Economic Research Service,
"Economic Indicators of the Farm Sector: State Financial Summary, 1990" (ECIFS 10-2, December 1991)

Farm Income: Livestock in 1990

National Total = $89,623,454,000*

RANK	STATE	FARM INCOME	%	RANK	STATE	FARM INCOME	%
1	Texas	$7,712,149,000	8.61%	26	Florida	$1,260,281,000	1.41%
2	Nebraska	6,037,490,000	6.74%	27	Idaho	1,153,678,000	1.29%
3	Iowa	5,882,149,000	6.56%	28	Tennessee	1,110,601,000	1.24%
4	California	5,515,159,000	6.15%	29	New Mexico	1,045,979,000	1.17%
5	Kansas	4,896,215,000	5.46%	30	Montana	863,679,000	0.96%
6	Wisconsin	4,581,226,000	5.11%	31	Maryland	828,464,000	0.92%
7	Minnesota	3,757,696,000	4.19%	32	Arizona	819,246,000	0.91%
8	Colorado	3,029,345,000	3.38%	33	North Dakota	813,451,000	0.91%
9	Pennsylvania	2,713,767,000	3.03%	34	Oregon	754,695,000	0.84%
10	Arkansas	2,706,429,000	3.02%	35	Louisiana	637,067,000	0.71%
11	North Carolina	2,652,798,000	2.96%	36	Wyoming	609,574,000	0.68%
12	Illinois	2,476,972,000	2.76%	37	South Carolina	576,522,000	0.64%
13	Oklahoma	2,363,125,000	2.64%	38	Utah	576,140,000	0.64%
14	South Dakota	2,312,649,000	2.58%	39	Delaware	459,832,000	0.51%
15	Missouri	2,270,615,000	2.53%	40	Vermont	397,771,000	0.44%
16	Georgia	2,268,105,000	2.53%	41	West Virginia	268,615,000	0.30%
17	Alabama	2,082,513,000	2.32%	42	Maine	219,895,000	0.25%
18	Indiana	2,059,601,000	2.30%	43	Nevada	218,350,000	0.24%
19	New York	1,983,159,000	2.21%	44	New Jersey	195,873,000	0.22%
20	Ohio	1,836,394,000	2.05%	45	Connecticut	195,833,000	0.22%
21	Kentucky	1,698,323,000	1.89%	46	Massachusetts	115,937,000	0.13%
22	Michigan	1,398,322,000	1.56%	47	Hawaii	88,444,000	0.10%
23	Washington	1,395,640,000	1.56%	48	New Hampshire	63,172,000	0.07%
24	Virginia	1,378,752,000	1.54%	49	Rhode Island	12,524,000	0.01%
25	Mississippi	1,321,676,000	1.47%	50	Alaska	7,562,000	0.01%

Source: U.S. Department of Agriculture, Economic Research Service,
  "Economic Indicators of the Farm Sector: State Financial Summary, 1990" (ECIFS 10–2, December 1991)
Includes livestock products.

State and Local Taxes Levied on Farm Real Estate in 1989

National Total = $4,422,400,000

RANK	STATE	TAXES	%	RANK	STATE	TAXES	%
1	Illinois	$451,800,000	10.22%	26	Tennessee	$46,200,000	1.04%
2	Iowa	353,600,000	8.00%	27	Arizona	45,500,000	1.03%
3	Michigan	325,800,000	7.37%	28	Idaho	41,700,000	0.94%
4	Texas	320,300,000	7.24%	29	Arkansas	40,600,000	0.92%
5	Nebraska	290,800,000	6.58%	30	Kentucky	32,200,000	0.73%
6	Wisconsin	272,700,000	6.17%	31	New Jersey	31,400,000	0.71%
7	California	240,000,000	5.43%	32	Hawaii	25,000,000	0.57%
8	Minnesota	162,100,000	3.67%	33	Maryland	21,900,000	0.50%
9	New York	147,600,000	3.34%	34	Mississippi	21,300,000	0.48%
10	Ohio	142,600,000	3.22%	35	Louisiana	19,600,000	0.44%
11	Pennsylvania	123,000,000	2.78%	36	Vermont	18,700,000	0.42%
12	Indiana	122,500,000	2.77%	37	Wyoming	16,200,000	0.37%
13	Kansas	118,100,000	2.67%	38	Massachusetts	15,300,000	0.35%
14	Florida	113,700,000	2.57%	39	South Carolina	15,100,000	0.34%
15	South Dakota	104,800,000	2.37%	40	New Mexico	12,900,000	0.29%
16	Montana	88,300,000	2.00%	41	Utah	11,700,000	0.26%
17	Oregon	82,300,000	1.86%	42	Maine	11,600,000	0.26%
18	North Dakota	79,800,000	1.80%	43	Alabama	11,400,000	0.26%
19	Missouri	70,300,000	1.59%	44	Connecticut	9,700,000	0.22%
20	Colorado	67,100,000	1.52%	45	New Hampshire	7,900,000	0.18%
21	Washington	60,800,000	1.37%	46	Nevada	3,600,000	0.08%
22	Oklahoma	55,400,000	1.25%	47	West Virginia	3,500,000	0.08%
23	Virginia	55,300,000	1.25%	48	Rhode Island	2,800,000	0.06%
24	Georgia	54,800,000	1.24%	49	Delaware	800,000	0.02%
25	North Carolina	52,000,000	1.18%	–	Alaska*	N/A	N/A

Source: U.S. Department of Agriculture, Economic Research Service,
   "Agricultural Resources: Situation and Outlook Report (AR-22, June 1991)
*Not available.

Average State and Local Taxes per Acre of Farmland in 1989

National Average = $5.06 per Acre

RANK	STATE	PER ACRE	RANK	STATE	PER ACRE
1	Rhode Island	$48.23	26	Oregon	$5.11
2	New Jersey	36.63	27	Washington	4.73
3	Michigan	32.31	28	Tennessee	3.98
4	Massachusetts	26.33	29	Idaho	3.70
5	Connecticut	24.76	30	South Carolina	3.20
6	New Hampshire	18.96	31	Arkansas	2.88
7	New York	18.30	32	South Dakota	2.83
8	Wisconsin	16.58	33	Kansas	2.55
9	Pennsylvania	16.18	34	Louisiana	2.52
10	Illinois	15.94	35	Texas	2.51
11	Hawaii	14.65	36	Missouri	2.43
12	Vermont	13.43	37	Kentucky	2.34
13	Iowa	11.21	38	Colorado	2.29
14	Florida	10.94	39	North Dakota	2.13
15	Maryland	9.81	40	Mississippi	2.10
16	Ohio	9.44	41	Oklahoma	1.83
17	California	9.36	42	Utah	1.67
18	Maine	8.74	43	Delaware	1.45
19	Indiana	7.51	44	Alabama	1.27
20	Nebraska	6.65	45	Montana	1.25
21	Virginia	6.48	46	West Virginia	1.06
22	Minnesota	6.12	47	Wyoming	0.69
23	North Carolina	5.82	48	Nevada	0.68
24	Arizona	5.41	49	New Mexico	0.42
25	Georgia	5.31	–	Alaska*	N/A

Source: U.S. Department of Agriculture, Economic Research Service,
   Agricultural Resources: Situation and Outlook Report (AR-22, June 1991)
*Not available.

Acres Planted in 1991

National Total = 314,342,000 Acres Planted

RANK	STATE	ACRES	%	RANK	STATE	ACRES	%
1	Iowa	23,852,000	7.59%	26	Georgia	3,849,000	1.22%
2	Illinois	23,391,000	7.44%	27	Louisiana	3,797,000	1.21%
3	North Dakota	21,600,000	6.87%	28	New York	3,494,000	1.11%
4	Kansas	21,036,000	6.69%	29	Virginia	2,715,000	0.86%
5	Texas	20,098,000	6.39%	30	Oregon	2,318,000	0.74%
6	Minnesota	19,307,000	6.14%	31	Alabama	2,306,000	0.73%
7	Nebraska	18,629,000	5.93%	32	Wyoming	1,925,000	0.61%
8	South Dakota	16,145,000	5.14%	33	South Carolina	1,885,000	0.60%
9	Missouri	13,054,000	4.15%	34	Maryland	1,587,000	0.50%
10	Indiana	11,661,000	3.71%	35	Florida	1,076,000	0.34%
11	Ohio	10,124,000	3.22%	36	New Mexico	1,061,000	0.34%
12	Montana	9,130,000	2.90%	37	Utah	1,030,000	0.33%
13	Oklahoma	8,810,000	2.80%	38	Arizona	777,000	0.25%
14	Wisconsin	8,735,000	2.78%	39	West Virginia	627,000	0.20%
15	Arkansas	8,010,000	2.55%	40	Delaware	565,000	0.18%
16	Michigan	6,781,000	2.16%	41	Nevada	500,000	0.16%
17	Colorado	5,700,000	1.81%	42	Vermont	442,000	0.14%
18	Kentucky	5,530,000	1.76%	43	New Jersey	388,000	0.12%
19	California	4,795,000	1.53%	44	Maine	369,000	0.12%
20	Mississippi	4,620,000	1.47%	45	Massachusetts	141,000	0.04%
21	North Carolina	4,539,000	1.44%	46	Connecticut	132,000	0.04%
22	Tennessee	4,447,000	1.41%	47	New Hampshire	94,000	0.03%
23	Idaho	4,280,000	1.36%	48	Hawaii	74,000	0.02%
24	Washington	4,157,000	1.32%	49	Rhode Island	10,000	0.00%
25	Pennsylvania	4,143,000	1.32%	–	Alaska*	N/A	N/A

Source: U.S. Department of Agriculture, National Agricultural Statistics Service,
   "Annual Crop Summary" (January 1992)
*Not available.

Acres Harvested in 1991

National Total = 304,894,000 Acres Harvested

RANK	STATE	ACRES	%	RANK	STATE	ACRES	%
1	Iowa	23,376,000	7.67%	26	Georgia	3,774,000	1.24%
2	Illinois	22,906,000	7.51%	27	Louisiana	3,571,000	1.17%
3	North Dakota	20,925,000	6.86%	28	New York	3,443,000	1.13%
4	Kansas	20,712,000	6.79%	29	Virginia	2,660,000	0.87%
5	Minnesota	18,719,000	6.14%	30	Oregon	2,260,000	0.74%
6	Nebraska	18,316,000	6.01%	31	Alabama	2,240,000	0.73%
7	Texas	17,608,000	5.78%	32	Wyoming	1,889,000	0.62%
8	South Dakota	15,640,000	5.13%	33	South Carolina	1,827,000	0.60%
9	Missouri	12,900,000	4.23%	34	Maryland	1,561,000	0.51%
10	Indiana	11,555,000	3.79%	35	New Mexico	1,047,000	0.34%
11	Ohio	9,972,000	3.27%	36	Florida	1,040,000	0.34%
12	Montana	8,687,000	2.85%	37	Utah	973,000	0.32%
13	Oklahoma	8,614,000	2.83%	38	Arizona	770,000	0.25%
14	Wisconsin	8,449,000	2.77%	39	West Virginia	615,000	0.20%
15	Arkansas	7,863,000	2.58%	40	Delaware	556,000	0.18%
16	Michigan	6,713,000	2.20%	41	Nevada	495,000	0.16%
17	Colorado	5,580,000	1.83%	42	Vermont	434,000	0.14%
18	Kentucky	5,495,000	1.80%	43	New Jersey	382,000	0.13%
19	Mississippi	4,481,000	1.47%	44	Maine	351,000	0.12%
20	North Carolina	4,428,000	1.45%	45	Massachusetts	136,000	0.04%
21	Tennessee	4,379,000	1.44%	46	Connecticut	125,000	0.04%
22	California	4,340,000	1.42%	47	New Hampshire	92,000	0.03%
23	Idaho	4,215,000	1.38%	48	Hawaii	74,000	0.02%
24	Pennsylvania	4,067,000	1.33%	49	Rhode Island	10,000	0.00%
25	Washington	4,046,000	1.33%	–	Alaska*	N/A	N/A

Source: U.S. Department of Agriculture, National Agricultural Statistics Service,
"Annual Crop Summary" (January 1992)
*Not available.

Acres Harvested: Corn in 1991

National Total = 68,790,000 Acres*

RANK	STATE	ACRES	%	RANK	STATE	ACRES	%
1	Iowa	11,800,000	17.15%	26	Delaware	168,000	0.24%
2	Illinois	11,100,000	16.14%	27	Mississippi	150,000	0.22%
3	Nebraska	7,900,000	11.48%	28	California	130,000	0.19%
4	Minnesota	5,900,000	8.58%	29	Oklahoma	95,000	0.14%
5	Indiana	5,650,000	8.21%	30	Washington	88,000	0.13%
6	Ohio	3,600,000	5.23%	31	Arkansas	80,000	0.12%
7	South Dakota	3,250,000	4.72%	32	New Jersey	78,000	0.11%
8	Wisconsin	3,100,000	4.51%	33	Florida	75,000	0.11%
9	Michigan	2,300,000	3.34%	34	New Mexico	60,000	0.09%
10	Missouri	2,050,000	2.98%	35	West Virginia	55,000	0.08%
11	Kansas	1,600,000	2.33%	36	Idaho	45,000	0.07%
11	Texas	1,600,000	2.33%	37	Wyoming	40,000	0.06%
13	Kentucky	1,250,000	1.82%	38	Oregon	22,000	0.03%
14	North Carolina	950,000	1.38%	39	Utah	20,000	0.03%
14	Pennsylvania	950,000	1.38%	40	Montana	14,000	0.02%
16	Colorado	850,000	1.24%	41	Arizona	5,000	0.01%
17	New York	690,000	1.00%	–	Alaska**	N/A	N/A
18	North Dakota	600,000	0.87%	–	Connecticut**	N/A	N/A
19	Georgia	550,000	0.80%	–	Hawaii**	N/A	N/A
20	Tennessee	510,000	0.74%	–	Maine**	N/A	N/A
21	Maryland	460,000	0.67%	–	Massachusetts**	N/A	N/A
22	Virginia	320,000	0.47%	–	Nevada**	N/A	N/A
23	South Carolina	245,000	0.36%	–	New Hampshire**	N/A	N/A
24	Alabama	220,000	0.32%	–	Rhode Island**	N/A	N/A
24	Louisiana	220,000	0.32%	–	Vermont**	N/A	N/A

Source: U.S. Department of Agriculture, National Agricultural Statistics Service,
"Crop Production" (Cr Pr 2-2, August 1991)

*Forecasted totals.

**Not available.

Acres Harvested: Soybeans in 1991

National Total = 58,733,000 Acres*

RANK	STATE	ACRES	%
1	Illinois	9,100,000	15.49%
2	Iowa	8,700,000	14.81%
3	Minnesota	5,450,000	9.28%
4	Missouri	4,450,000	7.58%
5	Indiana	4,430,000	7.54%
6	Ohio	3,880,000	6.61%
7	Arkansas	3,100,000	5.28%
8	Nebraska	2,450,000	4.17%
9	South Dakota	2,250,000	3.83%
10	Kansas	1,950,000	3.32%
11	Mississippi	1,800,000	3.06%
12	Louisiana	1,390,000	2.37%
12	Michigan	1,390,000	2.37%
14	North Carolina	1,300,000	2.21%
15	Kentucky	1,130,000	1.92%
16	Tennessee	1,050,000	1.79%
17	South Carolina	640,000	1.09%
18	Georgia	620,000	1.06%
19	North Dakota	590,000	1.00%
20	Wisconsin	550,000	0.94%
21	Virginia	515,000	0.88%
22	Maryland	500,000	0.85%
23	Alabama	370,000	0.63%
24	Pennsylvania	305,000	0.52%
25	Delaware	250,000	0.43%

RANK	STATE	ACRES	%
26	Oklahoma	230,000	0.39%
27	Texas	180,000	0.31%
28	New Jersey	123,000	0.21%
29	Florida	40,000	0.07%
30	Alaska	0	0.00%
30	Arizona	0	0.00%
30	California	0	0.00%
30	Colorado	0	0.00%
30	Connecticut	0	0.00%
30	Hawaii	0	0.00%
30	Idaho	0	0.00%
30	Maine	0	0.00%
30	Massachusetts	0	0.00%
30	Montana	0	0.00%
30	Nevada	0	0.00%
30	New Hampshire	0	0.00%
30	New Mexico	0	0.00%
30	New York	0	0.00%
30	Oregon	0	0.00%
30	Rhode Island	0	0.00%
30	Utah	0	0.00%
30	Vermont	0	0.00%
30	Washington	0	0.00%
30	West Virginia	0	0.00%
30	Wyoming	0	0.00%

Source: U.S. Department of Agriculture, National Agricultural Statistics Service,
"Crop Production" (Cr Pr 2-2, August 1991)

*Forecasted totals.

Acres Harvested: Wheat in 1991

National Total = 58,137,000 Acres*

RANK	STATE	ACRES	%	RANK	STATE	ACRES	%
1	Kansas	10,800,000	18.58%	26	Mississippi	250,000	0.43%
2	North Dakota	9,930,000	17.08%	27	Virginia	245,000	0.42%
3	Oklahoma	5,000,000	8.60%	28	Louisiana	220,000	0.38%
4	Montana	4,579,000	7.88%	29	Wyoming	201,000	0.35%
5	South Dakota	3,136,000	5.39%	30	Maryland	195,000	0.34%
6	Texas	2,800,000	4.82%	31	Pennsylvania	175,000	0.30%
7	Colorado	2,336,000	4.02%	32	Utah	158,000	0.27%
8	Washington	2,200,000	3.78%	33	Wisconsin	127,000	0.22%
9	Minnesota	2,165,000	3.72%	34	Alabama	120,000	0.21%
10	Nebraska	2,100,000	3.61%	35	New York	110,000	0.19%
11	Missouri	1,550,000	2.67%	36	Arizona	73,000	0.13%
12	Illinois	1,400,000	2.41%	37	Delaware	67,000	0.12%
13	Idaho	1,160,000	2.00%	38	Iowa	50,000	0.09%
14	Ohio	1,100,000	1.89%	39	New Jersey	27,000	0.05%
15	Arkansas	930,000	1.60%	40	Florida	25,000	0.04%
16	Oregon	846,000	1.46%	41	West Virginia	11,000	0.02%
17	Indiana	750,000	1.29%	42	Nevada	9,000	0.02%
18	Michigan	560,000	0.96%	43	Alaska	0	0.00%
19	North Carolina	500,000	0.86%	43	Connecticut	0	0.00%
20	Georgia	450,000	0.77%	43	Hawaii	0	0.00%
21	Kentucky	430,000	0.74%	43	Maine	0	0.00%
22	California	422,000	0.73%	43	Massachusetts	0	0.00%
23	Tennessee	330,000	0.57%	43	New Hampshire	0	0.00%
24	New Mexico	320,000	0.55%	43	Rhode Island	0	0.00%
25	South Carolina	280,000	0.48%	43	Vermont	0	0.00%

Source: U.S. Department of Agriculture, National Agricultural Statistics Service,
    "Crop Production" (Cr Pr 2-2, August 1991)
*Forecasted totals.

Cattle on Farms in 1991

National Total = 99,436,000 Cattle*

RANK	STATE	CATTLE	%	RANK	STATE	CATTLE	%
1	Texas	13,400,000	13.48%	26	Georgia	1,420,000	1.43%
2	Nebraska	6,000,000	6.03%	27	New Mexico	1,340,000	1.35%
3	Kansas	5,700,000	5.73%	27	Washington	1,340,000	1.35%
4	Oklahoma	5,550,000	5.58%	29	Mississippi	1,290,000	1.30%
5	California	4,750,000	4.78%	30	Indiana	1,225,000	1.23%
5	Iowa	4,750,000	4.78%	30	Michigan	1,225,000	1.23%
7	Missouri	4,500,000	4.53%	32	Wyoming	1,190,000	1.20%
8	Wisconsin	4,170,000	4.19%	33	Louisiana	1,020,000	1.03%
9	South Dakota	3,400,000	3.42%	34	North Carolina	950,000	0.96%
10	Colorado	2,800,000	2.82%	35	Arizona	840,000	0.84%
11	Minnesota	2,760,000	2.78%	36	Utah	810,000	0.81%
12	Kentucky	2,500,000	2.51%	37	South Carolina	575,000	0.58%
13	Montana	2,400,000	2.41%	38	Nevada	520,000	0.52%
14	Tennessee	2,250,000	2.26%	39	West Virginia	515,000	0.52%
15	Illinois	2,000,000	2.01%	40	Maryland	320,000	0.32%
16	Florida	1,900,000	1.91%	41	Vermont	280,000	0.28%
17	Pennsylvania	1,820,000	1.83%	42	Hawaii	214,000	0.22%
18	Alabama	1,800,000	1.81%	43	Maine	119,000	0.12%
19	Idaho	1,740,000	1.75%	44	Connecticut	74,000	0.07%
20	Virginia	1,730,000	1.74%	45	Massachusetts	70,000	0.07%
21	North Dakota	1,700,000	1.71%	45	New Jersey	70,000	0.07%
22	Arkansas	1,690,000	1.70%	47	New Hampshire	46,000	0.05%
23	Ohio	1,580,000	1.59%	48	Delaware	28,000	0.03%
24	New York	1,550,000	1.56%	49	Alaska	7,500	0.01%
25	Oregon	1,500,000	1.51%	50	Rhode Island	7,000	0.01%

Source: U.S. Department of Agriculture, National Agricultural Statistics Service,
"Meat Animals: Production, Disposition and Income 1990" (MtAn 1-1 (91), April 1991)
As of January 1, 1991.

Milk Cows on Farms in 1990

National Total = 10,127,000 Milk Cows

RANK	STATE	MILK COWS	%	RANK	STATE	MILK COWS	%
1	Wisconsin	1,753,000	17.31%	26	Kansas	99,000	0.98%
2	California	1,135,000	11.21%	26	Oregon	99,000	0.98%
3	New York	768,000	7.58%	28	Arizona	94,000	0.93%
4	Minnesota	710,000	7.01%	29	North Dakota	88,000	0.87%
5	Pennsylvania	683,000	6.74%	30	Louisiana	81,000	0.80%
6	Texas	386,000	3.81%	30	New Mexico	81,000	0.80%
7	Michigan	344,000	3.40%	32	Utah	80,000	0.79%
8	Ohio	342,000	3.38%	33	Colorado	77,000	0.76%
9	Iowa	305,000	3.01%	34	Arkansas	69,000	0.68%
10	Washington	237,000	2.34%	35	Mississippi	62,000	0.61%
11	Missouri	230,000	2.27%	36	Alabama	42,000	0.41%
12	Kentucky	206,000	2.03%	36	Maine	42,000	0.41%
13	Tennessee	196,000	1.94%	38	South Carolina	35,000	0.35%
14	Illinois	195,000	1.93%	39	Connecticut	33,000	0.33%
15	Florida	180,000	1.78%	40	Massachusetts	31,000	0.31%
16	Idaho	179,000	1.77%	41	New Jersey	26,000	0.26%
17	Vermont	163,000	1.61%	42	Montana	24,000	0.24%
18	Indiana	156,000	1.54%	42	West Virginia	24,000	0.24%
19	Virginia	141,000	1.39%	44	Nevada	20,000	0.20%
20	South Dakota	140,000	1.38%	44	New Hampshire	20,000	0.20%
21	Georgia	111,000	1.10%	46	Hawaii	11,100	0.11%
22	Nebraska	104,000	1.03%	47	Wyoming	10,100	0.10%
23	Maryland	103,000	1.02%	48	Delaware	8,900	0.09%
24	Oklahoma	101,000	1.00%	49	Rhode Island	2,200	0.02%
25	North Carolina	100,000	0.99%	50	Alaska	1,200	0.01%

Source: U.S. Department of Agriculture, National Agricultural Statistics Service,
"Milk: Production, Disposition and Income 1990" (Da 1-2 (91), May 1991)

Hogs and Pigs on Farms in 1990

National Total = 54,362,000 Hogs and Pigs

RANK	STATE	HOGS AND PIGS	%	RANK	STATE	HOGS AND PIGS	%
1	Iowa	13,800,000	25.39%	26	California	180,000	0.33%
2	Illinois	5,700,000	10.49%	27	Maryland	162,000	0.30%
3	Minnesota	4,500,000	8.28%	28	Mississippi	149,000	0.27%
4	Indiana	4,300,000	7.91%	29	Florida	130,000	0.24%
4	Nebraska	4,300,000	7.91%	30	Arizona	110,000	0.20%
6	Missouri	2,800,000	5.15%	31	New York	103,000	0.19%
6	North Carolina	2,800,000	5.15%	32	Oregon	80,000	0.15%
8	Ohio	2,000,000	3.68%	33	Idaho	60,000	0.11%
9	South Dakota	1,770,000	3.26%	34	Washington	56,000	0.10%
10	Kansas	1,500,000	2.76%	35	Louisiana	50,000	0.09%
11	Michigan	1,250,000	2.30%	36	Hawaii	36,000	0.07%
12	Wisconsin	1,200,000	2.21%	37	Massachusetts	33,000	0.06%
13	Georgia	1,100,000	2.02%	37	Utah	33,000	0.06%
14	Kentucky	920,000	1.69%	39	Delaware	31,000	0.06%
14	Pennsylvania	920,000	1.69%	40	West Virginia	30,000	0.06%
16	Arkansas	760,000	1.40%	41	New Mexico	27,000	0.05%
17	Tennessee	620,000	1.14%	42	New Jersey	25,000	0.05%
18	Texas	550,000	1.01%	43	Wyoming	20,000	0.04%
19	Virginia	430,000	0.79%	44	Nevada	14,000	0.03%
20	South Carolina	410,000	0.75%	45	Maine	9,900	0.02%
21	Alabama	400,000	0.74%	46	New Hampshire	9,300	0.02%
22	Colorado	300,000	0.55%	47	Connecticut	6,900	0.01%
23	North Dakota	265,000	0.49%	48	Rhode Island	5,300	0.01%
24	Oklahoma	215,000	0.40%	49	Vermont	5,000	0.01%
25	Montana	185,000	0.34%	50	Alaska	1,200	0.00%

Source: U.S. Department of Agriculture, National Agricultural Statistics Service,
"Meat Animals: Production, Disposition and Income 1990" (MtAn 1-1 (91), April 1991)

Chickens in 1990
(Leading States Only)
National Total = 5,864,650,000 Chickens*

RANK	STATE	CHICKENS	%		RANK	STATE	CHICKENS	%
1	Arkansas	951,200,000	16.22%		26	Hawaii	1,940,000	0.03%
2	Georgia	854,500,000	14.57%		27	Kentucky	1,520,000	0.03%
3	Alabama	846,900,000	14.44%		28	Michigan	780,000	0.01%
4	North Carolina	540,300,000	9.21%					
5	Mississippi	413,000,000	7.04%					
6	Texas	338,100,000	5.77%					
7	Maryland	265,400,000	4.53%					
8	Delaware	231,700,000	3.95%					
9	California	231,100,000	3.94%					
10	Virginia	195,900,000	3.34%					
11	Oklahoma	142,000,000	2.42%					
12	Florida	119,600,000	2.04%					
13	Pennsylvania	115,600,000	1.97%					
14	Tennessee	99,100,000	1.69%					
15	Missouri	88,200,000	1.50%					
16	South Carolina	83,600,000	1.43%					
17	Minnesota	41,300,000	0.70%					
18	West Virginia	41,000,000	0.70%					
19	Washington	33,300,000	0.57%					
20	Oregon	23,700,000	0.40%					
21	Ohio	20,500,000	0.35%					
22	Wisconsin	14,000,000	0.24%					
23	Iowa	9,450,000	0.16%					
24	Nebraska	2,950,000	0.05%					
25	New York	2,400,000	0.04%					

Source: U.S. Department of Agriculture, National Agricultural Statistics Service,
    "Poultry: Productions and Value, 1990 Summary" (Pou 3-1 (91), April 1991)
*Broilers. Total includes numbers for states not shown separately.

Eggs Produced in 1990

National Total = 67,832,000,000 Eggs

RANK	STATE	EGGS	%	RANK	STATE	EGGS	%
1	California	7,472,000,000	11.02%	26	Illinois	793,000,000	1.17%
2	Indiana	5,445,000,000	8.03%	27	Colorado	788,000,000	1.16%
3	Pennsylvania	4,976,000,000	7.34%	28	Oregon	652,000,000	0.96%
4	Ohio	4,667,000,000	6.88%	29	Utah	456,000,000	0.67%
5	Georgia	4,302,000,000	6.34%	30	New Jersey	442,000,000	0.65%
6	Arkansas	3,620,000,000	5.34%	31	South Dakota	435,000,000	0.64%
7	Texas	3,317,000,000	4.89%	32	Kentucky	407,000,000	0.60%
8	North Carolina	2,986,000,000	4.40%	33	Kansas	404,000,000	0.60%
9	Florida	2,586,000,000	3.81%	34	New Mexico	283,000,000	0.42%
10	Minnesota	2,499,000,000	3.68%	35	Tennessee	277,000,000	0.41%
11	Alabama	2,206,000,000	3.25%	36	Louisiana	273,000,000	0.40%
12	Iowa	2,151,000,000	3.17%	37	Massachusetts	235,000,000	0.35%
13	Missouri	1,580,000,000	2.33%	38	Hawaii	227,500,000	0.34%
14	Mississippi	1,434,000,000	2.11%	39	Idaho	187,000,000	0.28%
15	South Carolina	1,422,000,000	2.10%	40	Montana	172,000,000	0.25%
16	Michigan	1,404,000,000	2.07%	41	Delaware	170,000,000	0.25%
17	Washington	1,287,000,000	1.90%	42	West Virginia	136,000,000	0.20%
18	Nebraska	1,202,000,000	1.77%	43	Arizona	73,000,000	0.11%
19	Maine	1,069,000,000	1.58%	44	North Dakota	51,000,000	0.08%
20	Connecticut	1,023,000,000	1.51%	45	New Hampshire	43,000,000	0.06%
21	New York	975,000,000	1.44%	46	Rhode Island	42,000,000	0.06%
22	Maryland	954,000,000	1.41%	47	Vermont	31,000,000	0.05%
23	Wisconsin	910,000,000	1.34%	48	Nevada	2,200,000	0.00%
24	Virginia	894,000,000	1.32%	49	Wyoming	1,700,000	0.00%
25	Oklahoma	869,000,000	1.28%	50	Alaska	700,000	0.00%

Source: U.S. Department of Agriculture, National Agricultural Statistics Service,
"Poultry: Production and Value 1990" (Pou 3-1 (91), April 1991)

II. CRIME AND LAW ENFORCEMENT

II. CRIME AND LAW ENFORCEMENT (continued)

Crimes in 1990

National Total = 14,475,613 Crimes

RANK	STATE	CRIMES	%	RANK	STATE	CRIMES	%
1	California	1,965,237	13.58%	26	Connecticut	177,068	1.22%
2	Texas	1,329,494	9.18%	27	Oklahoma	176,111	1.22%
3	New York	1,144,874	7.91%	28	Oregon	160,478	1.11%
4	Florida	1,139,934	7.87%	29	Kansas	128,664	0.89%
5	Illinois	678,416	4.69%	30	Kentucky	121,594	0.84%
6	Michigan	557,232	3.85%	31	Arkansas	114,408	0.79%
7	Ohio	525,373	3.63%	32	Iowa	113,871	0.79%
8	Georgia	438,161	3.03%	33	New Mexico	101,269	0.70%
9	New Jersey	421,080	2.91%	34	Mississippi	99,561	0.69%
10	Pennsylvania	413,018	2.85%	35	Utah	97,512	0.67%
11	North Carolina	363,638	2.51%	36	Nevada	72,874	0.50%
12	Massachusetts	318,742	2.20%	37	Hawaii	67,676	0.47%
13	Washington	302,850	2.09%	38	Nebraska	66,499	0.46%
14	Arizona	289,140	2.00%	39	Rhode Island	53,712	0.37%
15	Maryland	278,782	1.93%	40	Maine	45,406	0.31%
16	Virginia	274,757	1.90%	41	West Virginia	44,891	0.31%
17	Louisiana	273,736	1.89%	42	Idaho	40,845	0.28%
18	Missouri	262,024	1.81%	43	New Hampshire	40,435	0.28%
19	Indiana	259,651	1.79%	44	Montana	35,975	0.25%
20	Tennessee	246,346	1.70%	45	Delaware	35,709	0.25%
21	Wisconsin	215,000	1.49%	46	Alaska	28,342	0.20%
22	South Carolina	210,779	1.46%	47	Vermont	24,429	0.17%
23	Colorado	199,434	1.38%	48	South Dakota	20,249	0.14%
24	Alabama	198,604	1.37%	49	Wyoming	19,099	0.13%
25	Minnesota	198,577	1.37%	50	North Dakota	18,668	0.13%
					District of Columbia	65,389	0.45%

Source: Federal Bureau of Investigation,
  "1990 Crime in the United States" (August 11, 1991)

Percent Change in Number of Crimes: 1989 to 1990

National Percent Change = 1.6% Increase

RANK	STATE	PERCENT CHANGE		RANK	STATE	PERCENT CHANGE
1	Alaska	12.5		26	Kansas	2.8
2	Montana	11.7		27	Idaho	2.5
3	Tennessee	10.5		28	West Virginia	2.3
4	North Dakota	10.4		29	Florida	2.2
5	Delaware	9.1		30	Pennsylvania	2.1
6	Mississippi	8.1		31	Ohio	1.8
7	Virginia	7.0		32	New Hampshire	1.6
8	Maryland	6.8		33	New York	1.3
8	South Carolina	6.8		34	Arizona	0.9
10	Wisconsin	6.1		34	Nebraska	0.9
11	South Dakota	5.5		36	New Mexico	0.8
12	Vermont	5.4		37	Michigan	0.7
13	North Carolina	5.3		38	Utah	0.5
14	Massachusetts	5.0		39	Louisiana	0.1
15	Indiana	4.6		40	California	0.0
15	Nevada	4.6		41	Colorado	(0.4)
17	Arkansas	4.4		42	Oklahoma	(0.7)
18	Alabama	4.2		43	Missouri	(0.9)
19	Minnesota	4.1		44	Texas	(1.3)
20	Connecticut	3.7		45	Kentucky	(1.6)
20	Maine	3.7		46	Iowa	(1.8)
22	Wyoming	3.4		47	Hawaii	(2.9)
23	New Jersey	3.3		48	Washington	(3.5)
24	Illinois	3.2		49	Georgia	(3.7)
25	Rhode Island	3.0		50	Oregon	(7.6)

District of Columbia   5.2

Source: Federal Bureau of Investigation,
    "1990 Crime in the United States" (August 11, 1991)

Crime Rate in 1990

National Rate = 5,820.3 Crimes per 100,000 Population

RANK	STATE	RATE	RANK	STATE	RATE
1	Florida	8,810.8	26	Kansas	5,193.1
2	Arizona	7,888.7	27	Alaska	5,152.7
3	Texas	7,826.8	28	Missouri	5,120.6
4	Georgia	6,763.6	29	Tennessee	5,051.0
5	New Mexico	6,684.1	30	Alabama	4,915.2
6	California	6,603.6	31	Arkansas	4,866.9
7	Louisiana	6,486.7	32	Ohio	4,843.4
8	New York	6,363.8	33	Indiana	4,683.3
9	Washington	6,222.9	34	Minnesota	4,538.8
10	Hawaii	6,106.7	35	Montana	4,502.1
11	Nevada	6,063.6	36	Virginia	4,440.6
12	Colorado	6,053.7	37	Wisconsin	4,395.1
13	South Carolina	6,045.2	38	Vermont	4,340.9
14	Michigan	5,994.8	39	Nebraska	4,213.1
15	Illinois	5,935.1	40	Wyoming	4,210.6
16	Maryland	5,830.5	41	Iowa	4,100.9
17	Utah	5,659.9	42	Idaho	4,057.1
18	Oregon	5,646.0	43	Mississippi	3,869.1
19	Oklahoma	5,598.7	44	Maine	3,697.8
20	North Carolina	5,485.9	45	New Hampshire	3,645.2
21	New Jersey	5,447.2	46	Pennsylvania	3,476.1
22	Connecticut	5,386.7	47	Kentucky	3,299.4
23	Delaware	5,360.4	48	North Dakota	2,922.4
24	Rhode Island	5,352.7	49	South Dakota	2,909.3
25	Massachusetts	5,297.9	50	West Virginia	2,503.0

District of Columbia 10,774.3

Source: Federal Bureau of Investigation,

"1990 Crime in the United States" (August 11, 1991)

Violent Crimes in 1990

National Total = 1,820,127 Violent Crimes*

RANK	STATE	CRIMES	%	RANK	STATE	CRIMES	%
1	California	311,051	17.09%	26	Oregon	14,405	0.79%
2	New York	212,458	11.67%	27	Kentucky	14,386	0.79%
3	Florida	160,990	8.84%	28	Minnesota	13,392	0.74%
4	Texas	129,343	7.11%	29	Wisconsin	12,948	0.71%
5	Illinois	110,575	6.08%	30	Arkansas	12,511	0.69%
6	Michigan	73,468	4.04%	31	New Mexico	11,821	0.65%
7	Ohio	54,904	3.02%	32	Kansas	11,093	0.61%
8	Pennsylvania	51,213	2.81%	33	Mississippi	8,758	0.48%
9	New Jersey	50,057	2.75%	34	Iowa	8,321	0.46%
10	Georgia	48,996	2.69%	35	Nevada	7,222	0.40%
11	Massachusetts	44,300	2.43%	36	Nebraska	5,209	0.29%
12	Maryland	43,940	2.41%	37	Utah	4,892	0.27%
13	North Carolina	41,332	2.27%	38	Delaware	4,365	0.24%
14	Louisiana	37,914	2.08%	39	Rhode Island	4,334	0.24%
15	Missouri	36,602	2.01%	40	Hawaii	3,113	0.17%
16	South Carolina	34,050	1.87%	41	West Virginia	3,036	0.17%
17	Tennessee	32,698	1.80%	42	Alaska	2,885	0.16%
18	Alabama	28,630	1.57%	43	Idaho	2,776	0.15%
19	Indiana	26,275	1.44%	44	Maine	1,759	0.10%
20	Washington	24,410	1.34%	45	New Hampshire	1,459	0.08%
21	Arizona	23,911	1.31%	46	Wyoming	1,367	0.08%
22	Virginia	21,694	1.19%	47	Montana	1,273	0.07%
23	Connecticut	18,201	1.00%	48	South Dakota	1,133	0.06%
24	Colorado	17,328	0.95%	49	Vermont	716	0.04%
25	Oklahoma	17,222	0.95%	50	North Dakota	472	0.03%
					District of Columbia	14,919	0.82%

Source: Federal Bureau of Investigation,
   "1990 Crime in the United States" (August 11, 1991)

*Violent crimes are offenses of murder, forcible rape, robbery and aggravated assault.

Percent Change in Number of Violent Crimes: 1989 to 1990

National Percent Change = 10.6% Increase*

RANK	STATE	PERCENT CHANGE	RANK	STATE	PERCENT CHANGE
1	Montana	36.1	26	Louisiana	10.7
2	Tennessee	20.6	27	Kansas	10.1
3	Wisconsin	19.5	28	Alaska	10.0
4	South Carolina	19.2	28	Iowa	10.0
5	Alabama	17.7	30	New Mexico	9.9
6	South Dakota	16.9	31	Arkansas	9.8
7	Delaware	16.6	31	Connecticut	9.8
8	Nebraska	15.7	33	California	9.5
9	Indiana	15.6	34	Maryland	9.4
9	Texas	15.6	35	Oklahoma	8.7
11	North Carolina	15.1	35	Washington	8.7
12	Rhode Island	14.9	37	Kentucky	8.1
13	Florida	14.5	38	Idaho	7.5
14	Virginia	13.8	39	Mississippi	7.4
15	North Dakota	13.2	39	Ohio	7.4
16	Pennsylvania	12.3	41	Minnesota	6.7
17	Arizona	12.2	42	New Jersey	6.3
17	Missouri	12.2	43	Maine	5.0
19	Illinois	12.1	44	New York	4.6
20	Michigan	11.7	45	Nevada	4.0
21	West Virginia	11.5	46	Hawaii	3.6
22	Wyoming	11.4	47	Georgia	3.5
23	Massachusetts	11.0	48	Oregon	(1.5)
24	Colorado	10.8	49	Vermont	(4.9)
24	Utah	10.8	50	New Hampshire	(21.8)

District of Columbia   15.3

Source: Federal Bureau of Investigation,
 "1990 Crime in the United States" (August 11, 1991)
*Violent crimes are offenses of murder, forcible rape, robbery and aggravated assault.

Violent Crime Rate in 1990

National Rate = 731.8 Violent Crimes per 100,000 Population*

RANK	STATE	RATE	RANK	STATE	RATE
1	Florida	1,244.3	26	Oregon	506.8
2	New York	1,180.9	27	Ohio	506.2
3	California	1,045.2	28	Washington	501.6
4	South Carolina	976.6	29	Indiana	473.9
5	Illinois	967.4	30	Kansas	447.7
6	Maryland	919.0	31	Rhode Island	431.9
7	Louisiana	898.4	32	Pennsylvania	431.0
8	Michigan	790.4	33	Kentucky	390.4
9	New Mexico	780.2	34	Virginia	350.6
10	Texas	761.4	35	Mississippi	340.4
11	Georgia	756.3	36	Nebraska	330.0
12	Massachusetts	736.3	37	Minnesota	306.1
13	Missouri	715.3	38	Wyoming	301.4
14	Alabama	708.6	39	Iowa	299.7
15	Tennessee	670.4	40	Utah	283.9
16	Delaware	655.2	41	Hawaii	280.9
17	Arizona	652.4	42	Idaho	275.7
18	New Jersey	647.6	43	Wisconsin	264.7
19	North Carolina	623.5	44	West Virginia	169.3
20	Nevada	600.9	45	South Dakota	162.8
21	Connecticut	553.7	46	Montana	159.3
22	Oklahoma	547.5	47	Maine	143.2
23	Arkansas	532.2	48	New Hampshire	131.5
24	Colorado	526.0	49	Vermont	127.2
25	Alaska	524.5	50	North Dakota	73.9

District of Columbia   2,458.2

Source: Federal Bureau of Investigation,
     "1990 Crime in the United States" (August 11, 1991)

*Violent crimes are offenses of murder, forcible rape, robbery and aggravated assault.

Murders in 1990

National Total = 23,438 Murders*

RANK	STATE	MURDERS	%		RANK	STATE	MURDERS	%
1	California	3,553	15.16%		26	Washington	238	1.02%
2	New York	2,605	11.11%		27	Wisconsin	225	0.96%
3	Texas	2,389	10.19%		28	Connecticut	166	0.71%
4	Florida	1,379	5.88%		29	New Mexico	139	0.59%
5	Illinois	1,182	5.04%		30	Colorado	138	0.59%
6	Michigan	971	4.14%		31	Minnesota	117	0.50%
7	Pennsylvania	801	3.42%		32	Nevada	116	0.49%
8	Georgia	767	3.27%		33	Oregon	108	0.46%
9	Louisiana	724	3.09%		34	West Virginia	102	0.44%
10	North Carolina	711	3.03%		35	Kansas	98	0.42%
11	Ohio	663	2.83%		36	Iowa	54	0.23%
12	Maryland	552	2.36%		37	Utah	52	0.22%
13	Virginia	545	2.33%		38	Rhode Island	48	0.20%
14	Tennessee	511	2.18%		39	Hawaii	44	0.19%
15	Alabama	467	1.99%		40	Nebraska	43	0.18%
16	Missouri	449	1.92%		41	Alaska	41	0.17%
17	New Jersey	432	1.84%		42	Montana	39	0.17%
18	South Carolina	390	1.66%		43	Delaware	33	0.14%
19	Indiana	344	1.47%		44	Maine	30	0.13%
20	Mississippi	313	1.34%		45	Idaho	27	0.12%
21	Arizona	284	1.21%		46	Wyoming	22	0.09%
22	Kentucky	264	1.13%		47	New Hampshire	21	0.09%
23	Oklahoma	253	1.08%		48	South Dakota	14	0.06%
24	Massachusetts	243	1.04%		49	Vermont	13	0.06%
25	Arkansas	241	1.03%		50	North Dakota	5	0.02%
						District of Columbia	472	2.01%

Source: Federal Bureau of Investigation,
    "1990 Crime in the United States" (August 11, 1991)
*Includes nonnegligent manslaughter.

Percent Change in Number of Murders: 1989 to 1990

National Percent Change = 9.0% Increase*

RANK	STATE	PERCENT CHANGE	RANK	STATE	PERCENT CHANGE
1	Montana	69.6	26	Pennsylvania	6.4
2	South Dakota	55.6	27	Minnesota	5.4
3	Wisconsin	27.8	28	New Mexico	5.3
4	Nevada	27.5	29	Wyoming	4.8
5	North Dakota	25.0	30	Idaho	3.8
6	Mississippi	23.7	31	Ohio	1.7
7	Tennessee	22.5	32	Maryland	1.5
8	South Carolina	21.9	33	Iowa	0.0
9	North Carolina	21.7	34	Florida	(1.9)
10	Oklahoma	20.5	35	Rhode Island	(2.0)
11	Arizona	19.8	36	Michigan	(2.2)
12	Arkansas	18.7	37	Alaska	(2.4)
13	Vermont	18.2	38	Indiana	(2.5)
14	Texas	17.7	39	Delaware	(2.9)
15	New York	16.0	40	Massachusetts	(4.3)
16	Utah	15.6	41	Colorado	(5.5)
17	Washington	13.9	42	Georgia	(6.5)
18	Virginia	13.5	43	Kentucky	(9.9)
19	California	12.5	44	Connecticut	(12.6)
19	Illinois	12.5	45	West Virginia	(15.7)
21	Alabama	10.9	46	Hawaii	(17.0)
21	Louisiana	10.9	47	Oregon	(19.4)
23	Missouri	9.8	48	Maine	(23.1)
24	New Jersey	9.6	49	Kansas	(29.0)
25	Nebraska	7.5	50	New Hampshire	(41.7)

District of Columbia   8.8

Source: Federal Bureau of Investigation,

    "1990 Crime in the United States" (August 11, 1991)

Includes nonnegligent manslaughter.

Murder Rate in 1990

National Murder Rate = 9.4 Murders per 100,000 Population*

RANK	STATE	RATE	RANK	STATE	RATE
1	Louisiana	17.2	26	Ohio	6.1
2	New York	14.5	27	West Virginia	5.7
3	Texas	14.1	28	New Jersey	5.6
4	Mississippi	12.2	29	Connecticut	5.1
5	California	11.9	30	Delaware	5.0
6	Georgia	11.8	31	Montana	4.9
7	Alabama	11.6	31	Washington	4.9
8	Maryland	11.5	31	Wyoming	4.9
9	South Carolina	11.2	34	Rhode Island	4.8
10	Florida	10.7	35	Wisconsin	4.6
10	North Carolina	10.7	36	Colorado	4.2
12	Tennessee	10.5	37	Hawaii	4.0
13	Michigan	10.4	37	Kansas	4.0
14	Arkansas	10.3	37	Massachusetts	4.0
14	Illinois	10.3	40	Oregon	3.8
16	Nevada	9.7	41	Utah	3.0
17	New Mexico	9.2	42	Idaho	2.7
18	Missouri	8.8	42	Minnesota	2.7
18	Virginia	8.8	42	Nebraska	2.7
20	Oklahoma	8.0	45	Maine	2.4
21	Arizona	7.7	46	Vermont	2.3
22	Alaska	7.5	47	South Dakota	2.0
23	Kentucky	7.2	48	Iowa	1.9
24	Pennsylvania	6.7	48	New Hampshire	1.9
25	Indiana	6.2	50	North Dakota	0.8

District of Columbia   77.8

Source: Federal Bureau of Investigation,
     "1990 Crime in the United States" (August 11, 1991)
*Includes nonnegligent manslaughter.

Rapes in 1990

National Total = 102,555 Rapes*

RANK	STATE	RAPES	%
1	California	12,688	12.37%
2	Texas	8,750	8.53%
3	Michigan	7,209	7.03%
4	Florida	6,781	6.61%
5	New York	5,368	5.23%
6	Ohio	5,075	4.95%
7	Illinois	4,505	4.39%
8	Georgia	3,472	3.39%
9	Washington	3,115	3.04%
10	Pennsylvania	3,068	2.99%
11	Tennessee	2,415	2.35%
12	New Jersey	2,307	2.25%
13	North Carolina	2,272	2.22%
14	Maryland	2,185	2.13%
15	Indiana	2,103	2.05%
16	Massachusetts	2,030	1.98%
17	Virginia	1,915	1.87%
18	South Carolina	1,873	1.83%
19	Louisiana	1,781	1.74%
20	Missouri	1,663	1.62%
21	Colorado	1,521	1.48%
22	Arizona	1,500	1.46%
23	Minnesota	1,487	1.45%
24	Oklahoma	1,479	1.44%
25	Oregon	1,332	1.30%

RANK	STATE	RAPES	%
26	Alabama	1,319	1.29%
27	Mississippi	1,134	1.11%
28	Kentucky	1,068	1.04%
29	Arkansas	1,019	0.99%
30	Wisconsin	1,013	0.99%
31	Kansas	1,002	0.98%
32	Connecticut	918	0.90%
33	New Mexico	753	0.73%
34	Nevada	748	0.73%
35	Utah	651	0.63%
36	Delaware	587	0.57%
37	Iowa	510	0.50%
38	Nebraska	473	0.46%
39	West Virginia	423	0.41%
40	Alaska	401	0.39%
41	New Hampshire	386	0.38%
42	Hawaii	360	0.35%
43	Idaho	275	0.27%
44	Rhode Island	248	0.24%
45	Maine	242	0.24%
46	South Dakota	239	0.23%
47	Montana	195	0.19%
48	Vermont	146	0.14%
49	Wyoming	134	0.13%
50	North Dakota	114	0.11%
	District of Columbia	303	0.30%

Source: Federal Bureau of Investigation,
"1990 Crime in the United States" (August 11, 1991)
*Forcible rape.

Percent Change in Number of Rapes: 1989 to 1990

National Percent Change = 8.5% Increase*

RANK	STATE	PERCENT CHANGE	RANK	STATE	PERCENT CHANGE
1	North Dakota	46.2	26	Minnesota	9.1
2	Alaska	43.7	27	Michigan	8.8
3	Montana	34.5	28	Illinois	8.3
4	Utah	33.1	29	Massachusetts	7.9
5	Colorado	26.5	30	Florida	7.7
6	Nebraska	24.1	31	New Mexico	7.3
7	Maryland	22.5	32	Tennessee	6.4
8	Oklahoma	22.3	33	Louisiana	6.3
9	West Virginia	21.9	34	California	6.0
10	New Hampshire	18.0	34	Washington	6.0
11	Virginia	16.9	36	Maine	5.7
12	Arizona	16.6	37	Missouri	4.8
12	Indiana	16.6	38	South Dakota	4.4
14	Idaho	16.5	39	Ohio	4.2
14	Kentucky	16.5	40	Pennsylvania	3.5
16	North Carolina	15.7	41	Alabama	3.4
17	South Carolina	14.8	42	Delaware	3.2
18	Nevada	13.0	43	Connecticut	2.9
19	Mississippi	11.5	44	New York	2.4
19	Vermont	11.5	45	Wisconsin	2.0
21	Iowa	11.1	46	Oregon	1.4
22	Arkansas	10.3	47	Wyoming	0.0
23	Georgia	10.2	48	New Jersey	(5.8)
24	Texas	10.0	49	Rhode Island	(6.8)
25	Kansas	9.3	50	Hawaii	(27.4)

District of Columbia   62.9

Source: Federal Bureau of Investigation,
    "1990 Crime in the United States" (August 11, 1991)
*Forcible rape.

Rape Rate in 1990

National Rate = 41.2 Rapes per 100,000 Population*

RANK	STATE	RATE		RANK	STATE	RATE
1	Delaware	88.1		26	New Hampshire	34.8
2	Michigan	77.6		27	North Carolina	34.3
3	Alaska	72.9		28	Minnesota	34.0
4	Washington	64.0		28	South Dakota	34.0
5	Nevada	62.2		30	Massachusetts	33.7
6	South Carolina	53.7		31	Alabama	32.6
7	Georgia	53.6		32	Hawaii	32.5
8	Florida	52.4		32	Missouri	32.5
9	Texas	51.5		34	Virginia	31.0
10	New Mexico	49.7		35	Nebraska	30.0
11	Tennessee	49.5		36	New Jersey	29.8
12	Oklahoma	47.0		36	New York	29.8
13	Oregon	46.9		38	Wyoming	29.5
14	Ohio	46.8		39	Kentucky	29.0
15	Colorado	46.2		40	Connecticut	27.9
16	Maryland	45.7		41	Idaho	27.3
17	Mississippi	44.1		42	Vermont	25.9
18	Arkansas	43.3		43	Pennsylvania	25.8
19	California	42.6		44	Rhode Island	24.7
20	Louisiana	42.2		45	Montana	24.4
21	Arizona	40.9		46	West Virginia	23.6
22	Kansas	40.4		47	Wisconsin	20.7
23	Illinois	39.4		48	Maine	19.7
24	Indiana	37.9		49	Iowa	18.4
25	Utah	37.8		50	North Dakota	17.8

District of Columbia   49.9

Source: Federal Bureau of Investigation,
    "1990 Crime in the United States" (August 11, 1991)
*Forcible rape.

Robberies in 1990

National Total = 639,271 Robberies*

RANK	STATE	ROBBERIES	%	RANK	STATE	ROBBERIES	%
1	New York	112,380	17.58%	26	Minnesota	4,057	0.63%
2	California	112,208	17.55%	27	Oklahoma	3,836	0.60%
3	Florida	53,928	8.44%	28	Colorado	2,985	0.47%
4	Illinois	45,038	7.05%	29	Kansas	2,914	0.46%
5	Texas	44,297	6.93%	30	Nevada	2,864	0.45%
6	New Jersey	23,269	3.64%	31	Arkansas	2,661	0.42%
7	Michigan	21,752	3.40%	32	Kentucky	2,545	0.40%
8	Pennsylvania	20,930	3.27%	33	Mississippi	2,217	0.35%
9	Ohio	20,451	3.20%	34	New Mexico	1,744	0.27%
10	Maryland	17,394	2.72%	35	Rhode Island	1,224	0.19%
11	Georgia	17,067	2.67%	36	Delaware	1,098	0.17%
12	Massachusetts	13,062	2.04%	37	Iowa	1,089	0.17%
13	Louisiana	11,387	1.78%	38	Hawaii	1,013	0.16%
14	Missouri	11,073	1.73%	39	Utah	980	0.15%
15	North Carolina	10,082	1.58%	40	Nebraska	807	0.13%
16	Tennessee	9,325	1.46%	41	West Virginia	680	0.11%
17	Connecticut	7,717	1.21%	42	Alaska	422	0.07%
18	Virginia	7,626	1.19%	43	Maine	308	0.05%
19	Washington	6,326	0.99%	44	New Hampshire	302	0.05%
20	Arizona	5,897	0.92%	45	Montana	173	0.03%
21	Alabama	5,805	0.91%	46	Idaho	151	0.02%
22	Indiana	5,619	0.88%	47	South Dakota	86	0.01%
23	Wisconsin	5,514	0.86%	48	Wyoming	72	0.01%
24	South Carolina	5,313	0.83%	49	Vermont	66	0.01%
25	Oregon	4,102	0.64%	50	North Dakota	50	0.01%

District of Columbia 7,365 1.15%

Source: Federal Bureau of Investigation,
   "1990 Crime in the United States" (August 11, 1991)
*Robbery is the taking of anything of value by force or threat of force.

Percent Change in Number of Robberies: 1989 to 1990

National Percent Change = 10.5% Increase*

RANK	STATE	PERCENT CHANGE	RANK	STATE	PERCENT CHANGE
1	Wisconsin	50.7	26	New Mexico	8.5
2	Montana	26.3	27	New York	8.1
3	Arizona	19.3	28	Mississippi	8.0
4	Alaska	18.5	29	Michigan	5.5
5	Tennessee	17.7	30	Florida	5.4
6	Delaware	17.6	31	Alabama	5.3
7	Virginia	17.4	32	Maine	5.1
8	Texas	16.8	33	Nevada	2.9
9	California	16.4	34	South Dakota	2.4
10	Kansas	16.2	35	Arkansas	0.0
10	South Carolina	16.2	35	Colorado	0.0
12	Pennsylvania	16.1	37	Idaho	(0.7)
13	Illinois	15.1	38	Indiana	(0.9)
14	North Carolina	15.0	39	Iowa	(1.7)
15	New Hampshire	14.4	39	Minnesota	(1.7)
16	Maryland	11.6	41	Georgia	(2.2)
17	Connecticut	10.9	42	Nebraska	(3.6)
18	Missouri	10.1	43	Oregon	(4.2)
18	New Jersey	10.1	44	Washington	(5.2)
20	Ohio	9.7	45	Oklahoma	(5.7)
21	Hawaii	9.5	46	Kentucky	(10.3)
21	Louisiana	9.5	47	Wyoming	(11.1)
23	Rhode Island	9.1	48	West Virginia	(14.2)
23	Utah	9.1	49	North Dakota	(18.0)
25	Massachusetts	9.0	50	Vermont	(35.3)

District of Columbia 12.6

Source: Federal Bureau of Investigation,
"1990 Crime in the United States" (August 11, 1991)
*Robbery is the taking of anything of value by force or threat of force.

Robbery Rate in 1990

National Rate = 257 Robberies per 100,000 Population*

RANK	STATE	RATE		RANK	STATE	RATE
1	New York	624.7		26	Rhode Island	122.0
2	Florida	416.8		27	Oklahoma	121.9
3	Illinois	394.0		28	Kansas	117.6
4	California	377.0		29	New Mexico	115.1
5	Maryland	363.8		30	Arkansas	113.2
6	New Jersey	301.0		31	Wisconsin	112.7
7	Louisiana	269.8		32	Indiana	101.3
8	Georgia	263.5		33	Minnesota	92.7
9	Texas	260.8		34	Hawaii	91.4
10	Nevada	238.3		35	Colorado	90.6
11	Connecticut	234.8		36	Mississippi	86.2
12	Michigan	234.0		37	Alaska	76.7
13	Massachusetts	217.1		38	Kentucky	69.1
14	Missouri	216.4		39	Utah	56.9
15	Tennessee	191.2		40	Nebraska	51.1
16	Ohio	188.5		41	Iowa	39.2
17	Pennsylvania	176.2		42	West Virginia	37.9
18	Delaware	164.8		43	New Hampshire	27.2
19	Arizona	160.9		44	Maine	25.1
20	South Carolina	152.4		45	Montana	21.7
21	North Carolina	152.1		46	Wyoming	15.9
22	Oregon	144.3		47	Idaho	15.0
23	Alabama	143.7		48	South Dakota	12.4
24	Washington	130.0		49	Vermont	11.7
25	Virginia	123.3		50	North Dakota	7.8

District of Columbia   1,213.5

Source: Federal Bureau of Investigation,
"1990 Crime in the United States" (August 11, 1991)
*Robbery is the taking of anything of value by force or threat of force.

Aggravated Assaults in 1990

National Total = 1,054,863 Aggravated Assaults*

RANK	STATE	ASSAULTS	%	RANK	STATE	ASSAULTS	%
1	California	182,602	17.31%	26	Connecticut	9,400	0.89%
2	Florida	98,902	9.38%	27	New Mexico	9,185	0.87%
3	New York	92,105	8.73%	28	Oregon	8,863	0.84%
4	Texas	73,907	7.01%	29	Arkansas	8,590	0.81%
5	Illinois	59,850	5.67%	30	Minnesota	7,731	0.73%
6	Michigan	43,536	4.13%	31	Kansas	7,079	0.67%
7	Massachusetts	28,965	2.75%	32	Iowa	6,668	0.63%
8	Ohio	28,715	2.72%	33	Wisconsin	6,196	0.59%
9	North Carolina	28,267	2.68%	34	Mississippi	5,094	0.48%
10	Georgia	27,690	2.62%	35	Nebraska	3,886	0.37%
11	South Carolina	26,474	2.51%	36	Nevada	3,494	0.33%
12	Pennsylvania	26,414	2.50%	37	Utah	3,209	0.30%
13	New Jersey	24,049	2.28%	38	Rhode Island	2,814	0.27%
14	Louisiana	24,022	2.28%	39	Delaware	2,647	0.25%
15	Maryland	23,809	2.26%	40	Idaho	2,323	0.22%
16	Missouri	23,417	2.22%	41	Alaska	2,021	0.19%
17	Alabama	21,039	1.99%	42	West Virginia	1,831	0.17%
18	Tennessee	20,447	1.94%	43	Hawaii	1,696	0.16%
19	Indiana	18,209	1.73%	44	Maine	1,179	0.11%
20	Arizona	16,230	1.54%	45	Wyoming	1,139	0.11%
21	Washington	14,731	1.40%	46	Montana	866	0.08%
22	Colorado	12,684	1.20%	47	South Dakota	794	0.08%
23	Oklahoma	11,654	1.10%	48	New Hampshire	750	0.07%
24	Virginia	11,608	1.10%	49	Vermont	491	0.05%
25	Kentucky	10,509	1.00%	50	North Dakota	303	0.03%
					District of Columbia	6,779	0.64%

Source: Federal Bureau of Investigation,

"1990 Crime in the United States" (August 11, 1991)

*Aggravated assault is an attack for the purpose of inflicting severe bodily injury.

Percent Change in Number of Aggravated Assaults: 1989 to 1990

National Percent Change = 10.8% Increase*

RANK	STATE	PERCENT CHANGE	RANK	STATE	PERCENT CHANGE
1	Montana	37.5	26	Virginia	11.1
2	West Virginia	25.2	27	Hawaii	10.8
3	Tennessee	23.9	27	Pennsylvania	10.8
4	Alabama	22.9	29	North Dakota	10.6
5	South Dakota	22.7	30	New Mexico	10.5
6	Indiana	22.2	31	Illinois	10.3
7	Florida	21.1	32	Connecticut	10.1
8	Rhode Island	20.5	33	Arizona	9.3
9	South Carolina	20.1	34	Kansas	8.7
10	Delaware	19.9	35	Utah	7.5
11	Nebraska	19.8	36	Idaho	7.1
12	Washington	16.5	36	Maryland	7.1
13	Michigan	16.0	38	Georgia	6.8
14	Texas	15.5	39	Ohio	6.5
15	North Carolina	15.0	40	California	5.8
16	Wyoming	14.9	41	Maine	5.7
17	Missouri	13.8	42	Mississippi	5.4
18	Kentucky	13.5	43	New Jersey	4.0
19	Arkansas	12.9	44	Alaska	3.9
20	Oklahoma	12.5	45	Wisconsin	3.2
21	Massachusetts	12.3	46	Nevada	2.5
22	Colorado	12.2	47	New York	0.6
22	Iowa	12.2	48	Oregon	(0.4)
24	Louisiana	11.6	49	Vermont	(3.5)
25	Minnesota	11.3	50	New Hampshire	(39.4)

District of Columbia   17.4

Source: Federal Bureau of Investigation,

"1990 Crime in the United States" (August 11, 1991)

*Aggravated assault is an attack for the purpose of inflicting severe bodily injury.

Aggravated Assault Rate in 1990

National Rate = 424.1 Aggravated Assaults per 100,000 Population*

RANK	STATE	RATE	RANK	STATE	RATE
1	Florida	764.4	26	Washington	302.7
2	South Carolina	759.3	27	Nevada	290.7
3	California	613.6	28	Connecticut	286.0
4	New Mexico	606.2	29	Kansas	285.7
5	Louisiana	569.2	30	Kentucky	285.2
6	Illinois	523.6	31	Rhode Island	280.4
7	Alabama	520.7	32	Ohio	264.7
8	New York	512.0	33	Wyoming	251.1
9	Maryland	497.9	34	Nebraska	246.2
10	Massachusetts	481.4	35	Iowa	240.1
11	Michigan	468.4	36	Idaho	230.7
12	Missouri	457.6	37	Pennsylvania	222.3
13	Arizona	442.8	38	Mississippi	198.0
14	Texas	435.1	39	Virginia	187.6
15	Georgia	427.4	40	Utah	186.3
16	North Carolina	426.4	41	Minnesota	176.7
17	Tennessee	419.2	42	Hawaii	153.0
18	Delaware	397.3	43	Wisconsin	126.7
19	Colorado	385.0	44	South Dakota	114.1
20	Oklahoma	370.5	45	Montana	108.4
21	Alaska	367.4	46	West Virginia	102.1
22	Arkansas	365.4	47	Maine	96.0
23	Indiana	328.4	48	Vermont	87.2
24	Oregon	311.8	49	New Hampshire	67.6
25	New Jersey	311.1	50	North Dakota	47.4

District of Columbia   1,117.0

Source: Federal Bureau of Investigation,
"1990 Crime in the United States" (August 11, 1991)

*Aggravated assault is an attack for the purpose of inflicting severe bodily injury.

Property Crimes in 1990

National Total = 12,655,486 Property Crimes*

RANK	STATE	CRIMES	%	RANK	STATE	CRIMES	%
1	California	1,654,186	13.07%	26	Oklahoma	158,889	1.26%
2	Texas	1,200,151	9.48%	27	Connecticut	158,867	1.26%
3	Florida	978,944	7.74%	28	Oregon	146,073	1.15%
4	New York	932,416	7.37%	29	Kansas	117,571	0.93%
5	Illinois	567,841	4.49%	30	Kentucky	107,208	0.85%
6	Michigan	483,764	3.82%	31	Iowa	105,550	0.83%
7	Ohio	470,469	3.72%	32	Arkansas	101,897	0.81%
8	Georgia	389,165	3.08%	33	Utah	92,620	0.73%
9	New Jersey	371,023	2.93%	34	Mississippi	90,803	0.72%
10	Pennsylvania	361,805	2.86%	35	New Mexico	89,448	0.71%
11	North Carolina	322,306	2.55%	36	Nevada	65,652	0.52%
12	Washington	278,440	2.20%	37	Hawaii	64,563	0.51%
13	Massachusetts	274,442	2.17%	38	Nebraska	61,290	0.48%
14	Arizona	265,229	2.10%	39	Rhode Island	49,378	0.39%
15	Virginia	253,063	2.00%	40	Maine	43,647	0.34%
16	Louisiana	235,822	1.86%	41	West Virginia	41,855	0.33%
17	Maryland	234,842	1.86%	42	New Hampshire	38,976	0.31%
18	Indiana	233,376	1.84%	43	Idaho	38,069	0.30%
19	Missouri	225,422	1.78%	44	Montana	34,702	0.27%
20	Tennessee	213,648	1.69%	45	Delaware	31,344	0.25%
21	Wisconsin	202,052	1.60%	46	Alaska	25,457	0.20%
22	Minnesota	185,185	1.46%	47	Vermont	23,713	0.19%
23	Colorado	182,106	1.44%	48	South Dakota	19,116	0.15%
24	South Carolina	176,729	1.40%	49	North Dakota	18,196	0.14%
25	Alabama	169,974	1.34%	50	Wyoming	17,732	0.14%

District of Columbia   50,470   0.40%

Source: Federal Bureau of Investigation,

"1990 Crime in the United States" (August 11, 1991)

*Property crimes are offenses of burglary, larceny-theft and motor vehicle theft.

Percent Change in Number of Property Crimes: 1989 to 1990

National Percent Change = 0.4% Increase*

RANK	STATE	RATE	RANK	STATE	RATE
1	Alaska	12.8	25	Kansas	2.1
2	Montana	10.9	25	Rhode Island	2.1
3	North Dakota	10.4	28	West Virginia	1.7
4	Tennessee	9.1	29	Illinois	1.6
5	Delaware	8.1	30	Ohio	1.1
5	Mississippi	8.1	31	Pennsylvania	0.8
7	Virginia	6.4	32	New York	0.6
8	Maryland	6.3	33	Florida	0.4
9	Vermont	5.7	34	Arizona	0.0
10	Wisconsin	5.3	34	Utah	0.0
11	South Dakota	4.9	36	Nebraska	(0.2)
12	Nevada	4.7	37	New Mexico	(0.3)
12	South Carolina	4.7	38	Michigan	(0.8)
14	North Carolina	4.2	39	Colorado	(1.4)
15	Massachusetts	4.0	39	Louisiana	(1.4)
16	Minnesota	3.9	41	California	(1.6)
17	Arkansas	3.8	42	Oklahoma	(1.7)
18	Maine	3.6	43	Iowa	(2.6)
19	Indiana	3.5	44	Kentucky	(2.8)
20	Connecticut	3.1	44	Missouri	(2.8)
21	New Jersey	2.9	44	Texas	(2.8)
22	Wyoming	2.8	47	Hawaii	(3.2)
23	New Hampshire	2.7	48	Washington	(4.5)
24	Alabama	2.2	49	Georgia	(4.6)
25	Idaho	2.1	50	Oregon	(8.2)

District of Columbia   2.5

Source: Federal Bureau of Investigation,

    "1990 Crime in the United States" (August 11, 1991)

*Property crimes are offenses of burglary, larceny-theft and motor vehicle theft.

Property Crime Rate in 1990

National Rate = 5,088.5 Property Crimes per 100,000 Population*

RANK	STATE	RATE	RANK	STATE	RATE
1	Florida	7,566.5	26	Alaska	4,628.2
2	Arizona	7,236.4	27	Massachusetts	4,561.5
3	Texas	7,065.3	28	Missouri	4,405.3
4	Georgia	6,007.3	29	Tennessee	4,380.6
5	New Mexico	5,903.9	30	Montana	4,342.8
6	Hawaii	5,825.8	31	Ohio	4,337.3
7	Washington	5,721.3	32	Arkansas	4,334.7
8	Louisiana	5,588.2	33	Minnesota	4,232.7
9	California	5,558.4	34	Vermont	4,213.7
10	Colorado	5,527.8	35	Indiana	4,209.4
11	Nevada	5,462.7	36	Alabama	4,206.7
12	Utah	5,376.0	37	Wisconsin	4,130.4
13	Michigan	5,204.4	38	Virginia	4,090.0
14	New York	5,182.8	39	Wyoming	3,909.3
15	Oregon	5,139.2	40	Nebraska	3,883.1
16	South Carolina	5,068.7	41	Iowa	3,801.2
17	Oklahoma	5,051.2	42	Idaho	3,781.4
18	Illinois	4,967.7	43	Maine	3,554.5
19	Rhode Island	4,920.8	44	Mississippi	3,528.8
20	Maryland	4,911.5	45	New Hampshire	3,513.7
21	North Carolina	4,862.3	46	Pennsylvania	3,045.1
22	Connecticut	4,833.0	47	Kentucky	2,909.1
23	New Jersey	4,799.7	48	North Dakota	2,848.5
24	Kansas	4,745.4	49	South Dakota	2,746.5
25	Delaware	4,705.1	50	West Virginia	2,333.7

District of Columbia   8,316.0

Source: Federal Bureau of Investigation,

    "1990 Crime in the United States" (August 11, 1991)

*Property crimes are offenses of burglary, larceny-theft and mother vehicle theft.

Burglaries in 1990

National Total = 3,073,909 Burglaries*

RANK	STATE	BURGLARIES	%	RANK	STATE	BURGLARIES	%
1	California	400,392	13.03%	26	Minnesota	39,691	1.29%
2	Texas	314,512	10.23%	27	Wisconsin	36,755	1.20%
3	Florida	280,832	9.14%	28	Oregon	32,273	1.05%
4	New York	208,813	6.79%	29	Mississippi	32,196	1.05%
5	Illinois	121,506	3.95%	30	Kansas	28,901	0.94%
6	Ohio	106,575	3.47%	31	Arkansas	28,464	0.93%
7	Michigan	106,275	3.46%	32	Kentucky	28,264	0.92%
8	Georgia	104,905	3.41%	33	New Mexico	26,343	0.86%
9	North Carolina	101,444	3.30%	34	Iowa	22,448	0.73%
10	Pennsylvania	86,624	2.82%	35	Nevada	16,434	0.53%
11	New Jersey	78,628	2.56%	36	Utah	15,172	0.49%
12	Massachusetts	66,942	2.18%	37	Hawaii	13,611	0.44%
13	Tennessee	61,646	2.01%	38	Rhode Island	12,755	0.41%
14	Washington	61,460	2.00%	39	West Virginia	11,785	0.38%
15	Arizona	61,206	1.99%	40	Nebraska	11,424	0.37%
16	Louisiana	60,677	1.97%	41	Maine	10,106	0.33%
17	Missouri	54,536	1.77%	42	Idaho	8,187	0.27%
18	Maryland	53,549	1.74%	43	New Hampshire	8,158	0.27%
19	Indiana	52,297	1.70%	44	Delaware	6,465	0.21%
20	South Carolina	48,132	1.57%	45	Vermont	6,119	0.20%
21	Oklahoma	45,531	1.48%	46	Montana	5,666	0.18%
22	Virginia	45,236	1.47%	47	Alaska	4,919	0.16%
23	Alabama	44,585	1.45%	48	South Dakota	3,671	0.12%
24	Connecticut	40,355	1.31%	49	Wyoming	2,862	0.09%
25	Colorado	39,822	1.30%	50	North Dakota	2,725	0.09%
					District of Columbia	12,035	0.39%

Source: Federal Bureau of Investigation,
   "1990 Crime in the United States" (August 11, 1991)
*Burglary is the unlawful entry of a structure to commit a felony or theft.

Percent Change in Number of Burglaries: 1989 to 1990

National Percent Change = 3.0% Decrease*

RANK	STATE	PERCENT CHANGE	RANK	STATE	PERCENT CHANGE
1	North Dakota	15.0	26	New York	(1.1)
2	Alaska	12.9	27	South Carolina	(1.6)
3	South Dakota	8.2	28	Virginia	(2.0)
4	Mississippi	7.3	29	California	(2.5)
5	Delaware	6.5	30	Florida	(2.9)
6	Massachusetts	6.3	31	Illinois	(3.1)
7	Rhode Island	5.9	32	Kansas	(3.2)
8	Nevada	5.3	33	Indiana	(3.5)
9	Vermont	4.9	34	Colorado	(4.0)
10	New Jersey	4.1	34	Ohio	(4.0)
11	Tennessee	3.4	36	Wyoming	(4.6)
12	Arizona	3.2	37	Georgia	(4.8)
13	Maine	3.0	38	Nebraska	(4.9)
13	Wisconsin	3.0	39	Louisiana	(5.5)
15	North Carolina	2.7	40	Alabama	(5.6)
16	Minnesota	1.7	41	Michigan	(6.4)
17	Montana	1.6	42	Iowa	(6.7)
18	Maryland	1.5	43	Missouri	(6.9)
19	West Virginia	1.3	44	Idaho	(7.4)
20	Connecticut	0.8	44	Kentucky	(7.4)
20	New Mexico	0.8	46	Texas	(8.1)
20	Pennsylvania	0.8	47	Hawaii	(8.9)
23	New Hampshire	0.0	48	Oklahoma	(9.7)
24	Utah	(0.9)	49	Washington	(16.5)
25	Arkansas	(1.0)	50	Oregon	(19.7)

District of Columbia   2.2

Source: Federal Bureau of Investigation,
   "1990 Crime in the United States" (August 11, 1991)
*Burglary is the unlawful entry of a structure to commit a felony or theft.

48

Burglary Rate in 1990

National Rate = 1,235.9 Burglaries per 100,000 Population*

RANK	STATE	RATE	RANK	STATE	RATE
1	Florida	2,170.6	26	Alabama	1,103.4
2	Texas	1,851.5	27	Vermont	1,087.3
3	New Mexico	1,738.7	28	Missouri	1,065.8
4	Arizona	1,669.9	29	Illinois	1,063.0
5	Georgia	1,619.4	30	New Jersey	1,017.2
6	North Carolina	1,530.4	31	Ohio	982.5
7	Oklahoma	1,447.5	32	Delaware	970.5
8	Louisiana	1,437.9	33	Indiana	943.3
9	South Carolina	1,380.4	34	Minnesota	907.2
10	Nevada	1,367.4	35	Alaska	894.3
11	California	1,345.4	36	Utah	880.6
12	Rhode Island	1,271.1	37	Maine	823.0
13	Tennessee	1,264.0	38	Idaho	813.2
14	Washington	1,262.9	39	Iowa	808.4
15	Mississippi	1,251.2	40	Kentucky	766.9
16	Hawaii	1,228.2	41	Wisconsin	751.4
17	Connecticut	1,227.7	42	New Hampshire	735.5
18	Arkansas	1,210.9	43	Virginia	731.1
19	Colorado	1,208.8	44	Pennsylvania	729.1
20	Kansas	1,166.5	45	Nebraska	723.8
21	New York	1,160.7	46	Montana	709.1
22	Michigan	1,143.3	47	West Virginia	657.1
23	Oregon	1,135.4	48	Wyoming	631.0
24	Maryland	1,119.9	49	South Dakota	527.4
25	Massachusetts	1,112.7	50	North Dakota	426.6

District of Columbia   1,983.0

Source: Federal Bureau of Investigation,

"1990 Crime in the United States" (August 11, 1991)

*Burglary is the unlawful entry of a structure to commit a felony or theft.

Larceny and Theft in 1990

National Total = 7,945,670 Larcenies and Thefts*

RANK	STATE	LARCENIES	%	RANK	STATE	LARCENIES	%
1	California	951,580	11.98%	26	Oregon	100,765	1.27%
2	Texas	731,224	9.20%	27	Connecticut	94,485	1.19%
3	Florida	591,210	7.44%	28	Oklahoma	94,432	1.19%
4	New York	536,012	6.75%	29	Kansas	80,361	1.01%
5	Illinois	372,862	4.69%	30	Iowa	78,384	0.99%
6	Michigan	311,153	3.92%	31	Utah	73,352	0.92%
7	Ohio	310,673	3.91%	32	Kentucky	71,594	0.90%
8	Georgia	240,623	3.03%	33	Arkansas	66,630	0.84%
9	New Jersey	219,767	2.77%	34	New Mexico	58,004	0.73%
10	Pennsylvania	215,119	2.71%	35	Mississippi	53,266	0.67%
11	North Carolina	202,059	2.54%	36	Nebraska	47,054	0.59%
12	Washington	195,221	2.46%	37	Hawaii	46,735	0.59%
13	Virginia	187,564	2.36%	38	Nevada	42,097	0.53%
14	Arizona	172,375	2.17%	39	Maine	31,372	0.39%
15	Indiana	156,741	1.97%	40	Idaho	28,216	0.36%
16	Massachusetts	151,933	1.91%	41	New Hampshire	28,111	0.35%
17	Louisiana	149,752	1.88%	42	West Virginia	27,310	0.34%
18	Maryland	147,407	1.86%	43	Montana	27,098	0.34%
19	Wisconsin	144,924	1.82%	44	Rhode Island	27,046	0.34%
20	Missouri	143,287	1.80%	45	Delaware	21,922	0.28%
21	Minnesota	129,500	1.63%	46	Alaska	17,428	0.22%
22	Colorado	128,172	1.61%	47	Vermont	16,424	0.21%
23	Tennessee	124,127	1.56%	48	South Dakota	14,678	0.18%
24	South Carolina	115,144	1.45%	49	North Dakota	14,621	0.18%
25	Alabama	111,336	1.40%	50	Wyoming	14,194	0.18%
					District of Columbia	30,326	0.38%

Source: Federal Bureau of Investigation,
   "1990 Crime in the United States" (August 11, 1991)
*Larceny and Theft is the unlawful taking of property.

Percent Change in Number of Larcenies and Thefts: 1989 to 1990

National Percent Change = 0.9% Increase*

RANK	STATE	PERCENT CHANGE	RANK	STATE	PERCENT CHANGE
1	Montana	13.4	26	Illinois	2.8
2	Tennessee	12.9	26	New Jersey	2.8
3	Alaska	10.2	28	West Virginia	2.6
4	North Dakota	9.4	29	Oklahoma	2.3
5	Virginia	8.6	30	Nebraska	1.4
6	Mississippi	8.1	31	Florida	1.3
7	Delaware	8.0	31	Michigan	1.3
8	Maryland	7.6	31	Ohio	1.3
9	South Carolina	6.8	34	Utah	0.2
10	Vermont	6.2	35	Colorado	0.0
11	Arkansas	5.6	35	Kentucky	0.0
11	Minnesota	5.6	37	Rhode Island	(0.2)
13	North Carolina	5.4	38	New Mexico	(0.3)
14	Idaho	5.2	39	Washington	(0.5)
15	Indiana	4.8	40	Pennsylvania	(0.7)
16	South Dakota	4.4	41	Hawaii	(1.3)
16	Wyoming	4.4	42	Texas	(1.4)
18	Alabama	4.3	43	Louisiana	(1.6)
18	Maine	4.3	43	New York	(1.6)
20	New Hampshire	3.8	45	Iowa	(1.8)
21	Nevada	3.5	46	Missouri	(2.0)
21	Wisconsin	3.5	47	California	(2.2)
23	Massachusetts	3.4	48	Oregon	(2.8)
24	Connecticut	3.3	49	Arizona	(5.1)
24	Kansas	3.3	50	Georgia	(5.9)

District of Columbia   4.0

Source: Federal Bureau of Investigation,
   "1990 Crime in the United States" (August 11, 1991)
*Larceny and Theft is the unlawful taking of property.

Larceny and Theft Rate in 1990

National Rate = 3,194.8 Larcenies and Thefts per 100,000 Population*

RANK	STATE	RATE	RANK	STATE	RATE
1	Arizona	4,703.0	26	Nebraska	2,981.1
2	Florida	4,569.6	27	New York	2,979.4
3	Texas	4,304.7	28	Wisconsin	2,962.6
4	Utah	4,257.6	29	Minnesota	2,959.9
5	Hawaii	4,217.1	30	Vermont	2,918.5
6	Washington	4,011.4	31	Connecticut	2,874.4
7	Colorado	3,890.6	32	Ohio	2,864.1
8	New Mexico	3,828.5	33	New Jersey	2,843.0
9	Georgia	3,714.3	34	Arkansas	2,834.4
10	Louisiana	3,548.6	35	Indiana	2,827.1
11	Oregon	3,545.2	36	Iowa	2,822.9
12	Nevada	3,502.7	37	Idaho	2,802.7
13	Montana	3,391.2	38	Missouri	2,800.2
14	Michigan	3,347.4	39	Alabama	2,755.4
15	South Carolina	3,302.4	40	Rhode Island	2,695.3
16	Delaware	3,290.8	41	Maine	2,554.9
17	Illinois	3,262.0	42	Tennessee	2,545.1
18	Kansas	3,243.5	43	New Hampshire	2,534.2
19	California	3,197.5	44	Massachusetts	2,525.3
20	Alaska	3,168.5	45	North Dakota	2,288.8
21	Wyoming	3,129.3	46	South Dakota	2,108.9
22	Maryland	3,082.9	47	Mississippi	2,070.0
23	North Carolina	3,048.3	48	Kentucky	1,942.7
24	Virginia	3,031.4	49	Pennsylvania	1,810.5
25	Oklahoma	3,002.0	50	West Virginia	1,522.7

District of Columbia 4,996.9

Source: Federal Bureau of Investigation,
   "1990 Crime in the United States" (August 11, 1991)
*Larceny and Theft is the unlawful taking of property.

Motor Vehicle Thefts in 1990

National Total = 1,635,907 Motor Vehicle Thefts

RANK	STATE	VEHICLE THEFTS	%	RANK	STATE	VEHICLE THEFTS	%
1	California	302,214	18.47%	26	Alabama	14,053	0.86%
2	New York	187,591	11.47%	27	South Carolina	13,453	0.82%
3	Texas	154,415	9.44%	28	Oregon	13,035	0.80%
4	Florida	106,902	6.53%	29	Rhode Island	9,577	0.59%
5	Illinois	73,473	4.49%	30	Kansas	8,309	0.51%
6	New Jersey	72,628	4.44%	31	Kentucky	7,350	0.45%
7	Michigan	66,336	4.05%	32	Nevada	7,121	0.44%
8	Pennsylvania	60,062	3.67%	33	Arkansas	6,803	0.42%
9	Massachusetts	55,567	3.40%	34	Mississippi	5,341	0.33%
10	Ohio	53,221	3.25%	35	New Mexico	5,101	0.31%
11	Georgia	43,637	2.67%	36	Iowa	4,718	0.29%
12	Maryland	33,886	2.07%	37	Hawaii	4,217	0.26%
13	Arizona	31,648	1.93%	38	Utah	4,096	0.25%
14	Tennessee	27,875	1.70%	39	Alaska	3,110	0.19%
15	Missouri	27,599	1.69%	40	Delaware	2,957	0.18%
16	Louisiana	25,393	1.55%	41	Nebraska	2,812	0.17%
17	Indiana	24,338	1.49%	42	West Virginia	2,760	0.17%
18	Connecticut	24,027	1.47%	43	New Hampshire	2,707	0.17%
19	Washington	21,759	1.33%	44	Maine	2,169	0.13%
20	Wisconsin	20,373	1.25%	45	Montana	1,938	0.12%
21	Virginia	20,263	1.24%	46	Idaho	1,666	0.10%
22	Oklahoma	18,926	1.16%	47	Vermont	1,170	0.07%
23	North Carolina	18,803	1.15%	48	North Dakota	850	0.05%
24	Minnesota	15,994	0.98%	49	South Dakota	767	0.05%
25	Colorado	14,112	0.86%	50	Wyoming	676	0.04%
					District of Columbia	8,109	0.50%

Source: Federal Bureau of Investigation,
"1990 Crime in the United States" (August 11, 1991)

Percent Change in Number of Motor Vehicle Thefts: 1989 to 1990

National Percent Change = 4.5% Increase

RANK	STATE	PERCENT CHANGE	RANK	STATE	PERCENT CHANGE
1	Alaska	29.7	26	Georgia	3.7
2	Arizona	29.6	26	Vermont	3.7
3	Wisconsin	26.2	26	Wyoming	3.7
4	Alabama	14.7	29	Idaho	3.5
5	North Dakota	13.9	30	Massachusetts	3.2
6	Mississippi	13.7	31	Texas	2.3
7	Delaware	12.3	32	Missouri	2.2
8	Ohio	12.1	33	New Jersey	2.1
9	South Carolina	12.0	34	California	1.3
10	Indiana	11.2	35	Utah	1.0
10	Kansas	11.2	36	North Carolina	0.3
10	Louisiana	11.2	36	Oklahoma	0.3
13	Nevada	10.6	38	New Hampshire	0.2
14	New York	9.7	39	Washington	(0.1)
15	Maryland	8.7	40	Michigan	(1.0)
16	Virginia	7.0	41	South Dakota	(1.5)
17	Montana	6.6	42	Maine	(3.1)
18	Arkansas	6.4	43	Minnesota	(3.3)
19	Connecticut	6.3	44	Hawaii	(4.4)
19	Pennsylvania	6.3	45	New Mexico	(4.6)
21	Tennessee	5.9	46	West Virginia	(5.2)
22	Iowa	4.9	47	Colorado	(6.1)
23	Florida	4.7	48	Nebraska	(6.3)
24	Illinois	3.8	49	Kentucky	(10.3)
24	Rhode Island	3.8	50	Oregon	(14.4)

District of Columbia   (2.2)

Source: Federal Bureau of Investigation,

"1990 Crime in the United States" (August 11, 1991)

Motor Vehicle Theft Rate in 1990

National Rate = 657.8 Motor Vehicle Thefts per 100,000 Population

RANK	STATE	RATE	RANK	STATE	RATE
1	New York	1,042.7	26	Colorado	428.4
2	California	1,015.5	27	Wisconsin	416.5
3	Rhode Island	954.4	28	South Carolina	385.8
4	New Jersey	939.5	29	Hawaii	380.5
5	Massachusetts	923.6	30	Minnesota	365.6
6	Texas	909.0	31	Alabama	347.8
7	Arizona	863.5	32	New Mexico	336.7
8	Florida	826.3	33	Kansas	335.4
9	Connecticut	730.9	34	Virginia	327.5
10	Michigan	713.7	35	Arkansas	289.4
11	Maryland	708.7	36	North Carolina	283.7
12	Georgia	673.6	37	New Hampshire	244.0
13	Illinois	642.8	38	Montana	242.5
14	Louisiana	601.7	39	Utah	237.7
14	Oklahoma	601.7	40	Vermont	207.9
16	Nevada	592.5	41	Mississippi	207.6
17	Tennessee	571.5	42	Kentucky	199.4
18	Alaska	565.4	43	Nebraska	178.2
19	Missouri	539.4	44	Maine	176.6
20	Pennsylvania	505.5	45	Iowa	169.9
21	Ohio	490.6	46	Idaho	165.5
22	Oregon	458.6	47	West Virginia	153.9
23	Washington	447.1	48	Wyoming	149.0
24	Delaware	443.9	49	North Dakota	133.1
25	Indiana	439.0	50	South Dakota	110.2

District of Columbia   1,336.1

Source: Federal Bureau of Investigation,
   "1990 Crime in the United States" (August 11, 1991)

Adults Under State Correctional Supervision in 1989*

National Total = 3,920,001 Adults**

RANK	STATE	ADULTS	%		RANK	STATE	ADULTS	%
1	California	498,550	12.72%		26	Oregon	46,751	1.19%
2	Texas	466,240	11.89%		27	Colorado	39,610	1.01%
3	Florida	266,738	6.80%		28	Oklahoma	38,989	0.99%
4	New York	245,720	6.27%		29	Kansas	34,264	0.87%
5	Georgia	182,554	4.66%		30	Arkansas	28,529	0.73%
6	Michigan	173,687	4.43%		31	Kentucky	23,631	0.60%
7	Pennsylvania	172,507	4.40%		32	Mississippi	21,829	0.56%
8	Illinois	144,399	3.68%		33	Iowa	21,260	0.54%
9	Ohio	124,032	3.16%		34	Nevada	18,089	0.46%
10	Maryland	119,277	3.04%		35	Nebraska	16,886	0.43%
11	New Jersey	116,113	2.96%		36	Rhode Island	15,098	0.39%
12	Massachusetts	106,429	2.72%		37	Hawaii	14,955	0.38%
13	North Carolina	104,554	2.67%		38	Delaware	13,787	0.35%
14	Washington	98,740	2.52%		39	New Mexico	12,034	0.31%
15	Indiana	84,074	2.14%		40	Utah	10,766	0.27%
16	Missouri	71,361	1.82%		41	Maine	9,880	0.25%
17	Minnesota	67,033	1.71%		42	West Virginia	9,531	0.24%
18	Louisiana	67,006	1.71%		43	Idaho	7,638	0.19%
19	Tennessee	60,898	1.55%		44	Montana	6,649	0.17%
20	South Carolina	52,534	1.34%		45	Vermont	6,499	0.17%
21	Connecticut	51,941	1.33%		46	Alaska	6,495	0.17%
22	Alabama	51,520	1.31%		47	New Hampshire	5,530	0.14%
23	Virginia	51,468	1.31%		48	South Dakota	4,936	0.13%
24	Arizona	49,108	1.25%		49	Wyoming	4,125	0.11%
25	Wisconsin	47,023	1.20%		50	North Dakota	2,590	0.07%

District of Columbia   26,144   0.67%

Source: U.S. Bureau of Justice Statistics,

"Correctional Populations in the United States, 1989" (November 1991)

*In prisons, jails, on parole or on probation.

**Does not include 133,945 under federal correctional supervision.

State Correctional Population as a Percent of Adult Resident Population in 1989

National Percent = 2.13% of Adult Population*

RANK	STATE	PERCENT		RANK	STATE	PERCENT
1	Georgia	3.94		26	Alaska	1.79
2	Texas	3.87		27	Alabama	1.71
3	Maryland	3.38		28	Illinois	1.66
4	Washington	2.79		29	Tennessee	1.65
5	Delaware	2.74		30	Oklahoma	1.64
6	Florida	2.72		31	Arkansas	1.62
7	Michigan	2.54		32	Colorado	1.61
8	California	2.34		33	Ohio	1.53
9	Massachusetts	2.33		33	Vermont	1.53
10	Oregon	2.20		35	Nebraska	1.42
11	Nevada	2.17		36	Wisconsin	1.30
12	Louisiana	2.16		37	Wyoming	1.22
13	North Carolina	2.12		38	Mississippi	1.18
14	Connecticut	2.10		39	Montana	1.13
15	Minnesota	2.08		40	New Mexico	1.12
16	South Carolina	2.05		40	Virginia	1.12
17	Indiana	2.03		42	Idaho	1.08
18	New Jersey	1.97		42	Maine	1.08
18	Rhode Island	1.97		44	Iowa	1.00
20	Arizona	1.91		44	Utah	1.00
21	Pennsylvania	1.88		46	South Dakota	0.95
22	Kansas	1.85		47	Kentucky	0.86
22	Missouri	1.85		48	West Virginia	0.68
24	Hawaii	1.81		49	New Hampshire	0.67
24	New York	1.81		50	North Dakota	0.54

District of Columbia   5.62

Source: U.S. Bureau of Justice Statistics,
   "Correctional Populations in the United States, 1989" (November 1991)
*In prisons, jails, on parole or on probation.

Prisoners in State Correctional Institutions in 1990

National Total = 705,717 State Prisoners*

RANK	STATE	PRISONERS	%
1	California	97,309	13.79%
2	New York	54,895	7.78%
3	Texas	50,042	7.09%
4	Florida	44,387	6.29%
5	Michigan	34,267	4.86%
6	Ohio	31,855	4.51%
7	Illinois	27,516	3.90%
8	Georgia	22,345	3.17%
9	Pennsylvania	22,290	3.16%
10	New Jersey	21,128	2.99%
11	Louisiana	18,599	2.64%
12	North Carolina	18,412	2.61%
13	Maryland	17,798	2.52%
14	South Carolina	17,319	2.45%
14	Virginia	17,319	2.45%
16	Alabama	15,665	2.22%
17	Missouri	14,919	2.11%
18	Arizona	14,261	2.02%
19	Indiana	12,732	1.80%
20	Oklahoma	12,322	1.75%
21	Connecticut	10,500	1.49%
22	Tennessee	10,388	1.47%
23	Kentucky	9,023	1.28%
24	Mississippi	8,375	1.19%
25	Massachusetts	8,273	1.17%

RANK	STATE	PRISONERS	%
26	Washington	7,995	1.13%
27	Wisconsin	7,362	1.04%
28	Colorado	7,018	0.99%
29	Arkansas	6,766	0.96%
30	Oregon	6,436	0.91%
31	Kansas	5,777	0.82%
32	Nevada	5,322	0.75%
33	Iowa	3,967	0.56%
34	Delaware	3,506	0.50%
35	Minnesota	3,176	0.45%
36	New Mexico	2,961	0.42%
37	Alaska	2,622	0.37%
38	Hawaii	2,533	0.36%
39	Utah	2,503	0.35%
40	Nebraska	2,403	0.34%
41	Rhode Island	2,394	0.34%
42	Idaho	2,074	0.29%
43	West Virginia	1,565	0.22%
44	Maine	1,523	0.22%
45	Montana	1,425	0.20%
46	South Dakota	1,345	0.19%
47	New Hampshire	1,342	0.19%
48	Wyoming	1,110	0.16%
49	Vermont	1,049	0.15%
50	North Dakota	483	0.07%

	District of Columbia	9,121	1.29%

Source: U.S. Bureau of Justice Statistics,

Prisoners in 1990 (Bulletin, May 1991)

*As of December 31, 1990. Excludes 65,526 federal prisoners.

Percent of Adult Population in State Prisons in 1990

National Percent = 0.38% of Adults are in State Prisons*

RANK	STATE	PERCENT		RANK	STATE	PERCENT
1	Delaware	0.70		26	Illinois	0.32
2	Alaska	0.69		26	Kansas	0.32
3	South Carolina	0.67		28	Hawaii	0.31
4	Louisiana	0.62		28	Indiana	0.31
5	Nevada	0.59		28	Rhode Island	0.31
6	Alabama	0.53		31	Idaho	0.30
6	Arizona	0.53		31	Oregon	0.30
6	Oklahoma	0.53		33	Colorado	0.29
9	Michigan	0.50		34	New Mexico	0.28
10	Maryland	0.49		34	Tennessee	0.28
11	Georgia	0.47		36	South Dakota	0.27
12	Mississippi	0.46		37	Montana	0.25
13	California	0.44		37	Pennsylvania	0.25
13	Florida	0.44		37	Vermont	0.25
15	Connecticut	0.41		40	Utah	0.23
15	Texas	0.41		41	Washington	0.22
17	New York	0.40		42	Nebraska	0.21
17	Ohio	0.40		43	Wisconsin	0.20
19	Arkansas	0.39		44	Iowa	0.19
19	Missouri	0.39		45	Massachusetts	0.18
21	North Carolina	0.37		46	Maine	0.17
21	Virginia	0.37		47	New Hampshire	0.16
23	New Jersey	0.36		48	West Virginia	0.12
24	Wyoming	0.35		49	Minnesota	0.10
25	Kentucky	0.33		49	North Dakota	0.10

District of Columbia   1.86

Source: U.S. Bureau of Justice Statistics,

"Prisoners in 1990" (Bulletin, May 1991) (Rates calculated by the editors using 1990 Census population numbers.)

*As of December 31, 1990. Prisoners with sentences of more than one year.

Percent Change in State Prison Population: 1989 to 1990

National Percent Change = 8.0% Increase*

RANK	STATE	PERCENT CHANGE		RANK	STATE	PERCENT CHANGE
1	Vermont	15.9		25	New York	7.2
2	Washington	15.4		27	North Dakota	7.1
3	New Hampshire	15.1		28	Georgia	7.0
4	Texas	13.7		29	Oklahoma	6.2
5	Connecticut	12.9		30	Mississippi	5.9
6	Alabama	12.6		31	Arkansas	5.6
7	Idaho	12.1		32	North Carolina	5.5
8	California	11.5		33	Virginia	5.1
9	Illinois	11.3		34	Maine	4.7
10	Florida	11.0		35	Utah	4.6
11	Iowa	10.7		36	Ohio	4.3
12	South Carolina	10.2		37	Nevada	4.1
13	Massachusetts	10.0		38	Indiana	3.2
14	Wyoming	9.3		39	Kansas	2.9
15	Kentucky	8.9		40	Hawaii	2.8
15	Pennsylvania	8.9		41	Minnesota	2.4
17	New Jersey	8.7		42	West Virginia	1.9
18	Wisconsin	8.5		43	Colorado	1.6
19	Michigan	8.3		44	Delaware	1.4
20	Louisiana	7.8		45	New Mexico	1.0
20	Maryland	7.8		46	Nebraska	0.4
22	Arizona	7.6		47	Tennessee	(2.3)
23	South Dakota	7.4		48	Rhode Island	(3.4)
24	Montana	7.3		49	Alaska	(4.4)
25	Missouri	7.2		50	Oregon	(4.6)

District of Columbia   (9.1)

Source: U.S. Bureau of Justice Statistics,

"Prisoners in 1990" (Bulletin, May 1991)

*Federal prison population increased by 10.7%. Federal and state prison populations combined increased by 8.2%.

Prisoners in State Correctional Institutions as a Percent of Capacity in 1990

National Rate = 115% of Capacity*

RANK	STATE	% OF CAPACITY		RANK	STATE	% OF CAPACITY
1	California	185		25	Idaho	104
2	Massachusetts	170		27	Arizona	103
3	Vermont	157		27	Kentucky	103
4	Pennsylvania	156		27	Oregon	103
5	Ohio	155		30	Montana	101
6	Oklahoma	150		31	Georgia	100
7	Nebraska	144		31	Missouri	100
8	Wyoming	140		33	Maryland	99
9	Wisconsin	139		33	Minnesota	99
10	New Jersey	137		35	Nevada	98
11	Iowa	131		35	Rhode Island	98
12	Michigan	130		37	New York	97
13	Maine	127		37	Tennessee	97
14	Washington	124		39	Louisiana	96
15	Illinois	121		40	North Carolina	95
16	Hawaii	118		41	Texas	94
17	Indiana	117		42	Alaska	93
18	Colorado	115		43	Arkansas	92
19	South Dakota	113		44	New Hampshire	90
20	Delaware	112		45	Florida	88
21	Virginia	111		45	Mississippi	88
22	South Carolina	109		47	West Virginia	85
23	Alabama	107		48	North Dakota	84
23	Kansas	107		49	Utah	83
25	Connecticut	104		50	New Mexico	82

District of Columbia   100

Source: U.S. Bureau of Justice Statistics,
"Prisoners in 1990" (Bulletin, May 1991)
*As of December 31, 1990. Based on highest rated capacity.

Prisoners Under Sentence of Death in 1990

National Total = 2,356 Prisoners*

RANK	STATE	PRISONERS	%	RANK	STATE	PRISONERS	%
1	Texas	320	13.58%	26	New Jersey	10	0.42%
2	Florida	299	12.69%	26	Oregon	10	0.42%
3	California	280	11.88%	26	Washington	10	0.42%
4	Illinois	128	5.43%	29	Delaware	6	0.25%
5	Pennsylvania	121	5.14%	29	Montana	6	0.25%
6	Oklahoma	118	5.01%	31	Colorado	3	0.13%
7	Alabama	117	4.97%	32	Connecticut	2	0.08%
8	Ohio	105	4.46%	32	Wyoming	2	0.08%
9	Georgia	98	4.16%	34	New Mexico	1	0.04%
10	Arizona	91	3.86%	35	New Hampshire	0	0.00%
11	North Carolina	84	3.57%	35	South Dakota	0	0.00%
11	Tennessee	84	3.57%	–	Alaska**	N/A	N/A
13	Missouri	72	3.06%	–	Hawaii**	N/A	N/A
14	Nevada	57	2.42%	–	Iowa**	N/A	N/A
15	Indiana	48	2.04%	–	Kansas**	N/A	N/A
16	Mississippi	47	1.99%	–	Maine**	N/A	N/A
17	Virginia	45	1.91%	–	Massachusetts**	N/A	N/A
18	South Carolina	42	1.78%	–	Michigan**	N/A	N/A
19	Arkansas	33	1.40%	–	Minnesota**	N/A	N/A
20	Louisiana	31	1.32%	–	New York**	N/A	N/A
21	Kentucky	26	1.10%	–	North Dakota**	N/A	N/A
22	Idaho	19	0.81%	–	Rhode Island**	N/A	N/A
22	Maryland	19	0.81%	–	Vermont**	N/A	N/A
24	Nebraska	11	0.47%	–	West Virginia**	N/A	N/A
24	Utah	11	0.47%	–	Wisconsin**	N/A	N/A

District of Columbia**   N/A   N/A

Source: U.S. Bureau of Justice Statistics,
   "Capital Punishment 1990" (Bulletin, September 1991)
*As of December 31, 1990.
**No death penalty.

Adults Under State Parole Supervision in 1989

National Total = 435,385 State Parolees*

RANK	STATE	PAROLEES	%	RANK	STATE	PAROLEES	%
1	Texas	91,294	20.97%	26	Kentucky	3,133	0.72%
2	California	57,508	13.21%	27	Nevada	2,417	0.56%
3	Pennsylvania	47,702	10.96%	28	Florida	2,318	0.53%
4	New York	36,685	8.43%	29	Arizona	2,048	0.47%
5	New Jersey	20,062	4.61%	30	Oklahoma	1,993	0.46%
6	Georgia	17,437	4.00%	31	Iowa	1,900	0.44%
7	Illinois	14,550	3.34%	32	Colorado	1,799	0.41%
8	Tennessee	10,700	2.46%	33	Minnesota	1,699	0.39%
9	Michigan	9,890	2.27%	34	Hawaii	1,287	0.30%
10	Maryland	9,862	2.27%	35	Utah	1,277	0.29%
11	Washington	9,832	2.26%	36	New Mexico	1,151	0.26%
12	Louisiana	9,177	2.11%	37	Delaware	1,013	0.23%
13	Missouri	7,638	1.75%	38	West Virginia	943	0.22%
14	North Carolina	7,559	1.74%	39	Montana	752	0.17%
15	Virginia	7,392	1.70%	40	Alaska	533	0.12%
16	Ohio	6,464	1.48%	41	South Dakota	510	0.12%
17	Oregon	5,794	1.33%	42	Nebraska	490	0.11%
18	Alabama	5,756	1.32%	43	New Hampshire	477	0.11%
19	Kansas	4,793	1.10%	44	Rhode Island	391	0.09%
20	Massachusetts	4,688	1.08%	45	Connecticut	322	0.07%
21	Wisconsin	4,392	1.01%	46	Wyoming	310	0.07%
22	South Carolina	3,630	0.83%	47	Idaho	238	0.05%
23	Arkansas	3,500	0.80%	48	Vermont	220	0.05%
24	Indiana	3,456	0.79%	49	North Dakota	139	0.03%
25	Mississippi	3,349	0.77%	50	Maine	0	0.00%
					District of Columbia	4,915	1.13%

Source: U.S. Bureau of Justice Statistics,
   "Correctional Populations in the United States, 1989" (November 1991)
*Includes all adults under state parole supervision who were sentenced to more than 1 year in prison. Excludes 21,412 adults under federal parole.

Adults on State Probation in 1989

National Total = 2,461,133 Adults*

RANK	STATE	ADULTS	%	RANK	STATE	ADULTS	%
1	Texas	291,156	11.83%	26	Colorado	26,378	1.07%
2	California	285,018	11.58%	27	Oklahoma	24,240	0.98%
3	Florida	192,495	7.82%	28	Kansas	22,525	0.92%
4	New York	128,707	5.23%	29	Virginia	19,085	0.78%
5	Georgia	125,441	5.10%	30	Arkansas	17,572	0.71%
6	Michigan	121,436	4.93%	31	Iowa	13,722	0.56%
7	Illinois	93,944	3.82%	32	Nebraska	12,627	0.51%
8	Pennsylvania	89,491	3.64%	33	Rhode Island	12,231	0.50%
9	Massachusetts	88,529	3.60%	34	Hawaii	11,377	0.46%
10	Maryland	84,456	3.43%	35	Delaware	9,701	0.39%
11	Ohio	78,223	3.18%	36	Kentucky	8,062	0.33%
12	Washington	74,254	3.02%	37	Mississippi	7,333	0.30%
13	North Carolina	72,325	2.94%	38	Nevada	7,324	0.30%
14	New Jersey	66,753	2.71%	39	Maine	6,851	0.28%
15	Indiana	61,861	2.51%	40	New Mexico	5,660	0.23%
16	Minnesota	58,648	2.38%	41	Utah	5,524	0.22%
17	Missouri	45,251	1.84%	42	Vermont	5,399	0.22%
18	Connecticut	42,842	1.74%	43	West Virginia	4,963	0.20%
19	Louisiana	32,295	1.31%	44	Idaho	4,025	0.16%
20	Oregon	31,878	1.30%	45	Montana	3,459	0.14%
21	Tennessee	30,906	1.26%	46	Alaska	3,335	0.14%
22	Wisconsin	30,160	1.23%	47	New Hampshire	2,991	0.12%
23	South Carolina	29,652	1.20%	48	South Dakota	2,716	0.11%
24	Arizona	27,650	1.12%	49	Wyoming	2,384	0.10%
25	Alabama	26,475	1.08%	50	North Dakota	1,652	0.07%
					District of Columbia	10,351	0.42%

Source: U.S. Bureau of Justice Statistics,
    "Correctional Populations in the United States, 1989" (November 1991)
*Excludes 59,146 adults on federal probation.

Full-Time State and Local Police in 1990

National Total = 697,974 Police*

RANK	STATE	POLICE	%	RANK	STATE	POLICE	%
1	California	85,514	12.25%	26	Oklahoma	8,520	1.22%
2	New York	66,348	9.51%	27	South Carolina	8,485	1.22%
3	Texas	43,802	6.28%	28	Kentucky	7,418	1.06%
4	Florida	43,685	6.26%	29	Kansas	6,631	0.95%
5	Illinois	39,346	5.64%	30	Oregon	6,515	0.93%
6	New Jersey	31,660	4.54%	31	Iowa	6,043	0.87%
7	Pennsylvania	29,602	4.24%	32	Mississippi	5,551	0.80%
8	Ohio	26,716	3.83%	33	Arkansas	4,984	0.71%
9	Michigan	21,884	3.14%	34	New Mexico	4,466	0.64%
10	Georgia	18,182	2.60%	35	Nevada	4,341	0.62%
11	Massachusetts	17,556	2.52%	36	Nebraska	3,780	0.54%
12	North Carolina	16,850	2.41%	37	Utah	3,720	0.53%
13	Virginia	14,992	2.15%	38	Hawaii	3,149	0.45%
14	Maryland	14,630	2.10%	39	New Hampshire	2,997	0.43%
15	Missouri	14,459	2.07%	40	Rhode Island	2,989	0.43%
16	Indiana	12,888	1.85%	41	West Virginia	2,898	0.42%
17	Wisconsin	12,603	1.81%	42	Maine	2,888	0.41%
18	Tennessee	12,333	1.77%	43	Idaho	2,600	0.37%
19	Louisiana	11,752	1.68%	44	Montana	1,932	0.28%
20	Arizona	10,887	1.56%	45	Delaware	1,874	0.27%
21	Washington	10,456	1.50%	46	Wyoming	1,577	0.23%
22	Alabama	10,023	1.44%	47	Alaska	1,533	0.22%
23	Connecticut	9,423	1.35%	48	South Dakota	1,471	0.21%
24	Colorado	9,012	1.29%	49	North Dakota	1,311	0.19%
25	Minnesota	8,884	1.27%	50	Vermont	1,223	0.18%
					District of Columbia	5,591	0.80%

Source: U.S. Bureau of the Census,
   "Public Employment in 1990" (GE-90, No. 1, October 1991)
*Includes non-officers.

Rate of Full-Time State and Local Police in 1990

National Rate = 28.1 Police per 10,000 Population*

RANK	STATE	RATE	RANK	STATE	RATE
1	New Jersey	41.0	24	Wisconsin	25.8
2	New York	36.9	27	North Carolina	25.4
3	Nevada	36.1	28	Tennessee	25.3
4	Wyoming	34.7	29	Pennsylvania	24.9
5	Illinois	34.4	30	Alabama	24.8
6	Florida	33.8	31	Ohio	24.6
7	Maryland	30.6	32	South Carolina	24.3
8	Rhode Island	29.8	33	Montana	24.2
9	Arizona	29.7	33	Virginia	24.2
10	New Mexico	29.5	35	Nebraska	24.0
11	Massachusetts	29.2	36	Maine	23.5
12	California	28.7	36	Michigan	23.5
12	Connecticut	28.7	38	Indiana	23.2
14	Hawaii	28.4	39	Oregon	22.9
15	Missouri	28.3	40	Iowa	21.8
16	Delaware	28.1	41	Vermont	21.7
16	Georgia	28.1	42	Mississippi	21.6
18	Alaska	27.9	42	Utah	21.6
19	Louisiana	27.8	44	Washington	21.5
20	Colorado	27.4	45	Arkansas	21.2
21	Oklahoma	27.1	46	South Dakota	21.1
22	New Hampshire	27.0	47	North Dakota	20.5
23	Kansas	26.8	48	Minnesota	20.3
24	Idaho	25.8	49	Kentucky	20.1
24	Texas	25.8	50	West Virginia	16.2

District of Columbia   92.1

Source: U.S. Bureau of the Census,

   "Public Employment in 1990" (GE-90, No. 1, October 1991)

Includes non-officers.

Full-Time State and Local Corrections Employment in 1990

National Total = 503,181 Corrections Employees

RANK	STATE	EMPLOYEES	%	RANK	STATE	EMPLOYEES	%
1	California	63,989	12.72%	26	Connecticut	5,364	1.07%
2	New York	59,157	11.76%	27	Oregon	5,088	1.01%
3	Florida	38,663	7.68%	28	Oklahoma	5,062	1.01%
4	Texas	37,429	7.44%	29	Minnesota	4,953	0.98%
5	Michigan	18,917	3.76%	30	Kansas	4,150	0.82%
6	Illinois	18,650	3.71%	31	Mississippi	3,675	0.73%
7	New Jersey	17,547	3.49%	32	New Mexico	3,438	0.68%
8	Pennsylvania	16,946	3.37%	33	Arkansas	3,097	0.62%
9	Georgia	16,751	3.33%	34	Nevada	2,795	0.56%
10	Ohio	15,351	3.05%	35	Iowa	2,785	0.55%
11	Virginia	14,869	2.96%	36	Nebraska	2,493	0.50%
12	North Carolina	13,704	2.72%	37	Utah	2,488	0.49%
13	Maryland	11,340	2.25%	38	Rhode Island	1,742	0.35%
14	Tennessee	10,281	2.04%	39	Delaware	1,687	0.34%
15	Louisiana	9,052	1.80%	40	Maine	1,656	0.33%
16	Arizona	8,880	1.76%	41	Hawaii	1,501	0.30%
17	Massachusetts	8,555	1.70%	42	New Hampshire	1,370	0.27%
18	Missouri	8,498	1.69%	43	Idaho	1,328	0.26%
19	Washington	8,445	1.68%	44	West Virginia	1,327	0.26%
20	Indiana	8,238	1.64%	45	Alaska	1,310	0.26%
21	South Carolina	8,181	1.63%	46	Montana	1,061	0.21%
22	Kentucky	6,568	1.31%	47	Wyoming	887	0.18%
23	Wisconsin	6,115	1.22%	48	South Dakota	746	0.15%
24	Alabama	6,053	1.20%	49	Vermont	681	0.14%
25	Colorado	5,431	1.08%	50	North Dakota	495	0.10%

	District of Columbia	4,392	0.87%

Source: U.S. Bureau of the Census,
"Public Employment in 1990" (GE-90, No. 1, October 1991)

Rate of Full–Time State and Local Government Corrections Employment in 1990

National Rate = 20.2 Corrections Employees per 10,000 Population

RANK	STATE	RATE	RANK	STATE	RATE
1	New York	32.9	26	Colorado	16.5
2	Florida	29.9	27	Connecticut	16.3
3	Georgia	25.9	27	Illinois	16.3
4	Delaware	25.3	29	Oklahoma	16.1
5	Arizona	24.2	30	Nebraska	15.8
6	Virginia	24.0	31	Alabama	15.0
7	Alaska	23.8	32	Indiana	14.9
8	Maryland	23.7	33	Utah	14.4
9	South Carolina	23.5	34	Mississippi	14.3
10	Nevada	23.3	34	Pennsylvania	14.3
11	New Jersey	22.7	36	Massachusetts	14.2
11	New Mexico	22.7	36	Ohio	14.2
13	Texas	22.0	38	Hawaii	13.5
14	California	21.5	38	Maine	13.5
14	Louisiana	21.5	40	Montana	13.3
16	Tennessee	21.1	41	Arkansas	13.2
17	North Carolina	20.7	41	Idaho	13.2
18	Michigan	20.4	43	Wisconsin	12.5
19	Wyoming	19.5	44	New Hampshire	12.4
20	Oregon	17.9	45	Vermont	12.1
21	Kentucky	17.8	46	Minnesota	11.3
22	Rhode Island	17.4	47	South Dakota	10.7
22	Washington	17.4	48	Iowa	10.0
24	Kansas	16.7	49	North Dakota	7.7
25	Missouri	16.6	50	West Virginia	7.4

District of Columbia   72.4

Source: U.S. Bureau of the Census,
"Public Employment in 1990" (GE–90, No. 1, October 1991)

State and Local Government Expenditures for Police Protection in 1990

National Total = $30,408,469,000*

RANK	STATE	EXPENDITURES	%	RANK	STATE	EXPENDITURES	%
1	California	$4,747,817,000	15.61%	26	Alabama	$317,016,000	1.04%
2	New York	3,391,355,000	11.15%	27	South Carolina	289,434,000	0.95%
3	Florida	1,904,096,000	6.26%	28	Kentucky	263,835,000	0.87%
4	Texas	1,705,197,000	5.61%	29	Oklahoma	251,075,000	0.83%
5	Illinois	1,522,424,000	5.01%	30	Iowa	232,738,000	0.77%
6	New Jersey	1,190,920,000	3.92%	31	Kansas	228,436,000	0.75%
7	Michigan	1,169,958,000	3.85%	32	Nevada	195,031,000	0.64%
8	Ohio	1,117,125,000	3.67%	33	New Mexico	184,232,000	0.61%
9	Pennsylvania	1,059,360,000	3.48%	34	Mississippi	166,883,000	0.55%
10	Massachusetts	809,371,000	2.66%	35	Utah	154,229,000	0.51%
11	Virginia	721,552,000	2.37%	36	Arkansas	144,939,000	0.48%
12	Maryland	663,521,000	2.18%	37	Hawaii	137,656,000	0.45%
13	Georgia	656,059,000	2.16%	38	Nebraska	127,663,000	0.42%
14	North Carolina	645,827,000	2.12%	39	Rhode Island	121,388,000	0.40%
15	Wisconsin	601,638,000	1.98%	40	New Hampshire	118,381,000	0.39%
16	Arizona	559,627,000	1.84%	41	Alaska	107,756,000	0.35%
17	Washington	497,240,000	1.64%	42	Maine	93,467,000	0.31%
18	Missouri	494,270,000	1.63%	43	Idaho	90,482,000	0.30%
19	Indiana	480,834,000	1.58%	44	West Virginia	89,466,000	0.29%
20	Louisiana	469,677,000	1.54%	45	Delaware	86,338,000	0.28%
21	Connecticut	457,735,000	1.51%	46	Wyoming	65,094,000	0.21%
22	Minnesota	449,893,000	1.48%	47	Montana	64,325,000	0.21%
23	Tennessee	416,825,000	1.37%	48	South Dakota	52,195,000	0.17%
24	Colorado	407,109,000	1.34%	49	Vermont	47,678,000	0.16%
25	Oregon	324,070,000	1.07%	50	North Dakota	39,504,000	0.13%
					District of Columbia	275,728,000	0.91%

Source: U.S. Bureau of the Census,
   "Government Finances: 1989-90 (Preliminary Report)" (GF-90-5P, September 1991)
*Preliminary.

Per Capita State and Local Government Expenditures for Police Protection in 1990

National Per Capita = $122.27*

RANK	STATE	PER CAPITA		RANK	STATE	PER CAPITA
1	Alaska	$195.90		26	Washington	$102.17
2	New York	188.51		27	Georgia	101.27
3	Nevada	162.28		28	Texas	100.39
4	California	159.54		29	North Carolina	97.43
5	New Jersey	154.06		30	Missouri	96.59
6	Arizona	152.69		31	Kansas	92.20
7	Florida	147.17		32	Idaho	89.88
8	Wyoming	143.51		33	Utah	89.52
9	Connecticut	139.25		34	Pennsylvania	89.16
10	Maryland	138.77		35	Indiana	86.73
11	Massachusetts	134.53		36	Tennessee	85.46
12	Illinois	133.19		37	Vermont	84.72
13	Delaware	129.60		38	Iowa	83.82
14	Michigan	125.87		39	South Carolina	83.01
15	Hawaii	124.21		40	Nebraska	80.88
16	Colorado	123.58		41	Montana	80.50
17	Wisconsin	122.99		42	Oklahoma	79.82
18	New Mexico	121.60		43	Alabama	78.46
19	Rhode Island	120.97		44	Maine	76.12
20	Virginia	116.62		45	South Dakota	74.99
21	Oregon	114.02		46	Kentucky	71.59
22	Louisiana	111.30		47	Mississippi	64.85
23	New Hampshire	106.72		48	North Dakota	61.84
24	Ohio	102.99		49	Arkansas	61.66
25	Minnesota	102.83		50	West Virginia	49.88

District of Columbia   454.32

Source: U.S. Bureau of the Census,
   "Government Finance: 1989-90 (Preliminary Report)" (GF-90-5P, 1990)
*Rates calculated by the editors using preliminary totals and 1990 Census numbers.

State and Local Government Expenditures for Corrections in 1990

National Total = $24,636,310,000*

RANK	STATE	EXPENDITURES	%	RANK	STATE	EXPENDITURES	%
1	California	$4,368,817,000	17.73%	26	Minnesota	$239,391,000	0.97%
2	New York	3,332,635,000	13.53%	27	Kentucky	233,474,000	0.95%
3	Florida	1,466,698,000	5.95%	28	Alabama	212,728,000	0.86%
4	Texas	1,410,975,000	5.73%	29	Oklahoma	211,305,000	0.86%
5	Michigan	958,387,000	3.89%	30	Kansas	210,011,000	0.85%
6	New Jersey	823,048,000	3.34%	31	Nevada	186,530,000	0.76%
7	Pennsylvania	770,944,000	3.13%	32	New Mexico	148,254,000	0.60%
8	Ohio	761,337,000	3.09%	33	Iowa	124,582,000	0.51%
9	Illinois	743,524,000	3.02%	34	Alaska	114,904,000	0.47%
10	Massachusetts	694,292,000	2.82%	35	Utah	107,446,000	0.44%
11	Georgia	681,289,000	2.77%	36	Mississippi	105,875,000	0.43%
12	Maryland	628,394,000	2.55%	37	Arkansas	100,953,000	0.41%
13	Virginia	593,138,000	2.41%	38	Nebraska	83,076,000	0.34%
14	North Carolina	531,094,000	2.16%	39	Rhode Island	80,165,000	0.33%
15	Arizona	456,535,000	1.85%	40	Hawaii	80,117,000	0.33%
16	Washington	411,107,000	1.67%	41	Maine	79,657,000	0.32%
17	Tennessee	402,634,000	1.63%	42	New Hampshire	78,643,000	0.32%
18	Colorado	370,581,000	1.50%	43	Delaware	70,994,000	0.29%
19	Wisconsin	348,578,000	1.41%	44	Idaho	52,151,000	0.21%
20	Connecticut	323,302,000	1.31%	45	West Virginia	46,528,000	0.19%
21	Indiana	318,716,000	1.29%	46	Wyoming	38,300,000	0.16%
22	South Carolina	300,386,000	1.22%	47	Montana	34,221,000	0.14%
23	Louisiana	291,250,000	1.18%	48	South Dakota	30,526,000	0.12%
24	Oregon	265,816,000	1.08%	49	Vermont	26,880,000	0.11%
25	Missouri	264,819,000	1.07%	50	North Dakota	20,593,000	0.08%
					District of Columbia	400,710,000	1.63%

Source: U.S. Bureau of the Census,
    "Government Finances: 1989-90 (Preliminary Report)" (GF-90-5P, September 1991)
*Preliminary.

Per Capita State and Local Government Expenditures for Corrections in 1990

National Per Capita = $99.06*

RANK	STATE	PER CAPITA
1	Alaska	$208.90
2	New York	185.24
3	Nevada	155.20
4	California	146.80
5	Maryland	131.42
6	Arizona	124.56
7	Massachusetts	115.40
8	Florida	113.36
9	Colorado	112.49
10	Delaware	106.57
11	New Jersey	106.47
12	Georgia	105.17
13	Michigan	103.10
14	Connecticut	98.35
15	New Mexico	97.85
16	Virginia	95.86
17	Oregon	93.52
18	South Carolina	86.15
19	Kansas	84.76
20	Washington	84.47
21	Wyoming	84.44
22	Texas	83.06
23	Tennessee	82.55
24	North Carolina	80.12
25	Rhode Island	79.89

RANK	STATE	PER CAPITA
26	Hawaii	$72.29
27	Wisconsin	71.26
28	New Hampshire	70.90
29	Ohio	70.19
30	Louisiana	69.02
31	Oklahoma	67.18
32	Illinois	65.05
33	Pennsylvania	64.89
34	Maine	64.87
35	Kentucky	63.35
36	Utah	62.37
37	Indiana	57.49
38	Minnesota	54.72
39	Alabama	52.65
40	Nebraska	52.63
41	Idaho	51.80
42	Missouri	51.75
43	Vermont	47.76
44	Iowa	44.87
45	South Dakota	43.86
46	Arkansas	42.95
47	Montana	42.83
48	Mississippi	41.15
49	North Dakota	32.24
50	West Virginia	25.94

	District of Columbia	660.26

Source: U.S. Bureau of the Census,

"Government Finances: 1989-90 (Preliminary Report)" (GF-90-5P, September 1991)

Rates calculated by the editors.

III. DEFENSE

U.S. Department of Defense Grants to State and Local Governments in 1990

National Total = $175,978,000

RANK	STATE	GRANTS	%
1	Alaska	$14,178,000	8.06%
2	Mississippi	13,527,000	7.69%
3	Virginia	9,700,000	5.51%
4	Minnesota	8,122,000	4.62%
5	New York	7,831,000	4.45%
6	Ohio	6,317,000	3.59%
7	New Jersey	6,258,000	3.56%
8	West Virginia	6,118,000	3.48%
9	Iowa	5,907,000	3.36%
10	Alabama	5,769,000	3.28%
11	Texas	5,751,000	3.27%
12	Idaho	5,326,000	3.03%
13	North Dakota	4,938,000	2.81%
14	Missouri	4,674,000	2.66%
15	South Carolina	3,959,000	2.25%
16	Kansas	3,552,000	2.02%
17	Vermont	3,530,000	2.01%
18	New Mexico	3,451,000	1.96%
19	Illinois	3,368,000	1.91%
20	Michigan	3,348,000	1.90%
21	Montana	2,801,000	1.59%
22	Oklahoma	2,759,000	1.57%
23	Indiana	2,711,000	1.54%
24	Arkansas	2,695,000	1.53%
25	Florida	2,685,000	1.53%

RANK	STATE	GRANTS	%
26	Tennessee	$2,625,000	1.49%
27	Washington	2,586,000	1.47%
28	Wisconsin	2,469,000	1.40%
29	Connecticut	1,981,000	1.13%
30	Kentucky	1,785,000	1.01%
31	Georgia	1,533,000	0.87%
32	California	1,530,000	0.87%
33	Arizona	1,480,000	0.84%
34	Hawaii	1,343,000	0.76%
35	South Dakota	1,301,000	0.74%
36	Utah	1,232,000	0.70%
37	North Carolina	1,222,000	0.69%
38	Oregon	1,202,000	0.68%
39	Nevada	1,171,000	0.67%
40	Louisiana	734,000	0.42%
41	Pennsylvania	733,000	0.42%
42	Nebraska	631,000	0.36%
43	Wyoming	562,000	0.32%
44	Colorado	513,000	0.29%
45	Maine	499,000	0.28%
46	Delaware	314,000	0.18%
47	Maryland	308,000	0.18%
48	New Hampshire	307,000	0.17%
49	Massachusetts	222,000	0.13%
50	Rhode Island	1,000	0.00%

District of Columbia		1,338,000	0.76%
Puerto Rico		2,973,000	1.69%

Source: U.S. Bureau of the Census,
  "Federal Expenditures by State for FY 1990" (April 1991)

U.S. Department of Defense Procurement Contract Awards in 1990

National Total = $135,259,039,000

RANK	STATE	CONTRACTS	%
1	California	$21,952,261,000	16.23%
2	Texas	8,825,869,000	6.53%
3	Massachusetts	7,927,809,000	5.86%
4	Virginia	7,831,697,000	5.79%
5	New York	6,698,138,000	4.95%
6	Missouri	6,025,346,000	4.45%
7	Florida	4,657,397,000	3.44%
8	Ohio	4,340,054,000	3.21%
9	Maryland	4,319,087,000	3.19%
10	Connecticut	4,251,160,000	3.14%
11	New Jersey	3,526,257,000	2.61%
12	Arizona	3,324,684,000	2.46%
13	Colorado	3,263,921,000	2.41%
14	Pennsylvania	2,787,707,000	2.06%
15	Washington	2,432,430,000	1.80%
16	Alabama	1,922,142,000	1.42%
17	Georgia	1,779,460,000	1.32%
18	Minnesota	1,747,790,000	1.29%
19	Indiana	1,674,885,000	1.24%
20	Louisiana	1,629,014,000	1.20%
21	Mississippi	1,406,598,000	1.04%
22	Illinois	1,301,927,000	0.96%
23	Michigan	1,265,474,000	0.94%
24	North Carolina	1,191,225,000	0.88%
25	Tennessee	1,138,861,000	0.84%

RANK	STATE	CONTRACTS	%
26	Kansas	$921,807,000	0.68%
27	Wisconsin	910,891,000	0.67%
28	Utah	883,014,000	0.65%
29	Maine	847,292,000	0.63%
30	South Carolina	697,750,000	0.52%
31	New Mexico	667,539,000	0.49%
32	Oklahoma	613,111,000	0.45%
33	Rhode Island	550,178,000	0.41%
34	Hawaii	508,351,000	0.38%
35	Iowa	486,707,000	0.36%
36	Alaska	440,864,000	0.33%
37	Kentucky	410,015,000	0.30%
38	New Hampshire	368,538,000	0.27%
39	Oregon	362,061,000	0.27%
40	Arkansas	310,034,000	0.23%
41	Nebraska	240,973,000	0.18%
42	West Virginia	222,976,000	0.16%
43	Nevada	182,114,000	0.13%
44	North Dakota	98,733,000	0.07%
45	Delaware	95,974,000	0.07%
46	Vermont	73,151,000	0.05%
47	Montana	69,497,000	0.05%
48	Wyoming	63,340,000	0.05%
49	Idaho	39,897,000	0.03%
50	South Dakota	35,179,000	0.03%

	CONTRACTS	%
District of Columbia	1,246,092,000	0.92%
Other*	892,411,000	0.66%
Undistributed**	15,799,357,000	11.68%

Source: U.S. Bureau of the Census,
"Federal Expenditures by State for FY 1990" (April 1991)

"Other" is American Samoa, Guam, Northern Marianas, Puerto Rico and the Virgin Islands.

Includes awards under $25,000 and classified location awards.

Per Capita U.S. Department of Defense Procurement Contracts in 1990

National Per Capita = $543.84

RANK	STATE	PER CAPITA	RANK	STATE	PER CAPITA
1	Massachusetts	$1,317.69	26	New Hampshire	$332.24
2	Connecticut	1,293.28	27	Indiana	302.10
3	Virginia	1,265.76	28	Georgia	274.68
4	Missouri	1,177.50	29	Pennsylvania	234.62
5	Colorado	990.75	30	Tennessee	233.51
6	Arizona	907.09	31	South Carolina	200.12
7	Maryland	903.30	32	Oklahoma	194.91
8	Alaska	801.51	33	Wisconsin	186.21
9	California	737.64	34	North Carolina	179.71
10	Maine	690.02	35	Iowa	175.28
11	Rhode Island	548.28	36	North Dakota	154.56
12	Mississippi	546.63	37	Nebraska	152.67
13	Texas	519.58	38	Nevada	151.53
14	Utah	512.53	39	Delaware	144.07
15	Washington	499.81	40	Wyoming	139.64
16	Alabama	475.71	41	Michigan	136.14
17	Hawaii	458.71	42	Arkansas	131.89
18	New Jersey	456.17	43	Vermont	129.99
19	New Mexico	440.60	44	Oregon	127.38
20	Ohio	400.11	45	West Virginia	124.33
21	Minnesota	399.49	46	Illinois	113.90
22	Louisiana	386.02	47	Kentucky	111.26
23	New York	372.32	48	Montana	86.97
24	Kansas	372.06	49	South Dakota	50.54
25	Florida	359.98	50	Idaho	39.63

District of Columbia   2,053.21

Source: U.S. Bureau of the Census,

"Federal Expenditures by State for FY 1990" (April 1991)

*Rates calculated by the editors using 1990 Census resident population.

U.S. Department of Defense Payroll in 1989

National Total = $66,180,000,000

RANK	STATE	PAYROLL	%
1	California	$10,529,000,000	15.91%
2	Virginia	7,634,000,000	11.54%
3	Texas	4,908,000,000	7.42%
4	Florida	3,246,000,000	4.90%
5	Georgia	2,762,000,000	4.17%
6	North Carolina	2,673,000,000	4.04%
7	Maryland	2,277,000,000	3.44%
8	Washington	2,172,000,000	3.28%
9	Hawaii	2,002,000,000	3.03%
10	South Carolina	1,912,000,000	2.89%
11	Pennsylvania	1,699,000,000	2.57%
12	Kentucky	1,444,000,000	2.18%
13	Ohio	1,434,000,000	2.17%
14	Alabama	1,378,000,000	2.08%
15	Colorado	1,362,000,000	2.06%
16	Oklahoma	1,358,000,000	2.05%
17	New York	1,293,000,000	1.95%
18	Illinois	1,290,000,000	1.95%
19	New Jersey	1,205,000,000	1.82%
20	Missouri	1,053,000,000	1.59%
21	Louisiana	925,000,000	1.40%
22	Arizona	894,000,000	1.35%
23	Kansas	803,000,000	1.21%
24	Utah	768,000,000	1.16%
25	Alaska	761,000,000	1.15%

RANK	STATE	PAYROLL	%
26	Mississippi	$692,000,000	1.05%
27	Massachusetts	650,000,000	0.98%
28	New Mexico	640,000,000	0.97%
29	Indiana	597,000,000	0.90%
30	Michigan	557,000,000	0.84%
31	Maine	490,000,000	0.74%
32	Nebraska	457,000,000	0.69%
33	Connecticut	452,000,000	0.68%
34	Tennessee	393,000,000	0.59%
35	Arkansas	336,000,000	0.51%
36	Rhode Island	287,000,000	0.43%
37	Nevada	281,000,000	0.42%
38	North Dakota	276,000,000	0.42%
39	South Dakota	182,000,000	0.28%
40	Idaho	147,000,000	0.22%
41	New Hampshire	145,000,000	0.22%
42	Delaware	143,000,000	0.22%
43	Montana	131,000,000	0.20%
44	Oregon	121,000,000	0.18%
45	Wisconsin	118,000,000	0.18%
46	Wyoming	114,000,000	0.17%
47	Minnesota	109,000,000	0.16%
48	West Virginia	58,000,000	0.09%
49	Iowa	47,000,000	0.07%
50	Vermont	20,000,000	0.03%
	District of Columbia	951,000,000	1.44%

Source: U.S. Department of Defense,
"Atlas/Data Abstract for the United States and Selected Areas" (annual)

U.S. Department of Defense Military Personnel in 1989

National Total = 1,342,100 Military Personnel

RANK	STATE	PERSONNEL	%	RANK	STATE	PERSONNEL	%
1	California	204,200	15.21%	26	Ohio	11,700	0.87%
2	Texas	127,000	9.46%	27	North Dakota	10,800	0.80%
3	Virginia	96,200	7.17%	28	Nevada	10,300	0.77%
4	North Carolina	92,300	6.88%	29	Tennessee	9,900	0.74%
5	Florida	77,800	5.80%	30	Massachusetts	9,700	0.72%
6	Georgia	63,300	4.72%	31	Arkansas	9,000	0.67%
7	Hawaii	43,800	3.26%	32	Michigan	8,600	0.64%
8	South Carolina	41,600	3.10%	33	South Dakota	7,000	0.52%
9	Washington	40,500	3.02%	34	Connecticut	6,700	0.50%
10	Colorado	40,000	2.98%	35	Pennsylvania	6,000	0.45%
11	Kentucky	38,800	2.89%	36	Utah	5,800	0.43%
12	Illinois	38,300	2.85%	37	Indiana	5,700	0.42%
13	Maryland	36,600	2.73%	38	Maine	5,600	0.42%
14	New York	28,900	2.15%	39	Idaho	5,200	0.39%
15	Oklahoma	28,200	2.10%	40	Delaware	4,600	0.34%
16	Arizona	26,200	1.95%	40	Montana	4,600	0.34%
17	Louisiana	25,300	1.89%	42	Rhode Island	4,100	0.31%
18	Alaska	22,800	1.70%	43	Wyoming	3,800	0.28%
19	Kansas	22,300	1.66%	44	New Hampshire	3,600	0.27%
20	Alabama	21,200	1.58%	45	Wisconsin	900	0.07%
21	New Jersey	18,000	1.34%	46	Minnesota	800	0.06%
22	Missouri	16,800	1.25%	47	Oregon	700	0.05%
23	New Mexico	15,000	1.12%	48	Iowa	400	0.03%
24	Mississippi	14,700	1.10%	48	West Virginia	400	0.03%
25	Nebraska	13,100	0.98%	50	Vermont	100	0.01%

	District of Columbia	13,600	1.01%

Source: U.S. Department of Defense,
 "Atlas/Data Abstract for the United States and Selected Areas" (annual)

U.S. Department of Defense Civilian Employees in 1989

National Total = 964,600 Civilian Employees

RANK	STATE	EMPLOYEES	%	RANK	STATE	EMPLOYEES	%
1	California	131,500	13.63%	26	Arizona	11,200	1.16%
2	Virginia	111,700	11.58%	27	Maine	10,700	1.11%
3	Texas	62,300	6.46%	28	Kansas	9,500	0.98%
4	Pennsylvania	52,000	5.39%	29	New Mexico	9,200	0.95%
5	Maryland	43,700	4.53%	30	Louisiana	8,500	0.88%
6	Georgia	39,900	4.14%	31	Tennessee	7,700	0.80%
7	Ohio	35,800	3.71%	32	Arkansas	5,200	0.54%
8	Florida	33,800	3.50%	33	Alaska	5,100	0.53%
9	Washington	29,400	3.05%	34	Connecticut	5,000	0.52%
10	Alabama	25,700	2.66%	35	Nebraska	4,800	0.50%
11	Oklahoma	24,400	2.53%	36	Rhode Island	4,500	0.47%
12	Missouri	23,500	2.44%	37	Minnesota	3,600	0.37%
13	Utah	22,000	2.28%	38	Wisconsin	3,300	0.34%
14	Illinois	21,700	2.25%	39	Oregon	3,200	0.33%
15	New Jersey	21,500	2.23%	40	Nevada	2,200	0.23%
16	South Carolina	20,700	2.15%	41	West Virginia	2,000	0.21%
17	Hawaii	20,200	2.09%	42	North Dakota	1,900	0.20%
17	New York	20,200	2.09%	43	Delaware	1,800	0.19%
19	Indiana	15,700	1.63%	43	New Hampshire	1,800	0.19%
20	North Carolina	15,500	1.61%	45	Iowa	1,500	0.16%
21	Colorado	14,400	1.49%	45	South Dakota	1,500	0.16%
22	Kentucky	14,000	1.45%	47	Montana	1,400	0.15%
23	Mississippi	13,300	1.38%	48	Idaho	1,300	0.13%
24	Michigan	13,100	1.36%	49	Wyoming	1,200	0.12%
25	Massachusetts	12,200	1.26%	50	Vermont	600	0.06%

District of Columbia 17,900 1.86%

Source: U.S. Department of Defense,
"Atlas/Data Abstract for the United States and Selected Areas" (annual)

Veterans in 1991

National Total = 26,506,500 Veterans

RANK	STATE	VETERANS	%	RANK	STATE	VETERANS	%
1	California	2,749,800	10.37%	26	Oklahoma	370,200	1.40%
2	Texas	1,740,300	6.57%	27	South Carolina	353,200	1.33%
3	New York	1,719,800	6.49%	28	Oregon	346,900	1.31%
4	Florida	1,550,200	5.85%	29	Kentucky	345,500	1.30%
5	Pennsylvania	1,462,000	5.52%	30	Iowa	314,400	1.19%
6	Ohio	1,254,000	4.73%	31	Kansas	273,800	1.03%
7	Illinois	1,173,800	4.43%	32	Arkansas	247,300	0.93%
8	Michigan	989,600	3.73%	33	Mississippi	225,500	0.85%
9	New Jersey	842,200	3.18%	34	West Virginia	209,000	0.79%
10	North Carolina	678,800	2.56%	35	Nebraska	172,700	0.65%
11	Georgia	668,100	2.52%	36	New Mexico	171,000	0.65%
12	Virginia	655,000	2.47%	37	Maine	152,200	0.57%
13	Massachusetts	637,700	2.41%	38	Nevada	147,600	0.56%
14	Indiana	621,500	2.34%	39	New Hampshire	145,500	0.55%
15	Missouri	616,700	2.33%	40	Utah	136,300	0.51%
16	Washington	590,700	2.23%	41	Rhode Island	114,100	0.43%
17	Wisconsin	549,400	2.07%	42	Idaho	106,000	0.40%
18	Maryland	532,100	2.01%	43	Hawaii	98,800	0.37%
19	Tennessee	522,300	1.97%	44	Montana	98,200	0.37%
20	Minnesota	481,900	1.82%	45	Delaware	78,800	0.30%
21	Arizona	427,800	1.61%	46	South Dakota	75,300	0.28%
22	Louisiana	407,100	1.54%	47	Alaska	64,200	0.24%
23	Alabama	396,700	1.50%	48	Vermont	63,500	0.24%
24	Colorado	390,700	1.47%	49	North Dakota	60,900	0.23%
25	Connecticut	371,600	1.40%	50	Wyoming	52,200	0.20%
					District of Columbia	53,300	0.20%

Source: U.S. Department of Veteran Affairs,
"Veteran Population Estimates" (September 30, 1991)

Male Veterans in 1991

National Total = 25,276,200 Male Veterans

RANK	STATE	VETERANS	%	RANK	STATE	VETERANS	%
1	California	2,603,400	10.30%	26	Oklahoma	354,500	1.40%
2	Texas	1,658,000	6.56%	27	South Carolina	336,300	1.33%
3	New York	1,644,400	6.51%	28	Kentucky	333,000	1.32%
4	Florida	1,461,700	5.78%	29	Oregon	329,300	1.30%
5	Pennsylvania	1,402,300	5.55%	30	Iowa	301,400	1.19%
6	Ohio	1,202,200	4.76%	31	Kansas	263,700	1.04%
7	Illinois	1,128,600	4.47%	32	Arkansas	236,400	0.94%
8	Michigan	947,100	3.75%	33	Mississippi	214,600	0.85%
9	New Jersey	808,200	3.20%	34	West Virginia	200,800	0.79%
10	North Carolina	648,100	2.56%	35	Nebraska	165,500	0.65%
11	Georgia	635,000	2.51%	36	New Mexico	161,700	0.64%
12	Virginia	618,500	2.45%	37	Maine	145,000	0.57%
13	Massachusetts	608,000	2.41%	38	Nevada	140,300	0.56%
14	Indiana	596,400	2.36%	39	New Hampshire	137,600	0.54%
15	Missouri	592,000	2.34%	40	Utah	131,000	0.52%
16	Washington	559,700	2.21%	41	Rhode Island	109,300	0.43%
17	Wisconsin	526,000	2.08%	42	Idaho	101,500	0.40%
18	Maryland	502,900	1.99%	43	Hawaii	93,300	0.37%
19	Tennessee	500,700	1.98%	43	Montana	93,300	0.37%
20	Minnesota	462,600	1.83%	45	Delaware	74,500	0.29%
21	Arizona	403,600	1.60%	46	South Dakota	72,300	0.29%
22	Louisiana	387,900	1.53%	47	Alaska	60,400	0.24%
23	Alabama	378,900	1.50%	48	Vermont	60,100	0.24%
24	Colorado	370,100	1.46%	49	North Dakota	58,500	0.23%
25	Connecticut	355,800	1.41%	50	Wyoming	50,000	0.20%
					District of Columbia	49,600	0.20%

Source: U.S. Department of Veteran Affairs,

"Veteran Population Estimates" (September 30, 1991)

Female Veterans in 1991

National Total = 1,230,400 Female Veterans

RANK	STATE	VETERANS	%		RANK	STATE	VETERANS	%
1	California	146,400	11.90%		26	South Carolina	17,000	1.38%
2	Florida	88,600	7.20%		27	Connecticut	15,800	1.28%
3	Texas	82,300	6.69%		28	Oklahoma	15,700	1.28%
4	New York	75,400	6.13%		29	Iowa	13,000	1.06%
5	Pennsylvania	59,700	4.85%		30	Kentucky	12,500	1.02%
6	Ohio	51,800	4.21%		31	Arkansas	10,900	0.89%
7	Illinois	45,200	3.67%		31	Mississippi	10,900	0.89%
8	Michigan	42,600	3.46%		33	Kansas	10,100	0.82%
9	Virginia	36,500	2.97%		34	New Mexico	9,200	0.75%
10	New Jersey	34,000	2.76%		35	West Virginia	8,200	0.67%
11	Georgia	33,100	2.69%		36	New Hampshire	7,900	0.64%
12	Washington	31,000	2.52%		37	Nevada	7,300	0.59%
13	North Carolina	30,700	2.50%		38	Maine	7,200	0.59%
14	Massachusetts	29,700	2.41%		38	Nebraska	7,200	0.59%
15	Maryland	29,300	2.38%		40	Hawaii	5,500	0.45%
16	Indiana	25,200	2.05%		41	Utah	5,300	0.43%
17	Missouri	24,700	2.01%		42	Montana	4,900	0.40%
18	Arizona	24,200	1.97%		42	Rhode Island	4,900	0.40%
19	Wisconsin	23,400	1.90%		44	Idaho	4,500	0.37%
20	Tennessee	21,600	1.76%		45	Delaware	4,300	0.35%
21	Colorado	20,600	1.67%		46	Alaska	3,800	0.31%
22	Minnesota	19,300	1.57%		47	Vermont	3,500	0.28%
23	Louisiana	19,200	1.56%		48	South Dakota	3,000	0.24%
24	Alabama	17,700	1.44%		49	North Dakota	2,400	0.20%
25	Oregon	17,600	1.43%		50	Wyoming	2,100	0.17%

District of Columbia   3,700   0.30%

Source: U.S. Department of Veteran Affairs,
"Veteran Population Estimates" (September 30, 1991)

IV. ECONOMY

Poverty Rate in 1990

National Poverty Rate = 13.1%*

RANK	STATE	PERCENT		RANK	STATE	PERCENT
1	Mississippi	25.0		26	Indiana	12.3
2	Louisiana	23.2		27	Maine	12.2
3	New Mexico	21.1		28	Minnesota	11.6
4	Arkansas	19.8		29	Ohio	11.5
5	Alabama	19.1		30	Hawaii	11.1
6	Tennessee	17.8		30	Nebraska	11.1
7	West Virginia	17.2		32	Alaska	11.0
8	Kentucky	17.0		33	Virginia	10.9
8	Texas	17.0		34	Pennsylvania	10.6
10	South Carolina	16.2		35	Wyoming	10.5
11	Oklahoma	15.9		36	Oregon	10.3
12	Montana	15.5		37	Iowa	10.0
13	Georgia	14.9		38	Kansas	9.7
14	Arizona	14.0		38	Nevada	9.7
15	South Dakota	13.6		40	Maryland	9.6
16	Florida	13.5		41	Massachusetts	9.3
17	New York	13.4		42	Washington	9.1
18	California	13.3		43	Vermont	9.0
18	Idaho	13.3		44	Utah	8.7
20	Michigan	13.2		45	Delaware	8.5
21	Illinois	13.0		45	Wisconsin	8.5
22	Missouri	12.9		47	Rhode Island	8.0
23	Colorado	12.8		48	New Jersey	7.9
24	North Carolina	12.6		49	New Hampshire	6.9
25	North Dakota	12.5		50	Connecticut	4.3

District of Columbia   18.1

Source: U.S. Bureau of the Census,

     "Poverty in the United States: 1990" (Series P-60, No. 175) and Press Release CB 91-287 (September 26, 1991)

*Estimates based on a three-year average (1988-1990). Census Bureau cautions against heavy reliance on state estimates because of relatively larger standard errors due to smaller sample sizes.

Personal Income in 1990

National Total = $4,662,698,000,000

RANK	STATE	INCOME	%
1	California	$619,381,000,000	13.28%
2	New York	397,602,000,000	8.53%
3	Texas	285,085,000,000	6.11%
4	Florida	241,713,000,000	5.18%
5	Illinois	233,661,000,000	5.01%
6	Pennsylvania	222,228,000,000	4.77%
7	New Jersey	192,893,000,000	4.14%
8	Ohio	190,720,000,000	4.09%
9	Michigan	171,003,000,000	3.67%
10	Massachusetts	135,861,000,000	2.91%
11	Virginia	122,215,000,000	2.62%
12	Georgia	110,886,000,000	2.38%
13	North Carolina	108,396,000,000	2.32%
14	Maryland	104,631,000,000	2.24%
15	Indiana	93,805,000,000	2.01%
16	Washington	92,174,000,000	1.98%
17	Missouri	89,572,000,000	1.92%
18	Wisconsin	86,147,000,000	1.85%
19	Connecticut	83,842,000,000	1.80%
20	Minnesota	82,223,000,000	1.76%
21	Tennessee	77,540,000,000	1.66%
22	Colorado	62,378,000,000	1.34%
23	Louisiana	61,237,000,000	1.31%
24	Alabama	60,776,000,000	1.30%
25	Arizona	58,946,000,000	1.26%

RANK	STATE	INCOME	%
26	Kentucky	$55,351,000,000	1.19%
27	South Carolina	53,006,000,000	1.14%
28	Oregon	49,198,000,000	1.06%
29	Oklahoma	48,620,000,000	1.04%
30	Iowa	47,870,000,000	1.03%
31	Kansas	45,050,000,000	0.97%
32	Arkansas	33,389,000,000	0.72%
33	Mississippi	33,009,000,000	0.71%
34	Nebraska	27,734,000,000	0.59%
35	West Virginia	24,622,000,000	0.53%
36	Utah	24,199,000,000	0.52%
37	Nevada	23,298,000,000	0.50%
38	New Hampshire	23,147,000,000	0.50%
39	Hawaii	22,663,000,000	0.49%
40	New Mexico	21,677,000,000	0.46%
41	Maine	21,146,000,000	0.45%
42	Rhode Island	18,894,000,000	0.41%
43	Idaho	15,423,000,000	0.33%
44	Delaware	13,397,000,000	0.29%
45	Montana	12,205,000,000	0.26%
46	Alaska	11,956,000,000	0.26%
47	South Dakota	10,997,000,000	0.24%
48	Vermont	9,889,000,000	0.21%
49	North Dakota	9,686,000,000	0.21%
50	Wyoming	7,378,000,000	0.16%

	District of Columbia	13,980,000,000	0.30%

Source: U.S. Department of Commerce, Bureau of Economic Analysis,
"Survey of Current Business" (August 1991, Vol. 71, No. 8)

Personal Income Per Capita in 1990

National Per Capita = $18,691

RANK	STATE	INCOME	RANK	STATE	INCOME
1	Connecticut	$25,484	26	Missouri	$17,472
2	New Jersey	24,936	27	Iowa	17,218
3	Massachusetts	22,569	28	Oregon	17,196
4	New York	22,086	29	Maine	17,175
5	Maryland	21,789	30	Georgia	17,049
6	Alaska	21,688	31	Indiana	16,890
7	New Hampshire	20,827	32	Texas	16,716
8	California	20,677	33	Wyoming	16,314
9	Illinois	20,419	34	North Carolina	16,293
10	Hawaii	20,356	35	Arizona	16,012
11	Delaware	20,022	36	Tennessee	15,866
12	Virginia	19,671	37	South Dakota	15,797
13	Nevada	19,035	38	Oklahoma	15,457
14	Colorado	18,890	39	Montana	15,270
15	Rhode Island	18,802	40	Idaho	15,249
16	Washington	18,775	41	North Dakota	15,215
17	Minnesota	18,731	42	South Carolina	15,151
18	Pennsylvania	18,686	43	Alabama	15,021
19	Florida	18,530	44	Kentucky	15,001
20	Michigan	18,360	45	Louisiana	14,542
21	Kansas	18,162	46	New Mexico	14,265
22	Ohio	17,564	47	Arkansas	14,188
23	Wisconsin	17,560	48	Utah	13,993
24	Nebraska	17,549	49	West Virginia	13,755
25	Vermont	17,511	50	Mississippi	12,823

District of Columbia   23,243

Source: U.S. Department of Commerce, Bureau of Economic Analysis,
"Survey of Current Business" (August 1991, Vol. 71, No. 8)

Annual Growth in Personal Income: 1989 to 1990

National Percentage Growth = 6.54% Increase

RANK	STATE	PERCENT GROWTH
1	Nevada	11.37
2	Hawaii	11.00
3	South Dakota	9.73
4	South Carolina	9.64
5	Washington	9.20
6	Idaho	8.97
7	Utah	8.58
8	Oregon	8.34
9	Texas	8.17
10	Wyoming	7.80
11	Louisiana	7.77
12	Nebraska	7.61
13	Kansas	7.48
14	California	7.44
15	Kentucky	7.28
16	Florida	7.26
17	Alabama	7.19
18	New Mexico	7.10
19	North Dakota	7.06
20	Colorado	6.97
21	North Carolina	6.86
21	West Virginia	6.86
23	Iowa	6.72
24	Arkansas	6.71
25	Maryland	6.52

RANK	STATE	PERCENT GROWTH
26	Georgia	6.51
27	Oklahoma	6.41
28	Wisconsin	6.38
29	Tennessee	6.35
30	Minnesota	6.32
31	Pennsylvania	6.23
32	Mississippi	6.18
33	New York	6.11
34	Alaska	6.03
35	Illinois	6.02
36	Arizona	5.92
37	Ohio	5.84
38	Virginia	5.77
39	Montana	5.69
40	Indiana	5.63
41	Delaware	5.55
42	New Jersey	5.47
43	Maine	5.30
44	Missouri	5.18
45	Vermont	4.82
46	Michigan	4.74
47	Rhode Island	4.43
48	Connecticut	4.40
49	Massachusetts	3.39
50	New Hampshire	2.67

District of Columbia   2.79

Source: U.S. Department of Commerce, Bureau of Economic Analysis,
"Survey of Current Business" (August 1991, Vol. 71, No. 8)

Adjusted Gross Income in 1989

National Total = $3,250,669,292,000

RANK	STATE	AGI	%
1	California	$428,913,735,000	13.19%
2	New York	275,422,642,000	8.47%
3	Texas	191,165,391,000	5.88%
4	Florida	169,688,336,000	5.22%
5	Illinois	162,700,520,000	5.01%
6	Pennsylvania	153,471,041,000	4.72%
7	New Jersey	137,226,542,000	4.22%
8	Ohio	133,501,983,000	4.11%
9	Michigan	121,711,417,000	3.74%
10	Massachusetts	96,339,542,000	2.96%
11	Virginia	88,219,678,000	2.71%
12	North Carolina	77,688,925,000	2.39%
13	Georgia	76,935,879,000	2.37%
14	Maryland	76,934,280,000	2.37%
15	Indiana	65,784,636,000	2.02%
16	Washington	65,106,425,000	2.00%
17	Connecticut	63,645,158,000	1.96%
18	Missouri	59,895,559,000	1.84%
19	Wisconsin	59,257,301,000	1.82%
20	Minnesota	57,353,862,000	1.76%
21	Tennessee	53,532,681,000	1.65%
22	Colorado	42,447,900,000	1.31%
23	Arizona	41,173,936,000	1.27%
24	Alabama	40,953,728,000	1.26%
25	Louisiana	38,354,213,000	1.18%

RANK	STATE	AGI	%
26	South Carolina	$36,548,640,000	1.12%
27	Kentucky	36,215,257,000	1.11%
28	Oregon	33,361,153,000	1.03%
29	Oklahoma	31,060,146,000	0.96%
30	Iowa	30,584,441,000	0.94%
31	Kansas	29,761,093,000	0.92%
32	Mississippi	20,784,199,000	0.64%
33	Arkansas	20,693,074,000	0.64%
34	Nebraska	17,773,115,000	0.55%
35	Nevada	17,175,259,000	0.53%
36	New Hampshire	17,145,954,000	0.53%
37	Utah	16,766,778,000	0.52%
38	West Virginia	16,192,043,000	0.50%
39	Hawaii	15,851,813,000	0.49%
40	New Mexico	14,547,845,000	0.45%
41	Maine	14,337,811,000	0.44%
42	Rhode Island	13,698,028,000	0.42%
43	Delaware	9,842,474,000	0.30%
44	Idaho	9,649,103,000	0.30%
45	Alaska	8,370,174,000	0.26%
46	Montana	7,517,874,000	0.23%
47	Vermont	7,102,811,000	0.22%
48	South Dakota	6,490,108,000	0.20%
49	North Dakota	6,154,756,000	0.19%
50	Wyoming	5,220,416,000	0.16%

	District of Columbia	10,030,094,000	0.31%
	Other*	20,372,527,000	0.63%

Source: Internal Revenue Service,
   "Statistics of Income Bulletin" (Winter 1990–1991)

*"Other" includes returns from military overseas, U.S. citizens abroad and residents of Puerto Rico with income from sources outside
   Puerto Rico or with income earned as U.S. Government employees.

Per Capita Adjusted Gross Income in 1989

National Per Capita = $13,095*

RANK	STATE	PER CAPITA AGI
1	Connecticut	$19,650
2	New Jersey	17,739
3	Maryland	16,390
4	Massachusetts	16,293
5	Alaska	15,883
6	New Hampshire	15,489
7	Nevada	15,459
8	New York	15,344
9	California	14,758
10	Delaware	14,625
11	Virginia	14,467
12	Hawaii	14,255
13	Illinois	13,956
14	Rhode Island	13,725
15	Washington	13,675
16	Florida	13,392
17	Minnesota	13,176
18	Michigan	13,125
19	Colorado	12,797
20	Pennsylvania	12,747
21	Vermont	12,527
22	Ohio	12,240
23	Wisconsin	12,175
24	Georgia	11,954
25	Kansas	11,843

RANK	STATE	PER CAPITA AGI
26	Oregon	$11,830
27	North Carolina	11,823
28	Indiana	11,762
29	Maine	11,733
30	Missouri	11,610
31	Arizona	11,579
32	Texas	11,251
33	Nebraska	11,032
34	Wyoming	10,990
35	Tennessee	10,837
36	Iowa	10,769
37	South Carolina	10,407
38	Alabama	9,945
39	Utah	9,822
40	Kentucky	9,717
41	Oklahoma	9,634
42	New Mexico	9,521
43	Idaho	9,516
44	Montana	9,327
45	North Dakota	9,325
46	South Dakota	9,077
47	Louisiana	8,753
48	West Virginia	8,719
49	Arkansas	8,601
50	Mississippi	7,930

District of Columbia   16,606

Source: Internal Revenue Service,

    "Statistics of Income Bulletin" (Winter 1990–1991)

*Calculated by the editors using 1989 Census figures.

Median Household Income in 1990

National Household Income = $30,163*

RANK	STATE	INCOME		RANK	STATE	INCOME
1	Connecticut	$41,162		26	Colorado	$29,316
2	New Jersey	40,019		27	Kansas	28,825
3	New Hampshire	39,540		28	Maine	28,793
4	Maryland	39,067		29	Georgia	28,647
5	Alaska	37,941		30	Indiana	27,758
6	Hawaii	37,445		31	Texas	27,697
7	Massachusetts	36,992		32	Nebraska	27,673
8	Virginia	35,702		33	Florida	27,416
9	California	33,848		34	South Carolina	27,343
10	Washington	33,838		35	Iowa	27,275
11	Delaware	32,769		36	Missouri	27,054
12	Illinois	32,717		37	North Carolina	27,045
13	New York	32,245		38	North Dakota	26,158
14	Rhode Island	32,230		39	Idaho	25,733
15	Vermont	32,037		40	Oklahoma	25,159
16	Minnesota	31,806		41	South Dakota	24,871
17	Michigan	31,645		42	Montana	24,303
18	Wisconsin	31,361		43	Kentucky	23,772
19	Nevada	31,288		44	New Mexico	23,394
20	Utah	30,530		45	Tennessee	23,156
21	Ohio	30,417		46	Louisiana	23,049
22	Oregon	30,003		47	Alabama	22,610
23	Wyoming	29,921		48	Arkansas	22,554
24	Pennsylvania	29,597		49	West Virginia	22,122
25	Arizona	29,508		50	Mississippi	20,414

District of Columbia 28,378

Source: U.S. Bureau of the Census,
   "Money Income of Households, Families, and Persons in the United States: 1990 (Series P-60, No. 174)
*Based on three-year average (1988-1990).

Insured Commercial Banks in 1989

National Total = 12,695 Banks*

RANK	STATE	BANKS	%		RANK	STATE	BANKS	%
1	Texas	1,318	10.38%		26	Montana	167	1.32%
2	Illinois	1,119	8.81%		27	North Dakota	158	1.24%
3	Minnesota	637	5.02%		28	South Dakota	129	1.02%
4	Iowa	576	4.54%		29	New Jersey	126	0.99%
5	Kansas	573	4.51%		30	Mississippi	123	0.97%
6	Missouri	551	4.34%		31	Maryland	106	0.83%
7	Wisconsin	510	4.02%		32	Massachusetts	99	0.78%
8	California	479	3.77%		33	New Mexico	93	0.73%
9	Colorado	451	3.55%		34	Washington	92	0.72%
10	Oklahoma	430	3.39%		35	South Carolina	82	0.65%
11	Florida	429	3.38%		36	North Carolina	78	0.61%
12	Georgia	392	3.09%		37	Wyoming	71	0.56%
12	Nebraska	392	3.09%		38	Connecticut	69	0.54%
14	Kentucky	335	2.64%		39	Utah	57	0.45%
15	Indiana	312	2.46%		40	Oregon	49	0.39%
16	Pennsylvania	298	2.35%		41	Delaware	48	0.38%
17	Ohio	293	2.31%		41	New Hampshire	48	0.38%
18	Michigan	268	2.11%		43	Arizona	43	0.34%
18	Tennessee	268	2.11%		44	Vermont	27	0.21%
20	Arkansas	257	2.02%		45	Idaho	23	0.18%
21	Louisiana	232	1.83%		46	Hawaii	21	0.17%
22	Alabama	221	1.74%		47	Maine	20	0.16%
23	New York	193	1.52%		48	Nevada	17	0.13%
24	West Virginia	188	1.48%		49	Rhode Island	13	0.10%
25	Virginia	182	1.43%		50	Alaska	7	0.06%
						District of Columbia	25	0.20%

Source: U.S. Federal Deposit Insurance Corporation,
    unpublished data
*As of December 31, 1989.

Assets of Insured Commercial Banks in 1989

National Total = $2,882,300,000,000*

RANK	STATE	ASSETS	%
1	New York	$392,100,000,000	13.60%
2	California	277,700,000,000	9.63%
3	Illinois	171,300,000,000	5.94%
4	Texas	170,800,000,000	5.93%
5	Pennsylvania	160,200,000,000	5.56%
6	Florida	131,400,000,000	4.56%
7	Ohio	107,200,000,000	3.72%
8	Massachusetts	101,400,000,000	3.52%
9	New Jersey	93,100,000,000	3.23%
10	Michigan	87,400,000,000	3.03%
11	North Carolina	73,300,000,000	2.54%
12	Virginia	67,100,000,000	2.33%
13	Delaware	66,400,000,000	2.30%
14	Georgia	64,300,000,000	2.23%
15	Missouri	58,100,000,000	2.02%
16	Indiana	56,100,000,000	1.95%
17	Maryland	52,000,000,000	1.80%
18	Minnesota	50,900,000,000	1.77%
19	Tennessee	44,800,000,000	1.55%
19	Wisconsin	44,800,000,000	1.55%
21	Connecticut	40,400,000,000	1.40%
22	Kentucky	39,300,000,000	1.36%
23	Washington	38,100,000,000	1.32%
24	Louisiana	36,300,000,000	1.26%
25	Alabama	36,200,000,000	1.26%

RANK	STATE	ASSETS	%
26	Iowa	$32,200,000,000	1.12%
27	Kansas	26,700,000,000	0.93%
28	Arizona	26,400,000,000	0.92%
29	Oklahoma	26,300,000,000	0.91%
30	Colorado	26,000,000,000	0.90%
31	South Carolina	23,700,000,000	0.82%
32	Oregon	22,000,000,000	0.76%
33	Mississippi	20,100,000,000	0.70%
33	South Dakota	20,100,000,000	0.70%
35	Arkansas	19,500,000,000	0.68%
36	Nebraska	18,600,000,000	0.65%
37	Nevada	17,000,000,000	0.59%
38	West Virginia	16,700,000,000	0.58%
39	Rhode Island	16,300,000,000	0.57%
40	Hawaii	14,300,000,000	0.50%
41	Utah	12,000,000,000	0.42%
42	New Mexico	10,700,000,000	0.37%
43	New Hampshire	10,400,000,000	0.36%
44	Idaho	8,300,000,000	0.29%
45	Maine	8,200,000,000	0.28%
46	Montana	7,000,000,000	0.24%
46	North Dakota	7,000,000,000	0.24%
48	Vermont	5,800,000,000	0.20%
49	Wyoming	4,400,000,000	0.15%
50	Alaska	4,300,000,000	0.15%

| | District of Columbia | 17,500,000,000 | 0.61% |

Source: U.S. Federal Deposit Insurance Corporation,
unpublished data
*As of December 31, 1989.

Deposits in Insured Commercial Banks in 1989

National Total = $2,223,600,000,000*

RANK	STATE	DEPOSITS	%	RANK	STATE	DEPOSITS	%
1	New York	$269,600,000,000	12.12%	26	Iowa	$27,400,000,000	1.23%
2	California	231,300,000,000	10.40%	27	Kansas	23,400,000,000	1.05%
3	Texas	140,700,000,000	6.33%	28	Arizona	23,100,000,000	1.04%
4	Illinois	128,000,000,000	5.76%	29	Oklahoma	23,000,000,000	1.03%
5	Pennsylvania	122,100,000,000	5.49%	30	Colorado	21,500,000,000	0.97%
6	Florida	110,000,000,000	4.95%	31	South Carolina	17,500,000,000	0.79%
7	Ohio	84,300,000,000	3.79%	32	Arkansas	17,200,000,000	0.77%
8	New Jersey	74,600,000,000	3.35%	32	Mississippi	17,200,000,000	0.77%
9	Michigan	72,300,000,000	3.25%	34	Oregon	16,800,000,000	0.76%
10	Massachusetts	71,200,000,000	3.20%	35	Nebraska	16,100,000,000	0.72%
11	Virginia	51,000,000,000	2.29%	36	West Virginia	14,200,000,000	0.64%
12	North Carolina	50,900,000,000	2.29%	37	Hawaii	12,800,000,000	0.58%
13	Georgia	49,300,000,000	2.22%	38	Rhode Island	10,800,000,000	0.49%
14	Missouri	48,300,000,000	2.17%	39	South Dakota	9,500,000,000	0.43%
15	Indiana	45,900,000,000	2.06%	40	Utah	9,300,000,000	0.42%
16	Minnesota	40,400,000,000	1.82%	41	New Mexico	9,000,000,000	0.40%
17	Maryland	39,000,000,000	1.75%	42	New Hampshire	8,600,000,000	0.39%
18	Tennessee	37,800,000,000	1.70%	43	Nevada	7,800,000,000	0.35%
19	Wisconsin	37,500,000,000	1.69%	44	Maine	7,000,000,000	0.31%
20	Louisiana	31,700,000,000	1.43%	45	Idaho	6,500,000,000	0.29%
21	Connecticut	31,400,000,000	1.41%	46	North Dakota	6,200,000,000	0.28%
21	Kentucky	31,400,000,000	1.41%	47	Montana	6,100,000,000	0.27%
23	Washington	31,000,000,000	1.39%	48	Vermont	5,200,000,000	0.23%
24	Alabama	29,100,000,000	1.31%	49	Wyoming	3,800,000,000	0.17%
25	Delaware	28,100,000,000	1.26%	50	Alaska	3,400,000,000	0.15%
					District of Columbia	13,200,000,000	0.59%

Source: U.S. Federal Deposit Insurance Corporation,
   unpublished data
*As of December 31, 1989.

Insured Commercial Banks Closed in 1989

National Total = 207 Banks Closed*

RANK	STATE	BANKS CLOSED	%	RANK	STATE	BANKS CLOSED	%
1	Texas	134	64.73%	20	Illinois	0	0.00%
2	Louisiana	21	10.14%	20	Indiana	0	0.00%
3	Oklahoma	12	5.80%	20	Iowa	0	0.00%
4	Colorado	7	3.38%	20	Kentucky	0	0.00%
5	Arizona	6	2.90%	20	Maine	0	0.00%
6	Florida	5	2.42%	20	Maryland	0	0.00%
6	Kansas	5	2.42%	20	Michigan	0	0.00%
8	New York	3	1.45%	20	Mississippi	0	0.00%
9	Alaska	2	0.97%	20	Nevada	0	0.00%
9	Montana	2	0.97%	20	New Hampshire	0	0.00%
9	North Dakota	2	0.97%	20	New Jersey	0	0.00%
12	California	1	0.48%	20	New Mexico	0	0.00%
12	Connecticut	1	0.48%	20	North Carolina	0	0.00%
12	Massachusetts	1	0.48%	20	Ohio	0	0.00%
12	Minnesota	1	0.48%	20	Oregon	0	0.00%
12	Missouri	1	0.48%	20	Pennsylvania	0	0.00%
12	Nebraska	1	0.48%	20	Rhode Island	0	0.00%
12	Virginia	1	0.48%	20	South Carolina	0	0.00%
12	West Virginia	1	0.48%	20	South Dakota	0	0.00%
20	Alabama	0	0.00%	20	Tennessee	0	0.00%
20	Arkansas	0	0.00%	20	Utah	0	0.00%
20	Delaware	0	0.00%	20	Vermont	0	0.00%
20	Georgia	0	0.00%	20	Washington	0	0.00%
20	Hawaii	0	0.00%	20	Wisconsin	0	0.00%
20	Idaho	0	0.00%	20	Wyoming	0	0.00%
					District of Columbia	0	0.00%

Source: U.S. Federal Deposit Insurance Corporation,
    unpublished data
*As of December 31, 1989.

Savings Institutions in 1989

National Total = 22,224 Savings Institutions*

RANK	STATE	INSTITUTIONS	%	RANK	STATE	INSTITUTIONS	%
1	California	3,164	14.24%	26	Minnesota	280	1.26%
2	Florida	1,937	8.72%	27	Alabama	270	1.21%
3	Texas	1,572	7.07%	28	Kentucky	259	1.17%
4	Ohio	1,317	5.93%	29	Arkansas	254	1.14%
5	Illinois	1,075	4.84%	30	Oklahoma	252	1.13%
6	Pennsylvania	1,050	4.72%	31	Nebraska	232	1.04%
7	New Jersey	907	4.08%	32	Mississippi	199	0.90%
8	New York	725	3.26%	33	Massachusetts	160	0.72%
9	North Carolina	645	2.90%	34	Hawaii	150	0.67%
10	Michigan	621	2.79%	35	New Mexico	124	0.56%
11	Virginia	580	2.61%	36	Connecticut	117	0.53%
12	Maryland	562	2.53%	37	Utah	90	0.40%
13	Wisconsin	543	2.44%	38	Nevada	89	0.40%
14	Missouri	486	2.19%	39	North Dakota	77	0.35%
15	Georgia	477	2.15%	40	West Virginia	75	0.34%
16	Indiana	418	1.88%	41	Idaho	62	0.28%
17	Louisiana	368	1.66%	42	South Dakota	61	0.27%
18	Washington	361	1.62%	43	Montana	60	0.27%
19	South Carolina	332	1.49%	44	Wyoming	44	0.20%
20	Arizona	315	1.42%	45	New Hampshire	41	0.18%
21	Colorado	310	1.39%	46	Maine	38	0.17%
22	Iowa	308	1.39%	47	Rhode Island	33	0.15%
23	Tennessee	301	1.35%	48	Delaware	22	0.10%
24	Oregon	293	1.32%	49	Vermont	19	0.09%
25	Kansas	286	1.29%	50	Alaska	16	0.07%
					District of Columbia	92	0.41%

Source: U.S. Office of Thrift Supervision,
   "Savings & Home Financing Source Book 1989" (March 1991)
*As of June, 1989. Insured by the Savings Association Insurance Fund (SAIF).

Deposits in Savings Institutions as of 1989

National Total = $937,435,000,000*

RANK	STATE	DEPOSITS	%	RANK	STATE	DEPOSITS	%
1	California	$225,573,000,000	24.06%	26	Oklahoma	$7,593,000,000	0.81%
2	Florida	78,470,000,000	8.37%	27	Massachusetts	7,411,000,000	0.79%
3	Texas	75,125,000,000	8.01%	28	Iowa	7,392,000,000	0.79%
4	Illinois	55,198,000,000	5.89%	29	Kentucky	6,814,000,000	0.73%
5	Ohio	44,211,000,000	4.72%	30	Arkansas	6,549,000,000	0.70%
6	New York	43,198,000,000	4.61%	31	Alabama	6,322,000,000	0.67%
7	New Jersey	42,862,000,000	4.57%	32	Nebraska	5,800,000,000	0.62%
8	Pennsylvania	35,497,000,000	3.79%	33	Hawaii	4,849,000,000	0.52%
9	Michigan	21,940,000,000	2.34%	34	Connecticut	4,811,000,000	0.51%
10	Maryland	19,329,000,000	2.06%	35	New Mexico	4,438,000,000	0.47%
11	Missouri	18,670,000,000	1.99%	36	Mississippi	3,992,000,000	0.43%
12	Virginia	18,523,000,000	1.98%	37	Nevada	3,201,000,000	0.34%
13	North Carolina	17,335,000,000	1.85%	38	North Dakota	2,284,000,000	0.24%
14	Arizona	16,717,000,000	1.78%	39	Rhode Island	2,102,000,000	0.22%
15	Kansas	15,738,000,000	1.68%	40	Utah	1,708,000,000	0.18%
16	Georgia	14,479,000,000	1.54%	41	West Virginia	1,684,000,000	0.18%
17	Wisconsin	14,052,000,000	1.50%	42	New Hampshire	1,409,000,000	0.15%
18	Colorado	13,747,000,000	1.47%	43	South Dakota	1,356,000,000	0.14%
19	Louisiana	12,888,000,000	1.37%	44	Idaho	1,179,000,000	0.13%
20	Indiana	11,591,000,000	1.24%	45	Montana	1,099,000,000	0.12%
21	Washington	11,488,000,000	1.23%	46	Wyoming	1,092,000,000	0.12%
22	Minnesota	10,247,000,000	1.09%	47	Maine	999,000,000	0.11%
23	Tennessee	9,722,000,000	1.04%	48	Delaware	483,000,000	0.05%
24	South Carolina	8,803,000,000	0.94%	49	Vermont	383,000,000	0.04%
25	Oregon	8,000,000,000	0.85%	50	Alaska	330,000,000	0.04%
					District of Columbia	4,104,000,000	0.44%

Source: U.S. Office of Thrift Supervision,
   "Savings & Home Financing Source Book 1989" (March 1991)
*As of June, 1989. Insured by the Savings Association Insurance Fund (SAIF).

Net Income After Taxes of Savings and Loans in 1989

National Total = –$14,083,000,000 Net Loss*

RANK	STATE	NET INCOME		RANK	STATE	NET INCOME
1	Ohio	$105,000,000		26	Illinois	($23,000,000)
2	Washington	85,000,000		27	Georgia	(26,000,000)
3	Indiana	66,000,000		28	North Carolina	(28,000,000)
4	Wisconsin	62,000,000		29	Rhode Island	(37,000,000)
5	Michigan	60,000,000		30	Oklahoma	(59,000,000)
6	Kentucky	47,000,000		31	Nebraska	(77,000,000)
7	Maryland	37,000,000		32	Alabama	(100,000,000)
8	Hawaii	30,000,000		33	Minnesota	(131,000,000)
9	Virginia	26,000,000		34	Mississippi	(139,000,000)
10	Nevada	19,000,000		35	Massachusetts	(181,000,000)
11	West Virginia	10,000,000		36	Utah	(232,000,000)
12	Montana	7,000,000		37	New Mexico	(248,000,000)
12	New Hampshire	7,000,000		38	Kansas	(302,000,000)
12	South Carolina	7,000,000		39	Arkansas	(333,000,000)
15	Maine	4,000,000		40	Louisiana	(339,000,000)
16	Connecticut	3,000,000		41	Oregon	(376,000,000)
17	Idaho	2,000,000		42	Missouri	(429,000,000)
18	Vermont	1,000,000		43	Colorado	(474,000,000)
19	Delaware	(1,000,000)		44	Pennsylvania	(670,000,000)
20	North Dakota	(7,000,000)		45	Florida	(823,000,000)
20	Wyoming	(7,000,000)		46	New Jersey	(940,000,000)
22	South Dakota	(11,000,000)		47	New York	(1,069,000,000)
23	Iowa	(14,000,000)		48	California	(1,168,000,000)
24	Tennessee	(17,000,000)		49	Arizona	(2,332,000,000)
25	Alaska	(19,000,000)		50	Texas	(4,074,000,000)

District of Columbia   25,000,000

Source: U.S. Office of Thrift Supervision,
   "Savings & Home Financing Source Book 1989" (March 1991)
Institutions insured by the Savings Association Insurance Fund (SAIF).

Return on Assets of Savings and Loans in 1989

National Return = −1.47% Loss*

RANK	STATE	PERCENT
1	Montana	0.65
2	Kentucky	0.62
3	Maine	0.51
4	West Virginia	0.48
5	Indiana	0.46
6	Hawaii	0.44
7	Washington	0.42
8	Nevada	0.37
8	New Hampshire	0.37
10	Wisconsin	0.36
11	Idaho	0.22
12	Ohio	0.17
13	Maryland	0.16
14	Vermont	0.13
15	Michigan	0.10
16	Virginia	0.03
17	Connecticut	0.01
17	South Carolina	0.01
19	Illinois	(0.02)
20	Tennessee	(0.14)
21	North Dakota	(0.16)
22	North Carolina	(0.20)
23	Delaware	(0.26)
24	Iowa	(0.31)
25	Wyoming	(0.55)

RANK	STATE	PERCENT
26	New Jersey	(0.57)
27	California	(0.66)
28	Georgia	(0.70)
29	South Dakota	(0.73)
30	Rhode Island	(1.00)
31	Alabama	(1.04)
32	Florida	(1.11)
33	Nebraska	(1.24)
34	Massachusetts	(1.80)
34	Missouri	(1.80)
36	New York	(1.85)
37	Kansas	(1.94)
38	Minnesota	(2.00)
39	Oklahoma	(2.63)
40	Pennsylvania	(2.69)
41	Louisiana	(3.07)
42	Oregon	(3.46)
43	Utah	(3.67)
44	Mississippi	(4.09)
45	Colorado	(4.10)
46	Texas	(6.27)
47	New Mexico	(6.97)
48	Arkansas	(7.37)
49	Arizona	(11.11)
50	Alaska	(13.37)

	District of Columbia	0.76

Source: U.S. Office of Thrift Supervision,
   "Savings & Home Financing Source Book 1989" (March 1991)
*Net income after taxes as a percent of average assets. Institutions insured by the Savings Association Insurance Fund (SAIF).

Savings and Loan Mortgages Foreclosed
as a Percent of Average Mortgage Balances in 1989
National Average = 2.50% of Mortgage Balances Foreclosed*

RANK	STATE	PERCENT	RANK	STATE	PERCENT
1	Arkansas	28.71	26	Montana	1.54
2	Arizona	19.61	27	New Jersey	1.45
3	Texas	14.99	28	West Virginia	1.39
4	Alaska	14.74	29	Virginia	1.17
5	Colorado	12.47	30	North Carolina	1.09
6	Kansas	8.29	30	South Carolina	1.09
7	New Mexico	8.11	32	California	1.03
8	Oklahoma	6.85	33	Maryland	0.99
9	Utah	3.60	34	Hawaii	0.96
10	Louisiana	3.44	35	South Dakota	0.86
11	Mississippi	3.39	35	Wisconsin	0.86
12	Tennessee	2.97	37	Idaho	0.82
13	Wyoming	2.87	38	New York	0.78
14	Minnesota	2.79	39	Ohio	0.75
15	Nebraska	2.78	40	Washington	0.74
16	North Dakota	2.75	41	New Hampshire	0.70
17	Alabama	2.46	42	Illinois	0.69
18	Iowa	2.42	43	Pennsylvania	0.60
19	Rhode Island	2.14	44	Michigan	0.51
20	Florida	2.07	45	Maine	0.50
21	Nevada	1.91	46	Indiana	0.44
22	Missouri	1.85	47	Kentucky	0.34
23	Massachusetts	1.78	48	Vermont	0.18
24	Georgia	1.73	49	Connecticut	0.17
25	Oregon	1.58	50	Delaware	0.00

District of Columbia   0.47

Source: U.S. Office of Thrift Supervision,
   "Savings & Home Financing Source Book 1989" (March 1991)
*At institutions insured by the Savings Association Insurance Fund (SAIF).

V. EDUCATION

V. EDUCATION (continued)

EDUCATION

School–Age Population as a Percent of Total Population in 1989

National Percent = 18.26% of Population is School–Age*

RANK	STATE	PERCENT		RANK	STATE	PERCENT
1	Utah	26.71		26	Wisconsin	18.47
2	Idaho	22.19		27	Minnesota	18.40
3	Mississippi	21.59		28	Iowa	18.27
4	Wyoming	21.05		29	Colorado	18.15
5	New Mexico	20.94		29	Illinois	18.15
6	Alaska	20.87		31	Missouri	18.14
7	Louisiana	20.79		32	Washington	18.04
8	Texas	20.45		33	Maine	18.00
9	Georgia	19.98		34	California	17.98
10	Arkansas	19.78		35	North Carolina	17.94
11	Alabama	19.69		36	Hawaii	17.90
12	South Carolina	19.65		37	Oregon	17.84
13	Montana	19.60		38	Vermont	17.81
14	South Dakota	19.58		39	Delaware	17.68
15	North Dakota	19.55		40	New Hampshire	17.62
16	Kentucky	19.21		41	Nevada	17.19
17	Oklahoma	19.20		42	Maryland	17.11
18	Indiana	19.04		43	Virginia	17.04
19	West Virginia	19.01		44	New York	16.96
20	Michigan	18.99		45	Pennsylvania	16.94
21	Nebraska	18.93		46	New Jersey	16.62
22	Arizona	18.87		47	Connecticut	16.42
23	Ohio	18.67		48	Rhode Island	16.23
24	Kansas	18.62		49	Florida	15.67
25	Tennessee	18.52		50	Massachusetts	15.63

District of Columbia   15.07

Source: U.S. Department of Education, National Center for Education Statistics,
"Digest of Education Statistics 1991" (NCES 91-697, November 1991)
*5 to 17-year olds. Total school-age population in 1989 was 45,330,000. Percentages calculated by the editors.

Public Elementary and Secondary Schools in 1990

National Total = 83,425 Schools*

RANK	STATE	SCHOOLS	%	RANK	STATE	SCHOOLS	%
1	California	7,433	8.91%	26	Colorado	1,337	1.60%
2	Texas	5,937	7.12%	27	Alabama	1,292	1.55%
3	Illinois	4,225	5.06%	28	Maryland	1,217	1.46%
4	New York	3,996	4.79%	29	Oregon	1,190	1.43%
5	Ohio	3,715	4.45%	30	South Carolina	1,103	1.32%
6	Michigan	3,314	3.97%	31	Arkansas	1,097	1.31%
7	Pennsylvania	3,276	3.93%	32	West Virginia	1,035	1.24%
8	Florida	2,505	3.00%	33	Arizona	1,026	1.23%
9	New Jersey	2,264	2.71%	34	Connecticut	983	1.18%
10	Missouri	2,151	2.58%	35	Mississippi	954	1.14%
11	Wisconsin	2,019	2.42%	36	South Dakota	799	0.96%
12	North Carolina	1,952	2.34%	37	Montana	758	0.91%
13	Indiana	1,923	2.31%	38	Maine	748	0.90%
14	Oklahoma	1,859	2.23%	39	Utah	718	0.86%
15	Washington	1,858	2.23%	40	North Dakota	679	0.81%
16	Massachusetts	1,817	2.18%	41	New Mexico	658	0.79%
17	Virginia	1,779	2.13%	42	Idaho	574	0.69%
18	Georgia	1,732	2.08%	43	Alaska	495	0.59%
19	Iowa	1,607	1.93%	44	New Hampshire	444	0.53%
20	Minnesota	1,564	1.87%	45	Wyoming	404	0.48%
21	Louisiana	1,536	1.84%	46	Vermont	336	0.40%
22	Tennessee	1,535	1.84%	47	Nevada	331	0.40%
23	Nebraska	1,524	1.83%	48	Rhode Island	294	0.35%
24	Kansas	1,459	1.75%	49	Hawaii	234	0.28%
25	Kentucky	1,385	1.66%	50	Delaware	170	0.20%

District of Columbia 184 0.22%

Source: U.S. Department of Education, National Center for Education Statistics,
"Digest of Education Statistics 1991" (NCES 91-697, November 1991)
*1989-90.

Public Elementary and Secondary School Districts in 1991

National Total = 15,203 School Districts*

RANK	STATE	DISTRICTS	%	RANK	STATE	DISTRICTS	%
1	Texas	1,076	7.08%	26	Georgia	185	1.22%
2	California	1,012	6.66%	27	South Dakota	183	1.20%
3	Illinois	956	6.29%	28	Colorado	176	1.16%
4	Nebraska	783	5.15%	28	Kentucky	176	1.16%
5	New York	718	4.72%	30	Connecticut	166	1.09%
6	Oklahoma	621	4.08%	31	New Hampshire	160	1.05%
7	Michigan	619	4.07%	32	Mississippi	151	0.99%
8	Ohio	612	4.03%	33	Tennessee	139	0.91%
9	New Jersey	592	3.89%	34	Virginia	137	0.90%
10	Missouri	543	3.57%	35	North Carolina	134	0.88%
11	Montana	528	3.47%	36	Alabama	130	0.86%
12	Pennsylvania	500	3.29%	37	Idaho	113	0.74%
13	Minnesota	433	2.85%	38	South Carolina	93	0.61%
14	Iowa	430	2.83%	39	New Mexico	88	0.58%
15	Wisconsin	428	2.82%	40	Florida	67	0.44%
16	Massachusetts	360	2.37%	41	Louisiana	66	0.43%
17	Arkansas	324	2.13%	42	West Virginia	55	0.36%
18	Kansas	304	2.00%	43	Alaska	54	0.36%
19	Vermont	303	1.99%	44	Wyoming	49	0.32%
20	Oregon	296	1.95%	45	Utah	40	0.26%
20	Washington	296	1.95%	46	Rhode Island	37	0.24%
22	Indiana	294	1.93%	47	Maryland	24	0.16%
23	North Dakota	268	1.76%	48	Delaware	19	0.12%
24	Maine	230	1.51%	49	Nevada	17	0.11%
25	Arizona	216	1.42%	50	Hawaii	1	0.01%

District of Columbia   1   0.01%

Source: National Education Association, Washington, D.C.,
    "Estimates of School Statistics 1990-91", (NEA, Reprinted by permission.)
*Estimate for 1990-91; operating school districts only.

Enrollment in Public Elementary and Secondary Schools in 1991

National Total = 41,047,643 Students*

RANK	STATE	STUDENTS	%	RANK	STATE	STUDENTS	%
1	California	4,950,474	12.06%	26	Oklahoma	577,000	1.41%
2	Texas	3,353,270	8.17%	27	Colorado	569,792	1.39%
3	New York	2,563,000	6.24%	28	Mississippi	500,122	1.22%
4	Florida	1,861,592	4.54%	29	Oregon	484,700	1.18%
5	Illinois	1,784,853	4.35%	30	Iowa	483,652	1.18%
6	Ohio	1,765,500	4.30%	31	Connecticut	472,970	1.15%
7	Pennsylvania	1,667,630	4.06%	32	Utah	444,732	1.08%
8	Michigan	1,582,321	3.85%	33	Arkansas	436,460	1.06%
9	Georgia	1,151,687	2.81%	34	Kansas	436,250	1.06%
10	New Jersey	1,082,561	2.64%	35	West Virginia	323,021	0.79%
11	North Carolina	1,082,558	2.64%	36	New Mexico	283,104	0.69%
12	Virginia	998,463	2.43%	37	Nebraska	273,002	0.67%
13	Indiana	949,133	2.31%	38	Idaho	220,840	0.54%
14	Washington	840,554	2.05%	39	Maine	210,200	0.51%
15	Massachusetts	834,159	2.03%	40	Nevada	201,310	0.49%
16	Tennessee	833,590	2.03%	41	New Hampshire	172,807	0.42%
17	Missouri	810,450	1.97%	42	Hawaii	171,056	0.42%
18	Wisconsin	790,900	1.93%	43	Montana	151,669	0.37%
19	Louisiana	779,161	1.90%	44	Rhode Island	137,946	0.34%
20	Minnesota	751,913	1.83%	45	South Dakota	128,635	0.31%
21	Alabama	726,158	1.77%	46	North Dakota	117,134	0.29%
22	Maryland	715,152	1.74%	47	Alaska	112,161	0.27%
23	Arizona	636,500	1.55%	48	Delaware	99,658	0.24%
24	Kentucky	630,091	1.54%	49	Wyoming	98,210	0.24%
25	South Carolina	622,618	1.52%	50	Vermont	96,230	0.23%
					District of Columbia	80,694	0.20%

Source: National Education Association, Washington, D.C.,

"Estimates of School Statistics 1990-91" (NEA, Reprinted by permission.)

*Estimate for 1990-91.

Public Elementary and Secondary School Enrollment Rate (Grades K–12) in 1990

National Rate = 90.71% of 5–17 Year Olds Enrolled in Public School*

RANK	STATE	RATE	RANK	STATE	RATE
1	Nevada	98.33	26	Iowa	92.01
2	Wyoming	97.48	27	North Dakota	91.84
3	Texas	97.32	28	Connecticut	90.74
4	Utah	97.14	29	Mississippi	90.70
5	Idaho	96.77	30	Minnesota	90.59
6	West Virginia	95.88	31	Michigan	90.10
7	Arkansas	95.62	32	Indiana	89.77
8	Alaska	95.50	33	Kentucky	89.60
9	Oklahoma	94.52	34	South Dakota	89.36
10	Vermont	94.51	35	New Hampshire	88.99
11	Tennessee	94.38	36	Maryland	88.90
12	North Carolina	94.37	37	Massachusetts	88.68
13	Maine	94.14	38	Nebraska	88.23
14	Virginia	94.05	38	New Mexico	88.23
15	Washington	93.96	40	Ohio	87.64
16	South Carolina	93.79	41	Louisiana	87.29
17	Colorado	93.66	42	Delaware	87.02
18	Alabama	93.64	43	Rhode Island	86.91
19	Georgia	93.50	44	Hawaii	86.87
20	Montana	93.14	45	Missouri	85.71
21	Oregon	92.73	46	New Jersey	85.45
22	Arizona	92.48	47	New York	85.33
22	California	92.48	48	Wisconsin	85.20
24	Florida	92.31	49	Illinois	85.06
25	Kansas	92.19	50	Pennsylvania	83.48

Source: U.S. Bureau of the Census (5-17 year old population) and National Education Association, Washington, D.C. (enrollment),
unpublished data and "Estimates of School Statistics 1990-91" (NEA, Reprinted by permission.)
*Rates calculated by the editors using 1990 Census population and 1990-91 estimated enrollment numbers.

Enrollment in Public Elementary Schools (Grades K–8) in 1991

National Total = 26,910,963 Students*

RANK	STATE	STUDENTS	%	RANK	STATE	STUDENTS	%
1	California	3,604,382	13.39%	26	Connecticut	344,328	1.28%
2	Texas	1,975,205	7.34%	27	Oklahoma	334,700	1.24%
3	New York	1,443,000	5.36%	28	Colorado	331,785	1.23%
4	Illinois	1,276,346	4.74%	29	Utah	322,736	1.20%
5	Michigan	1,140,564	4.24%	30	Oregon	321,500	1.19%
6	Ohio	1,139,619	4.23%	31	Mississippi	316,032	1.17%
7	Florida	1,099,976	4.09%	32	Kansas	291,019	1.08%
8	Pennsylvania	926,920	3.44%	33	Iowa	272,542	1.01%
9	Georgia	849,082	3.16%	34	Arkansas	245,652	0.91%
10	North Carolina	779,591	2.90%	35	West Virginia	191,555	0.71%
11	New Jersey	758,875	2.82%	36	Nebraska	167,310	0.62%
12	Indiana	672,665	2.50%	37	New Mexico	164,708	0.61%
13	Virginia	645,368	2.40%	38	Maine	154,526	0.57%
14	Massachusetts	601,493	2.24%	39	Idaho	125,037	0.46%
15	Tennessee	600,185	2.23%	40	Nevada	119,980	0.45%
16	Louisiana	580,275	2.16%	41	New Hampshire	113,648	0.42%
17	Missouri	579,118	2.15%	42	Montana	109,990	0.41%
18	Wisconsin	529,903	1.97%	43	Hawaii	100,071	0.37%
19	Washington	489,659	1.82%	44	South Dakota	94,287	0.35%
20	Arizona	474,000	1.76%	45	North Dakota	84,252	0.31%
21	South Carolina	452,968	1.68%	46	Alaska	83,584	0.31%
22	Kentucky	439,698	1.63%	47	Rhode Island	83,092	0.31%
23	Maryland	424,746	1.58%	48	Vermont	58,411	0.22%
24	Minnesota	423,350	1.57%	49	Delaware	57,669	0.21%
25	Alabama	409,571	1.52%	50	Wyoming	56,228	0.21%
					District of Columbia	49,762	0.18%

Source: National Education Association, Washington, D.C.,
    "Estimates of School Statistics 1990–91" (NEA, Reprinted by permission.)
*Estimate for 1990–91.

Enrollment in Public Secondary Schools (Grades 9–12) in 1991

National Total = 14,136,680 Students*

RANK	STATE	STUDENTS	%	RANK	STATE	STUDENTS	%
1	Texas	1,378,065	9.75%	26	Arkansas	190,808	1.35%
2	California	1,346,092	9.52%	27	Kentucky	190,393	1.35%
3	New York	1,120,000	7.92%	28	Mississippi	184,090	1.30%
4	Florida	761,616	5.39%	29	South Carolina	169,650	1.20%
5	Pennsylvania	740,710	5.24%	30	Oregon	163,200	1.15%
6	Ohio	625,881	4.43%	31	Arizona	162,500	1.15%
7	Illinois	508,507	3.60%	32	Kansas	145,231	1.03%
8	Michigan	441,757	3.12%	33	West Virginia	131,466	0.93%
9	Virginia	353,095	2.50%	34	Connecticut	128,642	0.91%
10	Washington	350,895	2.48%	35	Utah	121,996	0.86%
11	Minnesota	328,563	2.32%	36	New Mexico	118,396	0.84%
12	New Jersey	323,686	2.29%	37	Nebraska	105,692	0.75%
13	Alabama	316,587	2.24%	38	Idaho	95,803	0.68%
14	North Carolina	302,967	2.14%	39	Nevada	81,330	0.58%
15	Georgia	302,605	2.14%	40	Hawaii	70,985	0.50%
16	Maryland	290,406	2.05%	41	New Hampshire	59,159	0.42%
17	Indiana	276,468	1.96%	42	Maine	55,674	0.39%
18	Wisconsin	260,997	1.85%	43	Rhode Island	54,854	0.39%
19	Oklahoma	242,300	1.71%	44	Delaware	41,989	0.30%
20	Colorado	238,007	1.68%	45	Wyoming	41,982	0.30%
21	Tennessee	233,405	1.65%	46	Montana	41,679	0.29%
22	Massachusetts	232,666	1.65%	47	Vermont	37,819	0.27%
23	Missouri	231,332	1.64%	48	South Dakota	34,348	0.24%
24	Iowa	211,110	1.49%	49	North Dakota	32,882	0.23%
25	Louisiana	198,886	1.41%	50	Alaska	28,577	0.20%
					District of Columbia	30,932	0.22%

Source: National Education Association, Washington, D.C.,
"Estimates of School Statistics 1990-91" (NEA, Reprinted by permission.)
*Estimate for 1990-91.

Pupil–Teacher Ratio in 1989

National Ratio = 17.2 Pupils per Teacher*

RANK	STATE	RATIO	RANK	STATE	RATIO
1	Utah	24.8	25	Maryland	16.8
2	California	22.4	27	Texas	16.7
3	Nevada	20.4	28	Delaware	16.4
4	Idaho	20.1	29	New Hampshire	16.2
4	Washington	20.1	29	Oklahoma	16.2
6	Michigan	19.7	31	Virginia	15.9
7	Hawaii	19.1	31	Wisconsin	15.9
7	Tennessee	19.1	33	Missouri	15.8
9	Arizona	18.9	34	Iowa	15.7
10	Oregon	18.4	34	Montana	15.7
11	Georgia	18.3	34	Pennsylvania	15.7
11	New Mexico	18.3	37	South Dakota	15.5
13	Mississippi	18.2	38	North Dakota	15.1
14	Alabama	18.1	38	West Virginia	15.1
15	Kentucky	17.7	40	Kansas	15.0
16	Colorado	17.6	41	Nebraska	14.7
17	Indiana	17.5	41	New York	14.7
18	Ohio	17.4	43	Rhode Island	14.5
19	Minnesota	17.2	43	Wyoming	14.5
20	North Carolina	17.1	45	Maine	14.1
21	Arkansas	17.0	46	Massachusetts	14.0
21	Florida	17.0	47	Vermont	13.8
21	South Carolina	17.0	48	New Jersey	13.5
24	Illinois	16.9	49	Connecticut	13.1
25	Alaska	16.8	–	Louisiana**	N/A

District of Columbia 13.4

*Source: U.S. Department of Education, National Center for Education Statistics,
"Digest of Education Statistics 1991" (NCES 91-697, November 1991)*

*Fall 1989.

**Not available.

Teachers in Public Elementary and Secondary Schools in 1991

National Total = 2,408,836 Teachers*

RANK	STATE	TEACHERS	%	RANK	STATE	TEACHERS	%
1	California	214,900	8.92%	26	Arizona	35,278	1.46%
2	Texas	206,399	8.57%	27	Connecticut	35,164	1.46%
3	New York	188,900	7.84%	28	Colorado	32,461	1.35%
4	Florida	108,088	4.49%	29	Iowa	31,119	1.29%
5	Pennsylvania	104,800	4.35%	30	Kansas	29,086	1.21%
6	Illinois	104,543	4.34%	31	Mississippi	27,714	1.15%
7	Ohio	102,348	4.25%	32	Oregon	25,758	1.07%
8	New Jersey	81,934	3.40%	33	Arkansas	25,593	1.06%
9	Michigan	80,908	3.36%	34	West Virginia	21,476	0.89%
10	Georgia	68,859	2.86%	35	Nebraska	18,550	0.77%
11	North Carolina	64,335	2.67%	36	Utah	18,474	0.77%
12	Virginia	63,879	2.65%	37	New Mexico	16,233	0.67%
13	Massachusetts	59,040	2.45%	38	Maine	14,523	0.60%
14	Indiana	55,396	2.30%	39	Idaho	11,254	0.47%
15	Missouri	51,330	2.13%	40	New Hampshire	10,665	0.44%
16	Wisconsin	47,664	1.98%	41	Nevada	10,384	0.43%
17	Minnesota	43,771	1.82%	42	Hawaii	9,760	0.41%
18	Tennessee	43,640	1.81%	43	Montana	9,539	0.40%
19	Louisiana	43,610	1.81%	44	Rhode Island	9,437	0.39%
20	Maryland	42,143	1.75%	45	South Dakota	8,331	0.35%
21	Washington	41,816	1.74%	46	North Dakota	7,528	0.31%
22	Alabama	40,010	1.66%	47	Vermont	7,128	0.30%
23	Kentucky	36,651	1.52%	48	Alaska	6,586	0.27%
24	Oklahoma	36,600	1.52%	49	Wyoming	6,554	0.27%
25	South Carolina	35,600	1.48%	50	Delaware	5,951	0.25%

District of Columbia		7,126	0.30%

Source: National Education Association, Washington, D.C.,

   "Estimates of School Statistics 1990-91" (NEA, Reprinted by permission.)

*Estimate for 1990-91.

Average Salary of Classroom Teachers in 1991

National Average = $33,015*

RANK	STATE	SALARY	RANK	STATE	SALARY
1	Alaska	$43,861	26	Florida	$30,387
2	Connecticut	43,847	27	Kansas	29,923
3	New York	41,600	28	Kentucky	29,089
4	California	39,598	29	North Carolina	29,082
5	Maryland	38,806	30	Wyoming	28,988
6	New Jersey	38,790	31	Georgia	28,855
7	Michigan	37,682	32	Maine	28,700
8	Rhode Island	37,674	33	Missouri	28,607
9	Massachusetts	36,090	34	Texas	28,321
10	Pennsylvania	35,471	35	Tennessee	28,248
11	Delaware	35,200	36	South Carolina	28,174
12	Illinois	34,729	37	Iowa	27,949
13	Minnesota	33,284	38	Alabama	27,300
14	Wisconsin	33,100	39	Nebraska	26,592
15	Washington	32,975	40	Louisiana	26,240
16	Ohio	32,615	41	Montana	26,210
17	Hawaii	32,541	42	New Mexico	26,194
18	Virginia	32,382	43	West Virginia	25,958
19	Nevada	32,209	44	Idaho	25,485
20	Oregon	32,200	45	Utah	25,415
21	Indiana	32,178	46	Oklahoma	24,649
22	Colorado	32,020	47	Mississippi	24,443
23	New Hampshire	31,329	48	North Dakota	23,578
24	Vermont	30,986	49	Arkansas	23,040
25	Arizona	30,780	50	South Dakota	22,363
				District of Columbia	42,288

Source: National Education Association, Washington, D.C.,

"Estimates of School Statistics 1990-91" (NEA, Reprinted by permission.)

*Estimate for 1990-91.

Percent Increase in Average Teacher Salary: 1990 to 1991

National Percent = 5.4% Increase*

RANK	STATE	PERCENT		RANK	STATE	PERCENT
1	West Virginia	13.6		25	Virginia	4.6
2	Kentucky	10.6		27	Iowa	4.5
3	New Jersey	8.7		27	Montana	4.5
4	Connecticut	8.4		27	Ohio	4.5
5	Washington	8.3		27	Rhode Island	4.5
6	New Hampshire	8.1		31	Oregon	4.4
7	Louisiana	8.0		31	Tennessee	4.4
8	Alabama	7.9		33	New Mexico	4.3
9	Vermont	7.6		33	North Carolina	4.3
10	Utah	7.3		35	California	4.2
11	New York	6.9		35	Nebraska	4.2
12	Idaho	6.8		37	Colorado	4.1
12	Maine	6.8		37	Kansas	4.1
12	Oklahoma	6.8		39	Massachusetts	4.0
15	Pennsylvania	6.4		40	Wisconsin	3.7
16	Maryland	6.0		41	South Carolina	3.5
17	Illinois	5.9		42	Minnesota	3.4
17	Indiana	5.9		43	Arkansas	3.1
19	Delaware	5.5		44	Georgia	3.0
19	Florida	5.5		44	Texas	3.0
21	Nevada	5.3		46	Wyoming	2.8
22	Missouri	5.1		47	North Dakota	2.4
23	South Dakota	5.0		48	Alaska	1.6
24	Arizona	4.7		49	Hawaii	1.5
25	Michigan	4.6		50	Mississippi	0.3

District of Columbia   11.4

Source: National Education Association, Washington, D.C.,
    "Estimates of School Statistics 1990-91" (NEA, Reprinted by permission.)
*Estimated increase from 1989-90 school year to 1990-91 school year.

Public High School Graduates in 1991

National Total = 2,253,043 Students*

RANK	STATE	STUDENTS	%	RANK	STATE	STUDENTS	%
1	California	228,319	10.13%	26	Arizona	32,100	1.42%
2	Texas	184,060	8.17%	27	Colorado	31,800	1.41%
3	New York	133,800	5.94%	28	Connecticut	29,830	1.32%
4	Ohio	106,921	4.75%	29	Iowa	29,085	1.29%
5	Pennsylvania	103,200	4.58%	30	Arkansas	26,587	1.18%
6	Illinois	102,353	4.54%	31	Oregon	25,100	1.11%
7	Florida	89,276	3.96%	32	Kansas	24,094	1.07%
8	Michigan	89,122	3.96%	33	Utah	23,676	1.05%
9	New Jersey	64,460	2.86%	34	Mississippi	22,535	1.00%
10	North Carolina	62,005	2.75%	35	West Virginia	21,256	0.94%
11	Georgia	60,426	2.68%	36	Nebraska	17,664	0.78%
12	Virginia	58,154	2.58%	37	New Mexico	14,304	0.63%
13	Indiana	56,520	2.51%	38	Maine	12,754	0.57%
14	Massachusetts	50,866	2.26%	39	Idaho	11,594	0.51%
15	Wisconsin	50,700	2.25%	40	New Hampshire	10,191	0.45%
16	Missouri	46,297	2.05%	41	Nevada	9,622	0.43%
17	Minnesota	45,980	2.04%	42	Hawaii	9,578	0.43%
18	Washington	45,086	2.00%	43	Montana	9,000	0.40%
19	Tennessee	44,824	1.99%	44	North Dakota	7,960	0.35%
20	Maryland	39,110	1.74%	45	Rhode Island	7,523	0.33%
21	Louisiana	38,803	1.72%	46	South Dakota	6,649	0.30%
22	Alabama	38,663	1.72%	47	Delaware	6,230	0.28%
23	Kentucky	36,200	1.61%	48	Wyoming	5,741	0.25%
24	Oklahoma	36,000	1.60%	49	Vermont	5,436	0.24%
25	South Carolina	33,000	1.46%	50	Alaska	5,389	0.24%
					District of Columbia	3,200	0.14%

Source: U.S. Department of Education, National Center for Education Statistics,
   "Digest of Education Statistics 1991" (NCES 91-697, November 1991)
*Estimate for 1990-91.

Public High School Graduation Rate in 1989

National Rate = 71.4% Graduated

RANK	STATE	RATE	RANK	STATE	RATE
1	Minnesota	88.6	26	Oklahoma	74.4
2	North Dakota	87.9	27	New Hampshire	74.1
3	Iowa	86.4	28	Maryland	74.0
4	South Dakota	86.2	29	Missouri	73.5
5	Nebraska	86.1	30	Massachusetts	72.0
6	Montana	85.0	31	Nevada	71.9
7	Connecticut	83.2	31	Rhode Island	71.9
8	Kansas	82.1	33	Delaware	71.5
8	Utah	82.1	33	New Mexico	71.5
10	Wisconsin	81.8	35	Oregon	70.8
11	Hawaii	81.7	36	Michigan	70.7
12	Vermont	80.8	37	Arizona	68.8
13	New Jersey	79.6	37	North Carolina	68.8
14	Pennsylvania	79.2	39	Alabama	67.7
15	Arkansas	78.5	40	Tennessee	67.4
15	Illinois	78.5	41	California	67.3
17	Idaho	78.2	41	Kentucky	67.3
18	Maine	77.5	43	New York	65.0
19	West Virginia	76.7	43	South Carolina	65.0
20	Wyoming	76.5	45	Alaska	64.2
21	Washington	76.4	45	Texas	64.2
22	Indiana	76.2	47	Georgia	62.1
23	Colorado	75.9	48	Florida	61.5
24	Ohio	75.6	49	Mississippi	60.1
25	Virginia	74.7	50	Louisiana	56.9

District of Columbia 57.7

Source: U.S. Department of Education, National Center for Education Statistics,
unpublished data

Calculated by comparing numbers of public high school graduates in 1989 with 9th grade enrollment in Fall of 1985.

Percent of Population Graduated From High School in 1989

National Percent = 76.9% of Population*

RANK	STATE	PERCENT	RANK	STATE	PERCENT
1	Utah	88.2	26	Indiana	78.0
1	Washington	88.2	27	Florida	77.9
3	Alaska	86.9	28	Ohio	77.6
4	Wyoming	85.6	29	Idaho	77.3
5	Minnesota	85.5	30	Illinois	77.2
6	Nevada	84.0	31	Michigan	77.0
7	Oregon	83.9	32	Maine	76.9
8	Montana	83.6	33	Pennsylvania	76.8
9	Iowa	83.4	34	New York	76.7
10	Colorado	83.2	35	Missouri	75.9
11	Hawaii	82.3	36	Oklahoma	75.4
12	Kansas	82.2	37	New Mexico	74.6
12	Nebraska	82.2	38	Texas	74.3
12	New Hampshire	82.2	38	Virginia	74.3
15	Vermont	81.8	40	Rhode Island	72.7
16	North Dakota	81.1	41	North Carolina	71.3
16	Wisconsin	81.1	42	Georgia	71.1
18	Delaware	80.7	43	Louisiana	70.9
18	Maryland	80.7	44	South Carolina	69.8
18	Massachusetts	80.7	45	West Virginia	68.0
21	Arizona	80.6	46	Mississippi	67.7
21	Connecticut	80.6	47	Arkansas	67.6
23	New Jersey	79.4	48	Tennessee	65.4
24	California	78.6	49	Kentucky	64.7
25	South Dakota	78.3	50	Alabama	63.2

District of Columbia   72.9

Source: U.S. Bureau of the Census,

Press Release CB 91-317 (November 14, 1991)

*Persons age 25 and over.

Expenditure per Pupil in Public Elementary and Secondary Schools in 1991

National Average = $5,208 per Pupil*

RANK	STATE	PER PUPIL		RANK	STATE	PER PUPIL
1	New York	$8,680		26	Georgia	$4,852
2	Connecticut	8,455		27	California	4,826
3	New Jersey	8,451		28	Montana	4,794
4	Rhode Island	6,989		29	Colorado	4,702
5	Alaska	6,952		30	West Virginia	4,695
6	Pennsylvania	6,534		31	Nevada	4,677
7	Massachusetts	6,351		32	North Carolina	4,635
8	Maryland	6,184		33	Missouri	4,479
9	Delaware	6,016		34	New Mexico	4,446
10	Wisconsin	5,946		35	Indiana	4,398
11	Maine	5,894		36	Kentucky	4,390
12	Vermont	5,740		37	Texas	4,326
13	New Hampshire	5,474		38	Arizona	4,196
14	Minnesota	5,360		39	Nebraska	4,080
15	Virginia	5,335		40	Louisiana	4,041
16	Oregon	5,291		41	South Carolina	3,843
17	Ohio	5,269		42	Oklahoma	3,835
18	Michigan	5,257		43	South Dakota	3,730
19	Wyoming	5,255		44	Tennessee	3,707
20	Illinois	5,062		45	North Dakota	3,685
21	Kansas	5,044		46	Alabama	3,648
22	Washington	5,042		47	Arkansas	3,419
23	Hawaii	5,008		48	Mississippi	3,322
24	Florida	5,003		49	Idaho	3,211
25	Iowa	4,877		50	Utah	2,767

District of Columbia   8,221

Source: National Education Association, Washington, D.C.,

   "Estimates of School Statistics 1990-91" (NEA, Reprinted by permission.)

Pupil in average daily attendance; estimate for 1990-91.

Education Expenditures by State and Local Governments in 1990

National Total = $287,193,640,000*

RANK	STATE	EXPENDITURES	%	RANK	STATE	EXPENDITURES	%
1	California	$34,536,792,000	12.03%	26	South Carolina	$3,952,405,000	1.38%
2	New York	25,276,961,000	8.80%	27	Oregon	3,911,796,000	1.36%
3	Texas	19,445,275,000	6.77%	28	Iowa	3,434,456,000	1.20%
4	Florida	13,395,411,000	4.66%	29	Kentucky	3,380,647,000	1.18%
5	Pennsylvania	12,901,952,000	4.49%	30	Oklahoma	3,192,215,000	1.11%
6	Illinois	11,982,394,000	4.17%	31	Kansas	2,950,444,000	1.03%
7	Ohio	11,875,126,000	4.13%	32	Mississippi	2,518,653,000	0.88%
8	Michigan	11,838,308,000	4.12%	33	Arkansas	2,166,105,000	0.75%
9	New Jersey	9,830,579,000	3.42%	34	Utah	2,051,930,000	0.71%
10	Virginia	7,558,896,000	2.63%	35	Nebraska	1,970,573,000	0.69%
11	North Carolina	7,535,663,000	2.62%	36	New Mexico	1,867,257,000	0.65%
12	Georgia	7,000,015,000	2.44%	37	West Virginia	1,756,774,000	0.61%
13	Wisconsin	6,442,144,000	2.24%	38	Maine	1,462,560,000	0.51%
14	Indiana	6,268,221,000	2.18%	39	Alaska	1,246,090,000	0.43%
15	Washington	6,206,726,000	2.16%	40	Nevada	1,223,833,000	0.43%
16	Massachusetts	6,154,862,000	2.14%	41	New Hampshire	1,221,833,000	0.43%
17	Minnesota	5,792,887,000	2.02%	42	Rhode Island	1,194,861,000	0.42%
18	Maryland	5,670,421,000	1.97%	43	Hawaii	1,113,473,000	0.39%
19	Missouri	4,957,733,000	1.73%	44	Idaho	997,063,000	0.35%
20	Arizona	4,462,707,000	1.55%	45	Montana	944,740,000	0.33%
21	Tennessee	4,311,229,000	1.50%	46	Delaware	923,964,000	0.32%
22	Louisiana	4,132,113,000	1.44%	47	Vermont	873,562,000	0.30%
23	Alabama	4,126,795,000	1.44%	48	North Dakota	849,965,000	0.30%
24	Connecticut	4,070,818,000	1.42%	49	Wyoming	783,582,000	0.27%
25	Colorado	4,063,580,000	1.41%	50	South Dakota	693,353,000	0.24%
					District of Columbia	673,898,000	0.23%

Source: U.S. Bureau of the Census,
    "Government Finances: 1989-90 (Preliminary Report)" (GF-90-5P, September 1991)
*Preliminary data for 1989-90; direct general expenditures. Includes higher, secondary and elementary education.

Per Capita State and Local Government Expenditures for Education in 1990

National Per Capita = $1,154.73*

RANK	STATE	PER CAPITA		RANK	STATE	PER CAPITA
1	Alaska	$2,265.44		26	California	$1,160.51
2	Wyoming	1,727.52		27	Texas	1,144.75
3	Vermont	1,552.29		28	North Carolina	1,136.83
4	New York	1,405.02		29	South Carolina	1,133.57
5	Delaware	1,386.98		30	Indiana	1,130.60
6	Oregon	1,376.27		31	New Hampshire	1,101.49
7	North Dakota	1,330.57		32	Ohio	1,094.77
8	Minnesota	1,324.06		33	Pennsylvania	1,085.87
9	Wisconsin	1,316.94		34	Georgia	1,080.55
10	Washington	1,275.35		35	Illinois	1,048.27
11	Michigan	1,273.58		36	Florida	1,035.36
12	New Jersey	1,271.71		37	Massachusetts	1,023.01
13	Nebraska	1,248.47		38	Alabama	1,021.34
14	Connecticut	1,238.42		39	Nevada	1,018.31
15	Iowa	1,236.86		40	Oklahoma	1,014.82
16	Colorado	1,233.48		41	Hawaii	1,004.73
17	New Mexico	1,232.46		42	South Dakota	996.19
18	Virginia	1,221.67		43	Idaho	990.38
19	Arizona	1,217.58		44	West Virginia	979.54
20	Maine	1,191.08		45	Louisiana	979.18
21	Utah	1,191.01		46	Mississippi	978.80
22	Kansas	1,190.86		47	Missouri	968.86
23	Rhode Island	1,190.74		48	Arkansas	921.46
24	Maryland	1,185.92		49	Kentucky	917.33
25	Montana	1,182.31		50	Tennessee	883.96

District of Columbia   1,110.39

Source: U.S. Bureau of the Census,
    "Government Finances: 1989-90 (Preliminary Report)" (GF-90-5P, September 1991)
*Preliminary data for 1989-90; direct general expenditures. Includes higher, secondary and elementary education. Rates calculated by the editors using 1990 Census population counts.

Expenditures for Education as a Percent of All State and Local Government Expenditures in 1990

National Percent = 29.49% of All Expenditures*

RANK	STATE	PERCENT
1	Vermont	38.58
2	Indiana	37.31
3	Arkansas	36.44
4	North Dakota	35.60
5	Virginia	35.59
6	Texas	35.26
7	Wisconsin	35.19
8	Iowa	35.16
9	Kansas	35.15
10	Missouri	34.75
11	Oregon	34.39
12	New Mexico	34.04
13	Mississippi	33.95
14	North Carolina	33.90
15	Idaho	33.85
16	New Hampshire	33.48
17	Maine	33.27
18	South Carolina	33.17
19	Delaware	33.16
20	Wyoming	32.83
21	Oklahoma	32.75
22	Montana	32.33
23	West Virginia	32.31
24	Michigan	32.25
25	Alabama	32.19

RANK	STATE	PERCENT
26	Colorado	31.76
27	Utah	31.75
28	South Dakota	31.56
29	Pennsylvania	31.22
30	Kentucky	30.98
31	Ohio	30.84
32	Georgia	30.73
33	Maryland	30.67
34	Illinois	30.43
35	Minnesota	29.93
36	Nebraska	29.68
37	New Jersey	29.18
38	Arizona	28.97
39	Rhode Island	28.92
40	Florida	28.76
41	Louisiana	28.44
42	Washington	28.32
43	Connecticut	27.37
44	California	25.72
45	Nevada	25.35
46	Tennessee	25.32
47	New York	23.59
48	Hawaii	22.57
49	Massachusetts	22.24
50	Alaska	20.62

District of Columbia — 12.54

Source: U.S. Bureau of the Census,

"Government Finances: 1989-90 (Preliminary Report)" (GF-90-5P, September 1991)

*Preliminary data for 1989-90; education expenditures are for Secondary/Elementary and Higher Education and include capital outlays. Rates calculated by the editors.

Elementary and Secondary Education Expenditures by State and Local Governments in 1990

National Total = $201,055,002,000*

RANK	STATE	EXPENDITURES	%	RANK	STATE	EXPENDITURES	%
1	California	$23,322,724,000	11.60%	26	South Carolina	$2,624,114,000	1.31%
2	New York	19,598,333,000	9.75%	27	Alabama	2,326,422,000	1.16%
3	Texas	13,990,781,000	6.96%	28	Oklahoma	2,105,150,000	1.05%
4	Florida	10,024,231,000	4.99%	29	Iowa	2,083,630,000	1.04%
5	Pennsylvania	9,754,056,000	4.85%	30	Kentucky	1,998,623,000	0.99%
6	Illinois	8,362,723,000	4.16%	31	Kansas	1,915,439,000	0.95%
7	Ohio	8,323,076,000	4.14%	32	Mississippi	1,589,111,000	0.79%
8	Michigan	7,987,521,000	3.97%	33	Arkansas	1,395,445,000	0.69%
9	New Jersey	7,534,265,000	3.75%	34	Nebraska	1,287,156,000	0.64%
10	Virginia	5,186,687,000	2.58%	35	Utah	1,239,117,000	0.62%
11	Georgia	5,103,168,000	2.54%	36	West Virginia	1,203,072,000	0.60%
12	North Carolina	4,923,849,000	2.45%	37	New Mexico	1,134,259,000	0.56%
13	Massachusetts	4,689,021,000	2.33%	38	Maine	1,071,605,000	0.53%
14	Wisconsin	4,281,176,000	2.13%	39	New Hampshire	934,637,000	0.46%
15	Washington	4,278,770,000	2.13%	40	Nevada	922,791,000	0.46%
16	Indiana	4,122,711,000	2.05%	41	Alaska	913,873,000	0.45%
17	Minnesota	4,040,327,000	2.01%	42	Rhode Island	808,843,000	0.40%
18	Maryland	3,960,683,000	1.97%	43	Montana	698,402,000	0.35%
19	Missouri	3,658,078,000	1.82%	44	Hawaii	684,663,000	0.34%
20	Connecticut	3,232,778,000	1.61%	45	Idaho	647,111,000	0.32%
21	Louisiana	2,895,060,000	1.44%	46	Vermont	565,816,000	0.28%
22	Arizona	2,830,209,000	1.41%	47	Wyoming	541,794,000	0.27%
23	Oregon	2,777,210,000	1.38%	48	Delaware	519,084,000	0.26%
24	Colorado	2,725,673,000	1.36%	49	North Dakota	504,312,000	0.25%
25	Tennessee	2,663,607,000	1.32%	50	South Dakota	500,653,000	0.25%
					District of Columbia	573,163,000	0.29%

Source: U.S. Bureau of the Census,

"Government Finances: 1989-90 (Preliminary Report)" (GF-90-5P, September 1991)

*Preliminary data for 1989-90; direct general expenditures.

Per Capita State and Local Government Expenditures
For Elementary and Secondary Education in 1990
National Per Capita = $808.39*

RANK	STATE	PER CAPITA	RANK	STATE	PER CAPITA
1	Alaska	$1,661.46	26	Delaware	$779.21
2	Wyoming	1,194.46	27	Florida	774.79
3	New York	1,089.37	28	Kansas	773.11
4	Vermont	1,005.43	29	Arizona	772.18
5	Connecticut	983.47	30	Nevada	767.82
6	Oregon	977.09	31	Ohio	767.31
7	New Jersey	974.65	32	South Carolina	752.61
8	Minnesota	923.48	33	Iowa	750.38
9	Washington	879.19	34	New Mexico	748.65
10	Wisconsin	875.18	35	Indiana	743.61
11	Montana	874.02	36	North Carolina	742.81
12	Maine	872.69	37	Illinois	731.61
13	Michigan	859.31	38	South Dakota	719.32
14	New Hampshire	842.58	39	Utah	719.23
15	Virginia	838.27	40	Missouri	714.88
16	Maryland	828.34	41	Louisiana	686.04
17	Colorado	827.37	42	West Virginia	670.80
18	Texas	823.64	43	Oklahoma	669.24
19	Pennsylvania	820.94	44	Idaho	642.77
20	Nebraska	815.49	45	Hawaii	617.80
21	Rhode Island	806.05	46	Mississippi	617.56
22	North Dakota	789.47	47	Arkansas	593.62
23	Georgia	787.74	48	Alabama	575.76
24	California	783.69	49	Tennessee	546.14
25	Massachusetts	779.37	50	Kentucky	542.32

District of Columbia   944.41

Source: U.S. Bureau of the Census,
   "Government Finances: 1989–90 (Preliminary Report)" (GF-90-5P, September 1991)
*Preliminary data for 1989–90; direct general expenditures. Rates calculated by the editors using 1990 Census population counts.

Expenditures for Elementary and Secondary Education
As a Percent of All State and Local Government Expenditures in 1990
National Percent = 20.64% of All Expenditures*

RANK	STATE	PERCENT	RANK	STATE	PERCENT
1	Missouri	25.64	26	Florida	21.52
2	New Hampshire	25.61	27	Maryland	21.42
3	Texas	25.37	27	Mississippi	21.42
4	Vermont	24.99	29	Iowa	21.33
5	Indiana	24.54	30	Colorado	21.30
6	Oregon	24.42	31	Illinois	21.24
6	Virginia	24.42	32	North Dakota	21.12
8	Maine	24.37	33	Minnesota	20.88
9	Montana	23.90	34	New Mexico	20.68
10	Pennsylvania	23.61	35	Louisiana	19.93
11	Arkansas	23.48	36	Rhode Island	19.58
12	Wisconsin	23.38	37	Washington	19.52
13	Kansas	22.82	38	Nebraska	19.39
14	South Dakota	22.79	39	Utah	19.17
15	Wyoming	22.70	40	Nevada	19.12
16	Georgia	22.40	41	Delaware	18.63
17	New Jersey	22.36	42	Arizona	18.38
18	North Carolina	22.15	43	Kentucky	18.32
19	West Virginia	22.13	44	New York	18.29
20	South Carolina	22.02	45	Alabama	18.15
21	Idaho	21.97	46	California	17.37
22	Michigan	21.76	47	Massachusetts	16.95
23	Connecticut	21.73	48	Tennessee	15.64
24	Ohio	21.62	49	Alaska	15.12
25	Oklahoma	21.60	50	Hawaii	13.88
				District of Columbia	10.67

Source: U.S. Bureau of the Census,

"Government Finances: 1989-90 (Preliminary Report)" (GF-90-5P, September 1991)

Preliminary data for 1989-90; education expenditures include capital outlays. Rates calculated by the editors.

Higher Education Expenditures by State and Local Governments in 1990

National Total = $73,418,282,000*

RANK	STATE	EXPENDITURES	%	RANK	STATE	EXPENDITURES	%
1	California	$10,036,433,000	13.67%	26	Kentucky	$1,069,366,000	1.46%
2	Texas	5,041,828,000	6.87%	27	Oregon	1,027,753,000	1.40%
3	New York	4,454,665,000	6.07%	28	Louisiana	1,011,615,000	1.38%
4	Michigan	3,550,413,000	4.84%	29	Oklahoma	962,311,000	1.31%
5	Ohio	3,038,110,000	4.14%	30	Kansas	941,778,000	1.28%
6	Illinois	2,940,466,000	4.01%	31	Mississippi	791,684,000	1.08%
7	Florida	2,661,225,000	3.62%	32	Utah	738,494,000	1.01%
8	North Carolina	2,379,311,000	3.24%	33	New Mexico	666,392,000	0.91%
9	Pennsylvania	2,067,178,000	2.82%	34	Connecticut	652,528,000	0.89%
10	Virginia	2,064,283,000	2.81%	35	Nebraska	612,747,000	0.83%
11	New Jersey	2,026,998,000	2.76%	36	Arkansas	589,417,000	0.80%
12	Wisconsin	1,920,526,000	2.62%	37	West Virginia	467,062,000	0.64%
13	Indiana	1,797,911,000	2.45%	38	Hawaii	409,680,000	0.56%
14	Washington	1,705,599,000	2.32%	39	Delaware	332,634,000	0.45%
15	Minnesota	1,507,153,000	2.05%	40	Maine	331,254,000	0.45%
16	Arizona	1,502,430,000	2.05%	41	North Dakota	309,967,000	0.42%
17	Georgia	1,498,534,000	2.04%	42	Idaho	309,140,000	0.42%
18	Maryland	1,458,902,000	1.99%	43	Nevada	272,465,000	0.37%
19	Tennessee	1,371,459,000	1.87%	44	Rhode Island	270,403,000	0.37%
20	Alabama	1,344,408,000	1.83%	45	Vermont	254,755,000	0.35%
21	Colorado	1,257,335,000	1.71%	46	Alaska	245,536,000	0.33%
22	Iowa	1,203,961,000	1.64%	47	New Hampshire	239,874,000	0.33%
23	Massachusetts	1,172,786,000	1.60%	48	Wyoming	223,470,000	0.30%
24	Missouri	1,142,829,000	1.56%	49	Montana	183,188,000	0.25%
25	South Carolina	1,096,572,000	1.49%	50	South Dakota	162,719,000	0.22%
					District of Columbia	100,735,000	0.14%

Source: U.S. Bureau of the Census,
"Government Finances: 1989-90 (Preliminary Report)" (GF-90-5P, September 1991)
*Preliminary data for 1989-90; direct general expenditures.

Per Capita State and Local Government Expenditures for Higher Education in 1990

National Per Capita = $295.20*

RANK	STATE	PER CAPITA		RANK	STATE	PER CAPITA
1	Delaware	$499.32		26	Idaho	$307.07
2	Wyoming	492.67		27	Oklahoma	305.92
3	North Dakota	485.23		28	Maryland	305.12
4	Vermont	452.69		29	Texas	296.81
5	Alaska	446.39		30	Kentucky	290.17
6	New Mexico	439.84		31	Tennessee	281.20
7	Iowa	433.59		32	Ohio	280.08
8	Utah	428.65		33	Maine	269.77
9	Arizona	409.91		34	Rhode Island	269.47
10	Wisconsin	392.60		35	New Jersey	262.22
11	Nebraska	388.21		36	West Virginia	260.42
12	Michigan	381.96		37	Illinois	257.25
13	Colorado	381.66		38	Arkansas	250.74
14	Kansas	380.12		39	New York	247.61
15	Hawaii	369.67		40	Louisiana	239.72
16	Oregon	361.59		41	South Dakota	233.79
17	North Carolina	358.94		42	Georgia	231.32
18	Washington	350.46		43	Montana	229.25
19	Minnesota	344.48		44	Nevada	226.71
20	California	337.25		45	Missouri	223.34
21	Virginia	333.63		46	New Hampshire	216.25
22	Alabama	332.73		47	Florida	205.69
23	Indiana	324.29		48	Connecticut	198.51
24	South Carolina	314.50		49	Massachusetts	194.93
25	Mississippi	307.66		50	Pennsylvania	173.98
					District of Columbia	165.98

Source: U.S. Bureau of the Census,

"Government Finances: 1989-90 (Preliminary Report)" (GF-90-5P, September 1991)

*Preliminary data for 1989-90; direct general expenditures. Rates calculated by the editors using 1990 Census population counts.

Expenditures for Higher Education
As a Percent of All State and Local Government Expenditures in 1990
National Percent = 7.54% of All Expenditures*

RANK	STATE	PERCENT	RANK	STATE	PERCENT
1	North Dakota	12.98	26	West Virginia	8.59
2	Iowa	12.32	27	Hawaii	8.30
3	New Mexico	12.15	28	Tennessee	8.06
4	Delaware	11.94	29	Missouri	8.01
5	Utah	11.43	30	Maryland	7.89
6	Vermont	11.25	30	Ohio	7.89
7	Kansas	11.22	32	Minnesota	7.79
8	Indiana	10.70	33	Washington	7.78
8	North Carolina	10.70	34	Maine	7.53
10	Mississippi	10.67	35	California	7.47
11	Alabama	10.49	35	Illinois	7.47
11	Idaho	10.49	37	South Dakota	7.41
11	Wisconsin	10.49	38	Louisiana	6.96
14	Arkansas	9.92	39	Georgia	6.58
15	Oklahoma	9.87	40	New Hampshire	6.57
16	Colorado	9.83	41	Rhode Island	6.55
17	Kentucky	9.80	42	Montana	6.27
18	Arizona	9.75	43	New Jersey	6.02
19	Virginia	9.72	44	Florida	5.71
20	Michigan	9.67	45	Nevada	5.64
21	Wyoming	9.36	46	Pennsylvania	5.00
22	Nebraska	9.23	47	Connecticut	4.39
23	South Carolina	9.20	48	Massachusetts	4.24
24	Texas	9.14	49	New York	4.16
25	Oregon	9.04	50	Alaska	4.06

District of Columbia   1.87

Source: U.S. Bureau of the Census,

"Government Finances: 1989-90 (Preliminary Report)" (GF-90-5P, September 1991)

*Preliminary data for 1989-90; education expenditures include capital outlays. Rates calculated by the editors.

Public Institutions of Higher Education Revenue per FTE Student in 1987
From State and Local Governments
National Average = $4,570 per FTE Student*

RANK	STATE	PER STUDENT	RANK	STATE	PER STUDENT
1	Alaska	$8,795	26	Arizona	$4,283
2	Wyoming	6,788	27	North Dakota	4,256
3	Hawaii	6,117	27	Wisconsin	4,256
4	New York	5,513	29	Washington	4,239
5	North Carolina	5,497	30	Minnesota	4,235
6	California	5,384	31	Rhode Island	4,229
7	Kentucky	5,374	32	West Virginia	4,205
8	South Carolina	5,270	33	Nebraska	4,204
9	Georgia	5,217	34	Kansas	4,164
10	New Jersey	5,089	35	Michigan	4,132
11	Idaho	4,950	36	Virginia	4,042
12	Tennessee	4,949	37	Nevada	4,010
13	Arkansas	4,874	38	Ohio	3,999
14	Maryland	4,854	39	Delaware	3,939
15	Maine	4,828	40	Mississippi	3,933
16	Florida	4,731	41	Illinois	3,812
17	Texas	4,587	42	Louisiana	3,764
18	Indiana	4,574	43	Missouri	3,763
19	Utah	4,556	44	Pennsylvania	3,544
20	Massachusetts	4,532	45	Montana	3,427
21	New Mexico	4,521	46	South Dakota	3,388
22	Connecticut	4,461	47	Oklahoma	3,166
23	Iowa	4,420	48	Colorado	2,960
24	Alabama	4,419	49	New Hampshire	2,459
25	Oregon	4,322	50	Vermont	2,196

District of Columbia   10,329

Source: U.S. Department of Education, National Center for Education Statistics,
   "State Higher Education Profiles" (Third Edition)
*Full-time equivalent.

Average Undergraduate Tuition and Fees and Room and Board Rates
At Public Institutions of Higher Education in 1990
National Average = $4,979*

RANK	STATE	AVERAGE COST	RANK	STATE	AVERAGE COST
1	Vermont	$7,715	26	Hawaii	$4,529
2	Maryland	6,437	27	Wisconsin	4,411
3	New Jersey	6,396	28	North Dakota	4,360
4	Pennsylvania	6,366	29	Alaska	4,352
5	Rhode Island	6,340	30	Iowa	4,347
6	Delaware	6,196	31	Utah	4,342
7	Virginia	5,983	32	Louisiana	4,311
8	Michigan	5,854	33	Georgia	4,308
9	Ohio	5,805	34	Mississippi	4,241
10	Arizona	5,595	35	South Dakota	4,236
11	California	5,547	36	Arkansas	4,187
12	Illinois	5,495	37	Tennessee	4,172
13	New Hampshire	5,484	38	Texas	4,168
14	Massachusetts	5,478	39	Alabama	4,119
15	Connecticut	5,445	40	Missouri	4,098
16	Maine	5,429	41	Kentucky	4,047
17	West Virginia	5,128	42	New Mexico	4,018
18	New York	5,094	43	Nevada	4,007
19	South Carolina	5,089	44	Nebraska	3,944
20	Montana	5,047	45	Wyoming	3,880
21	Indiana	4,969	46	Idaho	3,792
22	Colorado	4,956	47	North Carolina	3,790
23	Oregon	4,776	48	Oklahoma	3,754
24	Minnesota	4,670	49	Kansas	3,509
25	Washington	4,634	–	Florida**	N/A

District of Columbia**   N/A

Source: U.S. Department of Education, National Center for Education Statistics,
   "Digest of Education Statistics 1991" (NCES 91-697, November 1991)

*Preliminary data for 1989-90.

**Data not reported or not applicable.

Average Undergraduate Tuition and Fees and Room and Board Rates
At Private Institutions of Higher Education in 1990
National Average = $12,348*

RANK	STATE	AVERAGE COST	RANK	STATE	AVERAGE COST
1	Massachusetts	$16,904	26	Virginia	$10,342
2	Connecticut	16,184	27	Georgia	10,244
3	New Hampshire	14,748	28	West Virginia	10,058
4	Vermont	14,691	29	Idaho	9,827
5	Maryland	14,621	30	Michigan	9,764
6	Maine	14,598	31	Tennessee	9,642
7	New Jersey	14,439	32	Texas	9,402
8	California	14,245	33	Nebraska	9,101
9	Rhode Island	14,126	34	Alaska	9,030
10	New York	14,076	35	Delaware	8,776
11	Louisiana	13,464	36	South Carolina	8,771
12	Pennsylvania	13,416	37	South Dakota	8,595
13	Colorado	12,920	38	Kansas	8,272
14	Illinois	12,209	39	Alabama	8,212
15	Oregon	12,074	40	Oklahoma	8,119
16	Minnesota	11,891	41	Montana	8,013
17	Indiana	11,461	42	North Dakota	7,939
18	Ohio	11,330	43	Kentucky	7,366
19	Washington	11,229	44	Mississippi	7,208
20	Wisconsin	11,021	45	Hawaii	6,997
21	Iowa	10,769	46	Arizona	6,432
22	Florida	10,738	47	Arkansas	6,110
23	Missouri	10,691	48	Utah	4,970
24	New Mexico	10,563	–	Nevada**	N/A
25	North Carolina	10,412	–	Wyoming**	N/A

District of Columbia   14,622

Source: U.S. Department of Education, National Center for Education Statistics,
    "Digest of Education Statistics 1991" (NCES 91-697, November 1991)

*Preliminary data for 1989-90.

**Data not reported or not applicable.

Institutions of Higher Education in 1990

National Total = 3,535 Institutions of Higher Education*

RANK	STATE	INSTITUTIONS	%	RANK	STATE	INSTITUTIONS	%
1	New York	326	9.22%	25	Kansas	54	1.53%
2	California	310	8.77%	27	Connecticut	48	1.36%
3	Pennsylvania	217	6.14%	28	Mississippi	47	1.33%
4	Texas	174	4.92%	28	Oklahoma	47	1.33%
5	Illinois	166	4.70%	30	Oregon	46	1.30%
6	Ohio	152	4.30%	31	Arizona	37	1.05%
7	North Carolina	126	3.56%	31	Arkansas	37	1.05%
8	Massachusetts	117	3.31%	33	Nebraska	36	1.02%
9	Michigan	97	2.74%	34	Louisiana	34	0.96%
10	Florida	95	2.69%	35	Maine	31	0.88%
10	Georgia	95	2.69%	36	New Hampshire	29	0.82%
12	Missouri	89	2.52%	37	West Virginia	28	0.79%
13	Alabama	87	2.46%	38	New Mexico	26	0.74%
14	Tennessee	86	2.43%	39	Vermont	22	0.62%
15	Minnesota	81	2.29%	40	North Dakota	20	0.57%
16	Indiana	78	2.21%	41	Montana	19	0.54%
16	Virginia	78	2.21%	41	South Dakota	19	0.54%
18	South Carolina	64	1.81%	43	Hawaii	14	0.40%
19	New Jersey	62	1.75%	43	Utah	14	0.40%
20	Wisconsin	61	1.73%	45	Idaho	11	0.31%
21	Kentucky	59	1.67%	45	Rhode Island	11	0.31%
22	Iowa	58	1.64%	47	Delaware	10	0.28%
23	Maryland	57	1.61%	48	Wyoming	9	0.25%
24	Washington	55	1.56%	49	Alaska	8	0.23%
25	Colorado	54	1.53%	49	Nevada	8	0.23%
					District of Columbia	17	0.48%

Source: U.S. Department of Education, National Center for Education Statistics,
"Digest of Education Statistics 1991" (NCES 91-697, November 1991)
*1989-90; consists of 2,127 4-year and 1408 2-year institutions. Excludes nine U.S. service schools.

Enrollment in Institutions of Higher Education in 1989

National Total = 13,457,855 Students*

RANK	STATE	ENROLLMENT	%	RANK	STATE	ENROLLMENT	%
1	California	1,746,743	12.98%	26	Connecticut	170,316	1.27%
2	New York	1,023,244	7.60%	27	Iowa	169,901	1.26%
3	Texas	877,859	6.52%	28	Kentucky	166,014	1.23%
4	Illinois	709,937	5.28%	29	Oregon	161,822	1.20%
5	Pennsylvania	610,357	4.54%	30	Kansas	161,639	1.20%
6	Florida	573,712	4.26%	31	South Carolina	145,730	1.08%
7	Michigan	560,320	4.16%	32	Mississippi	116,370	0.86%
8	Ohio	551,416	4.10%	33	Utah	114,815	0.85%
9	Massachusetts	426,476	3.17%	34	Nebraska	108,844	0.81%
10	North Carolina	345,401	2.57%	35	Arkansas	88,572	0.66%
11	Virginia	344,284	2.56%	36	West Virginia	82,455	0.61%
12	New Jersey	314,091	2.33%	37	New Mexico	81,350	0.60%
13	Wisconsin	290,672	2.16%	38	Rhode Island	76,503	0.57%
14	Missouri	278,505	2.07%	39	New Hampshire	58,600	0.44%
15	Indiana	275,821	2.05%	40	Maine	58,230	0.43%
16	Maryland	259,778	1.93%	41	Nevada	56,471	0.42%
17	Washington	255,760	1.90%	42	Hawaii	54,188	0.40%
18	Minnesota	253,097	1.88%	43	Idaho	48,969	0.36%
19	Arizona	252,614	1.88%	44	Delaware	40,562	0.30%
20	Alabama	245,599	1.82%	45	North Dakota	40,350	0.30%
21	Georgia	239,208	1.78%	46	Montana	37,660	0.28%
22	Tennessee	218,866	1.63%	47	Vermont	35,946	0.27%
23	Colorado	202,754	1.51%	48	South Dakota	32,666	0.24%
24	Louisiana	179,927	1.34%	49	Wyoming	29,159	0.22%
25	Oklahoma	175,855	1.31%	50	Alaska	28,627	0.21%
					District of Columbia	79,800	0.59%

Source: U.S. Department of Education, National Center for Education Statistics,
"Enrollment in Higher Education, Fall 1989" (NCES 91-217, July 1991)
*Fall 1989 enrollment; includes public and private institutions.

Enrollment in Public Institutions of Higher Education in 1989

National Total = 10,514,973 Students*

RANK	STATE	STUDENTS	%
1	California	1,536,073	14.61%
2	Texas	782,495	7.44%
3	New York	605,701	5.76%
4	Illinois	536,643	5.10%
5	Florida	480,869	4.57%
6	Michigan	479,714	4.56%
7	Ohio	412,760	3.93%
8	Pennsylvania	335,101	3.19%
9	Virginia	287,624	2.74%
10	North Carolina	277,062	2.63%
11	New Jersey	253,544	2.41%
12	Wisconsin	245,968	2.34%
13	Arizona	239,314	2.28%
14	Alabama	224,612	2.14%
15	Maryland	222,014	2.11%
16	Washington	221,362	2.11%
17	Indiana	216,433	2.06%
18	Minnesota	198,610	1.89%
19	Missouri	192,322	1.83%
20	Massachusetts	187,772	1.79%
21	Georgia	186,776	1.78%
22	Colorado	177,490	1.69%
23	Tennessee	167,056	1.59%
24	Louisiana	151,733	1.44%
25	Oklahoma	151,410	1.44%

RANK	STATE	STUDENTS	%
26	Kansas	148,276	1.41%
27	Oregon	141,311	1.34%
28	Kentucky	137,297	1.31%
29	South Carolina	118,639	1.13%
30	Iowa	116,889	1.11%
31	Connecticut	110,575	1.05%
32	Mississippi	103,035	0.98%
33	Nebraska	91,337	0.87%
34	Utah	79,623	0.76%
35	New Mexico	79,359	0.75%
36	Arkansas	76,416	0.73%
37	West Virginia	72,478	0.69%
38	Nevada	56,184	0.53%
39	Hawaii	43,644	0.42%
40	Rhode Island	40,604	0.39%
41	Maine	40,511	0.39%
42	Idaho	38,447	0.37%
43	North Dakota	37,501	0.36%
44	Montana	33,197	0.32%
45	Delaware	33,037	0.31%
46	New Hampshire	32,889	0.31%
47	Wyoming	28,553	0.27%
48	Alaska	26,274	0.25%
49	South Dakota	25,075	0.24%
50	Vermont	20,925	0.20%
	District of Columbia	12,439	0.12%

Source: U.S. Department of Education, National Center for Education Statistics,
"Enrollment in Higher Education, Fall 1989" (NCES 91-217, July 1991)
*Fall 1989 enrollment.

Enrollment in Private Institutions of Higher Education in 1989

National Total = 2,942,882 Students*

RANK	STATE	STUDENTS	%	RANK	STATE	STUDENTS	%
1	New York	417,543	14.19%	26	Louisiana	28,194	0.96%
2	Pennsylvania	275,256	9.35%	27	South Carolina	27,091	0.92%
3	Massachusetts	238,704	8.11%	28	New Hampshire	25,711	0.87%
4	California	210,670	7.16%	29	Colorado	25,264	0.86%
5	Illinois	173,294	5.89%	30	Oklahoma	24,445	0.83%
6	Ohio	138,656	4.71%	31	Alabama	20,987	0.71%
7	Texas	95,364	3.24%	32	Oregon	20,511	0.70%
8	Florida	92,843	3.15%	33	Maine	17,719	0.60%
9	Missouri	86,183	2.93%	34	Nebraska	17,507	0.59%
10	Michigan	80,606	2.74%	35	Vermont	15,021	0.51%
11	North Carolina	68,339	2.32%	36	Kansas	13,363	0.45%
12	New Jersey	60,547	2.06%	37	Mississippi	13,335	0.45%
13	Connecticut	59,741	2.03%	38	Arizona	13,300	0.45%
14	Indiana	59,388	2.02%	39	Arkansas	12,156	0.41%
15	Virginia	56,660	1.93%	40	Hawaii	10,544	0.36%
16	Minnesota	54,487	1.85%	41	Idaho	10,522	0.36%
17	Iowa	53,012	1.80%	42	West Virginia	9,977	0.34%
18	Georgia	52,432	1.78%	43	South Dakota	7,591	0.26%
19	Tennessee	51,810	1.76%	44	Delaware	7,525	0.26%
20	Wisconsin	44,704	1.52%	45	Montana	4,463	0.15%
21	Maryland	37,764	1.28%	46	North Dakota	2,849	0.10%
22	Rhode Island	35,899	1.22%	47	Alaska	2,353	0.08%
23	Utah	35,192	1.20%	48	New Mexico	1,991	0.07%
24	Washington	34,398	1.17%	49	Wyoming	606	0.02%
25	Kentucky	28,717	0.98%	50	Nevada	287	0.01%
					District of Columbia	67,361	2.29%

Source: U.S. Department of Education, National Center for Education Statistics,
"Enrollment in Higher Education, Fall 1989" (NCES 91-217, July 1991)
*Fall 1989 enrollment.

Male Enrollment in Institutions of Higher Education in 1989

National Total = 6,155,484 Male Students*

RANK	STATE	STUDENTS	%	RANK	STATE	STUDENTS	%
1	California	804,841	13.08%	26	Louisiana	79,162	1.29%
2	New York	455,937	7.41%	27	Oregon	75,843	1.23%
3	Texas	410,001	6.66%	28	Connecticut	74,412	1.21%
4	Illinois	324,571	5.27%	29	Kansas	72,657	1.18%
5	Pennsylvania	281,633	4.58%	30	Kentucky	70,340	1.14%
6	Ohio	265,891	4.32%	31	South Carolina	64,414	1.05%
7	Florida	259,448	4.21%	32	Utah	59,189	0.96%
8	Michigan	254,627	4.14%	33	Mississippi	50,686	0.82%
9	Massachusetts	191,404	3.11%	34	Nebraska	49,273	0.80%
10	Virginia	152,983	2.49%	35	Arkansas	38,111	0.62%
11	North Carolina	152,130	2.47%	36	New Mexico	36,720	0.60%
12	New Jersey	140,643	2.28%	37	West Virginia	36,612	0.59%
13	Wisconsin	133,103	2.16%	38	Rhode Island	34,587	0.56%
14	Indiana	130,987	2.13%	39	New Hampshire	27,378	0.44%
15	Missouri	127,273	2.07%	40	Hawaii	25,022	0.41%
16	Alabama	126,980	2.06%	41	Nevada	24,753	0.40%
17	Arizona	119,225	1.94%	42	Maine	23,852	0.39%
18	Maryland	115,318	1.87%	43	Idaho	22,595	0.37%
19	Washington	114,288	1.86%	44	North Dakota	20,778	0.34%
20	Minnesota	113,966	1.85%	45	Montana	17,805	0.29%
21	Georgia	110,068	1.79%	46	Delaware	17,568	0.29%
22	Tennessee	99,771	1.62%	47	Vermont	15,574	0.25%
23	Colorado	95,502	1.55%	48	South Dakota	14,621	0.24%
24	Oklahoma	81,648	1.33%	49	Wyoming	13,006	0.21%
25	Iowa	79,878	1.30%	50	Alaska	11,560	0.19%
					District of Columbia	36,850	0.60%

Source: U.S. Department of Education, National Center for Education Statistics,
"Enrollment in Higher Education, Fall 1989" (NCES 91-217, July 1991)
*Fall 1989 enrollment.

Female Enrollment in Institutions of Higher Education in 1989

National Total = 7,302,371 Female Students*

RANK	STATE	STUDENTS	%	RANK	STATE	STUDENTS	%
1	California	941,902	12.90%	26	Kentucky	95,674	1.31%
2	New York	567,307	7.77%	27	Oklahoma	94,207	1.29%
3	Texas	467,858	6.41%	28	Iowa	90,023	1.23%
4	Illinois	385,366	5.28%	29	Kansas	88,982	1.22%
5	Pennsylvania	328,724	4.50%	30	Oregon	85,979	1.18%
6	Florida	314,264	4.30%	31	South Carolina	81,316	1.11%
7	Michigan	305,693	4.19%	32	Mississippi	65,684	0.90%
8	Ohio	285,525	3.91%	33	Nebraska	59,571	0.82%
9	Massachusetts	235,072	3.22%	34	Utah	55,626	0.76%
10	North Carolina	193,271	2.65%	35	Arkansas	50,461	0.69%
11	Virginia	191,301	2.62%	36	West Virginia	45,843	0.63%
12	New Jersey	173,448	2.38%	37	New Mexico	44,630	0.61%
13	Wisconsin	157,569	2.16%	38	Rhode Island	41,916	0.57%
14	Missouri	151,232	2.07%	39	Maine	34,378	0.47%
15	Indiana	144,834	1.98%	40	Nevada	31,718	0.43%
16	Maryland	144,460	1.98%	41	New Hampshire	31,222	0.43%
17	Washington	141,472	1.94%	42	Hawaii	29,166	0.40%
18	Minnesota	139,131	1.91%	43	Idaho	26,374	0.36%
19	Arizona	133,389	1.83%	44	Delaware	22,994	0.31%
20	Georgia	129,140	1.77%	45	Vermont	20,372	0.28%
21	Tennessee	119,095	1.63%	46	Montana	19,855	0.27%
22	Alabama	118,619	1.62%	47	North Dakota	19,572	0.27%
23	Colorado	107,252	1.47%	48	South Dakota	18,045	0.25%
24	Louisiana	100,765	1.38%	49	Alaska	17,067	0.23%
25	Connecticut	95,904	1.31%	50	Wyoming	16,153	0.22%
					District of Columbia	42,950	0.59%

Source: U.S. Department of Education, National Center for Education Statistics,
"Enrollment in Higher Education, Fall 1989" (NCES 91-217, July 1991)
*Fall 1989 enrollment.

Percent of Population Completing Four or More Years of College in 1989

National Percent = 21.1% of Population*

RANK	STATE	PERCENT
1	Massachusetts	28.1
2	Connecticut	27.5
3	Maryland	27.4
4	Virginia	27.3
5	Colorado	27.0
6	Vermont	26.7
7	California	26.4
8	New Jersey	25.7
9	Utah	24.2
10	Washington	24.1
11	Hawaii	23.9
12	New Hampshire	23.5
13	Alaska	23.4
14	New York	22.8
15	Kansas	22.3
16	Arizona	22.2
16	North Dakota	22.2
18	Wyoming	21.9
19	Texas	21.7
20	Missouri	21.6
21	Minnesota	21.5
22	Illinois	21.1
22	Montana	21.1
24	New Mexico	20.6
25	Oregon	20.2

RANK	STATE	PERCENT
25	Rhode Island	20.2
27	Florida	19.8
28	Nebraska	19.7
29	Delaware	19.4
30	Wisconsin	18.9
31	Pennsylvania	18.6
32	Maine	18.5
33	South Dakota	18.4
34	North Carolina	18.3
35	Georgia	18.2
36	Ohio	17.6
37	Michigan	17.3
38	Nevada	17.2
39	Idaho	17.1
39	Iowa	17.1
39	Oklahoma	17.1
42	Louisiana	16.6
42	South Carolina	16.6
44	Tennessee	15.7
45	Mississippi	15.6
46	Kentucky	14.9
47	Arkansas	14.8
48	Indiana	13.8
49	Alabama	11.6
50	West Virginia	11.1

District of Columbia — 35.2

Source: U.S. Bureau of the Census,
    Press Release CB 91–317 (November 14, 1991)
*Persons age 25 or over.

Public Libraries and Branches in 1989

National Total = 15,481 Libraries and Branches*

RANK	STATE	LIBRARIES	%	RANK	STATE	LIBRARIES	%
1	New York	1,102	7.12%	26	Connecticut	249	1.61%
2	California	800	5.17%	27	Maine	244	1.58%
3	Illinois	737	4.76%	28	Colorado	241	1.56%
4	Texas	690	4.46%	29	New Hampshire	237	1.53%
5	Ohio	672	4.34%	30	Vermont	207	1.34%
6	Michigan	643	4.15%	31	Arkansas	202	1.30%
7	Pennsylvania	609	3.93%	31	Oregon	202	1.30%
8	Iowa	524	3.38%	33	Maryland	198	1.28%
9	Massachusetts	518	3.35%	34	Kentucky	185	1.20%
10	New Jersey	471	3.04%	35	Oklahoma	184	1.19%
11	Wisconsin	453	2.93%	36	West Virginia	179	1.16%
12	Indiana	400	2.58%	37	South Carolina	160	1.03%
13	Florida	377	2.44%	38	Idaho	147	0.95%
14	North Carolina	362	2.34%	39	Arizona	143	0.92%
15	Kansas	360	2.33%	40	South Dakota	131	0.85%
16	Minnesota	355	2.29%	41	Utah	112	0.72%
17	Georgia	341	2.20%	42	Montana	109	0.70%
18	Missouri	333	2.15%	43	North Dakota	103	0.67%
19	Louisiana	314	2.03%	44	Alaska	97	0.63%
20	Washington	313	2.02%	45	New Mexico	86	0.56%
21	Alabama	299	1.93%	46	Wyoming	81	0.52%
22	Nebraska	277	1.79%	47	Nevada	74	0.48%
23	Virginia	269	1.74%	47	Rhode Island	74	0.48%
24	Tennessee	266	1.72%	49	Hawaii	48	0.31%
25	Mississippi	250	1.61%	50	Delaware	32	0.21%
					District of Columbia	21	0.14%

Source: U.S. Department of Education, Office of Educational Research and Improvement,
   "Public Libraries in 50 States and the District of Columbia: 1989" (NCES 91-343, April 1991)
*Calculated by the editors. Consists of 8,968 main libraries and 6,513 branches.

Public Libraries and Branches per 10,000 Population in 1989

National Rate = 0.62 Libraries per 10,000 Population*

RANK	STATE	RATE	RANK	STATE	RATE
1	Vermont	3.65	26	Michigan	0.69
2	New Hampshire	2.14	27	Nevada	0.67
3	Maine	2.00	28	Utah	0.66
4	Iowa	1.85	28	Washington	0.66
5	Alaska	1.84	30	Missouri	0.65
6	South Dakota	1.83	31	Illinois	0.63
7	Nebraska	1.72	32	Ohio	0.62
8	Wyoming	1.71	33	New Jersey	0.61
9	North Dakota	1.56	33	New York	0.61
10	Idaho	1.45	35	Oklahoma	0.57
11	Kansas	1.43	36	New Mexico	0.56
12	Montana	1.35	37	North Carolina	0.55
13	West Virginia	0.96	38	Tennessee	0.54
14	Mississippi	0.95	39	Georgia	0.53
15	Wisconsin	0.93	40	Pennsylvania	0.51
16	Massachusetts	0.88	41	Kentucky	0.50
17	Arkansas	0.84	42	Delaware	0.48
18	Minnesota	0.82	43	South Carolina	0.46
19	Connecticut	0.77	44	Virginia	0.44
20	Rhode Island	0.74	45	Hawaii	0.43
21	Alabama	0.73	46	Maryland	0.42
21	Colorado	0.73	47	Texas	0.41
23	Indiana	0.72	48	Arizona	0.40
23	Louisiana	0.72	49	Florida	0.30
23	Oregon	0.72	50	California	0.28
				District of Columbia	0.35

Source: U.S. Department of Education, Office of Educational Research and Improvement,
"Public Libraries in 50 States and the District of Columbia: 1989" (NCES 91-343, April 1991)
*Rates calculated by the editors using 1989 Census population counts.

VI. EMPLOYMENT AND LABOR

Average Annual Pay in 1990

National Average = $23,602

RANK	STATE	ANNUAL PAY		RANK	STATE	ANNUAL PAY
1	Alaska	$29,946		26	Oregon	$21,332
2	Connecticut	28,995		27	Wisconsin	21,101
3	New York	28,873		28	Florida	21,032
4	New Jersey	28,449		29	West Virginia	20,715
5	Massachusetts	26,689		30	Louisiana	20,646
6	California	26,180		31	Tennessee	20,611
7	Michigan	25,376		32	Vermont	20,532
8	Illinois	25,312		33	Alabama	20,468
9	Maryland	24,730		34	Oklahoma	20,288
10	Delaware	24,423		35	Kansas	20,238
11	Pennsylvania	23,457		36	North Carolina	20,220
12	Hawaii	23,167		37	Maine	20,154
13	Minnesota	23,126		38	Utah	20,074
14	Colorado	22,908		39	Wyoming	20,049
15	Ohio	22,843		40	Kentucky	19,947
16	Virginia	22,750		41	South Carolina	19,669
17	Texas	22,700		42	New Mexico	19,347
18	Washington	22,646		43	Iowa	19,224
19	New Hampshire	22,609		44	Idaho	18,991
20	Rhode Island	22,388		45	Nebraska	18,577
21	Nevada	22,358		46	Arkansas	18,204
22	Georgia	22,114		47	Montana	17,895
23	Missouri	21,716		48	Mississippi	17,718
24	Indiana	21,699		49	North Dakota	17,626
25	Arizona	21,443		50	South Dakota	16,430
					District of Columbia	33,717

Source: U.S. Department of Labor, Bureau of Labor Statistics,
   Press Release USDL 91-390 (August 8, 1991)

Percent Change in Average Annual Pay: 1989 to 1990

National Percent Change = 4.6% Increase

RANK	STATE	PERCENT CHANGE	RANK	STATE	PERCENT CHANGE
1	Hawaii	7.1	26	Alabama	4.5
2	New Jersey	6.2	26	Arkansas	4.5
3	Rhode Island	6.0	26	Illinois	4.5
4	Massachusetts	5.8	26	Louisiana	4.5
4	New York	5.8	30	Colorado	4.4
6	Connecticut	5.4	30	Iowa	4.4
6	Maryland	5.4	30	Minnesota	4.4
8	Vermont	5.3	30	Texas	4.4
9	California	5.1	30	Wisconsin	4.4
9	Oregon	5.1	35	Wyoming	4.3
9	Pennsylvania	5.1	36	North Dakota	4.1
12	Delaware	5.0	37	Virginia	4.0
12	Kentucky	5.0	38	Kansas	3.9
12	Maine	5.0	38	Mississippi	3.9
12	Nebraska	5.0	38	Missouri	3.9
16	Georgia	4.9	38	Montana	3.9
16	New Hampshire	4.9	38	Ohio	3.9
18	Florida	4.8	38	Oklahoma	3.9
18	Nevada	4.8	38	South Dakota	3.9
18	Washington	4.8	45	Indiana	3.7
21	Idaho	4.7	45	Utah	3.7
21	North Carolina	4.7	47	New Mexico	3.6
21	West Virginia	4.7	48	Arizona	3.0
24	South Carolina	4.6	49	Michigan	2.5
24	Tennessee	4.6	50	Alaska	0.8

District of Columbia   5.0

Source: U.S. Department of Labor, Bureau of Labor Statistics,
Press Release USDL 91-390 (August 8, 1991)

State Minimum Wage Rates in 1992*

National Minimum Wage = $4.25 per Hour

RANK	STATE	MINIMUM WAGE	RANK	STATE	MINIMUM WAGE
1	New Jersey**	$5.05	8	Pennsylvania	$4.25
2	Alaska	4.75	8	South Dakota	4.25
2	Hawaii**	4.75	8	Utah	4.25
2	Oregon	4.75	8	Vermont	4.25
5	Iowa	4.65	8	Virginia***	4.25
6	Rhode Island	4.45	8	Washington	4.25
7	Connecticut	4.27	8	West Virginia**	4.25
8	California	4.25	33	Arkansas***	4.00
8	Delaware	4.25	34	North Carolina	3.80
8	Idaho	4.25	34	Wisconsin	3.80
8	Illinois	4.25	36	Indiana	3.35
8	Kentucky	4.25	36	Michigan	3.35
8	Maine	4.25	36	New Mexico	3.35
8	Maryland	4.25	36	Texas	3.35
8	Massachusetts	4.25	40	Georgia	3.25
8	Minnesota	4.25	41	Colorado	3.00
8	Missouri	4.25	42	Kansas	2.65
8	Montana	4.25	43	Wyoming	1.60
8	Nebraska	4.25	–	Alabama****	N/A
8	Nevada	4.25	–	Arizona****	N/A
8	New Hampshire	4.25	–	Florida****	N/A
8	New York	4.25	–	Louisiana****	N/A
8	North Dakota	4.25	–	Mississippi****	N/A
8	Ohio	4.25	–	South Carolina***	N/A
8	Oklahoma	4.25	–	Tennessee****	N/A

Source: U.S. Department of Labor, Employment Standards Administration,
    "Minimum Wage and Overtime Premium Pay Standards" (January 2, 1992)

*State minimum wage rates are for those employers and jobs not covered by the federal program.

**Effective April 1, 1992. ***Effective July 1, 1992.

****No separate state program.

Average Hourly Earnings of Production Workers on Manufacturing Payrolls in 1991

National Average = $11.28 per Hour

RANK	STATE	HOURLY WAGES	RANK	STATE	HOURLY WAGES
1	Michigan	$14.66	26	Oklahoma	$11.26
2	Ohio	13.33	27	Idaho	11.20
3	Washington	13.27	27	Nevada	11.20
4	Delaware	12.49	29	Maine	11.12
5	Indiana	12.47	30	Kentucky	11.07
6	Alaska	12.45	31	Missouri	11.06
7	New Jersey	12.33	32	Vermont	10.96
8	Maryland	12.14	33	New Hampshire	10.91
9	Connecticut	12.11	33	Texas	10.91
10	California	12.00	35	Arizona	10.75
11	Louisiana	11.91	35	Utah	10.75
11	Montana	11.91	37	Virginia	10.44
13	West Virginia	11.81	38	Tennessee	9.95
14	Illinois	11.75	39	Nebraska	9.90
15	Massachusetts	11.73	40	Alabama	9.80
16	Iowa	11.72	41	Rhode Island	9.66
17	Minnesota	11.54	42	Georgia	9.62
18	Pennsylvania	11.52	43	North Dakota	9.60
19	Oregon	11.51	44	New Mexico	9.33
20	New York	11.50	45	Florida	9.31
21	Wisconsin	11.44	46	North Carolina	9.22
22	Wyoming	11.40	47	South Carolina	9.19
23	Colorado	11.37	48	Arkansas	8.90
24	Kansas	11.36	49	South Dakota	8.82
25	Hawaii	11.34	50	Mississippi	8.73

District of Columbia   13.14

Source: U.S. Department of Labor, Bureau of Labor Statistics,
"Employment and Earnings" (November 1991)

*Preliminary; state averages not seasonally adjusted. As of September 1991.

Average Weekly Earnings of Production Workers on Manufacturing Payrolls in 1991

National Average = $466.99 per Week

RANK	STATE	WEEKLY WAGES	RANK	STATE	WEEKLY WAGES
1	Michigan	$628.91	26	Kansas	$457.81
2	Ohio	573.19	27	Maine	457.03
3	Alaska	545.31	28	Vermont	455.94
4	Washington	533.45	29	Missouri	455.67
5	Indiana	527.48	30	Idaho	454.72
6	Delaware	525.83	31	Nevada	451.36
7	Louisiana	515.70	32	Kentucky	450.55
8	New Jersey	511.70	33	Wyoming	450.30
9	Connecticut	507.41	34	Colorado	446.84
10	Maryland	501.38	35	Utah	437.53
11	California	490.80	36	Arizona	434.30
12	Massachusetts	484.45	37	Virginia	430.14
13	West Virginia	483.03	38	Nebraska	408.87
14	Illinois	482.93	39	Alabama	405.72
15	Iowa	482.86	40	Rhode Island	403.79
16	Wisconsin	481.62	41	Georgia	397.31
17	Minnesota	471.99	42	Tennessee	396.01
18	Pennsylvania	471.17	43	New Mexico	382.53
19	Texas	465.86	44	Florida	381.71
20	Hawaii	464.94	45	South Carolina	379.55
21	Montana	463.30	46	North Carolina	375.25
22	Oregon	462.70	47	Arkansas	374.69
23	New York	462.30	48	North Dakota	373.44
24	Oklahoma	461.66	49	South Dakota	372.20
25	New Hampshire	460.40	50	Mississippi	355.31

District of Columbia   517.72

Source: U.S. Department of Labor, Bureau of Labor Statistics,

   "Employment and Earnings" (November 1991)

Preliminary; state averages not seasonally adjusted. As of September 1991.

Average Work Week of Production Workers on Manufacturing Payrolls in 1991

National Average = 41.4 Hours per Week

RANK	STATE	HOURS	RANK	STATE	HOURS
1	Alaska	43.8	25	Maine	41.1
2	Louisiana	43.3	27	Florida	41.0
3	Ohio	43.0	27	Hawaii	41.0
4	Michigan	42.9	27	New Mexico	41.0
5	Texas	42.7	27	Oklahoma	41.0
6	Indiana	42.3	31	California	40.9
7	New Hampshire	42.2	31	Minnesota	40.9
7	South Dakota	42.2	31	Pennsylvania	40.9
9	Arkansas	42.1	31	West Virginia	40.9
9	Delaware	42.1	35	Kentucky	40.7
9	Wisconsin	42.1	35	Mississippi	40.7
12	Connecticut	41.9	35	North Carolina	40.7
13	Rhode Island	41.8	35	Utah	40.7
14	Vermont	41.6	39	Idaho	40.6
15	New Jersey	41.5	40	Arizona	40.4
16	Alabama	41.4	41	Kansas	40.3
17	Georgia	41.3	41	Nevada	40.3
17	Maryland	41.3	43	New York	40.2
17	Massachusetts	41.3	43	Oregon	40.2
17	Nebraska	41.3	43	Washington	40.2
17	South Carolina	41.3	46	Tennessee	39.8
22	Iowa	41.2	47	Wyoming	39.5
22	Missouri	41.2	48	Colorado	39.3
22	Virginia	41.2	49	Montana	38.9
25	Illinois	41.1	49	North Dakota	38.9

District of Columbia   39.4

Source: U.S. Department of Labor, Bureau of Labor Statistics,
   "Employment and Earnings" (November 1991)
*Preliminary; state averages not seasonally adjusted. As of September 1991.

Civilian Labor Force in 1991

National Total = 125,607,000 Workers*

RANK	STATE	WORKERS	%		RANK	STATE	WORKERS	%
1	California	14,968,600	11.92%		26	South Carolina	1,743,700	1.39%
2	New York	8,557,300	6.81%		27	Arizona	1,709,500	1.36%
3	Texas	8,524,800	6.79%		28	Oregon	1,526,300	1.22%
4	Florida	6,473,400	5.15%		29	Oklahoma	1,508,900	1.20%
5	Illinois	6,010,000	4.78%		30	Iowa	1,475,800	1.17%
6	Pennsylvania	5,915,100	4.71%		31	Kansas	1,302,400	1.04%
7	Ohio	5,434,700	4.33%		32	Mississippi	1,174,400	0.93%
8	Michigan	4,510,000	3.59%		33	Arkansas	1,112,500	0.89%
9	New Jersey	4,018,300	3.20%		34	Nebraska	854,800	0.68%
10	North Carolina	3,529,600	2.81%		35	Utah	816,000	0.65%
11	Virginia	3,329,500	2.65%		36	West Virginia	776,700	0.62%
12	Georgia	3,150,100	2.51%		37	New Mexico	711,900	0.57%
13	Massachusetts	3,124,900	2.49%		38	Nevada	652,200	0.52%
14	Indiana	2,806,400	2.23%		39	Maine	638,600	0.51%
15	Missouri	2,674,800	2.13%		40	New Hampshire	624,600	0.50%
16	Wisconsin	2,600,400	2.07%		41	Hawaii	556,100	0.44%
17	Maryland	2,586,200	2.06%		42	Rhode Island	510,300	0.41%
18	Washington	2,480,900	1.98%		43	Idaho	503,400	0.40%
19	Tennessee	2,420,700	1.93%		44	Montana	397,000	0.32%
20	Minnesota	2,409,900	1.92%		45	South Dakota	359,800	0.29%
21	Louisiana	1,939,300	1.54%		46	Delaware	358,600	0.29%
22	Alabama	1,894,500	1.51%		47	North Dakota	317,600	0.25%
23	Connecticut	1,798,500	1.43%		48	Vermont	306,200	0.24%
24	Kentucky	1,785,200	1.42%		49	Alaska	260,500	0.21%
25	Colorado	1,772,600	1.41%		50	Wyoming	244,700	0.19%
						District of Columbia	281,600	0.22%

Source: U.S. Department of Labor, Bureau of Labor Statistics,
   "Employment and Earnings" (November 1991)
*Preliminary; state totals not seasonally adjusted. As of September 1991.

Civilian Labor Force Unemployment in 1991

National Total = 8,442,000 Unemployed*

RANK	STATE	UNEMPLOYED	%	RANK	STATE	UNEMPLOYED	%
1	California	1,122,900	13.30%	26	Arizona	94,900	1.12%
2	New York	581,900	6.89%	27	Mississippi	94,300	1.12%
3	Texas	546,600	6.47%	28	Oklahoma	92,700	1.10%
4	Florida	519,100	6.15%	29	Oregon	82,600	0.98%
5	Michigan	416,700	4.94%	30	Arkansas	76,400	0.90%
6	Illinois	398,100	4.72%	31	West Virginia	74,000	0.88%
7	Pennsylvania	373,300	4.42%	32	Colorado	66,800	0.79%
8	Ohio	308,700	3.66%	33	Iowa	62,900	0.75%
9	Massachusetts	279,100	3.31%	34	Kansas	55,200	0.65%
10	New Jersey	241,000	2.85%	35	Rhode Island	47,200	0.56%
11	North Carolina	187,200	2.22%	36	New Mexico	44,200	0.52%
12	Virginia	172,300	2.04%	37	New Hampshire	43,100	0.51%
13	Missouri	163,400	1.94%	38	Maine	42,700	0.51%
14	Indiana	160,700	1.90%	39	Utah	40,200	0.48%
15	Georgia	157,600	1.87%	40	Nevada	34,700	0.41%
16	Tennessee	151,200	1.79%	41	Idaho	23,900	0.28%
17	Kentucky	134,600	1.59%	42	Montana	23,100	0.27%
18	Washington	133,900	1.59%	43	Delaware	22,200	0.26%
19	Maryland	133,200	1.58%	44	Nebraska	21,200	0.25%
20	Louisiana	131,600	1.56%	45	Alaska	19,600	0.23%
21	Alabama	126,000	1.49%	46	Hawaii	15,400	0.18%
22	Wisconsin	125,800	1.49%	46	Vermont	15,400	0.18%
23	Minnesota	125,600	1.49%	48	Wyoming	12,100	0.14%
24	Connecticut	115,700	1.37%	49	South Dakota	11,700	0.14%
25	South Carolina	96,700	1.15%	50	North Dakota	11,000	0.13%

District of Columbia   22,500   0.27%

Source: U.S. Department of Labor, Bureau of Labor Statistics,
   "Employment and Earnings" (November 1991)
*Preliminary; state totals not seasonally adjusted. As of September 1991.

Percent of Civilian Labor Force Unemployed in 1991

National Percent = 6.7%*

RANK	STATE	RATE		RANK	STATE	RATE
1	West Virginia	9.5		26	Montana	5.8
2	Michigan	9.2		27	Indiana	5.7
2	Rhode Island	9.2		27	Ohio	5.7
4	Massachusetts	8.9		29	Arizona	5.6
5	Florida	8.0		30	South Carolina	5.5
5	Mississippi	8.0		31	Oregon	5.4
7	Alaska	7.5		31	Washington	5.4
7	California	7.5		33	Nevada	5.3
7	Kentucky	7.5		33	North Carolina	5.3
10	Arkansas	6.9		35	Maryland	5.2
10	New Hampshire	6.9		35	Minnesota	5.2
12	Louisiana	6.8		35	Virginia	5.2
12	New York	6.8		38	Georgia	5.0
14	Maine	6.7		38	Vermont	5.0
15	Alabama	6.6		38	Wyoming	5.0
15	Illinois	6.6		41	Utah	4.9
17	Connecticut	6.4		42	Wisconsin	4.8
17	Texas	6.4		43	Idaho	4.7
19	Pennsylvania	6.3		44	Iowa	4.3
20	Delaware	6.2		45	Kansas	4.2
20	New Mexico	6.2		46	Colorado	3.8
20	Tennessee	6.2		47	North Dakota	3.5
23	Missouri	6.1		48	South Dakota	3.2
23	Oklahoma	6.1		49	Hawaii	2.8
25	New Jersey	6.0		50	Nebraska	2.5

District of Columbia   8.0

Source: U.S. Department of Labor, Bureau of Labor Statistics,
   "Employment and Earnings" (November 1991)

Preliminary; state rates not seasonally adjusted. As of September 1991. January 1992 national rate was 7.1%.

Employees in Construction in 1991

National Total = 4,697,000 Employees*

RANK	STATE	EMPLOYEES	%	RANK	STATE	EMPLOYEES	%
1	California	639,600	13.62%	26	Kentucky	69,300	1.48%
2	Texas	346,100	7.37%	27	Oregon	58,900	1.25%
3	New York	294,000	6.26%	28	Connecticut	54,700	1.16%
4	Florida	263,200	5.60%	29	Iowa	50,900	1.08%
5	Pennsylvania	233,600	4.97%	30	Nevada	46,900	1.00%
6	Illinois	227,600	4.85%	31	Kansas	44,800	0.95%
7	Ohio	216,300	4.61%	32	Arkansas	40,900	0.87%
8	Virginia	164,200	3.50%	33	Oklahoma	36,100	0.77%
9	North Carolina	157,000	3.34%	34	Mississippi	35,200	0.75%
10	Maryland	153,400	3.27%	35	Nebraska	35,000	0.75%
11	Michigan	137,200	2.92%	36	Utah	33,700	0.72%
12	New Jersey	132,600	2.82%	37	Hawaii	32,900	0.70%
13	Georgia	129,700	2.76%	38	West Virginia	30,600	0.65%
14	Indiana	125,500	2.67%	39	New Mexico	30,400	0.65%
15	Washington	123,500	2.63%	40	Maine	25,700	0.55%
16	Missouri	104,100	2.22%	41	Idaho	23,100	0.49%
17	Louisiana	97,000	2.07%	42	Delaware	19,600	0.42%
18	South Carolina	94,900	2.02%	43	New Hampshire	17,700	0.38%
19	Tennessee	88,400	1.88%	44	Rhode Island	14,700	0.31%
20	Wisconsin	86,000	1.83%	45	South Dakota	14,200	0.30%
21	Minnesota	85,600	1.82%	46	Wyoming	13,400	0.29%
22	Arizona	81,300	1.73%	47	Vermont	13,300	0.28%
23	Alabama	80,100	1.71%	48	Alaska	12,900	0.27%
24	Massachusetts	77,600	1.65%	49	Montana	12,400	0.26%
25	Colorado	71,800	1.53%	50	North Dakota	12,300	0.26%
					District of Columbia	12,500	0.27%

Source: U.S. Department of Labor, Bureau of Labor Statistics,
    "Employment and Earnings" (November 1991)
*Preliminary; state totals not seasonally adjusted. As of September 1991.

Employees in Finance, Insurance, and Real Estate in 1991

National Total = 6,691,000 Employees*

RANK	STATE	EMPLOYEES	%	RANK	STATE	EMPLOYEES	%
1	California	841,000	12.57%	26	Alabama	73,500	1.10%
2	New York	753,800	11.27%	27	Iowa	71,500	1.07%
3	Texas	427,500	6.39%	28	South Carolina	66,500	0.99%
4	Illinois	375,300	5.61%	29	Kentucky	61,200	0.91%
5	Florida	354,400	5.30%	30	Oklahoma	58,500	0.87%
6	Pennsylvania	303,100	4.53%	31	Kansas	57,900	0.87%
7	Ohio	257,900	3.85%	32	Nebraska	50,000	0.75%
8	New Jersey	231,600	3.46%	33	Arkansas	38,900	0.58%
9	Massachusetts	205,700	3.07%	33	Mississippi	38,900	0.58%
10	Michigan	193,100	2.89%	35	Hawaii	37,900	0.57%
11	Georgia	162,100	2.42%	36	Utah	35,900	0.54%
12	Virginia	150,800	2.25%	37	Delaware	32,100	0.48%
13	Connecticut	146,500	2.19%	38	New Hampshire	30,800	0.46%
14	Missouri	138,500	2.07%	39	Nevada	29,000	0.43%
15	North Carolina	135,000	2.02%	40	New Mexico	26,100	0.39%
16	Maryland	128,700	1.92%	41	Rhode Island	25,800	0.39%
17	Minnesota	127,100	1.90%	42	Maine	25,200	0.38%
18	Indiana	125,800	1.88%	43	West Virginia	24,800	0.37%
19	Wisconsin	122,800	1.84%	44	Idaho	20,600	0.31%
20	Washington	118,600	1.77%	45	South Dakota	16,500	0.25%
21	Tennessee	101,500	1.52%	46	Montana	13,600	0.20%
22	Colorado	97,600	1.46%	47	North Dakota	12,700	0.19%
23	Arizona	94,800	1.42%	48	Vermont	11,100	0.17%
24	Oregon	84,300	1.26%	49	Alaska	10,300	0.15%
25	Louisiana	79,100	1.18%	50	Wyoming	7,200	0.11%

	District of Columbia	32,200	0.48%

Source: U.S. Department of Labor, Bureau of Labor Statistics,
 "Employment and Earnings" (November 1991)

*Preliminary; state totals not seasonally adjusted. As of September 1991.

Employees in Government in 1991

National Total = 18,407,000 Employees*

RANK	STATE	EMPLOYEES	%
1	California	2,064,700	11.22%
2	New York	1,400,000	7.61%
3	Texas	1,302,700	7.08%
4	Florida	887,600	4.82%
5	Illinois	755,400	4.10%
6	Ohio	714,200	3.88%
7	Pennsylvania	677,100	3.68%
8	Michigan	608,600	3.31%
9	Virginia	577,400	3.14%
10	New Jersey	548,000	2.98%
11	Georgia	536,700	2.92%
12	North Carolina	506,700	2.75%
13	Maryland	412,800	2.24%
14	Washington	407,700	2.21%
15	Indiana	375,200	2.04%
16	Missouri	370,700	2.01%
17	Massachusetts	368,100	2.00%
18	Tennessee	354,600	1.93%
19	Wisconsin	342,800	1.86%
20	Louisiana	339,200	1.84%
21	Minnesota	328,500	1.78%
22	Alabama	324,300	1.76%
23	South Carolina	294,600	1.60%
24	Colorado	285,300	1.55%
25	Kentucky	271,000	1.47%

RANK	STATE	EMPLOYEES	%
26	Arizona	269,300	1.46%
27	Oklahoma	263,600	1.43%
28	Oregon	221,400	1.20%
29	Iowa	216,300	1.18%
30	Kansas	212,300	1.15%
31	Mississippi	208,600	1.13%
32	Connecticut	205,500	1.12%
33	Arkansas	166,400	0.90%
34	New Mexico	153,400	0.83%
35	Utah	152,800	0.83%
36	Nebraska	151,400	0.82%
37	West Virginia	122,500	0.67%
38	Hawaii	99,000	0.54%
39	Maine	93,700	0.51%
40	Idaho	85,000	0.46%
41	Nevada	83,600	0.45%
42	New Hampshire	72,700	0.39%
43	Montana	72,600	0.39%
44	Alaska	72,500	0.39%
45	North Dakota	65,200	0.35%
46	Rhode Island	64,000	0.35%
47	South Dakota	61,700	0.34%
48	Wyoming	55,600	0.30%
49	Vermont	45,000	0.24%
50	Delaware	44,200	0.24%
	District of Columbia	275,000	1.49%

Source: U.S. Department of Labor, Bureau of Labor Statistics,
   "Employment and Earnings" (November 1991)
*Preliminary; state totals not seasonally adjusted. As of September 1991. Includes federal, state and local government.

Employees in Manufacturing in 1991

National Total = 18,411,000 Employees*

RANK	STATE	EMPLOYEES	%	RANK	STATE	EMPLOYEES	%
1	California	2,050,900	11.14%	26	Iowa	232,900	1.27%
2	Ohio	1,089,300	5.92%	27	Oregon	218,800	1.19%
3	New York	1,075,200	5.84%	28	Maryland	198,500	1.08%
4	Texas	976,200	5.30%	29	Colorado	192,700	1.05%
5	Illinois	976,100	5.30%	30	Kansas	185,900	1.01%
6	Pennsylvania	971,700	5.28%	31	Louisiana	185,200	1.01%
7	Michigan	905,700	4.92%	32	Arizona	179,300	0.97%
8	North Carolina	839,700	4.56%	33	Oklahoma	166,900	0.91%
9	Indiana	631,300	3.43%	34	Utah	109,000	0.59%
10	Wisconsin	558,800	3.04%	35	Nebraska	103,700	0.56%
11	New Jersey	558,600	3.03%	36	New Hampshire	100,500	0.55%
12	Georgia	544,600	2.96%	37	Maine	96,700	0.53%
13	Tennessee	516,700	2.81%	38	Rhode Island	93,000	0.51%
14	Florida	496,700	2.70%	39	West Virginia	83,700	0.45%
15	Massachusetts	482,400	2.62%	40	Delaware	71,900	0.39%
16	Missouri	419,500	2.28%	41	Idaho	65,300	0.35%
17	Virginia	415,400	2.26%	42	Vermont	44,000	0.24%
18	Minnesota	400,000	2.17%	43	New Mexico	42,700	0.23%
19	Alabama	380,200	2.07%	44	South Dakota	36,300	0.20%
20	Washington	370,300	2.01%	45	Nevada	26,500	0.14%
21	South Carolina	367,800	2.00%	46	Montana	23,200	0.13%
22	Connecticut	324,500	1.76%	47	Hawaii	20,300	0.11%
23	Kentucky	283,800	1.54%	48	North Dakota	18,300	0.10%
24	Mississippi	248,100	1.35%	49	Alaska	17,100	0.09%
25	Arkansas	238,800	1.30%	50	Wyoming	10,100	0.05%

District of Columbia   15,200   0.08%

Source: U.S. Department of Labor, Bureau of Labor Statistics,
"Employment and Earnings" (November 1991)
*Preliminary; state totals not seasonally adjusted. As of September 1991.

Employees in Mining in 1991

National Total = 684,000 Employees*

RANK	STATE	EMPLOYEES	%	RANK	STATE	EMPLOYEES	%
1	Texas	178,400	26.08%	25	Tennessee	6,000	0.88%
2	Louisiana	55,000	8.04%	27	Mississippi	5,800	0.85%
3	Oklahoma	41,900	6.13%	28	New York	5,200	0.76%
4	California	37,700	5.51%	28	North Carolina	5,200	0.76%
5	Kentucky	34,200	5.00%	30	Missouri	4,900	0.72%
6	West Virginia	33,500	4.90%	31	North Dakota	4,800	0.70%
7	Pennsylvania	26,600	3.89%	32	Arkansas	3,900	0.57%
8	Illinois	19,800	2.89%	33	Washington	3,700	0.54%
9	Colorado	19,300	2.82%	34	Idaho	3,100	0.45%
10	Wyoming	19,100	2.79%	35	South Dakota	2,600	0.38%
11	Ohio	16,700	2.44%	36	Wisconsin	2,400	0.35%
12	New Mexico	15,700	2.30%	37	New Jersey	2,300	0.34%
13	Virginia	14,600	2.13%	38	Iowa	2,200	0.32%
14	Nevada	14,500	2.12%	38	Maryland	2,200	0.32%
15	Arizona	13,300	1.94%	40	Nebraska	1,900	0.28%
16	Alabama	12,700	1.86%	40	Oregon	1,900	0.28%
17	Alaska	12,100	1.77%	40	South Carolina	1,900	0.28%
18	Kansas	9,800	1.43%	43	Massachusetts	1,600	0.23%
19	Michigan	9,400	1.37%	44	Connecticut	800	0.12%
20	Minnesota	9,000	1.32%	45	Vermont	500	0.07%
21	Utah	8,700	1.27%	46	New Hampshire	400	0.06%
22	Georgia	8,400	1.23%	47	Maine	200	0.03%
23	Florida	7,700	1.13%	47	Rhode Island	200	0.03%
24	Indiana	7,500	1.10%	49	Delaware	100	0.01%
25	Montana	6,000	0.88%	–	Hawaii**	N/A	N/A

	District of Columbia	100	0.01%

Source: U.S. Department of Labor, Bureau of Labor Statistics,
   "Employment and Earnings" (November 1991)
Preliminary; state totals not seasonally adjusted. As of September 1991.
**Not available.*

Employees in Service Industries in 1991

National Total = 28,918,000 Employees*

RANK	STATE	EMPLOYEES	%	RANK	STATE	EMPLOYEES	%
1	California	3,575,500	12.36%	26	Alabama	329,200	1.14%
2	New York	2,365,900	8.18%	27	South Carolina	316,900	1.10%
3	Texas	1,751,600	6.06%	28	Oregon	311,200	1.08%
4	Florida	1,635,200	5.65%	29	Iowa	302,600	1.05%
5	Pennsylvania	1,495,100	5.17%	30	Oklahoma	280,200	0.97%
6	Illinois	1,375,100	4.76%	31	Nevada	279,500	0.97%
7	Ohio	1,262,600	4.37%	32	Kansas	251,100	0.87%
8	New Jersey	1,004,300	3.47%	33	Arkansas	206,800	0.72%
9	Michigan	957,800	3.31%	34	Utah	194,600	0.67%
10	Massachusetts	896,700	3.10%	35	Nebraska	194,300	0.67%
11	Virginia	757,300	2.62%	36	Mississippi	168,100	0.58%
12	Georgia	653,400	2.26%	37	Hawaii	160,400	0.55%
13	Maryland	627,900	2.17%	38	West Virginia	154,400	0.53%
14	North Carolina	619,600	2.14%	39	New Mexico	150,800	0.52%
15	Missouri	595,400	2.06%	40	New Hampshire	130,900	0.45%
16	Minnesota	576,600	1.99%	41	Maine	129,800	0.45%
17	Wisconsin	554,700	1.92%	42	Rhode Island	129,600	0.45%
18	Indiana	552,600	1.91%	43	Idaho	88,500	0.31%
19	Washington	538,600	1.86%	44	Delaware	84,900	0.29%
20	Tennessee	503,700	1.74%	45	Montana	79,500	0.27%
21	Connecticut	433,400	1.50%	46	South Dakota	75,500	0.26%
22	Arizona	423,900	1.47%	47	North Dakota	71,600	0.25%
23	Colorado	417,900	1.45%	48	Vermont	69,500	0.24%
24	Louisiana	385,100	1.33%	49	Alaska	55,000	0.19%
25	Kentucky	341,400	1.18%	50	Wyoming	41,900	0.14%

District of Columbia 261,900 0.91%

Source: U.S. Department of Labor, Bureau of Labor Statistics,
      "Employment and Earnings" (November 1991)
*Preliminary; state totals not seasonally adjusted. As of September 1991.

Employees in Transportation and Public Utilities in 1991

National Total = 5,825,000 Employees*

RANK	STATE	EMPLOYEES	%	RANK	STATE	EMPLOYEES	%
1	California	629,200	10.80%	26	Connecticut	72,500	1.24%
2	Texas	435,300	7.47%	27	Kansas	68,900	1.18%
3	New York	428,900	7.36%	28	Oklahoma	67,700	1.16%
4	Illinois	309,400	5.31%	29	South Carolina	67,200	1.15%
5	Pennsylvania	272,200	4.67%	30	Oregon	65,300	1.12%
6	Florida	266,400	4.57%	31	Arkansas	58,600	1.01%
7	New Jersey	233,700	4.01%	32	Iowa	55,000	0.94%
8	Ohio	223,000	3.83%	33	Nebraska	46,300	0.79%
9	Georgia	194,300	3.34%	34	Mississippi	45,400	0.78%
10	Michigan	158,300	2.72%	35	Utah	43,000	0.74%
11	Missouri	154,100	2.65%	36	Hawaii	42,200	0.72%
12	North Carolina	153,600	2.64%	37	West Virginia	37,000	0.64%
13	Virginia	148,500	2.55%	38	Nevada	33,800	0.58%
14	Indiana	134,800	2.31%	39	New Mexico	29,100	0.50%
15	Massachusetts	124,000	2.13%	40	Alaska	22,900	0.39%
16	Washington	116,600	2.00%	41	Maine	22,200	0.38%
17	Tennessee	116,500	2.00%	42	Idaho	20,900	0.36%
18	Wisconsin	111,500	1.91%	43	Montana	20,500	0.35%
19	Louisiana	111,000	1.91%	44	North Dakota	17,000	0.29%
20	Minnesota	110,300	1.89%	45	New Hampshire	16,900	0.29%
21	Maryland	101,500	1.74%	46	Delaware	15,400	0.26%
22	Colorado	97,700	1.68%	46	Rhode Island	15,400	0.26%
23	Alabama	84,500	1.45%	48	Wyoming	14,600	0.25%
24	Kentucky	82,100	1.41%	49	South Dakota	13,800	0.24%
25	Arizona	81,100	1.39%	50	Vermont	11,000	0.19%

District of Columbia		23,600	0.41%

Source: U.S. Department of Labor, Bureau of Labor Statistics,
   "Employment and Earnings" (November 1991)
Preliminary; state totals not seasonally adjusted. As of September 1991.

Employees in Wholesale and Retail Trade in 1991

National Total = 25,386,000 Employees*

RANK	STATE	EMPLOYEES	%	RANK	STATE	EMPLOYEES	%
1	California	2,996,900	11.81%	26	South Carolina	352,700	1.39%
2	Texas	1,718,000	6.77%	27	Alabama	351,100	1.38%
3	New York	1,609,000	6.34%	28	Oregon	323,300	1.27%
4	Florida	1,410,900	5.56%	29	Iowa	310,400	1.22%
5	Illinois	1,274,900	5.02%	30	Oklahoma	279,200	1.10%
6	Ohio	1,183,900	4.66%	31	Kansas	268,000	1.06%
7	Pennsylvania	1,175,800	4.63%	32	Arkansas	215,600	0.85%
8	Michigan	927,400	3.65%	33	Mississippi	204,300	0.80%
9	New Jersey	849,000	3.34%	34	Nebraska	195,100	0.77%
10	Georgia	723,400	2.85%	35	Utah	180,600	0.71%
11	North Carolina	712,300	2.81%	36	West Virginia	145,900	0.57%
12	Massachusetts	649,300	2.56%	37	New Mexico	138,800	0.55%
13	Virginia	642,600	2.53%	38	Hawaii	135,200	0.53%
14	Indiana	598,800	2.36%	39	Maine	130,700	0.51%
15	Missouri	556,400	2.19%	40	Nevada	130,400	0.51%
16	Wisconsin	541,300	2.13%	41	New Hampshire	119,500	0.47%
17	Maryland	526,400	2.07%	42	Idaho	102,100	0.40%
18	Washington	523,000	2.06%	43	Rhode Island	93,200	0.37%
19	Minnesota	522,500	2.06%	44	Montana	81,500	0.32%
20	Tennessee	518,700	2.04%	45	South Dakota	79,600	0.31%
21	Louisiana	378,800	1.49%	46	Delaware	75,800	0.30%
22	Arizona	377,500	1.49%	47	North Dakota	72,400	0.29%
23	Colorado	377,200	1.49%	48	Vermont	58,000	0.23%
24	Kentucky	355,000	1.40%	49	Alaska	47,800	0.19%
25	Connecticut	352,800	1.39%	50	Wyoming	46,900	0.18%
					District of Columbia	59,300	0.23%

Source: U.S. Department of Labor, Bureau of Labor Statistics,

   "Employment and Earnings" (November 1991)

*Preliminary; state totals not seasonally adjusted. As of September 1991.

VII. ENERGY AND ENVIRONMENT

Table	Title	Page

ENERGY AND
ENVIRONMENT

Energy Consumption in 1989

National Total = 81,342,000,000,000,000 Btu's*

RANK	STATE	BTU'S	%	RANK	STATE	BTU'S	%
1	Texas	9,690,000,000,000,000	11.91%	26	Kansas	1,027,000,000,000,000	1.26%
2	California	7,127,000,000,000,000	8.76%	27	Mississippi	989,000,000,000,000	1.22%
3	Ohio	3,863,000,000,000,000	4.75%	28	Iowa	925,000,000,000,000	1.14%
4	Pennsylvania	3,590,000,000,000,000	4.41%	29	Arizona	916,000,000,000,000	1.13%
5	New York	3,556,000,000,000,000	4.37%	30	Oregon	912,000,000,000,000	1.12%
6	Illinois	3,527,000,000,000,000	4.34%	31	Colorado	909,000,000,000,000	1.12%
7	Louisiana	3,523,000,000,000,000	4.33%	32	Arkansas	825,000,000,000,000	1.01%
8	Florida	2,995,000,000,000,000	3.68%	33	West Virginia	799,000,000,000,000	0.98%
9	Michigan	2,764,000,000,000,000	3.40%	34	Connecticut	768,000,000,000,000	0.94%
10	Indiana	2,494,000,000,000,000	3.07%	35	Alaska	567,000,000,000,000	0.70%
11	New Jersey	2,338,000,000,000,000	2.87%	36	New Mexico	559,000,000,000,000	0.69%
12	Georgia	2,030,000,000,000,000	2.50%	37	Utah	543,000,000,000,000	0.67%
13	North Carolina	1,939,000,000,000,000	2.38%	38	Nebraska	526,000,000,000,000	0.65%
14	Washington	1,883,000,000,000,000	2.31%	39	Nevada	383,000,000,000,000	0.47%
15	Virginia	1,839,000,000,000,000	2.26%	40	Wyoming	381,000,000,000,000	0.47%
16	Tennessee	1,763,000,000,000,000	2.17%	41	Idaho	372,000,000,000,000	0.46%
17	Alabama	1,643,000,000,000,000	2.02%	42	Montana	350,000,000,000,000	0.43%
18	Missouri	1,518,000,000,000,000	1.87%	43	Maine	341,000,000,000,000	0.42%
19	Kentucky	1,475,000,000,000,000	1.81%	44	North Dakota	319,000,000,000,000	0.39%
20	Wisconsin	1,413,000,000,000,000	1.74%	45	Hawaii	299,000,000,000,000	0.37%
21	Massachusetts	1,372,000,000,000,000	1.69%	46	New Hampshire	250,000,000,000,000	0.31%
22	Minnesota	1,335,000,000,000,000	1.64%	47	Delaware	233,000,000,000,000	0.29%
23	Oklahoma	1,291,000,000,000,000	1.59%	48	South Dakota	212,000,000,000,000	0.26%
24	Maryland	1,262,000,000,000,000	1.55%	49	Rhode Island	206,000,000,000,000	0.25%
25	South Carolina	1,163,000,000,000,000	1.43%	50	Vermont	131,000,000,000,000	0.16%

District of Columbia 175,000,000,000,000 0.22%

Source: U.S. Department of Energy, Energy Information Administration,
 "State Energy Data Report, 1960-1989" (May 1991)

*British Thermal Units: The amount of heat required to raise the temperature of one pound of water one degree.

Per Capita Energy Consumption in 1989

National Per Capita = 327,600,000 Btu's*

RANK	STATE	BTU'S PER CAPITA	RANK	STATE	BTU'S PER CAPITA
1	Alaska	1,075,200,000	26	Utah	318,300,000
2	Louisiana	804,000,000	27	Georgia	315,400,000
3	Wyoming	803,100,000	28	Minnesota	306,700,000
4	Texas	570,300,000	29	Illinois	302,600,000
5	North Dakota	483,300,000	30	New Jersey	302,300,000
6	Indiana	445,800,000	31	Virginia	301,600,000
7	Montana	434,100,000	32	Michigan	298,100,000
8	West Virginia	430,300,000	32	Pennsylvania	298,100,000
9	Kansas	408,800,000	34	South Dakota	296,500,000
10	Oklahoma	400,600,000	35	North Carolina	295,200,000
11	Alabama	398,900,000	36	Missouri	294,200,000
12	Kentucky	395,800,000	37	Wisconsin	290,200,000
13	Washington	395,600,000	38	Maine	279,400,000
14	Mississippi	377,300,000	39	Colorado	273,900,000
15	Idaho	366,700,000	40	Hawaii	268,900,000
16	New Mexico	365,800,000	40	Maryland	268,900,000
17	Tennessee	357,000,000	42	Arizona	257,600,000
18	Ohio	354,100,000	43	California	245,200,000
19	Delaware	346,100,000	44	Connecticut	237,100,000
20	Nevada	344,500,000	45	Florida	236,400,000
21	Arkansas	342,800,000	46	Massachusetts	232,000,000
22	South Carolina	331,200,000	47	Vermont	230,800,000
23	Nebraska	326,700,000	48	New Hampshire	226,200,000
24	Iowa	325,800,000	49	Rhode Island	206,100,000
25	Oregon	323,300,000	50	New York	198,100,000

	District of Columbia	289,700,000

Source: U.S. Department of Energy, Energy Information Administration,
   "State Energy Data Report, 1960-1989" (May 1991)

*British Thermal Units: The amount of heat required to raise the temperature of one pound of water one degree.

Percent Change in State Energy Consumption: 1988 to 1989

National Percent Change = 1.4% Increase

RANK	STATE	PERCENT CHANGE	RANK	STATE	PERCENT CHANGE
1	Hawaii	13.2	24	Texas	1.8
2	Alaska	9.0	24	Utah	1.8
3	Nevada	8.2	28	Delaware	1.7
4	New Mexico	6.8	28	Vermont	1.7
5	Kentucky	5.3	30	Wisconsin	1.5
6	Idaho	5.2	31	Maryland	1.2
6	Mississippi	5.2	31	Minnesota	1.2
8	Montana	5.1	33	Wyoming	0.9
9	Arkansas	5.0	34	Louisiana	0.8
10	South Dakota	4.3	35	Colorado	0.7
11	Washington	3.9	36	Indiana	0.6
12	Oregon	3.6	37	Michigan	0.5
13	New Hampshire	3.0	37	Virginia	0.5
14	North Dakota	2.8	39	Missouri	0.3
15	West Virginia	2.7	39	Oklahoma	0.3
16	Tennessee	2.6	41	Pennsylvania	0.1
17	Florida	2.4	42	Georgia	(0.3)
18	Arizona	2.3	43	New York	(0.8)
18	Ohio	2.3	44	North Carolina	(0.9)
20	Alabama	2.0	45	Iowa	(1.3)
20	California	2.0	46	Illinois	(2.0)
20	New Jersey	2.0	47	Nebraska	(2.1)
23	Massachusetts	1.9	48	Kansas	(3.1)
24	Connecticut	1.8	49	Rhode Island	(4.0)
24	South Carolina	1.8	50	Maine	(8.1)

	District of Columbia	1.3

Source: U.S. Department of Energy, Energy Information Administration,
"State Energy Data Report, 1960-1989" (May 1991)

Per Capita Average Annual Energy Consumption Change: 1973 Through 1989

National Average = –0.4% Annual Change

RANK	STATE	AVERAGE ANNUAL CHANGE
1	Alaska	3.9%
2	North Dakota	2.6%
3	South Dakota	0.9%
4	Kentucky	0.5%
4	Mississippi	0.5%
4	South Carolina	0.5%
7	North Carolina	0.4%
7	Oklahoma	0.4%
7	Virginia	0.4%
10	Georgia	0.3%
11	New Jersey	0.2%
12	Hawaii	0.1%
12	Wyoming	0.1%
14	Connecticut	0.0%
14	Missouri	0.0%
14	Wisconsin	0.0%
17	Alabama	–0.2%
17	Indiana	–0.2%
17	Iowa	–0.2%
17	Kansas	–0.2%
17	Minnesota	–0.2%
17	Nebraska	–0.2%
23	Florida	–0.3%
23	Louisiana	–0.3%
23	Washington	–0.3%

RANK	STATE	AVERAGE ANNUAL CHANGE
26	Maryland	–0.4%
26	Tennessee	–0.4%
28	Montana	–0.5%
29	Ohio	–0.6%
29	Oregon	–0.6%
31	Arkansas	–0.7%
31	New Hampshire	–0.7%
31	Vermont	–0.7%
34	Idaho	–0.8%
34	Massachusetts	–0.8%
34	Michigan	–0.8%
34	Rhode Island	–0.8%
38	California	–0.9%
38	Colorado	–0.9%
40	Delaware	–1.0%
40	Illinois	–1.0%
40	New Mexico	–1.0%
40	Texas	–1.0%
40	West Virginia	–1.0%
45	Maine	–1.1%
45	Nevada	–1.1%
45	Pennsylvania	–1.1%
48	Arizona	–1.2%
48	New York	–1.2%
48	Utah	–1.2%

District of Columbia	0.6%

Source: U.S. Department of Energy, Energy Information Administration,
"State Energy Data Report: 1960–1989" (May 1991)

Energy Prices in 1989

National Energy Price = $7.72 per Million Btu's*

RANK	STATE	ENERGY PRICE		RANK	STATE	ENERGY PRICE
1	Connecticut	$10.68		26	Pennsylvania	$7.88
2	New Hampshire	10.39		27	Wisconsin	7.80
3	Arizona	10.38		28	Michigan	7.78
4	Vermont	10.34		29	Minnesota	7.68
5	New York	9.94		29	Ohio	7.68
6	Florida	9.83		31	Nebraska	7.61
7	Massachusetts	9.66		32	Colorado	7.60
8	Rhode Island	9.59		33	Arkansas	7.56
9	North Carolina	9.31		34	Kentucky	7.47
10	Maine	9.13		35	Idaho	7.36
11	New Jersey	8.68		36	Kansas	7.25
12	Maryland	8.60		37	Iowa	7.16
13	Delaware	8.57		38	Mississippi	7.13
14	South Carolina	8.52		38	Montana	7.13
15	California	8.42		40	Alabama	7.04
16	Virginia	8.39		41	Washington	6.98
17	Hawaii	8.25		42	Oklahoma	6.73
18	Nevada	8.22		43	Utah	6.69
19	Georgia	8.15		44	Wyoming	6.45
20	New Mexico	8.13		45	Indiana	6.29
21	South Dakota	8.03		46	Alaska	6.25
21	Tennessee	8.03		47	West Virginia	6.13
23	Missouri	8.01		48	North Dakota	6.05
24	Illinois	7.99		49	Texas	5.70
25	Oregon	7.92		50	Louisiana	5.18

District of Columbia   10.58

Source: U.S. Department of Energy, Energy Information Administration,
    "State Energy Price and Expenditure Report 1989" (September 1991)
British Thermal Units: The amount of heat required to raise the temperature of one pound of water one degree.

Energy Expenditures in 1989

National Total = $436,643,000,000

RANK	STATE	EXPENDITURES	%
1	California	$43,619,000,000	9.99%
2	Texas	38,375,000,000	8.79%
3	New York	25,210,000,000	5.77%
4	Ohio	20,599,000,000	4.72%
5	Illinois	20,456,000,000	4.68%
6	Pennsylvania	20,365,000,000	4.66%
7	Florida	18,864,000,000	4.32%
8	Michigan	16,096,000,000	3.69%
9	New Jersey	15,343,000,000	3.51%
10	Louisiana	11,983,000,000	2.74%
11	Indiana	11,685,000,000	2.68%
12	Georgia	11,560,000,000	2.65%
13	North Carolina	11,530,000,000	2.64%
14	Virginia	10,513,000,000	2.41%
15	Massachusetts	9,838,000,000	2.25%
16	Tennessee	9,196,000,000	2.11%
17	Missouri	8,854,000,000	2.03%
18	Alabama	7,992,000,000	1.83%
19	Wisconsin	7,983,000,000	1.83%
20	Washington	7,756,000,000	1.78%
21	Maryland	7,587,000,000	1.74%
22	Minnesota	7,217,000,000	1.65%
23	Kentucky	7,195,000,000	1.65%
24	South Carolina	6,348,000,000	1.45%
25	Arizona	6,014,000,000	1.38%

RANK	STATE	EXPENDITURES	%
26	Connecticut	$5,948,000,000	1.36%
27	Oklahoma	5,570,000,000	1.28%
28	Kansas	5,062,000,000	1.16%
29	Iowa	4,971,000,000	1.14%
30	Colorado	4,869,000,000	1.12%
31	Mississippi	4,778,000,000	1.09%
32	Oregon	4,628,000,000	1.06%
33	Arkansas	4,376,000,000	1.00%
34	West Virginia	3,488,000,000	0.80%
35	Nebraska	2,942,000,000	0.67%
36	New Mexico	2,763,000,000	0.63%
37	Utah	2,595,000,000	0.59%
38	Maine	2,227,000,000	0.51%
39	Nevada	2,173,000,000	0.50%
40	New Hampshire	1,861,000,000	0.43%
41	Hawaii	1,856,000,000	0.43%
42	Alaska	1,772,000,000	0.41%
43	Idaho	1,696,000,000	0.39%
44	Montana	1,598,000,000	0.37%
45	North Dakota	1,525,000,000	0.35%
46	Rhode Island	1,505,000,000	0.34%
47	Wyoming	1,453,000,000	0.33%
48	Delaware	1,308,000,000	0.30%
48	South Dakota	1,308,000,000	0.30%
50	Vermont	983,000,000	0.23%
	District of Columbia	1,067,000,000	0.24%

Source: U.S. Department of Energy, Energy Information Administration,
"State Energy Price and Expenditure Report 1989" (September 1991)

156

Per Capita Energy Expenditures in 1989

National Per Capita = $1,759

RANK	STATE	PER CAPITA	RANK	STATE	PER CAPITA
1	Alaska	$3,362	26	Illinois	$1,755
2	Wyoming	3,060	26	North Carolina	1,755
3	Louisiana	2,735	28	Iowa	1,750
4	North Dakota	2,311	29	Michigan	1,736
5	Texas	2,259	30	Vermont	1,734
6	Indiana	2,089	31	Oklahoma	1,728
7	Kansas	2,014	32	Virginia	1,724
8	New Jersey	1,983	33	Missouri	1,716
9	Montana	1,982	34	Arizona	1,691
10	Nevada	1,956	34	Pennsylvania	1,691
11	Delaware	1,943	36	New Hampshire	1,681
12	Alabama	1,941	37	Idaho	1,673
13	Kentucky	1,931	38	Hawaii	1,669
14	Ohio	1,889	39	Massachusetts	1,664
15	West Virginia	1,878	40	Minnesota	1,658
16	Tennessee	1,862	41	Oregon	1,641
17	Connecticut	1,836	42	Wisconsin	1,640
18	South Dakota	1,830	43	Washington	1,629
19	Nebraska	1,826	44	Maryland	1,616
20	Mississippi	1,823	45	Utah	1,520
21	Maine	1,822	46	Rhode Island	1,508
22	Arkansas	1,819	47	California	1,501
23	New Mexico	1,808	48	Florida	1,489
23	South Carolina	1,808	49	Colorado	1,468
25	Georgia	1,796	50	New York	1,404
				District of Columbia	1,766

Source: U.S. Department of Energy, Energy Information Administration,
"State Energy Price and Expenditure Report 1989" (September 1991)

Expenditures on Coal in 1989

National Total = $28,101,000,000

RANK	STATE	EXPENDITURES	%	RANK	STATE	EXPENDITURES	%
1	Ohio	$2,208,000,000	7.86%	26	Colorado	$349,000,000	1.24%
2	Pennsylvania	2,200,000,000	7.83%	27	Oklahoma	346,000,000	1.23%
3	Indiana	1,953,000,000	6.95%	28	New Mexico	345,000,000	1.23%
4	Texas	1,910,000,000	6.80%	29	Louisiana	336,000,000	1.20%
5	Michigan	1,377,000,000	4.90%	30	Arkansas	333,000,000	1.19%
6	West Virginia	1,326,000,000	4.72%	31	Kansas	330,000,000	1.17%
7	Illinois	1,261,000,000	4.49%	32	Nevada	253,000,000	0.90%
8	Alabama	1,234,000,000	4.39%	33	Massachusetts	198,000,000	0.70%
9	Georgia	1,182,000,000	4.21%	34	Mississippi	161,000,000	0.57%
10	Florida	1,128,000,000	4.01%	35	Washington	157,000,000	0.56%
11	North Carolina	982,000,000	3.49%	36	New Jersey	153,000,000	0.54%
12	Kentucky	934,000,000	3.32%	37	Nebraska	113,000,000	0.40%
13	Tennessee	765,000,000	2.72%	38	California	112,000,000	0.40%
14	Missouri	740,000,000	2.63%	39	Montana	108,000,000	0.38%
15	New York	590,000,000	2.10%	40	Delaware	106,000,000	0.38%
15	Wisconsin	590,000,000	2.10%	41	New Hampshire	55,000,000	0.20%
17	Virginia	569,000,000	2.02%	42	Connecticut	51,000,000	0.18%
18	South Carolina	514,000,000	1.83%	43	South Dakota	35,000,000	0.12%
19	Arizona	494,000,000	1.76%	44	Idaho	18,000,000	0.06%
20	Maryland	473,000,000	1.68%	44	Maine	18,000,000	0.06%
21	Utah	452,000,000	1.61%	46	Alaska	9,000,000	0.03%
22	North Dakota	437,000,000	1.56%	46	Oregon	9,000,000	0.03%
23	Minnesota	406,000,000	1.44%	48	Rhode Island	2,000,000	0.01%
24	Iowa	398,000,000	1.42%	49	Hawaii	1,000,000	0.00%
25	Wyoming	375,000,000	1.33%	49	Vermont	1,000,000	0.00%
					District of Columbia	3,000,000	0.01%

Source: U.S. Department of Energy, Energy Information Administration,
"State Energy Price and Expenditure Report 1989" (September 1991)

Expenditures on Electricity in 1989

National Total = $169,340,000,000

RANK	STATE	EXPENDITURES	%	RANK	STATE	EXPENDITURES	%
1	California	$17,085,000,000	10.09%	26	Connecticut	$2,398,000,000	1.42%
2	Texas	12,782,000,000	7.55%	27	Oklahoma	2,040,000,000	1.20%
3	New York	11,353,000,000	6.70%	28	Mississippi	1,787,000,000	1.06%
4	Florida	9,661,000,000	5.71%	29	Colorado	1,775,000,000	1.05%
5	Pennsylvania	8,361,000,000	4.94%	30	Oregon	1,774,000,000	1.05%
6	Illinois	8,158,000,000	4.82%	31	Iowa	1,695,000,000	1.00%
7	Ohio	8,033,000,000	4.74%	32	Kansas	1,647,000,000	0.97%
8	New Jersey	5,583,000,000	3.30%	33	Arkansas	1,645,000,000	0.97%
9	Michigan	5,572,000,000	3.29%	34	West Virginia	1,085,000,000	0.64%
10	North Carolina	5,479,000,000	3.24%	35	Nebraska	972,000,000	0.57%
11	Georgia	4,885,000,000	2.88%	36	New Mexico	958,000,000	0.57%
12	Virginia	4,308,000,000	2.54%	37	Utah	854,000,000	0.50%
13	Tennessee	4,031,000,000	2.38%	38	Maryland	801,000,000	0.47%
14	Indiana	3,913,000,000	2.31%	39	Nevada	773,000,000	0.46%
15	Maine	3,801,000,000	2.24%	40	New Hampshire	759,000,000	0.45%
16	Louisiana	3,604,000,000	2.13%	41	Idaho	675,000,000	0.40%
17	Missouri	3,396,000,000	2.01%	42	Hawaii	630,000,000	0.37%
18	Alabama	3,140,000,000	1.85%	43	Rhode Island	526,000,000	0.31%
19	South Carolina	3,038,000,000	1.79%	44	Montana	519,000,000	0.31%
20	Arizona	3,030,000,000	1.79%	45	Delaware	504,000,000	0.30%
21	Washington	2,984,000,000	1.76%	46	Wyoming	467,000,000	0.28%
22	Massachusetts	2,946,000,000	1.74%	47	North Dakota	401,000,000	0.24%
23	Kentucky	2,792,000,000	1.65%	48	South Dakota	383,000,000	0.23%
24	Wisconsin	2,614,000,000	1.54%	49	Alaska	380,000,000	0.22%
25	Minnesota	2,410,000,000	1.42%	50	Vermont	366,000,000	0.22%
					District of Columbia	567,000,000	0.33%

Source: U.S. Department of Energy, Energy Information Administration,
"State Energy Price and Expenditure Report 1989" (September 1991)

Expenditures on Natural Gas in 1989

National Total = $65,419,000,000

RANK	STATE	EXPENDITURES	%	RANK	STATE	EXPENDITURES	%
1	Texas	$7,821,000,000	11.96%	26	North Carolina	$719,000,000	1.10%
2	California	7,426,000,000	11.35%	27	Kentucky	690,000,000	1.05%
3	New York	4,627,000,000	7.07%	28	Washington	628,000,000	0.96%
4	Illinois	4,359,000,000	6.66%	29	Connecticut	620,000,000	0.95%
5	Ohio	3,826,000,000	5.85%	30	Mississippi	525,000,000	0.80%
6	Michigan	3,517,000,000	5.38%	31	Arizona	511,000,000	0.78%
7	Pennsylvania	3,295,000,000	5.04%	32	South Carolina	495,000,000	0.76%
8	Louisiana	2,431,000,000	3.72%	33	West Virginia	475,000,000	0.73%
9	New Jersey	2,360,000,000	3.61%	34	Nebraska	437,000,000	0.67%
10	Indiana	2,045,000,000	3.13%	35	Oregon	430,000,000	0.66%
11	Wisconsin	1,491,000,000	2.28%	36	Utah	406,000,000	0.62%
12	Georgia	1,486,000,000	2.27%	37	New Mexico	355,000,000	0.54%
13	Massachusetts	1,367,000,000	2.09%	38	Nevada	246,000,000	0.38%
14	Oklahoma	1,353,000,000	2.07%	39	Rhode Island	216,000,000	0.33%
15	Missouri	1,161,000,000	1.77%	40	Alaska	187,000,000	0.29%
16	Minnesota	1,109,000,000	1.70%	41	Montana	165,000,000	0.25%
17	Maryland	990,000,000	1.51%	42	Idaho	149,000,000	0.23%
18	Florida	977,000,000	1.49%	43	Delaware	143,000,000	0.22%
19	Virginia	851,000,000	1.30%	44	Wyoming	135,000,000	0.21%
20	Alabama	838,000,000	1.28%	45	South Dakota	106,000,000	0.16%
21	Colorado	837,000,000	1.28%	46	North Dakota	105,000,000	0.16%
22	Kansas	829,000,000	1.27%	47	New Hampshire	86,000,000	0.13%
23	Tennessee	797,000,000	1.22%	48	Hawaii	33,000,000	0.05%
24	Iowa	778,000,000	1.19%	49	Vermont	28,000,000	0.04%
25	Arkansas	725,000,000	1.11%	50	Maine	21,000,000	0.03%
					District of Columbia	213,000,000	0.33%

Source: U.S. Department of Energy, Energy Information Administration,
"State Energy Price and Expenditure Report 1989" (September 1991)

Expenditures on Motor Gasoline in 1989

National Total = $112,585,000,000

RANK	STATE	EXPENDITURES	%
1	California	$12,504,000,000	11.11%
2	Texas	8,458,000,000	7.51%
3	Florida	5,732,000,000	5.09%
4	New York	5,480,000,000	4.87%
5	Ohio	4,994,000,000	4.44%
6	Illinois	4,853,000,000	4.31%
7	Pennsylvania	4,453,000,000	3.96%
8	Michigan	4,127,000,000	3.67%
9	New Jersey	3,626,000,000	3.22%
10	North Carolina	3,306,000,000	2.94%
11	Virginia	3,183,000,000	2.83%
12	Georgia	3,122,000,000	2.77%
13	Massachusetts	2,601,000,000	2.31%
13	Tennessee	2,601,000,000	2.31%
15	Missouri	2,493,000,000	2.21%
16	Indiana	2,461,000,000	2.19%
17	Maryland	2,279,000,000	2.02%
18	Washington	2,268,000,000	2.01%
19	Minnesota	2,225,000,000	1.98%
20	Wisconsin	2,139,000,000	1.90%
21	Alabama	2,067,000,000	1.84%
22	Louisiana	1,945,000,000	1.73%
23	Kentucky	1,841,000,000	1.64%
24	South Carolina	1,755,000,000	1.56%
25	Arizona	1,747,000,000	1.55%

RANK	STATE	EXPENDITURES	%
26	Oklahoma	$1,590,000,000	1.41%
27	Connecticut	1,576,000,000	1.40%
28	Colorado	1,513,000,000	1.34%
29	Iowa	1,436,000,000	1.28%
30	Oregon	1,423,000,000	1.26%
31	Mississippi	1,229,000,000	1.09%
32	Kansas	1,201,000,000	1.07%
33	Arkansas	1,188,000,000	1.06%
34	West Virginia	872,000,000	0.77%
35	New Mexico	817,000,000	0.73%
36	Nebraska	814,000,000	0.72%
37	Utah	749,000,000	0.67%
38	Maine	647,000,000	0.57%
39	Nevada	626,000,000	0.56%
40	New Hampshire	555,000,000	0.49%
41	Idaho	487,000,000	0.43%
42	Hawaii	479,000,000	0.43%
43	Montana	465,000,000	0.41%
44	Rhode Island	424,000,000	0.38%
45	South Dakota	408,000,000	0.36%
46	North Dakota	392,000,000	0.35%
47	Delaware	380,000,000	0.34%
48	Wyoming	309,000,000	0.27%
49	Vermont	304,000,000	0.27%
50	Alaska	231,000,000	0.21%
	District of Columbia	209,000,000	0.19%

Source: U.S. Department of Energy, Energy Information Administration,
"State Energy Price and Expenditure Report 1989" (September 1991)

Gasoline Used in 1990

National Total = 114,262,125,000 Gallons

RANK	STATE	GALLONS	%	RANK	STATE	GALLONS	%
1	California	13,166,741,000	11.52%	26	Arizona	1,694,334,000	1.48%
2	Texas	8,842,370,000	7.74%	27	Colorado	1,531,789,000	1.34%
3	Florida	6,137,213,000	5.37%	28	Oregon	1,365,524,000	1.20%
4	New York	5,971,939,000	5.23%	29	Iowa	1,362,766,000	1.19%
5	Illinois	5,200,780,000	4.55%	30	Connecticut	1,339,193,000	1.17%
6	Ohio	4,747,902,000	4.16%	31	Mississippi	1,252,411,000	1.10%
7	Pennsylvania	4,614,575,000	4.04%	32	Arkansas	1,248,553,000	1.09%
8	Michigan	4,293,491,000	3.76%	33	Kansas	1,233,131,000	1.08%
9	Georgia	3,573,671,000	3.13%	34	West Virginia	843,858,000	0.74%
10	New Jersey	3,364,597,000	2.94%	35	New Mexico	803,095,000	0.70%
11	North Carolina	3,333,266,000	2.92%	36	Nebraska	794,588,000	0.70%
12	Virginia	3,018,984,000	2.64%	37	Utah	721,491,000	0.63%
13	Missouri	2,749,492,000	2.41%	38	Nevada	645,271,000	0.56%
14	Indiana	2,668,046,000	2.34%	39	Maine	608,301,000	0.53%
15	Tennessee	2,494,386,000	2.18%	40	New Hampshire	505,919,000	0.44%
16	Massachusetts	2,406,598,000	2.11%	41	Idaho	492,689,000	0.43%
17	Washington	2,305,401,000	2.02%	42	Montana	447,364,000	0.39%
18	Alabama	2,114,554,000	1.85%	43	South Dakota	389,115,000	0.34%
19	Wisconsin	2,097,141,000	1.84%	44	Hawaii	382,770,000	0.33%
20	Minnesota	2,056,804,000	1.80%	45	Rhode Island	377,590,000	0.33%
21	Maryland	2,036,369,000	1.78%	46	North Dakota	350,707,000	0.31%
22	Louisiana	1,889,888,000	1.65%	47	Delaware	346,730,000	0.30%
23	South Carolina	1,859,473,000	1.63%	48	Wyoming	306,112,000	0.27%
24	Kentucky	1,847,847,000	1.62%	49	Vermont	287,733,000	0.25%
25	Oklahoma	1,695,341,000	1.48%	50	Alaska	270,832,000	0.24%
					District of Columbia	173,390,000	0.15%

Source: U.S. Department of Transportation, Federal Highway Administration,
"Highway Statistics 1990" (FHWA-PL-91-003)

Power Plants in 1990

National Total = 3,015 Power Plants*

RANK	STATE	POWER PLANTS	%	RANK	STATE	POWER PLANTS	%
1	California	293	9.72%	26	Idaho	45	1.49%
2	New York	183	6.07%	27	Indiana	43	1.43%
3	Michigan	143	4.74%	28	Virginia	38	1.26%
4	Texas	133	4.41%	29	Oklahoma	37	1.23%
5	Wisconsin	121	4.01%	29	Tennessee	37	1.23%
6	Alaska	117	3.88%	31	Louisiana	36	1.19%
7	Iowa	115	3.81%	32	Alabama	34	1.13%
8	Minnesota	106	3.52%	32	Connecticut	34	1.13%
9	Kansas	98	3.25%	32	Kentucky	34	1.13%
10	Missouri	83	2.75%	35	Arkansas	33	1.09%
11	Nebraska	82	2.72%	36	Arizona	31	1.03%
12	Illinois	70	2.32%	37	New Jersey	30	1.00%
13	Florida	67	2.22%	38	Montana	29	0.96%
14	Utah	66	2.19%	39	South Dakota	27	0.90%
15	Colorado	65	2.16%	40	Maryland	24	0.80%
15	Pennsylvania	65	2.16%	41	Wyoming	22	0.73%
17	Washington	64	2.12%	42	Nevada	21	0.70%
18	Vermont	63	2.09%	42	West Virginia	21	0.70%
19	North Carolina	61	2.02%	44	Mississippi	20	0.66%
20	Massachusetts	60	1.99%	44	North Dakota	20	0.66%
21	Maine	58	1.92%	46	New Hampshire	19	0.63%
21	Oregon	58	1.92%	47	New Mexico	18	0.60%
23	Ohio	56	1.86%	48	Hawaii	17	0.56%
24	Georgia	50	1.66%	49	Delaware	10	0.33%
24	South Carolina	50	1.66%	50	Rhode Island	6	0.20%
					District of Columbia	2	0.07%

Source: U.S. Department of Energy, Energy Information Administration,
    "Inventory of Power Plants in the United States 1990" (DOE/EIA-0095(90), October 1991)
*Each unique site reported by electric utilities, regardless of the number of generators at that site, is counted as a single plant.

Nuclear Power Plants in 1990

National Total = 71 Nuclear Power Plants*

RANK	STATE	PLANTS	%	RANK	STATE	PLANTS	%
1	Illinois	7	9.86%	21	Maryland	1	1.41%
2	New York	5	7.04%	21	Mississippi	1	1.41%
2	Pennsylvania	5	7.04%	21	Missouri	1	1.41%
4	Michigan	4	5.63%	21	New Hampshire	1	1.41%
4	South Carolina	4	5.63%	21	Oregon	1	1.41%
6	Florida	3	4.23%	21	Tennessee	1	1.41%
6	New Jersey	3	4.23%	21	Vermont	1	1.41%
6	North Carolina	3	4.23%	21	Washington	1	1.41%
9	Alabama	2	2.82%	34	Alaska	0	0.00%
9	California	2	2.82%	34	Colorado	0	0.00%
9	Connecticut	2	2.82%	34	Delaware	0	0.00%
9	Georgia	2	2.82%	34	Hawaii	0	0.00%
9	Louisiana	2	2.82%	34	Idaho	0	0.00%
9	Massachusetts	2	2.82%	34	Indiana	0	0.00%
9	Minnesota	2	2.82%	34	Kentucky	0	0.00%
9	Nebraska	2	2.82%	34	Montana	0	0.00%
9	Ohio	2	2.82%	34	Nevada	0	0.00%
9	Texas	2	2.82%	34	New Mexico	0	0.00%
9	Virginia	2	2.82%	34	North Dakota	0	0.00%
9	Wisconsin	2	2.82%	34	Oklahoma	0	0.00%
21	Arizona	1	1.41%	34	Rhode Island	0	0.00%
21	Arkansas	1	1.41%	34	South Dakota	0	0.00%
21	Iowa	1	1.41%	34	Utah	0	0.00%
21	Kansas	1	1.41%	34	West Virginia	0	0.00%
21	Maine	1	1.41%	34	Wyoming	0	0.00%
					District of Columbia	0	0.00%

Source: U.S. Department of Energy, Energy Information Administration,
    "Inventory of Power Plants in the United States 1990" (DOE/EIA-0095(90), October 1991)
*Each generator at a site is counted as a separate plant.

Hazardous Waste Sites on the National Priority List in 1991

National Total = 1,185 Sites*

RANK	STATE	SITES	%
1	New Jersey	109	9.20%
2	Pennsylvania	94	7.93%
3	California	87	7.34%
4	New York	83	7.00%
5	Michigan	77	6.50%
6	Florida	51	4.30%
7	Washington	45	3.80%
8	Minnesota	41	3.46%
9	Wisconsin	39	3.29%
10	Illinois	36	3.04%
11	Ohio	33	2.78%
12	Indiana	32	2.70%
13	Texas	28	2.36%
14	Massachusetts	25	2.11%
15	South Carolina	23	1.94%
16	Missouri	22	1.86%
16	North Carolina	22	1.86%
18	Delaware	20	1.69%
18	Iowa	20	1.69%
18	Virginia	20	1.69%
21	Kentucky	17	1.43%
22	Colorado	16	1.35%
22	New Hampshire	16	1.35%
24	Connecticut	15	1.27%
25	Tennessee	14	1.18%

RANK	STATE	SITES	%
26	Georgia	13	1.10%
27	Alabama	12	1.01%
28	Kansas	11	0.93%
28	Louisiana	11	0.93%
28	Rhode Island	11	0.93%
28	Utah	11	0.93%
32	Arizona	10	0.84%
32	Arkansas	10	0.84%
32	Maryland	10	0.84%
32	New Mexico	10	0.84%
32	Oklahoma	10	0.84%
37	Idaho	9	0.76%
37	Maine	9	0.76%
39	Montana	8	0.68%
39	Oregon	8	0.68%
39	Vermont	8	0.68%
42	Alaska	6	0.51%
42	Nebraska	6	0.51%
44	West Virginia	5	0.42%
45	South Dakota	3	0.25%
45	Wyoming	3	0.25%
47	Mississippi	2	0.17%
47	North Dakota	2	0.17%
49	Hawaii	1	0.08%
49	Nevada	1	0.08%

	STATE	SITES	%
	District of Columbia	0	0.00%
	Other**	10	0.84%

Source: Environmental Protection Agency, Hazardous Site Evaluation Division,
"National Priorities List" (Proposed and Final Rules, September 1991)

*Excludes 23 proposed sites.

**Other is Puerto Rico (9) and Guam (1).

Daily Water Withdrawals in 1985

National Total = 399,000,000,000 Gallons Per Day*

RANK	STATE	GALLONS	%
1	California	49,700,000,000	12.46%
2	Texas	25,300,000,000	6.34%
3	Idaho	22,300,000,000	5.59%
4	Florida	17,000,000,000	4.26%
5	New York	15,200,000,000	3.81%
6	Illinois	14,500,000,000	3.63%
7	Pennsylvania	14,300,000,000	3.58%
8	Colorado	13,600,000,000	3.41%
9	Ohio	12,700,000,000	3.18%
10	Michigan	11,400,000,000	2.86%
11	Louisiana	10,400,000,000	2.61%
12	Nebraska	10,000,000,000	2.51%
13	Massachusetts	9,660,000,000	2.42%
14	North Carolina	8,760,000,000	2.20%
15	Montana	8,650,000,000	2.17%
16	Alabama	8,600,000,000	2.16%
17	Tennessee	8,450,000,000	2.12%
18	Indiana	8,030,000,000	2.01%
19	Virginia	7,250,000,000	1.82%
20	Washington	7,030,000,000	1.76%
21	New Jersey	6,940,000,000	1.74%
22	South Carolina	6,820,000,000	1.71%
23	Wisconsin	6,740,000,000	1.69%
24	Maryland	6,710,000,000	1.68%
25	Oregon	6,540,000,000	1.64%

RANK	STATE	GALLONS	%
26	Arizona	6,430,000,000	1.61%
27	Wyoming	6,220,000,000	1.56%
28	Missouri	6,110,000,000	1.53%
29	Arkansas	5,910,000,000	1.48%
30	Kansas	5,670,000,000	1.42%
31	Georgia	5,450,000,000	1.37%
32	West Virginia	5,440,000,000	1.36%
33	Utah	4,320,000,000	1.08%
34	Kentucky	4,200,000,000	1.05%
35	Connecticut	3,780,000,000	0.95%
36	Nevada	3,740,000,000	0.94%
37	New Mexico	3,280,000,000	0.82%
38	Minnesota	2,830,000,000	0.71%
39	Iowa	2,770,000,000	0.69%
40	Mississippi	2,510,000,000	0.63%
41	Hawaii	2,150,000,000	0.54%
42	Delaware	1,650,000,000	0.41%
43	Maine	1,520,000,000	0.38%
44	Oklahoma	1,270,000,000	0.32%
45	North Dakota	1,160,000,000	0.29%
46	New Hampshire	894,000,000	0.22%
47	South Dakota	675,000,000	0.17%
48	Rhode Island	409,000,000	0.10%
49	Alaska	406,000,000	0.10%
50	Vermont	126,000,000	0.03%

	District of Columbia	348,000,000	0.09%
	Puerto Rico	2,600,000,000	0.65%

Source: U.S. Geological Survey,

"Estimated Use of Water in the United States in 1985" (circular 1004)

*State-by-state information on water withdrawls issued every five years. Update not expected until 1993.

Daily Per Capita Fresh Water Withdrawn in 1985

National Per Capita = 1,400 Gallons*

RANK	STATE	GALLONS	RANK	STATE	GALLONS
1	Idaho	22,200	26	Texas	1,230
2	Wyoming	12,200	27	Missouri	1,210
3	Montana	10,500	27	Pennsylvania	1,210
4	Nebraska	6,250	29	Ohio	1,180
5	Colorado	4,190	30	Kentucky	1,130
6	Nevada	3,860	31	Hawaii	1,100
7	West Virginia	2,810	32	Massachusetts	1,070
8	Utah	2,540	33	Iowa	960
9	Arkansas	2,500	34	South Dakota	956
10	Oregon	2,450	35	Georgia	899
11	New Mexico	2,320	36	Mississippi	885
12	Kansas	2,310	37	Virginia	853
13	Louisiana	2,210	38	Maine	733
14	Alabama	2,140	39	Alaska	727
15	South Carolina	2,040	40	New Hampshire	688
16	Arizona	1,960	41	Minnesota	676
17	Tennessee	1,770	42	Florida	554
18	North Dakota	1,690	43	New York	508
19	Washington	1,600	44	Oklahoma	386
20	Indiana	1,470	45	Connecticut	375
21	California	1,420	46	Maryland	321
22	Wisconsin	1,400	47	New Jersey	307
23	Michigan	1,270	48	Vermont	235
24	North Carolina	1,260	49	Delaware	222
25	Illinois	1,250	50	Rhode Island	152

District of Columbia		556
Puerto Rico		176

Source: U.S. Geological Survey,

"Estimated Use of Water in the United States in 1985" (circular 1004)

*State-by state information on water withdrawls issued every five years. Update not expected until 1993.

VIII. GEOGRAPHY

Total Area of States in Square Miles in 1990

National Total = 3,787,425 Square Miles*

RANK	STATE	SQUARE MILES	%	RANK	STATE	SQUARE MILES	%
1	Alaska	656,424	17.33%	26	Iowa	56,276	1.49%
2	Texas	268,601	7.09%	27	New York	54,475	1.44%
3	California	163,707	4.32%	28	North Carolina	53,821	1.42%
4	Montana	147,046	3.88%	29	Arkansas	53,182	1.40%
5	New Mexico	121,598	3.21%	30	Alabama	52,423	1.38%
6	Arizona	114,006	3.01%	31	Louisiana	51,843	1.37%
7	Nevada	110,567	2.92%	32	Mississippi	48,434	1.28%
8	Colorado	104,100	2.75%	33	Pennsylvania	46,058	1.22%
9	Oregon	98,386	2.60%	34	Ohio	44,828	1.18%
10	Wyoming	97,818	2.58%	35	Virginia	42,769	1.13%
11	Michigan	96,810	2.56%	36	Tennessee	42,146	1.11%
12	Minnesota	86,943	2.30%	37	Kentucky	40,411	1.07%
13	Utah	84,904	2.24%	38	Indiana	36,420	0.96%
14	Idaho	83,574	2.21%	39	Maine	35,387	0.93%
15	Kansas	82,282	2.17%	40	South Carolina	32,007	0.85%
16	Nebraska	77,358	2.04%	41	West Virginia	24,231	0.64%
17	South Dakota	77,121	2.04%	42	Maryland	12,407	0.33%
18	Washington	71,303	1.88%	43	Hawaii	10,932	0.29%
19	North Dakota	70,704	1.87%	44	Massachusetts	10,555	0.28%
20	Oklahoma	69,903	1.85%	45	Vermont	9,615	0.25%
21	Missouri	69,709	1.84%	46	New Hampshire	9,351	0.25%
22	Florida	65,758	1.74%	47	New Jersey	8,722	0.23%
23	Wisconsin	65,503	1.73%	48	Connecticut	5,544	0.15%
24	Georgia	59,441	1.57%	49	Delaware	2,489	0.07%
25	Illinois	57,918	1.53%	50	Rhode Island	1,545	0.04%
					District of Columbia	68	0.00%

Source: U.S. Bureau of the Census,
    unpublished data

*Total of land and water area. These totals are revised due to improved measuring capabilities.

Land Area of States in Square Miles in 1990

National Total = 3,536,342 Square Miles of Land Area*

RANK	STATE	SQUARE MILES	%	RANK	STATE	SQUARE MILES	%
1	Alaska	570,374	16.13%	26	Florida	53,997	1.53%
2	Texas	261,914	7.41%	27	Arkansas	52,075	1.47%
3	California	155,973	4.41%	28	Alabama	50,750	1.44%
4	Montana	145,556	4.12%	29	North Carolina	48,718	1.38%
5	New Mexico	121,365	3.43%	30	New York	47,224	1.34%
6	Arizona	113,642	3.21%	31	Mississippi	46,914	1.33%
7	Nevada	109,806	3.11%	32	Pennsylvania	44,820	1.27%
8	Colorado	103,730	2.93%	33	Louisiana	43,566	1.23%
9	Wyoming	97,105	2.75%	34	Tennessee	41,220	1.17%
10	Oregon	96,003	2.71%	35	Ohio	40,953	1.16%
11	Idaho	82,751	2.34%	36	Kentucky	39,732	1.12%
12	Utah	82,168	2.32%	37	Virginia	39,598	1.12%
13	Kansas	81,823	2.31%	38	Indiana	35,870	1.01%
14	Minnesota	79,617	2.25%	39	Maine	30,865	0.87%
15	Nebraska	76,878	2.17%	40	South Carolina	30,111	0.85%
16	South Dakota	75,898	2.15%	41	West Virginia	24,087	0.68%
17	North Dakota	68,994	1.95%	42	Maryland	9,775	0.28%
18	Missouri	68,898	1.95%	43	Vermont	9,249	0.26%
19	Oklahoma	68,679	1.94%	44	New Hampshire	8,969	0.25%
20	Washington	66,582	1.88%	45	Massachusetts	7,838	0.22%
21	Georgia	57,919	1.64%	46	New Jersey	7,419	0.21%
22	Michigan	56,809	1.61%	47	Hawaii	6,423	0.18%
23	Iowa	55,875	1.58%	48	Connecticut	4,845	0.14%
24	Illinois	55,593	1.57%	49	Delaware	1,955	0.06%
25	Wisconsin	54,314	1.54%	50	Rhode Island	1,045	0.03%
					District of Columbia	61	0.00%

Source: U.S. Bureau of the Census,
   unpublished data

*Includes dry land temporarily or partially covered by water, such as marshland, swamps, etc.; streams and canals under one-eighth mile wide; and lakes, reservoirs and ponds under 40 acres.

Water Area of States in Square Miles in 1990

National Total = 251,083 Square Miles of Water Area*

RANK	STATE	SQUARE MILES	%	RANK	STATE	SQUARE MILES	%
1	Alaska	86,051	34.27%	26	Montana	1,490	0.59%
2	Michigan	40,001	15.93%	27	New Jersey	1,303	0.52%
3	Florida	11,761	4.68%	28	Pennsylvania	1,239	0.49%
4	Wisconsin	11,190	4.46%	29	Oklahoma	1,224	0.49%
5	Louisiana	8,277	3.30%	29	South Dakota	1,224	0.49%
6	California	7,734	3.08%	31	Arkansas	1,107	0.44%
7	Minnesota	7,326	2.92%	32	Tennessee	926	0.37%
8	New York	7,251	2.89%	33	Idaho	823	0.33%
9	Texas	6,687	2.66%	34	Missouri	811	0.32%
10	North Carolina	5,103	2.03%	35	Nevada	761	0.30%
11	Washington	4,721	1.88%	36	Wyoming	714	0.28%
12	Maine	4,523	1.80%	37	Connecticut	698	0.28%
13	Hawaii	4,508	1.80%	38	Kentucky	679	0.27%
14	Ohio	3,875	1.54%	39	Indiana	550	0.22%
15	Virginia	3,171	1.26%	40	Delaware	535	0.21%
16	Utah	2,736	1.09%	41	Rhode Island	500	0.20%
17	Massachusetts	2,717	1.08%	42	Nebraska	481	0.19%
18	Maryland	2,633	1.05%	43	Kansas	459	0.18%
19	Oregon	2,383	0.95%	44	Iowa	401	0.16%
20	Illinois	2,325	0.93%	45	New Hampshire	382	0.15%
21	South Carolina	1,896	0.76%	46	Colorado	371	0.15%
22	North Dakota	1,710	0.68%	47	Vermont	366	0.15%
23	Alabama	1,673	0.67%	48	Arizona	364	0.14%
24	Georgia	1,522	0.61%	49	New Mexico	234	0.09%
25	Mississippi	1,520	0.61%	50	West Virginia	145	0.06%
					District of Columbia	7	0.00%

Source: U.S. Bureau of the Census,
unpublished data

*Includes permanent inland water surface, such as lakes, reservoirs, and ponds having an area of 40 acres or more, canals one-eighth mile or more in width; coastal waters behind or sheltered by headlands or islands separated by less than 1 nautical mile of water, and islands under 40 acres in area. Excludes areas of oceans, bays, etc., lying within U.S. jurisdiction but not defined as inland water.

Highest Point of Elevation in Feet

National High Point = 20,320 Feet Above Sea Level (Mt. McKinley--Alaska)

RANK	STATE	HIGH POINT	RANK	STATE	HIGH POINT
1	Alaska	20,320	26	Vermont	4,393
2	California	14,491	27	Kentucky	4,139
3	Colorado	14,433	28	Kansas	4,039
4	Washington	14,410	29	South Carolina	3,560
5	Wyoming	13,804	30	North Dakota	3,506
6	Hawaii	13,796	31	Massachusetts	3,487
7	Utah	13,528	32	Maryland	3,360
8	New Mexico	13,161	33	Pennsylvania	3,213
9	Nevada	13,140	34	Arkansas	2,753
10	Montana	12,799	35	Alabama	2,405
11	Idaho	12,662	36	Connecticut	2,380
12	Arizona	12,633	37	Minnesota	2,301
13	Oregon	11,239	38	Michigan	1,979
14	Texas	8,749	39	Wisconsin	1,951
15	South Dakota	7,242	40	New Jersey	1,803
16	North Carolina	6,684	41	Missouri	1,772
17	Tennessee	6,643	42	Iowa	1,670
18	New Hampshire	6,288	43	Ohio	1,549
19	Virginia	5,729	44	Indiana	1,257
20	Nebraska	5,426	45	Illinois	1,235
21	New York	5,344	46	Rhode Island	812
22	Maine	5,267	47	Mississippi	806
23	Oklahoma	4,973	48	Louisiana	535
24	West Virginia	4,861	49	Delaware	442
25	Georgia	4,784	50	Florida	345

District of Columbia   410

Source: U.S. Geological Survey,
   "Elevations and Distances in the United States, 1989"

Lowest Point of Elevation in Feet

National Low Point = 282 Feet Below Sea Level (Death Valley--California)*

RANK	STATE	LOWEST POINT		RANK	STATE	LOWEST POINT
1	California	-282		26	Arizona	70
2	Louisiana	-8		27	Vermont	95
3	Alabama*	0		28	Tennessee	178
3	Alaska	0		29	Missouri	230
3	Connecticut	0		30	West Virginia	240
3	Delaware	0		31	Kentucky	257
3	Florida	0		32	Illinois	279
3	Georgia	0		33	Oklahoma	289
3	Hawaii	0		34	Indiana	320
3	Maine	0		35	Ohio	455
3	Maryland	0		36	Nevada	479
3	Massachusetts	0		37	Iowa	480
3	Mississippi	0		38	Michigan	572
3	New Hampshire	0		39	Wisconsin	581
3	New Jersey	0		40	Minnesota	602
3	New York	0		41	Kansas	679
3	North Carolina	0		42	Idaho	710
3	Oregon	0		43	North Dakota	750
3	Pennsylvania	0		44	Nebraska	840
3	Rhode Island	0		45	South Dakota	966
3	South Carolina	0		46	Montana	1,800
3	Texas	0		47	Utah	2,000
3	Virginia	0		48	New Mexico	2,842
3	Washington	0		49	Wyoming	3,099
25	Arkansas	55		50	Colorado	3,350

District of Columbia   1

Source: U.S. Geological Survey,
    "Elevations and Distances in the United States, 1989"
*States with "0" have sea level as lowest point.

Approximate Mean Elevation in Feet

Approximate National Mean Elevation = 2,500 Feet Above Sea Level

RANK	STATE	FEET	RANK	STATE	FEET
1	Colorado	6,800	25	New York	1,000
2	Wyoming	6,700	25	Vermont	1,000
3	Utah	6,100	28	Virginia	950
4	New Mexico	5,700	29	Michigan	900
5	Nevada	5,500	29	Tennessee	900
6	Idaho	5,000	31	Ohio	850
7	Arizona	4,100	32	Missouri	800
8	Montana	3,400	33	Kentucky	750
9	Oregon	3,300	34	Indiana	700
10	Hawaii	3,030	34	North Carolina	700
11	California	2,900	36	Arkansas	650
12	Nebraska	2,600	37	Georgia	600
13	South Dakota	2,200	37	Illinois	600
14	Kansas	2,000	37	Maine	600
15	Alaska	1,900	40	Alabama	500
15	North Dakota	1,900	40	Connecticut	500
17	Texas	1,700	40	Massachusetts	500
17	Washington	1,700	43	Maryland	350
19	West Virginia	1,500	44	South Carolina	350
20	Oklahoma	1,300	45	Mississippi	300
21	Minnesota	1,200	46	New Jersey	250
22	Iowa	1,100	47	Rhode Island	200
22	Pennsylvania	1,100	48	Florida	100
24	Wisconsin	1,050	48	Louisiana	100
25	New Hampshire	1,000	50	Delaware	60

District of Columbia   150

Source: U.S. Geological Survey,
    "Elevations and Distances in the United States, 1989"

Land In Urban Areas in 1990

National Total = 87,376 Square Miles in Urban Area*

RANK	STATE	SQUARE MILES	%	RANK	STATE	SQUARE MILES	%
1	California	8,175	9.36%	26	Colorado	1,317	1.51%
2	Texas	7,671	8.78%	27	Connecticut	1,253	1.43%
3	Florida	5,128	5.87%	28	Arkansas	1,223	1.40%
4	Ohio	3,607	4.13%	29	Mississippi	1,129	1.29%
5	New York	3,386	3.87%	30	Iowa	1,101	1.26%
6	Illinois	3,033	3.47%	31	Kentucky	1,055	1.21%
7	Pennsylvania	3,016	3.45%	32	Nevada	941	1.08%
8	Georgia	2,812	3.22%	33	Kansas	933	1.07%
9	Alabama	2,678	3.06%	34	Oregon	829	0.95%
10	Michigan	2,664	3.05%	35	New Mexico	796	0.91%
11	New Jersey	2,428	2.78%	36	Utah	725	0.83%
12	Tennessee	2,360	2.70%	37	Maine	723	0.83%
13	North Carolina	2,262	2.59%	38	Hawaii	644	0.74%
14	Virginia	2,189	2.51%	39	Alaska	640	0.73%
15	Massachusetts	2,150	2.46%	40	New Hampshire	513	0.59%
16	Arizona	2,051	2.35%	41	Nebraska	393	0.45%
17	Missouri	1,888	2.16%	42	West Virginia	378	0.43%
18	Minnesota	1,839	2.10%	43	Idaho	322	0.37%
19	Oklahoma	1,824	2.09%	44	Rhode Island	298	0.34%
20	Indiana	1,781	2.04%	45	Montana	247	0.28%
21	Washington	1,775	2.03%	46	Wyoming	233	0.27%
22	Louisiana	1,597	1.83%	47	Delaware	209	0.24%
23	Maryland	1,578	1.81%	48	South Dakota	203	0.23%
24	Wisconsin	1,578	1.81%	49	North Dakota	169	0.19%
25	South Carolina	1,426	1.63%	50	Vermont	142	0.16%

District of Columbia 61 0.07%

Source: U.S. Bureau of the Census,

Press Release CB 91-334 (December 18, 1991)

*Urban areas are densely populated areas and include places located outside urbanized areas but with 2,500 or more population.

Percent of Land in Urban Areas in 1990

National Percent = 2.5% of Land is in Urban Area*

RANK	STATE	PERCENT	RANK	STATE	PERCENT
1	New Jersey	32.7	26	Kentucky	2.7
2	Rhode Island	28.5	26	Missouri	2.7
3	Massachusetts	27.4	26	Oklahoma	2.7
4	Connecticut	25.9	26	Washington	2.7
5	Maryland	16.1	30	Mississippi	2.4
6	Delaware	10.7	31	Arkansas	2.3
7	Hawaii	10.0	31	Maine	2.3
8	Florida	9.5	31	Minnesota	2.3
9	Ohio	8.8	34	Iowa	2.0
10	New York	7.2	35	Arizona	1.8
11	Pennsylvania	6.7	36	West Virginia	1.6
12	New Hampshire	5.7	37	Vermont	1.5
12	Tennessee	5.7	38	Colorado	1.3
14	Illinois	5.5	39	Kansas	1.1
14	Virginia	5.5	40	Nevada	0.9
16	Alabama	5.3	40	Oregon	0.9
17	California	5.2	40	Utah	0.9
18	Indiana	5.0	43	New Mexico	0.7
19	Georgia	4.9	44	Nebraska	0.5
20	Michigan	4.7	45	Idaho	0.4
20	South Carolina	4.7	46	South Dakota	0.3
22	North Carolina	4.6	47	Montana	0.2
23	Louisiana	3.7	47	North Dakota	0.2
24	Texas	2.9	47	Wyoming	0.2
24	Wisconsin	2.9	50	Alaska	0.1

District of Columbia   100.0

Source: U.S. Bureau of the Census,
   Press Release CB 91-334 (December 18, 1991)

*Urban areas are densely populated areas and include places located outside urbanized areas but with 2,500 or more population.

Land in Rural Areas in 1990

National Total = 3,448,902 Square Miles in Rural Areas*

RANK	STATE	SQUARE MILES	%	RANK	STATE	SQUARE MILES	%
1	Alaska	569,733	16.52%	26	Arkansas	50,852	1.47%
2	Texas	254,243	7.37%	27	Florida	48,809	1.42%
3	California	147,798	4.29%	28	Alabama	48,072	1.39%
4	Montana	145,309	4.21%	29	North Carolina	46,456	1.35%
5	New Mexico	120,568	3.50%	30	Mississippi	45,784	1.33%
6	Arizona	111,591	3.24%	31	New York	43,838	1.27%
7	Nevada	108,865	3.16%	32	Louisiana	41,969	1.22%
8	Colorado	102,412	2.97%	33	Pennsylvania	41,804	1.21%
9	Wyoming	96,871	2.81%	34	Tennessee	38,859	1.13%
10	Oregon	95,174	2.76%	35	Kentucky	38,677	1.12%
11	Idaho	82,429	2.39%	36	Virginia	37,409	1.08%
12	Utah	81,444	2.36%	37	Ohio	37,345	1.08%
13	Kansas	80,890	2.35%	38	Indiana	34,089	0.99%
14	Minnesota	77,778	2.26%	39	Maine	30,141	0.87%
15	Nebraska	76,484	2.22%	40	South Carolina	28,686	0.83%
16	South Dakota	75,693	2.19%	41	West Virginia	23,709	0.69%
17	North Dakota	68,825	2.00%	42	Vermont	9,108	0.26%
18	Missouri	67,010	1.94%	43	New Hampshire	8,456	0.25%
19	Oklahoma	66,855	1.94%	44	Maryland	8,196	0.24%
20	Washington	64,806	1.88%	45	Hawaii	5,779	0.17%
21	Georgia	55,107	1.60%	46	Massachusetts	5,688	0.16%
22	Iowa	54,774	1.59%	47	New Jersey	4,991	0.14%
23	Michigan	54,146	1.57%	48	Connecticut	3,592	0.10%
24	Wisconsin	52,736	1.53%	49	Delaware	1,746	0.05%
25	Illinois	52,561	1.52%	50	Rhode Island	747	0.02%
					District of Columbia	(1)	0.00%

Source: U.S. Bureau of the Census,
    Press Release CB 91-334 (December 18, 1991)

*Rural areas are those locations with less than 2,500 population or in the open countryside.

Percent of Land in Rural Areas in 1990

National Percent = 97.5% of Land is Rural*

RANK	STATE	PERCENT		RANK	STATE	PERCENT
1	Alaska	99.9		26	Texas	97.1
2	Montana	99.8		26	Wisconsin	97.1
2	North Dakota	99.8		28	Louisiana	96.3
2	Wyoming	99.8		29	North Carolina	95.4
5	South Dakota	99.7		30	Michigan	95.3
6	Idaho	99.6		30	South Carolina	95.3
7	Nebraska	99.5		32	Georgia	95.1
8	New Mexico	99.3		33	Indiana	95.0
9	Nevada	99.1		34	California	94.8
9	Oregon	99.1		35	Alabama	94.7
9	Utah	99.1		36	Illinois	94.5
12	Kansas	98.9		36	Virginia	94.5
13	Colorado	98.7		38	New Hampshire	94.3
14	Vermont	98.5		38	Tennessee	94.3
15	West Virginia	98.4		40	Pennsylvania	93.3
16	Arizona	98.2		41	New York	92.8
17	Iowa	98.0		42	Ohio	91.2
18	Arkansas	97.7		43	Florida	90.5
18	Maine	97.7		44	Hawaii	90.0
18	Minnesota	97.7		45	Delaware	89.3
21	Mississippi	97.6		46	Maryland	83.9
22	Kentucky	97.3		47	Connecticut	74.1
22	Missouri	97.3		48	Massachusetts	72.6
22	Oklahoma	97.3		49	Rhode Island	71.5
22	Washington	97.3		50	New Jersey	67.3
					District of Columbia	0.0

Source: U.S. Bureau of the Census,
   Press Release CB 91-334 (December 18, 1991)

*Rural areas are those locations with less than 2,500 population or in the open countryside.

Acres of Land Owned by the Federal Government in 1989

National Total = 662,158,197 Acres

RANK	STATE	ACRES	%
1	Alaska	247,802,245	37.42%
2	California	61,042,578	9.22%
3	Nevada	57,803,208	8.73%
4	Utah	33,611,396	5.08%
5	Idaho	33,121,959	5.00%
6	Arizona	31,491,365	4.76%
7	Wyoming	30,407,259	4.59%
8	Oregon	29,668,753	4.48%
9	Montana	25,862,496	3.91%
10	New Mexico	25,747,308	3.89%
11	Colorado	22,647,838	3.42%
12	Washington	12,373,150	1.87%
13	Louisiana	6,537,588	0.99%
14	Michigan	3,564,777	0.54%
15	Arkansas	3,421,061	0.52%
16	Florida	3,355,544	0.51%
17	Texas	2,844,943	0.43%
18	South Dakota	2,743,763	0.41%
19	Minnesota	2,386,684	0.36%
20	Georgia	2,292,379	0.35%
21	West Virginia	2,099,136	0.32%
22	Missouri	2,030,505	0.31%
23	North Dakota	1,964,786	0.30%
24	Virginia	1,918,344	0.29%
25	Wisconsin	1,905,815	0.29%

RANK	STATE	ACRES	%
26	Mississippi	1,670,524	0.25%
27	Kentucky	1,391,208	0.21%
28	Tennessee	1,322,215	0.20%
29	North Carolina	1,140,931	0.17%
30	Oklahoma	874,004	0.13%
31	New Hampshire	764,411	0.12%
32	Nebraska	718,604	0.11%
33	Kansas	689,845	0.10%
34	Hawaii	676,824	0.10%
35	Pennsylvania	640,939	0.10%
36	Alabama	549,858	0.08%
37	Illinois	493,878	0.07%
38	Indiana	469,794	0.07%
39	South Carolina	433,771	0.07%
40	Vermont	354,917	0.05%
41	Ohio	321,730	0.05%
42	New York	223,283	0.03%
43	Maryland	196,921	0.03%
44	Iowa	159,134	0.02%
45	Maine	152,678	0.02%
46	New Jersey	135,461	0.02%
47	Massachusetts	82,563	0.01%
48	Delaware	30,360	0.00%
49	Connecticut	13,910	0.00%
50	Rhode Island	4,686	0.00%
	District of Columbia	10,872	0.00%

Source: U.S. Department of Interior, Bureau of Land Management,
"Public Land Statistics 1990" (Volume 175, August 1991)

Percent of Land Owned by the Federal Government in 1989

National Percent = 29.15%

RANK	STATE	PERCENT
1	Nevada	82.27
2	Alaska	67.80
3	Utah	63.78
4	Idaho	62.57
5	California	60.92
6	Wyoming	48.77
7	Oregon	48.17
8	Arizona	43.32
9	Colorado	34.06
10	New Mexico	33.11
11	Washington	28.98
12	Montana	27.73
13	Louisiana	22.65
14	Hawaii	16.49
15	West Virginia	13.62
16	New Hampshire	13.08
17	Arkansas	10.18
18	Michigan	9.77
19	Florida	9.66
20	Virginia	7.52
21	Georgia	6.15
22	Vermont	5.98
23	South Dakota	5.61
24	Mississippi	5.53
25	Kentucky	5.45

RANK	STATE	PERCENT
26	Wisconsin	5.44
27	Tennessee	4.95
28	Minnesota	4.66
29	Missouri	4.59
30	North Dakota	4.42
31	North Carolina	3.63
32	Maryland	3.12
33	New Jersey	2.81
34	Delaware	2.40
35	South Carolina	2.24
36	Pennsylvania	2.23
37	Indiana	2.03
38	Oklahoma	1.98
39	Texas	1.69
40	Alabama	1.68
41	Massachusetts	1.64
42	Nebraska	1.47
43	Illinois	1.38
44	Kansas	1.31
45	Ohio	1.23
46	Maine	0.77
47	New York	0.73
48	Rhode Island	0.69
49	Connecticut	0.44
49	Iowa	0.44

District of Columbia   27.85

Source: U.S. Department of Interior, Bureau of Land Management,
"Public Land Statistics 1990" (Volume 175, August 1991)

IX. GOVERNMENT FINANCE: FEDERAL

Federal Tax Returns Filed in 1990

National Total = 201,714,638 Returns*

RANK	STATE	RETURNS	%	RANK	STATE	RETURNS	%
1	California	24,583,188	12.19%	26	Kentucky	2,547,926	1.26%
2	New York	15,081,928	7.48%	27	South Carolina	2,469,972	1.22%
3	Texas	12,612,868	6.25%	28	Oregon	2,449,320	1.21%
4	Florida	11,829,417	5.86%	29	Oklahoma	2,369,345	1.17%
5	Pennsylvania	9,646,214	4.78%	30	Iowa	2,351,663	1.17%
6	Illinois	9,338,961	4.63%	31	Kansas	2,068,294	1.03%
7	Ohio	8,441,961	4.19%	32	Arkansas	1,677,572	0.83%
8	New Jersey	7,138,846	3.54%	33	Mississippi	1,634,521	0.81%
9	Michigan	6,951,685	3.45%	34	Nebraska	1,358,535	0.67%
10	Massachusetts	5,403,403	2.68%	35	West Virginia	1,166,732	0.58%
11	North Carolina	5,093,807	2.53%	36	Utah	1,118,886	0.55%
12	Virginia	4,894,051	2.43%	37	New Mexico	1,092,426	0.54%
13	Georgia	4,692,495	2.33%	38	Maine	1,031,868	0.51%
14	Maryland**	4,643,829	2.30%	39	New Hampshire	1,002,922	0.50%
15	Indiana	4,198,873	2.08%	40	Nevada	982,709	0.49%
16	Washington	4,135,188	2.05%	41	Hawaii	964,868	0.48%
17	Missouri	4,109,035	2.04%	42	Rhode Island	857,615	0.43%
18	Wisconsin	3,948,233	1.96%	43	Idaho	753,649	0.37%
19	Minnesota	3,588,839	1.78%	44	Montana	701,553	0.35%
20	Tennessee	3,509,496	1.74%	45	South Dakota	588,471	0.29%
21	Connecticut	3,162,887	1.57%	46	Delaware	584,573	0.29%
22	Arizona	2,848,984	1.41%	47	North Dakota	562,564	0.28%
23	Colorado	2,825,657	1.40%	48	Vermont	530,429	0.26%
24	Louisiana	2,811,168	1.39%	49	Alaska	494,646	0.25%
25	Alabama	2,716,058	1.35%	50	Wyoming	389,500	0.19%

Source: U.S. Department of the Treasury, Internal Revenue Service,
"Highlights 1990" (Publication 1265, July 1991)

*Total includes returns from U.S. citizens and corporations abroad and other miscellaneous returns not shown separately.

**Maryland's total includes the District of Columbia.

Federal Individual Income Tax Returns Filed in 1990

National Total = 112,492,218 Returns*

RANK	STATE	RETURNS	%	RANK	STATE	RETURNS	%
1	California	13,290,080	11.81%	26	South Carolina	1,504,323	1.34%
2	New York	8,116,739	7.22%	27	Kentucky	1,491,363	1.33%
3	Texas	7,163,171	6.37%	28	Oklahoma	1,284,878	1.14%
4	Florida	5,940,093	5.28%	29	Oregon	1,258,240	1.12%
5	Pennsylvania	5,481,946	4.87%	30	Iowa	1,247,856	1.11%
6	Illinois	5,283,622	4.70%	31	Kansas	1,091,067	0.97%
7	Ohio	4,999,713	4.44%	32	Mississippi	992,119	0.88%
8	Michigan	4,122,060	3.66%	33	Arkansas	951,190	0.85%
9	New Jersey	3,814,693	3.39%	34	Nebraska	718,909	0.64%
10	North Carolina	2,999,591	2.67%	35	West Virginia	686,664	0.61%
11	Massachusetts	2,940,707	2.61%	36	Utah	655,075	0.58%
12	Virginia	2,847,754	2.53%	37	New Mexico	638,519	0.57%
13	Georgia	2,805,778	2.49%	38	Nevada	573,432	0.51%
14	Maryland**	2,609,750	2.32%	39	Maine	566,988	0.50%
15	Indiana	2,482,469	2.21%	40	New Hampshire	551,297	0.49%
16	Missouri	2,264,911	2.01%	41	Hawaii	535,785	0.48%
17	Wisconsin	2,219,440	1.97%	42	Rhode Island	473,788	0.42%
18	Washington	2,212,296	1.97%	43	Idaho	406,103	0.36%
19	Tennessee	2,129,127	1.89%	44	Montana	346,913	0.31%
20	Minnesota	1,990,443	1.77%	45	Delaware	321,582	0.29%
21	Connecticut	1,669,144	1.48%	46	Alaska	307,808	0.27%
22	Alabama	1,663,199	1.48%	47	South Dakota	303,850	0.27%
23	Louisiana	1,640,420	1.46%	48	North Dakota	278,574	0.25%
24	Arizona	1,556,196	1.38%	49	Vermont	266,700	0.24%
25	Colorado	1,518,409	1.35%	50	Wyoming	199,605	0.18%

Source: U.S. Department of the Treasury, Internal Revenue Service,

"Highlights 1990" (Publication 1265, July 1991)

*Total includes returns from U.S. citizens abroad and other miscellaneous returns not shown separately.

**Maryland's total includes the District of Columbia.

Federal Corporate Income Tax Returns Filed in 1990

National Total = 4,310,771 Returns*

RANK	STATE	RETURNS	%	RANK	STATE	RETURNS	%
1	New York	455,915	10.58%	26	South Carolina	47,587	1.10%
2	California	428,964	9.95%	27	Kentucky	47,448	1.10%
3	Florida	363,380	8.43%	28	Oregon	46,011	1.07%
4	Texas	242,218	5.62%	29	Alabama	45,776	1.06%
5	New Jersey	215,953	5.01%	30	Iowa	44,215	1.03%
6	Illinois	196,672	4.56%	31	Kansas	37,743	0.88%
7	Pennsylvania	155,191	3.60%	32	Arkansas	31,877	0.74%
8	Ohio	149,636	3.47%	33	Nebraska	29,324	0.68%
9	Michigan	149,504	3.47%	34	Mississippi	28,549	0.66%
10	Massachusetts	125,239	2.91%	35	Utah	25,128	0.58%
11	Georgia	101,896	2.36%	36	Rhode Island	24,315	0.56%
12	Maryland**	98,902	2.29%	37	Hawaii	23,188	0.54%
13	North Carolina	98,646	2.29%	38	Nevada	22,858	0.53%
14	Virginia	96,911	2.25%	39	New Hampshire	22,425	0.52%
15	Indiana	80,968	1.88%	40	Maine	21,486	0.50%
16	Missouri	80,371	1.86%	41	West Virginia	19,766	0.46%
17	Minnesota	76,114	1.77%	42	New Mexico	19,223	0.45%
18	Connecticut	74,830	1.74%	43	Delaware	16,575	0.38%
19	Washington	74,619	1.73%	44	Montana	15,172	0.35%
20	Colorado	74,360	1.72%	45	Idaho	15,014	0.35%
21	Louisiana	72,715	1.69%	46	Vermont	13,889	0.32%
22	Wisconsin	72,164	1.67%	47	South Dakota	9,652	0.22%
23	Arizona	60,379	1.40%	48	North Dakota	9,530	0.22%
24	Tennessee	55,544	1.29%	49	Wyoming	8,897	0.21%
25	Oklahoma	51,495	1.19%	50	Alaska	8,597	0.20%

Source: U.S. Department of the Treasury, Internal Revenue Service,
   "Highlights 1990" (Publication 1265, July 1991)

*Total includes returns from U.S. corporations abroad and other miscellaneous returns not shown separately.

**Maryland's total includes the District of Columbia.

Total Internal Revenue Service Collections in 1990

National Total = $1,056,365,652,000*

RANK	STATE	COLLECTIONS	%	RANK	STATE	COLLECTIONS	%
1	California	$127,795,725,000	12.10%	26	Kentucky	$9,803,571,000	0.93%
2	New York	109,694,335,000	10.38%	27	Oregon	9,683,100,000	0.92%
3	Texas	66,191,071,000	6.27%	28	Kansas	9,025,559,000	0.85%
4	Illinois	61,021,659,000	5.78%	29	Arizona	8,704,193,000	0.82%
5	Pennsylvania	51,062,367,000	4.83%	30	South Carolina	8,525,255,000	0.81%
6	New Jersey	48,867,251,000	4.63%	31	Iowa	7,802,387,000	0.74%
7	Ohio	47,522,201,000	4.50%	32	Arkansas	6,551,162,000	0.62%
8	Michigan	43,962,792,000	4.16%	33	Nebraska	6,479,162,000	0.61%
9	Florida	41,301,922,000	3.91%	34	Delaware	5,510,711,000	0.52%
10	Maryland**	31,181,676,000	2.95%	35	Mississippi	4,857,987,000	0.46%
11	Massachusetts	30,749,604,000	2.91%	36	Nevada	4,427,144,000	0.42%
12	Minnesota	25,574,997,000	2.42%	37	Utah	4,298,880,000	0.41%
13	Missouri	25,267,339,000	2.39%	38	Hawaii	4,264,127,000	0.40%
14	Connecticut	25,212,294,000	2.39%	39	Rhode Island	4,006,967,000	0.38%
15	Georgia	23,970,814,000	2.27%	40	New Hampshire	3,930,935,000	0.37%
16	Virginia	22,658,143,000	2.14%	41	West Virginia	3,532,952,000	0.33%
17	Indiana	22,094,484,000	2.09%	42	North Dakota	3,228,326,000	0.31%
18	North Carolina	20,681,755,000	1.96%	43	Maine	3,223,584,000	0.31%
19	Washington	19,278,594,000	1.82%	44	Idaho	2,997,111,000	0.28%
20	Wisconsin	17,953,867,000	1.70%	45	New Mexico	2,979,502,000	0.28%
21	Tennessee	16,087,585,000	1.52%	46	Alaska	2,051,568,000	0.19%
22	Colorado	14,744,185,000	1.40%	47	Montana	1,703,283,000	0.16%
23	Oklahoma	10,273,427,000	0.97%	48	Vermont	1,608,984,000	0.15%
24	Louisiana	10,050,666,000	0.95%	49	South Dakota	1,534,928,000	0.15%
25	Alabama	9,929,880,000	0.94%	50	Wyoming	1,237,898,000	0.12%

Source: U.S. Department of the Treasury, Internal Revenue Service,
"Highlights 1990" (Publication 1265, July 1991)

*Total includes collections from U.S. citizens and corporations abroad and other miscellaneous collections not shown separately.

**Maryland's total includes the District of Columbia.

Federal Individual Income and Employment Tax Collections in 1990

National Total = $907,447,729,000*

RANK	STATE	COLLECTIONS	%	RANK	STATE	COLLECTIONS	%
1	California	$110,328,131,000	12.16%	26	Kentucky	$8,136,174,000	0.90%
2	New York	93,070,426,000	10.26%	27	Arizona	8,001,854,000	0.88%
3	Texas	52,795,489,000	5.82%	28	Oklahoma	7,978,905,000	0.88%
4	Illinois	51,040,512,000	5.62%	29	Kansas	7,970,637,000	0.88%
5	Pennsylvania	44,416,497,000	4.89%	30	South Carolina	7,797,336,000	0.86%
6	New Jersey	41,659,623,000	4.59%	31	Iowa	6,821,743,000	0.75%
7	Ohio	40,269,085,000	4.44%	32	Nebraska	5,691,746,000	0.63%
8	Michigan	39,427,640,000	4.34%	33	Arkansas	5,148,749,000	0.57%
9	Florida	37,988,683,000	4.19%	34	Mississippi	4,149,090,000	0.46%
10	Maryland**	28,294,948,000	3.12%	35	Nevada	4,027,508,000	0.44%
11	Massachusetts	27,467,576,000	3.03%	36	Utah	3,708,056,000	0.41%
12	Minnesota	21,686,429,000	2.39%	37	Hawaii	3,670,041,000	0.40%
13	Connecticut	20,963,899,000	2.31%	38	New Hampshire	3,668,535,000	0.40%
14	Missouri	20,579,129,000	2.27%	39	Delaware	3,625,696,000	0.40%
15	Indiana	20,093,085,000	2.21%	40	Rhode Island	3,542,497,000	0.39%
16	Virginia	19,789,005,000	2.18%	41	West Virginia	3,163,900,000	0.35%
17	Georgia	19,083,821,000	2.10%	42	North Dakota	3,112,227,000	0.34%
18	North Carolina	18,082,275,000	1.99%	43	Maine	2,913,333,000	0.32%
19	Washington	16,925,626,000	1.87%	44	New Mexico	2,781,703,000	0.31%
20	Wisconsin	15,745,317,000	1.74%	45	Idaho	2,607,381,000	0.29%
21	Tennessee	14,133,555,000	1.56%	46	Alaska	1,901,262,000	0.21%
22	Colorado	13,533,208,000	1.49%	47	Montana	1,524,164,000	0.17%
23	Louisiana	9,220,243,000	1.02%	48	Vermont	1,479,608,000	0.16%
24	Alabama	8,938,510,000	0.99%	49	South Dakota	1,404,288,000	0.15%
25	Oregon	8,546,388,000	0.94%	50	Wyoming	1,053,786,000	0.12%

Source: U.S. Department of the Treasury, Internal Revenue Service,
    "Highlights 1990" (Publication 1265, July 1991)
*Total includes collections from U.S. citizens and corporations abroad and other miscellaneous collections not shown separately.
**Maryland's total includes the District of Columbia.

Average Federal Individual Income Tax Liability in 1989

National Average = $4,820

RANK	STATE	AVERAGE TAX	RANK	STATE	AVERAGE TAX
1	Connecticut	$6,756	26	Indiana	$4,226
2	New Jersey	6,163	27	Arizona	4,218
3	New York	5,730	28	Tennessee	4,195
4	California	5,526	29	Ohio	4,182
5	Illinois	5,407	30	Oregon	4,141
6	Massachusetts	5,375	31	Vermont	4,046
7	Nevada	5,240	32	North Carolina	4,037
8	Maryland	5,232	33	Louisiana	4,008
9	Florida	5,122	34	Wisconsin	3,999
10	New Hampshire	5,054	35	Alabama	3,947
11	Washington	4,913	36	Oklahoma	3,880
12	Texas	4,908	37	Nebraska	3,857
13	Virginia	4,896	38	Kentucky	3,856
14	Delaware	4,841	39	Iowa	3,761
15	Michigan	4,817	40	Maine	3,729
16	Hawaii	4,658	41	South Carolina	3,659
17	Pennsylvania	4,592	42	New Mexico	3,634
18	Alaska	4,555	43	West Virginia	3,619
19	Rhode Island	4,545	44	Idaho	3,603
20	Kansas	4,492	45	Utah	3,560
21	Colorado	4,484	46	Montana	3,526
22	Wyoming	4,471	47	South Dakota	3,447
23	Georgia	4,406	48	North Dakota	3,410
24	Minnesota	4,381	49	Mississippi	3,359
25	Missouri	4,307	50	Arkansas	2,798
				District of Columbia	5,642
				Other*	3,350

Source: Internal Revenue Service,

"Statistics of Income Bulletin" (Winter 1990–1991)

*"Other" includes returns from military overseas, U.S. citizens abroad and residents of Puerto Rico with income from sources outside Puerto Rico or with income earned as U.S. Government employees.

Federal Corporate Income Tax Collections in 1990

National Total = $110,016,539,000*

RANK	STATE	COLLECTIONS	%	RANK	STATE	COLLECTIONS	%
1	New York	$13,791,013,000	12.54%	26	Oklahoma	$881,800,000	0.80%
2	California	12,117,343,000	11.01%	27	Iowa	839,202,000	0.76%
3	Illinois	7,468,661,000	6.79%	28	Colorado	813,014,000	0.74%
4	Texas	6,983,762,000	6.35%	29	Alabama	736,591,000	0.67%
5	New Jersey	5,417,622,000	4.92%	30	Kansas	692,450,000	0.63%
6	Ohio	5,341,728,000	4.86%	31	Nebraska	618,723,000	0.56%
7	Pennsylvania	4,944,300,000	4.49%	32	Mississippi	602,301,000	0.55%
8	Michigan	3,935,282,000	3.58%	33	South Carolina	562,649,000	0.51%
9	Georgia	3,823,086,000	3.48%	34	Louisiana	502,637,000	0.46%
10	Connecticut	3,730,238,000	3.39%	35	Hawaii	461,579,000	0.42%
11	Missouri	3,725,911,000	3.39%	36	Utah	443,647,000	0.40%
12	Minnesota	3,217,338,000	2.92%	37	Arizona	442,325,000	0.40%
13	Massachusetts	2,684,689,000	2.44%	38	Rhode Island	369,455,000	0.34%
14	Maryland**	2,293,180,000	2.08%	39	Idaho	345,499,000	0.31%
15	North Carolina	2,208,919,000	2.01%	40	Nevada	328,121,000	0.30%
16	Virginia	2,058,260,000	1.87%	41	West Virginia	224,354,000	0.20%
17	Florida	1,962,771,000	1.78%	42	Maine	210,719,000	0.19%
18	Washington	1,908,115,000	1.73%	43	New Hampshire	203,215,000	0.18%
19	Wisconsin	1,890,623,000	1.72%	44	Alaska	120,019,000	0.11%
20	Delaware	1,685,618,000	1.53%	45	Montana	112,259,000	0.10%
21	Tennessee	1,469,657,000	1.34%	46	Vermont	104,664,000	0.10%
22	Indiana	1,442,438,000	1.31%	47	South Dakota	92,950,000	0.08%
23	Arkansas	1,180,879,000	1.07%	48	New Mexico	90,033,000	0.08%
24	Kentucky	1,088,426,000	0.99%	49	North Dakota	83,317,000	0.08%
25	Oregon	942,723,000	0.86%	50	Wyoming	35,637,000	0.03%

Source: U.S. Department of the Treasury, Internal Revenue Service,
"Highlights 1990" (Publication 1265, July 1991)

Total includes collections from U.S. corporations abroad and other miscellaneous collections not shown separately.

**Maryland's total includes the District of Columbia.*

Average Revenue Collection per Federal Corporate Income Tax Return in 1990

National Average = $25,521*

RANK	STATE	AVERAGE COLLECTION	RANK	STATE	AVERAGE COLLECTION
1	Delaware	$101,696	26	Oregon	$20,489
2	Connecticut	49,849	27	Hawaii	19,906
3	Missouri	46,359	28	Iowa	18,980
4	Minnesota	42,270	29	Kansas	18,346
5	Illinois	37,975	30	Indiana	17,815
6	Georgia	37,519	31	Utah	17,655
7	Arkansas	37,045	32	Oklahoma	17,124
8	Ohio	35,698	33	Alabama	16,091
9	Pennsylvania	31,859	34	Rhode Island	15,195
10	New York	30,249	35	Nevada	14,355
11	Texas	28,833	36	Alaska	13,961
12	California	28,248	37	South Carolina	11,824
13	Tennessee	26,459	38	West Virginia	11,351
14	Michigan	26,322	39	Colorado	10,933
15	Wisconsin	26,199	40	Maine	9,807
16	Washington	25,571	41	South Dakota	9,630
17	New Jersey	25,087	42	New Hampshire	9,062
18	Maryland**	23,186	43	North Dakota	8,743
19	Idaho	23,012	44	Vermont	7,536
20	Kentucky	22,939	45	Montana	7,399
21	North Carolina	22,392	46	Arizona	7,326
22	Massachusetts	21,437	47	Louisiana	6,912
23	Virginia	21,239	48	Florida	5,401
24	Nebraska	21,100	49	New Mexico	4,684
25	Mississippi	21,097	50	Wyoming	4,006

Source: U.S. Department of the Treasury, Internal Revenue Service,
"Highlights 1990" (Publication 1265, July 1991)

National average includes returns from U.S. corporations abroad and other miscellaneous returns not shown separately. Averages calculated by the editors.

**Maryland's total includes the District of Columbia.*

Income Tax Refunds Issued in 1990

National Total = 85,287,008 Refunds*

RANK	STATE	REFUNDS	%	RANK	STATE	REFUNDS	%
1	California	9,738,612	11.42%	26	Kentucky	1,141,749	1.34%
2	New York	6,059,294	7.10%	27	Arizona	1,138,092	1.33%
3	Texas	5,443,071	6.38%	28	Colorado	1,071,242	1.26%
4	Florida	4,402,221	5.16%	29	Oklahoma	921,139	1.08%
5	Pennsylvania	4,085,242	4.79%	30	Iowa	852,363	1.00%
6	Illinois	3,964,900	4.65%	31	Mississippi	768,186	0.90%
7	Ohio	3,914,939	4.59%	32	West Virginia	756,415	0.89%
8	Michigan	3,180,539	3.73%	33	Kansas	751,940	0.88%
9	New Jersey	2,934,941	3.44%	34	Arkansas	710,436	0.83%
10	North Carolina	2,271,427	2.66%	35	Nebraska	496,420	0.58%
11	Massachusetts	2,184,974	2.56%	36	Utah	477,127	0.56%
12	Georgia	2,164,263	2.54%	37	New Mexico	475,757	0.56%
13	Maryland**	2,119,861	2.49%	38	Maine	465,774	0.55%
14	Virginia	2,074,078	2.43%	39	New Hampshire	436,459	0.51%
15	Indiana	1,911,081	2.24%	40	Nevada	413,845	0.49%
16	Tennessee	1,778,717	2.09%	41	Hawaii	388,285	0.46%
17	Missouri	1,659,298	1.95%	42	Rhode Island	365,524	0.43%
18	Washington	1,590,497	1.86%	43	Idaho	281,689	0.33%
19	Wisconsin	1,589,664	1.86%	44	Delaware	244,180	0.29%
20	Connecticut	1,322,257	1.55%	45	Montana	238,370	0.28%
21	Minnesota	1,308,435	1.53%	46	South Dakota	214,070	0.25%
22	Oregon	1,284,038	1.51%	47	North Dakota	211,460	0.25%
23	Alabama	1,281,113	1.50%	48	Vermont	198,898	0.23%
24	Louisiana	1,242,776	1.46%	49	Alaska	172,595	0.20%
25	South Carolina	1,187,388	1.39%	50	Wyoming	145,963	0.17%

Source: U.S. Department of the Treasury, Internal Revenue Service,
    "Highlights 1990" (Publication 1265, July 1991)

*Total includes refunds to U.S. citizens and corporations abroad and others not shown separately.

**Maryland's total includes the District of Columbia.

Total Tax Refunds in 1990

National Total = $99,655,678,000*

RANK	STATE	REFUNDS	%	RANK	STATE	REFUNDS	%
1	California	$12,398,543,000	12.44%	26	South Carolina	$1,118,203,000	1.12%
2	New York	8,628,862,000	8.66%	27	Kentucky	1,081,367,000	1.09%
3	Texas	7,539,665,000	7.57%	28	Colorado	1,019,172,000	1.02%
4	Illinois	5,345,622,000	5.36%	29	Oklahoma	963,034,000	0.97%
5	New Jersey	4,401,830,000	4.42%	30	Iowa	771,376,000	0.77%
6	Florida	4,374,280,000	4.39%	31	West Virginia	704,710,000	0.71%
7	Ohio	4,199,021,000	4.21%	32	Kansas	693,804,000	0.70%
8	Pennsylvania	4,079,183,000	4.09%	33	Mississippi	671,604,000	0.67%
9	Michigan	3,540,053,000	3.55%	34	Arkansas	602,829,000	0.60%
10	Massachusetts	3,106,642,000	3.12%	35	New Hampshire	567,738,000	0.57%
11	Maryland**	2,589,573,000	2.60%	36	Utah	454,035,000	0.46%
12	Virginia	2,326,236,000	2.33%	37	Nebraska	436,979,000	0.44%
13	Connecticut	2,300,663,000	2.31%	38	Maine	435,156,000	0.44%
14	Georgia	2,222,804,000	2.23%	39	New Mexico	425,756,000	0.43%
15	North Carolina	2,063,792,000	2.07%	40	Rhode Island	416,514,000	0.42%
16	Indiana	1,928,653,000	1.94%	41	Nevada	405,214,000	0.41%
17	Tennessee	1,806,586,000	1.81%	42	Hawaii	360,411,000	0.36%
18	Washington	1,754,217,000	1.76%	43	Delaware	340,814,000	0.34%
19	Missouri	1,590,664,000	1.60%	44	Idaho	251,071,000	0.25%
20	Wisconsin	1,389,169,000	1.39%	45	Vermont	190,334,000	0.19%
21	Oregon	1,243,404,000	1.25%	46	Alaska	189,723,000	0.19%
22	Alabama	1,195,734,000	1.20%	47	Montana	182,329,000	0.18%
23	Louisiana	1,190,525,000	1.19%	48	North Dakota	179,495,000	0.18%
24	Arizona	1,185,412,000	1.19%	49	South Dakota	159,723,000	0.16%
25	Minnesota	1,180,229,000	1.18%	50	Wyoming	143,105,000	0.14%

Source: U.S. Department of the Treasury, Internal Revenue Service,
   "Highlights 1990" (Publication 1265, July 1991)

*Total includes refunds to U.S. citizens and corporations abroad and other miscellaneous refunds not shown separately.

**Maryland's total includes the District of Columbia.

Average Refund for All Types Federal Tax Refunds in 1990

National Average = $1,168.47*

RANK	STATE	AVERAGE REFUND	RANK	STATE	AVERAGE REFUND
1	Connecticut	$1,739.95	26	Oregon	$968.35
2	New Jersey	1,499.80	27	Missouri	958.64
3	New York	1,424.07	28	Louisiana	957.96
4	Massachusetts	1,421.82	29	Vermont	956.94
5	Delaware	1,395.75	30	Utah	951.60
6	Texas	1,385.19	31	Colorado	951.39
7	Illinois	1,348.24	32	Kentucky	947.11
8	New Hampshire	1,300.78	33	South Carolina	941.73
9	California	1,273.13	34	Maine	934.26
10	Maryland**	1,221.58	35	Alabama	933.36
11	Rhode Island	1,139.50	36	West Virginia	931.64
12	Virginia	1,121.58	37	Hawaii	928.21
13	Michigan	1,113.04	38	Kansas	922.69
14	Washington	1,102.94	39	North Carolina	908.59
15	Alaska	1,099.24	40	Iowa	904.99
16	Ohio	1,072.56	41	Minnesota	902.02
17	Oklahoma	1,045.48	42	New Mexico	894.90
18	Arizona	1,041.58	43	Idaho	891.31
19	Georgia	1,027.05	44	Nebraska	880.26
20	Tennessee	1,015.67	45	Mississippi	874.27
21	Indiana	1,009.19	46	Wisconsin	873.88
22	Pennsylvania	998.52	47	North Dakota	848.84
23	Florida	993.65	48	Arkansas	848.53
24	Wyoming	980.42	49	Montana	764.90
25	Nevada	979.14	50	South Dakota	746.13

Source: U.S. Department of the Treasury, Internal Revenue Service,
   "Highlights 1990" (Publication 1265, July 1991)

*National average includes refunds to U.S. citizens and corporations abroad and other miscellaneous refunds not shown separately. Averages
   calculated by the editors.

**Maryland's total includes the District of Columbia.

Individual Income Tax Refunds in 1990

National Total = $76,064,612,000*

RANK	STATE	REFUNDS	%	RANK	STATE	REFUNDS	%
1	California	$9,803,319,000	12.89%	26	Kentucky	$932,497,000	1.23%
2	New York	6,138,964,000	8.07%	27	Minnesota	916,700,000	1.21%
3	Texas	4,753,881,000	6.25%	28	Colorado	847,477,000	1.11%
4	Florida	3,817,426,000	5.02%	29	Oklahoma	719,968,000	0.95%
5	Illinois	3,723,974,000	4.90%	30	West Virginia	670,984,000	0.88%
6	Pennsylvania	3,442,385,000	4.53%	31	Iowa	635,018,000	0.83%
7	Ohio	3,255,770,000	4.28%	32	Mississippi	598,869,000	0.79%
8	New Jersey	3,183,506,000	4.19%	33	Kansas	587,869,000	0.77%
9	Michigan	2,786,048,000	3.66%	34	Arkansas	541,701,000	0.71%
10	Massachusetts	2,286,174,000	3.01%	35	New Hampshire	456,862,000	0.60%
11	Maryland**	1,985,086,000	2.61%	36	Maine	392,492,000	0.52%
12	Georgia	1,929,142,000	2.54%	37	Nevada	360,253,000	0.47%
13	Virginia	1,840,071,000	2.42%	38	New Mexico	359,826,000	0.47%
14	North Carolina	1,788,155,000	2.35%	39	Nebraska	358,223,000	0.47%
15	Indiana	1,664,684,000	2.19%	40	Rhode Island	342,643,000	0.45%
16	Connecticut	1,477,623,000	1.94%	41	Utah	329,491,000	0.43%
17	Tennessee	1,459,623,000	1.92%	42	Hawaii	308,040,000	0.40%
18	Missouri	1,350,395,000	1.78%	43	Delaware	206,430,000	0.27%
19	Washington	1,265,071,000	1.66%	44	Idaho	191,340,000	0.25%
20	Wisconsin	1,163,830,000	1.53%	45	Alaska	172,388,000	0.23%
21	Oregon	1,096,162,000	1.44%	46	Montana	164,265,000	0.22%
22	Alabama	1,065,020,000	1.40%	47	Vermont	161,514,000	0.21%
23	Louisiana	1,026,642,000	1.35%	48	North Dakota	150,591,000	0.20%
24	South Carolina	973,083,000	1.28%	49	South Dakota	141,957,000	0.19%
25	Arizona	970,844,000	1.28%	50	Wyoming	114,222,000	0.15%

Source: U.S. Department of the Treasury, Internal Revenue Service,

"Highlights 1990" (Publication 1265, July 1991)

*Total includes refunds to U.S. citizens abroad and other miscellaneous refunds not shown separately.

**Maryland's total includes the District of Columbia.

Average Federal Individual Income Tax Refund in 1990

National Average = $924.84*

RANK	STATE	AVERAGE REFUND		RANK	STATE	AVERAGE REFUND
1	Connecticut	$1,173.39		26	Vermont	$854.22
2	New Jersey	1,131.67		27	Louisiana	851.85
3	New Hampshire	1,089.97		28	Alabama	851.75
4	Massachusetts	1,087.36		29	South Carolina	843.86
5	New York	1,051.76		30	Missouri	842.21
6	California	1,051.28		31	Kentucky	839.55
7	Alaska	1,048.45		32	Washington	829.72
8	Maryland**	973.41		33	Hawaii	824.04
9	Illinois	972.85		34	Colorado	823.32
10	Rhode Island	970.23		35	Wyoming	819.79
11	Georgia	924.80		36	North Carolina	812.25
12	Virginia	912.94		37	Kansas	812.12
13	Florida	909.40		38	Oklahoma	808.27
14	Texas	907.67		39	Mississippi	800.11
15	West Virginia	905.47		40	Arkansas	788.34
16	Michigan	904.66		41	New Mexico	782.01
17	Nevada	904.17		42	Iowa	773.72
18	Indiana	892.45		43	Wisconsin	757.14
19	Arizona	883.04		44	Nebraska	752.49
20	Delaware	881.72		45	North Dakota	740.75
21	Oregon	880.62		46	Montana	724.97
22	Maine	874.52		47	Minnesota	723.32
23	Pennsylvania	869.98		48	Utah	715.71
24	Ohio	856.07		49	Idaho	709.60
25	Tennessee	854.44		50	South Dakota	690.51

Source: U.S. Department of the Treasury, Internal Revenue Service,
"Highlights 1990" (Publication 1265, July 1991)

*Total includes refunds to U.S. citizens abroad and other miscellaneous refunds not shown separately. Averages calculated by the editors.

**Maryland's total includes the District of Columbia.

Corporate Income Tax Refunds in 1990

National Total = $18,323,511,000*

RANK	STATE	REFUNDS	%	RANK	STATE	REFUNDS	%
1	California	$2,246,379,000	12.26%	26	Kentucky	$133,604,000	0.73%
2	New York	2,238,899,000	12.22%	27	Delaware	129,733,000	0.71%
3	Texas	1,930,519,000	10.54%	28	Iowa	123,338,000	0.67%
4	Illinois	1,472,698,000	8.04%	29	South Carolina	120,772,000	0.66%
5	New Jersey	1,086,165,000	5.93%	30	Oregon	119,016,000	0.65%
6	Ohio	849,162,000	4.63%	31	Utah	115,021,000	0.63%
7	Connecticut	758,599,000	4.14%	32	Alabama	112,632,000	0.61%
8	Massachusetts	740,032,000	4.04%	33	New Hampshire	97,715,000	0.53%
9	Michigan	665,427,000	3.63%	34	Kansas	72,761,000	0.40%
10	Pennsylvania	524,106,000	2.86%	35	Nebraska	69,115,000	0.38%
11	Washington	445,623,000	2.43%	36	Rhode Island	65,737,000	0.36%
12	Virginia	434,535,000	2.37%	37	Mississippi	63,203,000	0.34%
13	Maryland**	432,603,000	2.36%	38	New Mexico	58,162,000	0.32%
14	Florida	431,748,000	2.36%	39	Idaho	54,393,000	0.30%
15	Tennessee	293,898,000	1.60%	40	Arkansas	51,707,000	0.28%
16	Georgia	244,702,000	1.34%	41	Hawaii	41,109,000	0.22%
17	North Carolina	241,186,000	1.32%	42	Nevada	35,992,000	0.20%
18	Minnesota	238,973,000	1.30%	43	Maine	35,499,000	0.19%
19	Indiana	228,298,000	1.25%	44	West Virginia	29,047,000	0.16%
20	Missouri	200,198,000	1.09%	45	Wyoming	26,389,000	0.14%
21	Wisconsin	195,041,000	1.06%	46	North Dakota	25,732,000	0.14%
22	Arizona	193,887,000	1.06%	47	Vermont	24,434,000	0.13%
23	Oklahoma	191,598,000	1.05%	48	South Dakota	15,102,000	0.08%
24	Colorado	147,277,000	0.80%	49	Montana	14,422,000	0.08%
25	Louisiana	143,785,000	0.78%	50	Alaska	11,854,000	0.06%

Source: U.S. Department of the Treasury, Internal Revenue Service,
    "Highlights 1990" (Publication 1265, July 1991)

*Total includes refunds to U.S. corporations abroad and other miscellaneous refunds not shown separately.

**Maryland's total includes the District of Columbia.

Average Corporate Income Tax Refund in 1990

National Average = $26,009*

RANK	STATE	AVERAGE REFUND
1	New York	$50,481
2	Connecticut	48,183
3	Delaware	45,472
4	Illinois	43,708
5	New Jersey	42,730
6	Texas	42,087
7	Virginia	32,922
8	Utah	32,327
9	Massachusetts	30,956
10	Washington	30,856
11	Ohio	28,073
12	Oklahoma	26,925
13	California	24,947
14	Indiana	24,049
15	Maryland**	23,899
16	Pennsylvania	23,349
17	Michigan	23,080
18	New Hampshire	22,376
19	Minnesota	22,003
20	Arizona	21,091
21	Kentucky	20,460
22	Louisiana	20,073
23	Idaho	19,364
24	Rhode Island	18,549
25	Alabama	18,332

RANK	STATE	AVERAGE REFUND
26	New Mexico	$18,068
27	Tennessee	16,717
28	South Carolina	16,485
29	Colorado	15,330
30	Wyoming	15,271
31	Mississippi	15,120
32	North Carolina	13,283
33	Wisconsin	13,242
34	Georgia	12,871
35	North Dakota	12,509
36	Missouri	12,485
37	Oregon	11,971
38	Iowa	11,259
39	Nevada	11,174
40	Vermont	10,893
41	Florida	10,865
42	Nebraska	10,502
43	Arkansas	9,836
44	Hawaii	9,119
45	Kansas	8,820
46	West Virginia	8,725
47	Maine	8,179
48	Alaska	7,469
49	South Dakota	6,609
50	Montana	3,793

Source: U.S. Department of the Treasury, Internal Revenue Service,
    "Highlights 1990" (Publication 1265, July 1991)

*Total includes refunds to U.S. corporations abroad and other miscellaneous refunds not shown separately. Averages calculated by the editors.

**Maryland's total includes the District of Columbia.

Federal Government Expenditures in 1990

National Total = $1,002,703,000,000

RANK	STATE	EXPENDITURES	%	RANK	STATE	EXPENDITURES	%
1	California	$115,802,000,000	11.55%	26	South Carolina	$13,664,000,000	1.36%
2	New York	70,493,000,000	7.03%	27	Kentucky	13,524,000,000	1.35%
3	Texas	58,237,000,000	5.81%	28	Oklahoma	11,804,000,000	1.18%
4	Florida	51,359,000,000	5.12%	29	Mississippi	10,066,000,000	1.00%
5	Pennsylvania	45,424,000,000	4.53%	30	Iowa	9,962,000,000	0.99%
6	Ohio	37,920,000,000	3.78%	31	Oregon	9,826,000,000	0.98%
7	Illinois	36,696,000,000	3.66%	32	Kansas	9,538,000,000	0.95%
8	Virginia	36,346,000,000	3.62%	33	New Mexico	8,640,000,000	0.86%
9	Massachusetts	29,778,000,000	2.97%	34	Arkansas	8,250,000,000	0.82%
10	Michigan	29,205,000,000	2.91%	35	West Virginia	6,609,000,000	0.66%
11	New Jersey	28,322,000,000	2.82%	36	Utah	6,511,000,000	0.65%
12	Maryland	27,118,000,000	2.70%	37	Nebraska	6,092,000,000	0.61%
13	Missouri	24,258,000,000	2.42%	38	Hawaii	5,461,000,000	0.54%
14	Georgia	21,149,000,000	2.11%	39	Maine	4,925,000,000	0.49%
15	North Carolina	20,172,000,000	2.01%	40	Rhode Island	4,318,000,000	0.43%
16	Washington	20,149,000,000	2.01%	41	Nevada	4,144,000,000	0.41%
17	Tennessee	18,049,000,000	1.80%	42	Idaho	3,888,000,000	0.39%
18	Alabama	17,261,000,000	1.72%	43	New Hampshire	3,559,000,000	0.35%
19	Indiana	16,915,000,000	1.69%	44	Montana	3,345,000,000	0.33%
20	Louisiana	15,116,000,000	1.51%	45	Alaska	3,227,000,000	0.32%
21	Minnesota	15,073,000,000	1.50%	46	North Dakota	2,910,000,000	0.29%
22	Arizona	15,072,000,000	1.50%	47	South Dakota	2,863,000,000	0.29%
23	Wisconsin	14,928,000,000	1.49%	48	Delaware	2,149,000,000	0.21%
24	Connecticut	14,739,000,000	1.47%	49	Wyoming	1,855,000,000	0.18%
25	Colorado	14,586,000,000	1.45%	50	Vermont	1,772,000,000	0.18%

District of Columbia		17,353,000,000	1.73%
Puerto Rico		7,699,000,000	0.77%
Other*		24,589,000,000	2.45%

Source: U.S. Bureau of the Census,
  "Federal Expenditures by State for FY 1990" (Apirl 1991)
*"Other" is American Samoa, Guam, Northern Marianas, Virgin Islands and Undistributed Funds.

Per Capita Federal Government Expenditures in 1990

National Per Capita = $3,974.31

RANK	STATE	PER CAPITA	RANK	STATE	PER CAPITA
1	Virginia	$5,874.30	26	Kansas	$3,849.64
2	Alaska	5,866.65	27	Pennsylvania	3,823.04
3	New Mexico	5,702.65	28	Utah	3,779.23
4	Maryland	5,671.41	29	Oklahoma	3,752.69
5	Massachusetts	4,949.43	30	Tennessee	3,700.71
6	Hawaii	4,927.28	31	West Virginia	3,684.86
7	Missouri	4,740.65	32	Kentucky	3,669.70
8	North Dakota	4,554.95	33	New Jersey	3,663.76
9	Connecticut	4,483.79	34	Iowa	3,587.48
10	Colorado	4,427.63	35	Louisiana	3,581.97
11	Rhode Island	4,302.99	36	Arkansas	3,509.46
12	Alabama	4,271.79	37	Ohio	3,495.86
13	Montana	4,186.40	38	Oregon	3,457.19
14	Washington	4,140.11	39	Nevada	3,448.17
15	South Dakota	4,113.69	40	Minnesota	3,445.13
16	Arizona	4,112.18	41	Texas	3,428.43
17	Wyoming	4,089.12	42	Georgia	3,264.57
18	Maine	4,010.67	43	Delaware	3,225.57
19	Florida	3,969.61	44	Illinois	3,210.31
20	South Carolina	3,918.80	45	New Hampshire	3,208.56
21	New York	3,918.35	46	Vermont	3,147.99
22	Mississippi	3,911.71	47	Michigan	3,141.86
23	California	3,891.19	48	Wisconsin	3,051.63
24	Idaho	3,861.51	49	Indiana	3,050.92
25	Nebraska	3,859.53	50	North Carolina	3,043.19

District of Columbia   28,592.06

Source: U.S. Bureau of the Census,
    "Federal Expenditures by State for FY 1990" (April 1991)

Federal Government Procurement Contract Awards in 1990

National Total = $188,530,641,000

RANK	STATE	CONTRACTS	%
1	California	$29,499,571,000	15.65%
2	Texas	11,203,047,000	5.94%
3	Virginia	10,167,683,000	5.39%
4	Massachusetts	8,807,986,000	4.67%
5	New York	8,621,028,000	4.57%
6	Missouri	6,960,773,000	3.69%
7	Maryland	6,693,535,000	3.55%
8	Florida	6,616,097,000	3.51%
9	Ohio	6,037,689,000	3.20%
10	Connecticut	4,443,344,000	2.36%
11	New Jersey	4,306,983,000	2.28%
12	Pennsylvania	4,152,665,000	2.20%
13	Colorado	4,043,389,000	2.14%
14	Washington	3,942,511,000	2.09%
15	Arizona	3,667,045,000	1.95%
16	Alabama	3,388,260,000	1.80%
17	Tennessee	3,308,460,000	1.75%
18	New Mexico	3,256,469,000	1.73%
19	South Carolina	2,663,624,000	1.41%
20	Illinois	2,601,344,000	1.38%
21	Louisiana	2,384,117,000	1.26%
22	Georgia	2,227,821,000	1.18%
23	Minnesota	2,078,045,000	1.10%
24	Kentucky	2,010,279,000	1.07%
25	Indiana	1,971,190,000	1.05%

RANK	STATE	CONTRACTS	%
26	Michigan	$1,698,383,000	0.90%
27	Mississippi	1,616,057,000	0.86%
28	North Carolina	1,592,358,000	0.84%
29	Utah	1,543,171,000	0.82%
30	Wisconsin	1,263,372,000	0.67%
31	Kansas	1,131,487,000	0.60%
32	Maine	942,302,000	0.50%
33	Oklahoma	873,350,000	0.46%
34	Idaho	862,046,000	0.46%
35	Nevada	829,487,000	0.44%
36	Iowa	700,372,000	0.37%
37	Oregon	648,891,000	0.34%
38	Rhode Island	600,437,000	0.32%
39	Hawaii	547,303,000	0.29%
40	Alaska	529,188,000	0.28%
41	New Hampshire	430,293,000	0.23%
42	Nebraska	426,338,000	0.23%
43	Arkansas	390,631,000	0.21%
44	West Virginia	325,147,000	0.17%
45	Montana	166,912,000	0.09%
46	North Dakota	163,566,000	0.09%
47	Wyoming	145,929,000	0.08%
48	Delaware	138,357,000	0.07%
49	South Dakota	119,266,000	0.06%
50	Vermont	106,763,000	0.06%

	District of Columbia	2,935,517,000	1.56%
	Other*	975,589,000	0.52%
	Undistributed**	21,775,175,000	11.55%

Source: U.S. Bureau of the Census,
  "Federal Expenditures by State for FY 1990" (April 1991)

*"Other" is American Samoa, Guam, Northern Marianas, Puerto Rico and the Virgin Islands.

**Includes awards under $25,000 and Department of Defense classified location awards.

Per Capita Expenditures for Federal Government Procurement Contract Awards in 1990

National Per Capita Expenditure = $747.26

RANK	STATE	PER CAPITA
1	New Mexico	$2,149.39
2	Virginia	1,643.30
3	Massachusetts	1,463.99
4	Maryland	1,399.89
5	Missouri	1,360.30
6	Connecticut	1,351.75
7	Colorado	1,227.35
8	Arizona	1,000.50
9	California	991.25
10	Alaska	962.08
11	Utah	895.71
12	Idaho	856.27
13	Alabama	838.56
14	Washington	810.10
15	Maine	767.39
16	South Carolina	763.94
17	Nevada	690.18
18	Tennessee	678.35
19	Texas	659.53
20	Mississippi	628.03
21	Rhode Island	598.36
22	Louisiana	564.96
23	New Jersey	557.16
24	Ohio	556.62
25	Kentucky	545.49

RANK	STATE	PER CAPITA
26	Florida	$511.37
27	Hawaii	493.85
28	New York	479.20
29	Minnesota	474.97
30	Kansas	456.69
31	New Hampshire	387.91
32	Indiana	355.54
33	Pennsylvania	349.50
34	Georgia	343.89
35	Wyoming	321.72
36	Oklahoma	277.64
37	Nebraska	270.11
38	Wisconsin	258.26
39	North Dakota	256.05
40	Iowa	252.23
41	North Carolina	240.22
42	Oregon	228.30
43	Illinois	227.58
44	Montana	208.88
45	Delaware	207.69
46	Vermont	189.71
47	Michigan	182.71
48	West Virginia	181.29
49	South Dakota	171.36
50	Arkansas	166.17

	District of Columbia	4,836.90

Source: U.S. Bureau of the Census,
"Federal Expenditures by State for FY 1990" (April 1991)

Federal Government Direct Payments for Individuals in 1990

National Total = $497,695,773,000

RANK	STATE	PAYMENTS	%
1	California	$51,447,689,000	10.34%
2	New York	37,594,963,000	7.55%
3	Florida	32,881,651,000	6.61%
4	Texas	28,861,651,000	5.80%
5	Pennsylvania	28,814,802,000	5.79%
6	Illinois	22,686,780,000	4.56%
7	Ohio	21,784,864,000	4.38%
8	Michigan	19,670,962,000	3.95%
9	New Jersey	16,270,761,000	3.27%
10	Massachusetts	13,253,127,000	2.66%
11	Virginia	12,524,768,000	2.52%
12	North Carolina	11,540,089,000	2.32%
13	Georgia	10,838,938,000	2.18%
14	Missouri	10,791,022,000	2.17%
15	Indiana	10,024,118,000	2.01%
16	Maryland	9,816,051,000	1.97%
17	Tennessee	9,470,429,000	1.90%
18	Wisconsin	9,374,313,000	1.88%
19	Washington	9,328,182,000	1.87%
20	Alabama	8,588,930,000	1.73%
21	Louisiana	7,667,180,000	1.54%
22	Minnesota	7,543,750,000	1.52%
23	Arizona	7,381,716,000	1.48%
24	Kentucky	7,267,029,000	1.46%
25	Oklahoma	6,529,129,000	1.31%

RANK	STATE	PAYMENTS	%
26	Connecticut	$6,466,497,000	1.30%
27	South Carolina	6,196,502,000	1.25%
28	Oregon	5,960,331,000	1.20%
29	Iowa	5,703,754,000	1.15%
30	Colorado	5,686,892,000	1.14%
31	Arkansas	5,286,343,000	1.06%
32	Mississippi	5,252,745,000	1.06%
33	Kansas	5,062,523,000	1.02%
34	West Virginia	4,472,100,000	0.90%
35	Nebraska	3,146,205,000	0.63%
36	New Mexico	2,851,695,000	0.57%
37	Maine	2,566,075,000	0.52%
38	Utah	2,490,472,000	0.50%
39	Rhode Island	2,290,826,000	0.46%
40	Nevada	2,176,054,000	0.44%
41	Hawaii	2,034,097,000	0.41%
42	New Hampshire	1,924,945,000	0.39%
43	Idaho	1,802,541,000	0.36%
44	Montana	1,643,742,000	0.33%
45	South Dakota	1,385,289,000	0.28%
46	North Dakota	1,277,067,000	0.26%
47	Delaware	1,269,202,000	0.26%
48	Vermont	1,024,732,000	0.21%
49	Wyoming	770,044,000	0.15%
50	Alaska	612,092,000	0.12%

District of Columbia		1,960,715,000	0.39%
Puerto Rico		3,487,697,000	0.70%

Source: U.S. Bureau of the Census,
   "Federal Expenditures by State for FY 1990" (April 1991)

Per Capita Expenditures for Federal Government Direct Payments for Individuals in 1990

National Per Capita = $1,972.67

RANK	STATE	PER CAPITA	RANK	STATE	PER CAPITA
1	Florida	$2,541.49	26	Illinois	$1,984.74
2	West Virginia	2,493.54	27	Kentucky	1,971.90
3	Pennsylvania	2,425.15	28	Connecticut	1,967.23
4	Rhode Island	2,282.92	29	Tennessee	1,941.78
5	Arkansas	2,248.81	30	Washington	1,916.74
6	Massachusetts	2,202.82	31	Wisconsin	1,916.34
7	Alabama	2,125.66	32	Delaware	1,905.23
8	Michigan	2,116.23	33	New Mexico	1,882.22
9	Missouri	2,108.83	34	Hawaii	1,835.45
10	New Jersey	2,104.83	35	Vermont	1,820.91
11	Oregon	2,096.99	36	Louisiana	1,816.88
12	Maine	2,089.76	37	Nevada	1,810.61
13	New York	2,089.72	38	Indiana	1,808.05
14	Oklahoma	2,075.65	39	Idaho	1,790.46
15	Montana	2,057.08	40	South Carolina	1,777.18
16	Iowa	2,054.11	41	North Carolina	1,740.94
17	Maryland	2,052.94	42	New Hampshire	1,735.35
18	Kansas	2,043.34	43	California	1,728.75
19	Mississippi	2,041.32	44	Colorado	1,726.23
20	Virginia	2,024.25	45	Minnesota	1,724.25
21	Arizona	2,013.99	46	Texas	1,699.09
22	Ohio	2,008.36	47	Wyoming	1,697.67
23	North Dakota	1,999.17	48	Georgia	1,673.14
24	Nebraska	1,993.31	49	Utah	1,445.55
25	South Dakota	1,990.35	50	Alaska	1,112.81

District of Columbia		3,230.71
Puerto Rico		1,059.45

Source: U.S. Bureau of the Census,
   "Federal Expenditures by State for FY 1990" (April 1991)

Federal Salaries and Wages in 1990

National Total = $146,095,000,000

RANK	STATE	SALARIES	%		RANK	STATE	SALARIES	%
1	California	$17,746,000,000	12.15%		26	Indiana	$1,800,000,000	1.23%
2	Virginia	10,303,000,000	7.05%		27	Kansas	1,465,000,000	1.00%
3	Texas	9,060,000,000	6.20%		28	Utah	1,427,000,000	0.98%
4	Florida	6,596,000,000	4.51%		29	New Mexico	1,358,000,000	0.93%
5	New York	6,423,000,000	4.40%		30	Minnesota	1,348,000,000	0.92%
6	Maryland	6,101,000,000	4.18%		31	Mississippi	1,288,000,000	0.88%
7	Pennsylvania	5,142,000,000	3.52%		32	Connecticut	1,267,000,000	0.87%
8	Illinois	4,755,000,000	3.25%		33	Alaska	1,237,000,000	0.85%
9	Georgia	4,427,000,000	3.03%		34	Wisconsin	1,197,000,000	0.82%
10	Ohio	3,922,000,000	2.68%		35	Oregon	1,186,000,000	0.81%
11	Washington	3,584,000,000	2.45%		36	Nebraska	953,000,000	0.65%
12	North Carolina	3,564,000,000	2.44%		37	Arkansas	930,000,000	0.64%
13	New Jersey	3,396,000,000	2.32%		38	Iowa	733,000,000	0.50%
14	Missouri	2,858,000,000	1.96%		39	New Hampshire	692,000,000	0.47%
15	Colorado	2,757,000,000	1.89%		40	Nevada	646,000,000	0.44%
16	Alabama	2,756,000,000	1.89%		41	West Virginia	600,000,000	0.41%
17	Massachusetts	2,647,000,000	1.81%		42	Maine	561,000,000	0.38%
18	Michigan	2,432,000,000	1.66%		43	Rhode Island	558,000,000	0.38%
19	South Carolina	2,407,000,000	1.65%		44	Montana	523,000,000	0.36%
20	Oklahoma	2,281,000,000	1.56%		45	North Dakota	511,000,000	0.35%
21	Tennessee	2,225,000,000	1.52%		46	Idaho	508,000,000	0.35%
22	Hawaii	2,166,000,000	1.48%		47	South Dakota	503,000,000	0.34%
23	Arizona	2,047,000,000	1.40%		48	Delaware	384,000,000	0.26%
24	Kentucky	1,918,000,000	1.31%		49	Wyoming	315,000,000	0.22%
25	Louisiana	1,863,000,000	1.28%		50	Vermont	210,000,000	0.14%
					District of Columbia		9,439,000,000	6.46%
					Puerto Rico		516,000,000	0.35%

Source: U.S. Bureau of the Census,
   "Federal Expenditures by State for FY 1990" (April 1991)

Per Capita Expenditures for Federal Salaries and Wages in 1990

National Per Capita Expenditure = $579.06

RANK	STATE	PER CAPITA	RANK	STATE	PER CAPITA
1	Alaska	$2,249.45	26	Nevada	$537.29
2	Hawaii	1,954.29	27	Texas	533.38
3	Virginia	1,665.19	28	Kentucky	520.50
4	Maryland	1,275.88	29	Florida	509.79
5	New Mexico	896.57	30	Idaho	504.77
6	Colorado	836.98	31	Mississippi	500.44
7	Utah	828.49	32	Maine	456.51
8	North Dakota	799.51	33	Tennessee	456.15
9	Washington	736.35	34	Louisiana	441.56
10	Oklahoma	725.19	35	Massachusetts	439.95
11	South Dakota	722.11	36	New Jersey	439.34
12	Wyoming	694.18	37	Pennsylvania	432.81
13	South Carolina	690.29	38	Oregon	417.12
14	Georgia	683.31	39	Illinois	415.99
15	Alabama	682.15	40	Arkansas	395.57
16	Montana	654.31	41	Connecticut	385.39
17	New Hampshire	624.15	42	Vermont	373.41
18	Nebraska	603.48	43	Ohio	361.57
19	California	596.29	44	New York	357.04
20	Kansas	591.15	45	West Virginia	334.56
21	Delaware	575.93	46	Indiana	324.69
22	Missouri	558.46	47	Minnesota	308.20
23	Arizona	558.42	48	Iowa	264.09
24	Rhode Island	556.07	49	Michigan	261.63
25	North Carolina	537.68	50	Wisconsin	244.63

District of Columbia   15,552.34

Source: U.S. Bureau of the Census,
"Federal Expenditures by State for FY 1990" (April 1991)

Federal Employees in 1990

National Total = 3,105,000 Employees*

RANK	STATE	EMPLOYEES	%	RANK	STATE	EMPLOYEES	%
1	California	315,000	10.14%	26	Minnesota	32,000	1.03%
2	Texas	177,000	5.70%	26	South Carolina	32,000	1.03%
3	Virginia	161,000	5.19%	28	Oregon	29,000	0.93%
4	New York	152,000	4.90%	29	Wisconsin	27,000	0.87%
5	Maryland	133,000	4.28%	30	New Mexico	26,000	0.84%
6	Pennsylvania	129,000	4.15%	31	Hawaii	25,000	0.81%
7	Florida	112,000	3.61%	31	Kansas	25,000	0.81%
8	Illinois	104,000	3.35%	33	Connecticut	24,000	0.77%
9	Ohio	91,000	2.93%	33	Mississippi	24,000	0.77%
10	Georgia	88,000	2.83%	35	Arkansas	19,000	0.61%
11	New Jersey	75,000	2.42%	36	Iowa	18,000	0.58%
12	Missouri	66,000	2.13%	37	Maine	17,000	0.55%
13	Washington	65,000	2.09%	38	Alaska	15,000	0.48%
14	Massachusetts	60,000	1.93%	38	Nebraska	15,000	0.48%
15	Alabama	57,000	1.84%	38	West Virginia	15,000	0.48%
16	Michigan	56,000	1.80%	41	Montana	11,000	0.35%
16	Tennessee	56,000	1.80%	41	Nevada	11,000	0.35%
18	Colorado	53,000	1.71%	43	Idaho	10,000	0.32%
19	North Carolina	46,000	1.48%	43	Rhode Island	10,000	0.32%
20	Oklahoma	45,000	1.45%	45	South Dakota	9,000	0.29%
21	Indiana	41,000	1.32%	46	New Hampshire	8,000	0.26%
22	Arizona	39,000	1.26%	46	North Dakota	8,000	0.26%
23	Utah	36,000	1.16%	48	Wyoming	6,000	0.19%
24	Kentucky	35,000	1.13%	49	Delaware	5,000	0.16%
25	Louisiana	34,000	1.10%	49	Vermont	5,000	0.16%
					District of Columbia	212,000	6.83%

Source: U.S. Bureau of the Census,
   "Public Employment in 1990" (GE-90, No. 1, October 1991)
*Full-time and part time. Total includes federal civilian employment outside the 50 states and the District of Columbia as of October 1990.
   State distribution is as of December 31, 1990 and excludes employees based outside the United States.

X. GOVERNMENT FINANCE: STATE AND LOCAL

X. GOVERNMENT FINANCE: STATE AND LOCAL (continued)

Gross State Product in 1989

National Total = $5,164,671,000,000*

RANK	STATE	G.S.P.	%	RANK	STATE	G.S.P.	%
1	California	$697,381,000,000	13.50%	26	Arizona	$65,306,000,000	1.26%
2	New York	441,068,000,000	8.54%	27	South Carolina	60,150,000,000	1.16%
3	Texas	340,057,000,000	6.58%	28	Iowa	52,574,000,000	1.02%
4	Illinois	256,478,000,000	4.97%	29	Oklahoma	52,342,000,000	1.01%
5	Pennsylvania	227,898,000,000	4.41%	30	Oregon	52,118,000,000	1.01%
6	Florida	226,964,000,000	4.39%	31	Kansas	48,829,000,000	0.95%
7	Ohio	211,545,000,000	4.10%	32	Mississippi	38,135,000,000	0.74%
8	New Jersey	203,375,000,000	3.94%	33	Arkansas	37,169,000,000	0.72%
9	Michigan	181,827,000,000	3.52%	34	Nebraska	31,115,000,000	0.60%
10	Massachusetts	144,791,000,000	2.80%	35	Utah	28,135,000,000	0.54%
11	Virginia	136,497,000,000	2.64%	36	Nevada	27,960,000,000	0.54%
12	North Carolina	130,085,000,000	2.52%	37	West Virginia	27,922,000,000	0.54%
13	Georgia	129,776,000,000	2.51%	38	Hawaii	25,755,000,000	0.50%
14	Indiana	105,314,000,000	2.04%	39	New Mexico	25,414,000,000	0.49%
15	Missouri	100,081,000,000	1.94%	40	New Hampshire	24,504,000,000	0.47%
16	Maryland	99,074,000,000	1.92%	41	Maine	23,474,000,000	0.45%
17	Washington	96,233,000,000	1.86%	42	Alaska	19,582,000,000	0.38%
18	Wisconsin	93,978,000,000	1.82%	43	Rhode Island	18,807,000,000	0.36%
19	Minnesota	93,559,000,000	1.81%	44	Idaho	16,339,000,000	0.32%
20	Tennessee	92,267,000,000	1.79%	45	Delaware	15,418,000,000	0.30%
21	Connecticut	88,863,000,000	1.72%	46	Montana	13,104,000,000	0.25%
22	Louisiana	79,138,000,000	1.53%	47	Vermont	11,502,000,000	0.22%
23	Alabama	67,886,000,000	1.31%	48	North Dakota	11,231,000,000	0.22%
24	Colorado	66,180,000,000	1.28%	49	South Dakota	11,135,000,000	0.22%
25	Kentucky	65,858,000,000	1.28%	50	Wyoming	11,115,000,000	0.22%

District of Columbia   39,363,000,000   0.76%

Source: U.S. Department of Commerce, Bureau of Economic Analysis,
   Press Release BEA 91-51 (November 26, 1991)

*Gross state product is the market value of goods and services produced by labor and property located in a state. It is the state counterpart
of the nation's gross domestic product.

Per Capita State Gross Product in 1989

National Per Capita = $20,805*

RANK	STATE	PER CAPITA
1	Alaska	$37,157
2	Connecticut	27,435
3	New Jersey	26,289
4	Nevada	25,167
5	New York	24,572
6	Massachusetts	24,487
7	California	23,995
8	Wyoming	23,400
9	Hawaii	23,161
10	Delaware	22,909
11	Virginia	22,384
12	New Hampshire	22,136
13	Illinois	22,000
14	Minnesota	21,493
15	Maryland	21,107
16	Vermont	20,286
17	Washington	20,213
18	Georgia	20,164
19	Texas	20,014
20	Colorado	19,952
21	North Carolina	19,797
22	Michigan	19,608
23	Kansas	19,431
24	Missouri	19,399
25	Ohio	19,395

RANK	STATE	PER CAPITA
26	Nebraska	$19,314
27	Wisconsin	19,309
28	Maine	19,209
29	Pennsylvania	18,928
30	Rhode Island	18,845
31	Indiana	18,830
32	Tennessee	18,678
33	Iowa	18,512
34	Oregon	18,482
35	Arizona	18,365
36	Louisiana	18,060
37	Florida	17,912
38	Kentucky	17,671
39	South Carolina	17,127
40	North Dakota	17,017
41	New Mexico	16,632
42	Alabama	16,485
43	Utah	16,482
44	Montana	16,258
45	Oklahoma	16,235
46	Idaho	16,113
47	South Dakota	15,573
48	Arkansas	15,448
49	West Virginia	15,036
50	Mississippi	14,550

	District of Columbia	65,171

Source: U.S. Department of Commerce, Bureau of Economic Analysis,
   Press Release BEA 91-51 (November 26, 1991) (Rates calculated by the editors using 1989 Census population estimates.)
*Gross state product is the market value of goods and services produced by labor and property located in a state. It is the state counterpart of the nation's gross domestic product.

Average Annual Percent Change in Gross State Product: 1977 to 1989

National Average = 8.4% Increase

RANK	STATE	PERCENT CHANGE	RANK	STATE	PERCENT CHANGE
1	Nevada	12.0	26	Alaska	8.2
1	New Hampshire	12.0	26	Texas	8.2
3	Florida	11.1	28	Arkansas	8.0
4	Arizona	10.9	29	New Mexico	7.9
5	Vermont	10.6	30	Missouri	7.6
6	Georgia	10.2	31	Kansas	7.5
6	Virginia	10.2	31	Mississippi	7.5
8	California	9.9	31	Oregon	7.5
9	Maine	9.8	34	Idaho	7.4
9	New Jersey	9.8	35	Wisconsin	7.3
11	South Carolina	9.7	36	Kentucky	7.2
12	Connecticut	9.5	36	Pennsylvania	7.2
13	Massachusetts	9.4	38	Nebraska	7.0
13	North Carolina	9.4	39	Illinois	6.9
15	Maryland	9.3	40	Oklahoma	6.8
16	Hawaii	9.2	41	Indiana	6.7
17	Tennessee	8.9	41	Ohio	6.7
17	Utah	8.9	43	South Dakota	6.6
19	Delaware	8.8	44	North Dakota	6.3
20	Washington	8.7	45	Michigan	6.2
21	Colorado	8.6	45	Montana	6.2
22	Rhode Island	8.4	47	Louisiana	6.0
23	Alabama	8.3	47	Wyoming	6.0
23	Minnesota	8.3	49	Iowa	5.8
23	New York	8.3	50	West Virginia	5.5

District of Columbia   8.5

Source: U.S. Department of Commerce, Bureau of Economic Analysis,
Press Release BEA 91-51 (November 26, 1991)

State and Local Government Revenue in 1990

National Total = $1,031,653,095,000*

RANK	STATE	REVENUE	%	RANK	STATE	REVENUE	%
1	California	$147,334,480,000	14.28%	26	Oregon	$13,045,513,000	1.26%
2	New York	108,704,780,000	10.54%	27	South Carolina	12,559,271,000	1.22%
3	Texas	58,589,532,000	5.68%	28	Kentucky	11,794,128,000	1.14%
4	Florida	47,069,843,000	4.56%	29	Iowa	10,560,505,000	1.02%
5	Pennsylvania	43,714,999,000	4.24%	30	Oklahoma	10,554,311,000	1.02%
6	Illinois	43,541,721,000	4.22%	31	Kansas	9,043,469,000	0.88%
7	Ohio	42,542,588,000	4.12%	32	Mississippi	8,150,934,000	0.79%
8	Michigan	37,184,020,000	3.60%	33	Alaska	7,118,723,000	0.69%
9	New Jersey	35,133,978,000	3.41%	34	Nebraska	7,057,560,000	0.68%
10	Massachusetts	26,052,450,000	2.53%	35	Utah	6,939,307,000	0.67%
11	Georgia	24,059,769,000	2.33%	36	Arkansas	6,347,988,000	0.62%
12	Washington	23,323,180,000	2.26%	37	New Mexico	6,211,566,000	0.60%
13	North Carolina	23,176,554,000	2.25%	38	West Virginia	5,752,630,000	0.56%
14	Virginia	21,976,846,000	2.13%	39	Hawaii	5,661,258,000	0.55%
15	Wisconsin	21,766,102,000	2.11%	40	Nevada	5,083,835,000	0.49%
16	Minnesota	21,140,762,000	2.05%	41	Maine	4,520,883,000	0.44%
17	Maryland	19,527,993,000	1.89%	42	Rhode Island	4,103,968,000	0.40%
18	Indiana	18,168,010,000	1.76%	43	New Hampshire	3,507,170,000	0.34%
19	Tennessee	17,965,066,000	1.74%	44	Idaho	3,373,510,000	0.33%
20	Louisiana	15,528,717,000	1.51%	45	Montana	3,267,547,000	0.32%
21	Missouri	15,403,003,000	1.49%	46	Delaware	2,955,329,000	0.29%
22	Arizona	14,908,752,000	1.45%	47	Wyoming	2,730,761,000	0.26%
23	Connecticut	14,549,674,000	1.41%	48	North Dakota	2,472,001,000	0.24%
24	Colorado	14,160,973,000	1.37%	49	South Dakota	2,338,294,000	0.23%
25	Alabama	13,768,493,000	1.33%	50	Vermont	2,283,747,000	0.22%
					District of Columbia	4,926,602,000	0.48%

Source: U.S. Bureau of the Census,
   "Government Finances: 1989-90 (Preliminary Report)" (GF-90-5P, September 1991)
*Preliminary.

Per Capita State and Local Government Revenue in 1990

National Per Capita = $4,148*

RANK	STATE	PER CAPITA	RANK	STATE	PER CAPITA
1	Alaska	$12,942	26	North Dakota	$3,870
2	New York	6,042	27	Illinois	3,809
3	Wyoming	6,020	28	Iowa	3,803
4	Hawaii	5,108	29	Georgia	3,714
5	California	4,951	30	Tennessee	3,683
6	Minnesota	4,832	31	Maine	3,682
7	Washington	4,792	32	Louisiana	3,680
8	Oregon	4,590	33	Pennsylvania	3,679
9	New Jersey	4,545	34	Kansas	3,650
10	Nebraska	4,471	35	Florida	3,638
11	Wisconsin	4,450	36	South Carolina	3,602
12	Delaware	4,436	37	Virginia	3,552
13	Connecticut	4,426	38	North Carolina	3,496
14	Massachusetts	4,330	39	Texas	3,449
15	Colorado	4,299	40	Alabama	3,408
16	Nevada	4,230	41	South Dakota	3,360
17	New Mexico	4,100	42	Oklahoma	3,355
18	Rhode Island	4,090	43	Idaho	3,351
19	Montana	4,089	44	Indiana	3,277
20	Maryland	4,084	45	West Virginia	3,208
21	Arizona	4,068	46	Kentucky	3,200
22	Vermont	4,058	47	Mississippi	3,168
23	Utah	4,028	48	New Hampshire	3,162
24	Michigan	4,000	49	Missouri	3,010
25	Ohio	3,922	50	Arkansas	2,700

District of Columbia   8,118

Source: U.S. Bureau of the Census,

"Government Finances: 1989-90 (Preliminary Report)" (GF-90-5P, September 1991)

*Preliminary. Rates calculated by the editors using 1990 Census population counts.

State and Local Government Revenue from the Federal Government in 1990

National Total = $136,843,083,000*

RANK	STATE	REVENUE	%	RANK	STATE	REVENUE	%
1	California	$18,136,627,000	13.25%	26	South Carolina	$1,890,584,000	1.38%
2	New York	14,505,895,000	10.60%	27	Mississippi	1,691,703,000	1.24%
3	Texas	7,357,180,000	5.38%	28	Arizona	1,610,594,000	1.18%
4	Pennsylvania	6,139,854,000	4.49%	29	Colorado	1,599,261,000	1.17%
5	Ohio	5,529,527,000	4.04%	30	Iowa	1,513,107,000	1.11%
6	Illinois	5,424,729,000	3.96%	31	Oklahoma	1,499,209,000	1.10%
7	Florida	4,871,353,000	3.56%	32	Arkansas	1,230,684,000	0.90%
8	Michigan	4,662,566,000	3.41%	33	Utah	1,059,631,000	0.77%
9	New Jersey	4,032,955,000	2.95%	34	Kansas	1,025,100,000	0.75%
10	Massachusetts	3,872,687,000	2.83%	35	West Virginia	993,795,000	0.73%
11	Georgia	3,332,102,000	2.43%	36	New Mexico	936,679,000	0.68%
12	North Carolina	3,060,374,000	2.24%	37	Nebraska	778,794,000	0.57%
13	Minnesota	2,807,947,000	2.05%	38	Maine	757,169,000	0.55%
14	Tennessee	2,761,319,000	2.02%	39	Rhode Island	727,313,000	0.53%
15	Louisiana	2,672,203,000	1.95%	40	Alaska	713,238,000	0.52%
16	Washington	2,622,104,000	1.92%	41	Hawaii	700,208,000	0.51%
17	Wisconsin	2,595,012,000	1.90%	42	Montana	625,191,000	0.46%
18	Maryland	2,512,458,000	1.84%	43	Idaho	553,028,000	0.40%
19	Indiana	2,497,066,000	1.82%	44	Wyoming	533,055,000	0.39%
20	Virginia	2,472,341,000	1.81%	45	South Dakota	503,333,000	0.37%
21	Alabama	2,252,354,000	1.65%	46	North Dakota	496,696,000	0.36%
22	Missouri	2,122,867,000	1.55%	47	Nevada	474,593,000	0.35%
23	Oregon	1,997,663,000	1.46%	48	New Hampshire	425,362,000	0.31%
24	Kentucky	1,975,861,000	1.44%	49	Vermont	421,879,000	0.31%
25	Connecticut	1,922,362,000	1.40%	50	Delaware	346,242,000	0.25%
					District of Columbia	1,599,230,000	1.17%

Source: U.S. Bureau of the Census,
    "Government Finances: 1989-90 (Preliminary Report)" (September 1991)
*Preliminary.

Per Capita State and Local Government Revenue from the Federal Government in 1990

National Per Capita = $550.21 *

RANK	STATE	PER CAPITA		RANK	STATE	PER CAPITA
1	Alaska	$1,296.69		26	Washington	$538.79
2	Wyoming	1,175.20		27	Kentucky	536.15
3	New York	806.31		28	Wisconsin	530.49
4	Montana	782.40		29	Maryland	525.46
5	North Dakota	777.55		30	Arkansas	523.53
6	Vermont	749.66		31	New Jersey	521.71
7	Rhode Island	724.80		32	Delaware	519.75
8	South Dakota	723.18		33	Pennsylvania	516.75
9	Oregon	702.83		34	Georgia	514.35
10	Mississippi	657.43		35	Ohio	509.77
11	Massachusetts	643.69		36	Michigan	501.60
12	Minnesota	641.80		37	Nebraska	493.41
13	Louisiana	633.23		38	Colorado	485.45
14	Hawaii	631.83		39	Oklahoma	476.61
15	New Mexico	618.24		40	Illinois	474.58
16	Maine	616.62		41	North Carolina	461.69
17	Utah	615.05		42	Indiana	450.40
18	California	609.43		43	Arizona	439.43
19	Connecticut	584.82		44	Texas	433.12
20	Tennessee	566.17		45	Missouri	414.86
21	Alabama	557.43		46	Kansas	413.75
22	West Virginia	554.12		47	Virginia	399.58
23	Idaho	549.32		48	Nevada	394.89
24	Iowa	544.92		49	New Hampshire	383.47
25	South Carolina	542.23		50	Florida	376.52

District of Columbia   2,635.08

Source: U.S. Bureau of the Census,
   "Government Finances: 1989-90 (Preliminary Report)" (September 1991)
*Preliminary. Rates calculated by the editors.

State Government Revenue in 1990

National Total = $625,473,000,000

RANK	STATE	REVENUE	%
1	California	$88,704,000,000	14.18%
2	New York	64,253,000,000	10.27%
3	Texas	30,975,000,000	4.95%
4	Ohio	28,516,000,000	4.56%
5	Pennsylvania	27,223,000,000	4.35%
6	Illinois	24,313,000,000	3.89%
7	Florida	23,868,000,000	3.82%
8	Michigan	23,405,000,000	3.74%
9	New Jersey	22,624,000,000	3.62%
10	Massachusetts	17,034,000,000	2.72%
11	Washington	14,999,000,000	2.40%
12	North Carolina	14,485,000,000	2.32%
13	Virginia	13,607,000,000	2.18%
14	Wisconsin	13,388,000,000	2.14%
15	Minnesota	13,162,000,000	2.10%
16	Georgia	13,108,000,000	2.10%
17	Maryland	12,195,000,000	1.95%
18	Indiana	11,456,000,000	1.83%
19	Louisiana	10,096,000,000	1.61%
20	Connecticut	9,591,000,000	1.53%
21	Missouri	9,343,000,000	1.49%
22	Tennessee	9,110,000,000	1.46%
23	Alabama	9,041,000,000	1.45%
24	South Carolina	8,750,000,000	1.40%
25	Arizona	8,598,000,000	1.37%

RANK	STATE	REVENUE	%
26	Kentucky	$8,593,000,000	1.37%
27	Colorado	7,527,000,000	1.20%
28	Oklahoma	7,201,000,000	1.15%
29	Oregon	7,001,000,000	1.12%
30	Iowa	6,728,000,000	1.08%
31	Alaska	5,500,000,000	0.88%
32	Mississippi	5,344,000,000	0.85%
33	Kansas	5,136,000,000	0.82%
34	New Mexico	4,731,000,000	0.76%
35	Arkansas	4,511,000,000	0.72%
36	West Virginia	4,435,000,000	0.71%
37	Hawaii	4,326,000,000	0.69%
38	Utah	4,302,000,000	0.69%
39	Nevada	3,266,000,000	0.52%
40	Maine	3,246,000,000	0.52%
41	Nebraska	3,073,000,000	0.49%
42	Rhode Island	3,034,000,000	0.49%
43	Idaho	2,417,000,000	0.39%
44	Delaware	2,316,000,000	0.37%
45	Montana	2,225,000,000	0.36%
46	New Hampshire	1,922,000,000	0.31%
47	Wyoming	1,900,000,000	0.30%
48	North Dakota	1,810,000,000	0.29%
49	Vermont	1,592,000,000	0.25%
50	South Dakota	1,494,000,000	0.24%

Source: U.S. Bureau of the Census,
   "State Government Finance: 1990" (GF-90-3, August 1991)

Per Capita State Government Revenue in 1990

National Per Capita = $2,515*

RANK	STATE	PER CAPITA
1	Alaska	$9,999
2	Wyoming	4,189
3	Hawaii	3,904
4	New York	3,572
5	Delaware	3,477
6	New Mexico	3,123
7	Washington	3,082
8	Rhode Island	3,024
9	Minnesota	3,008
10	California	2,981
11	New Jersey	2,927
12	Connecticut	2,918
13	North Dakota	2,833
14	Massachusetts	2,831
15	Vermont	2,829
16	Montana	2,785
17	Wisconsin	2,737
18	Nevada	2,718
19	Maine	2,643
20	Ohio	2,629
21	Maryland	2,550
22	Michigan	2,518
23	South Carolina	2,510
24	Utah	2,497
25	West Virginia	2,473

RANK	STATE	PER CAPITA
26	Oregon	$2,463
27	Iowa	2,423
28	Idaho	2,401
29	Louisiana	2,392
30	Arizona	2,346
31	Kentucky	2,332
32	Pennsylvania	2,291
33	Oklahoma	2,289
34	Colorado	2,285
35	Alabama	2,238
36	Virginia	2,199
37	North Carolina	2,185
38	South Dakota	2,147
39	Illinois	2,127
40	Mississippi	2,077
41	Kansas	2,073
42	Indiana	2,066
43	Georgia	2,023
44	Nebraska	1,947
45	Arkansas	1,919
46	Tennessee	1,868
47	Florida	1,845
48	Missouri	1,826
49	Texas	1,824
50	New Hampshire	1,733

Source: U.S. Bureau of the Census,

"State Government Finance: 1990" (GF-90-3, August 1991)

*Rates calculated by the editors using 1990 Census population counts.

State Government Revenue from Federal Government in 1990

National Total = $118,352,725,000

RANK	STATE	REVENUE	%	RANK	STATE	REVENUE	%
1	California	$16,051,093,000	13.56%	26	Oregon	$1,637,681,000	1.38%
2	New York	12,902,385,000	10.90%	27	Mississippi	1,491,721,000	1.26%
3	Texas	6,499,293,000	5.49%	28	Colorado	1,361,971,000	1.15%
4	Pennsylvania	5,268,530,000	4.45%	29	Oklahoma	1,345,219,000	1.14%
5	Ohio	4,767,298,000	4.03%	30	Arizona	1,292,634,000	1.09%
6	Illinois	4,489,498,000	3.79%	31	Iowa	1,290,794,000	1.09%
7	Michigan	4,180,674,000	3.53%	32	Arkansas	1,142,632,000	0.97%
8	Florida	3,998,886,000	3.38%	33	Utah	966,344,000	0.82%
9	New Jersey	3,644,323,000	3.08%	34	Kansas	958,282,000	0.81%
10	Massachusetts	3,306,591,000	2.79%	35	West Virginia	941,961,000	0.80%
11	Georgia	2,876,781,000	2.43%	36	New Mexico	779,486,000	0.66%
12	North Carolina	2,648,279,000	2.24%	37	Maine	691,385,000	0.58%
13	Tennessee	2,478,513,000	2.09%	38	Nebraska	681,411,000	0.58%
14	Louisiana	2,399,015,000	2.03%	39	Rhode Island	667,218,000	0.56%
15	Wisconsin	2,365,079,000	2.00%	40	Alaska	622,581,000	0.53%
16	Minnesota	2,273,674,000	1.92%	41	Hawaii	610,424,000	0.52%
17	Indiana	2,255,261,000	1.91%	42	Montana	547,571,000	0.46%
18	Washington	2,245,605,000	1.90%	43	Wyoming	504,307,000	0.43%
19	Virginia	2,105,108,000	1.78%	44	Idaho	493,630,000	0.42%
20	Maryland	2,095,422,000	1.77%	45	South Dakota	450,866,000	0.38%
21	Alabama	2,060,142,000	1.74%	46	North Dakota	443,436,000	0.37%
22	Missouri	1,804,226,000	1.52%	47	Vermont	393,572,000	0.33%
23	Kentucky	1,794,233,000	1.52%	48	New Hampshire	373,603,000	0.32%
24	Connecticut	1,753,168,000	1.48%	49	Nevada	365,993,000	0.31%
25	South Carolina	1,728,124,000	1.46%	50	Delaware	306,802,000	0.26%

Source: U.S. Bureau of the Census,
    "State Government Finance: 1990" (GF-90-3, August 1991)

Local Government Revenue in 1990

National Total = $580,578,318,000*

RANK	STATE	REVENUE	%
1	California	$93,222,809,000	16.06%
2	New York	68,938,838,000	11.87%
3	Texas	34,650,811,000	5.97%
4	Florida	31,434,206,000	5.41%
5	Illinois	24,998,023,000	4.31%
6	Pennsylvania	23,259,625,000	4.01%
7	Ohio	20,422,242,000	3.52%
8	Michigan	20,092,045,000	3.46%
9	New Jersey	18,095,851,000	3.12%
10	Georgia	14,478,794,000	2.49%
11	North Carolina	13,516,138,000	2.33%
12	Massachusetts	13,490,671,000	2.32%
13	Tennessee	12,793,626,000	2.20%
14	Minnesota	12,307,189,000	2.12%
15	Washington	12,032,066,000	2.07%
16	Virginia	11,843,755,000	2.04%
17	Wisconsin	10,707,235,000	1.84%
18	Indiana	10,189,622,000	1.76%
19	Maryland	9,745,448,000	1.68%
20	Arizona	9,239,881,000	1.59%
21	Colorado	8,411,922,000	1.45%
22	Missouri	8,064,280,000	1.39%
23	Louisiana	7,582,194,000	1.31%
24	Connecticut	6,692,653,000	1.15%
25	Alabama	6,619,894,000	1.14%

RANK	STATE	REVENUE	%
26	Oregon	$6,267,745,000	1.08%
27	South Carolina	5,599,815,000	0.96%
28	Iowa	5,572,111,000	0.96%
29	Kansas	5,062,683,000	0.87%
30	Kentucky	4,932,928,000	0.85%
31	Oklahoma	4,869,538,000	0.84%
32	Nebraska	4,568,177,000	0.79%
33	Mississippi	4,310,795,000	0.74%
34	Utah	3,607,056,000	0.62%
35	Arkansas	2,894,518,000	0.50%
36	Nevada	2,846,587,000	0.49%
37	New Mexico	2,773,809,000	0.48%
38	Alaska	2,391,344,000	0.41%
39	West Virginia	2,181,903,000	0.38%
40	Maine	1,860,312,000	0.32%
41	New Hampshire	1,840,414,000	0.32%
42	Idaho	1,525,133,000	0.26%
43	Rhode Island	1,491,858,000	0.26%
44	Montana	1,428,479,000	0.25%
45	Hawaii	1,409,823,000	0.24%
46	Wyoming	1,355,661,000	0.23%
47	South Dakota	1,042,955,000	0.18%
48	Delaware	1,035,848,000	0.18%
49	North Dakota	1,020,466,000	0.18%
50	Vermont	931,940,000	0.16%
	District of Columbia	4,926,602,000	0.85%

Source: U.S. Bureau of the Census,
    "Government Finances: 1989-90 (Preliminary Report)" (GF-90-5P, September 1991)
*Preliminary.

Per Capita Local Government Revenue in 1990

National Per Capita = $2,334*

RANK	STATE	PER CAPITA		RANK	STATE	PER CAPITA
1	Alaska	$4,348		26	Iowa	$2,007
2	New York	3,832		27	Pennsylvania	1,958
3	California	3,132		28	Virginia	1,914
4	Wyoming	2,989		29	Ohio	1,883
5	Nebraska	2,894		30	Indiana	1,838
6	Minnesota	2,813		31	New Mexico	1,831
7	Tennessee	2,623		32	Louisiana	1,797
8	Colorado	2,553		33	Montana	1,788
9	Arizona	2,521		34	Mississippi	1,675
10	Washington	2,472		35	New Hampshire	1,659
11	Florida	2,430		36	Vermont	1,656
12	Nevada	2,369		37	Alabama	1,638
13	New Jersey	2,341		38	South Carolina	1,606
14	Massachusetts	2,242		39	North Dakota	1,597
15	Georgia	2,235		40	Missouri	1,576
16	Oregon	2,205		41	Delaware	1,555
17	Wisconsin	2,189		42	Oklahoma	1,548
18	Illinois	2,187		43	Idaho	1,515
19	Michigan	2,162		43	Maine	1,515
20	Utah	2,094		45	South Dakota	1,498
21	Kansas	2,043		46	Rhode Island	1,487
22	Texas	2,040		47	Kentucky	1,339
23	North Carolina	2,039		48	Hawaii	1,272
24	Maryland	2,038		49	Arkansas	1,231
25	Connecticut	2,036		50	West Virginia	1,217
					District of Columbia	8,118

Source: U.S. Bureau of the Census,
   "Government Finances: 1989-90 (Preliminary Report)" (GF-90-5P, September 1991)
*Preliminary. Rates calculated by the editors using 1990 Census population counts.

Local Government Revenue from Federal Government in 1990

National Total = $18,490,358,000*

RANK	STATE	REVENUE	%	RANK	STATE	REVENUE	%
1	California	$2,085,534,000	11.28%	26	Mississippi	$199,982,000	1.08%
2	New York	1,603,510,000	8.67%	27	Alabama	192,212,000	1.04%
3	Illinois	935,231,000	5.06%	28	Kentucky	181,628,000	0.98%
4	Florida	872,467,000	4.72%	29	Connecticut	169,194,000	0.92%
5	Pennsylvania	871,324,000	4.71%	30	South Carolina	162,460,000	0.88%
6	Texas	857,887,000	4.64%	31	New Mexico	157,193,000	0.85%
7	Ohio	762,229,000	4.12%	32	Oklahoma	153,989,000	0.83%
8	Massachusetts	566,096,000	3.06%	33	Nevada	108,600,000	0.59%
9	Minnesota	534,273,000	2.89%	34	Nebraska	97,383,000	0.53%
10	Michigan	481,892,000	2.61%	35	Utah	93,287,000	0.50%
11	Georgia	455,321,000	2.46%	36	Alaska	90,657,000	0.49%
12	Maryland	417,036,000	2.26%	37	Hawaii	89,784,000	0.49%
13	North Carolina	412,095,000	2.23%	38	Arkansas	88,052,000	0.48%
14	New Jersey	388,632,000	2.10%	39	Montana	77,620,000	0.42%
15	Washington	376,499,000	2.04%	40	Kansas	66,818,000	0.36%
16	Virginia	367,233,000	1.99%	41	Maine	65,784,000	0.36%
17	Oregon	359,982,000	1.95%	42	Rhode Island	60,095,000	0.33%
18	Missouri	318,641,000	1.72%	43	Idaho	59,398,000	0.32%
19	Arizona	317,960,000	1.72%	44	North Dakota	53,260,000	0.29%
20	Tennessee	282,806,000	1.53%	45	South Dakota	52,467,000	0.28%
21	Louisiana	273,188,000	1.48%	46	West Virginia	51,834,000	0.28%
22	Indiana	241,805,000	1.31%	47	New Hampshire	51,759,000	0.28%
23	Colorado	237,290,000	1.28%	48	Delaware	39,440,000	0.21%
24	Wisconsin	229,933,000	1.24%	49	Wyoming	28,748,000	0.16%
25	Iowa	222,313,000	1.20%	50	Vermont	28,307,000	0.15%
					District of Columbia	1,599,230,000	8.65%

Source: U.S. Bureau of the Census,

"Government Finances: 1989–90 (Preliminary Report)" (GF-90-5P, September 1991)

*Preliminary.

State and Local Government Expenditures in 1990

National Total = $973,987,525,000*

RANK	STATE	EXPENDITURES	%	RANK	STATE	EXPENDITURES	%
1	California	$134,300,484,000	13.79%	26	South Carolina	$11,914,918,000	1.22%
2	New York	107,134,608,000	11.00%	27	Oregon	11,374,341,000	1.17%
3	Texas	55,146,746,000	5.66%	28	Kentucky	10,910,723,000	1.12%
4	Florida	46,571,493,000	4.78%	29	Iowa	9,768,678,000	1.00%
5	Pennsylvania	41,321,595,000	4.24%	30	Oklahoma	9,746,128,000	1.00%
6	Illinois	39,377,152,000	4.04%	31	Kansas	8,393,453,000	0.86%
7	Ohio	38,500,549,000	3.95%	32	Mississippi	7,417,802,000	0.76%
8	Michigan	36,713,254,000	3.77%	33	Nebraska	6,638,927,000	0.68%
9	New Jersey	33,689,786,000	3.46%	34	Utah	6,462,190,000	0.66%
10	Massachusetts	27,671,436,000	2.84%	35	Alaska	6,042,700,000	0.62%
11	Georgia	22,778,173,000	2.34%	36	Arkansas	5,943,512,000	0.61%
12	North Carolina	22,226,475,000	2.28%	37	New Mexico	5,486,117,000	0.56%
13	Washington	21,915,529,000	2.25%	38	West Virginia	5,437,148,000	0.56%
14	Virginia	21,238,823,000	2.18%	39	Hawaii	4,934,322,000	0.51%
15	Minnesota	19,352,082,000	1.99%	40	Nevada	4,827,092,000	0.50%
16	Maryland	18,489,907,000	1.90%	41	Maine	4,396,543,000	0.45%
17	Wisconsin	18,308,078,000	1.88%	42	Rhode Island	4,131,377,000	0.42%
18	Tennessee	17,026,123,000	1.75%	43	New Hampshire	3,649,316,000	0.37%
19	Indiana	16,799,836,000	1.72%	44	Idaho	2,945,687,000	0.30%
20	Arizona	15,402,366,000	1.58%	45	Montana	2,921,877,000	0.30%
21	Connecticut	14,874,979,000	1.53%	46	Delaware	2,786,602,000	0.29%
22	Louisiana	14,529,192,000	1.49%	47	North Dakota	2,387,626,000	0.25%
23	Missouri	14,265,645,000	1.46%	48	Wyoming	2,386,709,000	0.25%
24	Alabama	12,820,208,000	1.32%	49	Vermont	2,264,541,000	0.23%
25	Colorado	12,793,673,000	1.31%	50	South Dakota	2,196,833,000	0.23%
					District of Columbia	5,374,171,000	0.55%

Source: U.S. Bureau of the Census,
"Government Finances: 1989-90 (Preliminary Report)" (GF-90-5P, September 1991)
*Preliminary.

Per Capita State and Local Government Expenditures in 1990

National Per Capita = $3,916*

RANK	STATE	PER CAPITA		RANK	STATE	PER CAPITA
1	Alaska	$10,986		26	Florida	$3,600
2	New York	5,955		27	Maine	3,580
3	Wyoming	5,262		28	Ohio	3,549
4	Massachusetts	4,599		29	Iowa	3,518
5	Connecticut	4,525		30	Georgia	3,516
6	California	4,513		31	Tennessee	3,491
7	Washington	4,503		32	Pennsylvania	3,478
8	Hawaii	4,452		33	Illinois	3,445
9	Minnesota	4,423		34	Louisiana	3,443
10	New Jersey	4,358		35	Virginia	3,433
11	Nebraska	4,206		36	South Carolina	3,417
12	Arizona	4,202		37	Kansas	3,388
13	Delaware	4,183		38	North Carolina	3,353
14	Rhode Island	4,117		39	New Hampshire	3,290
15	Vermont	4,024		40	Texas	3,247
16	Nevada	4,016		41	Alabama	3,173
17	Oregon	4,002		42	South Dakota	3,156
18	Michigan	3,950		43	Oklahoma	3,098
19	Colorado	3,883		44	West Virginia	3,032
20	Maryland	3,867		45	Indiana	3,030
21	Utah	3,751		46	Kentucky	2,961
22	Wisconsin	3,743		47	Idaho	2,926
23	North Dakota	3,738		48	Mississippi	2,883
24	Montana	3,657		49	Missouri	2,788
25	New Mexico	3,621		50	Arkansas	2,528

District of Columbia   8,855

Source: U.S. Bureau of the Census,

    "Government Finances: 1989-90 (Preliminary Report)" (GF-90-5P, September 1991)

Preliminary. Rates calculated by the editors using 1990 Census population counts.

State Government Expenditures in 1990

National Total = $571,909,000,000

RANK	STATE	EXPENDITURES	%	RANK	STATE	EXPENDITURES	%
1	California	$78,867,000,000	13.79%	26	Kentucky	$7,772,000,000	1.36%
2	New York	59,139,000,000	10.34%	27	Oklahoma	6,515,000,000	1.14%
3	Texas	26,027,000,000	4.55%	28	Colorado	6,510,000,000	1.14%
4	Ohio	25,237,000,000	4.41%	29	Oregon	6,352,000,000	1.11%
5	Pennsylvania	24,531,000,000	4.29%	30	Iowa	6,317,000,000	1.10%
6	Michigan	23,098,000,000	4.04%	31	Mississippi	4,838,000,000	0.85%
7	Illinois	22,072,000,000	3.86%	32	Kansas	4,705,000,000	0.82%
8	Florida	21,723,000,000	3.80%	33	Alaska	4,688,000,000	0.82%
9	New Jersey	21,454,000,000	3.75%	34	Arkansas	4,223,000,000	0.74%
10	Massachusetts	18,736,000,000	3.28%	35	West Virginia	4,212,000,000	0.74%
11	Washington	13,567,000,000	2.37%	36	New Mexico	4,172,000,000	0.73%
12	North Carolina	13,493,000,000	2.36%	37	Utah	3,857,000,000	0.67%
13	Virginia	12,632,000,000	2.21%	38	Hawaii	3,832,000,000	0.67%
14	Georgia	12,213,000,000	2.14%	39	Maine	3,044,000,000	0.53%
15	Wisconsin	11,416,000,000	2.00%	40	Rhode Island	3,014,000,000	0.53%
16	Minnesota	11,355,000,000	1.99%	41	Nevada	2,929,000,000	0.51%
17	Maryland	11,296,000,000	1.98%	42	Nebraska	2,885,000,000	0.50%
18	Indiana	10,414,000,000	1.82%	43	Delaware	2,128,000,000	0.37%
19	Connecticut	9,886,000,000	1.73%	44	Idaho	2,047,000,000	0.36%
20	Louisiana	9,420,000,000	1.65%	45	Montana	2,007,000,000	0.35%
21	Tennessee	8,403,000,000	1.47%	46	New Hampshire	1,972,000,000	0.34%
22	Missouri	8,326,000,000	1.46%	47	North Dakota	1,755,000,000	0.31%
23	Arizona	8,265,000,000	1.45%	48	Wyoming	1,641,000,000	0.29%
24	Alabama	8,108,000,000	1.42%	49	Vermont	1,565,000,000	0.27%
25	South Carolina	7,910,000,000	1.38%	50	South Dakota	1,344,000,000	0.24%

Source: U.S. Bureau of the Census,

"State Government Finance: 1990" (GF-90-3, August 1991)

Per Capita State Government Expenditures in 1990

National Per Capita = $2,300*

RANK	STATE	PER CAPITA	RANK	STATE	PER CAPITA
1	Alaska	$8,523	26	Arizona	$2,255
2	Wyoming	3,618	27	Utah	2,239
3	Hawaii	3,458	28	Oregon	2,235
4	New York	3,287	29	Louisiana	2,232
5	Delaware	3,194	30	Kentucky	2,109
6	Massachusetts	3,114	31	Oklahoma	2,071
7	Connecticut	3,007	32	Pennsylvania	2,065
8	Rhode Island	3,004	33	Virginia	2,042
9	Washington	2,788	34	North Carolina	2,036
10	Vermont	2,781	35	Idaho	2,033
11	New Jersey	2,775	36	Alabama	2,007
12	New Mexico	2,754	37	Colorado	1,976
13	North Dakota	2,747	38	Illinois	1,931
14	California	2,650	38	South Dakota	1,931
15	Minnesota	2,595	40	Kansas	1,899
16	Montana	2,512	41	Georgia	1,885
17	Michigan	2,485	42	Mississippi	1,880
18	Maine	2,479	43	Indiana	1,878
19	Nevada	2,437	44	Nebraska	1,828
20	Maryland	2,362	45	Arkansas	1,796
21	West Virginia	2,349	46	New Hampshire	1,778
22	Wisconsin	2,334	47	Tennessee	1,723
23	Ohio	2,327	48	Florida	1,679
24	Iowa	2,275	49	Missouri	1,627
25	South Carolina	2,269	50	Texas	1,532

Source: U.S. Bureau of the Census,
"State Government Finance: 1990" (GF-90-3, August 1991)
*Rates calculated by the editors using 1990 Census population counts.

Local Government Expenditures in 1990

National Total = $579,419,447,000*

RANK	STATE	EXPENDITURES	%	RANK	STATE	EXPENDITURES	%
1	California	$88,573,649,000	15.29%	26	Oregon	$6,505,962,000	1.12%
2	New York	70,388,586,000	12.15%	27	South Carolina	5,911,559,000	1.02%
3	Texas	36,531,460,000	6.30%	28	Iowa	5,445,901,000	0.94%
4	Florida	32,093,416,000	5.54%	29	Kentucky	5,054,394,000	0.87%
5	Pennsylvania	23,760,043,000	4.10%	30	Kansas	5,001,083,000	0.86%
6	Illinois	23,181,144,000	4.00%	31	Oklahoma	4,870,573,000	0.84%
7	Ohio	20,708,099,000	3.57%	32	Nebraska	4,529,362,000	0.78%
8	Michigan	20,047,764,000	3.46%	33	Mississippi	4,271,579,000	0.74%
9	New Jersey	18,169,750,000	3.14%	34	Utah	3,585,432,000	0.62%
10	Georgia	14,251,853,000	2.46%	35	Arkansas	2,896,882,000	0.50%
11	North Carolina	13,970,273,000	2.41%	36	Nevada	2,845,677,000	0.49%
12	Massachusetts	13,732,058,000	2.37%	37	New Mexico	2,797,230,000	0.48%
13	Minnesota	12,345,042,000	2.13%	38	Alaska	2,193,853,000	0.38%
14	Washington	12,123,581,000	2.09%	39	West Virginia	2,186,611,000	0.38%
15	Virginia	12,101,488,000	2.09%	40	Maine	2,009,089,000	0.35%
16	Wisconsin	11,119,705,000	1.92%	41	New Hampshire	1,929,113,000	0.33%
17	Tennessee	10,857,990,000	1.87%	42	Rhode Island	1,594,400,000	0.28%
18	Arizona	9,844,659,000	1.70%	43	Idaho	1,490,511,000	0.26%
19	Indiana	9,812,786,000	1.69%	44	Montana	1,343,380,000	0.23%
20	Maryland	9,687,903,000	1.67%	45	Wyoming	1,330,270,000	0.23%
21	Missouri	8,502,595,000	1.47%	46	Hawaii	1,193,459,000	0.21%
22	Colorado	8,113,893,000	1.40%	47	South Dakota	1,098,835,000	0.19%
23	Louisiana	7,463,133,000	1.29%	48	Delaware	1,028,530,000	0.18%
24	Connecticut	6,848,250,000	1.18%	49	North Dakota	1,013,168,000	0.17%
25	Alabama	6,733,301,000	1.16%	50	Vermont	956,002,000	0.16%
					District of Columbia	5,374,171,000	0.93%

Source: U.S. Bureau of the Census,

"Government Finances: 1989-90 (Preliminary Report)" (GF-90-5P, September 1991)

*Preliminary.

Per Capita Local Government Expenditures in 1990

National Per Capita = $2,330*

RANK	STATE	PER CAPITA		RANK	STATE	PER CAPITA
1	Alaska	$3,989		26	Pennsylvania	$2,000
2	New York	3,913		27	Iowa	1,961
3	California	2,976		28	Virginia	1,956
4	Wyoming	2,933		29	Ohio	1,909
5	Nebraska	2,870		30	New Mexico	1,846
6	Minnesota	2,822		31	Indiana	1,770
7	Arizona	2,686		32	Louisiana	1,769
8	Washington	2,491		33	New Hampshire	1,739
9	Florida	2,481		34	Vermont	1,699
10	Colorado	2,463		35	South Carolina	1,695
11	Nevada	2,368		36	Montana	1,681
12	New Jersey	2,350		37	Alabama	1,666
13	Oregon	2,289		38	Missouri	1,662
14	Massachusetts	2,282		39	Mississippi	1,660
15	Wisconsin	2,273		40	Maine	1,636
16	Tennessee	2,226		41	Rhode Island	1,589
17	Georgia	2,200		42	North Dakota	1,586
18	Michigan	2,157		43	South Dakota	1,579
19	Texas	2,151		44	Oklahoma	1,548
20	North Carolina	2,108		45	Delaware	1,544
21	Connecticut	2,083		46	Idaho	1,481
22	Utah	2,081		47	Kentucky	1,372
23	Illinois	2,028		48	Arkansas	1,232
24	Maryland	2,026		49	West Virginia	1,219
25	Kansas	2,019		50	Hawaii	1,077
					District of Columbia	8,855

Source: U.S. Bureau of the Census,

"Government Finances: 1989-90 (Preliminary Report)" (GF-90-5P, September 1991)

*Preliminary. Rates calculated by the editors using 1990 Census population counts.

State and Local Government Debt Outstanding in 1990

National Total = $857,844,113,000*

RANK	STATE	DEBT	%	RANK	STATE	DEBT	%
1	New York	$94,514,256,000	11.02%	26	Alabama	$10,221,077,000	1.19%
2	California	91,675,649,000	10.69%	27	Oregon	10,124,682,000	1.18%
3	Texas	64,224,248,000	7.49%	28	Missouri	10,081,516,000	1.18%
4	Florida	53,463,746,000	6.23%	29	Utah	10,009,728,000	1.17%
5	Pennsylvania	45,804,451,000	5.34%	30	South Carolina	9,722,520,000	1.13%
6	New Jersey	32,615,440,000	3.80%	31	Oklahoma	8,232,772,000	0.96%
7	Illinois	31,977,835,000	3.73%	32	Kansas	6,959,097,000	0.81%
8	Massachusetts	26,968,075,000	3.14%	33	West Virginia	6,286,062,000	0.73%
9	Washington	23,645,313,000	2.76%	34	Nebraska	6,090,160,000	0.71%
10	Ohio	23,190,853,000	2.70%	35	Iowa	5,250,070,000	0.61%
11	Louisiana	21,560,222,000	2.51%	36	New Mexico	4,992,834,000	0.58%
12	Michigan	21,442,579,000	2.50%	37	Mississippi	4,768,763,000	0.56%
13	Minnesota	17,528,100,000	2.04%	38	Arkansas	4,612,227,000	0.54%
14	Arizona	17,513,489,000	2.04%	39	Hawaii	4,428,745,000	0.52%
15	Georgia	17,396,934,000	2.03%	40	Nevada	4,352,294,000	0.51%
16	Maryland	16,288,012,000	1.90%	41	New Hampshire	4,337,522,000	0.51%
17	Virginia	15,804,025,000	1.84%	42	Rhode Island	4,329,395,000	0.50%
18	North Carolina	15,722,911,000	1.83%	43	Delaware	3,938,570,000	0.46%
19	Tennessee	14,403,306,000	1.68%	44	Maine	3,397,742,000	0.40%
20	Connecticut	14,331,255,000	1.67%	45	Montana	2,549,040,000	0.30%
21	Kentucky	13,258,468,000	1.55%	46	South Dakota	2,274,145,000	0.27%
22	Colorado	12,508,159,000	1.46%	47	Wyoming	2,257,534,000	0.26%
23	Wisconsin	12,090,190,000	1.41%	48	North Dakota	1,854,936,000	0.22%
24	Indiana	10,883,342,000	1.27%	49	Vermont	1,655,820,000	0.19%
25	Alaska	10,357,849,000	1.21%	50	Idaho	1,528,165,000	0.18%
					District of Columbia	4,419,990,000	0.52%

Source: U.S. Bureau of the Census,
"Government Finances: 1989-90 (Preliminary Report)" (GF-90-5P, September 1991)

*Preliminary.

223

Per Capita State and Local Government Debt Outstanding in 1990

National Per Capita = $3,449*

RANK	STATE	PER CAPITA	RANK	STATE	PER CAPITA
1	Alaska	$18,831	26	New Mexico	$3,295
2	Delaware	5,912	27	South Dakota	3,267
3	Utah	5,810	28	Montana	3,190
4	New York	5,254	29	California	3,080
5	Louisiana	5,109	30	Tennessee	2,953
6	Wyoming	4,977	31	Vermont	2,942
7	Washington	4,859	32	North Dakota	2,904
8	Arizona	4,778	33	Kansas	2,809
9	Massachusetts	4,482	34	Illinois	2,798
10	Connecticut	4,360	35	South Carolina	2,788
11	Rhode Island	4,314	36	Maine	2,767
12	New Jersey	4,219	37	Georgia	2,685
13	Florida	4,132	38	Oklahoma	2,617
14	Minnesota	4,006	39	Virginia	2,554
15	Hawaii	3,996	40	Alabama	2,530
16	New Hampshire	3,910	41	Wisconsin	2,472
17	Nebraska	3,858	42	North Carolina	2,372
18	Pennsylvania	3,855	43	Michigan	2,307
19	Colorado	3,797	44	Ohio	2,138
20	Texas	3,781	45	Missouri	1,970
21	Nevada	3,621	46	Indiana	1,963
22	Kentucky	3,598	47	Arkansas	1,962
23	Oregon	3,562	48	Iowa	1,891
24	West Virginia	3,505	49	Mississippi	1,853
25	Maryland	3,406	50	Idaho	1,518

District of Columbia 7,283

Source: U.S. Bureau of the Census,

"Government Finances: 1989-90 (Preliminary Report)" (GF-90-5P, September 1991)

*Preliminary. Rates calculated by the editors using 1990 Census population counts.

State Government Debt Outstanding in 1990

National Total = $318,237,000,000

RANK	STATE	DEBT	%
1	New York	$46,547,000,000	14.63%
2	California	28,866,000,000	9.07%
3	New Jersey	18,908,000,000	5.94%
4	Massachusetts	18,715,000,000	5.88%
5	Illinois	15,262,000,000	4.80%
6	Louisiana	12,770,000,000	4.01%
7	Ohio	11,209,000,000	3.52%
8	Connecticut	10,988,000,000	3.45%
9	Pennsylvania	10,926,000,000	3.43%
10	Florida	9,950,000,000	3.13%
11	Michigan	9,170,000,000	2.88%
12	Texas	7,864,000,000	2.47%
13	Maryland	6,644,000,000	2.09%
14	Oregon	6,558,000,000	2.06%
15	Wisconsin	6,119,000,000	1.92%
16	Virginia	6,083,000,000	1.91%
17	Washington	5,686,000,000	1.79%
18	Alaska	5,536,000,000	1.74%
19	Kentucky	5,295,000,000	1.66%
20	Missouri	5,250,000,000	1.65%
21	Indiana	4,140,000,000	1.30%
22	Alabama	3,979,000,000	1.25%
23	South Carolina	3,894,000,000	1.22%
24	Minnesota	3,764,000,000	1.18%
25	Oklahoma	3,714,000,000	1.17%

RANK	STATE	DEBT	%
26	Rhode Island	$3,616,000,000	1.14%
27	Hawaii	3,396,000,000	1.07%
28	New Hampshire	3,338,000,000	1.05%
29	Georgia	3,117,000,000	0.98%
30	North Carolina	3,071,000,000	0.97%
31	Delaware	2,978,000,000	0.94%
32	Tennessee	2,618,000,000	0.82%
33	West Virginia	2,471,000,000	0.78%
34	Colorado	2,422,000,000	0.76%
35	Arizona	2,193,000,000	0.69%
36	Maine	2,125,000,000	0.67%
37	Iowa	1,875,000,000	0.59%
38	New Mexico	1,830,000,000	0.58%
39	Utah	1,790,000,000	0.56%
40	South Dakota	1,787,000,000	0.56%
41	Arkansas	1,747,000,000	0.55%
42	Nevada	1,573,000,000	0.49%
43	Montana	1,396,000,000	0.44%
44	Nebraska	1,361,000,000	0.43%
45	Mississippi	1,343,000,000	0.42%
46	Vermont	1,259,000,000	0.40%
47	Idaho	977,000,000	0.31%
48	Wyoming	938,000,000	0.29%
49	North Dakota	872,000,000	0.27%
50	Kansas	306,000,000	0.10%

Source: U.S. Bureau of the Census,
"State Government Finance: 1990" (GF-90-3, August 1991)

Per Capita State Government Debt Outstanding in 1990

National Per Capita = $1,280*

RANK	STATE	PER CAPITA		RANK	STATE	PER CAPITA
1	Alaska	$10,065		26	Washington	$1,168
2	Delaware	4,470		27	South Carolina	1,117
3	Rhode Island	3,604		28	Utah	1,039
4	Connecticut	3,343		29	Ohio	1,033
5	Massachusetts	3,111		30	Missouri	1,026
6	Hawaii	3,064		31	Michigan	987
7	Louisiana	3,026		32	Alabama	985
8	New Hampshire	3,009		33	Virginia	983
9	New York	2,587		34	California	970
10	South Dakota	2,568		34	Idaho	970
11	New Jersey	2,446		36	Pennsylvania	920
12	Oregon	2,307		37	Nebraska	862
13	Vermont	2,237		38	Minnesota	860
14	Wyoming	2,068		39	Florida	769
15	Montana	1,747		40	Indiana	747
16	Maine	1,731		41	Arkansas	743
17	Kentucky	1,437		42	Colorado	735
18	Maryland	1,390		43	Iowa	675
19	West Virginia	1,378		44	Arizona	598
20	North Dakota	1,365		45	Tennessee	537
21	Illinois	1,335		46	Mississippi	522
22	Nevada	1,309		47	Georgia	481
23	Wisconsin	1,251		48	North Carolina	463
24	New Mexico	1,208		48	Texas	463
25	Oklahoma	1,181		50	Kansas	124

Source: U.S. Bureau of the Census,

"Government Finances: 1989-90 (Preliminary Report)" (GF-90-5P, September 1991)

*Rates calculated by the editors using 1990 Census population counts.

Per Capita Interest on State Government General Debt in 1990

National Per Capita = $86.79

RANK	STATE	PER CAPITA		RANK	STATE	PER CAPITA
1	Alaska	$941.31		26	New Mexico	$75.75
2	Delaware	327.61		27	Ohio	73.81
3	Rhode Island	257.92		28	Nebraska	72.81
4	Louisiana	226.24		29	Virginia	72.64
5	Connecticut	212.80		30	Idaho	71.51
6	South Dakota	206.27		31	Missouri	70.91
7	Massachusetts	201.88		32	Pennsylvania	66.60
8	New Hampshire	192.95		33	Michigan	66.35
9	New Jersey	188.00		34	California	65.88
10	Hawaii	176.89		35	Colorado	62.39
11	Vermont	170.66		36	Minnesota	62.00
12	Oregon	165.84		37	Arkansas	52.03
13	Wyoming	162.09		38	Indiana	51.61
14	New York	159.89		39	Florida	51.50
15	Maine	128.75		40	Alabama	51.49
16	Montana	125.73		41	Iowa	47.04
17	North Dakota	114.23		42	Oklahoma	46.62
18	West Virginia	95.87		43	South Carolina	44.29
19	Nevada	90.10		44	Tennessee	42.90
20	Kentucky	89.14		45	Arizona	41.34
21	Maryland	88.92		46	Mississippi	38.63
22	Wisconsin	88.27		47	Georgia	34.81
23	Illinois	84.87		48	North Carolina	32.99
24	Utah	77.36		49	Texas	27.51
25	Washington	76.48		50	Kansas	10.17

Source: U.S. Bureau of the Census,
"State Government Finance: 1990" (GF-90-3, August 1991)

Local Government Debt Outstanding in 1990

National Total = $539,607,122,000*

RANK	STATE	DEBT	%	RANK	STATE	DEBT	%
1	California	$62,809,343,000	11.64%	26	Wisconsin	$5,970,923,000	1.11%
2	Texas	56,360,691,000	10.44%	27	South Carolina	5,828,153,000	1.08%
3	New York	47,967,129,000	8.89%	28	Missouri	4,831,660,000	0.90%
4	Florida	43,513,675,000	8.06%	29	Alaska	4,822,323,000	0.89%
5	Pennsylvania	34,878,050,000	6.46%	30	Nebraska	4,729,104,000	0.88%
6	Washington	17,959,765,000	3.33%	31	Oklahoma	4,518,574,000	0.84%
7	Illinois	16,715,438,000	3.10%	32	West Virginia	3,814,989,000	0.71%
8	Arizona	15,320,533,000	2.84%	33	Oregon	3,566,667,000	0.66%
9	Georgia	14,279,568,000	2.65%	34	Mississippi	3,426,140,000	0.63%
10	Minnesota	13,764,029,000	2.55%	35	Iowa	3,374,887,000	0.63%
11	New Jersey	13,707,841,000	2.54%	36	Connecticut	3,343,590,000	0.62%
12	North Carolina	12,651,700,000	2.34%	37	New Mexico	3,162,506,000	0.59%
13	Michigan	12,272,940,000	2.27%	38	Arkansas	2,865,179,000	0.53%
14	Ohio	11,982,322,000	2.22%	39	Nevada	2,779,649,000	0.52%
15	Tennessee	11,785,212,000	2.18%	40	Wyoming	1,319,298,000	0.24%
16	Colorado	10,086,604,000	1.87%	41	Maine	1,272,596,000	0.24%
17	Virginia	9,721,461,000	1.80%	42	Montana	1,153,198,000	0.21%
18	Maryland	9,644,259,000	1.79%	43	Hawaii	1,032,796,000	0.19%
19	Louisiana	8,789,901,000	1.63%	44	New Hampshire	999,048,000	0.19%
20	Massachusetts	8,253,371,000	1.53%	45	North Dakota	982,777,000	0.18%
21	Utah	8,219,234,000	1.52%	46	Delaware	960,556,000	0.18%
22	Kentucky	7,963,098,000	1.48%	47	Rhode Island	713,590,000	0.13%
23	Indiana	6,743,304,000	1.25%	48	Idaho	550,994,000	0.10%
24	Kansas	6,652,800,000	1.23%	49	South Dakota	486,782,000	0.09%
25	Alabama	6,242,010,000	1.16%	50	Vermont	396,875,000	0.07%
					District of Columbia	4,419,990,000	0.82%

Source: U.S. Bureau of the Census,
    "Government Finances: 1989-90 (Preliminary Report)" (GF-90-5P, September 1991)
*Preliminary.

Per Capita Local Government Debt Outstanding in 1990

National Per Capita = $2,170*

RANK	STATE	PER CAPITA		RANK	STATE	PER CAPITA
1	Alaska	$8,767		26	Virginia	$1,571
2	Utah	4,771		27	Alabama	1,545
3	Arizona	4,180		28	North Dakota	1,538
4	Washington	3,690		29	Illinois	1,462
5	Florida	3,363		30	Montana	1,443
6	Texas	3,318		31	Delaware	1,442
7	Minnesota	3,146		32	Oklahoma	1,436
8	Colorado	3,062		33	Massachusetts	1,372
9	Nebraska	2,996		34	Mississippi	1,331
10	Pennsylvania	2,935		35	Michigan	1,320
11	Wyoming	2,909		36	Oregon	1,255
12	Kansas	2,685		37	Wisconsin	1,221
13	New York	2,666		38	Arkansas	1,219
14	Tennessee	2,416		39	Indiana	1,216
15	Nevada	2,313		40	Iowa	1,215
16	Georgia	2,204		41	Ohio	1,105
17	Kentucky	2,161		42	Maine	1,036
18	West Virginia	2,127		43	Connecticut	1,017
19	California	2,111		44	Missouri	944
20	New Mexico	2,087		45	Hawaii	932
21	Louisiana	2,083		46	New Hampshire	901
22	Maryland	2,017		47	Rhode Island	711
23	North Carolina	1,909		48	Vermont	705
24	New Jersey	1,773		49	South Dakota	699
25	South Carolina	1,672		50	Idaho	547
					District of Columbia	7,283

Source: U.S. Bureau of the Census,

"Government Finances: 1989-90 (Preliminary Report)" (GF-90-5P, September 1991)

*Preliminary. Rates calculated by the editors using 1990 Census population counts.

State and Local Property Tax Revenue in 1990

National Total = $155,758,980,000*

RANK	STATE	PROPERTY TAX	%	RANK	STATE	PROPERTY TAX	%
1	New York	$18,413,224,000	11.82%	26	Tennessee	$1,566,790,000	1.01%
2	California	18,005,900,000	11.56%	27	South Carolina	1,399,646,000	0.90%
3	Texas	11,051,863,000	7.10%	28	New Hampshire	1,279,527,000	0.82%
4	New Jersey	8,939,322,000	5.74%	29	Nebraska	1,183,506,000	0.76%
5	Illinois	8,626,242,000	5.54%	30	Louisiana	1,133,895,000	0.73%
6	Florida	7,916,723,000	5.08%	31	Kentucky	929,702,000	0.60%
7	Michigan	7,618,047,000	4.89%	32	Maine	886,541,000	0.57%
8	Pennsylvania	6,126,246,000	3.93%	33	Mississippi	877,163,000	0.56%
9	Ohio	5,594,600,000	3.59%	34	Oklahoma	872,770,000	0.56%
10	Massachusetts	4,671,998,000	3.00%	35	Rhode Island	807,279,000	0.52%
11	Virginia	3,698,150,000	2.37%	36	Utah	743,614,000	0.48%
12	Wisconsin	3,610,402,000	2.32%	37	Alaska	685,358,000	0.44%
13	Connecticut	3,469,768,000	2.23%	38	Montana	661,417,000	0.42%
14	Georgia	3,198,094,000	2.05%	39	Alabama	658,810,000	0.42%
15	Minnesota	3,095,007,000	1.99%	40	Arkansas	536,465,000	0.34%
16	Washington	2,841,487,000	1.82%	41	Nevada	508,458,000	0.33%
17	Maryland	2,822,266,000	1.81%	42	Vermont	464,940,000	0.30%
18	Indiana	2,619,156,000	1.68%	43	West Virginia	459,656,000	0.30%
19	Oregon	2,425,276,000	1.56%	44	Hawaii	425,552,000	0.27%
20	North Carolina	2,336,587,000	1.50%	45	Idaho	417,809,000	0.27%
21	Arizona	2,329,522,000	1.50%	46	Wyoming	411,597,000	0.26%
22	Colorado	2,254,745,000	1.45%	47	South Dakota	405,706,000	0.26%
23	Iowa	1,833,359,000	1.18%	48	New Mexico	331,030,000	0.21%
24	Missouri	1,748,824,000	1.12%	49	North Dakota	304,872,000	0.20%
25	Kansas	1,631,463,000	1.05%	50	Delaware	201,431,000	0.13%
					District of Columbia	727,175,000	0.47%

Source: U.S. Bureau of the Census,
    "Government Finances: 1989-90 (Preliminary Report)" (GF-90-5P, September 1991)
*Preliminary.

Per Capita State and Local Government Property Tax Revenue in 1990

National Per Capita = $626*

RANK	STATE	PER CAPITA	RANK	STATE	PER CAPITA
1	Alaska	$1,246	26	Maryland	$590
2	New Jersey	1,156	27	Washington	584
3	New Hampshire	1,154	28	South Dakota	583
4	Connecticut	1,056	29	Ohio	516
5	New York	1,023	29	Pennsylvania	516
6	Wyoming	907	31	Georgia	494
7	Oregon	853	32	North Dakota	477
8	Montana	828	33	Indiana	472
9	Vermont	826	34	Utah	432
10	Michigan	820	35	Nevada	423
11	Rhode Island	804	36	Idaho	415
12	Massachusetts	777	37	South Carolina	401
13	Illinois	755	38	Hawaii	384
14	Nebraska	750	39	North Carolina	352
15	Wisconsin	738	40	Missouri	342
16	Maine	722	41	Mississippi	341
17	Minnesota	707	42	Tennessee	321
18	Colorado	684	43	Delaware	302
19	Iowa	660	44	Oklahoma	277
20	Kansas	658	45	Louisiana	269
21	Texas	651	46	West Virginia	256
22	Arizona	636	47	Kentucky	252
23	Florida	612	48	Arkansas	228
24	California	605	49	New Mexico	218
25	Virginia	598	50	Alabama	163

	District of Columbia	1,198

Source: U.S. Bureau of the Census,

"Government Finances: 1989-90 (Preliminary Report)" (GF-90-5P, September 1991)

*Preliminary. Rates calculated by the editors using 1990 Census population counts.

State Tax Revenue in 1991*

National Total = $309,293,273,000**

RANK	STATE	STATE TAXES	%	RANK	STATE	STATE TAXES	%
1	California	$44,743,011,000	14.47%	26	Oklahoma	$3,872,552,000	1.25%
2	New York	28,954,556,000	9.36%	27	Iowa	3,432,553,000	1.11%
3	Texas	15,712,737,000	5.08%	28	Colorado	3,163,025,000	1.02%
4	Florida	13,389,595,000	4.33%	29	Oregon	3,033,502,000	0.98%
5	Pennsylvania	13,242,472,000	4.28%	30	Kansas	2,835,467,000	0.92%
6	Illinois	13,235,381,000	4.28%	31	Hawaii	2,618,956,000	0.85%
7	New Jersey	11,773,720,000	3.81%	32	Mississippi	2,486,588,000	0.80%
8	Ohio	11,555,042,000	3.74%	33	West Virginia	2,341,408,000	0.76%
9	Michigan	10,682,655,000	3.45%	34	Arkansas	2,332,617,000	0.75%
10	Massachusetts	9,382,269,000	3.03%	35	New Mexico	2,070,412,000	0.67%
11	Washington	7,948,830,000	2.57%	36	Utah	1,811,545,000	0.59%
12	North Carolina	7,847,725,000	2.54%	37	Nebraska	1,762,463,000	0.57%
13	Georgia	7,144,952,000	2.31%	38	Maine	1,525,208,000	0.49%
14	Minnesota	7,018,262,000	2.27%	39	Idaho	1,183,837,000	0.38%
15	Wisconsin	7,017,024,000	2.27%	40	Delaware	1,163,747,000	0.38%
16	Virginia	6,861,736,000	2.22%	41	Montana	856,323,000	0.28%
17	Maryland	6,401,426,000	2.07%	42	North Dakota	745,802,000	0.24%
18	Indiana	6,186,268,000	2.00%	43	Vermont	686,818,000	0.22%
19	Connecticut	5,268,657,000	1.70%	44	Wyoming	609,590,000	0.20%
20	Missouri	4,995,993,000	1.62%	45	New Hampshire	599,857,000	0.19%
21	Arizona	4,602,197,000	1.49%	46	South Dakota	516,187,000	0.17%
22	Louisiana	4,595,178,000	1.49%	–	Alaska***	N/A	N/A
23	Tennessee	4,264,169,000	1.38%	–	Kentucky***	N/A	N/A
24	South Carolina	3,944,548,000	1.28%	–	Nevada***	N/A	N/A
25	Alabama	3,939,403,000	1.27%	–	Rhode Island***	N/A	N/A

District of Columbia****   2,356,210,000   0.76%

Source: U.S. Bureau of the Census,
   "Quarterly Summary of Federal, State, and Local Tax Revenue" (GT-91Q2, Issued December 1991)
*For year ending June 30, 1991.
**Includes amounts not shown separately.
***Not Available.   ****DC is not included in national total but is shown for comparison purposes.

Per Capita State Tax Revenue in 1991*

National Per Capita = $1,226

RANK	STATE	PER CAPITA	RANK	STATE	PER CAPITA
1	Hawaii	$2,307	26	South Carolina	$1,108
2	Delaware	1,711	27	Pennsylvania	1,107
3	New York	1,603	28	Nebraska	1,106
4	Connecticut	1,601	29	Indiana	1,103
5	Minnesota	1,584	30	Virginia	1,092
5	Washington	1,584	31	Louisiana	1,081
7	Massachusetts	1,565	32	Georgia	1,079
8	New Jersey	1,517	33	Montana	1,060
9	California	1,473	34	Ohio	1,056
10	Wisconsin	1,416	35	Oregon	1,038
11	New Mexico	1,337	36	Utah	1,023
12	Wyoming	1,325	37	Florida	1,008
13	Maryland	1,317	38	Arkansas	983
14	West Virginia	1,300	39	Missouri	969
15	Maine	1,235	40	Alabama	963
16	Iowa	1,228	41	Mississippi	960
17	Arizona	1,227	42	Colorado	937
18	Oklahoma	1,220	43	Texas	906
19	Vermont	1,211	44	Tennessee	861
20	North Dakota	1,174	45	South Dakota	734
21	North Carolina	1,165	46	New Hampshire	543
22	Illinois	1,147	–	Alaska**	N/A
23	Michigan	1,140	–	Kentucky**	N/A
24	Idaho	1,139	–	Nevada**	N/A
25	Kansas	1,136	–	Rhode Island**	N/A

District of Columbia   3,940

Source: U.S. Bureau of the Census,

"Quarterly Summary of Federal, State, and Local Tax Revenue" (GT-91Q2, Issued December 1991)

*For year ending June 30, 1991. Determined by the editors using July 1, 1991 Census population estimate.

**Not Available.

State Individual Income Tax Revenue in 1991*

National Total = $98,661,328,000**

RANK	STATE	INCOME TAX	%
1	California	$16,817,244,000	17.05%
2	New York	14,502,334,000	14.70%
3	Massachusetts	5,064,256,000	5.13%
4	Illinois	4,538,544,000	4.60%
5	Ohio	4,216,655,000	4.27%
6	Michigan	3,639,563,000	3.69%
7	North Carolina	3,534,474,000	3.58%
8	New Jersey	3,391,026,000	3.44%
9	Pennsylvania	3,274,657,000	3.32%
10	Virginia	3,251,476,000	3.30%
11	Wisconsin	3,003,381,000	3.04%
12	Minnesota	2,974,553,000	3.01%
13	Georgia	2,947,681,000	2.99%
14	Maryland	2,931,020,000	2.97%
15	Indiana	2,183,972,000	2.21%
16	Oregon	1,983,705,000	2.01%
17	Missouri	1,829,224,000	1.85%
18	Colorado	1,461,191,000	1.48%
19	South Carolina	1,386,649,000	1.41%
20	Iowa	1,343,571,000	1.36%
21	Arizona	1,245,646,000	1.26%
22	Oklahoma	1,218,279,000	1.23%
23	Alabama	1,160,005,000	1.18%
24	Kansas	880,739,000	0.89%
25	Hawaii	872,734,000	0.88%

RANK	STATE	INCOME TAX	%
26	Louisiana	$798,459,000	0.81%
27	Arkansas	793,939,000	0.80%
28	Utah	646,274,000	0.66%
29	Nebraska	603,112,000	0.61%
30	West Virginia	587,474,000	0.60%
31	Maine	580,749,000	0.59%
32	Mississippi	479,602,000	0.49%
33	Connecticut	474,609,000	0.48%
34	Delaware	463,793,000	0.47%
35	Idaho	446,149,000	0.45%
36	New Mexico	392,401,000	0.40%
37	Montana	281,638,000	0.29%
38	Vermont	257,517,000	0.26%
39	North Dakota	114,298,000	0.12%
40	Tennessee	97,033,000	0.10%
41	New Hampshire	36,949,000	0.04%
42	Alaska	0	0.00%
42	Florida	0	0.00%
42	Nevada	0	0.00%
42	South Dakota	0	0.00%
42	Texas	0	0.00%
42	Washington	0	0.00%
42	Wyoming	0	0.00%
–	Kentucky***	N/A	N/A
–	Rhode Island***	N/A	N/A

District of Columbia****   619,657,000   0.63%

Source: U.S. Bureau of the Census,

"Quarterly Summary of Federal, State, and Local Tax Revenue" (GT-91Q2, Issued December 1991)

*For year ending June 30, 1991.

**Includes amounts not shown separately.

***Not Available.   ****DC is not included in national total but is shown for comparison purposes.

Per Capita State Individual Income Tax Revenue in 1991*

National Per Capita = $391.24

RANK	STATE	PER CAPITA		RANK	STATE	PER CAPITA
1	Massachusetts	$844.61		26	Utah	$365.13
2	New York	803.10		27	Missouri	354.64
3	Hawaii	768.93		28	Kansas	353.00
4	Delaware	682.05		29	Montana	348.56
5	Oregon	678.89		30	Arkansas	334.71
6	Minnesota	671.15		31	Arizona	332.17
7	Wisconsin	606.13		32	West Virginia	326.19
8	Maryland	603.09		33	Alabama	283.69
9	California	553.56		34	Pennsylvania	273.78
10	North Carolina	524.64		35	New Mexico	253.49
11	Virginia	517.26		36	Louisiana	187.78
12	Iowa	480.71		37	Mississippi	185.03
13	Maine	470.24		38	North Dakota	180.00
14	Vermont	454.17		39	Connecticut	144.21
15	Georgia	445.07		40	New Hampshire	33.44
16	New Jersey	436.99		41	Tennessee	19.59
17	Colorado	432.69		42	Alaska	0.00
18	Idaho	429.40		42	Florida	0.00
19	Illinois	393.19		42	Nevada	0.00
20	South Carolina	389.51		42	South Dakota	0.00
21	Indiana	389.30		42	Texas	0.00
22	Michigan	388.51		42	Washington	0.00
23	Ohio	385.47		42	Wyoming	0.00
24	Oklahoma	383.71		–	Kentucky**	N/A
25	Nebraska	378.60		–	Rhode Island**	N/A

District of Columbia   1,036.22

Source: U.S. Bureau of the Census,

"Quarterly Summary of Federal, State, and Local Tax Revenue" (GT-91Q2, Issued December 1991)

For year ending June 30, 1991. Determined by the editors using July 1, 1991 Census population estimate.

**Not Available.*

State Corporate Net Income Tax Revenue in 1991*

National Total = $20,757,632,000**

RANK	STATE	CORPORATE TAX	%	RANK	STATE	CORPORATE TAX	%
1	California	$4,440,479,000	21.39%	26	South Carolina	$151,434,000	0.73%
2	New York	2,242,160,000	10.80%	27	Oregon	149,074,000	0.72%
3	Michigan	1,686,064,000	8.12%	28	Mississippi	139,823,000	0.67%
4	Pennsylvania	1,157,394,000	5.58%	29	Oklahoma	137,581,000	0.66%
5	New Jersey	1,030,621,000	4.97%	30	Delaware	122,457,000	0.59%
6	Illinois	940,760,000	4.53%	31	Arkansas	122,234,000	0.59%
7	Massachusetts	719,568,000	3.47%	32	New Hampshire	122,205,000	0.59%
8	Ohio	630,183,000	3.04%	33	Colorado	117,345,000	0.57%
9	Connecticut	538,901,000	2.60%	34	Hawaii	116,380,000	0.56%
10	North Carolina	499,957,000	2.41%	35	Nebraska	81,947,000	0.39%
11	Florida	496,725,000	2.39%	36	Utah	80,510,000	0.39%
12	Minnesota	458,271,000	2.21%	37	Maine	76,052,000	0.37%
13	Wisconsin	440,918,000	2.12%	38	Montana	70,825,000	0.34%
14	Georgia	417,007,000	2.01%	39	Idaho	59,712,000	0.29%
15	Tennessee	345,542,000	1.66%	40	New Mexico	52,597,000	0.25%
16	Louisiana	333,936,000	1.61%	41	North Dakota	49,112,000	0.24%
17	Indiana	319,442,000	1.54%	42	South Dakota	38,778,000	0.19%
18	Virginia	285,106,000	1.37%	43	Vermont	27,386,000	0.13%
19	Maryland	255,486,000	1.23%	44	Nevada	0	0.00%
20	Missouri	224,759,000	1.08%	44	Texas	0	0.00%
21	Kansas	212,948,000	1.03%	44	Washington	0	0.00%
22	Iowa	201,930,000	0.97%	44	Wyoming	0	0.00%
23	Arizona	192,325,000	0.93%	–	Alaska***	N/A	N/A
24	West Virginia	191,214,000	0.92%	–	Kentucky***	N/A	N/A
25	Alabama	169,558,000	0.82%	–	Rhode Island***	N/A	N/A

District of Columbia****   131,878,000   0.64%

Source: U.S. Bureau of the Census,
   "Quarterly Summary of Federal, State, and Local Tax Revenue" (GT-91Q2, Issued December 1991)

*For year ending June 30, 1991.

**Includes amounts not shown separately.

***Not Available.   ****DC is not included in national total but is shown for comparison purposes.

Per Capita State Corporate Net Income Tax Revenue in 1991*

National Per Capita = $82.31

RANK	STATE	PER CAPITA		RANK	STATE	PER CAPITA
1	Delaware	$180.08		26	Indiana	$56.94
2	Michigan	179.98		27	South Dakota	55.16
3	Connecticut	163.75		28	Mississippi	53.94
4	California	146.16		29	Maryland	52.57
5	New Jersey	132.81		30	Arkansas	51.53
6	New York	124.16		31	Nebraska	51.44
7	Massachusetts	120.01		32	Arizona	51.29
8	New Hampshire	110.59		33	Oregon	51.02
9	West Virginia	106.17		34	Vermont	48.30
10	Minnesota	103.40		35	Utah	45.49
11	Hawaii	102.54		36	Virginia	45.36
12	Pennsylvania	96.76		37	Missouri	43.57
13	Wisconsin	88.98		38	Oklahoma	43.33
14	Montana	87.65		39	South Carolina	42.54
15	Kansas	85.35		40	Alabama	41.47
16	Illinois	81.50		41	Florida	37.41
17	Louisiana	78.54		42	Colorado	34.75
18	North Dakota	77.34		43	New Mexico	33.98
19	North Carolina	74.21		44	Nevada	0.00
20	Iowa	72.25		44	Texas	0.00
21	Tennessee	69.76		44	Washington	0.00
22	Georgia	62.96		44	Wyoming	0.00
23	Maine	61.58		–	Alaska**	N/A
24	Ohio	57.61		–	Kentucky**	N/A
25	Idaho	57.47		–	Rhode Island**	N/A

District of Columbia   220.53

Source: U.S. Bureau of the Census,
"Quarterly Summary of Federal, State, and Local Tax Revenue" (GT-91Q2, Issued December 1991)
*For year ending June 30, 1991. Determined by the editors using July 1, 1991 Census population estimate.
**Not Available.

State Sales Tax Revenue in 1991*

National Total = $103,273,986,000**

RANK	STATE	SALES TAX	%	RANK	STATE	SALES TAX	%
1	California	$14,294,104,000	13.84%	26	Mississippi	$1,120,155,000	1.08%
2	Texas	8,182,086,000	7.92%	27	Alabama	1,051,538,000	1.02%
3	Florida	8,107,647,000	7.85%	28	Iowa	977,057,000	0.95%
4	New York	6,063,535,000	5.87%	29	Oklahoma	963,579,000	0.93%
5	Washington	4,758,204,000	4.61%	30	Kansas	918,211,000	0.89%
6	Pennsylvania	4,197,700,000	4.06%	31	New Mexico	914,287,000	0.89%
7	Illinois	4,107,890,000	3.98%	32	Arkansas	882,676,000	0.85%
8	New Jersey	4,042,805,000	3.91%	33	Colorado	844,673,000	0.82%
9	Ohio	3,574,541,000	3.46%	34	West Virginia	817,256,000	0.79%
10	Michigan	2,963,228,000	2.87%	35	Utah	737,855,000	0.71%
11	Connecticut	2,670,308,000	2.59%	36	Nebraska	620,487,000	0.60%
12	Georgia	2,663,201,000	2.58%	37	Maine	497,069,000	0.48%
13	Indiana	2,537,926,000	2.46%	38	Idaho	404,164,000	0.39%
14	Tennessee	2,363,252,000	2.29%	39	North Dakota	264,790,000	0.26%
15	Wisconsin	2,026,710,000	1.96%	40	South Dakota	247,974,000	0.24%
16	Arizona	2,005,802,000	1.94%	41	Wyoming	170,873,000	0.17%
17	Minnesota	1,963,433,000	1.90%	42	Vermont	125,611,000	0.12%
18	Massachusetts	1,909,434,000	1.85%	43	Alaska	0	0.00%
19	Missouri	1,863,373,000	1.80%	43	Delaware	0	0.00%
20	North Carolina	1,688,321,000	1.63%	43	Montana	0	0.00%
21	Louisiana	1,554,795,000	1.51%	43	New Hampshire	0	0.00%
22	Virginia	1,550,098,000	1.50%	43	Oregon	0	0.00%
23	Maryland	1,540,887,000	1.49%	–	Kentucky***	N/A	N/A
24	South Carolina	1,437,473,000	1.39%	–	Nevada***	N/A	N/A
25	Hawaii	1,278,737,000	1.24%	–	Rhode Island***	N/A	N/A

District of Columbia**** 473,128,000 0.46%

Source: U.S. Bureau of the Census,

"Quarterly Summary of Federal, State, and Local Tax Revenue" (GT-91Q2, Issued December 1991)

*For year ending June 30, 1991.

**Includes amounts not shown separately.

***Not Available. ****DC is not included in national total but is shown for comparison purposes.

Per Capita State Sales Tax Revenue in 1991*

National Per Capita = $410

RANK	STATE	PER CAPITA
1	Hawaii	$1,127
2	Washington	948
3	Connecticut	811
4	Florida	611
5	New Mexico	591
6	Arizona	535
7	New Jersey	521
8	Tennessee	477
9	Texas	472
10	California	471
11	West Virginia	454
12	Indiana	452
13	Minnesota	443
14	Mississippi	432
15	North Dakota	417
15	Utah	417
17	Wisconsin	409
18	South Carolina	404
19	Georgia	402
19	Maine	402
21	Nebraska	390
22	Idaho	389
23	Arkansas	372
24	Wyoming	371
25	Kansas	368

RANK	STATE	PER CAPITA
26	Louisiana	$366
27	Missouri	361
28	Illinois	356
29	South Dakota	353
30	Pennsylvania	351
31	Iowa	350
32	New York	336
33	Ohio	327
34	Massachusetts	318
35	Maryland	317
36	Michigan	316
37	Oklahoma	303
38	Alabama	257
39	North Carolina	251
40	Colorado	250
41	Virginia	247
42	Vermont	222
43	Alaska	0
43	Delaware	0
43	Montana	0
43	New Hampshire	0
43	Oregon	0
–	Kentucky**	N/A
–	Nevada**	N/A
–	Rhode Island**	N/A

	District of Columbia	791

Source: U.S. Bureau of the Census,

"Quarterly Summary of Federal, State, and Local Tax Revenue" (GT-91Q2, Issued December 1991)

*For year ending June 30, 1991. Determined by the editors using July 1, 1991 Census population estimate.

**Not Available.

State Motor Fuel Sales Tax Revenue in 1991*

National Total = $20,573,203,000**

RANK	STATE	FUEL TAX	%	RANK	STATE	FUEL TAX	%
1	California	$2,002,286,000	9.73%	26	Colorado	$328,713,000	1.60%
2	Texas	1,500,607,000	7.29%	27	Oklahoma	321,232,000	1.56%
3	Ohio	1,035,493,000	5.03%	28	Mississippi	319,994,000	1.56%
4	Illinois	1,024,491,000	4.98%	29	Alabama	290,884,000	1.41%
5	North Carolina	825,424,000	4.01%	30	Oregon	258,969,000	1.26%
6	Florida	781,317,000	3.80%	31	Kansas	234,725,000	1.14%
7	Michigan	723,823,000	3.52%	32	Nebraska	222,715,000	1.08%
8	Pennsylvania	722,719,000	3.51%	33	Arkansas	222,287,000	1.08%
9	Tennessee	635,248,000	3.09%	34	West Virginia	205,981,000	1.00%
10	Virginia	620,273,000	3.01%	35	New Mexico	171,976,000	0.84%
11	Indiana	588,048,000	2.86%	36	Utah	163,300,000	0.79%
12	Washington	584,960,000	2.84%	37	Maine	130,004,000	0.63%
13	Wisconsin	546,507,000	2.66%	38	Idaho	111,537,000	0.54%
14	New York	494,042,000	2.40%	39	Montana	110,123,000	0.54%
15	Minnesota	457,572,000	2.22%	40	New Hampshire	90,718,000	0.44%
16	Georgia	451,102,000	2.19%	41	North Dakota	74,247,000	0.36%
17	Massachusetts	448,317,000	2.18%	42	South Dakota	72,855,000	0.35%
18	Louisiana	444,890,000	2.16%	43	Delaware	66,216,000	0.32%
19	Maryland	443,563,000	2.16%	44	Hawaii	53,188,000	0.26%
20	New Jersey	400,186,000	1.95%	45	Vermont	52,212,000	0.25%
21	Missouri	364,998,000	1.77%	46	Wyoming	38,047,000	0.18%
22	Connecticut	363,452,000	1.77%	–	Alaska***	N/A	N/A
23	Arizona	362,019,000	1.76%	–	Kentucky***	N/A	N/A
24	South Carolina	340,112,000	1.65%	–	Nevada***	N/A	N/A
25	Iowa	330,531,000	1.61%	–	Rhode Island***	N/A	N/A
					District of Columbia****	28,335,000	0.14%

Source: U.S. Bureau of the Census,

   "Quarterly Summary of Federal, State, and Local Tax Revenue" (GT-91Q2, Issued December 1991)

*For year ending June 30, 1991.

**Includes amounts not shown separately.

***Not Available.   ****DC is not included in national total but is shown for comparison purposes.

Per Capita State Motor Fuel Sales Tax Revenue in 1991*

National Per Capita = $82

RANK	STATE	PER CAPITA		RANK	STATE	PER CAPITA
1	Nebraska	$140		26	Arkansas	$94
2	Montana	136		26	Kansas	94
3	Tennessee	128		28	Utah	92
4	Mississippi	123		28	Vermont	92
4	North Carolina	123		30	Maryland	91
6	Iowa	118		31	Illinois	89
7	North Dakota	117		31	Oregon	89
7	Washington	117		33	Texas	86
9	West Virginia	114		34	Wyoming	83
10	New Mexico	111		35	New Hampshire	82
11	Connecticut	110		36	Michigan	77
11	Wisconsin	110		37	Massachusetts	75
13	Idaho	107		38	Alabama	71
14	Indiana	105		38	Missouri	71
14	Louisiana	105		40	Georgia	68
14	Maine	105		41	California	66
17	South Dakota	104		42	Pennsylvania	60
18	Minnesota	103		43	Florida	59
19	Oklahoma	101		44	New Jersey	52
20	Virginia	99		45	Hawaii	47
21	Arizona	97		46	New York	27
21	Colorado	97		–	Alaska**	N/A
21	Delaware	97		–	Kentucky**	N/A
24	South Carolina	96		–	Nevada**	N/A
25	Ohio	95		–	Rhode Island**	N/A

District of Columbia		47

Source: U.S. Bureau of the Census,

"Quarterly Summary of Federal, State, and Local Tax Revenue" (GT-91Q2, Issued December 1991)

*For year ending June 30, 1991. Determined by the editors using July 1, 1991 Census population estimate.

**Not Available.

State Tax Rates on Gasoline in 1990

National Weighted Average = 15.39 Cents per Gallon *

RANK	STATE	CENTS PER GALLON	RANK	STATE	CENTS PER GALLON
1	Connecticut	22.00	25	Maine	17.00
1	Washington	22.00	25	Massachusetts	17.00
3	Nebraska	21.70	25	New Mexico	17.00
4	North Carolina	21.50	25	North Dakota	17.00
4	Wisconsin	21.50	25	Oklahoma	17.00
6	West Virginia	20.35	31	New Hampshire	16.60
7	Colorado	20.00	32	Delaware	16.00
7	Iowa	20.00	32	Kansas	16.00
7	Louisiana	20.00	32	South Carolina	16.00
7	Minnesota	20.00	32	Vermont	16.00
7	Montana	20.00	36	Kentucky	15.40
7	Ohio	20.00	37	Indiana	15.00
7	Rhode Island	20.00	37	Michigan	15.00
7	Tennessee	20.00	37	Texas	15.00
15	Illinois	19.00	40	New York	14.375
15	Utah	19.00	41	Arkansas	13.50
17	Maryland	18.50	42	Alabama	13.00
18	Mississippi	18.20	43	Missouri	11.03
19	Idaho	18.00	44	Hawaii	11.00
19	Nevada	18.00	45	Florida	10.90
19	Oregon	18.00	46	New Jersey	10.50
19	South Dakota	18.00	47	California	9.00
23	Pennsylvania	17.80	47	Wyoming	9.00
24	Virginia	17.70	49	Alaska	8.00
25	Arizona	17.00	50	Georgia	7.50
				District of Columbia	18.00

Source: U.S. Department of Transportation, Federal Highway Administration,
"Highway Statistics 1990" (FHWA-PL-91-003)
*As of January 1, 1990. Includes any subsequent changes that occurred throughout 1990.

State Motor Vehicle and Operators' License Tax Revenue in 1991*

National Total = $10,860,257,000**

RANK	STATE	RECEIPTS	%
1	California	$1,298,012,000	11.95%
2	Texas	785,222,000	7.23%
3	Illinois	638,628,000	5.88%
4	New York	620,100,000	5.71%
5	Florida	609,806,000	5.62%
6	Michigan	480,284,000	4.42%
7	Pennsylvania	429,959,000	3.96%
8	Ohio	418,575,000	3.85%
9	Minnesota	389,479,000	3.59%
10	New Jersey	342,176,000	3.15%
11	Oklahoma	319,794,000	2.94%
12	Massachusetts	305,204,000	2.81%
13	Virginia	267,115,000	2.46%
14	North Carolina	255,754,000	2.35%
15	Oregon	255,703,000	2.35%
16	Iowa	229,836,000	2.12%
17	Arizona	216,867,000	2.00%
18	West Virginia	213,255,000	1.96%
19	Missouri	208,279,000	1.92%
20	Wisconsin	175,295,000	1.61%
21	Indiana	165,705,000	1.53%
22	Tennessee	163,087,000	1.50%
23	Connecticut	155,432,000	1.43%
24	Maryland	152,914,000	1.41%
25	Alabama	148,134,000	1.36%

RANK	STATE	RECEIPTS	%
26	Kansas	$113,220,000	1.04%
27	Colorado	103,125,000	0.95%
28	New Mexico	102,334,000	0.94%
29	Georgia	100,102,000	0.92%
30	Washington	86,408,000	0.80%
31	Mississippi	83,621,000	0.77%
32	South Carolina	81,952,000	0.75%
33	Louisiana	76,461,000	0.70%
34	Arkansas	68,773,000	0.63%
35	Nebraska	58,511,000	0.54%
36	Idaho	58,159,000	0.54%
37	New Hampshire	55,737,000	0.51%
38	Maine	54,808,000	0.50%
39	Utah	46,542,000	0.43%
40	South Dakota	41,821,000	0.39%
41	Wyoming	41,083,000	0.38%
42	Vermont	40,773,000	0.38%
43	North Dakota	40,452,000	0.37%
44	Montana	37,674,000	0.35%
45	Hawaii	20,935,000	0.19%
46	Delaware	20,628,000	0.19%
–	Alaska***	N/A	N/A
–	Kentucky***	N/A	N/A
–	Nevada***	N/A	N/A
–	Rhode Island***	N/A	N/A

District of Columbia****   18,026,000   0.17%

Source: U.S. Bureau of the Census,

"Quarterly Summary of Federal, State, and Local Tax Revenue" (GT–91Q2, Issued December 1991)

*For year ending June 30, 1991.

**Includes amounts not shown separately.

***Not Available.   ****DC is not included in national total but is shown for comparison purposes.

Per Capita State Motor Vehicle and Operators' License Tax Revenue in 1991*

National Per Capita = $43.07

RANK	STATE	PER CAPITA	RANK	STATE	PER CAPITA
1	West Virginia	$118.41	26	Missouri	$40.38
2	Oklahoma	100.72	27	Ohio	38.26
3	Wyoming	89.31	28	North Carolina	37.96
4	Minnesota	87.88	29	Nebraska	36.73
5	Oregon	87.51	30	Alabama	36.23
6	Iowa	82.23	31	Pennsylvania	35.95
7	Vermont	71.91	32	Wisconsin	35.38
8	New Mexico	66.11	33	New York	34.34
9	North Dakota	63.70	34	Tennessee	32.93
10	South Dakota	59.49	35	Mississippi	32.26
11	Arizona	57.83	36	Maryland	31.46
12	Idaho	55.98	37	Colorado	30.54
13	Illinois	55.33	38	Delaware	30.34
14	Michigan	51.27	39	Indiana	29.54
15	Massachusetts	50.90	40	Arkansas	28.99
16	New Hampshire	50.44	41	Utah	26.29
17	Connecticut	47.23	42	South Carolina	23.02
18	Montana	46.63	43	Hawaii	18.44
19	Florida	45.93	44	Louisiana	17.98
20	Kansas	45.38	45	Washington	17.22
21	Texas	45.26	46	Georgia	15.11
22	Maine	44.38	–	Alaska**	N/A
23	New Jersey	44.09	–	Kentucky**	N/A
24	California	42.73	–	Nevada**	N/A
25	Virginia	42.49	–	Rhode Island**	N/A

District of Columbia 30.14

Source: U.S. Bureau of the Census,

"Quarterly Summary of Federal, State, and Local Tax Revenue" (GT-91Q2, Issued December 1991)

*For year ending June 30, 1991. Determined by the editors using July 1, 1991 Census population estimate.

**Not Available.

State Tobacco Product Sales Tax Revenue in 1991*

National Total = $5,905,525,000**

RANK	STATE	TOBACCO TAX	%	RANK	STATE	TOBACCO TAX	%
1	California	$755,530,000	12.79%	26	Arkansas	$60,592,000	1.03%
2	New York	611,497,000	10.35%	27	Kansas	54,584,000	0.92%
3	Texas	594,756,000	10.07%	28	Arizona	51,796,000	0.88%
4	Florida	428,042,000	7.25%	29	Mississippi	50,914,000	0.86%
5	Illinois	319,033,000	5.40%	30	Maine	43,844,000	0.74%
6	New Jersey	275,833,000	4.67%	31	New Hampshire	39,923,000	0.68%
7	Michigan	255,939,000	4.33%	32	Nebraska	38,962,000	0.66%
8	Pennsylvania	213,419,000	3.61%	33	West Virginia	31,741,000	0.54%
9	Ohio	211,836,000	3.59%	34	South Carolina	30,335,000	0.51%
10	Minnesota	153,740,000	2.60%	35	Hawaii	26,262,000	0.44%
11	Massachusetts	144,423,000	2.45%	36	Utah	20,654,000	0.35%
12	Wisconsin	141,452,000	2.40%	37	New Mexico	17,560,000	0.30%
13	Washington	140,252,000	2.37%	38	Delaware	17,188,000	0.29%
14	Connecticut	122,356,000	2.07%	39	Idaho	17,158,000	0.29%
15	Indiana	102,450,000	1.73%	40	North Dakota	16,531,000	0.28%
16	Iowa	86,523,000	1.47%	41	Virginia	15,458,000	0.26%
17	Georgia	85,162,000	1.44%	42	North Carolina	15,191,000	0.26%
18	Louisiana	83,575,000	1.42%	43	South Dakota	13,890,000	0.24%
19	Oregon	83,231,000	1.41%	44	Montana	12,563,000	0.21%
20	Tennessee	78,390,000	1.33%	45	Vermont	12,094,000	0.20%
21	Missouri	78,063,000	1.32%	46	Wyoming	5,149,000	0.09%
22	Oklahoma	69,632,000	1.18%	–	Alaska***	N/A	N/A
23	Alabama	68,336,000	1.16%	–	Kentucky***	N/A	N/A
24	Maryland	61,320,000	1.04%	–	Nevada***	N/A	N/A
25	Colorado	61,259,000	1.04%	–	Rhode Island***	N/A	N/A
					District of Columbia****	8,804,000	0.15%

Source: U.S. Bureau of the Census,

"Quarterly Summary of Federal, State, and Local Tax Revenue" (GT-91Q2, Issued December 1991)

*For year ending June 30, 1991.

**Includes amounts not shown separately.

***Not Available.   ****DC is not included in national total but is shown for comparison purposes.

Per Capita State Tobacco Product Sales Tax Revenue in 1991*

National Per Capita = $23.42

RANK	STATE	PER CAPITA	RANK	STATE	PER CAPITA
1	Connecticut	$37.18	26	Louisiana	$19.66
2	New Hampshire	36.13	27	Mississippi	19.64
3	New Jersey	35.55	28	Ohio	19.37
4	Maine	35.50	29	Indiana	18.26
5	Minnesota	34.69	30	Colorado	18.14
6	Texas	34.28	31	Pennsylvania	17.84
7	New York	33.86	32	West Virginia	17.62
8	Florida	32.24	33	Alabama	16.71
9	Iowa	30.96	34	Idaho	16.51
10	Wisconsin	28.55	35	Tennessee	15.83
11	Oregon	28.48	36	Montana	15.55
12	Washington	27.95	37	Missouri	15.13
13	Illinois	27.64	38	Arizona	13.81
14	Michigan	27.32	39	Georgia	12.86
15	North Dakota	26.03	40	Maryland	12.62
16	Arkansas	25.54	41	Utah	11.67
17	Delaware	25.28	42	New Mexico	11.34
18	California	24.87	43	Wyoming	11.19
19	Nebraska	24.46	44	South Carolina	8.52
20	Massachusetts	24.09	45	Virginia	2.46
21	Hawaii	23.14	46	North Carolina	2.25
22	Oklahoma	21.93	–	Alaska**	N/A
23	Kansas	21.88	–	Kentucky**	N/A
24	Vermont	21.33	–	Nevada**	N/A
25	South Dakota	19.76	–	Rhode Island**	N/A

District of Columbia   15

Source: U.S. Bureau of the Census,

"Quarterly Summary of Federal, State, and Local Tax Revenue" (GT-91Q2, Issued December 1991)

*For year ending June 30, 1991. Determined by the editors using July 1, 1991 Census population estimate.

**Not Available.

State Alcoholic Beverage Sales Tax Revenue in 1991*

National Total = $3,389,654,000**

RANK	STATE	LIQUOR TAX	%	RANK	STATE	LIQUOR TAX	%
1	Florida	$542,002,000	15.99%	26	Maine	$34,934,000	1.03%
2	Texas	373,656,000	11.02%	27	Mississippi	33,710,000	0.99%
3	New York	247,716,000	7.31%	28	Indiana	33,257,000	0.98%
4	North Carolina	153,565,000	4.53%	29	Maryland	26,324,000	0.78%
5	Pennsylvania	142,908,000	4.22%	30	Arkansas	23,992,000	0.71%
6	California	128,730,000	3.80%	31	Missouri	23,442,000	0.69%
7	Washington	116,747,000	3.44%	32	Colorado	19,414,000	0.57%
8	Georgia	115,042,000	3.39%	33	New Mexico	17,183,000	0.51%
9	Michigan	114,653,000	3.38%	34	Nebraska	15,935,000	0.47%
10	South Carolina	114,187,000	3.37%	35	Vermont	13,975,000	0.41%
11	Alabama	109,068,000	3.22%	36	Utah	13,166,000	0.39%
12	Virginia	85,121,000	2.51%	37	Montana	13,016,000	0.38%
13	New Jersey	81,006,000	2.39%	38	New Hampshire	12,794,000	0.38%
14	Ohio	65,558,000	1.93%	39	Iowa	12,708,000	0.37%
15	Illinois	63,626,000	1.88%	40	Idaho	12,583,000	0.37%
16	Tennessee	62,195,000	1.83%	41	Oregon	10,471,000	0.31%
17	Massachusetts	57,718,000	1.70%	42	South Dakota	9,581,000	0.28%
18	Minnesota	55,573,000	1.64%	43	Delaware	8,896,000	0.26%
19	Oklahoma	55,514,000	1.64%	44	West Virginia	8,563,000	0.25%
20	Connecticut	52,790,000	1.56%	45	North Dakota	6,073,000	0.18%
21	Kansas	51,829,000	1.53%	46	Wyoming	992,000	0.03%
22	Louisiana	42,906,000	1.27%	–	Alaska***	N/A	N/A
23	Hawaii	40,795,000	1.20%	–	Kentucky***	N/A	N/A
24	Arizona	39,809,000	1.17%	–	Nevada***	N/A	N/A
25	Wisconsin	39,787,000	1.17%	–	Rhode Island***	N/A	N/A

District of Columbia****   6,203,000   0.18%

Source: U.S. Bureau of the Census,

"Quarterly Summary of Federal, State, and Local Tax Revenue" (GT-91Q2, Issued December 1991)

*For year ending June 30, 1991.

**Includes amounts not shown separately.

***Not Available.   ****DC is not included in national total but is shown for comparison purposes.

Per Capita State Alcoholic Beverage Sales Tax Revenue in 1991*

National Per Capita = $13.44

RANK	STATE	PER CAPITA	RANK	STATE	PER CAPITA
1	Florida	$40.82	26	New Mexico	$11.10
2	Hawaii	35.94	27	Arizona	10.62
3	South Carolina	32.08	28	New Jersey	10.44
4	Maine	28.29	29	Arkansas	10.11
5	Alabama	26.67	30	Louisiana	10.09
6	Vermont	24.65	31	Nebraska	10.00
7	Washington	23.27	32	Massachusetts	9.63
8	North Carolina	22.79	33	North Dakota	9.56
9	Texas	21.54	34	Wisconsin	8.03
10	Kansas	20.77	35	Utah	7.44
11	Oklahoma	17.48	36	Ohio	5.99
12	Georgia	17.37	37	Indiana	5.93
13	Montana	16.11	38	Colorado	5.75
14	Connecticut	16.04	39	Illinois	5.51
15	New York	13.72	40	Maryland	5.42
16	South Dakota	13.63	41	West Virginia	4.75
17	Virginia	13.54	42	Iowa	4.55
18	Delaware	13.08	43	Missouri	4.54
19	Mississippi	13.01	44	California	4.24
20	Tennessee	12.56	45	Oregon	3.58
21	Minnesota	12.54	46	Wyoming	2.16
22	Michigan	12.24	–	Alaska**	N/A
23	Idaho	12.11	–	Kentucky**	N/A
24	Pennsylvania	11.95	–	Nevada**	N/A
25	New Hampshire	11.58	–	Rhode Island**	N/A

District of Columbia   10.37

Source: U.S. Bureau of the Census,

  "Quarterly Summary of Federal, State, and Local Tax Revenue" (GT-91Q2, Issued December 1991)

*For year ending June 30, 1991. Determined by the editors using July 1, 1991 Census population estimate.

**Not Available.

State Lottery Revenue in 1990

National Total = $18,818,592,000

RANK	STATE	REVENUE	%
1	California	$2,350,102,000	12.49%
2	Florida	1,943,767,000	10.33%
3	New York	1,884,258,000	10.01%
4	Ohio	1,523,117,000	8.09%
5	Massachusetts	1,452,593,000	7.72%
6	Pennsylvania	1,442,121,000	7.66%
7	Illinois	1,424,150,000	7.57%
8	New Jersey	1,156,681,000	6.15%
9	Michigan	1,095,248,000	5.82%
10	Maryland	769,645,000	4.09%
11	Connecticut	497,721,000	2.64%
12	Virginia	454,234,000	2.41%
13	Indiana	378,623,000	2.01%
14	Wisconsin	293,836,000	1.56%
15	Arizona	270,654,000	1.44%
16	Washington	246,334,000	1.31%
17	Missouri	210,905,000	1.12%
18	Kentucky	187,410,000	1.00%
19	Oregon	153,568,000	0.82%
20	Iowa	152,250,000	0.81%
21	Colorado	131,560,000	0.70%
22	Maine	98,495,000	0.52%
23	New Hampshire	92,548,000	0.49%
24	Idaho	66,268,000	0.35%
25	Minnesota	63,960,000	0.34%

RANK	STATE	REVENUE	%
26	West Virginia	$63,839,000	0.34%
27	Delaware	62,317,000	0.33%
28	Kansas	61,213,000	0.33%
29	Rhode Island	58,728,000	0.31%
30	Vermont	40,744,000	0.22%
31	South Dakota	28,750,000	0.15%
32	Montana	21,485,000	0.11%
33	Alabama	0	0.00%
33	Alaska	0	0.00%
33	Arkansas	0	0.00%
33	Georgia	0	0.00%
33	Hawaii	0	0.00%
33	Louisiana	0	0.00%
33	Mississippi	0	0.00%
33	Nebraska	0	0.00%
33	Nevada	0	0.00%
33	New Mexico	0	0.00%
33	North Carolina	0	0.00%
33	North Dakota	0	0.00%
33	Oklahoma	0	0.00%
33	South Carolina	0	0.00%
33	Tennessee	0	0.00%
33	Texas	0	0.00%
33	Utah	0	0.00%
33	Wyoming	0	0.00%

	District of Columbia	141,468,000	0.75%

Source: U.S. Bureau of the Census,
"State Government Finance: 1990" (GF-90-3, August 1991)

Per Capita State Lottery Revenue in 1990

National Per Capita = $75.67*

RANK	STATE	PER CAPITA		RANK	STATE	PER CAPITA
1	Massachusetts	$241.44		26	South Dakota	$41.31
2	Maryland	160.96		27	Missouri	41.22
3	Connecticut	151.42		28	Colorado	39.93
4	Florida	150.24		29	West Virginia	35.60
5	New Jersey	149.63		30	Montana	26.89
6	Ohio	140.42		31	Kansas	24.71
7	Illinois	124.59		32	Minnesota	14.62
8	Pennsylvania	121.37		33	Alabama	0.00
9	Michigan	117.83		33	Alaska	0.00
10	New York	104.74		33	Arkansas	0.00
11	Delaware	93.55		33	Georgia	0.00
12	New Hampshire	83.43		33	Hawaii	0.00
13	Maine	80.21		33	Louisiana	0.00
14	California	78.97		33	Mississippi	0.00
15	Arizona	73.84		33	Nebraska	0.00
16	Virginia	73.41		33	Nevada	0.00
17	Vermont	72.40		33	New Mexico	0.00
18	Indiana	68.29		33	North Carolina	0.00
19	Idaho	65.82		33	North Dakota	0.00
20	Wisconsin	60.07		33	Oklahoma	0.00
21	Rhode Island	58.53		33	South Carolina	0.00
22	Iowa	54.83		33	Tennessee	0.00
23	Oregon	54.03		33	Texas	0.00
24	Kentucky	50.85		33	Utah	0.00
25	Washington	50.62		33	Wyoming	0.00

District of Columbia   233.10

Source: U.S. Bureau of the Census,
     "State Government Finance: 1990" (GF-90-3, August 1991)
*Rates calculated by the editors using 1990 Census counts.

Average Annual Earnings of Full-time State and Local Government Employees in 1990

National Average = $28,740*

RANK	STATE	EARNINGS		RANK	STATE	EARNINGS
1	Alaska	$42,216		26	Vermont	$26,184
2	California	37,248		27	Indiana	26,040
3	Connecticut	34,980		28	North Carolina	25,860
4	New York	34,152		29	Maine	25,272
5	New Jersey	32,904		30	North Dakota	25,248
6	Maryland	32,604		31	Wyoming	25,080
7	Michigan	32,496		32	Nebraska	25,008
8	Minnesota	31,848		33	Utah	24,624
9	Rhode Island	31,524		34	Missouri	24,312
10	Nevada	30,624		35	Kansas	24,132
11	Massachusetts	30,600		36	Texas	24,096
12	Washington	29,952		37	Montana	23,940
13	Arizona	29,832		38	Kentucky	23,256
14	Illinois	29,724		39	Tennessee	23,220
15	Colorado	28,956		40	Georgia	23,028
16	Pennsylvania	28,944		41	New Mexico	22,860
17	Wisconsin	28,848		42	Alabama	22,764
18	Hawaii	28,416		43	South Carolina	22,692
19	Delaware	28,104		44	West Virginia	22,584
20	Oregon	27,792		45	Idaho	22,512
21	Iowa	27,660		46	Oklahoma	22,020
22	Ohio	27,636		47	Louisiana	21,924
23	New Hampshire	27,108		48	South Dakota	21,840
24	Virginia	27,048		49	Arkansas	20,112
25	Florida	26,532		50	Mississippi	19,548

District of Columbia   36,288

Source: U.S. Bureau of the Census,
   "Public Employment in 1990" (GE-90, No. 1, October 1991)
*Annual figures calculated by editors using October 1990 monthly averages.

State Government Employees in 1990

National Total = 4,503,000 Employees

RANK	STATE	EMPLOYEES	%	RANK	STATE	EMPLOYEES	%
1	California	390,000	8.66%	26	Colorado	69,000	1.53%
2	New York	305,000	6.77%	27	Connecticut	67,000	1.49%
3	Texas	259,000	5.75%	28	Iowa	62,000	1.38%
4	Florida	181,000	4.02%	28	Oregon	62,000	1.38%
5	Michigan	178,000	3.95%	30	Arizona	61,000	1.35%
6	Ohio	172,000	3.82%	31	Hawaii	58,000	1.29%
7	Illinois	170,000	3.78%	31	Kansas	58,000	1.29%
8	Pennsylvania	150,000	3.33%	33	Mississippi	53,000	1.18%
9	Virginia	141,000	3.13%	34	New Mexico	52,000	1.15%
10	New Jersey	125,000	2.78%	35	Arkansas	49,000	1.09%
11	Georgia	123,000	2.73%	36	Utah	43,000	0.95%
12	North Carolina	122,000	2.71%	37	West Virginia	39,000	0.87%
13	Washington	112,000	2.49%	38	Nebraska	36,000	0.80%
14	Massachusetts	108,000	2.40%	39	Maine	27,000	0.60%
15	Indiana	107,000	2.38%	40	Alaska	25,000	0.56%
16	Maryland	102,000	2.27%	40	Delaware	25,000	0.56%
17	Louisiana	100,000	2.22%	42	Rhode Island	24,000	0.53%
18	Alabama	92,000	2.04%	43	Idaho	23,000	0.51%
18	Tennessee	92,000	2.04%	43	Montana	23,000	0.51%
20	Wisconsin	90,000	2.00%	45	Nevada	22,000 ·	0.49%
21	South Carolina	88,000	1.95%	46	New Hampshire	21,000	0.47%
22	Missouri	87,000	1.93%	47	North Dakota	20,000	0.44%
23	Minnesota	85,000	1.89%	48	South Dakota	17,000	0.38%
24	Kentucky	84,000	1.87%	49	Vermont	15,000	0.33%
25	Oklahoma	78,000	1.73%	50	Wyoming	13,000	0.29%

Source: U.S. Bureau of the Census,
   "Public Employment in 1990" (GE-90, No. 1, October 1991)
*Full-time and part-time. As of October 1990.

Rate of State Government Employees in 1990

National Rate = 154 State Government Employees per 10,000 Population*

RANK	STATE	RATE	RANK	STATE	RATE
1	Hawaii	445	26	Mississippi	183
2	Alaska	401	27	Arkansas	182
3	Delaware	314	28	Maine	179
4	New Mexico	262	29	Connecticut	178
5	Wyoming	239	30	Georgia	173
6	North Dakota	234	31	Colorado	165
7	Vermont	233	32	Tennessee	163
8	South Carolina	227	33	Indiana	161
9	Utah	216	33	North Carolina	161
10	Montana	211	35	Minnesota	160
11	Oklahoma	208	35	Nevada	160
12	Iowa	207	37	New York	158
13	Rhode Island	205	38	Massachusetts	155
14	Kentucky	204	38	Michigan	155
15	Kansas	200	40	Missouri	145
15	Louisiana	200	40	New Hampshire	145
17	Alabama	196	40	New Jersey	145
18	South Dakota	192	43	Arizona	137
19	Virginia	188	44	Wisconsin	136
19	West Virginia	188	45	Texas	131
21	Washington	187	46	Ohio	128
22	Idaho	186	47	Illinois	127
22	Maryland	186	48	Florida	123
22	Nebraska	186	49	California	109
25	Oregon	184	50	Pennsylvania	107

Source: U.S. Bureau of the Census,
   "Public Employment in 1990" (GE-90, No. 1, October 1991)
*Full-time equivalent employment. As of October 1990.

Local Government Employees in 1990

National Total = 10,760,000 Local Government Employees*

RANK	STATE	EMPLOYEES	%	RANK	STATE	EMPLOYEES	%
1	California	1,303,000	12.11%	26	Oklahoma	134,000	1.25%
2	New York	1,007,000	9.36%	27	Kansas	131,000	1.22%
3	Texas	770,000	7.16%	28	South Carolina	129,000	1.20%
4	Florida	554,000	5.15%	29	Kentucky	125,000	1.16%
5	Illinois	509,000	4.73%	29	Oregon	125,000	1.16%
6	Ohio	460,000	4.28%	31	Mississippi	119,000	1.11%
7	Pennsylvania	414,000	3.85%	32	Connecticut	111,000	1.03%
8	Michigan	394,000	3.66%	33	Arkansas	91,000	0.85%
9	New Jersey	340,000	3.16%	34	Nebraska	85,000	0.79%
10	Georgia	296,000	2.75%	35	Utah	66,000	0.61%
11	North Carolina	289,000	2.69%	36	West Virginia	65,000	0.60%
12	Virginia	246,000	2.29%	37	New Mexico	63,000	0.59%
13	Wisconsin	232,000	2.16%	38	Maine	54,000	0.50%
14	Indiana	230,000	2.14%	39	Idaho	47,000	0.44%
15	Massachusetts	222,000	2.06%	39	Nevada	47,000	0.44%
16	Minnesota	210,000	1.95%	41	Montana	44,000	0.41%
17	Missouri	203,000	1.89%	42	New Hampshire	42,000	0.39%
18	Tennessee	191,000	1.78%	43	South Dakota	37,000	0.34%
19	Washington	185,000	1.72%	44	North Dakota	33,000	0.31%
20	Maryland	181,000	1.68%	45	Wyoming	30,000	0.28%
21	Louisiana	169,000	1.57%	46	Rhode Island	29,000	0.27%
22	Alabama	162,000	1.51%	47	Alaska	25,000	0.23%
23	Arizona	154,000	1.43%	48	Vermont	22,000	0.20%
23	Colorado	154,000	1.43%	49	Delaware	18,000	0.17%
25	Iowa	138,000	1.28%	50	Hawaii	14,000	0.13%

	District of Columbia	59,000	0.55%

Source: U.S. Bureau of the Census,

"Public Employment in 1990" (GE-90, No. 1, October 1991)

*Full-time and part-time. As of October 1990.

Rate of Local Government Employees in 1990

National Rate = 371 Local Government Employees per 10,000 Population*

RANK	STATE	RATE		RANK	STATE	RATE
1	Wyoming	539		26	Virginia	356
2	New York	482		27	Ohio	355
3	Montana	434		28	Indiana	354
4	Nebraska	430		29	Oregon	353
5	Kansas	421		30	South Dakota	349
6	Georgia	418		31	Nevada	348
7	Texas	415		32	Maine	345
8	Mississippi	407		33	Michigan	340
9	Colorado	395		34	Washington	336
10	New Jersey	393		35	Missouri	334
11	Iowa	387		36	Maryland	333
12	Alaska	385		36	South Carolina	333
13	Florida	384		38	Arkansas	330
14	New Mexico	379		39	West Virginia	326
15	Wisconsin	375		40	Massachusetts	325
16	Minnesota	374		41	North Dakota	314
17	Idaho	372		42	Vermont	312
18	Arizona	370		43	Kentucky	310
19	Oklahoma	369		44	Pennsylvania	304
20	Louisiana	368		45	New Hampshire	301
20	North Carolina	368		46	Connecticut	299
22	Alabama	367		47	Utah	294
22	California	367		48	Rhode Island	266
24	Illinois	364		49	Delaware	250
25	Tennessee	358		50	Hawaii	120

District of Columbia   939

Source: U.S. Bureau of the Census,

    "Public Employment in 1990" (GE-90, No. 1, October 1991)

**Full-time equivalent employment. As of October 1990.*

State Lobbyists in 1991

National Total = 41,278 State Lobbyists

RANK	STATE	LOBBYISTS	%	RANK	STATE	LOBBYISTS	%
1	Missouri*	4,750	11.51%	26	Wisconsin	582	1.41%
2	Florida	3,115	7.55%	27	Massachusetts	575	1.39%
3	Arizona	2,520	6.10%	28	Utah	550	1.33%
4	New York	1,919	4.65%	29	New Jersey	534	1.29%
5	Ohio	1,750	4.24%	30	Colorado	525	1.27%
6	Minnesota	1,480	3.59%	31	Tennessee	517	1.25%
7	Connecticut	1,450	3.51%	32	North Dakota	493	1.19%
8	Oregon	1,368	3.31%	33	South Dakota	487	1.18%
9	Michigan	1,250	3.03%	34	Maryland	442	1.07%
10	Georgia	1,062	2.57%	35	North Carolina	433	1.05%
11	Virginia	986	2.39%	36	Louisiana	427	1.03%
12	California	979	2.37%	37	West Virginia	363	0.88%
13	Texas	850	2.06%	38	Maine	358	0.87%
14	Illinois	838	2.03%	39	Oklahoma	356	0.86%
15	Pennsylvania	814	1.97%	40	Alabama	336	0.81%
16	Washington	747	1.81%	41	Nebraska	328	0.79%
17	Montana	716	1.73%	42	Mississippi	322	0.78%
18	Indiana	659	1.60%	43	South Carolina	320	0.78%
19	Iowa	636	1.54%	44	Rhode Island	308	0.75%
20	Kansas	625	1.51%	45	Idaho	300	0.73%
21	Arkansas	621	1.50%	46	Alaska	282	0.68%
22	Kentucky	600	1.45%	46	Vermont	282	0.68%
23	Wyoming	598	1.45%	48	Delaware	250	0.61%
24	Nevada	597	1.45%	49	New Hampshire	206	0.50%
25	New Mexico	585	1.42%	50	Hawaii	187	0.45%

Source: Lobbying & Influence Alert Newsletter,

   "The Lobbification of America – 1991" (November 1991) (Copyright 1991 by Global Success Corporation, Naples, Florida)

*Missouri's figure is considered an aberration due to a surge in registrations caused by an overly-broad definition of lobbying in a recent law, since narrowed. Missouri's "usual" number is thought to be about 750, which would place it 16th in the United States.

Lobbyists per State Legislator in 1991

National Median = 4.47 Lobbyists per Legislator

RANK	STATE	AVERAGE		RANK	STATE	AVERAGE
1	Arizona	28.0		25	New Jersey	4.5
2	Missouri*	24.1		27	Indiana	4.4
3	Florida	19.5		27	Kentucky	4.4
4	Oregon	15.2		27	Wisconsin	4.4
5	Ohio	13.3		30	Iowa	4.2
6	Nevada	9.3		31	Delaware	4.0
7	New York	9.1		32	Tennessee	3.9
8	Michigan	8.5		33	Kansas	3.8
9	California	8.2		34	Pennsylvania	3.2
10	Connecticut	7.8		35	North Dakota	3.1
11	Minnesota	7.4		36	Louisiana	3.0
12	Virginia	7.0		37	Massachusetts	2.9
13	Nebraska	6.7		38	West Virginia	2.7
14	Wyoming	6.4		39	North Carolina	2.6
15	Colorado	5.3		40	Hawaii	2.5
15	Utah	5.3		41	Alabama	2.4
17	New Mexico	5.2		41	Idaho	2.4
18	Washington	5.1		41	Maryland	2.4
19	Montana	4.8		41	Oklahoma	2.4
20	Alaska	4.7		45	Rhode Island	2.1
20	Illinois	4.7		46	Maine	1.9
20	Texas	4.7		46	Mississippi	1.9
23	Arkansas	4.6		48	South Carolina	1.7
23	South Dakota	4.6		49	Vermont	1.6
25	Georgia	4.5		50	New Hampshire	0.5

Source: Lobbying & Influence Alert Newsletter,

"The Lobbification of America - 1991" (November 1991) (Copyright 1991 by Global Success Corporation, Naples, Florida)

*Missouri's figure is considered an aberration due to a surge in registrations caused by an overly-broad definition of lobbying in a recent law, since narrowed. Missouri's "usual" average is thought to be about 3.81, which would place it 34th in the United States.

XI. HEALTH

XI. HEALTH (continued)

Births in 1990

National Total = 4,179,000 Births*

RANK	STATE	BIRTHS	%
1	California	617,704	14.78%
2	Texas	329,976	7.90%
3	New York	302,084	7.23%
4	Florida	199,481	4.77%
5	Illinois	192,545	4.61%
6	Pennsylvania	172,145	4.12%
7	Ohio	165,546	3.96%
8	Michigan	157,674	3.77%
9	New Jersey	120,654	2.89%
10	Georgia	114,818	2.75%
11	North Carolina	105,230	2.52%
12	Virginia	96,665	2.31%
13	Massachusetts	95,066	2.27%
14	Indiana	85,202	2.04%
15	Missouri	83,085	1.99%
16	Tennessee	77,821	1.86%
17	Washington	77,034	1.84%
18	Maryland	75,557	1.81%
19	Wisconsin	72,490	1.73%
20	Louisiana	71,913	1.72%
21	Arizona	68,701	1.64%
22	Minnesota	68,353	1.64%
23	Alabama	66,935	1.60%
24	Kentucky	56,753	1.36%
25	South Carolina	56,521	1.35%

RANK	STATE	BIRTHS	%
26	Colorado	53,238	1.27%
27	Connecticut	52,230	1.25%
28	Oklahoma	46,119	1.10%
29	Oregon	45,851	1.10%
30	Mississippi	43,063	1.03%
31	Iowa	39,595	0.95%
32	Kansas	38,864	0.93%
33	Utah	37,175	0.89%
34	Arkansas	35,499	0.85%
35	New Mexico	28,252	0.68%
36	Nebraska	24,317	0.58%
37	West Virginia	23,202	0.56%
38	Nevada	21,109	0.51%
39	Hawaii	20,469	0.49%
40	New Hampshire	16,927	0.41%
41	Idaho	16,418	0.39%
42	Maine	16,211	0.39%
43	Rhode Island	15,666	0.37%
44	Delaware	11,728	0.28%
45	Alaska	11,506	0.28%
46	Montana	11,482	0.27%
47	South Dakota	10,912	0.26%
48	North Dakota	10,483	0.25%
49	Vermont	8,045	0.19%
50	Wyoming	6,517	0.16%
	District of Columbia	21,912	0.52%

Source: U.S. Department of Health and Human Services, Centers for Disease Control, National Center for Health Statistics,
"Monthly Vital Statistics Report" (August 28, 1991)

*Live births by state of occurrence.

Birth Rate in 1990

National Rate = 16.7 Births per 1,000 Population*

RANK	STATE	BIRTH RATE	RANK	STATE	BIRTH RATE
1	Alaska	21.8	26	North Carolina	15.8
2	Utah	21.6	26	Washington	15.8
3	California	20.7	28	Rhode Island	15.6
4	Texas	19.2	28	Tennessee	15.6
5	Arizona	18.9	28	Virginia	15.6
6	New Mexico	18.3	31	Minnesota	15.5
7	Hawaii	18.1	31	New Jersey	15.5
7	Nevada	18.1	33	Kansas	15.4
9	Georgia	17.6	34	Florida	15.3
10	Delaware	17.1	35	Kentucky	15.2
11	Michigan	16.9	35	South Dakota	15.2
12	New York	16.8	37	Indiana	15.1
13	Louisiana	16.5	37	Ohio	15.1
14	Illinois	16.4	39	Nebraska	15.0
14	Mississippi	16.4	39	New Hampshire	15.0
16	Alabama	16.2	41	Wisconsin	14.8
17	Connecticut	16.1	42	Arkansas	14.7
18	Colorado	16.0	43	Oklahoma	14.3
18	Idaho	16.0	44	Montana	14.2
18	Massachusetts	16.0	44	Pennsylvania	14.2
18	Missouri	16.0	46	Vermont	14.0
18	North Dakota	16.0	47	Iowa	13.9
23	Maryland	15.9	47	Wyoming	13.9
23	Oregon	15.9	49	Maine	13.1
23	South Carolina	15.9	50	West Virginia	12.6

District of Columbia 36.8

Source: U.S. Department of Health and Human Services, Centers for Disease Control, National Center for Health Statistics,
"Monthly Vital Statistics Report" (August 28, 1991)
*Live births by state of occurrence.

Births in 1980

National Total = 3,612,000 Births*

RANK	STATE	BIRTHS	%
1	California	403,000	11.16%
2	Texas	274,000	7.59%
3	New York	239,000	6.62%
4	Illinois	190,000	5.26%
5	Ohio	169,000	4.68%
6	Pennsylvania	159,000	4.40%
7	Michigan	146,000	4.04%
8	Florida	132,000	3.65%
9	New Jersey	97,000	2.69%
10	Georgia	92,000	2.55%
11	Indiana	88,000	2.44%
12	North Carolina	84,000	2.33%
13	Louisiana	82,000	2.27%
14	Missouri	79,000	2.19%
15	Virginia	78,000	2.16%
16	Wisconsin	75,000	2.08%
17	Massachusetts	73,000	2.02%
18	Tennessee	69,000	1.91%
19	Minnesota	68,000	1.88%
19	Washington	68,000	1.88%
21	Alabama	64,000	1.77%
22	Kentucky	60,000	1.66%
22	Maryland	60,000	1.66%
24	Oklahoma	52,000	1.44%
24	South Carolina	52,000	1.44%

RANK	STATE	BIRTHS	%
26	Arizona	50,000	1.38%
26	Colorado	50,000	1.38%
28	Iowa	48,000	1.33%
28	Mississippi	48,000	1.33%
30	Oregon	43,000	1.19%
31	Utah	42,000	1.16%
32	Kansas	41,000	1.14%
33	Connecticut	39,000	1.08%
34	Arkansas	37,000	1.02%
35	West Virginia	29,000	0.80%
36	Nebraska	27,000	0.75%
37	New Mexico	26,000	0.72%
38	Idaho	20,000	0.55%
39	Hawaii	18,000	0.50%
40	Maine	16,000	0.44%
41	Montana	14,000	0.39%
41	New Hampshire	14,000	0.39%
43	Nevada	13,000	0.36%
43	South Dakota	13,000	0.36%
45	North Dakota	12,000	0.33%
45	Rhode Island	12,000	0.33%
47	Wyoming	11,000	0.30%
48	Alaska	10,000	0.28%
49	Delaware	9,000	0.25%
50	Vermont	8,000	0.22%

	District of Columbia	9,000	0.25%

Source: U.S. Department of Health and Human Services, Centers for Disease Control, National Center for Health Statistics,
   "Vital Statistics of the United States, 1980" and "Monthly Vital Statistics Report"
*Live births by state of residence.

Birth Rate in 1980

National Rate = 15.9 Births per 1,000 Population*

RANK	STATE	RATE	RANK	STATE	RATE
1	Utah	28.6	24	Washington	16.4
2	Alaska	23.7	27	Alabama	16.3
3	Wyoming	22.5	27	Arkansas	16.3
4	Idaho	21.4	27	Kentucky	16.3
5	New Mexico	20.0	30	Indiana	16.1
6	Louisiana	19.5	30	Missouri	16.1
7	South Dakota	19.2	32	Wisconsin	15.9
7	Texas	19.2	33	Delaware	15.8
9	Mississippi	19.0	34	Michigan	15.7
10	Hawaii	18.8	34	Ohio	15.7
11	Arizona	18.4	36	Vermont	15.4
11	North Dakota	18.4	37	Tennessee	15.1
13	Montana	18.1	37	West Virginia	15.1
14	Nebraska	17.4	39	New Hampshire	14.9
15	Colorado	17.2	40	Virginia	14.7
15	Kansas	17.2	41	Maine	14.6
15	Oklahoma	17.2	42	North Carolina	14.4
18	California	17.0	43	Maryland	14.2
19	Georgia	16.9	44	New York	13.6
20	Illinois	16.6	45	Florida	13.5
20	Minnesota	16.6	46	Pennsylvania	13.4
20	Nevada	16.6	47	New Jersey	13.2
20	South Carolina	16.6	48	Rhode Island	12.9
24	Iowa	16.4	49	Massachusetts	12.7
24	Oregon	16.4	50	Connecticut	12.5
				District of Columbia	14.7

Source: U.S. Department of Health and Human Services, Centers for Disease Control, National Center for Health Statistics,
   "Vital Statistics of the United States, 1980" and "Monthly Vital Statistics Report"
* Live births by state of residence.

Male Births in 1988

National Total = 2,002,424 Male Births*

RANK	STATE	MALE BIRTHS	%	RANK	STATE	MALE BIRTHS	%
1	California	272,763	13.62%	26	Kentucky	26,237	1.31%
2	Texas	155,513	7.77%	27	Connecticut	24,646	1.23%
3	New York	144,255	7.20%	28	Oklahoma	24,316	1.21%
4	Illinois	94,869	4.74%	29	Mississippi	21,364	1.07%
5	Florida	94,493	4.72%	30	Oregon	20,497	1.02%
6	Pennsylvania	84,988	4.24%	31	Kansas	19,878	0.99%
7	Ohio	82,343	4.11%	32	Iowa	19,434	0.97%
8	Michigan	71,452	3.57%	33	Utah	18,453	0.92%
9	New Jersey	60,212	3.01%	34	Arkansas	17,955	0.90%
10	Georgia	54,238	2.71%	35	New Mexico	13,782	0.69%
11	North Carolina	49,717	2.48%	36	Nebraska	12,321	0.62%
12	Virginia	47,470	2.37%	37	West Virginia	11,251	0.56%
13	Massachusetts	44,930	2.24%	38	Hawaii	9,692	0.48%
14	Indiana	41,809	2.09%	39	Nevada	9,227	0.46%
15	Missouri	39,280	1.96%	40	New Hampshire	8,891	0.44%
16	Maryland	39,118	1.95%	41	Maine	8,832	0.44%
17	Louisiana	37,426	1.87%	42	Idaho	7,964	0.40%
18	Washington	37,156	1.86%	43	Rhode Island	7,328	0.37%
19	Tennessee	36,394	1.82%	44	Montana	6,025	0.30%
20	Wisconsin	36,350	1.82%	45	Alaska	5,788	0.29%
21	Minnesota	34,004	1.70%	46	South Dakota	5,774	0.29%
22	Arizona	33,608	1.68%	47	Delaware	5,359	0.27%
23	Alabama	31,225	1.56%	48	North Dakota	5,100	0.25%
24	South Carolina	28,290	1.41%	49	Vermont	4,154	0.21%
25	Colorado	27,165	1.36%	50	Wyoming	3,724	0.19%
					District of Columbia	5,364	0.27%

Source: U.S. Department of Health and Human Services, Centers for Disease Control, National Center for Health Statistics,
    "Vital Statistics of the United States, 1988" (Vol I–Natality, issued 1990)

*Live births by state of residence.

Female Births in 1988

National Total = 1,907,086 Female Births*

RANK	STATE	FEMALE BIRTHS	%	RANK	STATE	FEMALE BIRTHS	%
1	California	260,385	13.65%	26	Kentucky	24,821	1.30%
2	Texas	147,905	7.76%	27	Connecticut	23,431	1.23%
3	New York	136,395	7.15%	28	Oklahoma	23,092	1.21%
4	Illinois	89,972	4.72%	29	Mississippi	20,710	1.09%
5	Florida	89,626	4.70%	30	Oregon	19,555	1.03%
6	Pennsylvania	80,651	4.23%	31	Kansas	18,914	0.99%
7	Ohio	78,186	4.10%	32	Iowa	18,685	0.98%
8	Michigan	68,262	3.58%	33	Utah	17,602	0.92%
9	New Jersey	57,552	3.02%	34	Arkansas	17,080	0.90%
10	Georgia	51,685	2.71%	35	New Mexico	13,233	0.69%
11	North Carolina	47,862	2.51%	36	Nebraska	11,586	0.61%
12	Virginia	45,657	2.39%	37	West Virginia	10,595	0.56%
13	Massachusetts	43,264	2.27%	38	Hawaii	9,353	0.49%
14	Indiana	39,834	2.09%	39	Nevada	8,781	0.46%
15	Missouri	37,212	1.95%	40	New Hampshire	8,473	0.44%
16	Maryland	36,650	1.92%	41	Maine	8,340	0.44%
17	Louisiana	36,476	1.91%	42	Idaho	7,777	0.41%
18	Washington	35,347	1.85%	43	Rhode Island	6,896	0.36%
19	Wisconsin	34,467	1.81%	44	Montana	5,667	0.30%
20	Tennessee	34,317	1.80%	45	Alaska	5,444	0.29%
21	Minnesota	32,744	1.72%	46	South Dakota	5,420	0.28%
22	Arizona	32,015	1.68%	47	Delaware	5,047	0.26%
23	Alabama	29,520	1.55%	48	North Dakota	5,003	0.26%
24	South Carolina	26,824	1.41%	49	Vermont	3,957	0.21%
25	Colorado	26,202	1.37%	50	Wyoming	3,438	0.18%
					District of Columbia	5,176	0.27%

Source: U.S. Department of Health and Human Services, Centers for Disease Control, National Center for Health Statistics,
"Vital Statistics of the United States, 1988" (Vol I–Natality, issued 1990)
*Live births by state of residence.

White Births in 1989

National Total = 3,131,991 White Births*

RANK	STATE	BIRTHS	%	RANK	STATE	BIRTHS	%
1	California	448,489	14.32%	26	Alabama	40,125	1.28%
2	Texas	255,070	8.14%	27	Oregon	37,498	1.20%
3	New York	211,904	6.77%	28	Iowa	37,032	1.18%
4	Florida	143,309	4.58%	29	Oklahoma	35,589	1.14%
5	Illinois	139,435	4.45%	30	South Carolina	34,214	1.09%
6	Pennsylvania	138,442	4.42%	31	Kansas	33,786	1.08%
7	Ohio	135,177	4.32%	32	Utah	33,250	1.06%
8	Michigan	114,493	3.66%	33	Arkansas	26,787	0.86%
9	New Jersey	91,675	2.93%	34	New Mexico	22,068	0.70%
10	Massachusetts	78,089	2.49%	35	Mississippi	21,970	0.70%
11	Indiana	72,807	2.32%	36	Nebraska	21,941	0.70%
12	Virginia	69,636	2.22%	37	West Virginia	21,113	0.67%
13	Georgia	68,484	2.19%	38	New Hampshire	17,432	0.56%
14	North Carolina	68,449	2.19%	39	Maine	17,080	0.55%
15	Washington	64,337	2.05%	40	Nevada	16,313	0.52%
16	Missouri	63,185	2.02%	41	Idaho	15,157	0.48%
17	Wisconsin	62,035	1.98%	42	Rhode Island	12,825	0.41%
18	Minnesota	60,638	1.94%	43	Montana	9,871	0.32%
19	Arizona	56,208	1.79%	44	South Dakota	9,001	0.29%
20	Tennessee	54,539	1.74%	45	Vermont	8,388	0.27%
21	Maryland	50,209	1.60%	46	North Dakota	8,303	0.27%
22	Kentucky	47,614	1.52%	47	Delaware	7,955	0.25%
23	Colorado	47,476	1.52%	48	Alaska	7,457	0.24%
24	Louisiana	41,256	1.32%	49	Wyoming	6,447	0.21%
25	Connecticut	41,251	1.32%	50	Hawaii	4,477	0.14%
					District of Columbia	1,705	0.05%

Source: U.S. Department of Health and Human Services, Centers for Disease Control, National Center for Health Statistics,
    "Monthly Vital Statistics Report" (December 12, 1991)
*Live births by state of residence.

Black Births in 1989

National Total = 709,395 Black Births*

RANK	STATE	BIRTHS	%	RANK	STATE	BIRTHS	%
1	New York	66,286	9.34%	26	Kentucky	5,362	0.76%
2	California	56,631	7.98%	27	Washington	3,994	0.56%
3	Florida	46,617	6.57%	28	Kansas	3,734	0.53%
4	Texas	45,160	6.37%	29	Colorado	3,252	0.46%
5	Illinois	45,085	6.36%	30	Arizona	3,097	0.44%
6	Georgia	40,070	5.65%	31	Minnesota	2,951	0.42%
7	Michigan	30,856	4.35%	32	Delaware	2,589	0.36%
8	North Carolina	30,703	4.33%	33	Nevada	2,035	0.29%
9	Louisiana	29,995	4.23%	34	Nebraska	1,546	0.22%
10	Pennsylvania	27,308	3.85%	35	Rhode Island	1,275	0.18%
11	Ohio	26,836	3.78%	36	Iowa	1,260	0.18%
12	New Jersey	25,164	3.55%	37	Oregon	1,204	0.17%
13	Maryland	24,885	3.51%	38	Hawaii	936	0.13%
14	Virginia	24,104	3.40%	39	West Virginia	928	0.13%
15	South Carolina	22,516	3.17%	40	New Mexico	731	0.10%
16	Alabama	21,850	3.08%	41	Alaska	705	0.10%
17	Mississippi	20,544	2.90%	42	Utah	372	0.05%
18	Tennessee	17,867	2.52%	43	New Hampshire	184	0.03%
19	Missouri	13,360	1.88%	44	South Dakota	130	0.02%
20	Indiana	9,620	1.36%	45	Maine	124	0.02%
21	Massachusetts	9,513	1.34%	46	North Dakota	112	0.02%
22	Arkansas	8,588	1.21%	47	Wyoming	99	0.01%
23	Wisconsin	7,216	1.02%	48	Idaho	93	0.01%
24	Connecticut	7,006	0.99%	49	Montana	70	0.01%
25	Oklahoma	5,523	0.78%	50	Vermont	40	0.01%
					District of Columbia	9,269	1.31%

Source: U.S. Department of Health and Human Services, Centers for Disease Control, National Center for Health Statistics,
"Monthly Vital Statistics Report" (December 12, 1991)
*Live births by state of residence.

Births of Low Birth Weight in 1989

National Total = 284,391 Births of Low Birth Weight*

RANK	STATE	BIRTHS	%	RANK	STATE	BIRTHS	%
1	California	34,764	12.22%	26	Kentucky	3,657	1.29%
2	New York	22,282	7.83%	27	Connecticut	3,414	1.20%
3	Texas	21,462	7.55%	28	Minnesota	3,309	1.16%
4	Florida	14,808	5.21%	29	Oklahoma	3,068	1.08%
5	Illinois	14,645	5.15%	30	Arkansas	2,973	1.05%
6	Pennsylvania	11,943	4.20%	31	Kansas	2,370	0.83%
7	Ohio	11,512	4.05%	32	Oregon	2,151	0.76%
8	Michigan	11,275	3.96%	33	Iowa	2,116	0.74%
9	Georgia	9,202	3.24%	34	Utah	2,014	0.71%
10	New Jersey	8,902	3.13%	35	New Mexico	1,896	0.67%
11	North Carolina	8,270	2.91%	36	West Virginia	1,472	0.52%
12	Virginia	6,872	2.42%	37	Nevada	1,410	0.50%
13	Louisiana	6,626	2.33%	38	Nebraska	1,402	0.49%
14	Maryland	6,260	2.20%	39	Hawaii	1,378	0.48%
15	Tennessee	6,011	2.11%	40	New Hampshire	909	0.32%
16	Indiana	5,488	1.93%	40	Rhode Island	909	0.32%
17	Massachusetts	5,388	1.89%	42	Idaho	879	0.31%
18	Missouri	5,386	1.89%	43	Maine	851	0.30%
19	South Carolina	5,268	1.85%	44	Delaware	801	0.28%
20	Alabama	5,169	1.82%	45	Montana	647	0.23%
21	Arizona	4,262	1.50%	46	South Dakota	594	0.21%
22	Washington	4,219	1.48%	47	Alaska	572	0.20%
23	Wisconsin	4,141	1.46%	48	Wyoming	503	0.18%
24	Colorado	4,088	1.44%	49	North Dakota	481	0.17%
25	Mississippi	4,043	1.42%	50	Vermont	462	0.16%
					District of Columbia	1,867	0.66%

Source: U.S. Department of Health and Human Services, Centers for Disease Control, National Center for Health Statistics,
    "Monthly Vital Statistics Report" (December 12, 1991)

*Less than 2500 grams (5 pounds-8 ounces). By state of residence.

Births of Low Birth Weight as a Percent of Live Births in 1989

National Percent = 7.0% of Live Births*

RANK	STATE	PERCENT	RANK	STATE	PERCENT
1	Mississippi	9.4	25	Kentucky	6.9
2	South Carolina	9.2	25	Missouri	6.9
3	Louisiana	9.1	28	Indiana	6.6
4	Georgia	8.4	28	West Virginia	6.6
5	Alabama	8.3	30	Oklahoma	6.5
5	Arkansas	8.3	31	Arizona	6.3
7	Tennessee	8.2	32	Rhode Island	6.2
8	North Carolina	8.1	33	California	6.1
9	Maryland	8.0	33	Kansas	6.1
10	Colorado	7.8	35	Massachusetts	5.9
11	Florida	7.7	36	Nebraska	5.8
11	Illinois	7.7	36	Wisconsin	5.8
11	New York	7.7	38	Utah	5.7
14	Michigan	7.6	39	Washington	5.6
15	Delaware	7.5	40	Idaho	5.5
16	New Jersey	7.3	40	Montana	5.5
16	Wyoming	7.3	40	Vermont	5.5
18	Nevada	7.2	43	Iowa	5.4
19	Hawaii	7.1	43	South Dakota	5.4
19	Pennsylvania	7.1	45	Oregon	5.2
19	Virginia	7.1	46	New Hampshire	5.1
22	New Mexico	7.0	47	North Dakota	5.0
22	Ohio	7.0	48	Alaska	4.9
22	Texas	7.0	48	Maine	4.9
25	Connecticut	6.9	48	Minnesota	4.9

District of Columbia   15.9

Source: U.S. Department of Health and Human Services, Centers for Disease Control, National Center for Health Statistics,
   "Monthly Vital Statistics Report" (December 12, 1991)
*Less than 2500 grams (5 pounds–8 ounces). By state of residence.

Births of Low Birth Weight in 1980

National Total = 246,292 Births of Low Birth Weight*

RANK	STATE	BIRTHS	%	RANK	STATE	BIRTHS	%
1	California	23,734	9.64%	26	Washington	3,457	1.40%
2	Texas	18,959	7.70%	27	Minnesota	3,426	1.39%
3	New York	17,705	7.19%	28	Arizona	3,075	1.25%
4	Illinois	13,716	5.57%	29	Arkansas	2,834	1.15%
5	Ohio	11,401	4.63%	30	Connecticut	2,611	1.06%
6	Pennsylvania	10,323	4.19%	31	Iowa	2,408	0.98%
7	Florida	9,951	4.04%	32	Kansas	2,364	0.96%
8	Michigan	9,909	4.02%	33	Utah	2,161	0.88%
9	Georgia	7,928	3.22%	34	Oregon	2,132	0.87%
10	Louisiana	7,064	2.87%	35	West Virginia	1,968	0.80%
11	New Jersey	6,990	2.84%	36	New Mexico	1,643	0.67%
12	North Carolina	6,696	2.72%	37	Nebraska	1,533	0.62%
13	Virginia	5,849	2.37%	38	Hawaii	1,282	0.52%
14	Indiana	5,530	2.25%	39	Idaho	1,075	0.44%
15	Tennessee	5,524	2.24%	40	Maine	1,061	0.43%
16	Missouri	5,245	2.13%	41	Nevada	877	0.36%
17	Alabama	4,999	2.03%	42	Montana	797	0.32%
18	Maryland	4,905	1.99%	43	Rhode Island	769	0.31%
19	South Carolina	4,479	1.82%	43	Wyoming	769	0.31%
20	Massachusetts	4,410	1.79%	45	New Hampshire	738	0.30%
21	Mississippi	4,148	1.68%	46	Delaware	728	0.30%
22	Colorado	4,094	1.66%	47	South Dakota	678	0.28%
23	Kentucky	4,051	1.64%	48	North Dakota	591	0.24%
24	Wisconsin	4,022	1.63%	49	Alaska	511	0.21%
25	Oklahoma	3,517	1.43%	50	Vermont	465	0.19%

	District of Columbia	1,190	0.48%

Source: U.S. Department of Health and Human Services, Centers for Disease Control, National Center for Health Statistics,
   "Vital Statistics of the United States, 1980" (Vol. I-Natality, issued 1984)
*Less than 2500 grams (5 pounds-8 ounces). By state of residence.

Births of Low Birth Weight as a Percent of Live Births in 1980

National Percent = 6.8% of Live Births*

RANK	STATE	PERCENT	RANK	STATE	PERCENT
1	Mississippi	8.7	25	West Virginia	6.7
2	Georgia	8.6	27	Missouri	6.6
2	Louisiana	8.6	27	Nevada	6.6
2	South Carolina	8.6	29	Maine	6.5
5	Colorado	8.2	29	Pennsylvania	6.5
5	Maryland	8.2	31	Indiana	6.3
7	Tennessee	8.0	31	Rhode Island	6.3
8	Alabama	7.9	33	Arizona	6.2
8	North Carolina	7.9	34	Massachusetts	6.1
10	Delaware	7.7	35	California	5.9
11	Arkansas	7.6	35	Vermont	5.9
11	Florida	7.6	37	Kansas	5.8
11	New Mexico	7.6	38	Montana	5.6
14	Virginia	7.5	38	Nebraska	5.6
15	New York	7.4	40	Alaska	5.4
16	Wyoming	7.3	40	New Hampshire	5.4
17	Illinois	7.2	40	Wisconsin	5.4
17	New Jersey	7.2	43	Idaho	5.3
19	Hawaii	7.1	44	Utah	5.2
20	Michigan	6.9	45	Minnesota	5.1
20	Texas	6.9	45	South Dakota	5.1
22	Kentucky	6.8	45	Washington	5.1
22	Ohio	6.8	48	Iowa	5.0
22	Oklahoma	6.8	49	North Dakota	4.9
25	Connecticut	6.7	49	Oregon	4.9

District of Columbia   12.8

Source: U.S. Department of Health and Human Services, Centers for Disease Control, National Center for Health Statistics,
    "Vital Statistics of the United States, 1980" (Vol. I–Natality, issued 1984)
*Less than 2500 grams (5 pounds–8 ounces). By state of residence.

Births to Teenage Mothers in 1988

National Total = 488,941 Births

RANK	STATE	BIRTHS	%	RANK	STATE	BIRTHS	%
1	California	58,950	12.06%	26	Wisconsin	6,950	1.42%
2	Texas	46,113	9.43%	27	Arkansas	6,606	1.35%
3	New York	26,487	5.42%	28	Colorado	5,690	1.16%
4	Florida	25,292	5.17%	29	Minnesota	4,857	0.99%
5	Illinois	23,183	4.74%	30	Oregon	4,578	0.94%
6	Ohio	21,738	4.45%	31	Kansas	4,416	0.90%
7	Pennsylvania	18,137	3.71%	32	New Mexico	4,248	0.87%
8	Michigan	17,460	3.57%	33	Connecticut	4,124	0.84%
9	Georgia	17,457	3.57%	34	West Virginia	3,688	0.75%
10	North Carolina	15,629	3.20%	35	Iowa	3,541	0.72%
11	Louisiana	12,381	2.53%	36	Utah	3,358	0.69%
12	Tennessee	12,153	2.49%	37	Nevada	2,252	0.46%
13	Indiana	11,488	2.35%	38	Nebraska	2,213	0.45%
14	Alabama	10,597	2.17%	39	Maine	1,864	0.38%
15	New Jersey	10,515	2.15%	40	Idaho	1,827	0.37%
16	Missouri	10,456	2.14%	41	Hawaii	1,786	0.37%
17	Virginia	10,428	2.13%	42	Rhode Island	1,458	0.30%
18	South Carolina	9,248	1.89%	43	Delaware	1,329	0.27%
19	Arizona	9,059	1.85%	44	New Hampshire	1,301	0.27%
20	Kentucky	8,827	1.81%	45	South Dakota	1,191	0.24%
21	Mississippi	8,704	1.78%	46	Montana	1,156	0.24%
22	Maryland	8,451	1.73%	47	Alaska	1,049	0.21%
23	Washington	7,653	1.57%	48	Wyoming	858	0.18%
24	Oklahoma	7,581	1.55%	49	North Dakota	765	0.16%
25	Massachusetts	7,273	1.49%	50	Vermont	722	0.15%
					District of Columbia	1,854	0.38%

Source: U.S. Department of Health and Human Services, Centers for Disease Control, National Center for Health Statistics, unpublished data

Percent of Births to Teenage Mothers in 1988

National Percent = 12.5%

RANK	STATE	PERCENT
1	Mississippi	20.7
2	Arkansas	18.8
3	Alabama	17.5
4	Kentucky	17.3
5	Tennessee	17.1
6	West Virginia	16.9
7	South Carolina	16.8
8	Louisiana	16.7
9	Georgia	16.5
10	North Carolina	16.0
10	Oklahoma	16.0
12	New Mexico	15.7
13	Texas	15.2
14	Indiana	14.0
15	Arizona	13.8
16	Florida	13.7
17	Missouri	13.6
17	Ohio	13.6
19	Delaware	12.8
20	Illinois	12.5
20	Michigan	12.5
20	Nevada	12.5
23	Wyoming	12.0
24	Idaho	11.6
25	Kansas	11.4

RANK	STATE	PERCENT
25	Oregon	11.4
27	Virginia	11.2
28	California	11.1
29	Maryland	11.1
30	Maine	10.9
31	Pennsylvania	10.9
32	South Dakota	10.7
33	Colorado	10.6
34	Washington	10.5
35	Rhode Island	10.3
36	Montana	9.9
37	Wisconsin	9.8
38	Hawaii	9.4
39	New York	9.4
40	Alaska	9.3
40	Iowa	9.3
40	Utah	9.3
43	Nebraska	9.2
44	New Jersey	8.9
45	Vermont	8.9
46	Connecticut	8.6
47	Massachusetts	8.3
48	North Dakota	7.6
49	New Hampshire	7.5
50	Minnesota	7.3

District of Columbia		17.6

Source: U.S. Department of Health and Human Services, Centers for Disease Control, National Center for Health Statistics, unpublished data

Births to Teenage Mothers in 1980

National Total = 562,330 Births

RANK	STATE	BIRTHS	%	RANK	STATE	BIRTHS	%
1	California	56,138	9.98%	26	Arkansas	8,060	1.43%
2	Texas	50,125	8.91%	27	Massachusetts	7,765	1.38%
3	Illinois	29,798	5.30%	28	Minnesota	7,048	1.25%
4	New York	28,206	5.02%	29	Colorado	6,592	1.17%
5	Ohio	26,567	4.72%	30	Kansas	6,090	1.08%
6	Florida	24,042	4.28%	31	Iowa	5,962	1.06%
7	Pennsylvania	22,029	3.92%	32	West Virginia	5,911	1.05%
8	Michigan	20,401	3.63%	33	Oregon	5,731	1.02%
9	Georgia	19,137	3.40%	34	New Mexico	4,758	0.85%
10	Louisiana	16,504	2.93%	35	Utah	4,594	0.82%
11	North Carolina	16,192	2.88%	36	Connecticut	4,408	0.78%
12	Indiana	15,331	2.73%	37	Nebraska	3,313	0.59%
13	Tennessee	13,792	2.45%	38	Idaho	2,645	0.47%
14	Missouri	13,312	2.37%	39	Maine	2,522	0.45%
15	Alabama	13,096	2.33%	40	Hawaii	2,085	0.37%
16	Kentucky	12,559	2.23%	41	Nevada	2,048	0.36%
17	Virginia	12,138	2.16%	42	South Dakota	1,797	0.32%
18	New Jersey	11,904	2.12%	43	Montana	1,761	0.31%
19	Mississippi	11,079	1.97%	44	Wyoming	1,634	0.29%
20	South Carolina	10,282	1.83%	45	Delaware	1,572	0.28%
21	Oklahoma	10,206	1.81%	46	Rhode Island	1,502	0.27%
22	Wisconsin	9,220	1.64%	47	New Hampshire	1,475	0.26%
23	Maryland	8,885	1.58%	48	North Dakota	1,304	0.23%
24	Washington	8,495	1.51%	49	Alaska	1,123	0.20%
25	Arizona	8,235	1.46%	50	Vermont	1,024	0.18%
					District of Columbia	1,933	0.34%

Source: U.S. Department of Health and Human Services, Centers for Disease Control, National Center for Health Statistics,
"Vital Statistics of the United States, 1980" (Vol. I–Natality, issued 1984)

Percent of Births to Teenage Mothers in 1980

National Percent = 15.6%

RANK	STATE	PERCENT	RANK	STATE	PERCENT
1	Mississippi	23.2	26	Maryland	14.8
2	Arkansas	21.6	27	Michigan	14.0
3	Kentucky	21.1	28	California	13.9
4	Georgia	20.7	28	Pennsylvania	13.9
5	Alabama	20.6	30	South Dakota	13.5
6	Louisiana	20.1	31	Colorado	13.3
6	West Virginia	20.1	31	Oregon	13.3
8	Tennessee	19.9	33	Idaho	13.1
9	South Carolina	19.8	34	Vermont	13.0
10	Oklahoma	19.6	35	Iowa	12.5
11	North Carolina	19.2	35	Washington	12.5
12	Texas	18.3	37	Montana	12.4
13	Florida	18.2	38	New Jersey	12.3
13	New Mexico	18.2	38	Rhode Island	12.3
15	Indiana	17.3	38	Wisconsin	12.3
16	Missouri	16.9	41	Nebraska	12.1
17	Delaware	16.7	42	Alaska	11.8
18	Arizona	16.5	42	New York	11.8
19	Illinois	15.7	44	Hawaii	11.5
19	Ohio	15.7	45	Connecticut	11.4
21	Virginia	15.5	46	Utah	11.0
21	Wyoming	15.5	47	North Dakota	10.9
23	Nevada	15.4	48	Massachusetts	10.7
24	Maine	15.3	48	New Hampshire	10.7
25	Kansas	15.0	50	Minnesota	10.4

District of Columbia   20.7

Source: U.S. Department of Health and Human Services, Centers for Disease Control, National Center for Health Statistics, "Vital Statistics of the United States, 1980" (Vol. I–Natality, issued 1984)

Ratio of Births to Unmarried Women in 1989

National Total = 270.8 Births to Unmarried Women per 1,000 Live Births*

RANK	STATE	RATIO	RANK	STATE	RATIO
1	Mississippi	393.9	26	New Jersey	241.0
2	Louisiana	353.1	27	Indiana	238.4
3	New Mexico	345.4	28	Massachusetts	238.2
4	New York	319.1	29	Hawaii	238.0
5	Georgia	316.7	30	Oklahoma	237.6
6	South Carolina	316.0	31	West Virginia	235.2
7	Illinois	309.3	32	Nevada	235.0
8	Arizona	308.2	33	Washington	234.0
9	Florida	301.9	34	Wisconsin	233.5
10	California	300.3	35	Kentucky	225.5
11	Alabama	297.9	36	Maine	217.9
12	Delaware	291.2	37	South Dakota	217.8
13	Tennessee	290.8	38	Montana	217.4
14	Maryland	288.9	39	Colorado	204.6
15	Ohio	280.1	40	Vermont	198.4
16	Pennsylvania	279.0	41	Texas	196.0
17	North Carolina	277.3	42	Kansas	195.6
18	Arkansas	276.9	43	Minnesota	194.6
19	Missouri	271.3	44	Iowa	194.1
20	Connecticut	262.9	45	Nebraska	192.5
21	Oregon	252.8	46	Wyoming	184.9
22	Virginia	252.2	47	North Dakota	168.8
23	Rhode Island	249.5	48	Idaho	161.2
24	Alaska	245.9	49	New Hampshire	157.1
25	Michigan	245.4	50	Utah	126.6

District of Columbia   643.0

Source: U.S. Department of Health and Human Services, Centers for Disease Control, National Center for Health Statistics,
    "Monthly Vital Statistics Report" (December 12, 1991)

*By state of residence.

Ratio of Births to Unmarried Women in 1980

National Ratio = 184.3 Births to Unmarried Women per 1,000 Live Births*

RANK	STATE	RATIO
1	Mississippi	280.4
2	Maryland	251.5
3	Delaware	241.8
4	New York	238.1
5	Louisiana	233.6
6	Georgia	231.5
7	South Carolina	230.3
8	Florida	230.1
9	Illinois	225.3
10	Alabama	221.7
11	California	213.8
12	New Jersey	210.8
13	Arkansas	204.8
14	Tennessee	198.5
15	Virginia	191.9
16	North Carolina	190.0
17	Arizona	187.1
18	Connecticut	179.4
19	Ohio	178.1
20	Pennsylvania	176.9
21	Missouri	176.3
22	Hawaii	175.5
23	Michigan	161.8
24	New Mexico	160.8
25	Massachusetts	156.5

RANK	STATE	RATIO
25	Rhode Island	156.5
27	Alaska	156.2
28	Indiana	155.0
29	Kentucky	150.5
30	Oregon	147.9
31	Oklahoma	140.4
32	Wisconsin	138.7
33	Maine	138.6
34	Vermont	137.0
35	Washington	136.0
36	Nevada	134.5
37	South Dakota	134.1
38	Texas	133.1
39	West Virginia	130.5
40	Colorado	130.1
41	Montana	125.2
42	Kansas	122.5
43	Nebraska	116.0
44	Minnesota	114.1
45	New Hampshire	109.6
46	Iowa	102.5
47	North Dakota	92.4
48	Wyoming	82.1
49	Idaho	78.7
50	Utah	62.0

District of Columbia   564.5

Source: U.S. Department of Health and Human Services, Centers for Disease Control, National Center for Health Statistics,
"Vital Statistics of the United States, 1980" (Vol. I–Natality, issued 1984)
*By state of residence.

Ratio of Births to Unmarried White Women in 1989

National Ratio = 192.2 Births to Unmarried White Women per 1,000 Live Births*

RANK	STATE	RATIO		RANK	STATE	RATIO
1	New Mexico	292.9		26	Tennessee	163.2
2	California	287.3		27	Minnesota	162.2
3	Arizona	267.4		28	Delaware	161.7
4	Oregon	240.2		29	Montana	161.5
5	New York	231.2		30	Alaska	158.1
6	West Virginia	219.0		31	Kansas	157.2
7	Maine	216.1		32	New Hampshire	156.8
8	Rhode Island	213.4		33	Idaho	155.6
9	Washington	213.2		34	Maryland	153.6
10	Connecticut	201.6		34	Nebraska	153.6
11	Massachusetts	199.5		36	Arkansas	152.6
12	Vermont	198.1		37	New Jersey	149.5
13	Ohio	197.1		38	Hawaii	144.8
14	Pennsylvania	193.5		39	Texas	143.1
15	Florida	191.4		40	Louisiana	142.7
16	Nevada	190.3		41	Virginia	142.4
17	Colorado	186.1		42	Georgia	140.0
18	Indiana	181.5		43	South Carolina	136.6
19	Illinois	180.1		44	Michigan	135.2
20	Kentucky	178.6		45	South Dakota	133.5
21	Iowa	177.1		46	North Carolina	128.2
21	Missouri	177.1		47	North Dakota	126.8
23	Wyoming	174.4		48	Mississippi	123.8
24	Wisconsin	170.2		49	Utah	116.6
25	Oklahoma	169.7		50	Alabama	115.4

District of Columbia   129.8

Source: U.S. Department of Health and Human Services, Centers for Disease Control, National Center for Health Statistics,
   "Monthly Vital Statistics Report" (December 12, 1991)

*By state of residence.

Ratio of Births to Unmarried Black Women in 1989

National Ratio = 657.2 Births to Unmarried Black Women per 1,000 Live Births*

RANK	STATE	RATIO	RANK	STATE	RATIO
1	Wisconsin	799.2	26	Nevada	636.4
2	Pennsylvania	772.1	27	New Jersey	630.3
3	Iowa	767.3	28	North Carolina	621.7
4	Illinois	756.3	29	California	621.2
5	Missouri	749.8	30	Arizona	612.5
6	Ohio	740.4	31	Massachusetts	608.2
7	Minnesota	720.2	32	Kansas	606.5
8	Delaware	714.3	33	Virginia	603.8
9	Indiana	713.0	34	Maryland	600.9
10	Nebraska	701.7	35	South Carolina	600.3
11	Tennessee	700.9	36	New Mexico	558.9
12	Oregon	696.5	37	Texas	532.2
13	Mississippi	687.9	38	Colorado	532.0
14	Arkansas	682.1	39	Washington	530.4
15	Michigan	679.6	40	Utah	481.3
16	Kentucky	674.0	41	Wyoming	413.3
17	Florida	665.7	42	Maine	320.5
18	West Virginia	665.5	43	Alaska	296.4
19	Connecticut	661.4	44	New Hampshire	283.3
20	New York	657.9	45	Hawaii	151.2
21	Louisiana	655.3	–	Idaho**	–
22	Rhode Island	647.5	–	Montana**	–
23	Alabama	642.0	–	North Dakota**	–
23	Oklahoma	642.0	–	South Dakota**	–
25	Georgia	636.7	–	Vermont**	–

District of Columbia 759.3

Source: U.S. Department of Health and Human Services, Centers for Disease Control, National Center for Health Statistics,
 "Monthly Vital Statistics Report" (December 12, 1991)

*By state of residence.

**Insufficient frequency to determine ratio.

277

Infant Deaths in 1990

National Total = 38,100 Infant Deaths*

RANK	STATE	INFANT DEATHS	%	RANK	STATE	INFANT DEATHS	%
1	California	4,719	12.39%	26	Kentucky	456	1.20%
2	Texas	2,579	6.77%	27	Oklahoma	450	1.18%
3	Illinois	2,134	5.60%	28	Connecticut	401	1.05%
4	Florida	1,947	5.11%	29	Oregon	343	0.90%
5	Pennsylvania	1,759	4.62%	30	Arkansas	333	0.87%
6	Michigan	1,654	4.34%	31	Iowa	314	0.82%
7	Ohio	1,589	4.17%	32	Utah	302	0.79%
8	Georgia	1,242	3.26%	33	Kansas	282	0.74%
9	North Carolina	1,156	3.03%	34	New Mexico	237	0.62%
10	New Jersey	984	2.58%	35	West Virginia	223	0.59%
11	Virginia	960	2.52%	36	Nebraska	202	0.53%
12	Tennessee	864	2.27%	37	Nevada	181	0.48%
13	Indiana	818	2.15%	38	Hawaii	154	0.40%
14	Missouri	805	2.11%	39	Idaho	127	0.33%
15	Louisiana	774	2.03%	40	Rhode Island	120	0.31%
16	Massachusetts	772	2.03%	41	Alaska	112	0.29%
17	Alabama	670	1.76%	42	Delaware	104	0.27%
18	South Carolina	649	1.70%	43	Maine	103	0.27%
19	Washington	622	1.63%	44	New Hampshire	99	0.26%
20	Arizona	599	1.57%	45	South Dakota	97	0.25%
21	Maryland	594	1.56%	46	North Dakota	90	0.24%
21	Wisconsin	594	1.56%	47	Montana	84	0.22%
23	Minnesota	527	1.38%	48	Vermont	52	0.14%
24	Mississippi	491	1.29%	49	Wyoming	35	0.09%
25	Colorado	490	1.29%	–	New York**	N/A	N/A

District of Columbia   453   1.19%

Source: U.S. Department of Health and Human Services, Centers for Disease Control, National Center for Health Statistics,
"Monthly Vital Statistics Report" (August 28, 1991)

*Deaths of infants under 1 year old, exclusive of fetal deaths. By state of occurrence.

**Not available.

Infant Mortality Rate in 1990

National Rate = 9.12 Infant Deaths per 1,000 Live Births*

RANK	STATE	RATE	RANK	STATE	RATE
1	South Carolina	11.48	26	New Mexico	8.39
2	Mississippi	11.40	27	Nebraska	8.31
3	Tennessee	11.10	28	Wisconsin	8.19
4	Illinois	11.08	29	New Jersey	8.16
5	North Carolina	10.99	30	Massachusetts	8.12
6	Georgia	10.82	30	Utah	8.12
7	Louisiana	10.76	32	Washington	8.07
8	Michigan	10.49	33	Kentucky	8.03
9	Pennsylvania	10.22	34	Iowa	7.93
10	Alabama	10.01	35	Maryland	7.86
11	Virginia	9.93	36	Texas	7.82
12	Florida	9.76	37	Idaho	7.74
12	Oklahoma	9.76	38	Minnesota	7.71
14	Alaska	9.73	39	Connecticut	7.68
15	Missouri	9.69	40	Rhode Island	7.66
16	West Virginia	9.61	41	California	7.64
17	Indiana	9.60	42	Hawaii	7.52
17	Ohio	9.60	43	Oregon	7.48
19	Arkansas	9.38	44	Montana	7.32
20	Colorado	9.20	45	Kansas	7.26
21	South Dakota	8.89	46	Vermont	6.46
22	Delaware	8.87	47	Maine	6.35
23	Arizona	8.72	48	New Hampshire	5.85
24	North Dakota	8.59	49	Wyoming	5.37
25	Nevada	8.57	–	New York**	N/A

District of Columbia   20.67

Source: U.S. Department of Health and Human Services, Centers for Disease Control, National Center for Health Statistics,
   "Monthly Vital Statistics Report" (August 28, 1991)

*Deaths of infants under 1 year old, exclusive of fetal deaths. By state of occurrence. Rates calculated by the editors.

**Not available.

Infant Mortality Rate in 1980

National Rate = 12.6 Infant Deaths per 1,000 Live Births*

RANK	STATE	RATE		RANK	STATE	RATE
1	Mississippi	17.0		25	Texas	12.2
2	South Carolina	15.6		27	North Dakota	12.1
3	Alabama	15.1		28	Indiana	11.9
4	Illinois	14.8		29	Iowa	11.8
5	Florida	14.6		29	Washington	11.8
6	Georgia	14.5		29	West Virginia	11.8
6	North Carolina	14.5		32	Nebraska	11.5
8	Louisiana	14.3		32	New Mexico	11.5
9	Maryland	14.0		34	Connecticut	11.2
10	Delaware	13.9		35	California	11.1
11	Virginia	13.6		36	Rhode Island	11.0
12	Tennessee	13.5		37	South Dakota	10.9
13	Pennsylvania	13.2		38	Idaho	10.7
14	Kentucky	12.9		38	Nevada	10.7
15	Michigan	12.8		38	Vermont	10.7
15	Ohio	12.8		41	Massachusetts	10.5
17	Arkansas	12.7		42	Kansas	10.4
17	Oklahoma	12.7		42	Utah	10.4
19	New Jersey	12.5		44	Hawaii	10.3
19	New York	12.5		44	Wisconsin	10.3
21	Arizona	12.4		46	Colorado	10.1
21	Missouri	12.4		47	Minnesota	10.0
21	Montana	12.4		48	New Hampshire	9.9
24	Alaska	12.3		49	Wyoming	9.8
25	Oregon	12.2		50	Maine	9.2

District of Columbia   25.0

Source: U.S. Department of Health and Human Services, Centers for Disease Con
    "Vital Statistics of the United States, 1980" (Vol. I-Natality, issued 1984) and unpublished data
*Deaths of infants under 1 year old, exclusive of fetal deaths. By state of residence.

White Infant Mortality Rate in 1988

National Rate = 8.5 White Infant Deaths per 1,000 Live Births*

RANK	STATE	RATE	RANK	STATE	RATE
1	Kentucky	10.0	26	Florida	8.5
1	North Dakota	10.0	26	Idaho	8.5
3	Indiana	9.9	26	Maryland	8.5
4	Alaska	9.8	26	Oregon	8.5
5	New Mexico	9.7	26	West Virginia	8.5
5	South Dakota	9.7	31	New Hampshire	8.4
7	Colorado	9.6	32	Iowa	8.3
7	North Carolina	9.6	32	Texas	8.3
7	South Carolina	9.6	34	California	8.2
10	Arizona	9.4	34	Tennessee	8.2
11	Alabama	9.3	36	Nebraska	8.1
11	Oklahoma	9.3	36	Pennsylvania	8.1
13	Georgia	9.2	36	Virginia	8.1
14	Delaware	9.1	39	Connecticut	8.0
15	Louisiana	9.0	39	Maine	8.0
15	Missouri	9.0	41	New Jersey	7.9
17	New York	8.9	41	Utah	7.9
18	Montana	8.8	43	Nevada	7.5
18	Wyoming	8.8	43	Rhode Island	7.5
20	Arkansas	8.7	43	Wisconsin	7.5
20	Illinois	8.7	46	Massachusetts	7.3
20	Mississippi	8.7	47	Hawaii	7.2
20	Washington	8.7	47	Minnesota	7.2
24	Michigan	8.6	49	Kansas	7.0
24	Ohio	8.6	50	Vermont	6.7

District of Columbia 19.9

Source: U.S. Department of Health and Human Services, Centers for Disease Control, National Center for Health Statistics,
   "Vital Statistics of the United States, 1988" (Vol II, Part B, issued 1990)
*Deaths of infants under 1 year old, exclusive of fetal deaths. By state of residence.

White Infant Mortality Rate in 1980

National Rate = 11.0 White Infant Deaths per 1,000 Live Births*

RANK	STATE	RATE		RANK	STATE	RATE
1	Oregon	12.2		25	New York	10.8
2	North Carolina	12.1		25	South Carolina	10.8
2	Oklahoma	12.1		28	Idaho	10.7
4	Kentucky	12.0		28	Nebraska	10.7
5	Pennsylvania	11.9		28	Vermont	10.7
5	Tennessee	11.9		31	California	10.6
5	Virginia	11.9		31	Michigan	10.6
8	Arizona	11.8		33	Indiana	10.5
8	Florida	11.8		33	Louisiana	10.5
8	Montana	11.8		33	Utah	10.5
11	Illinois	11.7		36	Arkansas	10.3
11	North Dakota	11.7		36	New Jersey	10.3
13	Alabama	11.6		38	Connecticut	10.2
13	Hawaii	11.6		39	Massachusetts	10.1
13	Maryland	11.6		40	Nevada	10.0
16	Iowa	11.5		41	New Hampshire	9.9
16	Washington	11.5		42	Colorado	9.8
18	West Virginia	11.4		42	Delaware	9.8
19	New Mexico	11.3		44	Wisconsin	9.7
20	Ohio	11.2		45	Minnesota	9.6
20	Texas	11.2		46	Kansas	9.5
22	Mississippi	11.1		47	Alaska	9.4
22	Missouri	11.1		47	Maine	9.4
24	Rhode Island	10.9		49	Wyoming	9.3
25	Georgia	10.8		50	South Dakota	9.0

District of Columbia   17.8

Source: U.S. Department of Health and Human Services, Centers for Disease Control, National Center for Health Statistics,

 "Vital Statistics of the United States, 1980" (Vol. I-Natality, issued 1984) and unpublished data

*Deaths of infants under 1 year old, exclusive of fetal deaths. By state of residence.

Black Infant Mortality Rate in 1988

National Rate = 17.6 Black Infant Deaths per 1,000 Live Births*

RANK	STATE	RATE		RANK	STATE	RATE
1	Idaho**	25.0		26	South Carolina	16.6
2	Nebraska	22.4		27	Kansas	16.5
3	Michigan	21.9		28	Wisconsin	16.4
4	West Virginia	21.6		29	Missouri	16.2
5	Delaware	21.1		30	Mississippi	16.1
6	Illinois	20.7		30	Washington	16.1
7	Alaska**	20.2		32	California	15.9
8	Indiana	19.9		32	Ohio	15.9
8	Iowa	19.9		34	Connecticut	15.5
10	Pennsylvania	19.8		35	Massachusetts	15.4
11	Minnesota	19.5		36	Oregon**	14.7
11	North Carolina	19.5		37	Louisiana	14.3
13	Georgia	18.9		38	New Mexico**	14.2
14	Nevada	18.7		38	Texas	14.2
15	Tennessee	18.6		40	Rhode Island**	13.8
16	New Jersey	18.5		41	New Hampshire**	13.4
17	New York	18.1		42	Montana**	12.8
18	Arizona	17.9		43	Oklahoma	12.6
18	Virginia	17.9		44	Colorado	12.0
20	Maryland	17.8		45	Hawaii**	9.0
21	Arkansas	17.4		46	Utah**	6.2
21	Florida	17.4		47	Maine	0.0
21	Kentucky	17.4		47	North Dakota	0.0
24	Alabama	17.2		47	South Dakota	0.0
25	Wyoming**	16.8		47	Vermont	0.0

District of Columbia   26.0

Source: U.S. Department of Health and Human Services, Centers for Disease Control, National Center for Health Statistics,
   "Vital Statistics of the United States, 1988" (Vol II, Part B, issued 1990)

*Deaths of infants under 1 year old, exclusive of fetal deaths. By state of residence.

**Based on a frequency of less than 20 infant deaths.

Black Infant Mortality Rate in 1980

National Rate = 21.4 Black Infant Deaths per 1,000 Live Births*

RANK	STATE	RATE	RANK	STATE	RATE
1	Delaware	27.9	24	Nevada	20.6
2	North Dakota**	27.5	27	Maryland	20.4
3	Utah**	27.3	28	Arkansas	20.0
4	Iowa	27.2	28	Minnesota	20.0
5	Illinois	26.3	28	New York	20.0
6	Wyoming**	25.9	28	North Carolina	20.0
7	Nebraska	25.2	32	Virginia	19.8
8	Michigan	24.2	33	Alaska**	19.5
9	Mississippi	23.7	34	Tennessee	19.3
10	Indiana	23.4	35	Colorado	19.1
11	New Mexico**	23.1	35	Connecticut	19.1
11	Pennsylvania	23.1	37	Texas	18.8
13	Ohio	23.0	38	Wisconsin	18.5
14	South Carolina	22.9	39	Arizona	18.4
15	Florida	22.8	40	California	18.0
16	New Hampshire**	22.5	41	Rhode Island**	17.4
17	Kentucky	22.0	42	Massachusetts	16.8
18	New Jersey	21.9	43	Washington	16.4
19	Oklahoma	21.8	44	Oregon**	15.9
20	Alabama	21.6	45	Hawaii**	11.8
21	West Virginia	21.5	46	Idaho	0.0
22	Georgia	21.0	46	Maine	0.0
23	Missouri	20.7	46	Montana	0.0
24	Kansas	20.6	46	South Dakota	0.0
24	Louisiana	20.6	46	Vermont	0.0

District of Columbia   26.7

Source: U.S. Department of Health and Human Services, Centers for Disease Control, National Center for Health Statistics,
   "Vital Statistics of the United States, 1980" (Vol. I–Natality, issued 1984) and unpublished data
*Deaths of infants under 1 year old, exclusive of fetal deaths. By state of residence.
**Based on a frequency of less than 20 infant deaths.

Average Lifetime: 1979–1981

National Average = 73.88 Years*

RANK	STATE	YEARS	RANK	STATE	YEARS
1	Hawaii	77.02	26	Wyoming	73.85
2	Minnesota	76.15	27	Indiana	73.84
3	Iowa	75.81	27	Missouri	73.84
4	Utah	75.76	29	Arkansas	73.72
5	North Dakota	75.71	30	New York	73.70
6	Nebraska	75.49	31	Michigan	73.67
7	Wisconsin	75.35	31	Oklahoma	73.67
8	Kansas	75.31	33	Texas	73.64
9	Colorado	75.30	34	Pennsylvania	73.58
10	Idaho	75.19	35	Ohio	73.49
11	Washington	75.13	36	Virginia	73.43
12	Connecticut	75.12	37	Illinois	73.37
13	Massachusetts	75.01	38	Maryland	73.32
14	Oregon	74.99	39	Tennessee	73.30
15	New Hampshire	74.98	40	Delaware	73.21
16	South Dakota	74.97	41	Kentucky	73.06
17	Vermont	74.79	42	North Carolina	72.96
18	Rhode Island	74.76	43	West Virginia	72.84
19	Maine	74.59	44	Nevada	72.64
20	California	74.57	45	Alabama	72.53
21	Arizona	74.30	46	Alaska	72.24
22	New Mexico	74.01	47	Georgia	72.22
23	Florida	74.00	48	Mississippi	71.98
23	New Jersey	74.00	49	South Carolina	71.85
25	Montana	73.93	50	Louisiana	71.74

	District of Columbia	69.20

Source: U.S. Department of Health and Human Services, Centers for Disease Control, National Center for Health Statistics,
   "U.S. Decennial Life Tables for 1979-81" (Vol. II, State Life Tables, August 1985)

*The National Center for Health Statistics determines average lifetime by state every ten years. The national average lifetime for a child born in 1990 is 75.4 years.

Average Lifetime for Men: 1979-1981

National Average = 70.11 Years*

RANK	STATE	YEARS	RANK	STATE	YEARS
1	Hawaii	74.08	26	Michigan	70.07
2	Minnesota	72.52	27	New York	70.02
3	Utah	72.38	28	Wyoming	69.95
4	North Dakota	72.09	29	Missouri	69.92
5	Iowa	72.00	30	New Mexico	69.91
6	Wisconsin	71.86	31	Pennsylvania	69.90
7	Colorado	71.78	32	Ohio	69.85
8	Washington	71.74	33	Arkansas	69.73
9	Nebraska	71.73	34	Maryland	69.71
10	Kansas	71.60	35	Texas	69.70
11	Idaho	71.52	36	Oklahoma	69.63
12	Connecticut	71.51	37	Virginia	69.60
13	New Hampshire	71.43	38	Delaware	69.56
14	Oregon	71.35	39	Illinois	69.55
15	Massachusetts	71.27	40	Nevada	69.26
16	California	71.09	41	Tennessee	69.15
17	Vermont	71.06	42	Kentucky	69.14
18	South Dakota	71.03	43	West Virginia	68.86
19	Rhode Island	70.96	44	Alaska	68.71
20	Maine	70.78	45	North Carolina	68.60
21	New Jersey	70.48	46	Alabama	68.28
22	Montana	70.47	47	Georgia	68.01
23	Arizona	70.46	48	Louisiana	67.64
24	Indiana	70.16	48	Mississippi	67.64
25	Florida	70.08	50	South Carolina	67.56

District of Columbia   64.55

Source: U.S. Department of Health and Human Services, Centers for Disease Control, National Center for Health Statistics,

"U.S. Decennial Life Tables for 1979-81" (Vol. II, State Life Tables, August 1985)

*The National Center for Health Statistics determines average lifetime by state every ten years. The national average lifetime for a male child born in 1990 is 72.0 years.

Average Lifetime for Women: 1979–1981

National Average = 77.62 Years*

RANK	STATE	YEARS	RANK	STATE	YEARS
1	Hawaii	80.33	26	Oklahoma	77.81
2	Minnesota	79.82	27	Missouri	77.72
3	North Dakota	79.68	28	Montana	77.68
4	Iowa	79.60	29	Texas	77.67
5	Nebraska	79.29	30	Tennessee	77.47
6	South Dakota	79.21	31	Indiana	77.46
7	Utah	79.18	32	New Jersey	77.39
8	Idaho	79.15	33	North Carolina	77.35
9	Kansas	78.99	34	Michigan	77.29
10	Wisconsin	78.87	35	Virginia	77.27
11	Colorado	78.80	36	New York	77.18
12	Oregon	78.77	37	Pennsylvania	77.16
13	Connecticut	78.57	38	Illinois	77.13
13	Washington	78.57	39	Kentucky	77.12
15	Vermont	78.49	40	Ohio	77.06
16	Massachusetts	78.46	41	West Virginia	76.93
17	New Hampshire	78.42	42	Alaska	76.87
18	Maine	78.41	43	Maryland	76.83
19	Arizona	78.34	44	Alabama	76.79
19	New Mexico	78.34	45	Delaware	76.78
21	Rhode Island	78.33	46	Nevada	76.48
22	Wyoming	78.20	47	Mississippi	76.39
23	California	78.02	48	Georgia	76.35
24	Florida	77.98	49	South Carolina	76.12
25	Arkansas	77.83	50	Louisiana	75.89
				District of Columbia	73.70

Source: U.S. Department of Health and Human Services, Centers for Disease Control, National Center for Health Statistics,
   "U.S. Decennial Life Tables for 1979–81" (Vol. II, State Life Tables, August 1985)
*The National Center for Health Statistics determines average lifetime by state every ten years. The national average lifetime for a female child born in 1990 is 78.8 years.

Deaths in 1990

National Total = 2,162,000 Deaths*

RANK	STATE	DEATHS	%	RANK	STATE	DEATHS	%
1	California	215,269	9.96%	26	South Carolina	28,944	1.34%
2	New York	167,299	7.74%	27	Iowa	27,871	1.29%
3	Florida	135,736	6.28%	28	Connecticut	27,007	1.25%
4	Texas	128,361	5.94%	29	Oregon	25,811	1.19%
5	Pennsylvania	123,359	5.71%	30	Arkansas	24,735	1.14%
6	Illinois	100,648	4.66%	31	Mississippi	24,416	1.13%
7	Ohio	98,851	4.57%	32	Colorado	22,033	1.02%
8	Michigan	77,836	3.60%	33	Kansas	21,737	1.01%
9	New Jersey	68,841	3.18%	34	West Virginia	19,531	0.90%
10	North Carolina	57,884	2.68%	35	Nebraska	14,966	0.69%
11	Massachusetts	55,669	2.57%	36	Maine	11,114	0.51%
12	Georgia	53,337	2.47%	37	New Mexico	10,934	0.51%
13	Missouri	52,835	2.44%	38	Utah	9,668	0.45%
14	Indiana	50,312	2.33%	39	Nevada	9,659	0.45%
15	Tennessee	48,248	2.23%	40	Rhode Island	9,572	0.44%
16	Virginia	47,613	2.20%	41	New Hampshire	8,300	0.38%
17	Wisconsin	42,700	1.98%	42	Idaho	7,261	0.34%
18	Alabama	41,162	1.90%	43	Hawaii	7,063	0.33%
19	Maryland	38,403	1.78%	44	Montana	6,848	0.32%
20	Louisiana	37,155	1.72%	45	South Dakota	6,406	0.30%
21	Washington	36,670	1.70%	46	North Dakota	6,032	0.28%
22	Minnesota	35,041	1.62%	47	Delaware	5,879	0.27%
23	Kentucky	34,913	1.61%	48	Vermont	4,701	0.22%
24	Arizona	29,492	1.36%	49	Wyoming	3,069	0.14%
25	Oklahoma	29,368	1.36%	50	Alaska	2,210	0.10%
					District of Columbia	9,546	0.44%

Source: U.S. Department of Health and Human Services, Centers for Disease Control, National Center for Health Statistics,
"Monthly Vital Statistics Report" (August 28, 1991)
*By state of occurrence.

Death Rate in 1990

National Rate = 8.6 Deaths per 1,000 Population*

RANK	STATE	DEATH RATE
1	West Virginia	10.6
2	Florida	10.4
3	Arkansas	10.2
3	Missouri	10.2
3	Pennsylvania	10.2
6	Alabama	10.0
7	Iowa	9.8
8	Tennessee	9.7
9	Rhode Island	9.5
10	Kentucky	9.4
10	Massachusetts	9.4
12	Mississippi	9.3
12	New York	9.3
14	Nebraska	9.2
14	North Dakota	9.2
16	Oklahoma	9.1
17	Maine	9.0
17	Ohio	9.0
17	Oregon	9.0
20	Indiana	8.9
20	New Jersey	8.9
20	South Dakota	8.9
23	North Carolina	8.7
23	Wisconsin	8.7
25	Delaware	8.6

RANK	STATE	DEATH RATE
25	Illinois	8.6
25	Kansas	8.6
28	Louisiana	8.5
28	Montana	8.5
30	Michigan	8.4
31	Connecticut	8.3
31	Nevada	8.3
33	Georgia	8.2
33	Vermont	8.2
35	Arizona	8.1
35	Maryland	8.1
35	South Carolina	8.1
38	Minnesota	8.0
39	Virginia	7.7
40	Texas	7.5
40	Washington	7.5
42	New Hampshire	7.3
43	California	7.2
44	Idaho	7.1
44	New Mexico	7.1
46	Colorado	6.6
47	Wyoming	6.5
48	Hawaii	6.3
49	Utah	5.6
50	Alaska	4.2

District of Columbia   16.0

Source: U.S. Department of Health and Human Services, Centers for Disease Control, National Center for Health Statistics, "Monthly Vital Statistics Report" (August 28, 1991)

*By state of occurrence.

Deaths in 1980

National Total = 1,990,000 Deaths*

RANK	STATE	DEATHS	%	RANK	STATE	DEATHS	%
1	California	187,000	9.40%	25	Iowa	27,000	1.36%
2	New York	173,000	8.69%	27	South Carolina	25,000	1.26%
3	Pennsylvania	124,000	6.23%	28	Mississippi	24,000	1.21%
4	Texas	108,000	5.43%	29	Arkansas	23,000	1.16%
5	Florida	105,000	5.28%	30	Kansas	22,000	1.11%
6	Illinois	103,000	5.18%	30	Oregon	22,000	1.11%
7	Ohio	98,000	4.92%	32	Arizona	21,000	1.06%
8	Michigan	75,000	3.77%	33	Colorado	19,000	0.95%
9	New Jersey	69,000	3.47%	33	West Virginia	19,000	0.95%
10	Massachusetts	55,000	2.76%	35	Nebraska	14,000	0.70%
11	Missouri	50,000	2.51%	36	Maine	11,000	0.55%
12	North Carolina	48,000	2.41%	37	New Mexico	9,000	0.45%
13	Indiana	47,000	2.36%	37	Rhode Island	9,000	0.45%
14	Georgia	44,000	2.21%	39	New Hampshire	8,000	0.40%
15	Virginia	43,000	2.16%	39	Utah	8,000	0.40%
16	Tennessee	41,000	2.06%	41	Idaho	7,000	0.35%
16	Wisconsin	41,000	2.06%	41	Montana	7,000	0.35%
18	Alabama	36,000	1.81%	41	South Dakota	7,000	0.35%
18	Louisiana	36,000	1.81%	44	Nevada	6,000	0.30%
20	Kentucky	34,000	1.71%	44	North Dakota	6,000	0.30%
20	Maryland	34,000	1.71%	46	Delaware	5,000	0.25%
22	Minnesota	33,000	1.66%	46	Hawaii	5,000	0.25%
23	Washington	32,000	1.61%	46	Vermont	5,000	0.25%
24	Oklahoma	28,000	1.41%	49	Wyoming	3,000	0.15%
25	Connecticut	27,000	1.36%	50	Alaska	2,000	0.10%
					District of Columbia	7,000	0.35%

Source: U.S. Department of Health and Human Services, Centers for Disease Control, National Center for Health Statistics,
"Vital Statistics of the United States 1980" and "Monthly Vital Statistics Report"
*By state of residence.

Death Rate in 1980

National Rate = 8.8 Deaths per 1,000 Population*

RANK	STATE	RATE		RANK	STATE	RATE
1	Florida	10.7		25	North Dakota	8.6
2	Pennsylvania	10.4		27	Delaware	8.5
3	Missouri	10.1		27	Louisiana	8.5
4	Arkansas	9.9		27	Montana	8.5
4	West Virginia	9.9		30	New Hampshire	8.3
6	New York	9.8		30	Oregon	8.3
6	Rhode Island	9.8		32	Minnesota	8.2
8	Maine	9.6		32	North Carolina	8.2
8	Massachusetts	9.6		34	Georgia	8.1
10	South Dakota	9.5		34	Maryland	8.1
11	Mississippi	9.4		34	Michigan	8.1
11	New Jersey	9.4		34	South Carolina	8.1
13	Iowa	9.3		38	Virginia	8.0
13	Kansas	9.3		39	Arizona	7.9
13	Oklahoma	9.3		39	California	7.9
16	Kentucky	9.2		41	Washington	7.7
16	Nebraska	9.2		42	Texas	7.6
18	Alabama	9.1		43	Nevada	7.4
18	Ohio	9.1		44	Idaho	7.2
20	Illinois	9.0		45	New Mexico	7.0
20	Vermont	9.0		46	Wyoming	6.9
22	Tennessee	8.9		47	Colorado	6.6
23	Connecticut	8.8		48	Utah	5.6
24	Wisconsin	8.7		49	Hawaii	5.2
25	Indiana	8.6		50	Alaska	4.3

District of Columbia		11.1

Source: U.S. Department of Health and Human Services, Centers for Disease Control, National Center for Health Statistics,
    "Vital Statistics of the United States 1980" and "Monthly Vital Statistics Report"
*By state of residence.

Deaths by Atherosclerosis in 1988

National Total = 22,086 Deaths by Atherosclerosis*

RANK	STATE	DEATHS	%	RANK	STATE	DEATHS	%
1	California	2,353	10.65%	26	Colorado	357	1.62%
2	New York	1,562	7.07%	27	Kansas	337	1.53%
3	Florida	1,210	5.48%	28	Arizona	317	1.44%
4	Michigan	1,188	5.38%	29	Maryland	295	1.34%
5	Texas	1,163	5.27%	30	Nebraska	258	1.17%
6	Illinois	1,052	4.76%	31	Connecticut	256	1.16%
7	Pennsylvania	1,043	4.72%	32	Arkansas	208	0.94%
8	Ohio	1,017	4.60%	32	West Virginia	208	0.94%
9	Indiana	674	3.05%	34	Mississippi	196	0.89%
10	Massachusetts	631	2.86%	35	South Carolina	179	0.81%
11	New Jersey	619	2.80%	36	Maine	173	0.78%
12	Iowa	500	2.26%	37	New Hampshire	107	0.48%
13	Washington	473	2.14%	38	New Mexico	106	0.48%
14	Missouri	440	1.99%	39	North Dakota	98	0.44%
15	Tennessee	429	1.94%	40	Rhode Island	93	0.42%
16	Minnesota	423	1.92%	41	Montana	88	0.40%
16	Wisconsin	423	1.92%	42	Idaho	83	0.38%
18	North Carolina	416	1.88%	43	Utah	74	0.34%
19	Virginia	412	1.87%	44	South Dakota	69	0.31%
20	Georgia	394	1.78%	45	Nevada	67	0.30%
21	Oklahoma	389	1.76%	46	Vermont	49	0.22%
22	Oregon	388	1.76%	47	Delaware	38	0.17%
23	Alabama	382	1.73%	47	Hawaii	38	0.17%
24	Kentucky	379	1.72%	49	Wyoming	29	0.13%
25	Louisiana	375	1.70%	50	Alaska	5	0.02%

District of Columbia 23 0.10%

Source: U.S. Department of Health and Human Services, Centers for Disease Control, National Center for Health Statistics,
  "Vital Statistics of the United States, 1988" (Vol II, Part B, issued 1990)
By state of residence. Atherosclerosis is a form of hardening of the arteries.

Death Rate by Atherosclerosis in 1988

National Rate = 8.99 Deaths per 100,000 Population*

RANK	STATE	RATE	RANK	STATE	RATE
1	Iowa	17.64	26	Tennessee	8.76
2	Nebraska	16.10	27	New York	8.72
3	North Dakota	14.69	28	Wisconsin	8.71
4	Maine	14.36	29	Pennsylvania	8.69
5	Oregon	14.02	30	Arkansas	8.68
6	Kansas	13.51	31	Missouri	8.56
7	Michigan	12.86	32	Louisiana	8.51
8	Indiana	12.13	33	California	8.31
9	Oklahoma	12.00	34	Idaho	8.28
10	West Virginia	11.09	35	New Jersey	8.02
11	Montana	10.93	36	Connecticut	7.92
12	Colorado	10.81	37	Mississippi	7.48
13	Massachusetts	10.71	38	New Mexico	7.03
14	Washington	10.18	39	Texas	6.91
15	Kentucky	10.17	40	Virginia	6.85
16	New Hampshire	9.86	41	North Carolina	6.41
17	Minnesota	9.82	42	Maryland	6.38
18	Florida	9.81	43	Nevada	6.36
19	South Dakota	9.68	44	Georgia	6.21
20	Ohio	9.37	45	Wyoming	6.05
21	Rhode Island	9.37	46	Delaware	5.76
22	Alabama	9.31	47	South Carolina	5.16
23	Arizona	9.09	48	Utah	4.38
24	Illinois	9.06	49	Hawaii	3.46
25	Vermont	8.80	50	Alaska	0.95

District of Columbia   3.73

Source: U.S. Department of Health and Human Services, Centers for Disease Control, National Center for Health Statistics,
   "Vital Statistics of the United States, 1988" (Vol. II, Part B, issued 1990)
*By state of residence. Atherosclerosis is a form of hardening of the arteries. Rates calculated by the editors.

Deaths by Cerebrovascular Diseases in 1989

National Total = 145,551 Deaths by Cerebrovascular Diseases*

RANK	STATE	DEATHS	%	RANK	STATE	DEATHS	%
1	California	15,755	10.82%	26	Iowa	2,142	1.47%
2	New York	9,145	6.28%	27	Arkansas	2,035	1.40%
3	Florida	8,410	5.78%	28	Oregon	2,025	1.39%
4	Texas	8,380	5.76%	29	Mississippi	1,893	1.30%
5	Pennsylvania	7,729	5.31%	30	Connecticut	1,789	1.23%
6	Illinois	6,865	4.72%	31	Arizona	1,641	1.13%
7	Ohio	6,277	4.31%	32	Kansas	1,622	1.11%
8	Michigan	5,198	3.57%	33	Colorado	1,322	0.91%
9	North Carolina	4,613	3.17%	34	West Virginia	1,178	0.81%
10	New Jersey	4,111	2.82%	35	Nebraska	1,157	0.79%
11	Indiana	3,798	2.61%	36	Maine	726	0.50%
12	Georgia	3,755	2.58%	37	Utah	638	0.44%
13	Tennessee	3,550	2.44%	38	Rhode Island	606	0.42%
14	Missouri	3,460	2.38%	39	Idaho	577	0.40%
15	Massachusetts	3,430	2.36%	40	New Hampshire	566	0.39%
16	Virginia	3,319	2.28%	41	New Mexico	563	0.39%
17	Wisconsin	3,242	2.23%	42	South Dakota	511	0.35%
18	Alabama	2,869	1.97%	43	Hawaii	491	0.34%
19	Minnesota	2,846	1.96%	44	Nevada	450	0.31%
20	Washington	2,686	1.85%	45	Montana	431	0.30%
21	Kentucky	2,513	1.73%	46	North Dakota	403	0.28%
22	Louisiana	2,472	1.70%	47	Delaware	323	0.22%
23	South Carolina	2,462	1.69%	48	Vermont	298	0.20%
24	Maryland	2,284	1.57%	49	Wyoming	170	0.12%
25	Oklahoma	2,282	1.57%	50	Alaska	97	0.07%
					District of Columbia	446	0.31%

Source: U.S. Department of Health and Human Services, Centers for Disease Control, National Center for Health Statistics,
"Monthly Vital Statistics Report" (Vol. 40, No. 8(S)2, January 7, 1992)

*By state of residence. Cerebrovascular disease includes stroke and other disorders of the blood vessels of the brain.

Death Rate by Cerebrovascular Disease in 1989

National Rate = 58.6 Deaths per 100,000 Population*

RANK	STATE	RATE	RANK	STATE	RATE
1	Arkansas	84.6	26	Massachusetts	58.0
2	Iowa	75.4	27	Ohio	57.6
3	Mississippi	72.2	28	Idaho	56.9
4	Tennessee	71.9	29	Louisiana	56.4
5	Nebraska	71.8	29	Washington	56.4
5	Oregon	71.8	31	Michigan	56.1
7	South Dakota	71.5	32	Connecticut	55.2
8	Oklahoma	70.8	33	Virginia	54.4
9	North Carolina	70.2	34	California	54.2
10	South Carolina	70.1	35	Montana	53.5
11	Alabama	69.7	36	New Jersey	53.1
12	Indiana	67.9	37	Vermont	52.6
13	Kentucky	67.4	38	New Hampshire	51.1
14	Missouri	67.1	39	New York	50.9
15	Wisconsin	66.6	40	Texas	49.3
16	Florida	66.4	41	Maryland	48.7
17	Minnesota	65.4	42	Delaware	48.0
18	Kansas	64.5	43	Arizona	46.1
19	Pennsylvania	64.2	44	Hawaii	44.2
20	West Virginia	63.4	45	Nevada	40.5
21	North Dakota	61.1	46	Colorado	39.9
22	Rhode Island	60.7	47	Utah	37.4
23	Maine	59.4	48	New Mexico	36.8
24	Illinois	58.9	49	Wyoming	35.8
25	Georgia	58.3	50	Alaska	18.4

	District of Columbia	73.8

Source: U.S. Department of Health and Human Services, Centers for Disease Control, National Center for Health Statistics,
"Monthly Vital Statistics Report" (Vol. 40, No. 8(S)2, January 7, 1992)
*By state of residence. Cerebrovascular disease includes stroke and other disorders of the blood vessels of the brain.

Deaths by Chronic Liver Disease and Cirrhosis in 1988

National Total = 26,409 Deaths by Chronic Liver Diseases and Cirrhosis*

RANK	STATE	DEATHS	%	RANK	STATE	DEATHS	%
1	California	4,154	15.73%	26	Minnesota	295	1.12%
2	New York	2,549	9.65%	27	Oklahoma	288	1.09%
3	Florida	1,683	6.37%	28	Oregon	287	1.09%
4	Texas	1,417	5.37%	29	Colorado	275	1.04%
5	Illinois	1,255	4.75%	30	Mississippi	211	0.80%
6	Pennsylvania	1,235	4.68%	31	New Mexico	193	0.73%
7	Michigan	1,079	4.09%	32	Iowa	192	0.73%
8	New Jersey	1,043	3.95%	33	Nevada	180	0.68%
9	Ohio	965	3.65%	34	Kansas	178	0.67%
10	Massachusetts	728	2.76%	35	Arkansas	168	0.64%
11	North Carolina	702	2.66%	36	West Virginia	165	0.62%
12	Georgia	585	2.22%	37	Rhode Island	130	0.49%
13	Virginia	544	2.06%	38	Maine	127	0.48%
14	Indiana	461	1.75%	39	New Hampshire	120	0.45%
15	Maryland	455	1.72%	40	Nebraska	102	0.39%
15	Washington	455	1.72%	41	Montana	87	0.33%
17	Arizona	450	1.70%	42	Utah	81	0.31%
18	Tennessee	410	1.55%	43	Hawaii	79	0.30%
19	Alabama	404	1.53%	44	Idaho	65	0.25%
20	Wisconsin	394	1.49%	45	Delaware	64	0.24%
21	Missouri	373	1.41%	46	Vermont	61	0.23%
22	Connecticut	330	1.25%	47	North Dakota	58	0.22%
23	Louisiana	328	1.24%	48	South Dakota	52	0.20%
24	Kentucky	326	1.23%	49	Alaska	45	0.17%
24	South Carolina	326	1.23%	50	Wyoming	41	0.16%
					District of Columbia	214	0.81%

Source: U.S. Department of Health and Human Services, Centers for Disease Control, National Center for Health Statistics,
   "Vital Statistics of the United States, 1988" (Vol II, Part B, issued 1990)
*By state of residence.

Death Rate by Chronic Liver Disease and Cirrhosis in 1988

National Rate = 10.74 Deaths per 100,000 Population*

RANK	STATE	RATE	RANK	STATE	RATE
1	Nevada	17.08	26	Virginia	9.04
2	California	14.67	27	Ohio	8.89
3	New York	14.23	28	Oklahoma	8.88
4	Florida	13.64	29	West Virginia	8.80
5	New Jersey	13.51	30	Kentucky	8.75
6	Rhode Island	13.09	31	North Dakota	8.70
7	Arizona	12.90	32	Alaska	8.59
8	New Mexico	12.81	33	Wyoming	8.56
9	Massachusetts	12.36	34	Texas	8.41
10	Michigan	11.68	35	Tennessee	8.38
11	New Hampshire	11.06	36	Colorado	8.33
12	Vermont	10.95	37	Indiana	8.30
13	North Carolina	10.82	38	Wisconsin	8.12
14	Montana	10.81	39	Mississippi	8.05
15	Illinois	10.81	40	Louisiana	7.44
16	Maine	10.54	41	South Dakota	7.29
17	Oregon	10.37	42	Missouri	7.26
18	Pennsylvania	10.29	43	Hawaii	7.19
19	Connecticut	10.21	44	Kansas	7.13
20	Alabama	9.85	45	Arkansas	7.01
21	Maryland	9.84	46	Minnesota	6.85
22	Washington	9.79	47	Iowa	6.77
23	Delaware	9.70	48	Idaho	6.48
24	South Carolina	9.39	49	Nebraska	6.37
25	Georgia	9.22	50	Utah	4.79

District of Columbia   34.68

Source: U.S. Department of Health and Human Services, Centers for Disease Control, National Center for Health Statistics,
"Vital Statistics of the United States, 1988" (Vol. II, Part B, issued 1990) (Rates calculated by editors.)
*By state of residence. Rates calculated by the editors.

Deaths by Chronic Obstructive Pulmonary Diseases in 1988

National Total = 82,853 Deaths by Chronic Pulmonary Diseases*

RANK	STATE	DEATHS	%	RANK	STATE	DEATHS	%
1	California	9,684	11.69%	26	Iowa	1,205	1.45%
2	New York	5,549	6.70%	27	Oregon	1,195	1.44%
3	Florida	5,317	6.42%	28	Louisiana	1,140	1.38%
4	Pennsylvania	4,325	5.22%	29	Kansas	1,008	1.22%
5	Texas	4,092	4.94%	30	South Carolina	950	1.15%
6	Ohio	4,070	4.91%	31	Connecticut	946	1.14%
7	Illinois	3,529	4.26%	32	West Virginia	903	1.09%
8	Michigan	2,902	3.50%	33	Arkansas	866	1.05%
9	New Jersey	2,261	2.73%	34	Mississippi	804	0.97%
10	North Carolina	2,098	2.53%	35	Nebraska	583	0.70%
11	Missouri	2,081	2.51%	36	Nevada	557	0.67%
12	Indiana	2,078	2.51%	37	Maine	555	0.67%
13	Massachusetts	2,024	2.44%	38	New Mexico	471	0.57%
14	Washington	1,846	2.23%	39	Idaho	403	0.49%
15	Georgia	1,842	2.22%	40	Montana	383	0.46%
16	Tennessee	1,742	2.10%	41	Utah	374	0.45%
17	Virginia	1,641	1.98%	42	New Hampshire	364	0.44%
18	Wisconsin	1,589	1.92%	43	Rhode Island	341	0.41%
19	Kentucky	1,530	1.85%	44	Vermont	252	0.30%
20	Arizona	1,461	1.76%	45	South Dakota	240	0.29%
21	Alabama	1,439	1.74%	46	North Dakota	203	0.25%
22	Maryland	1,407	1.70%	47	Delaware	199	0.24%
23	Minnesota	1,297	1.57%	48	Wyoming	197	0.24%
24	Colorado	1,296	1.56%	49	Hawaii	192	0.23%
25	Oklahoma	1,206	1.46%	50	Alaska	71	0.09%
					District of Columbia	145	0.18%

Source: U.S. Department of Health and Human Services, Centers for Disease Control, National Center for Health Statistics,
   "Vital Statistics of the United States, 1988" (Vol. II, Part B, issued 1990)

*By state of residence. Includes allied conditions.

Death Rate by Chronic Obstructive Pulmonary Diseases in 1988

National Rate = 33.71 Deaths per 100,000 Population*

RANK	STATE	RATE	RANK	STATE	RATE
1	Nevada	52.85	26	Rhode Island	34.34
2	West Virginia	48.13	27	California	34.20
3	Montana	47.58	28	South Dakota	33.66
4	Maine	46.06	29	New Hampshire	33.55
5	Vermont	45.24	30	Wisconsin	32.73
6	Oregon	43.19	31	North Carolina	32.33
7	Florida	43.10	32	Michigan	31.41
8	Iowa	42.52	33	New Mexico	31.25
9	Arizona	41.87	34	New York	30.98
10	Wyoming	41.13	35	Mississippi	30.69
11	Kentucky	41.05	36	Maryland	30.44
12	Missouri	40.48	37	North Dakota	30.43
13	Kansas	40.40	38	Illinois	30.39
14	Idaho	40.18	39	Delaware	30.15
15	Washington	39.72	40	Minnesota	30.11
16	Colorado	39.26	41	New Jersey	29.28
17	Ohio	37.49	42	Connecticut	29.26
18	Indiana	37.40	43	Georgia	29.04
19	Oklahoma	37.20	44	South Carolina	27.38
20	Nebraska	36.39	45	Virginia	27.28
21	Arkansas	36.16	46	Louisiana	25.86
22	Pennsylvania	36.04	47	Texas	24.30
23	Tennessee	35.59	48	Utah	22.13
24	Alabama	35.08	49	Hawaii	17.49
25	Massachusetts	34.37	50	Alaska	13.55

District of Columbia   23.50

Source: U.S. Department of Health and Human Services, Centers for Disease Control, National Center for Health Statistics,
    "Vital Statistics of the United States, 1988" (Vol. II, Part B, issued 1990) (Rates calculated by editors.)
*By state of residence. Includes allied conditions. Rates calculated by the editors.

Deaths by Diabetes Mellitus in 1988

National Total = 40,368 Deaths by Diabetes Mellitus*

RANK	STATE	DEATHS	%	RANK	STATE	DEATHS	%
1	California	3,405	8.43%	26	Oklahoma	539	1.34%
2	New York	3,249	8.05%	27	Connecticut	530	1.31%
3	Pennsylvania	2,624	6.50%	28	Mississippi	498	1.23%
4	Florida	2,139	5.30%	29	Iowa	458	1.13%
5	Ohio	2,135	5.29%	30	Oregon	443	1.10%
6	Texas	2,058	5.10%	31	Arkansas	419	1.04%
7	Illinois	1,835	4.55%	32	Kansas	409	1.01%
8	New Jersey	1,532	3.80%	33	West Virginia	390	0.97%
9	Michigan	1,520	3.77%	34	Colorado	371	0.92%
10	North Carolina	1,326	3.28%	35	Rhode Island	284	0.70%
11	Indiana	1,222	3.03%	36	Maine	276	0.68%
12	Massachusetts	922	2.28%	37	New Mexico	258	0.64%
13	Georgia	912	2.26%	38	Nebraska	249	0.62%
14	Louisiana	863	2.14%	39	Utah	221	0.55%
15	Kentucky	847	2.10%	40	New Hampshire	178	0.44%
16	Missouri	824	2.04%	41	Idaho	163	0.40%
17	Alabama	792	1.96%	42	Montana	153	0.38%
18	Wisconsin	788	1.95%	43	Delaware	147	0.36%
19	Maryland	773	1.91%	43	Hawaii	147	0.36%
20	Virginia	753	1.87%	45	Nevada	123	0.30%
21	Tennessee	739	1.83%	46	North Dakota	115	0.28%
22	Washington	655	1.62%	47	South Dakota	95	0.24%
23	Minnesota	557	1.38%	48	Vermont	93	0.23%
24	South Carolina	550	1.36%	49	Wyoming	70	0.17%
25	Arizona	543	1.35%	50	Alaska	40	0.10%

District of Columbia   136   0.34%

Source: U.S. Department of Health and Human Services, Centers for Disease Control, National Center for Health Statistics,
"Vital Statistics of the United States, 1988" (Vol II, Part B, issued 1990)
*By state of residence.

Death Rate by Diabetes Mellitus in 1988

National Rate = 16.42 Deaths per 100,000 Population*

RANK	STATE	RATE	RANK	STATE	RATE
1	Rhode Island	28.60	26	Kansas	16.39
2	Maine	22.90	27	Idaho	16.25
3	Kentucky	22.73	28	Wisconsin	16.23
4	Delaware	22.27	29	Iowa	16.16
5	Indiana	21.99	30	Missouri	16.03
6	Pennsylvania	21.86	31	Oregon	16.01
7	West Virginia	20.79	32	South Carolina	15.85
8	North Carolina	20.43	33	Illinois	15.80
9	New Jersey	19.84	34	Massachusetts	15.66
10	Ohio	19.67	35	Arizona	15.56
11	Louisiana	19.58	36	Nebraska	15.54
12	Alabama	19.31	37	Tennessee	15.10
13	Mississippi	19.01	38	Wyoming	14.61
14	Montana	19.01	39	Georgia	14.38
15	New York	18.14	40	Washington	14.09
16	Arkansas	17.49	41	Hawaii	13.39
17	Florida	17.34	42	South Dakota	13.32
18	North Dakota	17.24	43	Utah	13.08
19	New Mexico	17.12	44	Minnesota	12.93
20	Maryland	16.72	45	Virginia	12.52
21	Vermont	16.70	46	Texas	12.22
22	Oklahoma	16.63	47	California	12.03
23	Michigan	16.45	48	Nevada	11.67
24	New Hampshire	16.41	49	Colorado	11.24
25	Connecticut	16.39	50	Alaska	7.63

District of Columbia   22.04

Source: U.S. Department of Health and Human Services, Centers for Disease Control, National Center for Health Statistics,
"Vital Statistics of the United States, 1988" (Vol. II, Part B, issued 1990)
*By state of residence. Rates calculated by the editors.

Deaths by Diseases of the Heart in 1989

National Total = 733,867 Deaths by Diseases of the Heart*

RANK	STATE	DEATHS	%	RANK	STATE	DEATHS	%
1	California	69,610	9.49%	26	Iowa	9,681	1.32%
2	New York	64,823	8.83%	27	Mississippi	9,627	1.31%
3	Florida	46,304	6.31%	28	South Carolina	9,556	1.30%
4	Pennsylvania	45,086	6.14%	29	Arizona	8,768	1.19%
5	Texas	40,287	5.49%	30	Arkansas	8,341	1.14%
6	Illinois	36,709	5.00%	31	Kansas	7,734	1.05%
7	Ohio	35,357	4.82%	32	Oregon	7,588	1.03%
8	Michigan	28,098	3.83%	33	West Virginia	7,332	1.00%
9	New Jersey	24,317	3.31%	34	Colorado	6,102	0.83%
10	North Carolina	18,980	2.59%	35	Nebraska	5,128	0.70%
11	Massachusetts	17,836	2.43%	36	Maine	3,814	0.52%
12	Missouri	17,704	2.41%	37	Rhode Island	3,417	0.47%
13	Indiana	17,112	2.33%	38	New Mexico	3,014	0.41%
14	Georgia	16,754	2.28%	39	New Hampshire	2,818	0.38%
15	Virginia	15,778	2.15%	40	Nevada	2,729	0.37%
16	Tennessee	15,467	2.11%	41	Utah	2,728	0.37%
17	Wisconsin	14,888	2.03%	42	South Dakota	2,401	0.33%
18	Alabama	13,182	1.80%	43	Idaho	2,315	0.32%
19	Louisiana	12,754	1.74%	44	Montana	2,041	0.28%
20	Kentucky	12,253	1.67%	45	Hawaii	1,994	0.27%
21	Maryland	12,108	1.65%	46	Delaware	1,961	0.27%
22	Washington	11,199	1.53%	47	North Dakota	1,874	0.26%
23	Minnesota	10,879	1.48%	48	Vermont	1,475	0.20%
24	Oklahoma	10,698	1.46%	49	Wyoming	968	0.13%
25	Connecticut	9,829	1.34%	50	Alaska	476	0.06%
					District of Columbia	1,973	0.27%

Source: U.S. Department of Health and Human Services, Centers for Disease Control, National Center for Health Statistics,
    "Monthly Vital Statistics Report" (Vol. 40, No. 8(S)2, January 7, 1992)

*By state of residence.

Death Rate by Diseases of the Heart in 1989

National Rate = 295.6 Deaths per 100,000 Population*

RANK	STATE	RATE	RANK	STATE	RATE
1	West Virginia	394.8	26	Delaware	291.4
2	Pennsylvania	374.5	27	Louisiana	291.1
3	Mississippi	367.3	28	North Carolina	288.8
4	Florida	365.4	29	North Dakota	283.9
5	New York	361.1	30	South Carolina	272.1
6	Arkansas	346.7	31	Oregon	269.1
7	Missouri	343.2	32	Georgia	260.3
8	Rhode Island	342.4	33	Vermont	260.1
9	Iowa	340.9	34	Virginia	258.7
10	South Dakota	335.8	35	Maryland	257.9
11	Oklahoma	331.8	36	New Hampshire	254.6
12	Kentucky	328.8	37	Montana	253.2
13	Ohio	324.2	38	Minnesota	249.9
14	Alabama	320.1	39	Arizona	246.6
15	Nebraska	318.3	40	Nevada	245.6
16	Illinois	314.9	41	California	239.5
17	New Jersey	314.3	42	Texas	237.1
18	Tennessee	313.1	43	Washington	235.2
19	Maine	312.1	44	Idaho	228.3
20	Kansas	307.8	45	Wyoming	203.8
21	Indiana	306.0	46	New Mexico	197.3
22	Wisconsin	305.9	47	Colorado	184.0
23	Connecticut	303.5	48	Hawaii	179.3
24	Michigan	303.0	49	Utah	159.8
25	Massachusetts	301.6	50	Alaska	90.3

District of Columbia 326.7

Source: U.S. Department of Health and Human Services, Centers for Disease Control, National Center for Health Statistics,
"Monthly Vital Statistics Report" (Vol. 40, No. 8(S)2, January 7, 1992)
*By state of residence.

Deaths by Leukemia in 1988

National Total = 17,577 Deaths by Leukemia*

RANK	STATE	DEATHS	%	RANK	STATE	DEATHS	%
1	California	1,800	10.24%	26	Connecticut	245	1.39%
2	New York	1,317	7.49%	27	Iowa	242	1.38%
3	Florida	1,082	6.16%	28	Oklahoma	229	1.30%
4	Texas	1,067	6.07%	29	Arkansas	222	1.26%
5	Pennsylvania	1,027	5.84%	30	South Carolina	210	1.19%
6	Illinois	837	4.76%	31	Kansas	201	1.14%
7	Ohio	796	4.53%	32	Mississippi	181	1.03%
8	Michigan	663	3.77%	33	Colorado	176	1.00%
9	New Jersey	563	3.20%	34	West Virginia	158	0.90%
10	North Carolina	453	2.58%	35	Nebraska	122	0.69%
11	Massachusetts	437	2.49%	36	New Mexico	97	0.55%
12	Missouri	414	2.36%	37	Maine	87	0.49%
13	Indiana	410	2.33%	38	Rhode Island	80	0.46%
14	Wisconsin	398	2.26%	39	Idaho	77	0.44%
15	Georgia	393	2.24%	40	Utah	76	0.43%
16	Virginia	368	2.09%	41	Nevada	71	0.40%
17	Tennessee	319	1.81%	42	New Hampshire	64	0.36%
18	Minnesota	318	1.81%	43	Montana	63	0.36%
19	Washington	311	1.77%	44	North Dakota	62	0.35%
20	Maryland	307	1.75%	45	South Dakota	60	0.34%
21	Alabama	289	1.64%	46	Delaware	50	0.28%
22	Louisiana	285	1.62%	47	Hawaii	49	0.28%
23	Oregon	261	1.48%	48	Vermont	40	0.23%
24	Arizona	249	1.42%	49	Wyoming	39	0.22%
24	Kentucky	249	1.42%	50	Alaska	14	0.08%
					District of Columbia	49	0.28%

Source: U.S. Department of Health and Human Services, Centers for Disease Control, National Center for Health Statistics,
"Vital Statistics of the United States, 1988" (Vol II, Part B, issued 1990)
*By state of residence.

Death Rate by Leukemia in 1988

National Rate = 7.15 Deaths per 100,000 Population*

RANK	STATE	RATE	RANK	STATE	RATE
1	Oregon	9.43	26	Illinois	7.21
2	North Dakota	9.30	27	Vermont	7.18
3	Arkansas	9.27	28	Michigan	7.18
4	Florida	8.77	29	Arizona	7.14
5	Pennsylvania	8.56	30	Oklahoma	7.06
6	Iowa	8.54	31	Alabama	7.05
7	West Virginia	8.42	32	North Carolina	6.98
8	South Dakota	8.42	33	Mississippi	6.91
9	Wisconsin	8.20	34	Nevada	6.74
10	Wyoming	8.14	35	Washington	6.69
11	Rhode Island	8.06	36	Kentucky	6.68
12	Kansas	8.06	37	Maryland	6.64
13	Missouri	8.05	38	Tennessee	6.52
14	Montana	7.83	39	Louisiana	6.47
15	Idaho	7.68	40	New Mexico	6.44
16	Nebraska	7.62	41	California	6.36
17	Connecticut	7.58	42	Texas	6.34
18	Delaware	7.58	43	Georgia	6.20
19	Massachusetts	7.42	44	Virginia	6.12
20	Minnesota	7.38	45	South Carolina	6.05
21	Indiana	7.38	46	New Hampshire	5.90
22	New York	7.35	47	Colorado	5.33
23	Ohio	7.33	48	Utah	4.50
24	New Jersey	7.29	49	Hawaii	4.46
25	Maine	7.22	50	Alaska	2.67

District of Columbia 7.94

Source: U.S. Department of Health and Human Services, Centers for Disease Control, National Center for Health Statistics,
    "Vital Statistics of the United States, 1988" (Vol. II, Part B, issued 1990)
*By state of residence. Rates calculated by the editors.

Deaths by Malignant Neoplasms in 1989

National Total = 496,152 Deaths by Malignant Neoplasms*

RANK	STATE	DEATHS	%	RANK	STATE	DEATHS	%
1	California	48,165	9.71%	26	South Carolina	6,495	1.31%
2	New York	38,093	7.68%	27	Arizona	6,458	1.30%
3	Florida	32,580	6.57%	28	Iowa	6,187	1.25%
4	Pennsylvania	29,211	5.89%	29	Oregon	5,821	1.17%
5	Texas	27,414	5.53%	30	Arkansas	5,526	1.11%
6	Illinois	23,929	4.82%	31	Mississippi	5,269	1.06%
7	Ohio	23,218	4.68%	32	Kansas	5,011	1.01%
8	Michigan	18,337	3.70%	33	Colorado	4,705	0.95%
9	New Jersey	17,990	3.63%	34	West Virginia	4,380	0.88%
10	Massachusetts	13,630	2.75%	35	Nebraska	3,308	0.67%
11	North Carolina	12,976	2.62%	36	Maine	2,815	0.57%
12	Missouri	11,623	2.34%	37	Rhode Island	2,449	0.49%
13	Indiana	11,361	2.29%	38	New Mexico	2,249	0.45%
14	Virginia	11,262	2.27%	39	New Hampshire	2,168	0.44%
15	Georgia	11,150	2.25%	40	Nevada	2,080	0.42%
16	Tennessee	10,151	2.05%	41	Utah	1,858	0.37%
17	Wisconsin	9,815	1.98%	42	Idaho	1,672	0.34%
18	Maryland	9,498	1.91%	43	Montana	1,578	0.32%
19	Washington	8,718	1.76%	44	Hawaii	1,574	0.32%
20	Alabama	8,608	1.73%	45	South Dakota	1,444	0.29%
21	Louisiana	8,508	1.71%	46	Delaware	1,429	0.29%
22	Kentucky	8,257	1.66%	47	North Dakota	1,357	0.27%
23	Minnesota	8,018	1.62%	48	Vermont	1,094	0.22%
24	Connecticut	7,135	1.44%	49	Wyoming	754	0.15%
25	Oklahoma	6,681	1.35%	50	Alaska	440	0.09%
					District of Columbia	1,703	0.34%

Source: U.S. Department of Health and Human Services, Centers for Disease Control, National Center for Health Statistics,
   "Monthly Vital Statistics Report" (Vol. 40, No. 8(S)2, January 7, 1992)
*By state of residence. Neoplasms are abnormal tissue, tumors. Includes many cancers.

Death Rate by Malignant Neoplasms in 1989

National Rate = 199.9 Deaths per 100,000 Population*

RANK	STATE	RATE	RANK	STATE	RATE
1	Florida	257.1	26	Wisconsin	201.7
2	Rhode Island	245.4	27	Mississippi	201.0
3	Pennsylvania	242.6	28	Kansas	199.4
4	West Virginia	235.9	29	Michigan	197.7
5	New Jersey	232.5	30	North Carolina	197.5
6	Massachusetts	230.5	31	Montana	195.8
7	Maine	230.4	31	New Hampshire	195.8
8	Arkansas	229.7	33	Louisiana	194.2
9	Missouri	225.3	34	Vermont	192.9
10	Kentucky	221.5	35	Nevada	187.2
11	Connecticut	220.3	36	South Carolina	184.9
12	Iowa	217.9	37	Virginia	184.7
13	Ohio	212.9	38	Minnesota	184.2
14	Delaware	212.3	39	Washington	183.1
15	New York	212.2	40	Arizona	181.6
16	Alabama	209.0	41	Georgia	173.2
17	Oklahoma	207.2	42	California	165.7
18	Oregon	206.4	43	Idaho	164.9
19	North Dakota	205.6	44	Texas	161.3
20	Tennessee	205.5	45	Wyoming	158.7
21	Illinois	205.3	46	New Mexico	147.2
21	Nebraska	205.3	47	Colorado	141.8
23	Indiana	203.1	48	Hawaii	141.5
24	Maryland	202.3	49	Utah	108.8
25	South Dakota	202.0	50	Alaska	83.5

District of Columbia   282.0

Source: U.S. Department of Health and Human Services, Centers for Disease Control, National Center for Health Statistics,
   "Monthly Vital Statistics Report" (Vol. 40, No. 8(S)2, January 7, 1992)
*By state of residence. Neoplasms are abnormal tissue, tumors. Includes many cancers.

Deaths by Pneumonia and Influenza in 1988

National Total = 77,662 Deaths by Pneumonia and Influenza*

RANK	STATE	DEATHS	%	RANK	STATE	DEATHS	%
1	California	9,344	12.03%	26	Louisiana	1,021	1.31%
2	New York	6,932	8.93%	27	Arizona	998	1.29%
3	Texas	3,999	5.15%	27	Arkansas	998	1.29%
4	Pennsylvania	3,996	5.15%	29	Colorado	984	1.27%
5	Illinois	3,849	4.96%	30	Kansas	950	1.22%
6	Florida	3,366	4.33%	31	Oregon	924	1.19%
7	Ohio	3,248	4.18%	32	South Carolina	745	0.96%
8	Michigan	2,691	3.47%	33	Nebraska	732	0.94%
9	Massachusetts	2,530	3.26%	34	Mississippi	710	0.91%
10	New Jersey	2,404	3.10%	35	West Virginia	689	0.89%
11	Missouri	1,937	2.49%	36	Utah	410	0.53%
12	North Carolina	1,927	2.48%	37	New Mexico	366	0.47%
13	Wisconsin	1,799	2.32%	38	Maine	355	0.46%
14	Virginia	1,745	2.25%	39	Idaho	343	0.44%
15	Georgia	1,653	2.13%	40	South Dakota	308	0.40%
16	Tennessee	1,626	2.09%	41	New Hampshire	306	0.39%
17	Indiana	1,601	2.06%	42	Nevada	263	0.34%
18	Minnesota	1,536	1.98%	43	Rhode Island	259	0.33%
19	Kentucky	1,338	1.72%	44	Montana	249	0.32%
20	Washington	1,316	1.69%	45	North Dakota	210	0.27%
21	Maryland	1,291	1.66%	46	Hawaii	197	0.25%
22	Iowa	1,259	1.62%	47	Vermont	186	0.24%
23	Alabama	1,181	1.52%	48	Delaware	151	0.19%
24	Oklahoma	1,167	1.50%	49	Wyoming	149	0.19%
25	Connecticut	1,102	1.42%	50	Alaska	46	0.06%
					District of Columbia	276	0.36%

Source: U.S. Department of Health and Human Services, Centers for Disease Control, National Center for Health Statistics,
   "Vital Statistics of the United States, 1988" (Vol II, Part B, issued 1990)
*By state of residence.

Death Rate by Pneumonia and Influenza in 1988

National Rate = 31.59 Deaths per 100,000 Population*

RANK	STATE	RATE	RANK	STATE	RATE
1	Nebraska	45.69	26	Ohio	29.92
2	Iowa	44.42	27	Colorado	29.81
3	South Dakota	43.20	28	North Carolina	29.70
4	Massachusetts	42.96	29	Maine	29.46
5	Arkansas	41.67	30	Michigan	29.12
6	New York	38.71	31	Virginia	29.01
7	Kansas	38.08	32	Indiana	28.82
8	Missouri	37.68	33	Alabama	28.79
9	Wisconsin	37.05	34	Arizona	28.60
10	West Virginia	36.73	35	Washington	28.31
11	Oklahoma	36.00	36	New Hampshire	28.20
12	Kentucky	35.90	37	Maryland	27.93
13	Minnesota	35.66	38	Florida	27.29
14	Idaho	34.20	39	Mississippi	27.10
15	Connecticut	34.09	40	Rhode Island	26.08
16	Oregon	33.39	41	Georgia	26.06
17	Vermont	33.39	42	Nevada	24.95
18	Pennsylvania	33.30	43	New Mexico	24.29
19	Tennessee	33.22	44	Utah	24.26
20	Illinois	33.14	45	Texas	23.75
21	California	33.00	46	Louisiana	23.16
22	North Dakota	31.48	47	Delaware	22.88
23	New Jersey	31.14	48	South Carolina	21.47
24	Wyoming	31.11	49	Hawaii	17.94
25	Montana	30.93	50	Alaska	8.78

District of Columbia		44.73

Source: U.S. Department of Health and Human Services, Centers for Disease Control, National Center for Health Statistics,
   "Vital Statistics of the United States, 1988" (Vol. II, Part B, issued 1990)
*By state of residence. Rates calculated by the editors.

Deaths by Complications of Pregnancy and Childbirth in 1988

National Total = 330 Deaths by Complications of Pregnancy and Childbirth*

RANK	STATE	DEATHS	%	RANK	STATE	DEATHS	%
1	California	50	15.15%	24	Minnesota	4	1.21%
2	New York	35	10.61%	24	Missouri	4	1.21%
3	Texas	24	7.27%	24	South Carolina	4	1.21%
4	Illinois	14	4.24%	29	Arizona	3	0.91%
5	Florida	12	3.64%	29	Maine	3	0.91%
5	North Carolina	12	3.64%	29	Massachusetts	3	0.91%
7	Michigan	11	3.33%	32	Connecticut	2	0.61%
8	Louisiana	10	3.03%	32	Hawaii	2	0.61%
8	New Jersey	10	3.03%	32	Nebraska	2	0.61%
8	Virginia	10	3.03%	32	New Mexico	2	0.61%
11	Georgia	9	2.73%	32	Oregon	2	0.61%
11	Tennessee	9	2.73%	32	Utah	2	0.61%
13	Alabama	8	2.42%	38	Delaware	1	0.30%
13	Pennsylvania	8	2.42%	38	Idaho	1	0.30%
15	Indiana	7	2.12%	38	Montana	1	0.30%
15	Mississippi	7	2.12%	38	Nevada	1	0.30%
15	Ohio	7	2.12%	38	New Hampshire	1	0.30%
18	Arkansas	6	1.82%	38	Rhode Island	1	0.30%
18	Oklahoma	6	1.82%	38	South Dakota	1	0.30%
18	Wisconsin	6	1.82%	38	Vermont	1	0.30%
21	Colorado	5	1.52%	38	Washington	1	0.30%
21	Iowa	5	1.52%	38	West Virginia	1	0.30%
21	Kentucky	5	1.52%	38	Wyoming	1	0.30%
24	Kansas	4	1.21%	49	Alaska	0	0.00%
24	Maryland	4	1.21%	49	North Dakota	0	0.00%
					District of Columbia	2	0.61%

Source: U.S. Department of Health and Human Services, Centers for Disease Control, National Center for Health Statistics,
   "Vital Statistics of the United States, 1988" (Vol II, Part B, issued 1990)
*By state of residence.

Death Rate by Complications of Pregnancy and Childbirth in 1988

National Rate = .134 Deaths per 100,000 Population*

RANK	STATE	RATE	RANK	STATE	RATE
1	Mississippi	0.267	26	Nebraska	0.125
2	Arkansas	0.251	27	Montana	0.124
3	Maine	0.249	28	Wisconsin	0.124
4	Louisiana	0.227	29	Illinois	0.121
5	Wyoming	0.209	30	Michigan	0.119
6	New York	0.195	31	Utah	0.118
7	Alabama	0.195	32	South Carolina	0.115
8	Oklahoma	0.185	33	Rhode Island	0.101
9	North Carolina	0.185	34	Idaho	0.100
10	Tennessee	0.184	35	Florida	0.097
11	Hawaii	0.182	36	Nevada	0.095
12	Vermont	0.180	37	Minnesota	0.093
13	California	0.177	38	New Hampshire	0.092
14	Iowa	0.176	39	Maryland	0.087
15	Virginia	0.166	40	Arizona	0.086
16	Kansas	0.160	41	Missouri	0.078
17	Delaware	0.152	42	Oregon	0.072
18	Colorado	0.151	43	Pennsylvania	0.067
19	Texas	0.143	44	Ohio	0.064
20	Georgia	0.142	45	Connecticut	0.062
21	South Dakota	0.140	46	West Virginia	0.053
22	Kentucky	0.134	47	Massachusetts	0.051
23	New Mexico	0.133	48	Washington	0.022
24	New Jersey	0.130	49	Alaska	0.000
25	Indiana	0.126	49	North Dakota	0.000
				District of Columbia	0.324

Source: U.S. Department of Health and Human Services, Centers for Disease Control, National Center for Health Statistics,
"Vital Statistics of the United States, 1988" (Vol. II, Part B, issued 1990)
*By state of residence. Rates calculated by the editors.

Deaths by Suicide in 1989

National Total = 30,232 Deaths by Suicide*

RANK	STATE	SUICIDES	%	RANK	STATE	SUICIDES	%
1	California	3,704	12.25%	26	Oregon	470	1.55%
2	Texas	2,126	7.03%	27	South Carolina	424	1.40%
3	Florida	2,076	6.87%	28	Oklahoma	416	1.38%
4	New York	1,519	5.02%	29	Iowa	315	1.04%
5	Pennsylvania	1,451	4.80%	30	Mississippi	314	1.04%
6	Ohio	1,235	4.09%	31	Connecticut	303	1.00%
7	Illinois	1,171	3.87%	32	New Mexico	298	0.99%
8	Michigan	1,045	3.46%	33	Kansas	285	0.94%
9	North Carolina	871	2.88%	34	Nevada	257	0.85%
10	Georgia	855	2.83%	35	Arkansas	246	0.81%
11	Virginia	814	2.69%	36	West Virginia	231	0.76%
12	Indiana	678	2.24%	37	Utah	211	0.70%
13	Arizona	671	2.22%	38	Nebraska	174	0.58%
14	Missouri	665	2.20%	39	Maine	170	0.56%
15	Tennessee	652	2.16%	40	Montana	161	0.53%
16	Washington	648	2.14%	41	Idaho	160	0.53%
17	Wisconsin	597	1.97%	42	New Hampshire	126	0.42%
18	Colorado	549	1.82%	43	Hawaii	109	0.36%
19	Louisiana	542	1.79%	44	Rhode Island	100	0.33%
20	Maryland	525	1.74%	45	Delaware	95	0.31%
21	Minnesota	515	1.70%	46	Vermont	94	0.31%
22	Alabama	506	1.67%	47	South Dakota	90	0.30%
23	New Jersey	503	1.66%	48	Alaska	89	0.29%
24	Massachusetts	491	1.62%	49	Wyoming	82	0.27%
25	Kentucky	482	1.59%	50	North Dakota	70	0.23%
					District of Columbia	51	0.17%

Source: U.S. Department of Health and Human Services, Centers for Disease Control, National Center for Health Statistics,
    "Monthly Vital Statistics Report" (Vol. 40, No. 8(S)2, January 7, 1992)

*By state of residence.

Death Rate by Suicide in 1989

National Rate = 12.2 Deaths by Suicide per 100,000 Population*

RANK	STATE	RATE	RANK	STATE	RATE
1	Nevada	23.1	25	Utah	12.4
2	Montana	20.0	25	West Virginia	12.4
3	New Mexico	19.5	28	Alabama	12.3
4	Arizona	18.9	28	Wisconsin	12.3
5	Wyoming	17.3	30	Indiana	12.1
6	Alaska	16.9	30	Pennsylvania	12.1
7	Oregon	16.7	30	South Carolina	12.1
8	Colorado	16.6	33	Mississippi	12.0
8	Vermont	16.6	34	Minnesota	11.8
10	Florida	16.4	35	New Hampshire	11.4
11	Idaho	15.8	36	Kansas	11.3
12	Delaware	14.1	36	Michigan	11.3
13	Maine	13.9	36	Ohio	11.3
14	Washington	13.6	39	Maryland	11.2
15	Georgia	13.3	40	Iowa	11.1
15	North Carolina	13.3	41	Nebraska	10.8
15	Virginia	13.3	42	North Dakota	10.6
18	Tennessee	13.2	43	Arkansas	10.2
19	Kentucky	12.9	44	Illinois	10.0
19	Missouri	12.9	44	Rhode Island	10.0
19	Oklahoma	12.9	46	Hawaii	9.8
22	California	12.7	47	Connecticut	9.4
23	South Dakota	12.6	48	New York	8.5
24	Texas	12.5	49	Massachusetts	8.3
25	Louisiana	12.4	50	New Jersey	6.5

	District of Columbia	8.4

Source: U.S. Department of Health and Human Services, Centers for Disease Control, National Center for Health Statistics,
   "Monthly Vital Statistics Report" (Vol. 40, No. 8(S)2, January 7, 1992)
*By state of residence.

Deaths by Syphilis in 1988

National Total = 85 Deaths by Syphilis*

RANK	STATE	DEATHS	%	RANK	STATE	DEATHS	%
1	Florida	11	12.94%	19	Washington	1	1.18%
2	California	10	11.76%	27	Alabama	0	0.00%
3	New York	9	10.59%	27	Alaska	0	0.00%
4	Texas	8	9.41%	27	Arkansas	0	0.00%
5	North Carolina	4	4.71%	27	Delaware	0	0.00%
6	Indiana	3	3.53%	27	Hawaii	0	0.00%
6	Louisiana	3	3.53%	27	Idaho	0	0.00%
6	Missouri	3	3.53%	27	Kansas	0	0.00%
6	Ohio	3	3.53%	27	Kentucky	0	0.00%
6	Pennsylvania	3	3.53%	27	Maine	0	0.00%
6	Virginia	3	3.53%	27	Minnesota	0	0.00%
12	Arizona	2	2.35%	27	Mississippi	0	0.00%
12	Colorado	2	2.35%	27	Montana	0	0.00%
12	Connecticut	2	2.35%	27	Nebraska	0	0.00%
12	Georgia	2	2.35%	27	Nevada	0	0.00%
12	Massachusetts	2	2.35%	27	New Hampshire	0	0.00%
12	Michigan	2	2.35%	27	New Mexico	0	0.00%
12	Tennessee	2	2.35%	27	North Dakota	0	0.00%
19	Illinois	1	1.18%	27	South Carolina	0	0.00%
19	Iowa	1	1.18%	27	South Dakota	0	0.00%
19	Maryland	1	1.18%	27	Utah	0	0.00%
19	New Jersey	1	1.18%	27	Vermont	0	0.00%
19	Oklahoma	1	1.18%	27	West Virginia	0	0.00%
19	Oregon	1	1.18%	27	Wisconsin	0	0.00%
19	Rhode Island	1	1.18%	27	Wyoming	0	0.00%

District of Columbia 3 3.53%

Source: U.S. Department of Health and Human Services, Centers for Disease Control, National Center for Health Statistics,
"Vital Statistics of the United States, 1988" (Vol II, Part B, issued 1990)
*By state of residence.

Death Rate by Syphilis in 1988

National Rate = .035 Deaths per 100,000 Population*

RANK	STATE	RATE	RANK	STATE	RATE
1	Rhode Island	0.101	26	Illinois	0.009
2	Florida	0.089	27	Alabama	0.000
3	Louisiana	0.068	27	Alaska	0.000
4	Connecticut	0.062	27	Arkansas	0.000
5	North Carolina	0.062	27	Delaware	0.000
6	Colorado	0.061	27	Hawaii	0.000
7	Missouri	0.058	27	Idaho	0.000
8	Arizona	0.057	27	Kansas	0.000
9	Indiana	0.054	27	Kentucky	0.000
10	New York	0.050	27	Maine	0.000
11	Virginia	0.050	27	Minnesota	0.000
12	Texas	0.048	27	Mississippi	0.000
13	Tennessee	0.041	27	Montana	0.000
14	Oregon	0.036	27	Nebraska	0.000
15	California	0.035	27	Nevada	0.000
16	Iowa	0.035	27	New Hampshire	0.000
17	Massachusetts	0.034	27	New Mexico	0.000
18	Georgia	0.032	27	North Dakota	0.000
19	Oklahoma	0.031	27	South Carolina	0.000
20	Ohio	0.028	27	South Dakota	0.000
21	Pennsylvania	0.025	27	Utah	0.000
22	Michigan	0.022	27	Vermont	0.000
23	Maryland	0.022	27	West Virginia	0.000
24	Washington	0.022	27	Wisconsin	0.000
25	New Jersey	0.013	27	Wyoming	0.000

District of Columbia   0.486

Source: U.S. Department of Health and Human Services, Centers for Disease Control, National Center for Health Statistics,
    "Vital Statistics of the United States, 1988" (Vol. II, Part B, issued 1990)
*By state of residence. Rates calculated by the editors.

Deaths by Tuberculosis in 1988

National Total = 1,921 Deaths by Tuberculosis*

RANK	STATE	DEATHS	%	RANK	STATE	DEATHS	%
1	New York	290	15.10%	26	Indiana	22	1.15%
2	California	232	12.08%	26	Washington	22	1.15%
3	Florida	145	7.55%	28	Wisconsin	17	0.88%
4	Texas	127	6.61%	29	Hawaii	16	0.83%
5	Illinois	78	4.06%	30	Oregon	14	0.73%
6	North Carolina	73	3.80%	31	Colorado	13	0.68%
7	Pennsylvania	71	3.70%	31	Connecticut	13	0.68%
8	New Jersey	70	3.64%	31	Iowa	13	0.68%
9	Georgia	69	3.59%	34	Nevada	10	0.52%
10	Tennessee	60	3.12%	35	Minnesota	7	0.36%
11	Louisiana	48	2.50%	35	New Mexico	7	0.36%
12	Ohio	47	2.45%	37	Kansas	6	0.31%
13	Missouri	43	2.24%	38	Delaware	5	0.26%
14	Michigan	42	2.19%	38	Maine	5	0.26%
15	Alabama	41	2.13%	40	Utah	4	0.21%
16	Virginia	37	1.93%	41	South Dakota	3	0.16%
17	Kentucky	36	1.87%	42	Alaska	2	0.10%
18	Mississippi	30	1.56%	42	Montana	2	0.10%
19	Maryland	29	1.51%	42	Nebraska	2	0.10%
20	Arkansas	28	1.46%	42	Rhode Island	2	0.10%
20	Oklahoma	28	1.46%	46	Idaho	1	0.05%
22	Massachusetts	26	1.35%	46	North Dakota	1	0.05%
23	Arizona	24	1.25%	46	Vermont	1	0.05%
24	South Carolina	23	1.20%	49	New Hampshire	0	0.00%
24	West Virginia	23	1.20%	49	Wyoming	0	0.00%

	District of Columbia	13	0.68%

Source: U.S. Department of Health and Human Services, Centers for Disease Control, National Center for Health Statistics,
"Vital Statistics of the United States, 1988" (Vol II, Part B, issued 1990)
*By state of residence.

Death Rate by Tuberculosis in 1988

National Rate = .78 Deaths per 100,000 Population*

RANK	STATE	RATE		RANK	STATE	RATE
1	New York	1.62		26	Oregon	0.51
2	Hawaii	1.46		27	Washington	0.47
3	West Virginia	1.23		28	New Mexico	0.46
4	Tennessee	1.23		29	Iowa	0.46
5	Florida	1.18		30	Michigan	0.45
6	Arkansas	1.17		31	Massachusetts	0.44
7	Mississippi	1.15		32	Ohio	0.43
8	North Carolina	1.12		33	South Dakota	0.42
9	Louisiana	1.09		34	Maine	0.41
10	Georgia	1.09		35	Connecticut	0.40
11	Alabama	1.00		36	Indiana	0.40
12	Kentucky	0.97		37	Colorado	0.39
13	Nevada	0.95		38	Alaska	0.38
14	New Jersey	0.91		39	Wisconsin	0.35
15	Oklahoma	0.86		40	Montana	0.25
16	Missouri	0.84		41	Kansas	0.24
17	California	0.82		42	Utah	0.24
18	Delaware	0.76		43	Rhode Island	0.20
19	Texas	0.75		44	Vermont	0.18
20	Arizona	0.69		45	Minnesota	0.16
21	Illinois	0.67		46	North Dakota	0.15
22	South Carolina	0.66		47	Nebraska	0.12
23	Maryland	0.63		48	Idaho	0.10
24	Virginia	0.62		49	New Hampshire	0.00
25	Pennsylvania	0.59		49	Wyoming	0.00

District of Columbia   2.11

Source: U.S. Department of Health and Human Services, Centers for Disease Control, National Center for Health Statistics,
"Vital Statistics of the United States, 1988" (Vol. II, Part B, issued 1990) (Rates calculated by editors.)
*By state of residence. Rates calculated by the editors.

AIDS Cases in 1991

National Total = 41,947 AIDS Cases Reported*

RANK	STATE	AIDS CASES	%	RANK	STATE	AIDS CASES	%
1	New York	8,083	19.27%	26	Arizona	242	0.58%
2	California	7,533	17.96%	27	Minnesota	208	0.50%
3	Florida	5,017	11.96%	28	Oklahoma	202	0.48%
4	Texas	3,108	7.41%	29	Mississippi	195	0.46%
5	New Jersey	2,304	5.49%	30	Wisconsin	191	0.46%
6	Illinois	1,406	3.35%	31	Arkansas	187	0.45%
7	Georgia	1,388	3.31%	32	Kentucky	175	0.42%
8	Pennsylvania	1,168	2.78%	33	Hawaii	165	0.39%
9	Massachusetts	957	2.28%	34	New Mexico	123	0.29%
10	Maryland	931	2.22%	35	Utah	100	0.24%
11	Virginia	694	1.65%	36	Iowa	97	0.23%
12	Louisiana	682	1.63%	37	Kansas	91	0.22%
13	Ohio	613	1.46%	38	Rhode Island	88	0.21%
14	Missouri	600	1.43%	39	Delaware	79	0.19%
15	Washington	558	1.33%	40	Nebraska	57	0.14%
16	Michigan	537	1.28%	41	Maine	54	0.13%
17	Connecticut	516	1.23%	42	West Virginia	48	0.11%
18	North Carolina	509	1.21%	43	New Hampshire	47	0.11%
19	Colorado	423	1.01%	44	Montana	31	0.07%
20	Tennessee	315	0.75%	45	Idaho	27	0.06%
21	Alabama	310	0.74%	46	Vermont	24	0.06%
22	Oregon	303	0.72%	47	Alaska	17	0.04%
23	South Carolina	295	0.70%	47	Wyoming	17	0.04%
24	Indiana	272	0.65%	49	South Dakota	9	0.02%
25	Nevada	246	0.59%	50	North Dakota	4	0.01%
					District of Columbia	701	1.67%

Source: U.S. Department of Health and Human Services, Centers for Disease Control, Division of HIV/AIDS,
   "HIV/AIDS Surveillance Report" (October 1991)
*October 1990 through September 1991.

AIDS Rate in 1991

National Rate = 16.7 AIDS Cases Reported per 100,000 Population*

RANK	STATE	AIDS RATE		RANK	STATE	AIDS RATE
1	New York	44.8		25	Mississippi	7.6
2	Florida	37.8		25	North Carolina	7.6
3	New Jersey	29.7		28	Arizona	6.4
4	California	24.8		28	Oklahoma	6.4
5	Georgia	21.1		28	Tennessee	6.4
6	Nevada	19.8		31	Michigan	5.8
7	Maryland	19.2		32	Utah	5.7
8	Texas	18.0		33	Ohio	5.6
9	Louisiana	16.2		34	Indiana	4.9
10	Massachusetts	15.8		35	Kentucky	4.7
11	Connecticut	15.6		35	Minnesota	4.7
12	Hawaii	14.7		37	Maine	4.4
13	Colorado	12.7		38	New Hampshire	4.2
14	Illinois	12.3		38	Vermont	4.2
15	Delaware	11.7		40	Montana	3.9
15	Missouri	11.7		40	Wisconsin	3.9
17	Washington	11.3		42	Wyoming	3.8
18	Virginia	11.1		43	Kansas	3.7
19	Oregon	10.6		44	Nebraska	3.6
20	Pennsylvania	9.8		45	Iowa	3.5
21	Rhode Island	8.7		46	Alaska	3.0
22	South Carolina	8.4		47	Idaho	2.7
23	New Mexico	8.0		47	West Virginia	2.7
24	Arkansas	7.9		49	South Dakota	1.3
25	Alabama	7.6		50	North Dakota	0.6

	District of Columbia	116.1

Source: U.S. Department of Health and Human Services, Centers for Disease Control, Division of HIV/AIDS,

"HIV/AIDS Surveillance Report" (October 1991)

*October 1990 through September 1991.

AIDS Cases as of September 1991

National Total = 189,323 AIDS Cases Reported*

RANK	STATE	AIDS CASES	%	RANK	STATE	AIDS CASES	%
1	New York	40,892	21.60%	26	Minnesota	981	0.52%
2	California	36,582	19.32%	27	Oklahoma	868	0.46%
3	Florida	18,272	9.65%	28	Nevada	824	0.44%
4	Texas	13,787	7.28%	29	Mississippi	814	0.43%
5	New Jersey	12,120	6.40%	30	Wisconsin	799	0.42%
6	Illinois	5,816	3.07%	31	Hawaii	763	0.40%
7	Georgia	5,408	2.86%	32	Kentucky	636	0.34%
8	Pennsylvania	5,343	2.82%	33	Arkansas	602	0.32%
9	Massachusetts	4,085	2.16%	34	Kansas	515	0.27%
10	Maryland	3,899	2.06%	35	Rhode Island	446	0.24%
11	Louisiana	2,850	1.51%	36	New Mexico	438	0.23%
12	Ohio	2,779	1.47%	37	Utah	423	0.22%
13	Washington	2,622	1.38%	38	Delaware	370	0.20%
14	Virginia	2,588	1.37%	39	Iowa	301	0.16%
15	Michigan	2,422	1.28%	40	Maine	255	0.13%
16	Missouri	2,335	1.23%	41	Nebraska	228	0.12%
17	Connecticut	2,286	1.21%	42	New Hampshire	226	0.12%
18	North Carolina	2,088	1.10%	43	West Virginia	224	0.12%
19	Colorado	1,929	1.02%	44	Alaska	114	0.06%
20	Arizona	1,487	0.79%	45	Idaho	98	0.05%
21	Tennessee	1,352	0.71%	46	Vermont	92	0.05%
22	South Carolina	1,300	0.69%	47	Montana	80	0.04%
23	Indiana	1,261	0.67%	48	Wyoming	51	0.03%
24	Oregon	1,230	0.65%	49	South Dakota	28	0.01%
25	Alabama	1,148	0.61%	50	North Dakota	24	0.01%
					District of Columbia	3,242	1.71%

Source: U.S. Department of Health and Human Services, Centers for Disease Control, Division of HIV/AIDS,
"HIV/AIDS Surveillance Report" (October 1991)

*Cumulative totals.

Deaths by AIDS in 1990

National Total = 12,294 Deaths

RANK	STATE	DEATHS	%
1	California	2,768	22.52%
2	Florida	1,423	11.57%
3	New York	1,183	9.62%
4	Texas	889	7.23%
5	New Jersey	674	5.48%
6	Illinois	487	3.96%
7	Georgia	456	3.71%
8	Pennsylvania	441	3.59%
9	Maryland	327	2.66%
10	Ohio	254	2.07%
11	Louisiana	249	2.03%
12	Massachusetts	235	1.91%
13	Michigan	216	1.76%
14	Colorado	195	1.59%
15	Missouri	175	1.42%
16	Washington	167	1.36%
17	North Carolina	145	1.18%
18	Connecticut	142	1.16%
19	Virginia	139	1.13%
20	Tennessee	131	1.07%
21	Indiana	114	0.93%
22	Arizona	111	0.90%
23	Oregon	110	0.89%
23	South Carolina	110	0.89%
25	Alabama	100	0.81%

RANK	STATE	DEATHS	%
26	Minnesota	95	0.77%
27	Nevada	72	0.59%
28	Oklahoma	71	0.58%
29	Kentucky	65	0.53%
30	Hawaii	62	0.50%
31	Wisconsin	57	0.46%
32	Kansas	53	0.43%
33	Mississippi	39	0.32%
34	Delaware	38	0.31%
35	Utah	36	0.29%
36	Arkansas	32	0.26%
37	Rhode Island	28	0.23%
37	West Virginia	28	0.23%
39	Maine	27	0.22%
40	New Mexico	25	0.20%
41	Nebraska	19	0.15%
42	Idaho	14	0.11%
43	New Hampshire	11	0.09%
44	Vermont	6	0.05%
45	Iowa	4	0.03%
45	Montana	4	0.03%
45	Wyoming	4	0.03%
48	Alaska	3	0.02%
49	North Dakota	0	0.00%
49	South Dakota	0	0.00%

	District of Columbia	260	2.11%

Source: U.S. Department of Health and Human Services, Centers for Disease Control, National Center for Health Statistics, "Health United States 1990" (PHS 91-1232, March 1991)

Death Rate by AIDS in 1990

National Rate = 4.94 Deaths by AIDS per 100,000 Population*

RANK	STATE	RATE		RANK	STATE	RATE
1	Florida	11.00		26	Michigan	2.32
2	California	9.30		27	Oklahoma	2.26
3	New Jersey	8.72		28	Virginia	2.25
4	Georgia	7.04		29	Maine	2.20
5	Maryland	6.84		30	North Carolina	2.19
6	New York	6.58		31	Minnesota	2.17
7	Nevada	5.99		32	Kansas	2.14
8	Colorado	5.92		33	Utah	2.09
9	Louisiana	5.90		34	Indiana	2.06
10	Delaware	5.70		35	Kentucky	1.76
11	Hawaii	5.59		36	New Mexico	1.65
12	Texas	5.23		37	West Virginia	1.56
13	Connecticut	4.32		38	Mississippi	1.52
14	Illinois	4.26		39	Idaho	1.39
15	Massachusetts	3.91		40	Arkansas	1.36
16	Oregon	3.87		41	Nebraska	1.20
17	Pennsylvania	3.71		42	Wisconsin	1.17
18	Washington	3.43		43	Vermont	1.07
19	Missouri	3.42		44	New Hampshire	0.99
20	South Carolina	3.15		45	Wyoming	0.88
21	Arizona	3.03		46	Alaska	0.55
22	Rhode Island	2.79		47	Montana	0.50
23	Tennessee	2.69		48	Iowa	0.14
24	Alabama	2.47		49	North Dakota	0.00
25	Ohio	2.34		49	South Dakota	0.00

District of Columbia   42.84

Source: U.S. Department of Health and Human Services, Centers for Disease Control, National Center for Health Statistics,
   "Health United States 1990" (PHS 91–1232, March 1991)
*Rates calculated by the editors using 1990 Census counts.

Deaths by AIDS: 1983 to 1990

National Total = 90,914 Deaths

RANK	STATE	DEATHS	%
1	New York	20,343	22.38%
2	California	18,634	20.50%
3	Florida	8,077	8.88%
4	Texas	6,658	7.32%
5	New Jersey	6,011	6.61%
6	Illinois	2,843	3.13%
7	Pennsylvania	2,749	3.02%
8	Georgia	2,407	2.65%
9	Maryland	1,799	1.98%
10	Massachusetts	1,793	1.97%
11	Louisiana	1,388	1.53%
12	Ohio	1,306	1.44%
13	Virginia	1,194	1.31%
14	Michigan	1,117	1.23%
15	Washington	1,111	1.22%
16	Connecticut	1,069	1.18%
17	North Carolina	950	1.04%
18	Missouri	948	1.04%
19	Colorado	944	1.04%
20	Arizona	726	0.80%
21	Tennessee	589	0.65%
22	Indiana	554	0.61%
23	South Carolina	552	0.61%
24	Oregon	532	0.59%
25	Alabama	506	0.56%

RANK	STATE	DEATHS	%
26	Minnesota	456	0.50%
27	Oklahoma	426	0.47%
28	Hawaii	353	0.39%
28	Nevada	353	0.39%
30	Mississippi	342	0.38%
31	Wisconsin	326	0.36%
32	Kentucky	311	0.34%
33	Kansas	269	0.30%
34	Arkansas	244	0.27%
35	Rhode Island	210	0.23%
36	Utah	187	0.21%
37	Delaware	174	0.19%
37	New Mexico	174	0.19%
39	Nebraska	111	0.12%
40	Maine	108	0.12%
41	West Virginia	107	0.12%
42	New Hampshire	96	0.11%
43	Iowa	89	0.10%
44	Idaho	43	0.05%
45	Alaska	40	0.04%
46	Vermont	34	0.04%
47	Montana	27	0.03%
48	Wyoming	20	0.02%
49	North Dakota	15	0.02%
50	South Dakota	9	0.01%

	District of Columbia	1,590	1.75%

Source: U.S. Department of Health and Human Services, Centers for Disease Control, National Center for Health Statistics, "Health United States 1990" (PHS 91-1232, March 1991)

XII. HOUSING

Housing Units in 1990

National Total = 102,263,678 Housing Units

RANK	STATE	HOUSING UNITS	%	RANK	STATE	HOUSING UNITS	%
1	California	11,182,882	10.94%	26	South Carolina	1,424,155	1.39%
2	New York	7,226,891	7.07%	27	Oklahoma	1,406,499	1.38%
3	Texas	7,008,999	6.85%	28	Connecticut	1,320,850	1.29%
4	Florida	6,100,262	5.97%	29	Oregon	1,193,567	1.17%
5	Pennsylvania	4,938,140	4.83%	30	Iowa	1,143,669	1.12%
6	Illinois	4,506,275	4.41%	31	Kansas	1,044,112	1.02%
7	Ohio	4,371,945	4.28%	32	Mississippi	1,010,423	0.99%
8	Michigan	3,847,926	3.76%	33	Arkansas	1,000,667	0.98%
9	New Jersey	3,075,310	3.01%	34	West Virginia	781,295	0.76%
10	North Carolina	2,818,193	2.76%	35	Nebraska	660,621	0.65%
11	Georgia	2,638,418	2.58%	36	New Mexico	632,058	0.62%
12	Virginia	2,496,334	2.44%	37	Utah	598,388	0.59%
13	Massachusetts	2,472,711	2.42%	38	Maine	587,045	0.57%
14	Indiana	2,246,046	2.20%	39	Nevada	518,858	0.51%
15	Missouri	2,199,129	2.15%	40	New Hampshire	503,904	0.49%
16	Wisconsin	2,055,774	2.01%	41	Rhode Island	414,572	0.41%
17	Washington	2,032,378	1.99%	42	Idaho	413,327	0.40%
18	Tennessee	2,026,067	1.98%	43	Hawaii	389,810	0.38%
19	Maryland	1,891,917	1.85%	44	Montana	361,155	0.35%
20	Minnesota	1,848,445	1.81%	45	South Dakota	292,436	0.29%
21	Louisiana	1,716,241	1.68%	46	Delaware	289,919	0.28%
22	Alabama	1,670,379	1.63%	47	North Dakota	276,340	0.27%
23	Arizona	1,659,430	1.62%	48	Vermont	271,214	0.27%
24	Kentucky	1,506,845	1.47%	49	Alaska	232,608	0.23%
25	Colorado	1,477,349	1.44%	50	Wyoming	203,411	0.20%
					District of Columbia	278,489	0.27%

Source: U.S. Bureau of the Census,
Press Release CB 91-334 (December 18, 1991)

Households in 1990

National Total = 91,947,410 Households

RANK	STATE	HOUSEHOLDS	%	RANK	STATE	HOUSEHOLDS	%
1	California	10,381,206	11.29%	26	South Carolina	1,258,044	1.37%
2	New York	6,639,322	7.22%	27	Connecticut	1,230,479	1.34%
3	Texas	6,070,937	6.60%	28	Oklahoma	1,206,135	1.31%
4	Florida	5,134,869	5.58%	29	Oregon	1,103,313	1.20%
5	Pennsylvania	4,495,966	4.89%	30	Iowa	1,064,325	1.16%
6	Illinois	4,202,240	4.57%	31	Kansas	944,726	1.03%
7	Ohio	4,087,546	4.45%	32	Mississippi	911,374	0.99%
8	Michigan	3,419,331	3.72%	33	Arkansas	891,179	0.97%
9	New Jersey	2,794,711	3.04%	34	West Virginia	688,557	0.75%
10	North Carolina	2,517,026	2.74%	35	Nebraska	602,363	0.66%
11	Georgia	2,366,615	2.57%	36	New Mexico	542,709	0.59%
12	Virginia	2,291,830	2.49%	37	Utah	537,273	0.58%
13	Massachusetts	2,247,110	2.44%	38	Nevada	466,297	0.51%
14	Indiana	2,065,355	2.25%	39	Maine	465,312	0.51%
15	Missouri	1,961,206	2.13%	40	New Hampshire	411,186	0.45%
16	Washington	1,872,431	2.04%	41	Rhode Island	377,977	0.41%
17	Tennessee	1,853,725	2.02%	42	Idaho	360,723	0.39%
18	Wisconsin	1,822,118	1.98%	43	Hawaii	356,267	0.39%
19	Maryland	1,748,991	1.90%	44	Montana	306,163	0.33%
20	Minnesota	1,647,853	1.79%	45	South Dakota	259,034	0.28%
21	Alabama	1,506,790	1.64%	46	Delaware	247,497	0.27%
22	Louisiana	1,499,269	1.63%	47	North Dakota	240,878	0.26%
23	Kentucky	1,379,782	1.50%	48	Vermont	210,650	0.23%
24	Arizona	1,368,843	1.49%	49	Alaska	188,915	0.21%
25	Colorado	1,282,489	1.39%	50	Wyoming	168,839	0.18%
					District of Columbia	249,634	0.27%

Source: U.S. Bureau of the Census,
Press Release CB 91-217 (June 11, 1991)

Households in 1980

National Total = 80,390,000

RANK	STATE	HOUSEHOLDS	%	RANK	STATE	HOUSEHOLDS	%
1	California	8,630,000	10.74%	26	Colorado	1,061,000	1.32%
2	New York	6,340,000	7.89%	27	Iowa	1,053,000	1.31%
3	Texas	4,929,000	6.13%	28	South Carolina	1,030,000	1.28%
4	Pennsylvania	4,220,000	5.25%	29	Oregon	992,000	1.23%
5	Illinois	4,045,000	5.03%	30	Arizona	957,000	1.19%
6	Ohio	3,834,000	4.77%	31	Kansas	872,000	1.08%
7	Florida	3,744,000	4.66%	32	Mississippi	827,000	1.03%
8	Michigan	3,195,000	3.97%	33	Arkansas	816,000	1.02%
9	New Jersey	2,549,000	3.17%	34	West Virginia	686,000	0.85%
10	North Carolina	2,043,000	2.54%	35	Nebraska	571,000	0.71%
11	Massachusetts	2,033,000	2.53%	36	Utah	449,000	0.56%
12	Indiana	1,927,000	2.40%	37	New Mexico	441,000	0.55%
13	Georgia	1,872,000	2.33%	38	Maine	395,000	0.49%
14	Virginia	1,863,000	2.32%	39	Rhode Island	339,000	0.42%
15	Missouri	1,793,000	2.23%	40	Idaho	324,000	0.40%
16	Wisconsin	1,652,000	2.05%	41	New Hampshire	323,000	0.40%
17	Tennessee	1,619,000	2.01%	42	Nevada	304,000	0.38%
18	Washington	1,541,000	1.92%	43	Hawaii	294,000	0.37%
19	Maryland	1,461,000	1.82%	44	Montana	284,000	0.35%
20	Minnesota	1,445,000	1.80%	45	South Dakota	243,000	0.30%
21	Louisiana	1,412,000	1.76%	46	North Dakota	228,000	0.28%
22	Alabama	1,342,000	1.67%	47	Delaware	207,000	0.26%
23	Kentucky	1,263,000	1.57%	48	Vermont	178,000	0.22%
24	Oklahoma	1,119,000	1.39%	49	Wyoming	166,000	0.21%
25	Connecticut	1,094,000	1.36%	50	Alaska	131,000	0.16%
					District of Columbia	253,000	0.31%

Source: U.S. Bureau of the Census,
   "Current Population Reports" (Series P-25, No. 1024)

Persons per Household in 1990

National Figure = 2.63 Persons per Household

RANK	STATE	PERSONS		RANK	STATE	PERSONS
1	Utah	3.15		26	Connecticut	2.59
2	Hawaii	3.01		26	Ohio	2.59
3	Alaska	2.80		26	South Dakota	2.59
4	California	2.79		29	Massachusetts	2.58
5	Mississippi	2.75		29	Minnesota	2.58
6	Louisiana	2.74		31	Arkansas	2.57
6	New Mexico	2.74		31	Pennsylvania	2.57
8	Idaho	2.73		31	Vermont	2.57
8	Texas	2.73		34	Maine	2.56
10	New Jersey	2.70		34	Tennessee	2.56
11	South Carolina	2.68		36	North Dakota	2.55
12	Maryland	2.67		36	Rhode Island	2.55
13	Georgia	2.66		36	West Virginia	2.55
13	Michigan	2.66		39	Missouri	2.54
15	Illinois	2.65		39	Nebraska	2.54
16	New York	2.63		39	North Carolina	2.54
16	Wyoming	2.63		42	Kansas	2.53
18	Alabama	2.62		42	Montana	2.53
18	Arizona	2.62		42	Nevada	2.53
18	New Hampshire	2.62		42	Oklahoma	2.53
21	Delaware	2.61		42	Washington	2.53
21	Indiana	2.61		47	Iowa	2.52
21	Virginia	2.61		47	Oregon	2.52
21	Wisconsin	2.61		49	Colorado	2.51
25	Kentucky	2.60		50	Florida	2.46

District of Columbia   2.26

Source: U.S. Bureau of the Census,

Press Release CB 91–217 (June 11, 1991)

Persons per Household in 1980

National Average = 2.75 Persons

RANK	STATE	PERSONS	RANK	STATE	PERSONS
1	Utah	3.20	25	Illinois	2.76
2	Hawaii	3.15	25	Ohio	2.76
3	Mississippi	2.97	28	Maine	2.75
4	Alaska	2.93	28	New Hampshire	2.75
4	South Carolina	2.93	28	North Dakota	2.75
6	Louisiana	2.91	28	Vermont	2.75
7	New Mexico	2.90	32	Arkansas	2.74
8	Idaho	2.85	32	Minnesota	2.74
9	Alabama	2.84	32	Pennsylvania	2.74
9	Georgia	2.84	32	South Dakota	2.74
9	Michigan	2.84	36	Massachusetts	2.72
9	New Jersey	2.84	37	Montana	2.70
13	Kentucky	2.82	37	New York	2.70
13	Maryland	2.82	37	Rhode Island	2.70
13	Texas	2.82	40	California	2.68
16	Arizona	2.79	40	Iowa	2.68
16	Delaware	2.79	42	Missouri	2.67
16	West Virginia	2.79	43	Nebraska	2.66
19	North Carolina	2.78	44	Colorado	2.65
19	Wyoming	2.78	45	Kansas	2.62
21	Indiana	2.77	45	Oklahoma	2.62
21	Tennessee	2.77	47	Washington	2.61
21	Virginia	2.77	48	Oregon	2.60
21	Wisconsin	2.77	49	Nevada	2.59
25	Connecticut	2.76	50	Florida	2.55

District of Columbia   2.40

Source: U.S. Bureau of the Census,
"Current Population Reports" (Series P-25, No. 1024)

Family Households in 1990

National Total = 64,517,947 Family Households*

RANK	STATE	HOUSEHOLDS	%	RANK	STATE	HOUSEHOLDS	%
1	California	7,139,394	11.07%	26	Connecticut	864,493	1.34%
2	New York	4,489,312	6.96%	27	Oklahoma	855,321	1.33%
3	Texas	4,343,878	6.73%	28	Colorado	854,214	1.32%
4	Florida	3,511,825	5.44%	29	Oregon	750,844	1.16%
5	Pennsylvania	3,155,989	4.89%	30	Iowa	740,819	1.15%
6	Illinois	2,924,880	4.53%	31	Mississippi	674,378	1.05%
7	Ohio	2,895,223	4.49%	32	Kansas	658,600	1.02%
8	Michigan	2,439,171	3.78%	33	Arkansas	651,555	1.01%
9	New Jersey	2,021,346	3.13%	34	West Virginia	500,259	0.78%
10	North Carolina	1,812,053	2.81%	35	Nebraska	415,427	0.64%
11	Georgia	1,713,072	2.66%	36	Utah	410,862	0.64%
12	Virginia	1,629,490	2.53%	37	New Mexico	391,487	0.61%
13	Massachusetts	1,514,746	2.35%	38	Maine	328,685	0.51%
14	Indiana	1,480,351	2.29%	39	Nevada	307,400	0.48%
15	Missouri	1,368,334	2.12%	40	New Hampshire	292,601	0.45%
16	Tennessee	1,348,019	2.09%	41	Hawaii	263,456	0.41%
17	Wisconsin	1,275,172	1.98%	42	Idaho	263,194	0.41%
18	Washington	1,264,934	1.96%	43	Rhode Island	258,886	0.40%
19	Maryland	1,245,814	1.93%	44	Montana	211,666	0.33%
20	Minnesota	1,130,683	1.75%	45	South Dakota	180,306	0.28%
21	Alabama	1,103,835	1.71%	46	Delaware	175,867	0.27%
22	Louisiana	1,089,882	1.69%	47	North Dakota	166,270	0.26%
23	Kentucky	1,015,998	1.57%	48	Vermont	144,895	0.22%
24	Arizona	940,106	1.46%	49	Alaska	132,837	0.21%
25	South Carolina	928,206	1.44%	50	Wyoming	119,825	0.19%
					District of Columbia	122,087	0.19%

Source: U.S. Bureau of the Census,
Press Release CB 91-217 (June 11, 1991)

*Includes a householder and one or more other persons living in the same household who are related to the householder.
The number of family households always equals the number of families.

Married–Couple Family Households in 1990

National Total = 50,708,322 Married–Couple Family Households*

RANK	STATE	HOUSEHOLDS	%	RANK	STATE	HOUSEHOLDS	%
1	California	5,469,522	10.79%	26	Oklahoma	695,961	1.37%
2	Texas	3,435,540	6.78%	27	Colorado	690,292	1.36%
3	New York	3,315,845	6.54%	28	Connecticut	684,660	1.35%
4	Florida	2,791,734	5.51%	29	Iowa	629,893	1.24%
5	Pennsylvania	2,502,072	4.93%	30	Oregon	613,297	1.21%
6	Ohio	2,294,111	4.52%	31	Kansas	552,495	1.09%
7	Illinois	2,271,962	4.48%	32	Arkansas	527,358	1.04%
8	Michigan	1,883,143	3.71%	33	Mississippi	498,240	0.98%
9	New Jersey	1,578,702	3.11%	34	West Virginia	406,105	0.80%
10	North Carolina	1,424,206	2.81%	35	Nebraska	350,514	0.69%
11	Georgia	1,306,756	2.58%	36	Utah	348,029	0.69%
12	Virginia	1,302,219	2.57%	37	New Mexico	303,789	0.60%
13	Indiana	1,202,020	2.37%	38	Maine	270,565	0.53%
14	Massachusetts	1,170,275	2.31%	39	New Hampshire	245,307	0.48%
15	Missouri	1,104,723	2.18%	40	Nevada	239,573	0.47%
16	Tennessee	1,059,569	2.09%	41	Idaho	224,198	0.44%
17	Wisconsin	1,048,010	2.07%	42	Hawaii	210,468	0.42%
18	Washington	1,029,267	2.03%	43	Rhode Island	202,283	0.40%
19	Maryland	948,563	1.87%	44	Montana	176,526	0.35%
20	Minnesota	942,524	1.86%	45	South Dakota	152,519	0.30%
21	Alabama	858,327	1.69%	46	North Dakota	142,374	0.28%
22	Kentucky	816,732	1.61%	47	Delaware	137,983	0.27%
23	Louisiana	803,282	1.58%	48	Vermont	118,905	0.23%
24	Arizona	747,806	1.47%	49	Alaska	106,079	0.21%
25	South Carolina	710,089	1.40%	50	Wyoming	100,800	0.20%
					District of Columbia	63,110	0.12%

Source: U.S. Bureau of the Census,

Press Release CB 91-217 (June 11, 1991)

*The number of married-couple family households always equals the number of married-couple families.

Married–Couple Families as a Percent of Households in 1990

National Total = 55.1% of Households are Married–Couple Families

RANK	STATE	PERCENT	RANK	STATE	PERCENT
1	Utah	64.8	26	South Carolina	56.4
2	Idaho	62.2	26	Vermont	56.4
3	New Hampshire	59.7	28	Missouri	56.3
3	Wyoming	59.7	29	Alaska	56.2
5	Arkansas	59.2	30	Ohio	56.1
5	Iowa	59.2	31	New Mexico	56.0
5	Kentucky	59.2	32	Delaware	55.8
8	Hawaii	59.1	33	Pennsylvania	55.7
8	North Dakota	59.1	34	Connecticut	55.6
10	West Virginia	59.0	34	Oregon	55.6
11	South Dakota	58.9	36	Georgia	55.2
12	Kansas	58.5	37	Michigan	55.1
13	Indiana	58.2	38	Washington	55.0
13	Nebraska	58.2	39	Mississippi	54.7
15	Maine	58.1	40	Arizona	54.6
16	Montana	57.7	41	Florida	54.4
16	Oklahoma	57.7	42	Maryland	54.2
18	Wisconsin	57.5	43	Illinois	54.1
19	Minnesota	57.2	44	Colorado	53.8
19	Tennessee	57.2	45	Louisiana	53.6
21	Alabama	57.0	46	Rhode Island	53.5
22	Virginia	56.8	47	California	52.7
23	North Carolina	56.6	48	Massachusetts	52.1
23	Texas	56.6	49	Nevada	51.4
25	New Jersey	56.5	50	New York	49.9

District of Columbia   25.3

Source: U.S. Bureau of the Census,
    Press Release CB 91-217 (June 11, 1991)

Nonfamily Households in 1990

National Total = 27,429,463 Nonfamily Households

RANK	STATE	HOUSEHOLDS	%	RANK	STATE	HOUSEHOLDS	%
1	California	3,241,812	11.82%	26	Kentucky	363,784	1.33%
2	New York	2,150,010	7.84%	27	Oregon	352,469	1.29%
3	Texas	1,727,059	6.30%	28	Oklahoma	350,814	1.28%
4	Florida	1,623,044	5.92%	29	South Carolina	329,838	1.20%
5	Pennsylvania	1,339,977	4.89%	30	Iowa	323,506	1.18%
6	Illinois	1,277,360	4.66%	31	Kansas	286,126	1.04%
7	Ohio	1,192,323	4.35%	32	Arkansas	239,624	0.87%
8	Michigan	980,160	3.57%	33	Mississippi	236,996	0.86%
9	New Jersey	773,365	2.82%	34	West Virginia	188,298	0.69%
10	Massachusetts	732,364	2.67%	35	Nebraska	186,936	0.68%
11	North Carolina	704,973	2.57%	36	Nevada	158,897	0.58%
12	Virginia	662,340	2.41%	37	New Mexico	151,222	0.55%
13	Georgia	653,543	2.38%	38	Maine	136,627	0.50%
14	Washington	607,497	2.21%	39	Utah	126,411	0.46%
15	Missouri	592,872	2.16%	40	Rhode Island	119,091	0.43%
16	Indiana	585,004	2.13%	41	New Hampshire	118,585	0.43%
17	Wisconsin	546,946	1.99%	42	Idaho	97,529	0.36%
18	Minnesota	517,170	1.89%	43	Montana	94,497	0.34%
19	Tennessee	505,706	1.84%	44	Hawaii	92,811	0.34%
20	Maryland	503,177	1.83%	45	South Dakota	78,728	0.29%
21	Arizona	428,737	1.56%	46	North Dakota	74,608	0.27%
22	Colorado	428,275	1.56%	47	Delaware	71,630	0.26%
23	Louisiana	409,387	1.49%	48	Vermont	65,755	0.24%
24	Alabama	402,955	1.47%	49	Alaska	56,078	0.20%
25	Connecticut	365,986	1.33%	50	Wyoming	49,014	0.18%
					District of Columbia	127,547	0.46%

Source: U.S. Bureau of the Census,
Press Release CB 91-217 (June 11, 1991)

Median Value of a House in 1990

National Median = $79,100

RANK	STATE	MEDIAN VALUE	RANK	STATE	MEDIAN VALUE
1	Hawaii	$245,300	26	Oregon	$67,100
2	California	195,500	27	North Carolina	65,800
3	Connecticut	177,800	28	Ohio	63,500
4	Massachusetts	162,800	29	Wisconsin	62,500
5	New Jersey	162,300	30	Wyoming	61,600
6	Rhode Island	133,500	31	South Carolina	61,100
7	New York	131,600	32	Michigan	60,600
8	New Hampshire	129,400	33	Missouri	59,800
9	Maryland	116,500	34	Texas	59,600
10	Delaware	100,100	35	Louisiana	58,500
11	Nevada	95,700	36	Tennessee	58,400
12	Vermont	95,500	37	Idaho	58,200
13	Alaska	94,400	38	Montana	56,600
14	Washington	93,400	39	Indiana	53,900
15	Virginia	91,000	40	Alabama	53,700
16	Maine	87,400	41	Kansas	52,200
17	Colorado	82,700	42	North Dakota	50,800
18	Illinois	80,900	43	Kentucky	50,500
19	Arizona	80,100	44	Nebraska	50,400
20	Florida	77,100	45	Oklahoma	48,100
21	Minnesota	74,000	46	West Virginia	47,900
22	Georgia	71,300	47	Arkansas	46,300
23	New Mexico	70,100	48	Iowa	45,900
24	Pennsylvania	69,700	49	Mississippi	45,600
25	Utah	68,900	50	South Dakota	45,200
				District of Columbia	123,900

Source: U.S. Bureau of the Census,
Press Release CB 91-217 (June 11, 1991)

Mobile Homes and Trailers in 1990

National Total = 8,521,009 Mobile Homes and Trailers

RANK	STATE	MOBILE HOMES	%	RANK	STATE	MOBILE HOMES	%
1	Florida	821,048	9.64%	26	West Virginia	128,168	1.50%
2	California	679,940	7.98%	27	New Mexico	112,370	1.32%
3	Texas	630,661	7.40%	28	Minnesota	111,605	1.31%
4	North Carolina	454,159	5.33%	29	Colorado	102,269	1.20%
5	Georgia	327,888	3.85%	30	Kansas	78,396	0.92%
6	Pennsylvania	320,213	3.76%	31	New Jersey	76,705	0.90%
7	New York	302,759	3.55%	32	Nevada	75,617	0.89%
8	Michigan	288,840	3.39%	33	Iowa	68,479	0.80%
9	Arizona	274,867	3.23%	34	Maine	68,019	0.80%
10	South Carolina	253,375	2.97%	35	Idaho	60,246	0.71%
11	Ohio	246,519	2.89%	36	Montana	58,556	0.69%
12	Alabama	239,530	2.81%	37	Maryland	55,992	0.66%
13	Louisiana	217,523	2.55%	38	Massachusetts	51,119	0.60%
14	Tennessee	207,444	2.43%	39	Nebraska	42,057	0.49%
15	Washington	207,197	2.43%	40	New Hampshire	41,943	0.49%
16	Kentucky	199,567	2.34%	41	Utah	41,044	0.48%
17	Illinois	189,093	2.22%	42	Delaware	37,066	0.43%
18	Virginia	182,100	2.14%	43	Wyoming	35,855	0.42%
19	Missouri	181,957	2.14%	44	South Dakota	34,210	0.40%
20	Indiana	176,086	2.07%	45	Connecticut	30,954	0.36%
21	Mississippi	149,255	1.75%	46	North Dakota	29,616	0.35%
22	Oregon	145,144	1.70%	47	Vermont	28,593	0.34%
23	Oklahoma	143,701	1.69%	48	Alaska	24,702	0.29%
24	Arkansas	141,443	1.66%	49	Rhode Island	8,844	0.10%
25	Wisconsin	129,327	1.52%	50	Hawaii	6,101	0.07%

	District of Columbia	2,847	0.03%

Source: U.S. Bureau of the Census,
   Press Release CB 91-217 (June 11, 1991)

XIII. POPULATION

POPULATION

(continued on the next page)

Resident State Population in 1991

National Total = 252,177,000*

RANK	STATE	POPULATION	%	RANK	STATE	POPULATION	%
1	California	30,380,000	12.05%	26	Colorado	3,377,000	1.34%
2	New York	18,058,000	7.16%	27	Connecticut	3,291,000	1.31%
3	Texas	17,349,000	6.88%	28	Oklahoma	3,175,000	1.26%
4	Florida	13,277,000	5.26%	29	Oregon	2,922,000	1.16%
5	Pennsylvania	11,961,000	4.74%	30	Iowa	2,795,000	1.11%
6	Illinois	11,543,000	4.58%	31	Mississippi	2,592,000	1.03%
7	Ohio	10,939,000	4.34%	32	Kansas	2,495,000	0.99%
8	Michigan	9,368,000	3.71%	33	Arkansas	2,372,000	0.94%
9	New Jersey	7,760,000	3.08%	34	West Virginia	1,801,000	0.71%
10	North Carolina	6,737,000	2.67%	35	Utah	1,770,000	0.70%
11	Georgia	6,623,000	2.63%	36	Nebraska	1,593,000	0.63%
12	Virginia	6,286,000	2.49%	37	New Mexico	1,548,000	0.61%
13	Massachusetts	5,996,000	2.38%	38	Nevada	1,284,000	0.51%
14	Indiana	5,610,000	2.22%	39	Maine	1,235,000	0.49%
15	Missouri	5,158,000	2.05%	40	Hawaii	1,135,000	0.45%
16	Washington	5,018,000	1.99%	41	New Hampshire	1,105,000	0.44%
17	Wisconsin	4,955,000	1.96%	42	Idaho	1,039,000	0.41%
18	Tennessee	4,953,000	1.96%	43	Rhode Island	1,004,000	0.40%
19	Maryland	4,860,000	1.93%	44	Montana	808,000	0.32%
20	Minnesota	4,432,000	1.76%	45	South Dakota	703,000	0.28%
21	Louisiana	4,252,000	1.69%	46	Delaware	680,000	0.27%
22	Alabama	4,089,000	1.62%	47	North Dakota	635,000	0.25%
23	Arizona	3,750,000	1.49%	48	Alaska	570,000	0.23%
24	Kentucky	3,713,000	1.47%	49	Vermont	567,000	0.22%
25	South Carolina	3,560,000	1.41%	50	Wyoming	460,000	0.18%

	District of Columbia	598,000	0.24%

Source: U.S. Bureau of the Census,
   Press Release CB 91-346 (December 30, 1991)
*Estimate as of July 1, 1991.

Population (Resident and Overseas) in 1990

National Total = 249,632,692

RANK	STATE	POPULATION	%
1	California	29,839,250	11.95%
2	New York	18,044,505	7.23%
3	Texas	17,059,805	6.83%
4	Florida	13,003,362	5.21%
5	Pennsylvania	11,924,710	4.78%
6	Illinois	11,466,682	4.59%
7	Ohio	10,887,325	4.36%
8	Michigan	9,328,784	3.74%
9	New Jersey	7,748,634	3.10%
10	North Carolina	6,657,630	2.67%
11	Georgia	6,508,419	2.61%
12	Virginia	6,216,568	2.49%
13	Massachusetts	6,029,051	2.42%
14	Indiana	5,564,228	2.23%
15	Missouri	5,137,804	2.06%
16	Wisconsin	4,906,745	1.97%
17	Tennessee	4,896,641	1.96%
18	Washington	4,887,941	1.96%
19	Maryland	4,798,622	1.92%
20	Minnesota	4,387,029	1.76%
21	Louisiana	4,238,216	1.70%
22	Alabama	4,062,608	1.63%
23	Kentucky	3,698,969	1.48%
24	Arizona	3,677,985	1.47%
25	South Carolina	3,505,707	1.40%

RANK	STATE	POPULATION	%
26	Colorado	3,307,912	1.33%
27	Connecticut	3,295,669	1.32%
28	Oklahoma	3,157,604	1.26%
29	Oregon	2,853,733	1.14%
30	Iowa	2,787,424	1.12%
31	Mississippi	2,586,443	1.04%
32	Kansas	2,485,600	1.00%
33	Arkansas	2,362,239	0.95%
34	West Virginia	1,801,625	0.72%
35	Utah	1,727,784	0.69%
36	Nebraska	1,584,617	0.63%
37	New Mexico	1,521,779	0.61%
38	Maine	1,233,223	0.49%
39	Nevada	1,206,152	0.48%
40	Hawaii	1,115,274	0.45%
41	New Hampshire	1,113,915	0.45%
42	Idaho	1,011,986	0.41%
43	Rhode Island	1,005,984	0.40%
44	Montana	803,655	0.32%
45	South Dakota	699,999	0.28%
46	Delaware	668,696	0.27%
47	North Dakota	641,364	0.26%
48	Vermont	564,964	0.23%
49	Alaska	551,947	0.22%
50	Wyoming	455,975	0.18%

	District of Columbia	609,909	0.24%

Source: U.S. Bureau of the Census,
Press Release CB 91-07 (January 7, 1991)

Resident State Population in 1990

National Total = 248,709,873

RANK	STATE	POPULATION	%	RANK	STATE	POPULATION	%
1	California	29,760,021	11.97%	26	Colorado	3,294,394	1.32%
2	New York	17,990,455	7.23%	27	Connecticut	3,287,116	1.32%
3	Texas	16,986,510	6.83%	28	Oklahoma	3,145,585	1.26%
4	Florida	12,937,926	5.20%	29	Oregon	2,842,321	1.14%
5	Pennsylvania	11,881,632	4.78%	30	Iowa	2,776,755	1.12%
6	Illinois	11,430,602	4.60%	31	Mississippi	2,573,216	1.03%
7	Ohio	10,847,115	4.36%	32	Kansas	2,477,574	1.00%
8	Michigan	9,295,297	3.74%	33	Arkansas	2,350,725	0.95%
9	New Jersey	7,730,188	3.11%	34	West Virginia	1,793,477	0.72%
10	North Carolina	6,628,637	2.67%	35	Utah	1,722,850	0.69%
11	Georgia	6,478,216	2.60%	36	Nebraska	1,578,385	0.63%
12	Virginia	6,187,358	2.49%	37	New Mexico	1,515,069	0.61%
13	Massachusetts	6,016,425	2.42%	38	Maine	1,227,928	0.49%
14	Indiana	5,544,159	2.23%	39	Nevada	1,201,833	0.48%
15	Missouri	5,117,073	2.06%	40	New Hampshire	1,109,252	0.45%
16	Wisconsin	4,891,769	1.97%	41	Hawaii	1,108,229	0.45%
17	Tennessee	4,877,185	1.96%	42	Idaho	1,006,749	0.40%
18	Washington	4,866,692	1.96%	43	Rhode Island	1,003,464	0.40%
19	Maryland	4,781,468	1.92%	44	Montana	799,065	0.32%
20	Minnesota	4,375,099	1.76%	45	South Dakota	696,004	0.28%
21	Louisiana	4,219,973	1.70%	46	Delaware	666,168	0.27%
22	Alabama	4,040,587	1.62%	47	North Dakota	638,800	0.26%
23	Kentucky	3,685,296	1.48%	48	Vermont	562,758	0.23%
24	Arizona	3,665,228	1.47%	49	Alaska	550,043	0.22%
25	South Carolina	3,486,703	1.40%	50	Wyoming	453,588	0.18%
					District of Columbia	606,900	0.24%

Source: U.S. Bureau of the Census,

Press Release CB 91-100 (March 11, 1991)

U.S. Population Living Overseas in 1990

National Total = 922,819

RANK	STATE	OVERSEAS	%	RANK	STATE	OVERSEAS	%
1	California	79,229	8.59%	26	Massachusetts	12,626	1.37%
2	Texas	73,295	7.94%	27	Oklahoma	12,019	1.30%
3	Florida	65,436	7.09%	28	Minnesota	11,930	1.29%
4	New York	54,050	5.86%	29	Arkansas	11,514	1.25%
5	Pennsylvania	43,067	4.67%	30	Oregon	11,412	1.24%
6	Ohio	40,210	4.36%	31	Iowa	10,669	1.16%
7	Illinois	36,080	3.91%	32	Connecticut	8,553	0.93%
8	Michigan	33,487	3.63%	33	West Virginia	8,148	0.88%
9	Georgia	30,203	3.27%	34	Kansas	8,026	0.87%
10	Virginia	29,210	3.17%	35	Hawaii	7,045	0.76%
11	North Carolina	28,993	3.14%	36	New Mexico	6,710	0.73%
12	Alabama	22,021	2.39%	37	Nebraska	6,232	0.68%
13	Washington	21,249	2.30%	38	Maine	5,295	0.57%
14	Missouri	20,731	2.25%	39	Idaho	5,237	0.57%
15	Indiana	20,069	2.17%	40	Utah	4,934	0.53%
16	Tennessee	19,456	2.11%	41	New Hampshire	4,663	0.51%
17	South Carolina	19,004	2.06%	42	Montana	4,590	0.50%
18	New Jersey	18,446	2.00%	43	Nevada	4,319	0.47%
19	Louisiana	18,243	1.98%	44	South Dakota	3,995	0.43%
20	Maryland	17,154	1.86%	45	North Dakota	2,564	0.28%
21	Wisconsin	14,976	1.62%	46	Delaware	2,528	0.27%
22	Kentucky	13,673	1.48%	47	Rhode Island	2,520	0.27%
23	Colorado	13,518	1.46%	48	Wyoming	2,387	0.26%
24	Mississippi	13,227	1.43%	49	Vermont	2,206	0.24%
25	Arizona	12,757	1.38%	50	Alaska	1,904	0.21%

District of Columbia   3,009   0.33%

Source: U.S. Bureau of the Census,
Press Release CB 91-07 (January 7, 1991)

Resident State Population in 1989

National Total = 248,243,000

RANK	STATE	POPULATION	%	RANK	STATE	POPULATION	%
1	California	29,063,000	11.71%	26	Colorado	3,317,000	1.34%
2	New York	17,950,000	7.23%	27	Connecticut	3,239,000	1.30%
3	Texas	16,991,000	6.84%	28	Oklahoma	3,224,000	1.30%
4	Florida	12,671,000	5.10%	29	Iowa	2,840,000	1.14%
5	Pennsylvania	12,040,000	4.85%	30	Oregon	2,820,000	1.14%
6	Illinois	11,658,000	4.70%	31	Mississippi	2,621,000	1.06%
7	Ohio	10,907,000	4.39%	32	Kansas	2,513,000	1.01%
8	Michigan	9,273,000	3.74%	33	Arkansas	2,406,000	0.97%
9	New Jersey	7,736,000	3.12%	34	West Virginia	1,857,000	0.75%
10	North Carolina	6,571,000	2.65%	35	Utah	1,707,000	0.69%
11	Georgia	6,436,000	2.59%	36	Nebraska	1,611,000	0.65%
12	Virginia	6,098,000	2.46%	37	New Mexico	1,528,000	0.62%
13	Massachusetts	5,913,000	2.38%	38	Maine	1,222,000	0.49%
14	Indiana	5,593,000	2.25%	39	Hawaii	1,112,000	0.45%
15	Missouri	5,159,000	2.08%	40	Nevada	1,111,000	0.45%
16	Tennessee	4,940,000	1.99%	41	New Hampshire	1,107,000	0.45%
17	Wisconsin	4,867,000	1.96%	42	Idaho	1,014,000	0.41%
18	Washington	4,761,000	1.92%	43	Rhode Island	998,000	0.40%
19	Maryland	4,694,000	1.89%	44	Montana	806,000	0.32%
20	Louisiana	4,382,000	1.77%	45	South Dakota	715,000	0.29%
21	Minnesota	4,353,000	1.75%	46	Delaware	673,000	0.27%
22	Alabama	4,118,000	1.66%	47	North Dakota	660,000	0.27%
23	Kentucky	3,727,000	1.50%	48	Vermont	567,000	0.23%
24	Arizona	3,556,000	1.43%	49	Alaska	527,000	0.21%
25	South Carolina	3,512,000	1.41%	50	Wyoming	475,000	0.19%
					District of Columbia	604,000	0.24%

Source: U.S. Bureau of the Census,
"Federal Expenditures by State for FY 1989" (March 1990)

Resident State Population in 1980

National Total = 226,504,825

RANK	STATE	POPULATION	%	RANK	STATE	POPULATION	%
1	California	23,667,902	10.45%	26	Oklahoma	3,025,290	1.34%
2	New York	17,558,072	7.75%	27	Iowa	2,913,808	1.29%
3	Texas	14,229,191	6.28%	28	Colorado	2,889,964	1.28%
4	Pennsylvania	11,863,895	5.24%	29	Arizona	2,718,215	1.20%
5	Illinois	11,426,518	5.04%	30	Oregon	2,633,105	1.16%
6	Ohio	10,797,630	4.77%	31	Mississippi	2,520,638	1.11%
7	Florida	9,746,324	4.30%	32	Kansas	2,363,679	1.04%
8	Michigan	9,262,078	4.09%	33	Arkansas	2,286,435	1.01%
9	New Jersey	7,364,823	3.25%	34	West Virginia	1,949,644	0.86%
10	North Carolina	5,881,766	2.60%	35	Nebraska	1,569,825	0.69%
11	Massachusetts	5,737,037	2.53%	36	Utah	1,461,037	0.65%
12	Indiana	5,490,224	2.42%	37	New Mexico	1,302,894	0.58%
13	Georgia	5,463,105	2.41%	38	Maine	1,124,660	0.50%
14	Virginia	5,346,818	2.36%	39	Hawaii	964,691	0.43%
15	Missouri	4,916,686	2.17%	40	Rhode Island	947,154	0.42%
16	Wisconsin	4,705,767	2.08%	41	Idaho	943,935	0.42%
17	Tennessee	4,591,120	2.03%	42	New Hampshire	920,610	0.41%
18	Maryland	4,216,975	1.86%	43	Nevada	800,493	0.35%
19	Louisiana	4,205,900	1.86%	44	Montana	786,690	0.35%
20	Washington	4,132,156	1.82%	45	South Dakota	690,768	0.30%
21	Minnesota	4,075,970	1.80%	46	North Dakota	652,717	0.29%
22	Alabama	3,893,888	1.72%	47	Delaware	594,338	0.26%
23	Kentucky	3,660,777	1.62%	48	Vermont	511,456	0.23%
24	South Carolina	3,121,820	1.38%	49	Wyoming	469,557	0.21%
25	Connecticut	3,107,576	1.37%	50	Alaska	401,851	0.18%
					District of Columbia	638,333	0.28%

Source: U.S. Bureau of the Census,
Press Release CB 91-100 (March 11, 1991)

Resident State Population in 1970

National Total = 203,302,000

RANK	STATE	POPULATION	%
1	California	19,971,000	9.82%
2	New York	18,241,000	8.97%
3	Pennsylvania	11,801,000	5.80%
4	Texas	11,199,000	5.51%
5	Illinois	11,110,000	5.46%
6	Ohio	10,657,000	5.24%
7	Michigan	8,882,000	4.37%
8	New Jersey	7,171,000	3.53%
9	Florida	6,791,000	3.34%
10	Massachusetts	5,689,000	2.80%
11	Indiana	5,195,000	2.56%
12	North Carolina	5,084,000	2.50%
13	Missouri	4,678,000	2.30%
14	Virginia	4,651,000	2.29%
15	Georgia	4,588,000	2.26%
16	Wisconsin	4,418,000	2.17%
17	Tennessee	3,926,000	1.93%
18	Maryland	3,924,000	1.93%
19	Minnesota	3,806,000	1.87%
20	Louisiana	3,645,000	1.79%
21	Alabama	3,444,000	1.69%
22	Washington	3,413,000	1.68%
23	Kentucky	3,221,000	1.58%
24	Connecticut	3,032,000	1.49%
25	Iowa	2,825,000	1.39%

RANK	STATE	POPULATION	%
26	South Carolina	2,591,000	1.27%
27	Oklahoma	2,559,000	1.26%
28	Kansas	2,249,000	1.11%
29	Mississippi	2,217,000	1.09%
30	Colorado	2,210,000	1.09%
31	Oregon	2,092,000	1.03%
32	Arkansas	1,923,000	0.95%
33	Arizona	1,775,000	0.87%
34	West Virginia	1,744,000	0.86%
35	Nebraska	1,485,000	0.73%
36	Utah	1,059,000	0.52%
37	New Mexico	1,017,000	0.50%
38	Maine	994,000	0.49%
39	Rhode Island	950,000	0.47%
40	Hawaii	770,000	0.38%
41	New Hampshire	738,000	0.36%
42	Idaho	713,000	0.35%
43	Montana	694,000	0.34%
44	South Dakota	666,000	0.33%
45	North Dakota	618,000	0.30%
46	Delaware	548,000	0.27%
47	Nevada	489,000	0.24%
48	Vermont	445,000	0.22%
49	Wyoming	332,000	0.16%
50	Alaska	303,000	0.15%

	District of Columbia	757,000	0.37%

Source: U.S. Bureau of the Census,
"Census of Population: 1970" (vol. 1)

Resident State Population in 1960

National Total = 179,323,000

RANK	STATE	POPULATION	%	RANK	STATE	POPULATION	%
1	New York	16,782,000	9.36%	26	South Carolina	2,383,000	1.33%
2	California	15,717,000	8.76%	27	Oklahoma	2,328,000	1.30%
3	Pennsylvania	11,319,000	6.31%	28	Kansas	2,179,000	1.22%
4	Illinois	10,081,000	5.62%	29	Mississippi	2,178,000	1.21%
5	Ohio	9,706,000	5.41%	30	West Virginia	1,860,000	1.04%
6	Texas	9,580,000	5.34%	31	Arkansas	1,786,000	1.00%
7	Michigan	7,823,000	4.36%	32	Oregon	1,769,000	0.99%
8	New Jersey	6,067,000	3.38%	33	Colorado	1,754,000	0.98%
9	Massachusetts	5,149,000	2.87%	34	Nebraska	1,411,000	0.79%
10	Florida	4,952,000	2.76%	35	Arizona	1,302,000	0.73%
11	Indiana	4,662,000	2.60%	36	Maine	969,000	0.54%
12	North Carolina	4,556,000	2.54%	37	New Mexico	951,000	0.53%
13	Missouri	4,320,000	2.41%	38	Utah	891,000	0.50%
14	Virginia	3,967,000	2.21%	39	Rhode Island	859,000	0.48%
15	Wisconsin	3,952,000	2.20%	40	South Dakota	681,000	0.38%
16	Georgia	3,943,000	2.20%	41	Montana	675,000	0.38%
17	Tennessee	3,567,000	1.99%	42	Idaho	667,000	0.37%
18	Minnesota	3,414,000	1.90%	43	Hawaii	633,000	0.35%
19	Alabama	3,267,000	1.82%	44	North Dakota	632,000	0.35%
20	Louisiana	3,257,000	1.82%	45	New Hampshire	607,000	0.34%
21	Maryland	3,101,000	1.73%	46	Delaware	446,000	0.25%
22	Kentucky	3,038,000	1.69%	47	Vermont	390,000	0.22%
23	Washington	2,853,000	1.59%	48	Wyoming	330,000	0.18%
24	Iowa	2,758,000	1.54%	49	Nevada	285,000	0.16%
25	Connecticut	2,535,000	1.41%	50	Alaska	226,000	0.13%
					District of Columbia	764,000	0.43%

Source: U.S. Bureau of the Census,
"Census of Population: 1970" (vol. 1)

Resident State Population in 1950

National Total = 151,325,798

RANK	STATE	POPULATION	%	RANK	STATE	POPULATION	%
1	New York	14,830,192	9.80%	26	Mississippi	2,178,914	1.44%
2	California	10,586,223	7.00%	27	South Carolina	2,117,027	1.40%
3	Pennsylvania	10,498,012	6.94%	28	Connecticut	2,007,280	1.33%
4	Illinois	8,712,176	5.76%	29	West Virginia	2,005,552	1.33%
5	Ohio	7,946,627	5.25%	30	Arkansas	1,909,511	1.26%
6	Texas	7,711,194	5.10%	31	Kansas	1,905,299	1.26%
7	Michigan	6,371,766	4.21%	32	Oregon	1,521,341	1.01%
8	New Jersey	4,835,329	3.20%	33	Nebraska	1,325,510	0.88%
9	Massachusetts	4,690,514	3.10%	34	Colorado	1,325,089	0.88%
10	North Carolina	4,061,929	2.68%	35	Maine	913,774	0.60%
11	Missouri	3,954,653	2.61%	36	Rhode Island	791,896	0.52%
12	Indiana	3,934,224	2.60%	37	Arizona	749,587	0.50%
13	Georgia	3,444,578	2.28%	38	Utah	688,862	0.46%
14	Wisconsin	3,434,575	2.27%	39	New Mexico	681,187	0.45%
15	Virginia	3,318,680	2.19%	40	South Dakota	652,740	0.43%
16	Tennessee	3,291,718	2.18%	41	North Dakota	619,636	0.41%
17	Alabama	3,061,743	2.02%	42	Montana	591,024	0.39%
18	Minnesota	2,982,483	1.97%	43	Idaho	588,637	0.39%
19	Kentucky	2,944,806	1.95%	44	New Hampshire	533,242	0.35%
20	Florida	2,771,305	1.83%	45	Hawaii	499,794	0.33%
21	Louisiana	2,683,516	1.77%	46	Vermont	377,747	0.25%
22	Iowa	2,621,073	1.73%	47	Delaware	318,085	0.21%
23	Washington	2,378,963	1.57%	48	Wyoming	290,529	0.19%
24	Maryland	2,343,001	1.55%	49	Nevada	160,083	0.11%
25	Oklahoma	2,233,351	1.48%	50	Alaska	128,643	0.09%
					District of Columbia	802,178	0.53%

Source: U.S. Bureau of the Census,
Press Release CB 91-07 (March 11, 1991)

Projected Resident State Population in 2000

National Total = 267,747,000

RANK	STATE	POPULATION	%
1	California	33,500,000	12.51%
2	Texas	20,211,000	7.55%
3	New York	17,986,000	6.72%
4	Florida	15,415,000	5.76%
5	Illinois	11,580,000	4.32%
6	Pennsylvania	11,503,000	4.30%
7	Ohio	10,629,000	3.97%
8	Michigan	9,250,000	3.45%
9	New Jersey	8,546,000	3.19%
10	Georgia	7,957,000	2.97%
11	North Carolina	7,483,000	2.79%
12	Virginia	6,877,000	2.57%
13	Massachusetts	6,087,000	2.27%
14	Indiana	5,502,000	2.05%
15	Missouri	5,383,000	2.01%
16	Maryland	5,274,000	1.97%
17	Tennessee	5,266,000	1.97%
18	Washington	4,991,000	1.86%
19	Wisconsin	4,784,000	1.79%
20	Arizona	4,618,000	1.72%
21	Louisiana	4,516,000	1.69%
22	Minnesota	4,490,000	1.68%
23	Alabama	4,410,000	1.65%
24	South Carolina	3,906,000	1.46%
25	Colorado	3,813,000	1.42%

RANK	STATE	POPULATION	%
26	Kentucky	3,733,000	1.39%
27	Connecticut	3,445,000	1.29%
28	Oklahoma	3,376,000	1.26%
29	Mississippi	2,877,000	1.07%
29	Oregon	2,877,000	1.07%
31	Iowa	2,549,000	0.95%
32	Arkansas	2,529,000	0.94%
32	Kansas	2,529,000	0.94%
34	Utah	1,991,000	0.74%
35	New Mexico	1,968,000	0.74%
36	West Virginia	1,722,000	0.64%
37	Nebraska	1,556,000	0.58%
38	Hawaii	1,345,000	0.50%
39	New Hampshire	1,333,000	0.50%
40	Nevada	1,303,000	0.49%
41	Maine	1,271,000	0.47%
42	Rhode Island	1,049,000	0.39%
43	Idaho	1,047,000	0.39%
44	Montana	794,000	0.30%
45	Delaware	734,000	0.27%
46	South Dakota	714,000	0.27%
47	Alaska	687,000	0.26%
48	North Dakota	629,000	0.23%
49	Vermont	591,000	0.22%
50	Wyoming	489,000	0.18%

	District of Columbia	634,000	0.24%

Source: U.S. Bureau of the Census,
   "Current Population Reports" (series P-25, No. 1017)

Population Change: 1990 to 1991

National Total = 3,467,000 Increase*

RANK	STATE	POPULATION	%	RANK	STATE	POPULATION	%
1	California	620,000	17.88%	26	Idaho	33,000	0.95%
2	Texas	363,000	10.47%	26	New Mexico	33,000	0.95%
3	Florida	339,000	9.78%	28	Louisiana	32,000	0.92%
4	Washington	151,000	4.36%	29	New Jersey	30,000	0.87%
5	Georgia	144,000	4.15%	30	Oklahoma	29,000	0.84%
6	Illinois	112,000	3.23%	31	Kentucky	28,000	0.81%
7	North Carolina	108,000	3.12%	32	Hawaii	27,000	0.78%
8	Virginia	99,000	2.86%	33	Arkansas	21,000	0.61%
9	Ohio	92,000	2.65%	34	Alaska	20,000	0.58%
10	Arizona	84,000	2.42%	35	Mississippi	19,000	0.55%
11	Colorado	82,000	2.37%	36	Iowa	18,000	0.52%
11	Nevada	82,000	2.37%	37	Kansas	17,000	0.49%
13	Oregon	80,000	2.31%	38	Delaware	14,000	0.40%
14	Pennsylvania	79,000	2.28%	38	Nebraska	14,000	0.40%
15	Maryland	78,000	2.25%	40	Montana	9,000	0.26%
16	Tennessee	76,000	2.19%	41	Maine	7,000	0.20%
17	South Carolina	73,000	2.11%	41	South Dakota	7,000	0.20%
18	Michigan	72,000	2.08%	41	West Virginia	7,000	0.20%
19	New York	67,000	1.93%	44	Wyoming	6,000	0.17%
20	Indiana	65,000	1.87%	45	Connecticut	4,000	0.12%
21	Wisconsin	63,000	1.82%	45	Vermont	4,000	0.12%
22	Minnesota	57,000	1.64%	47	Rhode Island	1,000	0.03%
23	Alabama	49,000	1.41%	48	North Dakota	(4,000)	
24	Utah	47,000	1.36%	49	New Hampshire	(5,000)	
25	Missouri	41,000	1.18%	50	Massachusetts	(20,000)	

District of Columbia (9,000)

Source: U.S. Bureau of the Census,
   Press Release CB 91-346 (December 30, 1991)
*Estimated change from April 1, 1990 to July 1, 1991

Percent Change in Population: 1990 to 1991

National Percent Change = 1.4% Increase*

RANK	STATE	PERCENT CHANGE
1	Nevada	6.8
2	Alaska	3.7
3	Idaho	3.2
4	Washington	3.1
5	Oregon	2.8
6	Utah	2.7
7	Florida	2.6
8	Colorado	2.5
9	Hawaii	2.4
10	Arizona	2.3
11	Georgia	2.2
11	New Mexico	2.2
13	California	2.1
13	Delaware	2.1
13	South Carolina	2.1
13	Texas	2.1
17	Maryland	1.6
17	North Carolina	1.6
17	Virginia	1.6
20	Tennessee	1.5
21	Minnesota	1.3
21	Wisconsin	1.3
21	Wyoming	1.3
24	Alabama	1.2
24	Indiana	1.2

RANK	STATE	PERCENT CHANGE
24	Montana	1.2
27	Illinois	1.0
27	South Dakota	1.0
29	Arkansas	0.9
29	Nebraska	0.9
29	Oklahoma	0.9
32	Kentucky	0.8
32	Michigan	0.8
32	Missouri	0.8
32	Ohio	0.8
36	Iowa	0.7
36	Kansas	0.7
36	Louisiana	0.7
36	Mississippi	0.7
36	Pennsylvania	0.7
36	Vermont	0.7
42	Maine	0.5
43	New Jersey	0.4
43	New York	0.4
43	West Virginia	0.4
46	Connecticut	0.1
46	Rhode Island	0.1
48	Massachusetts	(0.3)
49	New Hampshire	(0.4)
50	North Dakota	(0.7)

District of Columbia   (1.4)

Source: U.S. Bureau of the Census,
    Press Release CB 91–346 (December 30, 1991)
*Estimated change from April 1, 1990 to July 1, 1991

Population Change: 1980 to 1990

National Total = 22,205,048 Increase*

RANK	STATE	GAIN/LOSS
1	California	6,092,119
2	Florida	3,191,602
3	Texas	2,757,319
4	Georgia	1,015,111
5	Arizona	947,013
6	Virginia	840,540
7	North Carolina	746,871
8	Washington	734,536
9	Maryland	564,493
10	New York	432,383
11	Colorado	404,430
12	Nevada	401,340
13	New Jersey	365,365
14	South Carolina	364,883
15	Minnesota	299,129
16	Tennessee	286,065
17	Massachusetts	279,388
18	Utah	261,813
19	New Mexico	212,175
20	Oregon	209,216
21	Missouri	200,387
22	New Hampshire	188,642
23	Wisconsin	186,002
24	Connecticut	179,540
25	Alaska	148,192

RANK	STATE	GAIN/LOSS
26	Alabama	146,699
27	Hawaii	143,538
28	Oklahoma	120,295
29	Kansas	113,895
30	Maine	103,268
31	Delaware	71,830
32	Arkansas	64,290
33	Idaho	62,814
34	Rhode Island	56,310
35	Indiana	53,935
36	Mississippi	52,578
37	Vermont	51,302
38	Ohio	49,485
39	Michigan	33,219
40	Kentucky	24,519
41	Pennsylvania	17,748
42	Louisiana	14,073
43	Montana	12,375
44	Nebraska	8,560
45	South Dakota	5,236
46	Illinois	4,084
47	North Dakota	(13,917)
48	Wyoming	(15,969)
49	Iowa	(31,433)
50	West Virginia	(137,053)

District of Columbia (156,167)

Source: U.S. Bureau of the Census,
Press Release CB 91-100 (March 11, 1991)
*Resident population.

Percent Change in Population: 1980 to 1990

National Change = 9.78% Increase*

RANK	STATE	PERCENT CHANGE		RANK	STATE	PERCENT CHANGE
1	Nevada	50.10		26	Connecticut	5.80
2	Alaska	36.90		27	New Jersey	5.00
3	Arizona	34.80		28	Massachusetts	4.90
4	Florida	32.70		29	Kansas	4.80
5	California	25.70		30	Missouri	4.10
6	New Hampshire	20.50		31	Oklahoma	4.00
7	Texas	19.40		31	Wisconsin	4.00
8	Georgia	18.60		33	Alabama	3.80
9	Utah	17.90		34	Arkansas	2.80
10	Washington	17.80		35	New York	2.50
11	New Mexico	16.30		36	Mississippi	2.10
12	Virginia	15.70		37	Montana	1.60
13	Hawaii	14.90		38	Indiana	1.00
14	Colorado	14.00		39	South Dakota	0.80
15	Maryland	13.40		40	Kentucky	0.70
16	North Carolina	12.70		41	Nebraska	0.50
17	Delaware	12.10		41	Ohio	0.50
18	South Carolina	11.70		43	Michigan	0.40
19	Vermont	10.00		44	Louisiana	0.30
20	Maine	9.20		45	Pennsylvania	0.10
21	Oregon	7.90		46	Illinois	0.00
22	Minnesota	7.30		47	North Dakota	(2.10)
23	Idaho	6.70		48	Wyoming	(3.40)
24	Tennessee	6.20		49	Iowa	(4.70)
25	Rhode Island	5.90		50	West Virginia	(8.00)

District of Columbia   (4.90)

Source: U.S. Bureau of the Census,

    Press Release CB 91–100 (March 11, 1991)

*Resident population.

Population Change: 1950 to 1990

National Change = 97,384,075 Increase*

RANK	STATE	GAIN/LOSS	RANK	STATE	GAIN/LOSS
1	California	19,173,798	26	Missouri	1,162,420
2	Florida	10,166,621	27	Nevada	1,041,750
3	Texas	9,275,316	28	Utah	1,033,988
4	New York	3,160,263	29	Alabama	978,844
5	Georgia	3,033,638	30	Oklahoma	912,234
6	Michigan	2,923,531	31	New Mexico	833,882
7	Arizona	2,915,641	32	Kentucky	740,490
8	Ohio	2,900,488	33	Hawaii	608,435
9	New Jersey	2,894,859	34	New Hampshire	576,010
10	Virginia	2,868,678	35	Kansas	572,275
11	Illinois	2,718,426	36	Arkansas	441,214
12	North Carolina	2,566,708	37	Alaska	421,400
13	Washington	2,487,729	38	Idaho	418,112
14	Maryland	2,438,467	39	Mississippi	394,302
15	Colorado	1,969,305	40	Delaware	348,083
16	Indiana	1,609,935	41	Maine	314,154
17	Tennessee	1,585,467	42	Nebraska	252,875
18	Louisiana	1,536,457	43	Rhode Island	211,568
19	Wisconsin	1,457,194	44	Montana	208,041
20	Minnesota	1,392,616	45	Vermont	185,011
21	Pennsylvania	1,383,631	46	Wyoming	163,059
22	South Carolina	1,369,676	47	Iowa	155,682
23	Massachusetts	1,325,911	48	South Dakota	43,264
24	Oregon	1,320,980	49	North Dakota	19,164
25	Connecticut	1,279,836	50	West Virginia	(212,075)

District of Columbia   (195,278)

Source: U.S. Bureau of the Census,
Press Release CB 91-07 (January 7, 1991)
*Resident population.

Percent Change in Population: 1950 to 1990

National Change = 64.35% Increase*

RANK	STATE	PERCENT CHANGE	RANK	STATE	PERCENT CHANGE
1	Nevada	650.76	26	Tennessee	48.17
2	Arizona	388.97	27	Minnesota	46.69
3	Florida	366.85	28	Michigan	45.88
4	Alaska	327.57	29	Wisconsin	42.43
5	California	181.12	30	Indiana	40.92
6	Utah	150.10	31	Oklahoma	40.85
7	Colorado	148.62	32	Ohio	36.50
8	New Mexico	122.42	33	Montana	35.20
9	Hawaii	121.74	34	Maine	34.38
10	Texas	120.28	35	Alabama	31.97
11	Delaware	109.43	36	Illinois	31.20
12	New Hampshire	108.02	37	Kansas	30.04
13	Washington	104.57	38	Missouri	29.39
14	Maryland	104.07	39	Massachusetts	28.27
15	Georgia	88.07	40	Rhode Island	26.72
16	Oregon	86.83	41	Kentucky	25.15
17	Virginia	86.44	42	Arkansas	23.11
18	Idaho	71.03	43	New York	21.31
19	South Carolina	64.70	44	Nebraska	19.08
20	Connecticut	63.76	45	Mississippi	18.10
21	North Carolina	63.19	46	Pennsylvania	13.18
22	New Jersey	59.87	47	South Dakota	6.63
23	Louisiana	57.26	48	Iowa	5.94
24	Wyoming	56.12	49	North Dakota	3.09
25	Vermont	48.98	50	West Virginia	(10.57)

District of Columbia   (24.34)

Source: U.S. Bureau of the Census,
   Press Release CB 91-07 (January 7, 1991)

*Resident population.

350

Projected Population Change: 1990 to 2000

National Change = 19,037,012 Increase*

RANK	STATE	GAIN/LOSS		RANK	STATE	GAIN/LOSS
1	California	3,739,979		26	Washington	124,308
2	Texas	3,224,490		27	Minnesota	114,901
3	Florida	2,477,074		28	Nevada	101,167
4	Georgia	1,478,784		29	Massachusetts	70,575
5	Arizona	952,772		30	Delaware	67,832
6	North Carolina	854,363		31	Kansas	51,426
7	New Jersey	815,812		32	Kentucky	47,704
8	Virginia	689,642		33	Rhode Island	45,536
9	Colorado	518,606		34	Maine	43,072
10	Maryland	492,532		35	Idaho	40,251
11	New Mexico	452,931		36	Wyoming	35,412
12	South Carolina	419,297		37	Oregon	34,679
13	Tennessee	388,815		38	Vermont	28,242
14	Alabama	369,413		39	South Dakota	17,996
15	Mississippi	303,784		40	New York	(4,455)
16	Louisiana	296,027		41	Montana	(5,065)
17	Utah	268,150		42	North Dakota	(9,800)
18	Missouri	265,927		43	Nebraska	(22,385)
19	Hawaii	236,771		44	Indiana	(42,159)
20	Oklahoma	230,415		45	Michigan	(45,297)
21	New Hampshire	223,748		46	West Virginia	(71,477)
22	Arkansas	178,275		47	Wisconsin	(107,769)
23	Connecticut	157,884		48	Ohio	(218,115)
24	Illinois	149,398		49	Iowa	(227,755)
25	Alaska	136,957		50	Pennsylvania	(378,632)
					District of Columbia	27,100

Source: U.S. Bureau of the Census,
     "Current Population Reports" (series P-25, No. 1017)
*Projected resident population. Calculated by the editors using 1990 Census counts.

Projected Percent Change in Population: 1990 to 2000

National Change = 7.1% Increase*

RANK	STATE	RCENT CHANGE		RANK	STATE	RCENT CHANGE
1	Arizona	23.1		26	Rhode Island	4.6
2	Nevada	21.1		27	Arkansas	4.2
3	New Mexico	20.5		28	Oregon	4.0
4	Florida	20.3		29	Minnesota	3.8
5	Georgia	19.4		30	Missouri	3.7
6	Alaska	19.2		31	Massachusetts	3.5
7	Hawaii	17.9		32	Idaho	3.0
8	New Hampshire	16.7		33	Oklahoma	2.8
9	California	15.0		34	Kansas	1.5
10	Texas	14.1		35	New York	1.2
11	Utah	12.1		36	South Dakota	0.8
12	North Carolina	11.8		37	Louisiana	0.1
13	Virginia	11.7		38	Illinois	(0.3)
14	Maryland	11.5		38	Kentucky	(0.3)
15	Colorado	11.0		40	Michigan	(0.5)
16	Delaware	10.2		40	Wisconsin	(0.5)
17	South Carolina	10.1		42	Indiana	(0.9)
18	New Jersey	8.2		43	Montana	(1.4)
19	Washington	7.2		44	Ohio	(1.5)
20	Mississippi	6.6		45	Nebraska	(2.0)
21	Tennessee	5.9		46	Wyoming	(2.6)
22	Alabama	5.5		47	Pennsylvania	(2.7)
23	Connecticut	5.1		48	North Dakota	(4.7)
23	Vermont	5.1		49	West Virginia	(7.3)
25	Maine	4.9		50	Iowa	(7.6)

District of Columbia   3.2

Source: U.S. Bureau of the Census,
   "Current Population Reports" (series P-25, No. 1017)

*Projected resident population. Calculated by the editors using 1990 Census counts.

Population per Square Mile in 1991

National Rate = 71.31 Persons per Square Mile*

RANK	STATE	POPULATION
1	New Jersey	1,045.96
2	Rhode Island	960.77
3	Massachusetts	764.99
4	Connecticut	679.26
5	Maryland	497.19
6	New York	382.39
7	Delaware	347.83
8	Ohio	267.11
9	Pennsylvania	266.87
10	Florida	245.88
11	Illinois	207.63
12	California	194.78
13	Hawaii	176.71
14	Michigan	164.90
15	Virginia	158.75
16	Indiana	156.40
17	North Carolina	138.29
18	New Hampshire	123.20
19	Tennessee	120.16
20	South Carolina	118.23
21	Georgia	114.35
22	Louisiana	97.60
23	Kentucky	93.45
24	Wisconsin	91.23
25	Alabama	80.57

RANK	STATE	POPULATION
26	Washington	75.37
27	Missouri	74.86
28	West Virginia	74.77
29	Texas	66.24
30	Vermont	61.30
31	Minnesota	55.67
32	Mississippi	55.25
33	Iowa	50.02
34	Oklahoma	46.23
35	Arkansas	45.55
36	Maine	40.01
37	Arizona	33.00
38	Colorado	32.56
39	Kansas	30.49
40	Oregon	30.44
41	Utah	21.54
42	Nebraska	20.72
43	New Mexico	12.75
44	Idaho	12.56
45	Nevada	11.69
46	South Dakota	9.26
47	North Dakota	9.20
48	Montana	5.55
49	Wyoming	4.74
50	Alaska	1.00

	District of Columbia	9,803.28

Source: U.S. Bureau of the Census,
    unpublished data

*Rates calculated by the editors using 1991 Census population estimates and land area of states.

Population per Square Mile in 1990

National Rate = 70.33 Persons per Square Mile*

RANK	STATE	POPULATION	RANK	STATE	POPULATION
1	New Jersey	1,041.94	26	West Virginia	74.46
2	Rhode Island	960.25	27	Missouri	74.27
3	Massachusetts	767.60	28	Washington	73.09
4	Connecticut	678.46	29	Texas	64.86
5	Maryland	489.15	30	Vermont	60.85
6	New York	380.96	31	Minnesota	54.95
7	Delaware	340.75	32	Mississippi	54.85
8	Pennsylvania	265.10	33	Iowa	49.70
9	Ohio	264.87	34	Oklahoma	45.80
10	Florida	239.60	35	Arkansas	45.14
11	Illinois	205.61	36	Maine	39.78
12	California	190.80	37	Arizona	32.25
13	Hawaii	172.54	38	Colorado	31.76
14	Michigan	163.62	39	Kansas	30.28
15	Virginia	156.25	40	Oregon	29.61
16	Indiana	154.56	41	Utah	20.97
17	North Carolina	136.06	42	Nebraska	20.53
18	New Hampshire	123.68	43	New Mexico	12.48
19	Tennessee	118.32	44	Idaho	12.17
20	South Carolina	115.79	45	Nevada	10.95
21	Georgia	111.85	46	North Dakota	9.26
22	Louisiana	96.86	47	South Dakota	9.17
23	Kentucky	92.75	48	Montana	5.49
24	Wisconsin	90.06	49	Wyoming	4.67
25	Alabama	79.62	50	Alaska	0.96

District of Columbia   9,949.18

Source: U.S. Bureau of the Census,
   unpublished data

*Rates calculated by the editors using 1990 Census counts and state land area.

Population per Square Mile in 1980

National Rate = 64.0 Persons per Square Mile

RANK	STATE	POPULATION	RANK	STATE	POPULATION
1	New Jersey	986.2	26	Alabama	76.7
2	Rhode Island	897.8	27	Missouri	71.3
3	Massachusetts	733.3	28	Washington	62.1
4	Connecticut	637.8	29	Vermont	55.2
5	Maryland	428.7	30	Texas	54.3
6	New York	370.6	31	Mississippi	53.4
7	Delaware	307.6	32	Iowa	52.1
8	Pennsylvania	264.3	33	Minnesota	51.2
9	Ohio	263.3	34	Oklahoma	44.1
10	Illinois	205.3	35	Arkansas	43.9
11	Florida	180.0	36	Maine	36.3
12	Michigan	162.6	37	Kansas	28.9
13	Indiana	152.8	38	Colorado	27.9
14	California	151.4	39	Oregon	27.4
15	Hawaii	150.1	40	Arizona	23.9
16	Virginia	134.7	41	Nebraska	20.5
17	North Carolina	120.4	42	Utah	17.8
18	Tennessee	111.6	43	Idaho	11.5
19	South Carolina	103.4	44	New Mexico	10.7
20	New Hampshire	102.4	45	North Dakota	9.4
21	Louisiana	94.5	46	South Dakota	9.1
22	Georgia	94.1	47	Nevada	7.3
23	Kentucky	92.3	48	Montana	5.4
24	Wisconsin	86.5	49	Wyoming	4.8
25	West Virginia	80.8	50	Alaska	0.7

District of Columbia   10,132.0

Source: U.S. Bureau of the Census,
"1980 Census of Population" (vol. 1, part A, PC80-1-A)

Population per Square Mile in 1970

National Rate = 57.4 Persons per Square Mile

RANK	STATE	POPULATION		RANK	STATE	POPULATION
1	New Jersey	953.1		26	Alabama	67.9
2	Rhode Island	902.5		27	Missouri	67.8
3	Massachusetts	727.0		28	Washington	51.2
4	Connecticut	623.6		29	Iowa	50.5
5	Maryland	396.6		30	Minnesota	48.0
6	New York	381.3		31	Vermont	47.9
7	Delaware	276.5		32	Mississippi	46.9
8	Pennsylvania	262.3		33	Texas	42.7
9	Ohio	260.0		34	Oklahoma	37.2
10	Illinois	199.4		35	Arkansas	37.0
11	Michigan	156.2		36	Maine	32.1
12	Indiana	143.9		37	Kansas	27.5
13	California	127.6		38	Oregon	21.7
14	Florida	125.5		39	Colorado	21.3
15	Hawaii	119.6		40	Nebraska	19.4
16	Virginia	116.9		41	Arizona	15.6
17	North Carolina	104.1		42	Utah	12.9
18	Tennessee	94.9		43	North Dakota	8.9
19	South Carolina	85.7		44	South Dakota	8.8
20	New Hampshire	81.7		45	Idaho	8.6
21	Kentucky	81.2		46	New Mexico	8.4
22	Wisconsin	81.1		47	Montana	4.8
23	Louisiana	81.0		48	Nevada	4.4
24	Georgia	79.0		49	Wyoming	3.4
25	West Virginia	72.5		50	Alaska	0.5

District of Columbia   12,402.0

Source: U.S. Bureau of the Census,
    "Census of Population: 1970" (vol. 1)

Population per Square Mile in 1960

National Rate = 50.6 Persons per Square Mile

RANK	STATE	POPULATION		RANK	STATE	POPULATION
1	Rhode Island	819.3		26	Alabama	64.2
2	New Jersey	805.5		27	Missouri	62.6
3	Massachusetts	657.3		28	Iowa	49.2
4	Connecticut	520.6		29	Mississippi	46.0
5	New York	350.6		30	Minnesota	43.1
6	Maryland	313.5		31	Washington	42.8
7	Pennsylvania	251.4		32	Vermont	42.0
8	Ohio	236.6		33	Texas	36.4
9	Delaware	225.2		34	Arkansas	34.2
10	Illinois	180.4		35	Oklahoma	33.8
11	Michigan	137.7		36	Maine	31.3
12	Indiana	128.8		37	Kansas	26.6
13	California	100.4		38	Nebraska	18.4
14	Virginia	99.6		38	Oregon	18.4
15	Hawaii	98.5		40	Colorado	16.9
16	North Carolina	93.2		41	Arizona	11.5
17	Florida	91.5		42	Utah	10.8
18	Tennessee	86.2		43	North Dakota	9.1
19	South Carolina	78.7		44	South Dakota	9.0
20	West Virginia	77.2		45	Idaho	8.1
21	Kentucky	76.2		46	New Mexico	7.8
22	Wisconsin	72.6		47	Montana	4.6
23	Louisiana	72.2		48	Wyoming	3.4
24	Georgia	67.8		49	Nevada	2.6
25	New Hampshire	67.2		50	Alaska	0.4

District of Columbia   12,524.0

Source: U.S. Bureau of the Census,
"Census of Population: 1970" (vol. 1)

Population per Square Mile in 1950

National Rate = 42.6 Persons per Square Mile

RANK	STATE	POPULATION		RANK	STATE	POPULATION
1	Rhode Island	748.5		26	Missouri	57.1
2	New Jersey	642.8		27	Florida	51.1
3	Massachusetts	596.2		28	Iowa	46.8
4	Connecticut	409.7		29	Mississippi	46.1
5	New York	309.3		30	Vermont	40.7
6	Maryland	237.1		31	Minnesota	37.3
7	Pennsylvania	233.1		32	Arkansas	36.3
8	Ohio	193.8		33	Washington	35.6
9	Delaware	160.8		34	Oklahoma	32.4
10	Illinois	155.8		35	Maine	29.4
11	Michigan	111.7		36	Texas	29.3
12	Indiana	108.7		37	Kansas	23.2
13	West Virginia	83.3		38	Nebraska	17.3
14	Virginia	83.2		39	Oregon	15.8
15	North Carolina	82.7		40	Colorado	12.8
16	Tennessee	78.8		41	North Dakota	8.8
17	Hawaii	78.0		42	South Dakota	8.5
18	Kentucky	73.9		43	Utah	8.4
19	South Carolina	69.9		44	Idaho	7.1
20	California	67.5		45	Arizona	6.6
21	Wisconsin	62.8		46	New Mexico	5.6
22	Alabama	59.9		47	Montana	4.1
23	Louisiana	59.4		48	Wyoming	3.0
24	New Hampshire	59.1		49	Nevada	1.5
25	Georgia	58.9		50	Alaska	0.2

District of Columbia   13,151.0

Source: U.S. Bureau of the Census,
    "Census of Population: 1970" (vol. 1)

Urban Population in 1990

National Total = 187,053,487 Urban Population*

RANK	STATE	POPULATION	%		RANK	STATE	POPULATION	%
1	California	27,571,321	14.74%		26	Oklahoma	2,130,139	1.14%
2	New York	15,164,047	8.11%		27	Oregon	2,003,271	1.07%
3	Texas	13,634,517	7.29%		28	Kentucky	1,910,325	1.02%
4	Florida	10,967,328	5.86%		29	South Carolina	1,905,378	1.02%
5	Illinois	9,668,552	5.17%		30	Kansas	1,712,564	0.92%
6	Pennsylvania	8,188,295	4.38%		31	Iowa	1,683,065	0.90%
7	Ohio	8,039,409	4.30%		32	Utah	1,499,081	0.80%
8	New Jersey	6,910,220	3.69%		33	Arkansas	1,258,021	0.67%
9	Michigan	6,555,842	3.50%		34	Mississippi	1,210,729	0.65%
10	Massachusetts	5,069,603	2.71%		35	New Mexico	1,105,651	0.59%
11	Virginia	4,293,443	2.30%		36	Nevada	1,061,444	0.57%
12	Georgia	4,097,339	2.19%		37	Nebraska	1,043,984	0.56%
13	Maryland	3,888,429	2.08%		38	Hawaii	986,171	0.53%
14	Washington	3,717,948	1.99%		39	Rhode Island	863,381	0.46%
15	Indiana	3,598,099	1.92%		40	West Virginia	648,184	0.35%
16	Missouri	3,516,009	1.88%		41	Idaho	578,214	0.31%
17	North Carolina	3,337,778	1.78%		42	New Hampshire	565,670	0.30%
18	Wisconsin	3,211,956	1.72%		43	Maine	547,824	0.29%
19	Arizona	3,206,973	1.71%		44	Delaware	486,501	0.26%
20	Minnesota	3,056,474	1.63%		45	Montana	419,826	0.22%
21	Tennessee	2,969,948	1.59%		46	Alaska	371,235	0.20%
22	Louisiana	2,871,759	1.54%		47	South Dakota	347,903	0.19%
23	Colorado	2,715,517	1.45%		48	North Dakota	340,339	0.18%
24	Connecticut	2,601,548	1.39%		49	Wyoming	294,635	0.16%
25	Alabama	2,439,549	1.30%		50	Vermont	181,149	0.10%
						District of Columbia	606,900	0.32%

Source: U.S. Bureau of the Census,
Press Release CB 91-334 (December 18, 1991)

*Urban population is composed of persons living in densely populated areas and in places of 2,500 or more outside urbanized areas.

Percent of Population Urban in 1990

National Percent = 75.2% of Population is Urban*

RANK	STATE	PERCENT		RANK	STATE	PERCENT
1	California	92.6		26	Missouri	68.7
2	New Jersey	89.4		27	Louisiana	68.1
3	Hawaii	89.0		28	Oklahoma	67.7
4	Nevada	88.3		29	Alaska	67.5
5	Arizona	87.5		30	Nebraska	66.1
6	Utah	87.0		31	Wisconsin	65.7
7	Rhode Island	86.0		32	Wyoming	65.0
8	Florida	84.8		33	Indiana	64.9
9	Illinois	84.6		34	Georgia	63.2
10	Massachusetts	84.3		35	Tennessee	60.9
10	New York	84.3		36	Iowa	60.6
12	Colorado	82.4		37	Alabama	60.4
13	Maryland	81.3		38	Idaho	57.4
14	Texas	80.3		39	South Carolina	54.6
15	Connecticut	79.1		40	Arkansas	53.5
16	Washington	76.4		41	North Dakota	53.3
17	Ohio	74.1		42	Montana	52.5
18	Delaware	73.0		43	Kentucky	51.8
18	New Mexico	73.0		44	New Hampshire	51.0
20	Michigan	70.5		45	North Carolina	50.4
20	Oregon	70.5		46	South Dakota	50.0
22	Minnesota	69.9		47	Mississippi	47.1
23	Virginia	69.4		48	Maine	44.6
24	Kansas	69.1		49	West Virginia	36.1
25	Pennsylvania	68.9		50	Vermont	32.2

District of Columbia   100.0

Source: U.S. Bureau of the Census,
    Press Release CB 91-334 (December 18, 1991)

*Urban population is composed of persons living in densely populated areas and in places of 2,500 or more outside urbanized areas.

Rural Population in 1990

National Total = 61,656,386 Rural Population*

RANK	STATE	POPULATION	%	RANK	STATE	POPULATION	%
1	Pennsylvania	3,693,348	5.99%	26	Oklahoma	1,015,446	1.65%
2	Texas	3,351,993	5.44%	27	Massachusetts	946,822	1.54%
3	North Carolina	3,290,859	5.34%	28	Maryland	893,039	1.45%
4	New York	2,826,408	4.58%	29	Oregon	839,050	1.36%
5	Ohio	2,807,706	4.55%	30	New Jersey	819,968	1.33%
6	Michigan	2,739,455	4.44%	31	Kansas	765,010	1.24%
7	Georgia	2,380,877	3.86%	32	Connecticut	685,568	1.11%
8	California	2,188,700	3.55%	33	Maine	680,104	1.10%
9	Florida	1,970,598	3.20%	34	Colorado	578,877	0.94%
10	Indiana	1,946,060	3.16%	35	New Hampshire	543,582	0.88%
11	Tennessee	1,907,237	3.09%	36	Nebraska	534,401	0.87%
12	Virginia	1,893,915	3.07%	37	Arizona	458,255	0.74%
13	Kentucky	1,774,971	2.88%	38	Idaho	428,535	0.70%
14	Illinois	1,762,050	2.86%	39	New Mexico	409,418	0.66%
15	Wisconsin	1,679,813	2.72%	40	Vermont	381,609	0.62%
16	Missouri	1,601,064	2.60%	41	Montana	379,239	0.62%
17	Alabama	1,601,038	2.60%	42	South Dakota	348,101	0.56%
18	South Carolina	1,581,325	2.56%	43	North Dakota	298,461	0.48%
19	Mississippi	1,362,487	2.21%	44	Utah	223,769	0.36%
20	Louisiana	1,348,214	2.19%	45	Delaware	179,667	0.29%
21	Minnesota	1,318,625	2.14%	46	Alaska	178,808	0.29%
22	Washington	1,148,744	1.86%	47	Wyoming	158,953	0.26%
23	West Virginia	1,145,293	1.86%	48	Nevada	140,389	0.23%
24	Iowa	1,093,690	1.77%	49	Rhode Island	140,083	0.23%
25	Arkansas	1,092,704	1.77%	50	Hawaii	122,058	0.20%
					District of Columbia	0	0.00%

Source: U.S. Bureau of the Census,

Press Release CB 91–334 (December 18, 1991)

*Rural population is composed of persons living outside urbanized areas and places of less than 2,500 or in the open countryside.

Percent of Population Rural in 1990

National Percent = 24.8% of Population is Rural*

RANK	STATE	PERCENT	RANK	STATE	PERCENT
1	Vermont	67.8	26	Pennsylvania	31.1
2	West Virginia	63.9	27	Kansas	30.9
3	Maine	55.4	28	Virginia	30.6
4	Mississippi	52.9	29	Minnesota	30.1
5	South Dakota	50.0	30	Michigan	29.5
6	North Carolina	49.6	30	Oregon	29.5
7	New Hampshire	49.0	32	Delaware	27.0
8	Kentucky	48.2	32	New Mexico	27.0
9	Montana	47.5	34	Ohio	25.9
10	North Dakota	46.7	35	Washington	23.6
11	Arkansas	46.5	36	Connecticut	20.9
12	South Carolina	45.4	37	Texas	19.7
13	Idaho	42.6	38	Maryland	18.7
14	Alabama	39.6	39	Colorado	17.6
15	Iowa	39.4	40	Massachusetts	15.7
16	Tennessee	39.1	40	New York	15.7
17	Georgia	36.8	42	Illinois	15.4
18	Indiana	35.1	43	Florida	15.2
19	Wyoming	35.0	44	Rhode Island	14.0
20	Wisconsin	34.3	45	Utah	13.0
21	Nebraska	33.9	46	Arizona	12.5
22	Alaska	32.5	47	Nevada	11.7
23	Oklahoma	32.3	48	Hawaii	11.0
24	Louisiana	31.9	49	New Jersey	10.6
25	Missouri	31.3	50	California	7.4

District of Columbia   0.0

Source: U.S. Bureau of the Census,
   Press Release CB 91–334 (December 18, 1991)

*Rural population is composed of persons living outside urbanized areas and places of less than 2,500 or in the open countryside.

Male Population in 1990

National Total = 121,239,418 Males

RANK	STATE	MALES	%	RANK	STATE	MALES	%
1	California	14,897,627	12.29%	26	Colorado	1,631,295	1.35%
2	New York	8,625,673	7.11%	27	Connecticut	1,592,873	1.31%
3	Texas	8,365,963	6.90%	28	Oklahoma	1,530,819	1.26%
4	Florida	6,261,719	5.16%	29	Oregon	1,397,073	1.15%
5	Pennsylvania	5,694,265	4.70%	30	Iowa	1,344,802	1.11%
6	Illinois	5,552,233	4.58%	31	Mississippi	1,230,617	1.02%
7	Ohio	5,226,340	4.31%	32	Kansas	1,214,645	1.00%
8	Michigan	4,512,781	3.72%	33	Arkansas	1,133,076	0.93%
9	New Jersey	3,735,685	3.08%	34	West Virginia	861,536	0.71%
10	North Carolina	3,214,290	2.65%	35	Utah	855,759	0.71%
11	Georgia	3,144,503	2.59%	36	Nebraska	769,439	0.63%
12	Virginia	3,033,974	2.50%	37	New Mexico	745,253	0.61%
13	Massachusetts	2,888,745	2.38%	38	Nevada	611,880	0.50%
14	Indiana	2,688,281	2.22%	39	Maine	597,850	0.49%
15	Missouri	2,464,315	2.03%	40	Hawaii	563,891	0.47%
16	Washington	2,413,747	1.99%	41	New Hampshire	543,544	0.45%
17	Wisconsin	2,392,935	1.97%	42	Idaho	500,956	0.41%
18	Tennessee	2,348,928	1.94%	43	Rhode Island	481,496	0.40%
19	Maryland	2,318,671	1.91%	44	Montana	395,769	0.33%
20	Minnesota	2,145,183	1.77%	45	South Dakota	342,498	0.28%
21	Louisiana	2,031,386	1.68%	46	Delaware	322,968	0.27%
22	Alabama	1,936,162	1.60%	47	North Dakota	318,201	0.26%
23	Arizona	1,810,691	1.49%	48	Alaska	289,867	0.24%
24	Kentucky	1,785,235	1.47%	49	Vermont	275,492	0.23%
25	South Carolina	1,688,510	1.39%	50	Wyoming	227,007	0.19%
					District of Columbia	282,970	0.23%

Source: U.S. Bureau of the Census,
Press Release CB 91-217 (June 11, 1991)

Female Population in 1990

National Total = 127,470,455 Females

RANK	STATE	FEMALES	%	RANK	STATE	FEMALES	%
1	California	14,862,394	11.66%	26	Connecticut	1,694,243	1.33%
2	New York	9,364,782	7.35%	27	Colorado	1,663,099	1.30%
3	Texas	8,620,547	6.76%	28	Oklahoma	1,614,766	1.27%
4	Florida	6,676,207	5.24%	29	Oregon	1,445,248	1.13%
5	Pennsylvania	6,187,378	4.85%	30	Iowa	1,431,953	1.12%
6	Illinois	5,878,369	4.61%	31	Mississippi	1,342,599	1.05%
7	Ohio	5,620,775	4.41%	32	Kansas	1,262,929	0.99%
8	Michigan	4,782,516	3.75%	33	Arkansas	1,217,649	0.96%
9	New Jersey	3,994,503	3.13%	34	West Virginia	931,941	0.73%
10	North Carolina	3,414,347	2.68%	35	Utah	867,091	0.68%
11	Georgia	3,333,713	2.62%	36	Nebraska	808,946	0.63%
12	Virginia	3,153,384	2.47%	37	New Mexico	769,816	0.60%
13	Massachusetts	3,127,680	2.45%	38	Maine	630,078	0.49%
14	Indiana	2,855,878	2.24%	39	Nevada	589,953	0.46%
15	Missouri	2,652,758	2.08%	40	New Hampshire	565,708	0.44%
16	Tennessee	2,528,257	1.98%	41	Hawaii	544,338	0.43%
17	Wisconsin	2,498,834	1.96%	42	Rhode Island	521,968	0.41%
18	Maryland	2,462,797	1.93%	43	Idaho	505,793	0.40%
19	Washington	2,452,945	1.92%	44	Montana	403,296	0.32%
20	Minnesota	2,229,916	1.75%	45	South Dakota	353,506	0.28%
21	Louisiana	2,188,587	1.72%	46	Delaware	343,200	0.27%
22	Alabama	2,104,425	1.65%	47	North Dakota	320,599	0.25%
23	Kentucky	1,900,061	1.49%	48	Vermont	287,266	0.23%
24	Arizona	1,854,537	1.45%	49	Alaska	260,176	0.20%
25	South Carolina	1,798,193	1.41%	50	Wyoming	226,581	0.18%
					District of Columbia	323,930	0.25%

Source: U.S. Bureau of the Census,
Press Release CB 91-217 (June 11, 1991)

White Population in 1990

National Total = 199,686,070 White Persons

RANK	STATE	WHITES	%	RANK	STATE	WHITES	%
1	California	20,524,327	10.28%	26	Louisiana	2,839,138	1.42%
2	New York	13,385,255	6.70%	27	Iowa	2,683,090	1.34%
3	Texas	12,774,762	6.40%	28	Oregon	2,636,787	1.32%
4	Florida	10,749,285	5.38%	29	Oklahoma	2,583,512	1.29%
5	Pennsylvania	10,520,201	5.27%	30	South Carolina	2,406,974	1.21%
6	Ohio	9,521,756	4.77%	31	Kansas	2,231,986	1.12%
7	Illinois	8,952,978	4.48%	32	Arkansas	1,944,744	0.97%
8	Michigan	7,756,086	3.88%	33	West Virginia	1,725,523	0.86%
9	New Jersey	6,130,465	3.07%	34	Mississippi	1,633,461	0.82%
10	Massachusetts	5,405,374	2.71%	35	Utah	1,615,845	0.81%
11	Indiana	5,020,700	2.51%	36	Nebraska	1,480,558	0.74%
12	North Carolina	5,008,491	2.51%	37	Maine	1,208,360	0.61%
13	Virginia	4,791,739	2.40%	38	New Mexico	1,146,028	0.57%
14	Georgia	4,600,148	2.30%	39	New Hampshire	1,087,433	0.54%
15	Wisconsin	4,512,523	2.26%	40	Nevada	1,012,695	0.51%
16	Missouri	4,486,228	2.25%	41	Idaho	950,451	0.48%
17	Washington	4,308,937	2.16%	42	Rhode Island	917,375	0.46%
18	Minnesota	4,130,395	2.07%	43	Montana	741,111	0.37%
19	Tennessee	4,048,068	2.03%	44	South Dakota	637,515	0.32%
20	Maryland	3,393,964	1.70%	45	North Dakota	604,142	0.30%
21	Kentucky	3,391,832	1.70%	46	Vermont	555,088	0.28%
22	Alabama	2,975,797	1.49%	47	Delaware	535,094	0.27%
23	Arizona	2,963,186	1.48%	48	Wyoming	427,061	0.21%
24	Colorado	2,905,474	1.46%	49	Alaska	415,492	0.21%
25	Connecticut	2,859,353	1.43%	50	Hawaii	369,616	0.19%
					District of Columbia	179,667	0.09%

Source: U.S. Bureau of the Census,
    Press Release CB 91-100 (March 11, 1991)

Percent of Population White in 1990

National Percent = 80.3% White

RANK	STATE	PERCENT		RANK	STATE	PERCENT
1	Vermont	98.6		26	Connecticut	87.0
2	Maine	98.4		27	Nevada	84.3
3	New Hampshire	98.0		28	Michigan	83.4
4	Iowa	96.6		29	Florida	83.1
5	West Virginia	96.2		30	Tennessee	83.0
6	North Dakota	94.6		31	Arkansas	82.7
7	Idaho	94.4		32	Oklahoma	82.1
7	Minnesota	94.4		33	Arizona	80.8
9	Wyoming	94.2		34	Delaware	80.3
10	Nebraska	93.8		35	New Jersey	79.3
10	Utah	93.8		36	Illinois	78.3
12	Oregon	92.8		37	Virginia	77.4
13	Montana	92.7		38	New Mexico	75.6
14	Wisconsin	92.2		38	North Carolina	75.6
15	Kentucky	92.0		40	Alaska	75.5
16	South Dakota	91.6		41	Texas	75.2
17	Rhode Island	91.4		42	New York	74.4
18	Indiana	90.6		43	Alabama	73.6
19	Kansas	90.1		44	Georgia	71.0
20	Massachusetts	89.8		44	Maryland	71.0
21	Pennsylvania	88.5		46	California	69.0
21	Washington	88.5		46	South Carolina	69.0
23	Colorado	88.2		48	Louisiana	67.3
24	Ohio	87.8		49	Mississippi	63.5
25	Missouri	87.7		50	Hawaii	33.4

District of Columbia   29.6

Source: U.S. Bureau of the Census,
    Press Release CB 91–100 (March 11, 1991)

Black Population in 1990

National Total = 29,986,060 Black Persons

RANK	STATE	BLACKS	%	RANK	STATE	BLACKS	%
1	New York	2,859,055	9.53%	26	Oklahoma	233,801	0.78%
2	California	2,208,801	7.37%	27	Washington	149,801	0.50%
3	Texas	2,021,632	6.74%	28	Kansas	143,076	0.48%
4	Florida	1,759,534	5.87%	29	Colorado	133,146	0.44%
5	Georgia	1,746,565	5.82%	30	Delaware	112,460	0.38%
6	Illinois	1,694,273	5.65%	31	Arizona	110,524	0.37%
7	North Carolina	1,456,323	4.86%	32	Minnesota	94,944	0.32%
8	Louisiana	1,299,281	4.33%	33	Nevada	78,771	0.26%
9	Michigan	1,291,706	4.31%	34	Nebraska	57,404	0.19%
10	Maryland	1,189,899	3.97%	35	West Virginia	56,295	0.19%
11	Virginia	1,162,994	3.88%	36	Iowa	48,090	0.16%
12	Ohio	1,154,826	3.85%	37	Oregon	46,178	0.15%
13	Pennsylvania	1,089,795	3.63%	38	Rhode Island	38,861	0.13%
14	South Carolina	1,039,884	3.47%	39	New Mexico	30,210	0.10%
15	New Jersey	1,036,825	3.46%	40	Hawaii	27,195	0.09%
16	Alabama	1,020,705	3.40%	41	Alaska	22,451	0.07%
17	Mississippi	915,057	3.05%	42	Utah	11,576	0.04%
18	Tennessee	778,035	2.59%	43	New Hampshire	7,198	0.02%
19	Missouri	548,208	1.83%	44	Maine	5,138	0.02%
20	Indiana	432,092	1.44%	45	Wyoming	3,606	0.01%
21	Arkansas	373,912	1.25%	46	North Dakota	3,524	0.01%
22	Massachusetts	300,130	1.00%	47	Idaho	3,370	0.01%
23	Connecticut	274,269	0.91%	48	South Dakota	3,258	0.01%
24	Kentucky	262,907	0.88%	49	Montana	2,381	0.01%
25	Wisconsin	244,539	0.82%	50	Vermont	1,951	0.01%
					District of Columbia	399,604	1.33%

Source: U.S. Bureau of the Census,
Press Release CB 91–100 (March 11, 1991)

Percent of Population Black in 1990

National Percent = 12.1% Black

RANK	STATE	PERCENT
1	Mississippi	35.6
2	Louisiana	30.8
3	South Carolina	29.8
4	Georgia	27.0
5	Alabama	25.3
6	Maryland	24.9
7	North Carolina	22.0
8	Virginia	18.8
9	Delaware	16.9
10	Tennessee	16.0
11	Arkansas	15.9
11	New York	15.9
13	Illinois	14.8
14	Michigan	13.9
15	Florida	13.6
16	New Jersey	13.4
17	Texas	11.9
18	Missouri	10.7
19	Ohio	10.6
20	Pennsylvania	9.2
21	Connecticut	8.3
22	Indiana	7.8
23	California	7.4
23	Oklahoma	7.4
25	Kentucky	7.1

RANK	STATE	PERCENT
26	Nevada	6.6
27	Kansas	5.8
28	Massachusetts	5.0
28	Wisconsin	5.0
30	Alaska	4.1
31	Colorado	4.0
32	Rhode Island	3.9
33	Nebraska	3.6
34	Washington	3.1
34	West Virginia	3.1
36	Arizona	3.0
37	Hawaii	2.5
38	Minnesota	2.2
39	New Mexico	2.0
40	Iowa	1.7
41	Oregon	1.6
42	Wyoming	0.8
43	Utah	0.7
44	New Hampshire	0.6
44	North Dakota	0.6
46	South Dakota	0.5
47	Maine	0.4
48	Idaho	0.3
48	Montana	0.3
48	Vermont	0.3

District of Columbia   65.8

Source: U.S. Bureau of the Census,
  Press Release CB 91–100 (March 11, 1991)

American Indian Population in 1990

National Total = 1,959,234 American Indians*

RANK	STATE	INDIANS	%	RANK	STATE	INDIANS	%
1	Oklahoma	252,420	12.88%	26	Alabama	16,506	0.84%
2	California	242,164	12.36%	27	Virginia	15,282	0.78%
3	Arizona	203,527	10.39%	28	New Jersey	14,970	0.76%
4	New Mexico	134,355	6.86%	29	Pennsylvania	14,733	0.75%
5	Alaska	85,698	4.37%	30	Idaho	13,780	0.70%
6	Washington	81,483	4.16%	31	Georgia	13,348	0.68%
7	North Carolina	80,155	4.09%	32	Maryland	12,972	0.66%
8	Texas	65,877	3.36%	33	Arkansas	12,773	0.65%
9	New York	62,651	3.20%	34	Indiana	12,720	0.65%
10	Michigan	55,638	2.84%	35	Nebraska	12,410	0.63%
11	South Dakota	50,575	2.58%	36	Massachusetts	12,241	0.62%
12	Minnesota	49,909	2.55%	37	Tennessee	10,039	0.51%
13	Montana	47,679	2.43%	38	Wyoming	9,479	0.48%
14	Wisconsin	39,387	2.01%	39	Mississippi	8,525	0.44%
15	Oregon	38,496	1.96%	40	South Carolina	8,246	0.42%
16	Florida	36,335	1.85%	41	Iowa	7,349	0.38%
17	Colorado	27,776	1.42%	42	Connecticut	6,654	0.34%
18	North Dakota	25,917	1.32%	43	Maine	5,998	0.31%
19	Utah	24,283	1.24%	44	Kentucky	5,769	0.29%
20	Kansas	21,965	1.12%	45	Hawaii	5,099	0.26%
21	Illinois	21,836	1.11%	46	Rhode Island	4,071	0.21%
22	Ohio	20,358	1.04%	47	West Virginia	2,458	0.13%
23	Missouri	19,835	1.01%	48	New Hampshire	2,134	0.11%
24	Nevada	19,637	1.00%	49	Delaware	2,019	0.10%
25	Louisiana	18,541	0.95%	50	Vermont	1,696	0.09%
					District of Columbia	1,466	0.07%

Source: U.S. Bureau of the Census,

   Press Release CB 91-100 (March 11, 1991)

*Includes Eskimo and Aleut.

Percent of Population American Indian in 1990

National Percent = 0.8% American Indian*

RANK	STATE	PERCENT
1	Alaska	15.6
2	New Mexico	8.9
3	Oklahoma	8.0
4	South Dakota	7.3
5	Montana	6.0
6	Arizona	5.6
7	North Dakota	4.1
8	Wyoming	2.1
9	Washington	1.7
10	Nevada	1.6
11	Idaho	1.4
11	Oregon	1.4
11	Utah	1.4
14	North Carolina	1.2
15	Minnesota	1.1
16	Kansas	0.9
17	California	0.8
17	Colorado	0.8
17	Nebraska	0.8
17	Wisconsin	0.8
21	Michigan	0.6
22	Arkansas	0.5
22	Hawaii	0.5
22	Maine	0.5
25	Alabama	0.4

RANK	STATE	PERCENT
25	Louisiana	0.4
25	Missouri	0.4
25	Rhode Island	0.4
25	Texas	0.4
30	Delaware	0.3
30	Florida	0.3
30	Iowa	0.3
30	Maryland	0.3
30	Mississippi	0.3
30	New York	0.3
30	Vermont	0.3
37	Connecticut	0.2
37	Georgia	0.2
37	Illinois	0.2
37	Indiana	0.2
37	Kentucky	0.2
37	Massachusetts	0.2
37	New Hampshire	0.2
37	New Jersey	0.2
37	Ohio	0.2
37	South Carolina	0.2
37	Tennessee	0.2
37	Virginia	0.2
49	Pennsylvania	0.1
49	West Virginia	0.1

	District of Columbia	0.2

Source: U.S. Bureau of the Census,
   Press Release CB 91-100 (March 11, 1991)
*Includes Eskimo and Aleut.

Asian Population in 1990

National Total = 7,273,662 Asians*

RANK	STATE	ASIANS	%	RANK	STATE	ASIANS	%
1	California	2,845,659	39.12%	26	Indiana	37,617	0.52%
2	New York	693,760	9.54%	27	Oklahoma	33,563	0.46%
3	Hawaii	685,236	9.42%	28	Utah	33,371	0.46%
4	Texas	319,459	4.39%	29	Tennessee	31,839	0.44%
5	Illinois	285,311	3.92%	30	Kansas	31,750	0.44%
6	New Jersey	272,521	3.75%	31	Iowa	25,476	0.35%
7	Washington	210,958	2.90%	32	South Carolina	22,382	0.31%
8	Virginia	159,053	2.19%	33	Alabama	21,797	0.30%
9	Florida	154,302	2.12%	34	Alaska	19,728	0.27%
10	Massachusetts	143,392	1.97%	35	Rhode Island	18,325	0.25%
11	Maryland	139,719	1.92%	36	Kentucky	17,812	0.24%
12	Pennsylvania	137,438	1.89%	37	New Mexico	14,124	0.19%
13	Michigan	104,983	1.44%	38	Mississippi	13,016	0.18%
14	Ohio	91,179	1.25%	39	Arkansas	12,530	0.17%
15	Minnesota	77,886	1.07%	40	Nebraska	12,422	0.17%
16	Georgia	75,781	1.04%	41	Idaho	9,365	0.13%
17	Oregon	69,269	0.95%	42	New Hampshire	9,343	0.13%
18	Colorado	59,862	0.82%	43	Delaware	9,057	0.12%
19	Arizona	55,206	0.76%	44	West Virginia	7,459	0.10%
20	Wisconsin	53,583	0.74%	45	Maine	6,683	0.09%
21	North Carolina	52,166	0.72%	46	Montana	4,259	0.06%
22	Connecticut	50,698	0.70%	47	North Dakota	3,462	0.05%
23	Missouri	41,277	0.57%	48	Vermont	3,215	0.04%
24	Louisiana	41,099	0.57%	49	South Dakota	3,123	0.04%
25	Nevada	38,127	0.52%	50	Wyoming	2,806	0.04%
					District of Columbia	11,214	0.15%

Source: U.S. Bureau of the Census,
    Press Release CB 91-100 (March 11, 1991)
*Includes Pacific Islanders.

Percent of Population Asian in 1990

National Percent = 2.9% Asian*

RANK	STATE	PERCENT		RANK	STATE	PERCENT
1	Hawaii	61.8		25	Oklahoma	1.1
2	California	9.6		25	Wisconsin	1.1
3	Washington	4.3		28	Louisiana	1.0
4	New York	3.9		29	Idaho	0.9
5	Alaska	3.6		29	Iowa	0.9
6	New Jersey	3.5		29	New Mexico	0.9
7	Nevada	3.2		32	Missouri	0.8
8	Maryland	2.9		32	Nebraska	0.8
9	Virginia	2.6		32	New Hampshire	0.8
10	Illinois	2.5		32	North Carolina	0.8
11	Massachusetts	2.4		32	Ohio	0.8
11	Oregon	2.4		37	Indiana	0.7
13	Texas	1.9		37	Tennessee	0.7
13	Utah	1.9		39	South Carolina	0.6
15	Colorado	1.8		39	Vermont	0.6
15	Minnesota	1.8		39	Wyoming	0.6
15	Rhode Island	1.8		42	Alabama	0.5
18	Arizona	1.5		42	Arkansas	0.5
18	Connecticut	1.5		42	Kentucky	0.5
20	Delaware	1.4		42	Maine	0.5
21	Kansas	1.3		42	Montana	0.5
22	Florida	1.2		42	North Dakota	0.5
22	Georgia	1.2		48	South Dakota	0.4
22	Pennsylvania	1.2		48	West Virginia	0.4
25	Michigan	1.1		50	Mississippi	0.1

District of Columbia   1.8

Source: U.S. Bureau of the Census,
  Press Release CB 91–100 (March 11, 1991)
*Includes Pacific Islanders.

Hispanic Population in 1990

National Total = 22,354,059 Hispanics*

RANK	STATE	HISPANICS	%	RANK	STATE	HISPANICS	%
1	California	7,687,938	34.39%	26	Utah	84,597	0.38%
2	Texas	4,339,905	19.41%	27	Hawaii	81,390	0.36%
3	New York	2,214,026	9.90%	28	North Carolina	76,726	0.34%
4	Florida	1,574,143	7.04%	29	Missouri	61,702	0.28%
5	Illinois	904,446	4.05%	30	Minnesota	53,884	0.24%
6	New Jersey	739,861	3.31%	31	Idaho	52,927	0.24%
7	Arizona	688,338	3.08%	32	Rhode Island	45,752	0.20%
8	New Mexico	579,224	2.59%	33	Nebraska	36,969	0.17%
9	Colorado	424,302	1.90%	34	Tennessee	32,741	0.15%
10	Massachusetts	287,549	1.29%	35	Iowa	32,647	0.15%
11	Pennsylvania	232,262	1.04%	36	South Carolina	30,551	0.14%
12	Washington	214,570	0.96%	37	Wyoming	25,751	0.12%
13	Connecticut	213,116	0.95%	38	Alabama	24,629	0.11%
14	Michigan	201,596	0.90%	39	Kentucky	21,984	0.10%
15	Virginia	160,288	0.72%	40	Arkansas	19,876	0.09%
16	Ohio	139,696	0.62%	41	Alaska	17,803	0.08%
17	Maryland	125,102	0.56%	42	Mississippi	15,931	0.07%
18	Nevada	124,419	0.56%	43	Delaware	15,820	0.07%
19	Oregon	112,707	0.50%	44	Montana	12,174	0.05%
20	Georgia	108,922	0.49%	45	New Hampshire	11,333	0.05%
21	Indiana	98,788	0.44%	46	West Virginia	8,489	0.04%
22	Kansas	93,670	0.42%	47	Maine	6,829	0.03%
23	Wisconsin	93,194	0.42%	48	South Dakota	5,252	0.02%
24	Louisiana	93,044	0.42%	49	North Dakota	4,665	0.02%
25	Oklahoma	86,160	0.39%	50	Vermont	3,661	0.02%
					District of Columbia	32,710	0.15%

Source: U.S. Bureau of the Census,
   Press Release CB 91–100 (March 11, 1991)
*Persons of Hispanic origin may be of any race.

Percent of Population Hispanic in 1990

National Percent = 9.0% Hispanic*

RANK	STATE	PERCENT
1	New Mexico	38.2
2	California	25.8
3	Texas	25.5
4	Arizona	18.8
5	Colorado	12.9
6	New York	12.3
7	Florida	12.2
8	Nevada	10.4
9	New Jersey	9.6
10	Illinois	7.9
11	Hawaii	7.3
12	Connecticut	6.5
13	Wyoming	5.7
14	Idaho	5.3
15	Utah	4.9
16	Massachusetts	4.8
17	Rhode Island	4.6
18	Washington	4.4
19	Oregon	4.0
20	Kansas	3.8
21	Alaska	3.2
22	Oklahoma	2.7
23	Maryland	2.6
23	Virginia	2.6
25	Delaware	2.4

RANK	STATE	PERCENT
26	Nebraska	2.3
27	Louisiana	2.2
27	Michigan	2.2
29	Pennsylvania	2.0
30	Wisconsin	1.9
31	Indiana	1.8
32	Georgia	1.7
33	Montana	1.5
34	Ohio	1.3
35	Minnesota	1.2
35	Missouri	1.2
35	North Carolina	1.2
38	Iowa	1.0
38	New Hampshire	1.0
40	South Carolina	0.9
41	Arkansas	0.8
41	South Dakota	0.8
43	North Dakota	0.7
43	Tennessee	0.7
43	Vermont	0.7
46	Alabama	0.6
46	Kentucky	0.6
46	Maine	0.6
46	Mississippi	0.6
50	West Virginia	0.5

District of Columbia   5.4

Source: U.S. Bureau of the Census,
    Press Release CB 91–100 (March 11, 1991)
*Persons of Hispanic origin can be of any race.

Projected White Population in 2000

National Total = 221,144,000 White Persons

RANK	STATE	WHITES	%		RANK	STATE	WHITES	%
1	California	26,641,000	12.05%		26	Louisiana	2,978,000	1.35%
2	Texas	17,311,000	7.83%		27	Oklahoma	2,810,000	1.27%
3	New York	14,062,000	6.36%		28	South Carolina	2,694,000	1.22%
4	Florida	12,870,000	5.82%		29	Oregon	2,674,000	1.21%
5	Pennsylvania	10,193,000	4.61%		30	Iowa	2,462,000	1.11%
6	Ohio	9,226,000	4.17%		31	Kansas	2,292,000	1.04%
7	Illinois	9,173,000	4.15%		32	Arkansas	2,093,000	0.95%
8	Michigan	7,543,000	3.41%		33	Utah	1,879,000	0.85%
9	New Jersey	6,855,000	3.10%		34	Mississippi	1,812,000	0.82%
10	Georgia	5,698,000	2.58%		35	New Mexico	1,711,000	0.77%
11	North Carolina	5,653,000	2.56%		36	West Virginia	1,664,000	0.75%
12	Massachusetts	5,595,000	2.53%		37	Nebraska	1,470,000	0.66%
13	Virginia	5,346,000	2.42%		38	New Hampshire	1,300,000	0.59%
14	Indiana	4,922,000	2.23%		39	Maine	1,252,000	0.57%
15	Missouri	4,705,000	2.13%		40	Nevada	1,125,000	0.51%
16	Washington	4,488,000	2.03%		41	Idaho	1,013,000	0.46%
17	Wisconsin	4,417,000	2.00%		42	Rhode Island	974,000	0.44%
18	Tennessee	4,331,000	1.96%		43	Montana	734,000	0.33%
19	Minnesota	4,250,000	1.92%		44	South Dakota	635,000	0.29%
20	Arizona	4,108,000	1.86%		45	North Dakota	592,000	0.27%
21	Maryland	3,597,000	1.63%		46	Vermont	580,000	0.26%
22	Colorado	3,535,000	1.60%		47	Delaware	561,000	0.25%
23	Kentucky	3,414,000	1.54%		48	Alaska	519,000	0.23%
24	Alabama	3,225,000	1.46%		49	Wyoming	467,000	0.21%
25	Connecticut	3,069,000	1.39%		50	Hawaii	432,000	0.20%
						District of Columbia	193,000	0.09%

Source: U.S. Bureau of the Census,
"Current Population Reports" (series P-25, No. 1017)

Projected Percent of Population White in 2000

National Percent = 82.6% White

RANK	STATE	PERCENT
1	Maine	98.5
2	Vermont	98.2
3	New Hampshire	97.5
4	Idaho	96.7
5	Iowa	96.6
5	West Virginia	96.6
7	Wyoming	95.4
8	Minnesota	94.7
9	Nebraska	94.5
10	Utah	94.4
11	North Dakota	94.0
12	Oregon	92.9
12	Rhode Island	92.9
14	Colorado	92.7
15	Montana	92.5
16	Wisconsin	92.3
17	Massachusetts	91.9
18	Kentucky	91.5
19	Kansas	90.6
20	Washington	89.9
21	Indiana	89.5
22	Connecticut	89.1
23	Arizona	89.0
23	South Dakota	89.0
25	Pennsylvania	88.6

RANK	STATE	PERCENT
26	Missouri	87.4
27	New Mexico	87.0
28	Ohio	86.8
29	Nevada	86.3
30	Texas	85.7
31	Florida	83.5
32	Oklahoma	83.2
33	Arkansas	82.8
34	Tennessee	82.2
35	Michigan	81.5
36	New Jersey	80.2
37	California	79.5
38	Illinois	79.2
39	New York	78.2
40	Virginia	77.7
41	Delaware	76.5
42	Alaska	75.6
43	North Carolina	75.5
44	Alabama	73.1
45	Georgia	71.6
46	South Carolina	69.0
47	Maryland	68.2
48	Louisiana	65.9
49	Mississippi	63.0
50	Hawaii	32.1

District of Columbia 30.5

Source: U.S. Bureau of the Census,
    "Current Population Reports" (series P-25, No. 1017)

Projected Black Population in 2000

National Total = 35,006,000 Black Persons

RANK	STATE	BLACKS	%	RANK	STATE	BLACKS	%
1	New York	3,180,000	9.08%	26	Oklahoma	231,000	0.66%
2	California	2,909,000	8.31%	27	Kansas	158,000	0.45%
3	Texas	2,439,000	6.97%	28	Colorado	156,000	0.45%
4	Florida	2,279,000	6.51%	29	Delaware	155,000	0.44%
5	Georgia	2,151,000	6.14%	30	Arizona	123,000	0.35%
6	Illinois	2,029,000	5.80%	31	Washington	116,000	0.33%
7	North Carolina	1,641,000	4.69%	32	Nevada	94,000	0.27%
8	Michigan	1,497,000	4.28%	33	Minnesota	77,000	0.22%
9	Maryland	1,469,000	4.20%	34	Iowa	58,000	0.17%
10	Louisiana	1,452,000	4.15%	34	Nebraska	58,000	0.17%
11	New Jersey	1,349,000	3.85%	36	Oregon	50,000	0.14%
12	Virginia	1,332,000	3.81%	37	Rhode Island	45,000	0.13%
13	Ohio	1,274,000	3.64%	37	West Virginia	45,000	0.13%
14	South Carolina	1,170,000	3.34%	39	New Mexico	34,000	0.10%
15	Alabama	1,136,000	3.25%	40	Hawaii	24,000	0.07%
16	Pennsylvania	1,131,000	3.23%	41	Alaska	23,000	0.07%
17	Mississippi	1,037,000	2.96%	42	Utah	13,000	0.04%
18	Tennessee	887,000	2.53%	43	New Hampshire	10,000	0.03%
19	Missouri	600,000	1.71%	44	Idaho	6,000	0.02%
20	Indiana	513,000	1.47%	45	Maine	4,000	0.01%
21	Arkansas	398,000	1.14%	45	North Dakota	4,000	0.01%
22	Massachusetts	327,000	0.93%	45	Wyoming	4,000	0.01%
23	Connecticut	313,000	0.89%	48	Vermont	3,000	0.01%
24	Kentucky	294,000	0.84%	49	Montana	2,000	0.01%
25	Wisconsin	273,000	0.78%	49	South Dakota	2,000	0.01%

	District of Columbia	430,000	1.23%

Source: U.S. Bureau of the Census,
   "Current Population Reports" (series P-25, No. 1017)

Projected Percent of State Population Black in 2000

National Percent = 13.1% Black

RANK	STATE	PERCENT
1	Mississippi	36.1
2	Louisiana	32.1
3	South Carolina	30.0
4	Maryland	27.9
5	Georgia	27.0
6	Alabama	25.8
7	North Carolina	21.9
8	Delaware	21.1
9	Virginia	19.4
10	New York	17.7
11	Illinois	17.5
12	Tennessee	16.8
13	Michigan	16.2
14	New Jersey	15.8
15	Arkansas	15.7
16	Florida	14.8
17	Texas	12.1
18	Ohio	12.0
19	Missouri	11.2
20	Pennsylvania	9.8
21	Indiana	9.3
22	Connecticut	9.1
23	California	8.7
24	Kentucky	7.9
25	Nevada	7.2

RANK	STATE	PERCENT
26	Oklahoma	6.8
27	Kansas	6.2
28	Wisconsin	5.7
29	Massachusetts	5.4
30	Rhode Island	4.3
31	Colorado	4.1
32	Nebraska	3.7
33	Alaska	3.4
34	Arizona	2.7
35	West Virginia	2.6
36	Iowa	2.3
36	Washington	2.3
38	Hawaii	1.8
39	Minnesota	1.7
39	New Mexico	1.7
39	Oregon	1.7
42	New Hampshire	0.8
42	Wyoming	0.8
44	Utah	0.7
45	North Dakota	0.6
46	Idaho	0.5
46	Vermont	0.5
48	Maine	0.4
49	South Dakota	0.3
50	Montana	0.2

District of Columbia   67.8

Source: U.S. Bureau of the Census,
    "Current Population Reports" (series P-25, No. 1017)

Population Under 5 Years Old in 1990

National Total = 18,354,443 Under 5 Years Old

RANK	STATE	POPULATION	%	RANK	STATE	POPULATION	%
1	California	2,397,715	13.06%	26	Kentucky	250,871	1.37%
2	Texas	1,390,054	7.57%	27	Connecticut	228,356	1.24%
3	New York	1,255,764	6.84%	28	Oklahoma	226,523	1.23%
4	Florida	849,596	4.63%	29	Oregon	201,421	1.10%
5	Illinois	848,141	4.62%	30	Mississippi	195,365	1.06%
6	Pennsylvania	797,058	4.34%	31	Iowa	193,203	1.05%
7	Ohio	785,149	4.28%	32	Kansas	188,390	1.03%
8	Michigan	702,554	3.83%	33	Utah	169,633	0.92%
9	New Jersey	532,637	2.90%	34	Arkansas	164,667	0.90%
10	Georgia	495,535	2.70%	35	New Mexico	125,878	0.69%
11	North Carolina	458,955	2.50%	36	Nebraska	119,606	0.65%
12	Virginia	443,155	2.41%	37	West Virginia	106,659	0.58%
13	Massachusetts	412,473	2.25%	38	Nevada	92,217	0.50%
14	Indiana	398,656	2.17%	39	Maine	85,722	0.47%
15	Missouri	369,244	2.01%	40	New Hampshire	84,565	0.46%
16	Washington	366,780	2.00%	41	Hawaii	83,223	0.45%
17	Wisconsin	360,730	1.97%	42	Idaho	80,193	0.44%
18	Maryland	357,818	1.95%	43	Rhode Island	66,969	0.36%
19	Minnesota	336,800	1.83%	44	Montana	59,257	0.32%
20	Louisiana	334,650	1.82%	45	Alaska	54,897	0.30%
21	Tennessee	333,415	1.82%	46	South Dakota	54,504	0.30%
22	Arizona	292,859	1.60%	47	Delaware	48,824	0.27%
23	Alabama	283,295	1.54%	48	North Dakota	47,845	0.26%
24	South Carolina	256,337	1.40%	49	Vermont	41,261	0.22%
25	Colorado	252,893	1.38%	50	Wyoming	34,780	0.19%
					District of Columbia	37,351	0.20%

Source: U.S. Bureau of the Census,
   Press Release CB 91-217 (June 11, 1991)

Population 5 to 17 Years Old in 1990

National Total = 45,249,989 Population 5 to 17 Years Old

RANK	STATE	POPULATION	%	RANK	STATE	POPULATION	%
1	California	5,353,010	11.83%	26	Oklahoma	610,484	1.35%
2	Texas	3,445,785	7.61%	27	Colorado	608,373	1.34%
3	New York	3,003,785	6.64%	28	Mississippi	551,396	1.22%
4	Illinois	2,098,225	4.64%	29	Iowa	525,677	1.16%
5	Florida	2,016,641	4.46%	30	Oregon	522,709	1.16%
6	Ohio	2,014,595	4.45%	31	Connecticut	521,225	1.15%
7	Pennsylvania	1,997,752	4.41%	32	Kansas	473,224	1.05%
8	Michigan	1,756,211	3.88%	33	Utah	457,811	1.01%
9	New Jersey	1,266,825	2.80%	34	Arkansas	456,464	1.01%
10	Georgia	1,231,768	2.72%	35	West Virginia	336,918	0.74%
11	North Carolina	1,147,194	2.54%	36	New Mexico	320,863	0.71%
12	Virginia	1,061,583	2.35%	37	Nebraska	309,406	0.68%
13	Indiana	1,057,308	2.34%	38	Idaho	228,212	0.50%
14	Missouri	945,582	2.09%	39	Maine	223,280	0.49%
15	Massachusetts	940,602	2.08%	40	Nevada	204,731	0.45%
16	Wisconsin	928,252	2.05%	41	Hawaii	196,903	0.44%
17	Washington	894,607	1.98%	42	New Hampshire	194,190	0.43%
18	Louisiana	892,619	1.97%	43	Montana	162,847	0.36%
19	Tennessee	883,189	1.95%	44	Rhode Island	158,721	0.35%
20	Minnesota	829,983	1.83%	45	South Dakota	143,958	0.32%
21	Maryland	804,423	1.78%	46	North Dakota	127,540	0.28%
22	Alabama	775,493	1.71%	47	Alaska	117,447	0.26%
23	Kentucky	703,223	1.55%	48	Delaware	114,517	0.25%
24	Arizona	688,260	1.52%	49	Vermont	101,822	0.23%
25	South Carolina	663,870	1.47%	50	Wyoming	100,745	0.22%

District of Columbia 79,741 0.18%

Source: U.S. Bureau of the Census,
Press Release CB 91–217 (June 11, 1991)

Population 18 to 20 Years Old in 1990

National Total = 11,726,868 Population 18 to 20 Years Old

RANK	STATE	POPULATION	%	RANK	STATE	POPULATION	%
1	California	1,411,200	12.03%	26	Colorado	148,197	1.26%
2	New York	839,066	7.16%	27	Oklahoma	148,115	1.26%
3	Texas	836,698	7.13%	28	Connecticut	145,274	1.24%
4	Pennsylvania	551,216	4.70%	29	Mississippi	141,847	1.21%
5	Illinois	531,971	4.54%	30	Iowa	131,299	1.12%
6	Florida	522,755	4.46%	31	Oregon	119,327	1.02%
7	Ohio	511,421	4.36%	32	Kansas	113,717	0.97%
8	Michigan	449,966	3.84%	33	Arkansas	109,879	0.94%
9	North Carolina	348,346	2.97%	34	Utah	90,245	0.77%
10	New Jersey	326,079	2.78%	35	West Virginia	87,263	0.74%
11	Georgia	325,159	2.77%	36	Nebraska	70,495	0.60%
12	Virginia	308,105	2.63%	37	New Mexico	68,168	0.58%
13	Massachusetts	302,128	2.58%	38	Maine	56,232	0.48%
14	Indiana	279,864	2.39%	39	Rhode Island	54,930	0.47%
15	Tennessee	238,948	2.04%	40	New Hampshire	52,399	0.45%
16	Missouri	234,368	2.00%	41	Hawaii	48,549	0.41%
17	Wisconsin	225,390	1.92%	42	Nevada	47,863	0.41%
18	Washington	210,809	1.80%	43	Idaho	47,064	0.40%
19	Louisiana	210,010	1.79%	44	Delaware	33,586	0.29%
20	Maryland	208,411	1.78%	45	Montana	32,703	0.28%
21	Alabama	205,557	1.75%	46	South Dakota	31,014	0.26%
22	Minnesota	192,809	1.64%	47	North Dakota	30,750	0.26%
23	South Carolina	185,514	1.58%	48	Vermont	29,671	0.25%
24	Kentucky	182,178	1.55%	49	Alaska	22,934	0.20%
25	Arizona	172,063	1.47%	50	Wyoming	20,025	0.17%
					District of Columbia	35,291	0.30%

Source: U.S. Bureau of the Census,
Press Release CB 91-217 (June 11, 1991)

Population 21 to 24 Years Old in 1990

National Total = 15,010,898 Population 21 to 24 Years Old

RANK	STATE	POPULATION	%		RANK	STATE	POPULATION	%
1	California	2,001,057	13.33%		26	Connecticut	200,159	1.33%
2	New York	1,114,358	7.42%		27	Colorado	187,328	1.25%
3	Texas	1,054,146	7.02%		28	Oklahoma	173,274	1.15%
4	Florida	692,902	4.62%		29	Iowa	152,414	1.02%
5	Illinois	680,979	4.54%		30	Mississippi	151,499	1.01%
6	Pennsylvania	675,559	4.50%		31	Oregon	148,201	0.99%
7	Ohio	624,997	4.16%		32	Kansas	140,776	0.94%
8	Michigan	554,561	3.69%		33	Arkansas	127,177	0.85%
9	New Jersey	453,105	3.02%		34	Utah	109,741	0.73%
10	North Carolina	432,707	2.88%		35	West Virginia	92,728	0.62%
11	Georgia	413,425	2.75%		36	Nebraska	85,392	0.57%
12	Virginia	411,626	2.74%		37	New Mexico	83,656	0.56%
13	Massachusetts	406,971	2.71%		38	Hawaii	72,636	0.48%
14	Indiana	325,018	2.17%		39	Nevada	71,082	0.47%
15	Maryland	296,962	1.98%		40	Maine	67,540	0.45%
16	Tennessee	288,707	1.92%		41	Rhode Island	65,428	0.44%
17	Wisconsin	286,936	1.91%		42	New Hampshire	65,203	0.43%
18	Missouri	282,823	1.88%		43	Idaho	51,183	0.34%
19	Washington	277,730	1.85%		44	Delaware	42,647	0.28%
20	Louisiana	254,501	1.70%		45	Montana	37,308	0.25%
21	Minnesota	250,000	1.67%		46	North Dakota	37,103	0.25%
22	Alabama	237,778	1.58%		47	South Dakota	37,099	0.25%
23	South Carolina	221,012	1.47%		48	Vermont	33,495	0.22%
24	Arizona	220,617	1.47%		49	Alaska	32,913	0.22%
25	Kentucky	217,811	1.45%		50	Wyoming	21,361	0.14%
						District of Columbia	47,267	0.31%

Source: U.S. Bureau of the Census,
   Press Release CB 91–217 (June 11, 1991)

Population 25 to 44 Years Old in 1990

National Total = 80,754,835 Population 25 to 44 Years Old

RANK	STATE	POPULATION	%	RANK	STATE	POPULATION	%
1	California	10,325,692	12.79%	26	South Carolina	1,114,643	1.38%
2	New York	5,862,873	7.26%	27	Connecticut	1,094,878	1.36%
3	Texas	5,625,196	6.97%	28	Oklahoma	961,560	1.19%
4	Florida	3,927,400	4.86%	29	Oregon	926,395	1.15%
5	Illinois	3,693,329	4.57%	30	Iowa	823,940	1.02%
6	Pennsylvania	3,657,323	4.53%	31	Kansas	774,499	0.96%
7	Ohio	3,411,043	4.22%	32	Mississippi	749,584	0.93%
8	Michigan	2,980,702	3.69%	33	Arkansas	685,748	0.85%
9	New Jersey	2,557,310	3.17%	34	West Virginia	532,807	0.66%
10	Georgia	2,190,594	2.71%	35	Utah	499,570	0.62%
11	North Carolina	2,151,486	2.66%	36	Nebraska	486,020	0.60%
12	Virginia	2,132,444	2.64%	37	New Mexico	484,466	0.60%
13	Massachusetts	2,019,817	2.50%	38	Nevada	414,292	0.51%
14	Indiana	1,734,270	2.15%	39	Maine	398,580	0.49%
15	Maryland	1,677,104	2.08%	40	New Hampshire	387,455	0.48%
16	Washington	1,658,951	2.05%	41	Hawaii	379,035	0.47%
17	Missouri	1,586,813	1.96%	42	Rhode Island	321,241	0.40%
18	Tennessee	1,553,309	1.92%	43	Idaho	301,968	0.37%
19	Wisconsin	1,546,832	1.92%	44	Montana	249,826	0.31%
20	Minnesota	1,445,827	1.79%	45	Delaware	217,981	0.27%
21	Louisiana	1,309,858	1.62%	46	Alaska	216,062	0.27%
22	Alabama	1,232,067	1.53%	47	South Dakota	204,629	0.25%
23	Colorado	1,179,936	1.46%	48	North Dakota	194,035	0.24%
24	Arizona	1,163,607	1.44%	49	Vermont	187,689	0.23%
25	Kentucky	1,159,182	1.44%	50	Wyoming	148,495	0.18%
					District of Columbia	216,472	0.27%

Source: U.S. Bureau of the Census,
   Press Release CB 91-217 (June 11, 1991)

Population 45 to 54 Years Old in 1990

National Total = 25,223,086 Population 45 to 54 Years Old

RANK	STATE	POPULATION	%	RANK	STATE	POPULATION	%
1	California	2,902,569	11.51%	26	Arizona	349,516	1.39%
2	New York	1,913,920	7.59%	27	Colorado	336,671	1.33%
3	Texas	1,628,634	6.46%	28	Oklahoma	322,975	1.28%
4	Florida	1,291,611	5.12%	29	Oregon	296,595	1.18%
5	Pennsylvania	1,213,845	4.81%	30	Iowa	274,428	1.09%
6	Illinois	1,166,727	4.63%	31	Mississippi	247,745	0.98%
7	Ohio	1,113,443	4.41%	32	Arkansas	243,337	0.96%
8	Michigan	948,119	3.76%	33	Kansas	235,388	0.93%
9	New Jersey	843,009	3.34%	34	West Virginia	191,318	0.76%
10	North Carolina	698,705	2.77%	35	Nebraska	149,389	0.59%
11	Georgia	668,951	2.65%	36	New Mexico	147,448	0.58%
12	Virginia	663,332	2.63%	37	Utah	138,481	0.55%
13	Massachusetts	600,095	2.38%	38	Nevada	136,000	0.54%
14	Indiana	570,791	2.26%	39	Maine	124,751	0.49%
15	Tennessee	526,210	2.09%	40	New Hampshire	112,215	0.44%
16	Missouri	523,177	2.07%	41	Hawaii	108,775	0.43%
17	Maryland	521,801	2.07%	42	Idaho	98,907	0.39%
18	Washington	501,543	1.99%	43	Rhode Island	96,425	0.38%
19	Wisconsin	478,882	1.90%	44	Montana	82,306	0.33%
20	Minnesota	428,460	1.70%	45	Delaware	68,114	0.27%
21	Alabama	419,421	1.66%	46	South Dakota	62,669	0.25%
22	Louisiana	406,440	1.61%	47	Vermont	57,389	0.23%
23	Kentucky	382,366	1.52%	48	North Dakota	57,084	0.23%
24	Connecticut	356,042	1.41%	49	Alaska	53,929	0.21%
25	South Carolina	355,610	1.41%	50	Wyoming	45,497	0.18%
					District of Columbia	62,031	0.25%

Source: U.S. Bureau of the Census,

Press Release CB 91-217 (June 11, 1991)

Population 55 to 59 Years Old in 1990

National Total = 10,531,756 Population 55 to 59 Years Old

RANK	STATE	POPULATION	%	RANK	STATE	POPULATION	%
1	California	1,133,907	10.77%	26	Arizona	146,658	1.39%
2	New York	811,857	7.71%	27	Oklahoma	141,214	1.34%
3	Texas	661,590	6.28%	28	Colorado	130,193	1.24%
4	Florida	588,552	5.59%	29	Iowa	122,335	1.16%
5	Pennsylvania	552,378	5.24%	30	Oregon	116,011	1.10%
6	Illinois	485,581	4.61%	31	Mississippi	107,784	1.02%
7	Ohio	482,526	4.58%	32	Arkansas	105,811	1.00%
8	Michigan	392,787	3.73%	33	Kansas	103,821	0.99%
9	New Jersey	355,677	3.38%	34	West Virginia	85,265	0.81%
10	North Carolina	295,739	2.81%	35	Nebraska	67,281	0.64%
11	Georgia	259,735	2.47%	36	New Mexico	62,038	0.59%
12	Virginia	257,207	2.44%	37	Utah	54,930	0.52%
13	Massachusetts	253,458	2.41%	38	Nevada	54,681	0.52%
14	Indiana	239,692	2.28%	39	Maine	54,216	0.51%
15	Missouri	228,556	2.17%	40	Hawaii	45,375	0.43%
16	Tennessee	220,952	2.10%	41	New Hampshire	44,703	0.42%
17	Wisconsin	204,647	1.94%	42	Rhode Island	42,077	0.40%
18	Maryland	202,170	1.92%	43	Idaho	39,407	0.37%
19	Washington	191,602	1.82%	44	Montana	34,005	0.32%
20	Alabama	183,677	1.74%	45	Delaware	29,861	0.28%
21	Minnesota	173,066	1.64%	46	South Dakota	29,218	0.28%
22	Louisiana	171,927	1.63%	47	North Dakota	26,268	0.25%
23	Kentucky	162,821	1.55%	48	Vermont	22,787	0.22%
24	South Carolina	148,762	1.41%	49	Wyoming	17,893	0.17%
25	Connecticut	147,022	1.40%	50	Alaska	16,595	0.16%
					District of Columbia	25,441	0.24%

Source: U.S. Bureau of the Census,
Press Release CB 91-217 (June 11, 1991)

Population 60 to 64 Years Old in 1990

National Total = 10,616,167 Population 60 to 64 Years Old

RANK	STATE	POPULATION	%	RANK	STATE	POPULATION	%
1	California	1,099,319	10.36%	26	South Carolina	144,020	1.36%
2	New York	825,110	7.77%	27	Oklahoma	137,227	1.29%
3	Florida	679,038	6.40%	28	Iowa	127,353	1.20%
4	Texas	627,831	5.91%	29	Colorado	121,360	1.14%
5	Pennsylvania	607,406	5.72%	30	Oregon	120,338	1.13%
6	Ohio	496,980	4.68%	31	Arkansas	107,584	1.01%
7	Illinois	489,104	4.61%	32	Mississippi	106,712	1.01%
8	Michigan	401,936	3.79%	33	Kansas	105,188	0.99%
9	New Jersey	363,521	3.42%	34	West Virginia	91,622	0.86%
10	North Carolina	291,164	2.74%	35	Nebraska	67,728	0.64%
11	Massachusetts	261,597	2.46%	36	New Mexico	59,490	0.56%
12	Virginia	245,436	2.31%	37	Maine	54,234	0.51%
13	Indiana	242,364	2.28%	38	Nevada	53,336	0.50%
14	Georgia	238,779	2.25%	39	Utah	52,481	0.49%
15	Missouri	228,829	2.16%	40	Hawaii	48,728	0.46%
16	Tennessee	213,637	2.01%	41	Rhode Island	47,126	0.44%
17	Wisconsin	208,879	1.97%	42	New Hampshire	43,493	0.41%
18	Maryland	195,297	1.84%	43	Idaho	38,550	0.36%
19	Washington	189,382	1.78%	44	Montana	34,316	0.32%
20	Alabama	180,310	1.70%	45	South Dakota	30,582	0.29%
21	Minnesota	171,220	1.61%	46	Delaware	29,903	0.28%
22	Louisiana	170,977	1.61%	47	North Dakota	27,120	0.26%
23	Kentucky	159,999	1.51%	48	Vermont	22,481	0.21%
24	Arizona	152,874	1.44%	49	Wyoming	17,597	0.17%
25	Connecticut	148,253	1.40%	50	Alaska	12,897	0.12%
					District of Columbia	25,459	0.24%

Source: U.S. Bureau of the Census,
Press Release CB 91-217 (June 11, 1991)

Population 65 to 74 Years Old in 1990

National Total = 18,106,558 Population 65 to 74 Years Old

RANK	STATE	POPULATION	%	RANK	STATE	POPULATION	%
1	California	1,857,221	10.26%	26	South Carolina	246,305	1.36%
2	Florida	1,369,652	7.56%	27	Oklahoma	235,135	1.30%
3	New York	1,348,279	7.45%	28	Iowa	226,961	1.25%
4	Pennsylvania	1,070,021	5.91%	29	Oregon	224,438	1.24%
5	Texas	998,239	5.51%	30	Arkansas	195,961	1.08%
6	Ohio	828,028	4.57%	31	Colorado	194,527	1.07%
7	Illinois	821,940	4.54%	32	Kansas	184,664	1.02%
8	Michigan	655,838	3.62%	33	Mississippi	180,149	0.99%
9	New Jersey	610,192	3.37%	34	West Virginia	155,743	0.86%
10	North Carolina	483,105	2.67%	35	Nebraska	117,643	0.65%
11	Massachusetts	459,881	2.54%	36	New Mexico	97,607	0.54%
12	Indiana	402,041	2.22%	37	Maine	91,600	0.51%
13	Virginia	400,622	2.21%	38	Utah	88,187	0.49%
14	Missouri	394,202	2.18%	39	Nevada	85,785	0.47%
15	Georgia	388,051	2.14%	40	Rhode Island	85,616	0.47%
16	Wisconsin	358,419	1.98%	41	Hawaii	78,653	0.43%
17	Tennessee	357,423	1.97%	42	New Hampshire	71,471	0.39%
18	Washington	336,034	1.86%	43	Idaho	69,755	0.39%
19	Maryland	314,491	1.74%	44	Montana	60,884	0.34%
20	Alabama	301,218	1.66%	45	South Dakota	54,471	0.30%
21	Minnesota	294,522	1.63%	46	Delaware	49,596	0.27%
22	Arizona	290,044	1.60%	47	North Dakota	47,541	0.26%
23	Louisiana	275,008	1.52%	48	Vermont	37,072	0.20%
24	Kentucky	268,226	1.48%	49	Wyoming	27,759	0.15%
25	Connecticut	256,237	1.42%	50	Alaska	15,548	0.09%
					District of Columbia	44,553	0.25%

Source: U.S. Bureau of the Census,
Press Release CB 91–217 (June 11, 1991)

Population 75 to 84 Years Old in 1990

National Total = 10,055,108 Population 75 to 84 Years Old

RANK	STATE	POPULATION	%	RANK	STATE	POPULATION	%
1	California	979,224	9.74%	26	Oklahoma	143,230	1.42%
2	Florida	789,669	7.85%	27	Connecticut	142,677	1.42%
3	New York	767,270	7.63%	28	Oregon	128,071	1.27%
4	Pennsylvania	587,249	5.84%	29	South Carolina	119,881	1.19%
5	Texas	551,732	5.49%	30	Arkansas	118,881	1.18%
6	Illinois	467,056	4.64%	31	Kansas	115,666	1.15%
7	Ohio	440,903	4.38%	32	Mississippi	108,800	1.08%
8	Michigan	345,716	3.44%	33	Colorado	101,963	1.01%
9	New Jersey	326,286	3.24%	34	West Virginia	87,703	0.87%
10	Massachusetts	267,194	2.66%	35	Nebraska	76,223	0.76%
11	North Carolina	251,267	2.50%	36	Maine	53,547	0.53%
12	Missouri	242,262	2.41%	37	New Mexico	51,223	0.51%
13	Indiana	222,404	2.21%	38	Rhode Island	48,915	0.49%
14	Wisconsin	218,509	2.17%	39	Utah	48,160	0.48%
15	Georgia	208,975	2.08%	40	New Hampshire	40,272	0.40%
16	Virginia	204,139	2.03%	41	Idaho	40,112	0.40%
17	Tennessee	202,601	2.01%	42	Hawaii	35,955	0.36%
18	Minnesota	183,577	1.83%	43	Montana	34,937	0.35%
19	Washington	182,953	1.82%	44	South Dakota	34,517	0.34%
20	Alabama	173,264	1.72%	45	Nevada	34,383	0.34%
21	Maryland	156,495	1.56%	46	North Dakota	32,274	0.32%
22	Kentucky	152,252	1.51%	47	Delaware	23,997	0.24%
23	Arizona	151,013	1.50%	48	Vermont	21,568	0.21%
24	Louisiana	150,350	1.50%	49	Wyoming	14,886	0.15%
25	Iowa	143,890	1.43%	50	Alaska	5,570	0.06%

District of Columbia		25,447	0.25%

Source: U.S. Bureau of the Census,
Press Release CB 91-217 (June 11, 1991)

Population 85 Years and Older in 1990

National Total = 3,080,165 Population 85 Years and Older

RANK	STATE	POPULATION	%	RANK	STATE	POPULATION	%
1	California	299,107	9.71%	26	Louisiana	43,633	1.42%
2	New York	248,173	8.06%	27	Kansas	42,241	1.37%
3	Florida	210,110	6.82%	28	Oregon	38,815	1.26%
4	Pennsylvania	171,836	5.58%	29	Arizona	37,717	1.22%
5	Texas	166,605	5.41%	30	Arkansas	35,216	1.14%
6	Illinois	147,549	4.79%	31	Colorado	32,953	1.07%
7	Ohio	138,030	4.48%	32	Mississippi	32,335	1.05%
8	Michigan	106,907	3.47%	33	South Carolina	30,749	1.00%
9	New Jersey	95,547	3.10%	34	Nebraska	29,202	0.95%
10	Massachusetts	92,209	2.99%	35	West Virginia	25,451	0.83%
11	Missouri	81,217	2.64%	36	Maine	18,226	0.59%
12	Wisconsin	74,293	2.41%	37	Rhode Island	16,016	0.52%
13	Indiana	71,751	2.33%	38	New Mexico	14,232	0.46%
14	North Carolina	69,969	2.27%	39	Utah	13,611	0.44%
15	Minnesota	68,835	2.23%	40	South Dakota	13,343	0.43%
16	Virginia	59,709	1.94%	41	New Hampshire	13,286	0.43%
17	Tennessee	58,794	1.91%	42	Idaho	11,398	0.37%
18	Georgia	57,244	1.86%	43	North Dakota	11,240	0.36%
19	Washington	56,301	1.83%	44	Montana	10,676	0.35%
20	Iowa	55,255	1.79%	45	Hawaii	10,397	0.34%
21	Alabama	48,507	1.57%	46	Vermont	7,523	0.24%
22	Connecticut	46,993	1.53%	47	Nevada	7,463	0.24%
23	Maryland	46,496	1.51%	48	Delaware	7,142	0.23%
24	Kentucky	46,367	1.51%	49	Wyoming	4,550	0.15%
25	Oklahoma	45,848	1.49%	50	Alaska	1,251	0.04%
					District of Columbia	7,847	0.25%

Source: U.S. Bureau of the Census,
   Press Release CB 91-217 (June 11, 1991)

Median Age in 1990

National Median Age = 32.9 Years Old

RANK	STATE	MEDIAN AGE
1	Florida	36.4
2	West Virginia	35.4
3	Pennsylvania	35.0
4	New Jersey	34.5
4	Oregon	34.5
6	Connecticut	34.4
7	Iowa	34.0
7	Rhode Island	34.0
9	Maine	33.9
9	New York	33.9
11	Arkansas	33.8
11	Montana	33.8
13	Massachusetts	33.6
13	Tennessee	33.6
15	Missouri	33.5
16	Nevada	33.3
16	Ohio	33.3
18	Oklahoma	33.2
19	North Carolina	33.1
19	Washington	33.1
21	Alabama	33.0
21	Kentucky	33.0
21	Maryland	33.0
21	Nebraska	33.0
21	Vermont	33.0

RANK	STATE	MEDIAN AGE
26	Delaware	32.9
26	Kansas	32.9
26	Wisconsin	32.9
29	Illinois	32.8
29	Indiana	32.8
29	New Hampshire	32.8
32	Hawaii	32.6
32	Michigan	32.6
32	Virginia	32.6
35	Colorado	32.5
35	Minnesota	32.5
35	South Dakota	32.5
38	North Dakota	32.4
39	Arizona	32.2
40	South Carolina	32.0
40	Wyoming	32.0
42	Georgia	31.6
43	California	31.5
43	Idaho	31.5
45	New Mexico	31.3
46	Mississippi	31.2
47	Louisiana	31.0
48	Texas	30.8
49	Alaska	29.4
50	Utah	26.2

	District of Columbia	33.5

Source: U.S. Bureau of the Census,
Press Release CB 91-217 (June 11, 1991)

Population Under 18 Years Old in 1990

National Total = 63,604,432 Population Under 18 Years Old

RANK	STATE	POPULATION	%		RANK	STATE	POPULATION	%
1	California	7,750,725	12.19%		26	Colorado	861,266	1.35%
2	Texas	4,835,839	7.60%		27	Oklahoma	837,007	1.32%
3	New York	4,259,549	6.70%		28	Connecticut	749,581	1.18%
4	Illinois	2,946,366	4.63%		29	Mississippi	746,761	1.17%
5	Florida	2,866,237	4.51%		30	Oregon	724,130	1.14%
6	Ohio	2,799,744	4.40%		31	Iowa	718,880	1.13%
7	Pennsylvania	2,794,810	4.39%		32	Kansas	661,614	1.04%
8	Michigan	2,458,765	3.87%		33	Utah	627,444	0.99%
9	New Jersey	1,799,462	2.83%		34	Arkansas	621,131	0.98%
10	Georgia	1,727,303	2.72%		35	New Mexico	446,741	0.70%
11	North Carolina	1,606,149	2.53%		36	West Virginia	443,577	0.70%
12	Virginia	1,504,738	2.37%		37	Nebraska	429,012	0.67%
13	Indiana	1,455,964	2.29%		38	Maine	309,002	0.49%
14	Massachusetts	1,353,075	2.13%		39	Idaho	308,405	0.48%
15	Missouri	1,314,826	2.07%		40	Nevada	296,948	0.47%
16	Wisconsin	1,288,982	2.03%		41	Hawaii	280,126	0.44%
17	Washington	1,261,387	1.98%		42	New Hampshire	278,755	0.44%
18	Louisiana	1,227,269	1.93%		43	Rhode Island	225,690	0.35%
19	Tennessee	1,216,604	1.91%		44	Montana	222,104	0.35%
20	Minnesota	1,166,783	1.83%		45	South Dakota	198,462	0.31%
21	Maryland	1,162,241	1.83%		46	North Dakota	175,385	0.28%
22	Alabama	1,058,788	1.66%		47	Alaska	172,344	0.27%
23	Arizona	981,119	1.54%		48	Delaware	163,341	0.26%
24	Kentucky	954,094	1.50%		49	Vermont	143,083	0.22%
25	South Carolina	920,207	1.45%		50	Wyoming	135,525	0.21%
						District of Columbia	117,092	0.18%

Source: U.S. Bureau of the Census,
Press Release CB 91-217 (June 11, 1991)

Percent of Population Under 18 Years Old in 1990

National Percent = 25.6% of Population Under 18 Years Old

RANK	STATE	PERCENT		RANK	STATE	PERCENT
1	Utah	36.4		26	Iowa	25.9
2	Alaska	31.3		26	Kentucky	25.9
3	Idaho	30.6		26	Washington	25.9
4	Wyoming	29.9		29	Illinois	25.8
5	New Mexico	29.5		29	Ohio	25.8
6	Louisiana	29.1		31	Missouri	25.7
7	Mississippi	29.0		32	Oregon	25.5
8	South Dakota	28.5		33	Vermont	25.4
8	Texas	28.5		34	Hawaii	25.3
10	Montana	27.8		35	Maine	25.2
11	North Dakota	27.5		36	New Hampshire	25.1
12	Nebraska	27.2		37	Tennessee	24.9
13	Arizona	26.8		38	Nevada	24.7
14	Georgia	26.7		38	West Virginia	24.7
14	Kansas	26.7		40	Delaware	24.5
14	Minnesota	26.7		41	Maryland	24.3
17	Oklahoma	26.6		41	Virginia	24.3
18	Michigan	26.5		43	North Carolina	24.2
19	Arkansas	26.4		44	New York	23.7
19	South Carolina	26.4		45	Pennsylvania	23.5
19	Wisconsin	26.4		46	New Jersey	23.3
22	Indiana	26.3		47	Connecticut	22.8
23	Alabama	26.2		48	Massachusetts	22.5
24	Colorado	26.1		48	Rhode Island	22.5
25	California	26.0		50	Florida	22.2

District of Columbia   19.3

Source: U.S. Bureau of the Census,
   Press Release CB 91-217 (June 11, 1991)

Population 18 Years Old and Older in 1990

National Total = 185,105,441 Adults*

RANK	STATE	POPULATION	%		RANK	STATE	POPULATION	%
1	California	22,009,296	11.89%		26	Connecticut	2,537,535	1.37%
2	New York	13,730,906	7.42%		27	Colorado	2,433,128	1.31%
3	Texas	12,150,671	6.56%		28	Oklahoma	2,308,578	1.25%
4	Florida	10,071,689	5.44%		29	Oregon	2,118,191	1.14%
5	Pennsylvania	9,086,822	4.91%		30	Iowa	2,057,875	1.11%
6	Illinois	8,484,236	4.58%		31	Mississippi	1,826,455	0.99%
7	Ohio	8,047,371	4.35%		32	Kansas	1,815,960	0.98%
8	Michigan	6,836,532	3.69%		33	Arkansas	1,729,594	0.93%
9	New Jersey	5,930,726	3.20%		34	West Virginia	1,349,900	0.73%
10	North Carolina	5,022,488	2.71%		35	Nebraska	1,149,373	0.62%
11	Georgia	4,750,913	2.57%		36	Utah	1,095,406	0.59%
12	Virginia	4,682,620	2.53%		37	New Mexico	1,068,328	0.58%
13	Massachusetts	4,663,350	2.52%		38	Maine	918,926	0.50%
14	Indiana	4,088,195	2.21%		39	Nevada	904,885	0.49%
15	Missouri	3,802,247	2.05%		40	New Hampshire	830,497	0.45%
16	Tennessee	3,660,581	1.98%		41	Hawaii	828,103	0.45%
17	Maryland	3,619,227	1.96%		42	Rhode Island	777,774	0.42%
18	Washington	3,605,305	1.95%		43	Idaho	698,344	0.38%
19	Wisconsin	3,602,787	1.95%		44	Montana	576,961	0.31%
20	Minnesota	3,208,316	1.73%		45	Delaware	502,827	0.27%
21	Louisiana	2,992,704	1.62%		46	South Dakota	497,542	0.27%
22	Alabama	2,981,799	1.61%		47	North Dakota	463,415	0.25%
23	Kentucky	2,731,202	1.48%		48	Vermont	419,675	0.23%
24	Arizona	2,684,109	1.45%		49	Alaska	377,699	0.20%
25	South Carolina	2,566,496	1.39%		50	Wyoming	318,063	0.17%
						District of Columbia	489,808	0.26%

Source: U.S. Bureau of the Census,
   Press Release CB 91-217 (June 11, 1991)
*Calculated by the editors.

Percent of Population 18 Years Old and Older in 1990

National Percent = 74.4% of Population*

RANK	STATE	PERCENT	RANK	STATE	PERCENT
1	Florida	77.8	26	California	74.0
2	Massachusetts	77.5	27	Colorado	73.9
2	Rhode Island	77.5	28	Alabama	73.8
4	Connecticut	77.2	29	Indiana	73.7
5	New Jersey	76.7	30	Arkansas	73.6
6	Pennsylvania	76.5	30	South Carolina	73.6
7	New York	76.3	30	Wisconsin	73.6
8	North Carolina	75.8	33	Michigan	73.5
9	Maryland	75.7	34	Oklahoma	73.4
9	Virginia	75.7	35	Georgia	73.3
11	Delaware	75.5	35	Kansas	73.3
12	Nevada	75.3	35	Minnesota	73.3
12	West Virginia	75.3	38	Arizona	73.2
14	Tennessee	75.1	39	Nebraska	72.8
15	New Hampshire	74.9	40	North Dakota	72.5
16	Maine	74.8	41	Montana	72.2
17	Hawaii	74.7	42	South Dakota	71.5
18	Vermont	74.6	42	Texas	71.5
19	Oregon	74.5	44	Mississippi	71.0
20	Missouri	74.3	45	Louisiana	70.9
21	Illinois	74.2	46	New Mexico	70.5
21	Ohio	74.2	47	Wyoming	70.1
23	Iowa	74.1	48	Idaho	69.4
23	Kentucky	74.1	49	Alaska	68.7
23	Washington	74.1	50	Utah	63.6

District of Columbia   80.7

Source: U.S. Bureau of the Census,
    Press Release CB 91–217 (June 11, 1991)
*Rates calculated by the editors.

Population 65 Years and Older in 1990

National Total = 31,241,831 Population 65 Years and Older

RANK	STATE	POPULATION	%	RANK	STATE	POPULATION	%
1	California	3,135,552	10.04%	26	Iowa	426,106	1.36%
2	Florida	2,369,431	7.58%	27	Oklahoma	424,213	1.36%
3	New York	2,363,722	7.57%	28	South Carolina	396,935	1.27%
4	Pennsylvania	1,829,106	5.85%	29	Oregon	391,324	1.25%
5	Texas	1,716,576	5.49%	30	Arkansas	350,058	1.12%
6	Illinois	1,436,545	4.60%	31	Kansas	342,571	1.10%
7	Ohio	1,406,961	4.50%	32	Colorado	329,443	1.05%
8	Michigan	1,108,461	3.55%	33	Mississippi	321,284	1.03%
9	New Jersey	1,032,025	3.30%	34	West Virginia	268,897	0.86%
10	Massachusetts	819,284	2.62%	35	Nebraska	223,068	0.71%
11	North Carolina	804,341	2.57%	36	Maine	163,373	0.52%
12	Missouri	717,681	2.30%	37	New Mexico	163,062	0.52%
13	Indiana	696,196	2.23%	38	Rhode Island	150,547	0.48%
14	Virginia	664,470	2.13%	39	Utah	149,958	0.48%
15	Georgia	654,270	2.09%	40	Nevada	127,631	0.41%
16	Wisconsin	651,221	2.08%	41	New Hampshire	125,029	0.40%
17	Tennessee	618,818	1.98%	42	Hawaii	125,005	0.40%
18	Washington	575,288	1.84%	43	Idaho	121,265	0.39%
19	Minnesota	546,934	1.75%	44	Montana	106,497	0.34%
20	Alabama	522,989	1.67%	45	South Dakota	102,331	0.33%
21	Maryland	517,482	1.66%	46	North Dakota	91,055	0.29%
22	Arizona	478,774	1.53%	47	Delaware	80,735	0.26%
23	Louisiana	468,991	1.50%	48	Vermont	66,163	0.21%
24	Kentucky	466,845	1.49%	49	Wyoming	47,195	0.15%
25	Connecticut	445,907	1.43%	50	Alaska	22,369	0.07%
					District of Columbia	77,847	0.25%

Source: U.S. Bureau of the Census,
   Press Release CB 91-217 (June 11, 1991)

Percent of Population 65 Years and Older in 1990

National Percent = 12.5% of Population 65 Years and Older

RANK	STATE	PERCENT	RANK	STATE	PERCENT
1	Florida	18.3	26	Illinois	12.6
2	Pennsylvania	15.4	26	Indiana	12.6
3	Iowa	15.3	28	Minnesota	12.5
4	Rhode Island	15.0	28	Mississippi	12.5
4	West Virginia	15.0	30	Delaware	12.1
6	Arkansas	14.9	30	North Carolina	12.1
7	South Dakota	14.7	32	Idaho	12.0
8	North Dakota	14.3	33	Michigan	11.9
9	Nebraska	14.1	34	Vermont	11.8
10	Missouri	14.0	34	Washington	11.8
11	Kansas	13.8	36	South Carolina	11.4
11	Oregon	13.8	37	Hawaii	11.3
13	Connecticut	13.6	37	New Hampshire	11.3
13	Massachusetts	13.6	39	Louisiana	11.1
15	Oklahoma	13.5	40	Maryland	10.8
16	New Jersey	13.4	40	New Mexico	10.8
17	Maine	13.3	42	Virginia	10.7
17	Montana	13.3	43	Nevada	10.6
17	Wisconsin	13.3	44	California	10.5
20	Arizona	13.1	45	Wyoming	10.4
20	New York	13.1	46	Georgia	10.1
22	Ohio	13.0	46	Texas	10.1
23	Alabama	12.9	48	Colorado	10.0
24	Kentucky	12.7	49	Utah	8.7
24	Tennessee	12.7	50	Alaska	4.1

District of Columbia   12.8

Source: U.S. Bureau of the Census,
Press Release CB 91–217 (June 11, 1991)

Marriages in 1990

National Total = 2,448,000 Marriages*

RANK	STATE	MARRIAGES	%	RANK	STATE	MARRIAGES	%
1	California	236,693	9.67%	26	Oklahoma	33,162	1.35%
2	Texas	182,831	7.47%	27	Colorado	31,512	1.29%
3	New York	169,264	6.91%	28	Connecticut	27,806	1.14%
4	Florida	142,292	5.81%	29	Oregon	25,211	1.03%
5	Ohio	95,827	3.91%	30	Iowa	24,813	1.01%
6	Pennsylvania	86,794	3.55%	31	Mississippi	24,322	0.99%
7	Michigan	76,137	3.11%	32	Kansas	23,385	0.96%
8	Virginia	71,257	2.91%	33	Utah	19,012	0.78%
9	Tennessee	66,597	2.72%	34	Hawaii	18,144	0.74%
10	Georgia	64,359	2.63%	35	Idaho	14,977	0.61%
11	New Jersey	58,012	2.37%	36	New Mexico	13,175	0.54%
12	South Carolina	55,837	2.28%	37	West Virginia	13,166	0.54%
13	Indiana	54,295	2.22%	38	Nebraska	12,484	0.51%
14	North Carolina	52,070	2.13%	39	Maine	11,773	0.48%
15	Kentucky	51,291	2.10%	40	New Hampshire	10,582	0.43%
16	Missouri	49,251	2.01%	41	Rhode Island	8,113	0.33%
17	Washington	48,642	1.99%	42	South Dakota	7,727	0.32%
18	Massachusetts	47,822	1.95%	43	Montana	7,025	0.29%
19	Maryland	46,081	1.88%	44	Vermont	6,144	0.25%
20	Alabama	43,263	1.77%	45	Alaska	5,730	0.23%
21	Louisiana	41,161	1.68%	46	Delaware	5,628	0.23%
22	Wisconsin	41,160	1.68%	47	Wyoming	4,843	0.20%
23	Arizona	37,007	1.51%	48	North Dakota	4,779	0.20%
24	Arkansas	35,703	1.46%	–	Illinois**	N/A	N/A
25	Minnesota	33,695	1.38%	–	Nevada**	N/A	N/A

District of Columbia	4,716	0.19%

Source: U.S. Department of Health and Human Services, Centers for Disease Control, National Center for Health Statistics,
"Monthly Vital Statistics Report" (August 28, 1991)

*By state of ocurrence.

**Not available.

Marriage Rate in 1990

National Rate = 9.8 Marriages per 1,000 Population*

RANK	STATE	RATE	RANK	STATE	RATE
1	Hawaii	16.1	24	New Hampshire	9.4
2	South Carolina	15.7	24	New York	9.4
3	Arkansas	14.8	28	Mississippi	9.3
4	Idaho	14.6	29	Kansas	9.2
5	Kentucky	13.8	30	Oregon	8.8
6	Tennessee	13.4	31	Iowa	8.7
7	Virginia	11.5	31	Montana	8.7
8	Utah	11.0	31	Ohio	8.7
9	Florida	10.9	34	Connecticut	8.6
10	Alaska	10.8	35	New Mexico	8.5
10	South Dakota	10.8	36	Wisconsin	8.4
12	Texas	10.7	37	Delaware	8.2
12	Vermont	10.7	37	Michigan	8.2
14	Alabama	10.5	39	Massachusetts	8.1
15	Oklahoma	10.3	39	Rhode Island	8.1
15	Wyoming	10.3	41	California	7.9
17	Arizona	10.2	42	North Carolina	7.8
18	Washington	10.0	43	Minnesota	7.7
19	Georgia	9.8	43	Nebraska	7.7
20	Maryland	9.7	45	New Jersey	7.5
21	Indiana	9.6	46	North Dakota	7.3
22	Maine	9.5	47	Pennsylvania	7.2
22	Missouri	9.5	47	West Virginia	7.2
24	Colorado	9.4	–	Illinois**	N/A
24	Louisiana	9.4	–	Nevada**	N/A

District of Columbia   7.9

Source: U.S. Department of Health and Human Services, Centers for Disease Control, National Center for Health Statistics,
   "Monthly Vital Statistics Report" (August 28, 1991)
*By state of occurrence.
**Not available. Illinois' rate in 1989 was 7.4, Nevada's 106.3.

Divorces in 1990

National Total = 1,175,000 Divorces*

RANK	STATE	DIVORCES	%	RANK	STATE	DIVORCES	%
1	Texas	95,139	8.10%	26	Mississippi	14,444	1.23%
2	Florida	81,655	6.95%	27	Nevada	13,290	1.13%
3	New York	57,863	4.92%	28	Kansas	12,623	1.07%
4	Ohio	50,989	4.34%	29	Iowa	11,060	0.94%
5	Michigan	40,219	3.42%	30	Connecticut	10,301	0.88%
6	Pennsylvania	40,123	3.41%	31	West Virginia	9,658	0.82%
7	Georgia	35,672	3.04%	32	Utah	8,786	0.75%
8	North Carolina	34,017	2.90%	33	New Mexico	7,652	0.65%
9	Tennessee	32,295	2.75%	34	Idaho	6,634	0.56%
10	Washington	28,773	2.45%	35	Nebraska	6,488	0.55%
11	Virginia	27,266	2.32%	36	New Hampshire	5,279	0.45%
12	Missouri	26,351	2.24%	37	Maine	5,275	0.45%
13	Alabama	25,280	2.15%	38	Hawaii	5,168	0.44%
14	Arizona	25,096	2.14%	39	Montana	4,093	0.35%
15	Oklahoma	24,919	2.12%	40	Rhode Island	3,754	0.32%
16	New Jersey	23,612	2.01%	41	Wyoming	3,095	0.26%
17	Kentucky	21,790	1.85%	42	Delaware	2,985	0.25%
18	Colorado	18,385	1.56%	43	Alaska	2,921	0.25%
19	Wisconsin	17,832	1.52%	44	South Dakota	2,648	0.23%
20	Massachusetts	16,781	1.43%	45	Vermont	2,616	0.22%
21	Arkansas	16,765	1.43%	46	North Dakota	2,326	0.20%
22	South Carolina	16,080	1.37%	–	California**	N/A	N/A
23	Maryland	16,055	1.37%	–	Illinois**	N/A	N/A
24	Oregon	15,884	1.35%	–	Indiana**	N/A	N/A
25	Minnesota	15,421	1.31%	–	Louisiana**	N/A	N/A

District of Columbia	3,257	0.28%

Source: U.S. Department of Health and Human Services, Centers for Disease Control, National Center for Health Statistics,
"Monthly Vital Statistics Report" (August 28, 1991)

*By state of occurrence.

**Not available.

Divorce Rate in 1990

National Rate = 4.7 Divorces per 1,000 Population*

RANK	STATE	RATE		RANK	STATE	RATE
1	Nevada	11.4		25	Ohio	4.7
2	Oklahoma	7.7		27	Hawaii	4.6
3	Arizona	6.9		28	South Carolina	4.5
3	Arkansas	6.9		28	Vermont	4.5
5	Wyoming	6.6		30	Delaware	4.4
6	Idaho	6.5		30	Virginia	4.4
6	Tennessee	6.5		32	Maine	4.3
8	Florida	6.3		32	Michigan	4.3
9	Alabama	6.1		34	Nebraska	4.0
10	Washington	5.9		35	Iowa	3.9
11	Kentucky	5.8		36	Rhode Island	3.7
12	Alaska	5.5		36	South Dakota	3.7
12	Colorado	5.5		38	North Dakota	3.6
12	Georgia	5.5		38	Wisconsin	3.6
12	Mississippi	5.5		40	Minnesota	3.5
12	Oregon	5.5		41	Maryland	3.4
12	Texas	5.5		42	Pennsylvania	3.3
18	West Virginia	5.3		43	Connecticut	3.2
19	Missouri	5.1		43	New York	3.2
19	Montana	5.1		45	New Jersey	3.0
19	North Carolina	5.1		46	Massachusetts	2.8
19	Utah	5.1		–	California**	N/A
23	Kansas	5.0		–	Illinois**	N/A
24	New Mexico	4.9		–	Indiana**	N/A
25	New Hampshire	4.7		–	Louisiana**	N/A

District of Columbia   5.5

Source: U.S. Department of Health and Human Services, Centers for Disease Control, National Center for Health Statistics,
    "Monthly Vital Statistics Report" (August 28, 1991)

By state of occurrence.

**Not available. Illinois' divorce rate was 3.9 in 1989; California's 4.3; Indiana's and Louisiana's rate were not available.*

Percent of Eligible Voters Reported Registered in 1990

National Percent = 62.2% of Eligible Voters Reported Registered

RANK	STATE	PERCENT	RANK	STATE	PERCENT
1	North Dakota	90.6	26	Wyoming	62.7
2	Minnesota	82.7	27	North Carolina	62.6
3	Maine	81.3	28	Ohio	62.4
4	Wisconsin	78.0	29	Washington	61.8
5	Vermont	74.4	30	Arkansas	61.0
6	South Dakota	74.1	31	Indiana	60.9
7	Louisiana	73.2	31	New Jersey	60.9
8	Montana	73.1	31	Utah	60.9
9	Alabama	72.6	34	Idaho	60.6
10	Alaska	71.0	35	Kentucky	60.4
11	Mississippi	70.9	35	Texas	60.4
12	Michigan	70.8	37	Virginia	60.0
13	Nebraska	70.2	38	New Mexico	59.3
14	Massachusetts	69.3	39	Pennsylvania	59.0
15	Iowa	67.4	40	Florida	58.1
16	Missouri	66.2	41	South Carolina	58.0
16	Oklahoma	66.2	42	Georgia	57.4
18	Oregon	66.1	43	Hawaii	57.2
19	Illinois	65.6	44	New York	57.0
20	Colorado	65.4	45	West Virginia	56.6
21	Connecticut	64.8	46	Arizona	56.3
22	Kansas	64.2	47	California	54.8
23	Tennessee	63.9	48	Maryland	54.7
24	New Hampshire	62.9	49	Delaware	53.5
25	Rhode Island	62.8	50	Nevada	52.1

District of Columbia   62.2

Source: U.S. Bureau of the Census,
   "Voting Registration in the Election of November 1990" (P-20, No. 453) (October 1991)

Percent of Eligible Voters Reported as Having Voted in 1990

National Percent = 45.0% of Eligible Voters Reported as Having Voted

RANK	STATE	PERCENT	RANK	STATE	PERCENT
1	Maine	64.7	26	Utah	47.1
2	Minnesota	62.9	27	Arkansas	46.4
3	Montana	62.7	28	Arizona	46.2
4	North Dakota	60.1	29	New Mexico	45.6
5	Alaska	59.2	30	Michigan	45.4
6	Massachusetts	58.8	31	New Hampshire	44.3
7	Nebraska	57.8	32	Indiana	44.2
8	South Dakota	57.2	33	Florida	43.4
9	Vermont	55.0	34	Washington	43.3
10	Oregon	53.9	35	South Carolina	42.8
11	Wyoming	53.5	36	Nevada	42.5
12	Rhode Island	53.4	37	California	42.4
13	Kansas	52.4	38	Georgia	42.3
14	Hawaii	51.6	39	Pennsylvania	42.0
15	Louisiana	51.4	40	New Jersey	41.8
16	Alabama	51.0	41	New York	41.5
17	Colorado	50.6	42	Texas	41.4
18	Iowa	50.5	43	Missouri	40.9
19	Connecticut	49.4	44	Maryland	39.4
20	North Carolina	49.3	45	Kentucky	39.0
21	Oklahoma	49.2	46	Delaware	38.4
22	Ohio	48.5	47	Virginia	37.4
23	Illinois	48.3	48	Mississippi	34.7
24	Idaho	48.2	48	West Virginia	34.7
25	Wisconsin	48.0	50	Tennessee	30.5

District of Columbia   48.6

Source: U.S. Bureau of the Census,
"Voting Registration in the Election of November 1990" (P-20, No. 453) (October 1991)

XIV. SOCIAL WELFARE

State and Local Government Expenditures for Public Welfare Programs in 1990

National Total = $107,153,832,000*

RANK	STATE	EXPENDITURES	%	RANK	STATE	EXPENDITURES	%
1	New York	$15,607,605,000	14.57%	26	Oklahoma	$1,102,345,000	1.03%
2	California	14,911,353,000	13.92%	27	South Carolina	1,080,098,000	1.01%
3	Ohio	5,362,942,000	5.00%	28	Alabama	1,073,215,000	1.00%
4	Pennsylvania	5,143,347,000	4.80%	29	Colorado	1,026,233,000	0.96%
5	Michigan	4,601,779,000	4.29%	30	Oregon	959,603,000	0.90%
6	Illinois	4,535,598,000	4.23%	31	Arkansas	789,248,000	0.74%
7	Massachusetts	4,432,447,000	4.14%	32	Wyoming	783,582,000	0.73%
8	Texas	4,304,196,000	4.02%	33	Kansas	758,018,000	0.71%
9	Florida	3,728,163,000	3.48%	34	Mississippi	710,712,000	0.66%
10	New Jersey	3,571,609,000	3.33%	35	Maine	689,658,000	0.64%
11	Wisconsin	2,594,922,000	2.42%	36	West Virginia	633,184,000	0.59%
12	Minnesota	2,565,745,000	2.39%	37	Rhode Island	538,161,000	0.50%
13	Georgia	2,159,874,000	2.02%	38	Nebraska	526,755,000	0.49%
14	Indiana	1,974,586,000	1.84%	39	Utah	459,944,000	0.43%
15	Washington	1,945,136,000	1.82%	40	New Mexico	459,737,000	0.43%
16	North Carolina	1,919,163,000	1.79%	41	Hawaii	429,521,000	0.40%
17	Maryland	1,900,652,000	1.77%	42	New Hampshire	368,805,000	0.34%
18	Connecticut	1,791,436,000	1.67%	43	Alaska	302,599,000	0.28%
19	Virginia	1,589,876,000	1.48%	44	Montana	292,069,000	0.27%
20	Missouri	1,438,744,000	1.34%	45	Vermont	265,649,000	0.25%
21	Kentucky	1,432,253,000	1.34%	46	Nevada	250,643,000	0.23%
22	Tennessee	1,384,414,000	1.29%	47	Idaho	250,456,000	0.23%
23	Louisiana	1,351,962,000	1.26%	48	North Dakota	250,176,000	0.23%
24	Arizona	1,284,246,000	1.20%	49	Delaware	227,886,000	0.21%
25	Iowa	1,198,957,000	1.12%	50	South Dakota	196,308,000	0.18%
					District of Columbia	672,426,000	0.63%

Source: U.S. Bureau of the Census,

"Government Finances: 1989-90 (Preliminary Report)" (GF-90-5P, September 1991)

*Preliminary.

Per Capita State and Local Government Expenditures for Public Welfare Programs in 1990

National Per Capita = $430.84*

RANK	STATE	PER CAPITA	RANK	STATE	PER CAPITA
1	Wyoming	$1,727.52	26	Oklahoma	$350.44
2	New York	867.55	27	Arizona	350.39
3	Massachusetts	736.72	28	Delaware	342.08
4	Minnesota	586.44	29	Oregon	337.61
5	Maine	561.64	30	Arkansas	335.75
6	Alaska	550.14	31	Nebraska	333.73
7	Connecticut	544.99	32	Georgia	333.41
8	Rhode Island	536.30	33	New Hampshire	332.48
9	Wisconsin	530.47	34	Louisiana	320.37
10	California	501.05	35	Colorado	311.51
11	Michigan	495.07	36	South Carolina	309.78
12	Ohio	494.41	37	Kansas	305.95
13	Vermont	472.05	38	New Mexico	303.44
14	New Jersey	462.03	39	North Carolina	289.53
15	Pennsylvania	432.88	40	Florida	288.16
16	Iowa	431.78	41	Tennessee	283.86
17	Washington	399.68	42	South Dakota	282.05
18	Maryland	397.50	43	Missouri	281.17
19	Illinois	396.79	44	Mississippi	276.20
20	North Dakota	391.63	45	Utah	266.97
21	Kentucky	388.64	46	Alabama	265.61
22	Hawaii	387.57	47	Virginia	256.96
23	Montana	365.51	48	Texas	253.39
24	Indiana	356.16	49	Idaho	248.78
25	West Virginia	353.05	50	Nevada	208.55

District of Columbia   1,107.97

Source: U.S. Bureau of the Census,

"Government Finances: 1989-90 (Preliminary Report)" (GF-90-5P, September 1991)

*Preliminary. Rates calculated by the editors.

State and Local Government Spending for Welfare as a Percent of All Spending in 1990

National Average = 11.07 Percent*

RANK	STATE	PERCENT		RANK	STATE	PERCENT
1	Wyoming	32.83		26	Montana	10.00
2	Massachusetts	16.02		27	Mississippi	9.58
3	Maine	15.69		28	Georgia	9.48
4	New York	14.57		29	Louisiana	9.31
5	Wisconsin	14.17		30	South Carolina	9.07
6	Ohio	13.93		31	Kansas	9.03
7	Arkansas	13.28		32	South Dakota	8.94
8	Minnesota	13.26		33	Washington	8.88
9	Kentucky	13.13		34	Hawaii	8.70
10	Rhode Island	13.03		35	North Carolina	8.63
11	Michigan	12.53		36	Idaho	8.50
12	Pennsylvania	12.45		37	Oregon	8.44
13	Iowa	12.27		38	New Mexico	8.38
14	Connecticut	12.04		39	Alabama	8.37
15	Indiana	11.75		40	Arizona	8.34
16	Vermont	11.73		41	Delaware	8.18
17	West Virginia	11.65		42	Tennessee	8.13
18	Illinois	11.52		43	Colorado	8.02
19	Oklahoma	11.31		44	Florida	8.01
20	California	11.10		45	Nebraska	7.93
21	New Jersey	10.60		46	Texas	7.80
22	North Dakota	10.48		47	Virginia	7.49
23	Maryland	10.28		48	Utah	7.12
24	New Hampshire	10.11		49	Nevada	5.19
25	Missouri	10.09		50	Alaska	5.01

District of Columbia   12.51

Source: U.S. Bureau of the Census,

"Government Finances: 1989-90 (Preliminary Report)" (GF-90-5P, September 1991)

*Preliminary. Rates calculated by the editors.

Social Security (OASDI) Payments in 1990

National Total = $243,606,965,000*

RANK	STATE	PAYMENTS	%	RANK	STATE	PAYMENTS	%
1	California	$23,138,797,000	9.50%	26	Iowa	$3,272,674,000	1.34%
2	New York	18,890,463,000	7.75%	27	Oregon	3,114,225,000	1.28%
3	Florida	16,367,115,000	6.72%	28	Oklahoma	3,109,102,000	1.28%
4	Pennsylvania	14,515,645,000	5.96%	29	South Carolina	3,087,275,000	1.27%
5	Texas	12,906,806,000	5.30%	30	Kansas	2,591,564,000	1.06%
6	Illinois	11,606,095,000	4.76%	31	Arkansas	2,561,551,000	1.05%
7	Ohio	11,484,151,000	4.71%	32	Colorado	2,546,051,000	1.05%
8	Michigan	9,884,814,000	4.06%	33	Mississippi	2,356,245,000	0.97%
9	New Jersey	8,424,341,000	3.46%	34	West Virginia	2,220,723,000	0.91%
10	North Carolina	6,144,126,000	2.52%	35	Nebraska	1,637,175,000	0.67%
11	Massachusetts	6,141,502,000	2.52%	36	Maine	1,234,158,000	0.51%
12	Indiana	5,946,060,000	2.44%	37	New Mexico	1,225,854,000	0.50%
13	Missouri	5,535,544,000	2.27%	38	Utah	1,170,665,000	0.48%
14	Wisconsin	5,355,877,000	2.20%	39	Rhode Island	1,138,436,000	0.47%
15	Georgia	5,017,444,000	2.06%	40	Nevada	1,045,443,000	0.43%
16	Virginia	4,868,538,000	2.00%	41	New Hampshire	1,016,960,000	0.42%
17	Tennessee	4,693,761,000	1.93%	42	Idaho	937,893,000	0.39%
18	Washington	4,591,173,000	1.88%	43	Hawaii	886,248,000	0.36%
19	Minnesota	4,058,949,000	1.67%	44	Montana	824,631,000	0.34%
20	Alabama	3,955,764,000	1.62%	45	South Dakota	717,316,000	0.29%
21	Maryland	3,827,714,000	1.57%	46	Delaware	677,697,000	0.28%
22	Arizona	3,664,614,000	1.50%	47	North Dakota	631,110,000	0.26%
23	Louisiana	3,653,741,000	1.50%	48	Vermont	532,569,000	0.22%
24	Connecticut	3,613,712,000	1.48%	49	Wyoming	383,388,000	0.16%
25	Kentucky	3,603,489,000	1.48%	50	Alaska	201,345,000	0.08%

District of Columbia	417,718,000	0.17%
Puerto Rico	2,100,042,000	0.86%

Source: U.S. Bureau of the Census,
"Federal Expenditures by State for FY 1990" (April 1991)
*"OASDI" is Old Age, Survivors and Disability Insurance.

Per Capita Federal Expenditures for Social Security (OASDI) in 1990

National Per Capita = $965.56*

RANK	STATE	PER CAPITA		RANK	STATE	PER CAPITA
1	Florida	$1,265.05		26	North Dakota	$987.96
2	West Virginia	1,238.23		27	Alabama	979.00
3	Pennsylvania	1,221.68		28	Kentucky	977.80
4	Iowa	1,178.60		29	Tennessee	962.39
5	Rhode Island	1,134.51		30	Vermont	946.35
6	Connecticut	1,099.36		31	Washington	943.39
7	Oregon	1,095.66		32	Idaho	931.61
8	Wisconsin	1,094.87		33	Minnesota	927.74
9	New Jersey	1,089.80		34	North Carolina	926.91
10	Arkansas	1,089.68		35	New Hampshire	916.80
11	Missouri	1,081.78		36	Mississippi	915.69
12	Indiana	1,072.49		37	South Carolina	885.44
13	Michigan	1,063.43		38	Nevada	869.87
14	Ohio	1,058.72		39	Louisiana	865.81
15	New York	1,050.03		40	Wyoming	845.24
16	Kansas	1,046.01		41	New Mexico	809.11
17	Nebraska	1,037.25		42	Maryland	800.53
18	Montana	1,032.00		43	Hawaii	799.69
19	South Dakota	1,030.62		44	Virginia	786.86
20	Massachusetts	1,020.79		45	California	777.51
21	Delaware	1,017.31		46	Georgia	774.51
22	Illinois	1,015.35		47	Colorado	772.85
23	Maine	1,005.08		48	Texas	759.83
24	Arizona	999.84		49	Utah	679.50
25	Oklahoma	988.40		50	Alaska	366.06

District of Columbia		688.28
Puerto Rico		637.93

Source: U.S. Bureau of the Census,
   "Federal Expenditures by State for FY 1990" (April 1991)
"OASDI" is Old Age, Survivors and Disability Insurance.

Social Security (OASDI) Beneficiaries in 1990

National Total = 39,829,430 Beneficiaries*

RANK	STATE	BENEFICIARIES	%	RANK	STATE	BENEFICIARIES	%
1	California	3,664,978	9.20%	26	Oklahoma	531,802	1.34%
2	New York	2,831,823	7.11%	27	Connecticut	526,628	1.32%
3	Florida	2,652,666	6.66%	28	Iowa	524,185	1.32%
4	Pennsylvania	2,237,286	5.62%	29	Oregon	492,394	1.24%
5	Texas	2,193,405	5.51%	30	Arkansas	469,897	1.18%
6	Ohio	1,803,385	4.53%	31	Mississippi	450,776	1.13%
7	Illinois	1,752,823	4.40%	32	Colorado	421,905	1.06%
8	Michigan	1,490,300	3.74%	33	Kansas	407,382	1.02%
9	New Jersey	1,229,396	3.09%	34	West Virginia	370,321	0.93%
10	North Carolina	1,074,614	2.70%	35	Nebraska	267,966	0.67%
11	Massachusetts	970,043	2.44%	36	New Mexico	218,915	0.55%
12	Missouri	914,020	2.29%	37	Maine	214,790	0.54%
13	Indiana	912,833	2.29%	38	Utah	191,542	0.48%
14	Georgia	883,636	2.22%	39	Rhode Island	180,905	0.45%
15	Wisconsin	838,345	2.10%	40	Nevada	168,229	0.42%
16	Virginia	834,421	2.09%	41	New Hampshire	161,655	0.41%
17	Tennessee	824,680	2.07%	42	Idaho	157,257	0.39%
18	Washington	714,463	1.79%	43	Hawaii	148,522	0.37%
19	Alabama	708,711	1.78%	44	Montana	137,738	0.35%
20	Minnesota	669,450	1.68%	45	South Dakota	128,243	0.32%
21	Louisiana	651,881	1.64%	46	North Dakota	112,605	0.28%
22	Kentucky	646,268	1.62%	47	Delaware	104,382	0.26%
23	Maryland	609,208	1.53%	48	Vermont	87,560	0.22%
24	Arizona	590,551	1.48%	49	Wyoming	61,947	0.16%
25	South Carolina	541,171	1.36%	50	Alaska	33,656	0.08%
					District of Columbia	77,363	0.19%
					Other**	940,508	2.36%

Source: U.S. Department of Health and Human Services, Social Security Administration,
   "Social Security Bulletin" (Vol. 54, No. 9, September 1991)

*"OASDI" is Old Age, Survivors and Disability Insurance.

**"Other" is for persons in outlying areas, in foreign countries or whose residence is unknown.

Social Security (OASDI) Monthly Benefit Payments in 1990

National Total = $21,684,924,000 per Month*

RANK	STATE	PAYMENTS	%	RANK	STATE	PAYMENTS	%
1	California	$2,048,747,000	9.45%	26	Iowa	$288,985,000	1.33%
2	New York	1,674,442,000	7.72%	27	Oregon	278,008,000	1.28%
3	Florida	1,475,328,000	6.80%	28	Oklahoma	275,405,000	1.27%
4	Pennsylvania	1,282,597,000	5.91%	29	South Carolina	271,849,000	1.25%
5	Texas	1,134,174,000	5.23%	30	Kansas	229,097,000	1.06%
6	Illinois	1,024,886,000	4.73%	31	Colorado	225,655,000	1.04%
7	Ohio	1,007,531,000	4.65%	32	Arkansas	225,109,000	1.04%
8	Michigan	868,130,000	4.00%	33	Mississippi	204,653,000	0.94%
9	New Jersey	749,141,000	3.45%	34	West Virginia	192,238,000	0.89%
10	Massachusetts	546,471,000	2.52%	35	Nebraska	145,647,000	0.67%
11	North Carolina	544,748,000	2.51%	36	Maine	109,395,000	0.50%
12	Indiana	522,564,000	2.41%	37	New Mexico	108,440,000	0.50%
13	Missouri	489,698,000	2.26%	38	Utah	104,320,000	0.48%
14	Wisconsin	473,950,000	2.19%	39	Rhode Island	101,706,000	0.47%
15	Georgia	440,248,000	2.03%	40	Nevada	94,662,000	0.44%
16	Virginia	430,114,000	1.98%	41	New Hampshire	91,208,000	0.42%
17	Tennessee	412,241,000	1.90%	42	Idaho	83,484,000	0.38%
18	Washington	408,534,000	1.88%	43	Hawaii	79,859,000	0.37%
19	Minnesota	361,158,000	1.67%	44	Montana	72,905,000	0.34%
20	Alabama	344,812,000	1.59%	45	South Dakota	63,804,000	0.29%
21	Maryland	338,874,000	1.56%	46	Delaware	60,100,000	0.28%
22	Arizona	328,404,000	1.51%	47	North Dakota	57,171,000	0.26%
23	Connecticut	323,530,000	1.49%	48	Vermont	47,204,000	0.22%
24	Louisiana	315,665,000	1.46%	49	Wyoming	34,151,000	0.16%
25	Kentucky	314,429,000	1.45%	50	Alaska	17,750,000	0.08%
					District of Columbia	36,897,000	0.17%
					Other**	324,490,000	1.50%

Source: U.S. Department of Health and Human Services, Social Security Administration,

"OASDI Beneficiaries by State and County" (December 1990)

*"OASDI" is Old Age, Survivors and Disability Insurance. Based on December 1990.

**"Other" is for persons in outlying areas, in foreign countries or whose residence is unknown.

Average Monthly Social Security (OASDI) Payment in 1990

National Average = $544.45 each Month per Beneficiary*

RANK	STATE	AVERAGE BENEFIT		RANK	STATE	AVERAGE BENEFIT
1	Connecticut	$614.34		26	Minnesota	$539.48
2	New Jersey	609.36		27	Vermont	539.10
3	New York	591.29		28	Hawaii	537.69
4	Illinois	584.71		29	Missouri	535.76
5	Michigan	582.52		30	Colorado	534.85
6	Delaware	575.77		31	Idaho	530.88
7	Pennsylvania	573.28		32	Montana	529.30
8	Indiana	572.46		33	Alaska	527.39
9	Washington	571.81		34	West Virginia	519.11
10	Wisconsin	565.34		35	Oklahoma	517.87
11	Oregon	564.60		36	Texas	517.08
12	New Hampshire	564.21		37	Virginia	515.46
13	Massachusetts	563.35		38	Maine	509.31
14	Nevada	562.70		39	North Dakota	507.71
15	Kansas	562.36		40	North Carolina	506.92
16	Rhode Island	562.21		41	South Carolina	502.33
17	California	559.01		42	Tennessee	499.88
18	Ohio	558.69		43	Georgia	498.22
19	Maryland	556.25		44	South Dakota	497.52
20	Florida	556.17		45	New Mexico	495.35
21	Arizona	556.10		46	Alabama	486.53
22	Iowa	551.30		46	Kentucky	486.53
23	Wyoming	551.29		48	Louisiana	484.24
24	Utah	544.63		49	Arkansas	479.06
25	Nebraska	543.53		50	Mississippi	454.00
					District of Columbia	476.93
					Other**	345.02

Source: U.S. Department of Health and Human Services, Social Security Administration,
    "Social Security Bulletin" (Vol. 54, No. 9, September 1991)

*"OASDI" is Old Age, Survivors and Disability Insurance. Averages calculated by the editors.

**"Other" is for persons in outlying areas, in foreign countries or whose residence is unknown.

Medicare Beneficiaries in 1990

National Total = 34,203,383 Beneficiaries*

RANK	STATE	BENEFICIARIES	%	RANK	STATE	BENEFICIARIES	%
1	California	3,279,233	9.59%	26	Iowa	456,800	1.34%
2	New York	2,508,901	7.34%	27	Oklahoma	451,115	1.32%
3	Florida	2,339,154	6.84%	28	South Carolina	441,923	1.29%
4	Pennsylvania	1,955,931	5.72%	29	Oregon	423,578	1.24%
5	Texas	1,823,921	5.33%	30	Arkansas	390,738	1.14%
6	Ohio	1,543,122	4.51%	31	Mississippi	365,704	1.07%
7	Illinois	1,533,653	4.48%	32	Kansas	363,496	1.06%
8	Michigan	1,232,672	3.60%	33	Colorado	357,826	1.05%
9	New Jersey	1,092,067	3.19%	34	West Virginia	307,766	0.90%
10	North Carolina	892,183	2.61%	35	Nebraska	237,334	0.69%
11	Massachusetts	866,869	2.53%	36	Maine	182,941	0.53%
12	Missouri	781,126	2.28%	37	New Mexico	179,433	0.52%
13	Indiana	761,946	2.23%	38	Utah	159,793	0.47%
14	Georgia	731,969	2.14%	39	Rhode Island	158,843	0.46%
15	Virginia	721,796	2.11%	40	Nevada	140,948	0.41%
16	Wisconsin	713,581	2.09%	41	New Hampshire	137,215	0.40%
17	Tennessee	691,803	2.02%	42	Idaho	132,110	0.39%
18	Washington	615,148	1.80%	43	Hawaii	126,934	0.37%
19	Minnesota	588,204	1.72%	44	Montana	117,381	0.34%
20	Alabama	582,062	1.70%	45	South Dakota	110,159	0.32%
21	Maryland	541,481	1.58%	46	North Dakota	98,396	0.29%
22	Kentucky	533,604	1.56%	47	Delaware	88,278	0.26%
23	Louisiana	531,018	1.55%	48	Vermont	74,552	0.22%
24	Arizona	498,116	1.46%	49	Wyoming	51,847	0.15%
25	Connecticut	468,975	1.37%	50	Alaska	24,958	0.07%
					District of Columbia	77,866	0.23%

Source: U.S. Department of Health and Human Services, Health Care Financing Administration,
   unpublished data (March 29, 1991)

*Aged and disabled beneficiaries. Includes 693,598 beneficiaries in outlying areas or whose residence unknown.

Average Annual Medicare Payment in 1990

National Average = $3,178 Annual Payment*

RANK	STATE	AVERAGE PAYMENT	RANK	STATE	AVERAGE PAYMENT
1	Maryland	$4,020	26	Kentucky	$2,965
2	New York	3,834	26	Virginia	2,965
3	Pennsylvania	3,787	28	Indiana	2,952
4	Michigan	3,746	29	Arkansas	2,879
5	Louisiana	3,736	30	Kansas	2,861
6	Massachusetts	3,636	31	Wisconsin	2,822
7	California	3,583	32	West Virginia	2,742
8	Alaska	3,566	33	Maine	2,739
9	Texas	3,304	34	Montana	2,701
10	Florida	3,282	35	Utah	2,685
11	Tennessee	3,225	36	Washington	2,682
12	Connecticut	3,222	37	New Mexico	2,642
13	Georgia	3,206	38	North Dakota	2,612
14	Delaware	3,194	39	North Carolina	2,607
15	New Jersey	3,191	40	Iowa	2,590
16	Alabama	3,185	41	Colorado	2,588
17	Arizona	3,142	42	South Carolina	2,548
18	Ohio	3,139	43	Vermont	2,522
19	Illinois	3,110	44	New Hampshire	2,507
20	Nevada	3,100	45	South Dakota	2,469
21	Rhode Island	3,079	46	Idaho	2,445
22	Missouri	3,061	47	Oregon	2,356
23	Mississippi	2,997	48	Nebraska	2,330
24	Wyoming	2,990	49	Minnesota	2,234
25	Oklahoma	2,984	50	Hawaii	2,064

District of Columbia   5,111

Source: U.S. Department of Health and Human Services, Health Care Financing Administration,
        unpublished data

*Averages calculated by the editors.

Medicare Benefit Payments in 1990

National Total = $108,707,000,000*

RANK	STATE	PAYMENTS	%	RANK	STATE	PAYMENTS	%
1	California	$11,751,000,000	10.81%	26	Minnesota	$1,314,000,000	1.21%
2	New York	9,619,000,000	8.85%	27	Iowa	1,183,000,000	1.09%
3	Florida	7,677,000,000	7.06%	28	South Carolina	1,126,000,000	1.04%
4	Pennsylvania	7,408,000,000	6.81%	29	Arkansas	1,125,000,000	1.03%
5	Texas	6,027,000,000	5.54%	30	Mississippi	1,096,000,000	1.01%
6	Ohio	4,844,000,000	4.46%	31	Kansas	1,040,000,000	0.96%
7	Illinois	4,770,000,000	4.39%	32	Oregon	998,000,000	0.92%
8	Michigan	4,618,000,000	4.25%	33	Colorado	926,000,000	0.85%
9	New Jersey	3,485,000,000	3.21%	34	West Virginia	844,000,000	0.78%
10	Massachusetts	3,152,000,000	2.90%	35	Nebraska	553,000,000	0.51%
11	Missouri	2,391,000,000	2.20%	36	Maine	501,000,000	0.46%
12	Georgia	2,347,000,000	2.16%	37	Rhode Island	489,000,000	0.45%
13	North Carolina	2,326,000,000	2.14%	38	New Mexico	474,000,000	0.44%
14	Indiana	2,249,000,000	2.07%	39	Nevada	437,000,000	0.40%
15	Tennessee	2,231,000,000	2.05%	40	Utah	429,000,000	0.39%
16	Maryland	2,177,000,000	2.00%	41	New Hampshire	344,000,000	0.32%
17	Virginia	2,140,000,000	1.97%	42	Idaho	323,000,000	0.30%
18	Wisconsin	2,014,000,000	1.85%	43	Montana	317,000,000	0.29%
19	Louisiana	1,984,000,000	1.83%	44	Delaware	282,000,000	0.26%
20	Alabama	1,854,000,000	1.71%	45	South Dakota	272,000,000	0.25%
21	Washington	1,650,000,000	1.52%	46	Hawaii	262,000,000	0.24%
22	Kentucky	1,582,000,000	1.46%	47	North Dakota	257,000,000	0.24%
23	Arizona	1,565,000,000	1.44%	48	Vermont	188,000,000	0.17%
24	Connecticut	1,511,000,000	1.39%	49	Wyoming	155,000,000	0.14%
25	Oklahoma	1,346,000,000	1.24%	50	Alaska	89,000,000	0.08%
					District of Columbia	398,000,000	0.37%

Source: U.S. Department of Health and Human Services, Health Care Financing Administration,
unpublished data (January 13, 1992)

*Includes $579,000,000 to persons in outlying areas, foreign countries and those whose residence is unknown.

Per Capita Federal Expenditures for Medicare in 1990

National Per Capita = $445.29*

RANK	STATE	PER CAPITA		RANK	STATE	PER CAPITA
1	Pennsylvania	$624.04		26	Mississippi	$399.61
2	Florida	602.97		27	Tennessee	398.47
3	Massachusetts	588.68		28	Montana	393.62
4	New York	556.77		29	Indiana	389.39
5	New Jersey	543.32		30	Vermont	384.40
6	Michigan	520.34		31	Delaware	383.85
7	North Dakota	518.50		32	Arizona	378.34
8	Illinois	514.47		33	Minnesota	370.58
9	Rhode Island	503.32		34	Kentucky	367.96
10	Missouri	495.01		35	Texas	366.61
11	Connecticut	480.65		36	Louisiana	361.61
12	West Virginia	480.30		37	New Hampshire	350.08
13	Arkansas	474.70		38	Washington	331.16
14	Kansas	474.21		39	Virginia	321.85
15	Iowa	464.57		40	Colorado	315.85
16	Ohio	458.01		41	Idaho	313.82
17	Maine	451.14		42	North Carolina	313.72
18	California	448.13		43	Georgia	313.58
19	Wisconsin	443.89		44	Nevada	312.74
20	Nebraska	438.29		45	New Mexico	308.80
21	Oklahoma	426.44		46	Wyoming	304.18
22	Oregon	422.28		47	Hawaii	284.56
23	South Dakota	421.73		48	South Carolina	281.35
24	Maryland	416.97		49	Utah	199.50
25	Alabama	412.92		50	Alaska	115.92

District of Columbia		746.18
Puerto Rico		120.44

Source: U.S. Bureau of the Census,
   "Federal Expenditures by State for FY 1990" (April 1991)
*Total of Per Capita Hospital Insurance Payments and Supplementary Medical Insurance Payments.

Medicaid Recipients in 1990

National Total = 25,255,067 Recipients*

RANK	STATE	RECIPIENTS	%	RANK	STATE	RECIPIENTS	%
1	California	3,624,247	14.35%	26	Oklahoma	273,255	1.08%
2	New York	2,329,456	9.22%	27	Arkansas	264,296	1.05%
3	Texas	1,442,074	5.71%	28	West Virginia	250,261	0.99%
4	Ohio	1,220,780	4.83%	29	Connecticut	249,589	0.99%
5	Pennsylvania	1,177,161	4.66%	30	Iowa	239,584	0.95%
6	Illinois	1,067,465	4.23%	31	Oregon	227,198	0.90%
7	Michigan	1,047,963	4.15%	32	Kansas	194,380	0.77%
8	Florida	1,038,443	4.11%	33	Colorado	190,636	0.75%
9	Georgia	650,871	2.58%	34	Maine	133,020	0.53%
10	Tennessee	613,323	2.43%	35	New Mexico	129,860	0.51%
11	Massachusetts	590,733	2.34%	36	Nebraska	119,177	0.47%
12	Louisiana	585,101	2.32%	37	Rhode Island	117,045	0.46%
13	New Jersey	566,825	2.24%	38	Utah	108,250	0.43%
14	North Carolina	563,330	2.23%	39	Hawaii	84,973	0.34%
15	Kentucky	467,714	1.85%	40	Montana	61,058	0.24%
16	Missouri	448,243	1.77%	41	Vermont	60,421	0.24%
17	Washington	447,630	1.77%	42	Idaho	54,554	0.22%
18	Mississippi	432,855	1.71%	43	South Dakota	49,302	0.20%
19	Wisconsin	392,733	1.56%	44	North Dakota	49,003	0.19%
20	Minnesota	380,291	1.51%	45	Nevada	47,008	0.19%
21	Virginia	379,456	1.50%	46	New Hampshire	44,819	0.18%
22	Alabama	351,996	1.39%	47	Delaware	41,009	0.16%
23	Indiana	347,872	1.38%	48	Alaska	39,053	0.15%
24	Maryland	330,382	1.31%	49	Wyoming	28,941	0.11%
25	South Carolina	317,128	1.26%	–	Arizona**	N/A	N/A

	RECIPIENTS	%
District of Columbia	93,482	0.37%
Puerto Rico	1,279,743	5.07%

Source: U.S. Department of Health and Human Services, Health Care Financing Administration,

"Statistical Report on Medical Care: Eligibles, Recipients, Payments and Services" (HCFA-2082, May 31, 1991)

*For fiscal year ending September 30, 1990.

**Not applicable.

Medicaid Expenditures in 1990

National Total = $64,858,936,389*

RANK	STATE	EXPENDITURES	%
1	New York	$11,877,391,639	18.31%
2	California	6,506,935,389	10.03%
3	Ohio	3,131,995,800	4.83%
4	Pennsylvania	2,883,103,154	4.45%
5	Texas	2,781,039,389	4.29%
6	Massachusetts	2,730,269,482	4.21%
7	Illinois	2,424,020,123	3.74%
8	Florida	2,360,690,819	3.64%
9	New Jersey	2,298,047,462	3.54%
10	Michigan	2,194,769,823	3.38%
11	Georgia	2,076,110,455	3.20%
12	North Carolina	1,426,023,968	2.20%
13	Minnesota	1,410,378,421	2.17%
14	Indiana	1,342,522,406	2.07%
15	Louisiana	1,314,751,735	2.03%
16	Wisconsin	1,248,362,579	1.92%
17	Connecticut	1,205,196,560	1.86%
18	Tennessee	1,162,751,849	1.79%
19	Maryland	1,090,293,054	1.68%
20	Virginia	985,072,923	1.52%
21	Kentucky	976,854,576	1.51%
22	Washington	952,446,621	1.47%
23	Missouri	897,284,259	1.38%
24	South Carolina	743,067,788	1.15%
25	Oklahoma	687,545,249	1.06%

RANK	STATE	EXPENDITURES	%
26	Iowa	$620,251,758	0.96%
27	Alabama	609,299,292	0.94%
28	Arkansas	599,200,357	0.92%
29	Mississippi	586,120,804	0.90%
30	Oregon	518,795,346	0.80%
31	Colorado	515,696,297	0.80%
32	Kansas	490,588,410	0.76%
33	Rhode Island	442,184,277	0.68%
34	Maine	432,013,154	0.67%
35	West Virginia	361,079,816	0.56%
36	Nebraska	309,306,033	0.48%
37	New Mexico	275,239,802	0.42%
38	Utah	246,653,927	0.38%
39	New Hampshire	243,047,411	0.37%
40	North Dakota	193,805,446	0.30%
41	Hawaii	191,320,487	0.29%
42	Montana	170,550,465	0.26%
43	South Dakota	166,059,514	0.26%
44	Idaho	162,190,978	0.25%
45	Vermont	152,893,458	0.24%
46	Nevada	148,590,658	0.23%
47	Alaska	139,120,001	0.21%
48	Delaware	123,175,346	0.19%
49	Wyoming	58,930,138	0.09%
–	Arizona**	N/A	N/A

District of Columbia		245,740,555	0.38%
Puerto Rico		146,380,495	0.23%

Source: U.S. Department of Health and Human Services, Health Care Financing Administration,
"Statistical Report on Medical Care: Eligibles, Recipients, Payments and Services" (HCFA-2082, May 31, 1991)
*For fiscal year ending September 30, 1990.
**Not applicable.

Cost per Medicaid Recipient in 1990

National Cost = $2,568 per Recipient*

RANK	STATE	COST PER RECIPIENT	RANK	STATE	COST PER RECIPIENT
1	New Hampshire	$5,423	26	Vermont	$2,530
2	New York	5,099	27	Kansas	2,524
3	Connecticut	4,829	28	Oklahoma	2,516
4	Massachusetts	4,622	29	Pennsylvania	2,449
5	New Jersey	4,054	30	South Carolina	2,343
6	North Dakota	3,955	31	Oregon	2,283
7	Indiana	3,859	32	Utah	2,279
8	Rhode Island	3,778	33	Florida	2,273
9	Minnesota	3,709	34	Illinois	2,271
10	Alaska	3,562	35	Arkansas	2,267
11	South Dakota	3,368	36	Hawaii	2,252
12	Maryland	3,300	37	Louisiana	2,247
13	Maine	3,248	38	Washington	2,128
14	Georgia	3,190	39	New Mexico	2,120
15	Wisconsin	3,179	40	Michigan	2,094
16	Nevada	3,161	41	Kentucky	2,089
17	Delaware	3,004	42	Wyoming	2,036
18	Idaho	2,973	43	Missouri	2,002
19	Montana	2,793	44	Texas	1,928
20	Colorado	2,705	45	Tennessee	1,896
21	Virginia	2,596	46	California	1,795
22	Nebraska	2,595	47	Alabama	1,731
23	Iowa	2,589	48	West Virginia	1,443
24	Ohio	2,566	49	Mississippi	1,354
25	North Carolina	2,531	–	Arizona**	N/A

District of Columbia		2,629
Puerto Rico		114

Source: U.S. Department of Health and Human Services, Health Care Financing Administration,

"Statistical Report on Medical Care: Eligibles, Recipients, Payments and Services" (HCFA-2082, May 31, 1991)

*For fiscal year ending September 30, 1990.

**Not applicable.

Food Stamp Recipients in 1989

National Total = 18,957,000 Recipients*

RANK	STATE	RECIPIENTS	%	RANK	STATE	RECIPIENTS	%
1	California	1,793,000	9.46%	26	Oklahoma	251,000	1.32%
2	Texas	1,702,000	8.98%	27	Maryland	248,000	1.31%
3	New York	1,447,000	7.63%	27	Minnesota	248,000	1.31%
4	Ohio	1,060,000	5.59%	29	Arkansas	223,000	1.18%
5	Illinois	966,000	5.10%	30	Colorado	208,000	1.10%
6	Pennsylvania	908,000	4.79%	31	Oregon	204,000	1.08%
7	Michigan	875,000	4.62%	32	Iowa	163,000	0.86%
8	Louisiana	720,000	3.80%	33	New Mexico	147,000	0.78%
9	Florida	696,000	3.67%	34	Kansas	134,000	0.71%
10	Tennessee	496,000	2.62%	35	Connecticut	118,000	0.62%
11	Georgia	493,000	2.60%	36	Utah	94,000	0.50%
12	Mississippi	492,000	2.60%	37	Nebraska	90,000	0.47%
13	South Carolina**	455,000	2.40%	38	Maine	82,000	0.43%
14	Kentucky	445,000	2.35%	39	Hawaii	77,000	0.41%
15	Alabama	438,000	2.31%	40	Rhode Island	58,000	0.31%
16	Missouri	405,000	2.14%	41	Idaho	57,000	0.30%
17	North Carolina	388,000	2.05%	42	Montana	53,000	0.28%
18	New Jersey	361,000	1.90%	43	South Dakota	49,000	0.26%
19	Virginia	327,000	1.72%	44	Nevada	45,000	0.24%
20	Massachusetts	322,000	1.70%	45	North Dakota	37,000	0.20%
21	Indiana	284,000	1.50%	46	Vermont	34,000	0.18%
22	Arizona	283,000	1.49%	47	Delaware	30,000	0.16%
22	Wisconsin	283,000	1.49%	48	Wyoming	26,000	0.14%
24	Washington	255,000	1.35%	49	Alaska	23,000	0.12%
24	West Virginia	255,000	1.35%	49	New Hampshire	23,000	0.12%
					District of Columbia	59,000	0.31%

Source: U.S. Department of Agriculture, Food and Nutrition Service,
"Agricultural Statistics 1990" (April 1991); and unpublished data
*Includes 28,000 recipients in outlying areas and Department of Defense overseas.
**Participation at yearend 1989 was atypical due to Hurricane Hugo disaster relief.

Households Receiving Food Stamps in 1989

National Total = 7,217,000 Households*

RANK	STATE	HOUSEHOLDS	%	RANK	STATE	HOUSEHOLDS	%
1	New York	650,000	9.01%	26	South Carolina	95,000	1.32%
2	California	624,000	8.65%	27	West Virginia	94,000	1.30%
3	Texas	542,000	7.51%	28	Oregon	91,000	1.26%
4	Ohio	449,000	6.22%	29	Arizona	90,000	1.25%
5	Illinois	402,000	5.57%	30	Arkansas	83,000	1.15%
6	Pennsylvania	389,000	5.39%	31	Colorado	82,000	1.14%
7	Michigan	363,000	5.03%	32	Iowa	67,000	0.93%
8	Florida	261,000	3.62%	33	Kansas	49,000	0.68%
9	Louisiana	245,000	3.39%	33	New Mexico	49,000	0.68%
10	Tennessee	193,000	2.67%	35	Connecticut	43,000	0.60%
11	Georgia	181,000	2.51%	36	Maine	37,000	0.51%
12	Mississippi	172,000	2.38%	37	Nebraska	36,000	0.50%
13	Kentucky	161,000	2.23%	38	Utah	34,000	0.47%
14	Alabama	157,000	2.18%	39	Hawaii	31,000	0.43%
15	North Carolina	154,000	2.13%	40	Rhode Island	25,000	0.35%
16	Missouri	153,000	2.12%	41	Idaho	21,000	0.29%
17	Virginia	138,000	1.91%	41	Montana	21,000	0.29%
18	New Jersey	137,000	1.90%	43	Nevada	19,000	0.26%
19	Massachusetts	136,000	1.88%	44	South Dakota	17,000	0.24%
20	Washington	118,000	1.64%	45	Vermont	15,000	0.21%
21	Maryland	106,000	1.47%	46	North Dakota	14,000	0.19%
22	Oklahoma	102,000	1.41%	47	Delaware	11,000	0.15%
23	Indiana	100,000	1.39%	48	New Hampshire	10,000	0.14%
24	Wisconsin	99,000	1.37%	48	Wyoming	10,000	0.14%
25	Minnesota	98,000	1.36%	50	Alaska	9,000	0.12%
					District of Columbia	25,000	0.35%

Source: U.S. Department of Agriculture, Food and Nutrition Service,
   "Agricultural Statistics 1990" (April 1991); and unpublished data
*Includes 8,000 households in outlying areas and Department of Defense overseas.

Households Receiving Food Stamps as a Percent of All Households in 1989

National Percent = 7.8% of All Households

RANK	STATE	PERCENT		RANK	STATE	PERCENT
1	Mississippi	18.5		26	Colorado	6.4
2	Louisiana	15.7		26	Utah	6.4
3	West Virginia	13.3		28	South Dakota	6.3
4	Kentucky	11.5		28	Washington	6.3
5	Ohio	10.8		30	North Carolina	6.2
6	Michigan	10.6		31	Iowa	6.1
7	Alabama	10.3		31	Maryland	6.1
7	Tennessee	10.3		31	Massachusetts	6.1
9	New York	9.5		31	Virginia	6.1
10	Illinois	9.2		35	Minnesota	6.0
11	Arkansas	9.1		36	California	5.9
12	New Mexico	8.9		37	Nebraska	5.8
13	Texas	8.8		38	Idaho	5.7
14	Hawaii	8.6		38	North Dakota	5.7
14	Pennsylvania	8.6		40	Wyoming	5.6
16	Oklahoma	8.2		41	Wisconsin	5.4
17	Oregon	8.1		42	Florida	5.1
18	Maine	7.9		42	Kansas	5.1
19	Georgia	7.7		44	Alaska	5.0
19	Missouri	7.7		45	Indiana	4.8
21	South Carolina	7.6		45	New Jersey	4.8
22	Arizona	6.9		47	Delaware	4.4
22	Vermont	6.9		48	Nevada	4.3
24	Montana	6.8		49	Connecticut	3.6
25	Rhode Island	6.6		50	New Hampshire	2.4

District of Columbia   10.4

Source: U.S. Department of Agriculture, Food and Nutrition Service,
"Agricultural Statistics 1990" (April 1991); and unpublished data

Federal Payments to Individuals for Food Stamps in 1990

National Total = $13,998,950,000

RANK	STATE	PAYMENTS	%	RANK	STATE	PAYMENTS	%
1	Texas	$1,428,181,000	10.20%	26	Wisconsin	$180,984,000	1.29%
2	New York	1,075,722,000	7.68%	27	Washington	171,078,000	1.22%
3	California	947,076,000	6.77%	28	Oregon	167,226,000	1.19%
4	Ohio	841,863,000	6.01%	29	Minnesota	164,868,000	1.18%
5	Illinois	823,862,000	5.89%	30	Arkansas	154,978,000	1.11%
6	Pennsylvania	665,207,000	4.75%	31	Colorado	152,980,000	1.09%
7	Michigan	661,884,000	4.73%	32	New Mexico	118,052,000	0.84%
8	Florida	605,058,000	4.32%	33	Iowa	109,045,000	0.78%
9	Louisiana	549,555,000	3.93%	34	Kansas	95,933,000	0.69%
10	Georgia	382,664,000	2.73%	35	Hawaii	80,775,000	0.58%
11	Tennessee	371,844,000	2.66%	36	Utah	71,050,000	0.51%
12	Mississippi	349,370,000	2.50%	37	Maine	62,622,000	0.45%
13	Kentucky	333,992,000	2.39%	38	Nebraska	58,655,000	0.42%
14	Alabama	320,749,000	2.29%	39	Connecticut	55,238,000	0.39%
15	Missouri	310,390,000	2.22%	40	Montana	40,638,000	0.29%
16	New Jersey	286,555,000	2.05%	41	Nevada	40,430,000	0.29%
17	North Carolina	279,436,000	2.00%	42	Idaho	39,270,000	0.28%
18	Virginia	246,023,000	1.76%	43	South Dakota	34,661,000	0.25%
19	Arizona	239,352,000	1.71%	44	Rhode Island	30,876,000	0.22%
20	South Carolina	224,726,000	1.61%	45	Alaska	25,170,000	0.18%
21	Indiana	223,641,000	1.60%	46	North Dakota	24,778,000	0.18%
22	Massachusetts	204,939,000	1.46%	47	Delaware	24,761,000	0.18%
23	Maryland	204,715,000	1.46%	48	Vermont	22,066,000	0.16%
24	West Virginia	192,413,000	1.37%	49	Wyoming	20,555,000	0.15%
25	Oklahoma	185,437,000	1.32%	50	New Hampshire	20,245,000	0.14%

District of Columbia		41,822,000	0.30%
Puerto Rico*		0	0.00%
Other**		35,540,000	0.25%

Source: U.S. Bureau of the Census,

"Federal Expenditures by State for FY 1990" (April 1991)

*Puerto Rico was dropped from the Food Stamp program in 1982 and transferred to a nutritional assistance grant program.

**"Other" is Guam, Northern Marianas and the Virgin Islands.

Per Capita Federal Expenditures for Food Stamps in 1990

National Per Capita = $55.49*

RANK	STATE	PER CAPITA		RANK	STATE	PER CAPITA
1	Mississippi	$135.77		26	Colorado	$46.44
2	Louisiana	130.23		27	Alaska	45.76
3	West Virginia	107.28		28	Wyoming	45.32
4	Kentucky	90.63		29	Maryland	42.81
5	Texas	84.08		30	North Carolina	42.16
6	Alabama	79.38		31	Utah	41.24
7	New Mexico	77.92		32	Indiana	40.34
8	Ohio	77.61		33	Virginia	39.76
9	Tennessee	76.24		34	Iowa	39.27
10	Hawaii	72.89		35	Vermont	39.21
11	Illinois	72.08		36	Idaho	39.01
12	Michigan	71.21		37	North Dakota	38.79
13	Arkansas	65.93		38	Kansas	38.72
14	Arizona	65.30		39	Minnesota	37.68
15	South Carolina	64.45		40	Delaware	37.17
16	Missouri	60.66		41	Nebraska	37.16
17	New York	59.79		42	New Jersey	37.07
18	Georgia	59.07		43	Wisconsin	37.00
19	Oklahoma	58.95		44	Washington	35.15
20	Oregon	58.83		45	Massachusetts	34.06
21	Pennsylvania	55.99		46	Nevada	33.64
22	Maine	51.00		47	California	31.82
23	Montana	50.86		48	Rhode Island	30.77
24	South Dakota	49.80		49	New Hampshire	18.25
25	Florida	46.77		50	Connecticut	16.80

District of Columbia		68.91
Puerto Rico**		0.00

Source: U.S. Bureau of the Census,
   "Federal Expenditures by State for FY 1990" (April 1991)

*Per capita of total direct federal payments to individuals for food stamps.

**Puerto Rico was dropped from the Food Stamp program in 1982 and transferred to a nutritional assistance grant program.

Federal Grants to State and Local Governments for Food Stamp Program Administration in 1990

National Total = $2,230,286,000

RANK	STATE	GRANTS	%	RANK	STATE	GRANTS	%
1	California	$159,982,000	7.17%	26	Oklahoma	$16,994,000	0.76%
2	New York	128,806,000	5.78%	27	Mississippi	16,519,000	0.74%
3	Texas	102,320,000	4.59%	28	Wisconsin	15,946,000	0.71%
4	Pennsylvania	76,832,000	3.44%	29	Arkansas	12,986,000	0.58%
5	Washington	61,219,000	2.74%	30	Colorado	10,791,000	0.48%
6	Illinois	47,848,000	2.15%	31	Iowa	9,533,000	0.43%
7	Florida	45,107,000	2.02%	32	New Mexico	9,226,000	0.41%
8	Michigan	43,132,000	1.93%	33	Kansas	7,675,000	0.34%
9	Georgia	42,738,000	1.92%	34	Utah	7,552,000	0.34%
10	Ohio	40,098,000	1.80%	35	Rhode Island	6,770,000	0.30%
11	New Jersey	37,644,000	1.69%	36	Montana	6,581,000	0.30%
12	Massachusetts	32,913,000	1.48%	37	Connecticut	6,488,000	0.29%
13	Alabama	27,681,000	1.24%	38	Vermont	6,219,000	0.28%
14	North Carolina	27,360,000	1.23%	39	Alaska	5,289,000	0.24%
15	Tennessee	26,706,000	1.20%	40	West Virginia	4,991,000	0.22%
16	Louisiana	24,545,000	1.10%	41	Maine	4,582,000	0.21%
17	Virginia	24,462,000	1.10%	42	Nebraska	4,125,000	0.18%
18	Kentucky	24,379,000	1.09%	43	Hawaii	4,029,000	0.18%
19	Indiana	22,620,000	1.01%	44	Idaho	3,463,000	0.16%
20	Arizona	20,857,000	0.94%	45	Nevada	3,427,000	0.15%
21	Missouri	20,386,000	0.91%	46	South Dakota	3,064,000	0.14%
22	Maryland	19,881,000	0.89%	47	North Dakota	2,964,000	0.13%
23	South Carolina	19,165,000	0.86%	48	Delaware	2,930,000	0.13%
24	Minnesota	18,435,000	0.83%	49	Wyoming	2,317,000	0.10%
25	Oregon	18,232,000	0.82%	50	New Hampshire	2,158,000	0.10%

District of Columbia	5,364,000	0.24%
Puerto Rico*	931,131,000	41.75%
Other**	3,824,000	0.17%

Source: U.S. Bureau of the Census,

 "Federal Expenditures by State for FY 1990" (April 1991)

*Amount shown is for nutritional assistance grant program.

**"Other" is Guam, Northern Marianas and the Virgin Islands.

Aid to Families with Dependent Children (AFDC) Recipients in 1990

National Total = 11,794,968 Recipients

RANK	STATE	RECIPIENTS	%	RANK	STATE	RECIPIENTS	%
1	California	1,962,260	16.64%	26	Alabama	128,960	1.09%
2	New York	1,003,678	8.51%	27	South Carolina	117,073	0.99%
3	Michigan	660,211	5.60%	28	Oklahoma	115,997	0.98%
4	Ohio	653,030	5.54%	29	West Virginia	108,730	0.92%
5	Illinois	649,117	5.50%	30	Colorado	102,268	0.87%
6	Texas	638,837	5.42%	31	Iowa	99,429	0.84%
7	Pennsylvania	540,126	4.58%	32	Oregon	87,395	0.74%
8	Florida	395,874	3.36%	33	Kansas	76,445	0.65%
9	New Jersey	319,874	2.71%	34	Arkansas	71,998	0.61%
10	Georgia	304,441	2.58%	35	New Mexico	61,424	0.52%
11	Massachusetts	285,410	2.42%	36	Maine	59,125	0.50%
12	Louisiana	278,489	2.36%	37	Rhode Island	49,374	0.42%
13	Wisconsin	237,155	2.01%	38	Utah	45,951	0.39%
14	North Carolina	236,094	2.00%	39	Hawaii	44,256	0.38%
15	Washington	230,139	1.95%	40	Nebraska	43,925	0.37%
16	Tennessee	221,788	1.88%	41	Montana	27,741	0.24%
17	Missouri	213,770	1.81%	42	Vermont	23,183	0.20%
18	Maryland	192,897	1.64%	43	Nevada	22,857	0.19%
19	Kentucky	179,878	1.53%	44	Alaska	21,384	0.18%
20	Mississippi	179,457	1.52%	45	Delaware	21,275	0.18%
21	Minnesota	175,438	1.49%	46	South Dakota	19,017	0.16%
22	Indiana	159,464	1.35%	47	New Hampshire	18,282	0.15%
23	Virginia	151,784	1.29%	48	Idaho	16,797	0.14%
24	Arizona	135,417	1.15%	49	North Dakota	15,364	0.13%
25	Connecticut	129,816	1.10%	50	Wyoming	13,579	0.12%
					District of Columbia	50,432	0.43%
					Puerto Rico	190,779	1.62%
					Other*	7,484	0.06%

Source: U.S. Department of Health and Human Services, Social Security Administration,
"Social Security Bulletin" (Vol. 54, No. 10, October 1991)
*Other is Guam and the Virgin Islands.

Average AFDC Monthly Payment per Family in 1989

National Average = $383

RANK	STATE	PAYMENT	RANK	STATE	PAYMENT
1	California	$620	26	Illinois	$320
2	Alaska	619	27	Ohio	314
3	Massachusetts	559	28	Wyoming	307
4	Hawaii	546	29	Oklahoma	288
5	Connecticut	534	30	Delaware	283
6	New York	530	31	Nevada	277
7	Minnesota	523	32	Missouri	272
8	Vermont	500	33	Arizona	271
9	Rhode Island	483	33	South Dakota	271
10	Michigan	480	35	Indiana	263
11	Wisconsin	461	36	Georgia	261
12	Washington	449	37	Virginia	260
13	New Hampshire	417	38	Florida	253
14	Maine	408	38	West Virginia	253
15	North Dakota	366	40	Idaho	251
16	Oregon	361	41	North Carolina	238
17	Iowa	360	42	New Mexico	225
18	New Jersey	357	43	Kentucky	223
19	Maryland	356	44	South Carolina	208
19	Montana	356	45	Arkansas	193
19	Pennsylvania	356	46	Tennessee	170
22	Utah	352	47	Texas	168
23	Kansas	349	48	Louisiana	167
24	Nebraska	333	49	Mississippi	118
25	Colorado	324	50	Alabama	114
				District of Columbia	363

Source: U.S. Department of Health and Human Services, Family Support Administration,
"Quarterly Public Assistance Statistics" (annual)

Aid to Families with Dependent Children (AFDC) Payments in 1989

National Total = $17,466,000,000*

RANK	STATE	PAYMENTS	%
1	California	$4,553,000,000	26.07%
2	New York	2,146,000,000	12.29%
3	Michigan	1,223,000,000	7.00%
4	Ohio	837,000,000	4.79%
5	Illinois	789,000,000	4.52%
6	Pennsylvania	743,000,000	4.25%
7	Massachusetts	600,000,000	3.44%
8	Wisconsin	447,000,000	2.56%
9	New Jersey	441,000,000	2.52%
10	Washington	424,000,000	2.43%
11	Texas	377,000,000	2.16%
12	Florida	371,000,000	2.12%
13	Minnesota	343,000,000	1.96%
14	Georgia	295,000,000	1.69%
15	Maryland	272,000,000	1.56%
16	Connecticut	252,000,000	1.44%
17	North Carolina	225,000,000	1.29%
18	Missouri	223,000,000	1.28%
19	Louisiana	186,000,000	1.06%
20	Virginia	169,000,000	0.97%
21	Indiana	163,000,000	0.93%
22	Kentucky	161,000,000	0.92%
23	Iowa	149,000,000	0.85%
24	Tennessee	146,000,000	0.84%
25	Oregon	139,000,000	0.80%

RANK	STATE	PAYMENTS	%
26	Colorado	$133,000,000	0.76%
27	Oklahoma	125,000,000	0.72%
28	Arizona	122,000,000	0.70%
29	West Virginia	109,000,000	0.62%
30	Kansas	107,000,000	0.61%
31	South Carolina	93,000,000	0.53%
32	Hawaii	92,000,000	0.53%
33	Maine	90,000,000	0.52%
34	Rhode Island	88,000,000	0.50%
35	Mississippi	85,000,000	0.49%
36	Utah	64,000,000	0.37%
37	Alabama	61,000,000	0.35%
38	Nebraska	57,000,000	0.33%
39	Alaska	55,000,000	0.31%
39	Arkansas	55,000,000	0.31%
39	New Mexico	55,000,000	0.31%
42	Vermont	43,000,000	0.25%
43	Montana	40,000,000	0.23%
44	Delaware	26,000,000	0.15%
44	New Hampshire	26,000,000	0.15%
46	Nevada	25,000,000	0.14%
47	North Dakota	24,000,000	0.14%
48	South Dakota	22,000,000	0.13%
49	Idaho	19,000,000	0.11%
49	Wyoming	19,000,000	0.11%
	District of Columbia	79,000,000	0.45%

Source: U.S. Department of Health and Human Services, Family Support Administration,
"Quarterly Public Assistance Statistics" (annual)
*Includes $78,000,000 in payments to Puerto Rico and other outlying areas.

Federal Expenditures for Aid to Families with Dependent Children (AFDC) Payments in 1990*

National Total = $12,246,000,000*

RANK	STATE	GRANTS	%	RANK	STATE	GRANTS	%
1	New York	$2,880,984,000	23.53%	26	South Carolina	$102,741,000	0.84%
2	California	1,830,187,000	14.95%	27	Oklahoma	99,653,000	0.81%
3	Michigan	681,672,000	5.57%	28	Mississippi	91,039,000	0.74%
4	Ohio	519,677,000	4.24%	29	Iowa	89,881,000	0.73%
5	Pennsylvania	482,675,000	3.94%	30	West Virginia	81,659,000	0.67%
6	Illinois	405,782,000	3.31%	31	Colorado	80,045,000	0.65%
7	Massachusetts	370,925,000	3.03%	32	Kansas	67,092,000	0.55%
8	Wisconsin	358,665,000	2.93%	33	Maine	62,750,000	0.51%
9	Texas	346,255,000	2.83%	34	Nebraska	56,311,000	0.46%
10	Washington	336,318,000	2.75%	35	Alabama	54,224,000	0.44%
11	New Jersey	319,114,000	2.61%	36	Hawaii	53,968,000	0.44%
12	Florida	272,923,000	2.23%	37	Rhode Island	53,006,000	0.43%
13	Georgia	221,613,000	1.81%	38	Utah	52,845,000	0.43%
14	Minnesota	200,809,000	1.64%	39	Arkansas	43,941,000	0.36%
15	Louisiana	178,664,000	1.46%	40	New Mexico	42,600,000	0.35%
16	North Carolina	170,023,000	1.39%	41	Alaska	39,187,000	0.32%
17	Maryland	159,787,000	1.30%	42	Montana	34,731,000	0.28%
18	Tennessee	152,216,000	1.24%	43	Vermont	28,430,000	0.23%
19	Connecticut	145,686,000	1.19%	44	Nevada	24,196,000	0.20%
20	Virginia	141,103,000	1.15%	45	North Dakota	22,715,000	0.19%
21	Indiana	140,609,000	1.15%	46	Idaho	21,119,000	0.17%
22	Missouri	139,583,000	1.14%	47	South Dakota	20,862,000	0.17%
23	Oregon	139,073,000	1.14%	48	Delaware	19,279,000	0.16%
24	Kentucky	128,882,000	1.05%	49	Wyoming	17,373,000	0.14%
25	Arizona	109,100,000	0.89%	50	New Hampshire	17,231,000	0.14%
					District of Columbia	51,359,000	0.42%
					Puerto Rico	78,625,000	0.64%

Source: U.S. Bureau of the Census,

"Federal Expenditures by State for FY 1990" (April 1991)

*U.S. Department of Health and Human Services, Family Support Administration grants to state and local governments.

Per Capita Federal Expenditures for Aid to Families with Dependent Children Program (AFDC) in 1990

National Per Capita = $48.54*

RANK	STATE	PER CAPITA		RANK	STATE	PER CAPITA
1	New York	$160.14		26	Kentucky	$34.97
2	Michigan	73.34		27	Georgia	34.21
3	Wisconsin	73.32		28	Maryland	33.42
4	Alaska	71.24		29	Iowa	32.37
5	Washington	69.11		30	Oklahoma	31.68
6	Massachusetts	61.65		31	Tennessee	31.21
7	California	61.50		32	Utah	30.67
8	Rhode Island	52.82		33	South Dakota	29.97
9	Maine	51.10		34	Arizona	29.77
10	Vermont	50.52		35	South Carolina	29.47
11	Oregon	48.93		36	Delaware	28.94
12	Hawaii	48.70		37	New Mexico	28.12
13	Ohio	47.91		38	Missouri	27.28
14	Minnesota	45.90		39	Kansas	27.08
15	West Virginia	45.53		40	North Carolina	25.65
16	Connecticut	44.32		41	Indiana	25.36
17	Montana	43.46		42	Colorado	24.30
18	Louisiana	42.34		43	Virginia	22.81
19	New Jersey	41.28		44	Florida	21.09
20	Pennsylvania	40.62		45	Idaho	20.98
21	Wyoming	38.30		46	Texas	20.38
22	Nebraska	35.68		47	Nevada	20.13
23	North Dakota	35.56		48	Arkansas	18.69
24	Illinois	35.50		49	New Hampshire	15.53
25	Mississippi	35.38		50	Alabama	13.42

District of Columbia		84.63
Puerto Rico		23.88

Source: U.S. Bureau of the Census,
   "Federal Expenditures by State for FY 1990" (April 1991)
*U.S. Department of Health and Human Services, Family Support Administration grants to state and local governments.

Persons in National School Lunch Program in 1989

National Total = 24,773,000*

RANK	STATE	PERSONS	%	RANK	STATE	PERSONS	%
1	California	2,111,000	8.52%	26	Maryland	357,000	1.44%
2	Texas	1,959,000	7.91%	26	Washington	357,000	1.44%
3	New York	1,547,000	6.24%	28	Arizona	325,000	1.31%
4	Florida	1,089,000	4.40%	29	Kansas	303,000	1.22%
5	Pennsylvania	1,007,000	4.06%	30	Arkansas	296,000	1.19%
6	Illinois	936,000	3.78%	31	Colorado	290,000	1.17%
7	Georgia	932,000	3.76%	32	Utah	261,000	1.05%
8	Ohio	905,000	3.65%	33	Oregon	240,000	0.97%
9	North Carolina	774,000	3.12%	34	Connecticut	238,000	0.96%
10	Michigan	748,000	3.02%	35	West Virginia	211,000	0.85%
11	Louisiana	716,000	2.89%	36	Nebraska	192,000	0.78%
12	Indiana	628,000	2.54%	37	New Mexico	181,000	0.73%
13	Virginia	614,000	2.48%	38	Hawaii	149,000	0.60%
14	Tennessee	607,000	2.45%	39	Idaho	131,000	0.53%
15	Alabama	582,000	2.35%	40	Maine	111,000	0.45%
16	Missouri	556,000	2.24%	41	South Dakota	101,000	0.41%
17	New Jersey	516,000	2.08%	42	North Dakota	94,000	0.38%
18	Kentucky	506,000	2.04%	43	New Hampshire	93,000	0.38%
19	Minnesota	487,000	1.97%	44	Montana	85,000	0.34%
20	Massachusetts	474,000	1.91%	45	Nevada	66,000	0.27%
21	Wisconsin	467,000	1.89%	46	Delaware	59,000	0.24%
22	South Carolina	465,000	1.88%	47	Rhode Island	57,000	0.23%
23	Mississippi	437,000	1.76%	48	Wyoming	54,000	0.22%
24	Iowa	377,000	1.52%	49	Vermont	46,000	0.19%
25	Oklahoma	363,000	1.47%	50	Alaska	38,000	0.15%

District of Columbia   51,000   0.21%

Source: U.S. Department of Agriculture, Food and Nutrition Service,
    "Agricultural Statistics 1990" (April 1991)
*Includes 584,000 in outlying areas and Department of Defense overseas.

National School Lunch Program Cost in 1989

National Total = $3,006,000,000*

RANK	STATE	COST	%	RANK	STATE	COST	%
1	California	$354,000,000	11.78%	26	Arkansas	$39,000,000	1.30%
2	Texas	278,000,000	9.25%	26	Minnesota	39,000,000	1.30%
3	New York	219,000,000	7.29%	28	Maryland	37,000,000	1.23%
4	Florida	141,000,000	4.69%	29	Colorado	30,000,000	1.00%
5	Illinois	124,000,000	4.13%	29	Iowa	30,000,000	1.00%
6	Ohio	105,000,000	3.49%	31	New Mexico	29,000,000	0.96%
7	Louisiana	100,000,000	3.33%	32	West Virginia	28,000,000	0.93%
8	Georgia	99,000,000	3.29%	33	Kansas	27,000,000	0.90%
8	Pennsylvania	99,000,000	3.29%	34	Oregon	25,000,000	0.83%
10	North Carolina	85,000,000	2.83%	35	Utah	22,000,000	0.73%
11	Michigan	81,000,000	2.69%	36	Connecticut	21,000,000	0.70%
12	Alabama	74,000,000	2.46%	37	Nebraska	17,000,000	0.57%
13	Mississippi	72,000,000	2.40%	38	Hawaii	14,000,000	0.47%
14	Tennessee	66,000,000	2.20%	39	Idaho	13,000,000	0.43%
15	Kentucky	58,000,000	1.93%	40	Maine	11,000,000	0.37%
15	New Jersey	58,000,000	1.93%	40	South Dakota	11,000,000	0.37%
17	South Carolina	57,000,000	1.90%	42	Montana	9,000,000	0.30%
18	Missouri	56,000,000	1.86%	43	North Dakota	8,000,000	0.27%
18	Virginia	56,000,000	1.86%	44	Alaska	7,000,000	0.23%
20	Indiana	50,000,000	1.66%	44	Nevada	7,000,000	0.23%
21	Oklahoma	43,000,000	1.43%	44	Rhode Island	7,000,000	0.23%
22	Arizona	42,000,000	1.40%	47	New Hampshire	6,000,000	0.20%
22	Massachusetts	42,000,000	1.40%	48	Delaware	5,000,000	0.17%
22	Wisconsin	42,000,000	1.40%	48	Wyoming	5,000,000	0.17%
25	Washington	40,000,000	1.33%	50	Vermont	4,000,000	0.13%
					District of Columbia	9,000,000	0.30%

Source: U.S. Department of Agriculture, Food and Nutrition Service,
   "Agricultural Statistics 1990" (April 1991)
*Includes $106,000,000 cost for Puerto Rico, outlying areas and Department of Defense overseas.

Federal Grants to State and Local Governments for WIC Program in 1990

National Total = $2,111,431,000*

RANK	STATE	GRANTS	%	RANK	STATE	GRANTS	%
1	California	$193,289,000	9.15%	26	Connecticut	$29,720,000	1.41%
2	New York	165,965,000	7.86%	27	Washington	28,324,000	1.34%
3	Texas	149,360,000	7.07%	28	Arkansas	27,943,000	1.32%
4	Ohio	86,882,000	4.11%	29	Maryland	26,449,000	1.25%
5	Florida	84,949,000	4.02%	30	Oregon	21,798,000	1.03%
6	Illinois	84,580,000	4.01%	31	Colorado	21,434,000	1.02%
7	Pennsylvania	79,267,000	3.75%	32	Iowa	21,164,000	1.00%
8	Michigan	70,703,000	3.35%	33	Utah	21,002,000	0.99%
9	Georgia	65,794,000	3.12%	34	West Virginia	18,371,000	0.87%
10	North Carolina	65,598,000	3.11%	35	Kansas	17,789,000	0.84%
11	Louisiana	57,819,000	2.74%	36	New Mexico	17,715,000	0.84%
12	New Jersey	45,046,000	2.13%	37	Nebraska	11,882,000	0.56%
13	Missouri	43,520,000	2.06%	38	Hawaii	10,945,000	0.52%
14	Tennessee	41,368,000	1.96%	39	Maine	10,891,000	0.52%
15	Mississippi	40,923,000	1.94%	40	Idaho	10,733,000	0.51%
16	Alabama	40,900,000	1.94%	41	South Dakota	9,457,000	0.45%
17	Virginia	40,806,000	1.93%	42	Rhode Island	8,395,000	0.40%
18	South Carolina	40,749,000	1.93%	43	Montana	7,831,000	0.37%
19	Kentucky	40,390,000	1.91%	44	Nevada	7,749,000	0.37%
20	Indiana	38,043,000	1.80%	45	New Hampshire	7,681,000	0.36%
21	Arizona	36,760,000	1.74%	46	North Dakota	7,516,000	0.36%
22	Massachusetts	33,612,000	1.59%	47	Vermont	6,753,000	0.32%
23	Oklahoma	32,471,000	1.54%	48	Alaska	6,190,000	0.29%
24	Wisconsin	31,835,000	1.51%	49	Delaware	5,089,000	0.24%
25	Minnesota	31,772,000	1.50%	50	Wyoming	4,870,000	0.23%
					District of Columbia	6,783,000	0.32%
					Puerto Rico	87,567,000	4.15%

Source: U.S. Bureau of the Census,
   "Federal Expenditures by State for FY 1990" (April 1991)
*Women, Infants and Children Special Supplemental Food Program

XV. TRANSPORTATION

Federal Subsidies for Amtrak Railroad in 1990

National Total = $665,000,000

RANK	STATE	SUBSIDY	%	RANK	STATE	SUBSIDY	%
1	New York	$167,000,000	25.11%	26	Nevada	$2,276,000	0.34%
2	Pennsylvania	96,426,000	14.50%	27	Minnesota	1,786,000	0.27%
3	California	70,998,000	10.68%	28	Montana	1,536,000	0.23%
4	Illinois	37,147,000	5.59%	29	Alabama	1,384,000	0.21%
5	New Jersey	35,521,000	5.34%	30	Vermont	1,360,000	0.20%
6	Maryland	33,889,000	5.10%	31	Mississippi	1,336,000	0.20%
7	Massachusetts	28,564,000	4.30%	32	Utah	1,330,000	0.20%
8	Connecticut	26,121,000	3.93%	33	Arizona	1,259,000	0.19%
9	Virginia	17,922,000	2.70%	34	New Mexico	1,095,000	0.16%
10	Delaware	13,212,000	1.99%	35	North Dakota	1,012,000	0.15%
11	Florida	12,966,000	1.95%	36	Nebraska	786,000	0.12%
12	Rhode Island	8,577,000	1.29%	37	Iowa	651,000	0.10%
13	Michigan	8,252,000	1.24%	38	West Virginia	547,000	0.08%
14	Washington	7,587,000	1.14%	39	Idaho	507,000	0.08%
15	Missouri	6,074,000	0.91%	40	Tennessee	475,000	0.07%
16	Oregon	6,013,000	0.90%	41	Kansas	467,000	0.07%
17	Wisconsin	4,934,000	0.74%	42	Arkansas	352,000	0.05%
18	Colorado	3,579,000	0.54%	43	Kentucky	131,000	0.02%
19	North Carolina	3,447,000	0.52%	44	New Hampshire	57,000	0.01%
20	Texas	3,428,000	0.52%	45	Alaska	0	0.00%
21	South Carolina	3,095,000	0.47%	45	Hawaii	0	0.00%
22	Louisiana	2,617,000	0.39%	45	Maine	0	0.00%
23	Georgia	2,575,000	0.39%	45	Oklahoma	0	0.00%
24	Ohio	2,506,000	0.38%	45	South Dakota	0	0.00%
25	Indiana	2,459,000	0.37%	45	Wyoming	0	0.00%

	District of Columbia	41,741,000	6.28%

Source: U.S. Bureau of the Census,
  "Federal Expenditures by State for FY 1990" (April 1991)

Federal Highway Funding in 1992

National Total = $16,151,362,985*

RANK	STATE	FUNDING	%	RANK	STATE	FUNDING	%
1	California	$1,512,172,691	9.36%	26	Kentucky	$221,434,032	1.37%
2	Texas	1,047,822,018	6.49%	27	Arkansas	212,292,512	1.31%
3	New York	794,630,507	4.92%	28	Alaska	206,883,786	1.28%
4	Pennsylvania	788,396,450	4.88%	29	Oregon	194,108,519	1.20%
5	Massachusetts	692,160,759	4.29%	30	Kansas	186,542,875	1.15%
6	Florida	680,307,732	4.21%	31	Colorado	186,204,515	1.15%
7	Ohio	590,183,618	3.65%	32	Mississippi	184,377,966	1.14%
8	Illinois	570,943,174	3.53%	33	South Carolina	176,499,732	1.09%
9	Georgia	479,631,948	2.97%	34	New Mexico	175,849,601	1.09%
10	New Jersey	467,610,267	2.90%	35	Iowa	172,665,136	1.07%
11	Michigan	448,965,645	2.78%	36	West Virginia	171,361,395	1.06%
12	North Carolina	435,516,891	2.70%	37	Montana	152,177,599	0.94%
13	Virginia	375,042,406	2.32%	38	Hawaii	144,758,862	0.90%
14	Indiana	358,063,064	2.22%	39	Nebraska	132,048,870	0.82%
15	Missouri	356,498,277	2.21%	40	Utah	127,366,789	0.79%
16	Tennessee	333,033,096	2.06%	41	Idaho	117,660,141	0.73%
17	Washington	329,058,809	2.04%	42	South Dakota	111,349,959	0.69%
18	Wisconsin	315,845,840	1.96%	43	Wyoming	105,970,322	0.66%
19	Connecticut	311,758,617	1.93%	44	North Dakota	104,155,776	0.64%
20	Maryland	287,647,911	1.78%	45	Rhode Island	100,360,778	0.62%
21	Alabama	276,007,706	1.71%	46	Nevada	95,737,758	0.59%
22	Minnesota	247,856,983	1.53%	47	Maine	94,496,865	0.59%
23	Arizona	238,077,550	1.47%	48	New Hampshire	79,889,047	0.49%
24	Oklahoma	232,228,640	1.44%	49	Vermont	71,655,410	0.44%
25	Louisiana	227,690,657	1.41%	50	Delaware	65,318,682	0.40%
					District of Columbia	94,800,450	0.59%

*Source: U.S. Department of Transportation, Federal Highway Administration,
unpublished data (December 17, 1991)*

For fiscal year ending September 30, 1992. Total includes $68,244,352 for Puerto Rico.

Per Capita Federal Highway Funds in 1992

National Per Capita = $63.78*

RANK	STATE	PER CAPITA
1	Alaska	$362.95
2	Wyoming	230.37
3	Montana	188.34
4	North Dakota	164.02
5	South Dakota	158.39
6	Hawaii	127.54
7	Vermont	126.38
8	Massachusetts	115.44
9	New Mexico	113.60
10	Idaho	113.24
11	Rhode Island	99.96
12	Delaware	96.06
13	West Virginia	95.15
14	Connecticut	94.73
15	Arkansas	89.50
16	Nebraska	82.89
17	Maine	76.52
18	Kansas	74.77
19	Nevada	74.56
20	Oklahoma	73.14
21	Georgia	72.42
22	New Hampshire	72.30
23	Utah	71.96
24	Mississippi	71.13
25	Missouri	69.12

RANK	STATE	PER CAPITA
26	Alabama	$67.50
27	Tennessee	67.24
28	Oregon	66.43
29	Pennsylvania	65.91
30	Washington	65.58
31	North Carolina	64.65
32	Indiana	63.83
33	Wisconsin	63.74
34	Arizona	63.49
35	Iowa	61.78
36	Texas	60.40
37	New Jersey	60.26
38	Virginia	59.66
39	Kentucky	59.64
40	Maryland	59.19
41	Minnesota	55.92
42	Colorado	55.14
43	Ohio	53.95
44	Louisiana	53.55
45	Florida	51.24
46	California	49.78
47	South Carolina	49.58
48	Illinois	49.46
49	Michigan	47.93
50	New York	44.00

District of Columbia   158.53

Source: U.S. Department of Transportation, Federal Highway Administration,
    unpublished data (December 17, 1991)

*For fiscal year ending September 30, 1992. Rates calculated by the editors using 1991 population estimates and excluding highway
    funds for Puerto Rico.

Public Road and Street Mileage in 1990

National Total = 3,880,151 Miles

RANK	STATE	MILES	%
1	Texas	305,951	7.89%
2	California	163,574	4.22%
3	Illinois	135,944	3.50%
4	Kansas	133,578	3.44%
5	Minnesota	129,397	3.33%
6	Missouri	120,527	3.11%
7	Michigan	117,449	3.03%
8	Pennsylvania	116,508	3.00%
9	Ohio	113,600	2.93%
10	Iowa	112,541	2.90%
11	Oklahoma	111,765	2.88%
12	New York	111,242	2.87%
13	Wisconsin	109,876	2.83%
14	Georgia	109,601	2.82%
15	Florida	108,085	2.79%
16	Oregon	94,969	2.45%
17	North Carolina	94,690	2.44%
18	Nebraska	92,403	2.38%
19	Indiana	91,908	2.37%
20	Alabama	90,672	2.34%
21	North Dakota	86,517	2.23%
22	Tennessee	84,639	2.18%
23	Washington	81,299	2.10%
24	Colorado	77,680	2.00%
25	Arkansas	77,085	1.99%

RANK	STATE	MILES	%
26	South Dakota	74,696	1.93%
27	Mississippi	72,520	1.87%
28	Montana	71,387	1.84%
29	Kentucky	69,668	1.80%
30	Virginia	67,700	1.74%
31	South Carolina	64,046	1.65%
32	Idaho	62,435	1.61%
33	Louisiana	58,620	1.51%
34	New Mexico	54,736	1.41%
35	Arizona	51,612	1.33%
36	Nevada	45,524	1.17%
37	Utah	43,244	1.11%
38	Wyoming	39,213	1.01%
39	West Virginia	34,592	0.89%
40	New Jersey	34,252	0.88%
41	Massachusetts	34,076	0.88%
42	Maryland	28,752	0.74%
43	Maine	22,389	0.58%
44	Connecticut	19,991	0.52%
45	New Hampshire	14,836	0.38%
46	Vermont	14,121	0.36%
47	Alaska	13,485	0.35%
48	Rhode Island	6,111	0.16%
49	Delaware	5,444	0.14%
50	Hawaii	4,099	0.11%

	District of Columbia	1,102	0.03%

Source: U.S. Department of Transportation, Federal Highway Administration,
"Highway Statistics 1990" (FHWA-PL-91-003)

Interstate Highway Mileage in 1990

National Total = 45,074 Interstate Highway Miles

RANK	STATE	MILES	%	RANK	STATE	MILES	%
1	Texas	3,229	7.16%	26	Louisiana	844	1.87%
2	California	2,399	5.32%	27	South Carolina	791	1.75%
3	Illinois	1,961	4.35%	28	Iowa	782	1.73%
4	Ohio	1,572	3.49%	29	Kentucky	763	1.69%
5	Pennsylvania	1,569	3.48%	30	Washington	759	1.68%
6	New York	1,500	3.33%	31	Oregon	727	1.61%
7	Florida	1,426	3.16%	32	Mississippi	684	1.52%
8	Georgia	1,245	2.76%	33	South Dakota	678	1.50%
9	Michigan	1,227	2.72%	34	Wisconsin	640	1.42%
10	Montana	1,191	2.64%	35	Idaho	605	1.34%
11	Missouri	1,177	2.61%	36	North Dakota	570	1.26%
12	Arizona	1,169	2.59%	37	Massachusetts	567	1.26%
13	Indiana	1,148	2.55%	38	Nevada	545	1.21%
14	Alaska	1,089	2.42%	39	Arkansas	542	1.20%
15	Virginia	1,076	2.39%	40	West Virginia	517	1.15%
16	Tennessee	1,062	2.36%	41	Nebraska	481	1.07%
17	New Mexico	1,000	2.22%	42	Maryland	400	0.89%
18	Colorado	942	2.09%	43	New Jersey	396	0.88%
19	Utah	938	2.08%	44	Maine	366	0.81%
20	North Carolina	937	2.08%	45	Connecticut	341	0.76%
21	Oklahoma	930	2.06%	46	Vermont	320	0.71%
22	Wyoming	913	2.03%	47	New Hampshire	224	0.50%
23	Minnesota	905	2.01%	48	Rhode Island	70	0.16%
24	Alabama	889	1.97%	49	Hawaii	43	0.10%
25	Kansas	872	1.93%	50	Delaware	41	0.09%

District of Columbia   12   0.03%

Source: U.S. Department of Transportation, Federal Highway Administration,
    "Highway Statistics 1990" (FHWA-PL-91-003)

Federal–Aid Primary Road Mileage in 1990

National Total = 260,273 Miles*

RANK	STATE	MILES	%	RANK	STATE	MILES	%
1	Texas	16,774	6.44%	26	Oregon	5,046	1.94%
2	California	11,078	4.26%	27	Washington	5,023	1.93%
3	Georgia	10,122	3.89%	28	Indiana	5,005	1.92%
4	Pennsylvania	9,913	3.81%	29	North Carolina	4,444	1.71%
5	Illinois	9,877	3.79%	30	Colorado	4,305	1.65%
6	Wisconsin	9,326	3.58%	31	Arizona	4,107	1.58%
7	Minnesota	9,303	3.57%	32	New Mexico	3,888	1.49%
8	Iowa	8,753	3.36%	33	Kentucky	3,846	1.48%
9	New York	8,446	3.25%	34	Louisiana	3,132	1.20%
10	Kansas	8,050	3.09%	35	Wyoming	2,990	1.15%
11	Florida	8,010	3.08%	36	Idaho	2,757	1.06%
12	Michigan	7,227	2.78%	37	Utah	2,615	1.00%
13	Nebraska	7,194	2.76%	38	West Virginia	2,447	0.94%
14	Missouri	7,020	2.70%	39	Massachusetts	2,210	0.85%
15	Alabama	6,762	2.60%	40	Maryland	2,205	0.85%
16	Ohio	6,589	2.53%	41	Maine	2,010	0.77%
17	Tennessee	6,165	2.37%	42	Nevada	1,856	0.71%
18	South Dakota	5,799	2.23%	43	New Jersey	1,479	0.57%
19	Mississippi	5,777	2.22%	44	Connecticut	1,270	0.49%
20	South Carolina	5,682	2.18%	45	New Hampshire	1,133	0.44%
21	North Dakota	5,540	2.13%	46	Vermont	1,124	0.43%
22	Montana	5,454	2.10%	47	Alaska	1,019	0.39%
23	Virginia	5,413	2.08%	48	Hawaii	511	0.20%
24	Oklahoma	5,307	2.04%	49	Delaware	443	0.17%
25	Arkansas	5,215	2.00%	50	Rhode Island	434	0.17%
					District of Columbia	178	0.07%

Source: U.S. Department of Transportation, Federal Highway Administration,
   "Highway Statistics 1990" (FHWA-PL-91-003)
*Excludes 45,074 miles of Interstate Highways which technically are primary roads.

Federal-Aid Secondary Road Mileage in 1990

National Total = 399,974 Miles*

RANK	STATE	MILES	%	RANK	STATE	MILES	%
1	Texas	32,638	8.16%	26	Washington	7,320	1.83%
2	Kansas	22,655	5.66%	27	Kentucky	7,172	1.79%
3	Missouri	18,093	4.52%	28	West Virginia	6,351	1.59%
4	Michigan	17,059	4.27%	29	New York	6,293	1.57%
5	Minnesota	16,604	4.15%	30	Tennessee	5,456	1.36%
6	Georgia	14,011	3.50%	31	Montana	4,744	1.19%
7	Iowa	13,566	3.39%	32	Florida	4,396	1.10%
8	Wisconsin	13,040	3.26%	33	Idaho	4,057	1.01%
9	Illinois	12,922	3.23%	34	New Mexico	3,640	0.91%
10	Oklahoma	11,809	2.95%	35	Colorado	3,410	0.85%
11	Ohio	11,793	2.95%	36	Arizona	3,256	0.81%
12	Mississippi	11,695	2.92%	37	Maine	2,742	0.69%
13	Alabama	11,581	2.90%	38	Utah	2,706	0.68%
14	Nebraska	11,458	2.86%	39	Nevada	2,315	0.58%
15	California	11,176	2.79%	40	Wyoming	2,266	0.57%
16	South Dakota	11,094	2.77%	41	Massachusetts	2,007	0.50%
17	North Dakota	10,628	2.66%	42	Vermont	1,913	0.48%
18	North Carolina	10,325	2.58%	43	Maryland	1,911	0.48%
19	Virginia	10,200	2.55%	44	Alaska	1,816	0.45%
20	Indiana	9,740	2.44%	45	New Jersey	1,687	0.42%
21	South Carolina	8,534	2.13%	46	New Hampshire	1,232	0.31%
22	Pennsylvania	7,980	2.00%	47	Connecticut	902	0.23%
23	Oregon	7,817	1.95%	48	Delaware	605	0.15%
24	Arkansas	7,374	1.84%	49	Hawaii	435	0.11%
25	Louisiana	7,349	1.84%	50	Rhode Island	201	0.05%
					District of Columbia	0	0.00%

Source: U.S. Department of Transportation, Federal Highway Administration,
"Highway Statistics 1990" (FHWA-PL-91-003)

*Secondary Roads are principal and feeder roads linking farms, distribution outlets and smaller communities with the federal-aid primary road system.

Federal–Aid Urban Road Mileage in 1990

National Total = 147,680 Miles

RANK	STATE	MILES	%
1	California	17,791	12.05%
2	New York	8,733	5.91%
3	Texas	8,198	5.55%
4	Ohio	7,866	5.33%
5	Pennsylvania	7,053	4.78%
6	Illinois	6,645	4.50%
7	Massachusetts	5,905	4.00%
8	Michigan	5,466	3.70%
9	New Jersey	5,388	3.65%
10	Indiana	4,714	3.19%
11	Florida	4,603	3.12%
12	Washington	4,236	2.87%
13	Georgia	3,982	2.70%
14	Virginia	3,450	2.34%
15	Tennessee	3,168	2.15%
16	North Carolina	2,995	2.03%
16	Oklahoma	2,995	2.03%
18	Wisconsin	2,982	2.02%
19	Connecticut	2,955	2.00%
20	Alabama	2,792	1.89%
21	Missouri	2,483	1.68%
22	Iowa	2,443	1.65%
23	Colorado	2,394	1.62%
24	Minnesota	2,256	1.53%
25	Louisiana	2,167	1.47%

RANK	STATE	MILES	%
26	Maryland	2,155	1.46%
27	Oregon	2,056	1.39%
28	Kentucky	2,008	1.36%
29	Arizona	1,833	1.24%
30	Mississippi	1,719	1.16%
31	Kansas	1,651	1.12%
32	South Carolina	1,168	0.79%
33	Arkansas	1,160	0.79%
34	Nebraska	1,064	0.72%
35	Rhode Island	930	0.63%
36	Utah	927	0.63%
37	West Virginia	808	0.55%
38	New Hampshire	726	0.49%
39	Idaho	725	0.49%
40	Maine	706	0.48%
41	New Mexico	573	0.39%
42	Wyoming	558	0.38%
43	Nevada	557	0.38%
44	North Dakota	501	0.34%
45	South Dakota	390	0.26%
46	Vermont	349	0.24%
47	Montana	342	0.23%
48	Hawaii	322	0.22%
49	Delaware	321	0.22%
50	Alaska	238	0.16%
	District of Columbia	233	0.16%

*Source: U.S. Department of Transportation, Federal Highway Administration,
"Highway Statistics 1990" (FHWA–PL–91–003)*

Bridges in 1990

National Total = 576,665 Highway Bridges

RANK	STATE	BRIDGES	%	RANK	STATE	BRIDGES	%
1	Texas	46,017	7.98%	26	South Carolina	8,919	1.55%
2	Ohio	29,218	5.07%	27	Colorado	7,700	1.34%
3	Iowa	25,603	4.44%	28	Washington	6,938	1.20%
4	Kansas	25,594	4.44%	29	Oregon	6,798	1.18%
5	Illinois	24,836	4.31%	30	South Dakota	6,638	1.15%
6	Missouri	23,262	4.03%	31	West Virginia	6,439	1.12%
7	Pennsylvania	22,981	3.99%	32	New Jersey	6,041	1.05%
8	Oklahoma	22,786	3.95%	33	Arizona	5,807	1.01%
9	California	22,398	3.88%	34	North Dakota	5,174	0.90%
10	Tennessee	18,700	3.24%	35	Massachusetts	5,035	0.87%
11	Indiana	17,586	3.05%	36	Montana	4,579	0.79%
12	New York	17,304	3.00%	37	Maryland	4,557	0.79%
13	Mississippi	17,153	2.97%	38	Connecticut	4,083	0.71%
14	North Carolina	16,181	2.81%	39	Idaho	3,719	0.64%
15	Nebraska	15,682	2.72%	40	New Mexico	3,418	0.59%
16	Alabama	15,405	2.67%	41	Wyoming	2,776	0.48%
17	Wisconsin	15,014	2.60%	42	Vermont	2,660	0.46%
18	Georgia	14,201	2.46%	43	Utah	2,629	0.46%
19	Louisiana	13,761	2.39%	44	Maine	2,572	0.45%
20	Minnesota	13,024	2.26%	45	New Hampshire	2,568	0.45%
21	Arkansas	12,846	2.23%	46	Nevada	1,102	0.19%
22	Kentucky	12,688	2.20%	47	Hawaii	1,047	0.18%
23	Virginia	12,369	2.14%	48	Alaska	816	0.14%
24	Michigan	10,664	1.85%	49	Delaware	740	0.13%
25	Florida	10,410	1.81%	50	Rhode Island	696	0.12%
					District of Columbia	237	0.04%

Source: U.S. Department of Transportation, Federal Highway Administration,
"Highway Bridge Replacement, Rehabilitation Program 1991"

Deficient Bridges in 1990

National Total = 225,826 Deficient Bridges*

RANK	STATE	BRIDGES	%	RANK	STATE	BRIDGES	%
1	Texas	13,548	6.00%	26	New Jersey	3,066	1.36%
2	Missouri	12,433	5.51%	27	Massachusetts	2,865	1.27%
3	New York	12,201	5.40%	28	Colorado	2,784	1.23%
4	Pennsylvania	10,921	4.84%	29	Florida	2,721	1.20%
5	Oklahoma	10,857	4.81%	30	South Dakota	2,507	1.11%
6	Ohio	10,355	4.59%	31	North Dakota	2,234	0.99%
7	Kansas	10,161	4.50%	32	Washington	2,187	0.97%
8	Iowa	8,783	3.89%	33	South Carolina	2,008	0.89%
9	Mississippi	8,356	3.70%	34	Connecticut	1,878	0.83%
10	Illinois	7,808	3.46%	35	Oregon	1,858	0.82%
11	Tennessee	7,412	3.28%	36	Maryland	1,758	0.78%
12	North Carolina	7,084	3.14%	37	Vermont	1,364	0.60%
13	Nebraska	6,970	3.09%	38	Montana	1,187	0.53%
14	California	6,715	2.97%	39	New Hampshire	1,092	0.48%
15	Louisiana	6,701	2.97%	40	Maine	1,018	0.45%
16	Alabama	6,395	2.83%	41	Idaho	1,006	0.45%
17	Indiana	6,347	2.81%	42	Arizona	737	0.33%
18	Kentucky	6,095	2.70%	43	Utah	717	0.32%
19	Arkansas	5,346	2.37%	44	Wyoming	639	0.28%
20	Georgia	4,352	1.93%	45	New Mexico	628	0.28%
21	Virginia	4,331	1.92%	46	Hawaii	515	0.23%
22	Wisconsin	4,265	1.89%	47	Rhode Island	373	0.17%
23	Michigan	4,261	1.89%	48	Nevada	259	0.11%
24	West Virginia	3,782	1.67%	49	Delaware	231	0.10%
25	Minnesota	3,303	1.46%	50	Alaska	210	0.09%
					District of Columbia	179	0.08%

Source: U.S. Department of Transportation, Federal Highway Administration,
   "Highway Bridge Replacement, Rehabilitation Program 1991"

*Bridges classified as deficient are either functionally obsolete or structurally deficient and are not necessarily unsafe.

Deficient Bridges as a Percent of Total Bridges in 1990

National Percent = 39.16% of Bridges Deficient*

RANK	STATE	PERCENT		RANK	STATE	PERCENT
1	New York	70.51		26	South Dakota	37.77
2	West Virginia	58.74		27	Colorado	36.16
3	Massachusetts	56.90		28	Indiana	36.09
4	Rhode Island	53.59		29	Ohio	35.44
5	Missouri	53.45		30	Virginia	35.01
6	Vermont	51.28		31	Iowa	34.30
7	New Jersey	50.75		32	Washington	31.52
8	Hawaii	49.19		33	Illinois	31.44
9	Mississippi	48.71		34	Delaware	31.22
10	Louisiana	48.70		35	Georgia	30.65
11	Kentucky	48.04		36	California	29.98
12	Oklahoma	47.65		37	Texas	29.44
13	Pennsylvania	47.52		38	Wisconsin	28.41
14	Connecticut	46.00		39	Oregon	27.33
15	Nebraska	44.45		40	Utah	27.27
16	North Carolina	43.78		41	Idaho	27.05
17	North Dakota	43.18		42	Florida	26.14
18	New Hampshire	42.52		43	Montana	25.92
19	Arkansas	41.62		44	Alaska	25.74
20	Alabama	41.51		45	Minnesota	25.36
21	Michigan	39.96		46	Nevada	23.50
22	Kansas	39.70		47	Wyoming	23.02
23	Tennessee	39.64		48	South Carolina	22.51
24	Maine	39.58		49	New Mexico	18.37
25	Maryland	38.58		50	Arizona	12.69

District of Columbia   75.53

Source: U.S. Department of Transportation, Federal Highway Administration,
   "Highway Bridge Replacement, Rehabilitation Program 1991"
*Bridges classified as deficient are either functionally obsolete or structurally deficient and are not necessarily unsafe.

Vehicle Miles of Travel in 1990

National Total = 2,147,501,000,000 Miles

RANK	STATE	MILES	%	RANK	STATE	MILES	%
1	California	258,926,000,000	12.06%	26	Oklahoma	33,081,000,000	1.54%
2	Texas	162,232,000,000	7.55%	27	Colorado	27,178,000,000	1.27%
3	Florida	109,997,000,000	5.12%	28	Oregon	26,738,000,000	1.25%
4	New York	106,902,000,000	4.98%	29	Connecticut	26,303,000,000	1.22%
5	Ohio	86,972,000,000	4.05%	30	Mississippi	24,398,000,000	1.14%
6	Pennsylvania	85,708,000,000	3.99%	31	Iowa	22,993,000,000	1.07%
7	Illinois	83,334,000,000	3.88%	32	Kansas	22,849,000,000	1.06%
8	Michigan	81,091,000,000	3.78%	33	Arkansas	21,011,000,000	0.98%
9	Georgia	72,746,000,000	3.39%	34	New Mexico	16,148,000,000	0.75%
10	North Carolina	62,707,000,000	2.92%	35	West Virginia	15,418,000,000	0.72%
11	Virginia	60,178,000,000	2.80%	36	Utah	14,646,000,000	0.68%
12	New Jersey	58,923,000,000	2.74%	37	Nebraska	13,958,000,000	0.65%
13	Indiana	53,697,000,000	2.50%	38	Maine	11,871,000,000	0.55%
14	Missouri	50,883,000,000	2.37%	39	Nevada	10,215,000,000	0.48%
15	Tennessee	46,710,000,000	2.18%	40	Idaho	9,849,000,000	0.46%
16	Massachusetts	46,130,000,000	2.15%	41	New Hampshire	9,844,000,000	0.46%
17	Washington	44,695,000,000	2.08%	42	Montana	8,332,000,000	0.39%
18	Wisconsin	44,277,000,000	2.06%	43	Hawaii	8,066,000,000	0.38%
19	Alabama	42,347,000,000	1.97%	44	Rhode Island	7,024,000,000	0.33%
20	Maryland	40,536,000,000	1.89%	45	South Dakota	6,989,000,000	0.33%
21	Minnesota	38,946,000,000	1.81%	46	Delaware	6,548,000,000	0.30%
22	Louisiana	37,667,000,000	1.75%	47	North Dakota	5,910,000,000	0.28%
23	Arizona	35,456,000,000	1.65%	48	Vermont	5,838,000,000	0.27%
24	South Carolina	34,376,000,000	1.60%	49	Wyoming	5,833,000,000	0.27%
25	Kentucky	33,639,000,000	1.57%	50	Alaska	3,979,000,000	0.19%
					District of Columbia	3,407,000,000	0.16%

Source: U.S. Department of Transportation, Federal Highway Administration,
"Highway Statistics 1990" (FHWA-PL-91-003)

Highway Fatalities in 1990

National Total = 44,529 Fatalities

RANK	STATE	FATALITIES	%	RANK	STATE	FATALITIES	%
1	California	5,189	11.65%	26	Massachusetts	605	1.36%
2	Texas	3,241	7.28%	27	Arkansas	604	1.36%
3	Florida	2,892	6.49%	28	Oregon	579	1.30%
4	New York	2,212	4.97%	29	Minnesota	566	1.27%
5	Pennsylvania	1,646	3.70%	30	Colorado	544	1.22%
6	Ohio	1,636	3.67%	31	New Mexico	499	1.12%
7	Illinois	1,589	3.57%	32	West Virginia	481	1.08%
8	Michigan	1,566	3.52%	33	Iowa	465	1.04%
9	Georgia	1,562	3.51%	34	Kansas	444	1.00%
10	North Carolina	1,385	3.11%	35	Connecticut	384	0.86%
11	Tennessee	1,176	2.64%	36	Nevada	343	0.77%
12	Alabama	1,118	2.51%	37	Utah	272	0.61%
13	Missouri	1,097	2.46%	38	Nebraska	262	0.59%
14	Virginia	1,077	2.42%	39	Idaho	244	0.55%
15	Indiana	1,050	2.36%	40	Maine	213	0.48%
16	South Carolina	979	2.20%	41	Montana	212	0.48%
17	Louisiana	956	2.15%	42	Hawaii	177	0.40%
18	New Jersey	886	1.99%	43	New Hampshire	158	0.35%
19	Arizona	869	1.95%	44	South Dakota	153	0.34%
20	Kentucky	846	1.90%	45	Delaware	138	0.31%
21	Washington	825	1.85%	46	Wyoming	125	0.28%
22	Wisconsin	769	1.73%	47	North Dakota	112	0.25%
23	Mississippi	746	1.68%	48	Alaska	95	0.21%
24	Maryland	682	1.53%	49	Vermont	88	0.20%
25	Oklahoma	640	1.44%	50	Rhode Island	84	0.19%
					District of Columbia	48	0.11%

Source: U.S. Department of Transportation, National Highway Traffic Safety Administration,
   "Fatal Accident Reporting System 1990"

Highway Fatality Rate in 1990

National Rate = 2.1 Fatalities per 100 Million Vehicle Miles of Travel

RANK	STATE	RATE		RANK	STATE	RATE
1	Nevada	3.4		25	Colorado	2.0
2	Mississippi	3.1		25	Indiana	2.0
2	New Mexico	3.1		25	Iowa	2.0
2	West Virginia	3.1		25	Texas	2.0
5	Arkansas	2.9		30	Illinois	1.9
6	South Carolina	2.8		30	Kansas	1.9
7	Alabama	2.6		30	Michigan	1.9
7	Florida	2.6		30	Nebraska	1.9
9	Arizona	2.5		30	North Dakota	1.9
9	Idaho	2.5		30	Ohio	1.9
9	Kentucky	2.5		30	Oklahoma	1.9
9	Louisiana	2.5		30	Pennsylvania	1.9
9	Montana	2.5		30	Utah	1.9
9	Tennessee	2.5		39	Maine	1.8
15	Alaska	2.4		39	Virginia	1.8
16	Hawaii	2.2		39	Washington	1.8
16	Missouri	2.2		42	Maryland	1.7
16	North Carolina	2.2		42	Wisconsin	1.7
16	Oregon	2.2		44	New Hampshire	1.6
16	South Dakota	2.2		45	Connecticut	1.5
21	Delaware	2.1		45	Minnesota	1.5
21	Georgia	2.1		45	New Jersey	1.5
21	New York	2.1		45	Vermont	1.5
21	Wyoming	2.1		49	Massachusetts	1.3
25	California	2.0		50	Rhode Island	1.2

District of Columbia   1.4

Source: U.S. Department of Transportation, National Highway Traffic Safety Administration,
  "Fatal Accident Reporting System 1990"

Percent of Highway Fatalities Where Victim Used a Seat Belt: 1990

National Rate = 27% of Highway Fatalities Occured with Belt Usage*

RANK	STATE	PERCENT		RANK	STATE	PERCENT
1	Hawaii	49		24	Pennsylvania	25
2	Michigan	35		27	Nebraska	24
2	North Carolina	35		28	Colorado	23
2	South Carolina	35		28	Iowa	23
5	New York	34		28	Missouri	23
6	Alaska	33		28	Ohio	23
6	Wisconsin	33		28	Utah	23
8	California	32		33	Kansas	22
8	Texas	32		34	Arizona	21
8	Washington	32		34	Louisiana	21
11	Delaware	31		34	Nevada	21
12	Illinois	30		37	Georgia	20
12	Maryland	30		37	Tennessee	20
14	Florida	29		37	West Virginia	20
14	Indiana	29		40	Maine	19
14	New Mexico	29		41	Kentucky	17
14	Oklahoma	29		42	Arkansas	16
18	Montana	28		42	Massachusetts	16
18	New Jersey	28		44	Rhode Island	15
20	Vermont	27		44	Wyoming	15
21	Minnesota	26		46	North Dakota	13
21	Oregon	26		47	Alabama	12
21	Virginia	26		47	New Hampshire	12
24	Connecticut	25		49	South Dakota	11
24	Idaho	25		50	Mississippi	7

District of Columbia   8

Source: U.S. Department of Transportation, National Highway Traffic Safety Administration,
    "Fatal Accident Reporting System 1990"
*Usage rates are based on fatalities where belt use is known.

Percent of Driver Fatalities Where Driver Is Legally Drunk in 1990

National Percent = 42.3% of Driver Fatalities are Legally Drunk*

RANK	STATE	PERCENT	RANK	STATE	PERCENT
1	Vermont	60.9	26	West Virginia	43.1
2	Wyoming	60.0	27	Kansas	42.8
3	North Dakota	55.3	28	Illinois	42.5
4	Texas	54.6	28	Wisconsin	42.5
5	Louisiana	53.9	30	Indiana	41.5
6	New Mexico	52.9	31	Minnesota	41.4
7	Alabama	51.2	32	Tennessee	41.3
8	Rhode Island	50.9	33	Arizona	40.9
9	South Dakota	50.6	33	South Carolina	40.9
10	Iowa	49.5	35	Massachusetts	40.8
11	Nevada	49.1	36	Georgia	40.0
12	Mississippi	48.3	37	Missouri	39.8
13	Michigan	48.1	38	Maine	39.7
14	Ohio	47.8	39	Kentucky	39.3
15	Pennsylvania	47.2	40	California	39.1
16	Washington	47.0	40	Maryland	39.1
17	Montana	46.9	42	Colorado	38.4
17	New Hampshire	46.9	43	North Carolina	36.0
19	Florida	46.5	44	Oregon	35.7
20	Connecticut	46.3	45	Virginia	34.7
21	Alaska	45.3	46	Oklahoma	33.4
22	Arkansas	45.2	47	Nebraska	31.9
23	Delaware	44.9	48	New York	30.7
24	Idaho	44.8	49	New Jersey	27.3
25	Hawaii	44.3	50	Utah	21.4
				District of Columbia	50.0

Source: U.S. Department of Transportation, National Highway Traffic Safety Administration,
     "Fatal Accident Reporting System 1990"

*Drivers with Blood Alcohol Content (BAC) of .10 or more where BAC is known. "Legally drunk" BAC differs from state to state.

Average Time for Emergency Medical Service to Arrive at Scene of Crash in Urban Areas in 1990

National Average = 6.40 Minutes*

RANK	STATE	MINUTES	RANK	STATE	MINUTES
1	Ohio	13.58	26	West Virginia	5.78
2	Tennessee	9.23	27	Wisconsin	5.74
3	Alabama	8.93	28	California	5.70
3	Texas	8.93	29	Montana	5.67
5	New Jersey	8.22	30	Arkansas	5.52
6	South Carolina	8.13	30	Kansas	5.52
7	Hawaii	7.45	30	Nebraska	5.52
8	Mississippi	7.37	33	Michigan	5.50
9	Arizona	7.36	34	Oregon	5.47
10	Nevada	7.21	35	Florida	5.46
11	New York	6.83	36	New Hampshire	5.41
12	Louisiana	6.72	37	Wyoming	5.27
13	Massachusetts	6.67	38	Connecticut	5.14
14	Pennsylvania	6.46	39	Iowa	5.11
15	Oklahoma	6.33	40	New Mexico	5.10
16	Delaware	6.15	41	Illinois	5.06
17	Idaho	6.06	42	Utah	5.05
17	Maryland	6.06	43	Indiana	4.93
19	Missouri	6.05	44	South Dakota	4.88
20	Georgia	6.03	45	North Dakota	4.57
21	Colorado	6.02	46	Washington	4.50
21	Minnesota	6.02	47	Maine	3.55
23	Vermont	6.00	48	Rhode Island	3.27
24	Kentucky	5.96	–	North Carolina**	N/A
25	Alaska	5.93	–	Virginia**	N/A

	District of Columbia	7.35

Source: U.S. Department of Transportation, National Highway Traffic Safety Administration,
   "Fatal Accident Reporting System 1990"

*From notification of accident.

**Not Available.

448

Average Time for Emergency Medical Service to Arrive at Scene of Crash in Rural Areas in 1990

National Average = 11.31 Minutes*

RANK	STATE	MINUTES	RANK	STATE	MINUTES
1	Nevada	23.00	26	South Carolina	11.30
2	Massachusetts	19.40	27	Oregon	11.13
3	Wyoming	18.88	28	Kentucky	10.58
4	Arizona	16.54	29	Pennsylvania	10.19
5	Montana	15.49	30	California	10.17
6	New Mexico	14.85	30	New Jersey	10.17
7	North Dakota	14.84	32	Wisconsin	9.86
8	Alaska	14.65	33	Maine	9.84
9	South Dakota	14.56	34	Michigan	9.74
10	Colorado	14.32	35	Iowa	9.62
11	Ohio	14.30	36	Nebraska	9.57
12	Texas	14.29	37	Hawaii	9.38
13	Idaho	13.83	38	Georgia	9.37
14	Utah	13.69	39	Florida	9.26
15	Alabama	13.55	40	New York	9.20
16	Illinois	12.87	41	Washington	9.04
17	Louisiana	12.67	42	North Carolina	8.95
18	Tennessee	12.45	43	Indiana	8.87
19	Arkansas	12.26	44	New Hampshire	8.69
20	Kansas	12.10	45	Maryland	8.49
21	Vermont	11.81	46	Connecticut	7.94
22	Oklahoma	11.71	47	Mississippi	7.29
23	Minnesota	11.70	48	Rhode Island	7.16
24	West Virginia	11.55	49	Delaware	6.51
25	Missouri	11.42	–	Virginia**	N/A

Source: U.S. Department of Transportation, National Highway Traffic Safety Administration,
   "Fatal Accident Reporting System 1990"

*From notification of accident.

**Not available.

Licensed Drivers in 1990

National Total = 167,015,250 Licensed Drivers

RANK	STATE	DRIVERS	%
1	California	19,845,906	11.88%
2	Texas	11,136,694	6.67%
3	New York	10,254,229	6.14%
4	Florida	9,231,405	5.53%
5	Pennsylvania	7,899,052	4.73%
6	Ohio	7,427,409	4.45%
7	Illinois	7,294,732	4.37%
8	Michigan	6,440,390	3.86%
9	New Jersey	5,584,727	3.34%
10	North Carolina	4,550,644	2.72%
11	Georgia	4,478,260	2.68%
12	Virginia	4,388,805	2.63%
13	Massachusetts	4,229,311	2.53%
14	Missouri	3,688,081	2.21%
15	Indiana	3,601,354	2.16%
16	Washington	3,376,671	2.02%
17	Maryland	3,361,936	2.01%
18	Tennessee	3,334,425	2.00%
19	Wisconsin	3,327,872	1.99%
20	Alabama	2,752,590	1.65%
21	Louisiana	2,575,460	1.54%
22	Minnesota	2,528,941	1.51%
23	Kentucky	2,401,661	1.44%
24	Arizona	2,392,618	1.43%
25	South Carolina	2,372,825	1.42%
26	Oklahoma	2,277,540	1.36%
27	Connecticut	2,214,146	1.33%
28	Oregon	2,211,551	1.32%
29	Colorado	2,043,003	1.22%
30	Mississippi	1,884,544	1.13%
31	Iowa	1,872,486	1.12%
32	Arkansas	1,722,021	1.03%
33	Kansas	1,714,507	1.03%
34	West Virginia	1,283,703	0.77%
35	Nebraska	1,088,677	0.65%
36	New Mexico	1,073,816	0.64%
37	Utah	1,046,106	0.63%
38	Maine	887,042	0.53%
39	Nevada	846,410	0.51%
40	New Hampshire	843,470	0.51%
41	Idaho	704,184	0.42%
42	Hawaii	677,626	0.41%
43	Rhode Island	670,651	0.40%
44	Montana	603,614	0.36%
45	South Dakota	492,378	0.29%
46	Delaware	484,801	0.29%
47	North Dakota	424,898	0.25%
48	Vermont	411,920	0.25%
49	Wyoming	333,546	0.20%
50	Alaska	314,300	0.19%
	District of Columbia	412,312	0.25%

Source: U.S. Department of Transportation, Federal Highway Administration, "Highway Statistics 1990" (FHWA-PL-91-003)

Licensed Male Drivers in 1990

National Total = 85,792,450 Male Drivers

RANK	STATE	DRIVERS	%	RANK	STATE	DRIVERS	%
1	California	10,535,859	12.28%	26	Oregon	1,159,013	1.35%
2	Texas	5,736,644	6.69%	27	Oklahoma	1,137,074	1.33%
3	New York	5,449,157	6.35%	28	Connecticut	1,054,539	1.23%
4	Florida	4,778,636	5.57%	29	Colorado	1,026,200	1.20%
5	Pennsylvania	4,116,337	4.80%	30	Mississippi	960,865	1.12%
6	Ohio	3,760,666	4.38%	31	Iowa	927,958	1.08%
7	Illinois	3,717,715	4.33%	32	Arkansas	878,710	1.02%
8	Michigan	3,218,771	3.75%	33	Kansas	848,702	0.99%
9	New Jersey	2,938,968	3.43%	34	West Virginia	671,929	0.78%
10	North Carolina	2,303,537	2.69%	35	New Mexico	558,383	0.65%
11	Georgia	2,255,799	2.63%	36	Nebraska	548,345	0.64%
12	Virginia	2,213,348	2.58%	37	Utah	521,799	0.61%
13	Massachusetts	2,176,846	2.54%	38	Nevada	444,505	0.52%
14	Missouri	1,863,591	2.17%	39	Maine	440,502	0.51%
15	Indiana	1,850,007	2.16%	40	New Hampshire	425,025	0.50%
16	Washington	1,724,508	2.01%	41	Hawaii	366,208	0.43%
17	Maryland	1,710,144	1.99%	42	Idaho	361,253	0.42%
18	Wisconsin	1,702,803	1.98%	43	Rhode Island	341,610	0.40%
19	Tennessee	1,658,225	1.93%	44	Montana	330,899	0.39%
20	Alabama	1,392,026	1.62%	45	South Dakota	248,878	0.29%
21	Louisiana	1,290,566	1.50%	46	Delaware	243,426	0.28%
22	Minnesota	1,283,189	1.50%	47	North Dakota	215,465	0.25%
23	Arizona	1,227,297	1.43%	48	Vermont	210,920	0.25%
24	Kentucky	1,225,596	1.43%	49	Wyoming	173,803	0.20%
25	South Carolina	1,182,475	1.38%	50	Alaska	172,950	0.20%
					District of Columbia	210,778	0.25%

Source: U.S. Department of Transportation, Federal Highway Administration,
"Highway Statistics 1990" (FHWA-PL-91-003)

Licensed Female Drivers in 1990

National Total = 81,222,800 Female Drivers

RANK	STATE	DRIVERS	%	RANK	STATE	DRIVERS	%
1	California	9,310,047	11.46%	26	Connecticut	1,159,607	1.43%
2	Texas	5,400,050	6.65%	27	Oklahoma	1,140,466	1.40%
3	New York	4,805,072	5.92%	28	Oregon	1,052,537	1.30%
4	Florida	4,452,769	5.48%	29	Colorado	1,016,803	1.25%
5	Pennsylvania	3,782,715	4.66%	30	Iowa	944,528	1.16%
6	Ohio	3,666,743	4.51%	31	Mississippi	923,679	1.14%
7	Illinois	3,577,017	4.40%	32	Kansas	865,805	1.07%
8	Michigan	3,221,619	3.97%	33	Arkansas	843,311	1.04%
9	New Jersey	2,645,759	3.26%	34	West Virginia	611,774	0.75%
10	North Carolina	2,247,107	2.77%	35	Nebraska	540,332	0.67%
11	Georgia	2,222,461	2.74%	36	Utah	524,307	0.65%
12	Virginia	2,175,457	2.68%	37	New Mexico	515,433	0.63%
13	Massachusetts	2,052,465	2.53%	38	Maine	446,540	0.55%
14	Missouri	1,824,490	2.25%	39	New Hampshire	418,445	0.52%
15	Indiana	1,751,347	2.16%	40	Nevada	401,905	0.49%
16	Tennessee	1,676,200	2.06%	41	Idaho	342,931	0.42%
17	Washington	1,652,163	2.03%	42	Rhode Island	329,041	0.41%
18	Maryland	1,651,792	2.03%	43	Hawaii	311,418	0.38%
19	Wisconsin	1,625,069	2.00%	44	Montana	272,715	0.34%
20	Alabama	1,360,564	1.68%	45	South Dakota	243,500	0.30%
21	Louisiana	1,284,894	1.58%	46	Delaware	241,375	0.30%
22	Minnesota	1,245,752	1.53%	47	North Dakota	209,433	0.26%
23	South Carolina	1,190,350	1.47%	48	Vermont	201,000	0.25%
24	Kentucky	1,176,065	1.45%	49	Wyoming	159,743	0.20%
25	Arizona	1,165,321	1.43%	50	Alaska	141,350	0.17%

	District of Columbia	201,534	0.25%

Source: U.S. Department of Transportation, Federal Highway Administration,
"Highway Statistics 1990" (FHWA-PL-91-003)

Licensed Drivers per 1,000 Driving Age Population in 1990

National Average = 873 Licensed Drivers per 1,000 Driving Age Population

RANK	STATE	RATE		RANK	STATE	RATE
1	Oregon	999		26	South Carolina	896
2	Montana	997		27	Florida	894
3	Wyoming	991		28	Alabama	893
4	Mississippi	990		29	Ohio	888
5	New Hampshire	981		29	Texas	888
6	New Mexico	967		31	Wisconsin	884
7	Arkansas	962		32	North Carolina	881
8	Idaho	956		32	Tennessee	881
9	Oklahoma	947		34	Massachusetts	880
10	Vermont	941		35	North Dakota	879
11	Delaware	938		36	California	878
11	South Dakota	938		37	Arizona	869
13	Missouri	930		38	Iowa	867
14	Maine	926		39	Connecticut	851
15	Georgia	919		40	Indiana	845
16	Utah	916		40	Kentucky	845
16	West Virginia	916		42	Rhode Island	841
18	New Jersey	914		43	Pennsylvania	840
19	Nevada	910		44	Illinois	826
20	Kansas	906		44	Louisiana	826
21	Virginia	905		46	Colorado	810
22	Michigan	904		47	Alaska	801
23	Maryland	902		48	Hawaii	797
23	Nebraska	902		49	Minnesota	754
25	Washington	900		50	New York	727

District of Columbia 860

Source: U.S. Department of Transportation, Federal Highway Administration,
"Highway Statistics 1990" (FHWA-PL-91-003)

Motor Vehicle Registrations in 1990

National Total = 188,655,462 Motor Vehicles*

RANK	STATE	VEHICLES	%	RANK	STATE	VEHICLES	%
1	California	21,925,878	11.62%	26	Oklahoma	2,649,051	1.40%
2	Texas	12,799,815	6.78%	27	Iowa	2,631,973	1.40%
3	Florida	10,949,806	5.80%	28	Connecticut	2,622,966	1.39%
4	New York	10,196,153	5.40%	29	South Carolina	2,519,737	1.34%
5	Ohio	8,410,466	4.46%	30	Oregon	2,445,487	1.30%
6	Pennsylvania	7,971,470	4.23%	31	Kansas	2,012,353	1.07%
7	Illinois	7,873,189	4.17%	32	Mississippi	1,875,445	0.99%
8	Michigan	7,209,217	3.82%	33	Arkansas	1,447,660	0.77%
9	New Jersey	5,652,382	3.00%	34	Nebraska	1,383,846	0.73%
10	Georgia	5,489,144	2.91%	35	New Mexico	1,301,261	0.69%
11	North Carolina	5,162,005	2.74%	36	West Virginia	1,224,947	0.65%
12	Virginia	4,938,062	2.62%	37	Utah	1,205,517	0.64%
13	Tennessee	4,444,108	2.36%	38	Idaho	1,053,538	0.56%
14	Indiana	4,365,760	2.31%	39	Maine	976,610	0.52%
15	Washington	4,256,866	2.26%	40	New Hampshire	945,743	0.50%
16	Missouri	3,904,679	2.07%	41	Nevada	853,444	0.45%
17	Alabama	3,744,491	1.98%	42	Montana	783,153	0.42%
18	Massachusetts	3,725,798	1.97%	43	Hawaii	771,478	0.41%
19	Wisconsin	3,671,859	1.95%	44	South Dakota	703,786	0.37%
20	Maryland	3,606,520	1.91%	45	Rhode Island	671,807	0.36%
21	Minnesota	3,507,937	1.86%	46	North Dakota	629,839	0.33%
22	Colorado	3,155,371	1.67%	47	Wyoming	528,421	0.28%
23	Louisiana	2,994,763	1.59%	48	Delaware	526,089	0.28%
24	Kentucky	2,909,408	1.54%	49	Alaska	477,325	0.25%
25	Arizona	2,825,112	1.50%	50	Vermont	461,796	0.24%
					District of Columbia	261,931	0.14%

Source: U.S. Department of Transportation, Federal Highway Administration,
"Highway Statistics 1990" (FHWA-PL-91-003)
*Includes automobiles, trucks and buses. Does not include motorcycles.

Per Capita Motor Vehicle Registrations in 1990

National Per Capita = 0.76 Motor Vehicles per Person*

RANK	STATE	PER CAPITA
1	Wyoming	1.16
2	Idaho	1.05
3	South Dakota	1.01
4	North Dakota	0.99
5	Montana	0.98
6	Colorado	0.96
7	Iowa	0.95
8	Alabama	0.93
9	Tennessee	0.91
10	Nebraska	0.88
11	Alaska	0.87
11	Washington	0.87
13	New Mexico	0.86
13	Oregon	0.86
15	Florida	0.85
15	Georgia	0.85
15	New Hampshire	0.85
18	Oklahoma	0.84
19	Vermont	0.82
20	Kansas	0.81
21	Connecticut	0.80
21	Maine	0.80
21	Minnesota	0.80
21	Virginia	0.80
25	Delaware	0.79

RANK	STATE	PER CAPITA
25	Indiana	0.79
25	Kentucky	0.79
28	Michigan	0.78
28	North Carolina	0.78
28	Ohio	0.78
31	Arizona	0.77
32	Missouri	0.76
33	Maryland	0.75
33	Texas	0.75
33	Wisconsin	0.75
36	California	0.74
37	Mississippi	0.73
37	New Jersey	0.73
39	South Carolina	0.72
40	Louisiana	0.71
40	Nevada	0.71
42	Hawaii	0.70
42	Utah	0.70
44	Illinois	0.69
45	West Virginia	0.68
46	Pennsylvania	0.67
46	Rhode Island	0.67
48	Arkansas	0.62
48	Massachusetts	0.62
50	New York	0.57

	District of Columbia	0.43

Source: U.S. Department of Transportation, Federal Highway Administration,
"Highway Statistics 1990" (FHWA-PL-91-003)

*Rates calculated by the editors. Includes automobiles, trucks and buses. Does not include motorcylces.

Automobile Registrations in 1990

National Total = 143,549,627 Automobiles

RANK	STATE	AUTOMOBILES	%	RANK	STATE	AUTOMOBILES	%
1	California	16,971,853	11.82%	26	Kentucky	1,915,091	1.33%
2	New York	8,831,316	6.15%	27	Iowa	1,880,368	1.31%
3	Texas	8,714,154	6.07%	28	South Carolina	1,877,508	1.31%
4	Florida	8,694,852	6.06%	29	Oregon	1,838,995	1.28%
5	Ohio	6,817,973	4.75%	30	Oklahoma	1,710,717	1.19%
6	Pennsylvania	6,384,121	4.45%	31	Mississippi	1,434,111	1.00%
7	Illinois	6,299,676	4.39%	32	Kansas	1,404,743	0.98%
8	Michigan	5,612,877	3.91%	33	Arkansas	934,337	0.65%
9	New Jersey	5,179,511	3.61%	34	Nebraska	912,688	0.64%
10	Georgia	3,833,915	2.67%	35	New Mexico	806,207	0.56%
11	Virginia	3,775,728	2.63%	36	Utah	789,347	0.55%
12	North Carolina	3,676,785	2.56%	37	West Virginia	752,762	0.52%
13	Tennessee	3,552,828	2.47%	38	New Hampshire	751,347	0.52%
14	Massachusetts	3,223,859	2.25%	39	Maine	741,797	0.52%
15	Indiana	3,196,573	2.23%	40	Hawaii	671,926	0.47%
16	Washington	2,979,369	2.08%	41	Idaho	636,250	0.44%
17	Maryland	2,970,320	2.07%	42	Nevada	592,118	0.41%
18	Missouri	2,759,818	1.92%	43	Rhode Island	563,333	0.39%
19	Wisconsin	2,756,994	1.92%	44	Montana	457,263	0.32%
20	Minnesota	2,741,763	1.91%	45	South Dakota	424,785	0.30%
21	Alabama	2,733,066	1.90%	46	Delaware	406,240	0.28%
22	Connecticut	2,471,504	1.72%	47	North Dakota	371,543	0.26%
23	Colorado	2,300,119	1.60%	48	Vermont	341,552	0.24%
24	Arizona	2,001,736	1.39%	49	Wyoming	308,731	0.22%
25	Louisiana	1,998,158	1.39%	50	Alaska	302,121	0.21%
					District of Columbia	244,879	0.17%

Source: U.S. Department of Transportation, Federal Highway Administration,
"Highway Statistics 1990" (FHWA-PL-91-003)

Bus Registrations in 1990

National Total = 626,987 Buses

RANK	STATE	BUSES	%	RANK	STATE	BUSES	%
1	Texas	61,286	9.77%	26	Connecticut	8,716	1.39%
2	California	40,127	6.40%	27	Mississippi	8,675	1.38%
3	Florida	36,846	5.88%	28	Alabama	8,234	1.31%
4	North Carolina	34,560	5.51%	29	Washington	7,064	1.13%
5	New York	32,456	5.18%	30	Colorado	5,526	0.88%
6	Pennsylvania	30,841	4.92%	31	Arkansas	5,179	0.83%
7	Ohio	30,681	4.89%	32	Nebraska	5,026	0.80%
8	Michigan	22,865	3.65%	33	Arizona	4,399	0.70%
9	Indiana	21,493	3.43%	34	Hawaii	4,251	0.68%
10	Louisiana	19,866	3.17%	35	Idaho	3,825	0.61%
11	New Jersey	18,004	2.87%	36	West Virginia	3,783	0.60%
12	Illinois	17,099	2.73%	37	Kansas	3,771	0.60%
13	Virginia	16,810	2.68%	38	New Mexico	3,415	0.54%
14	Minnesota	14,488	2.31%	39	Maine	2,876	0.46%
15	Georgia	14,377	2.29%	40	Wyoming	2,413	0.38%
16	Tennessee	13,867	2.21%	41	Montana	2,355	0.38%
17	South Carolina	13,829	2.21%	42	Delaware	2,204	0.35%
18	Oklahoma	13,197	2.10%	43	North Dakota	2,161	0.34%
19	Wisconsin	12,312	1.96%	44	Alaska	2,144	0.34%
20	Missouri	11,863	1.89%	45	South Dakota	2,063	0.33%
21	Massachusetts	10,940	1.74%	46	Nevada	1,757	0.28%
22	Maryland	10,937	1.74%	47	New Hampshire	1,675	0.27%
23	Oregon	10,612	1.69%	48	Rhode Island	1,607	0.26%
24	Kentucky	10,027	1.60%	49	Vermont	1,431	0.23%
25	Iowa	9,077	1.45%	50	Utah	1,164	0.19%
					District of Columbia	2,813	0.45%

Source: U.S. Department of Transportation, Federal Highway Administration,
"Highway Statistics 1990" (FHWA-PL-91-003)

Truck Registrations in 1990

National Total = 44,478,848 Trucks

RANK	STATE	TRUCKS	%	RANK	STATE	TRUCKS	%
1	California	4,913,898	11.05%	26	Maryland	625,263	1.41%
2	Texas	4,024,375	9.05%	27	Kansas	603,839	1.36%
3	Florida	2,218,108	4.99%	28	Oregon	595,880	1.34%
4	Georgia	1,640,852	3.69%	29	Arkansas	508,144	1.14%
5	Michigan	1,573,475	3.54%	30	New Mexico	491,639	1.11%
6	Ohio	1,561,812	3.51%	31	Massachusetts	490,999	1.10%
7	Pennsylvania	1,556,508	3.50%	32	West Virginia	468,402	1.05%
8	Illinois	1,556,414	3.50%	33	Nebraska	466,132	1.05%
9	North Carolina	1,450,660	3.26%	34	New Jersey	454,867	1.02%
10	New York	1,332,381	3.00%	35	Mississippi	432,659	0.97%
11	Washington	1,270,433	2.86%	36	Utah	415,006	0.93%
12	Indiana	1,147,694	2.58%	37	Idaho	413,463	0.93%
13	Virginia	1,145,524	2.58%	38	Montana	323,535	0.73%
14	Missouri	1,132,998	2.55%	39	South Dakota	276,938	0.62%
15	Alabama	1,003,191	2.26%	40	Nevada	259,569	0.58%
16	Kentucky	984,290	2.21%	41	North Dakota	256,135	0.58%
17	Louisiana	976,739	2.20%	42	Maine	231,937	0.52%
18	Oklahoma	925,137	2.08%	43	Wyoming	217,277	0.49%
19	Wisconsin	902,553	2.03%	44	New Hampshire	192,721	0.43%
20	Tennessee	877,413	1.97%	45	Alaska	173,060	0.39%
21	Colorado	849,726	1.91%	46	Connecticut	142,746	0.32%
22	Arizona	818,977	1.84%	47	Vermont	118,813	0.27%
23	Minnesota	751,686	1.69%	48	Delaware	117,645	0.26%
24	Iowa	742,528	1.67%	49	Rhode Island	106,867	0.24%
25	South Carolina	628,400	1.41%	50	Hawaii	95,301	0.21%
					District of Columbia	14,239	0.03%

Source: U.S. Department of Transportation, Federal Highway Administration,
"Highway Statistics 1990" (FHWA-PL-91-003)

Motorcycle Registrations in 1990

National Total = 4,259,462 Motorcycles*

RANK	STATE	MOTORCYCLES	%	RANK	STATE	MOTORCYCLES	%
1	California	640,554	15.04%	26	Massachusetts	55,730	1.31%
2	Ohio	228,408	5.36%	27	Connecticut	51,443	1.21%
3	Florida	205,827	4.83%	28	Alabama	43,871	1.03%
4	New York	197,935	4.65%	29	Idaho	41,974	0.99%
5	Wisconsin	189,102	4.44%	30	New Hampshire	39,533	0.93%
6	Illinois	179,962	4.22%	31	Maine	37,795	0.89%
7	Michigan	176,524	4.14%	32	Kentucky	34,509	0.81%
8	Texas	174,334	4.09%	33	New Mexico	33,464	0.79%
9	Iowa	173,367	4.07%	34	South Carolina	31,087	0.73%
10	Pennsylvania	173,301	4.07%	35	Louisiana	30,065	0.71%
11	Minnesota	122,476	2.88%	36	South Dakota	29,959	0.70%
12	Washington	119,318	2.80%	37	Utah	28,172	0.66%
13	Colorado	108,433	2.55%	38	Mississippi	26,090	0.61%
14	Indiana	96,712	2.27%	39	Rhode Island	23,605	0.55%
15	New Jersey	86,439	2.03%	40	West Virginia	22,138	0.52%
16	Tennessee	80,478	1.89%	41	Nebraska	22,105	0.52%
17	Arizona	79,554	1.87%	42	Montana	21,994	0.52%
18	Kansas	75,696	1.78%	43	Hawaii	20,424	0.48%
19	Georgia	74,463	1.75%	44	Wyoming	20,310	0.48%
20	Missouri	67,751	1.59%	45	North Dakota	20,176	0.47%
21	Oregon	64,088	1.50%	46	Nevada	19,257	0.45%
22	Virginia	61,884	1.45%	47	Vermont	17,590	0.41%
23	Oklahoma	60,838	1.43%	48	Arkansas	14,556	0.34%
24	North Carolina	57,079	1.34%	49	Alaska	11,541	0.27%
25	Maryland	56,124	1.32%	50	Delaware	8,867	0.21%
					District of Columbia	2,560	0.06%

Source: U.S. Department of Transportation, Federal Highway Administration,
"Highway Statistics 1990" (FHWA-PL-91-003)

*Includes private, commerical and publicly owned motorcycles but excludes those owned by the military.

XVI. SOURCES OF INFORMATION

Bureau of the Census
 US Department of Commerce
 Washington, DC 20233
 Public Information: (301) 763-4040
 Publications Information: (301) 763-4100

Bureau of Economic Analysis
 US Department of Commerce
 1401 K Street, NW
 Washington, DC 20230
 Information and Publications: (202) 523-0777

Bureau of Justice Statistics
 US Department of Justice
 633 Indiana Ave., NW
 Washington, DC 20530
 Information and Publications: (202) 307-6100

Bureau of Labor Statistics
 US Department of Labor
 Office of Publications and Information Services
 441 G St., NW
 Washington, DC 20212
 Information and Publications: (202) 523-1221

Bureau of Land Management
 US Department of Interior
 Office of Public Affairs
 1849 C Street, NW
 Washington, DC 20240
 Information: (202) 208-3435

Centers for Disease Control
 Office of Public Affairs
 1600 Clifton Road, NE
 Atlanta, GA 30333
 Public Inquiries: (404) 639-3286

Economic Research Service
 US Department of Agriculture
 1301 New York Ave., NW
 Washington, DC 20005
 Information and Publications: (202) 219-0515

Employment Standards Administration
 US Department of Labor
 Office of Public Affairs
 200 Constitution Avenue, NW
 Washington, DC 20210
 Information: (202) 523-8743

Energy Information Administration
 US Department of Energy
 1000 Independence Avenue, SW
 Washington, DC 20585
 Information and Publications: (202) 586-8800

Environmental Protection Agency
 Public Affairs Division
 401 M St., SW
 Washington, DC 20460
 Information: (202) 382-2080
 Publications: (202) 382-4359

Family Support Administration
 US Department of Health and Human Services
 370 L'Enfant Promenade, SW
 Washington, DC 20447
 Information and Publications: (202) 401-9215

Federal Bureau of Investigation
 US Department of Justice
 9th and Pennsylvania Avenue, NW
 Washington, DC 20535
 Public Information: (202) 324-3000

XVI. SOURCES OF INFORMATION (continued)

Federal Deposit Insurance Corporation
550 17th Street, NW
Washington, DC 20429
Information and Publications: (202) 898-6996

Federal Highway Administration
US Department of Transportation
Office of Public Affairs
400 7th St., SW
Washington, DC 20590
Information and Publications: (202) 366-0660

Food and Nutrition Service
US Department of Agriculture
3101 Park Center Drive
Alexandria, VA 22302
Information: (703) 756-4264

Health Care Financing Administration
US Department of Health and Human Services
Office of Public Affairs
200 Independence Ave., SW
Washington, DC 20201
Information: (202) 245-6133
Publications: (301) 966-7843

Internal Revenue Service
US Department of the Treasury
Statistics of Income Division
TR:S Room 401
1111 Constitution Ave., NW
Washington, DC 20224
Information and Publications: (202) 233-1634

National Agricultural Statistics Service
US Department of Agriculture
14th Street and Independence Ave., SW
Washington, DC 20250
Information and Publications: (202) 720-4020

National Center for Education Statistics
US Department of Education
555 New Jersey Avenue, NW
Washington, DC 20208
Information: (202) 401-1576
Publications: (202) 357-6651

National Center For Health Statistics
Centers for Disease Control
US Department of Health and Human Services
6525 Belcrest Road
Hyattsville, MD 20782
Information and Publications: (301) 436-7107

National Highway Traffic Safety Administration
US Department of Transportation
400 7th Street, SW
Washington, DC 20590
Information: (202) 366-9550
Publications: (202) 366-2588

Social Security Administration
US Department of Health and Human Services
6401 Security Boulevard
Baltimore, MD 21235
Information: 1-800-234-5772
Publications: (301) 965-5952

US Department of Defense
Office of Assistant Secretary for Public Affairs
ATTN: Directorate for Public Correspondence
The Pentagon 2E777
Washington, DC 20301-1400
Information and Publications: (202) 697-5737

US Department of Veterans Affairs
Office of Public Affairs
US Department of Veterans Affairs
810 Vermont Ave., NW
Washington, DC 20420
Information: (202) 233-2741
Publications: (202) 233-3056

US Geological Survey
US Department of Interior
12201 Sunrise Valley Drive
Reston, VA 22092
Information: (703) 648-4000

XVII. INDEX

XVII. INDEX (CONTINUED)